The Bilingual
Special Education
Interface

The Bilingual Special Education Interface

Leonard M. Baca

Director, BUENO Center for Multicultural Education
University of Colorado, Boulder

Hermes T. Cervantes

Section 504 School Psychologist
Socorro Independent School District
El Paso, Texas

MERRILL,
an imprint of Prentice Hall
Upper Saddle River, New Jersey   Columbus, Ohio

Library of Congress Cataloging-in-Publication Data

Baca, Leonard.
    The bilingual special education interface / Leonard M. Baca,
Hermes T. Cervantes. —3rd ed.
        p. cm.
    Includes bibliographical references and index.
    ISBN 0-13-769373-7
    1. Special education—United States.   2. Education, Bilingual—
United States.   3. Minorities—Education—United States.
4. Language arts—United States.   I. Cervantes, Hermes T.
II. Title.
LC3981.B32   1998   97-39969
370.117—dc21   CIP

Cover art: Jason Barbour, West Central School, Columbus, Ohio, Franklin County
    Board of Mental Retardation and Developmental Disabilities
Editor: Ann Castel Davis
Production Editor: Linda H. Bayma
Design Coordinator: Karrie M. Converse
Photo Coordinator: Anthony Magnacca
Cover Designer: Brian Deep
Production Manager: Pamela D. Bennett
Illustrations: Clarinda Company
Director of Marketing: Kevin Flanagan
Marketing Manager: Suzanne Stanton
Advertising/Marketing Coordinator: Julie Shough

This book was set in Sabon by Clarinda Company and was printed and bound by R.R.
Donnelley & Sons Company. The cover was printed by Phoenix Color Corp.

© 1998, 1989 by Prentice-Hall Inc.
Simon & Schuster/A Viacom Company
Upper Saddle River, New Jersey 07458

Photo Credits: pp. 1, 168, 326, and 350: Scott Cunningham/Merrill; pp. 26, 188, 214: Anthony
Magnacca/Merrill; p. 46: Julie Peters/Merrill; pp. 76, 98, 144, 290, 372: Anne
Vega/Merrill; p. 120: Todd Yarrington/Merrill; p. 264: Robert Vega/Merrill; Figure 13-4, p. 340, from *Behaivor
Modification in the Natural Environment* by R. G. Tharp and R. J. Wetzel, 1969, New York. Copyright © 1969 by
Harcourt Brace & Company. Adapted and reprinted by permission of the publisher.

ISBN 0-13-769373-7

Printed in the United States of America

10 9 8 7 6 5 4 3 2 1

Prentice-Hall International (UK) Limited, *London*
Prentice-Hall of Australia Pty. Limited, *Sydney*
Prentice-Hall of Canada Inc., *Toronto*
Prentice-Hall Hispanoamericana, S.A., *Mexico*
Prentice-Hall of India Private Limited, *New Delhi*
Prentice-Hall of Japan, Inc., *Tokyo*
Simon & Schuster Asia Pte. Ltd., *Singapore*
Editora Prentice-Hall do Brasil, Ltda., *Rio de Janeiro*

This book is affectionately dedicated to
our own bilingual exceptional families,
including our parents Marcus and Victoria and Jesus and Esther;
our spouses Eleanor and Cecilia;
and our children Elena, Carmela, Julianna, Michelle,
Rosalinda, Rafael, and Ziomara.

con cariño y amor,
Leonard and Hermes

CONTENTS

CHAPTER 11
Methods and Materials for Bilingual Special Education   264
John J. Hoover and Catherine Collier

CHAPTER 12
Including Bilingual Exceptional Children in the General Education Classroom   290
Catherine Collier

CHAPTER 13
How Educational Consultation Can Enhance Instruction for Culturally and Linguistically Diverse Exceptional (CLDE) Students   326
Kathleen C. Harris

CHAPTER 14
Family Involvement in Bilingual Special Education: Challenging the Norm   350
J. A. de Valenzuela, R. L. Torres, and Rudolfo L. Chavez

This book is about children who are learners at risk. They are bilingual or from bilingual homes and sometimes have legitimate special education needs. We see a tremendous need for a meaningful interface between bilingual education and special education. During the 1960s, 1970s, and 1980s, special education classes were over-promoted and misused for these students in many parts of the United States. Declaring a student "mentally retarded," "learning disabled," or otherwise in need of special education and placing the child in a special class or resource room became an accepted method of educating ethnically, linguistically, and socioeconomically different children. In some cases these children had authentic disabilities, but in other cases their linguistic or cultural background was the primary factor in their low test scores and subsequent special education placement. Because of the strong emphasis on inclusion and whole school programs, the decade of the 1990s has presented new challenges in properly identifying and serving these students.

Because of the tremendous increase in the numbers of Asian, Hispanic, and Native American students, school districts have been unable to ignore the need for adjusting instructional programs and service delivery models to better serve these groups and other linguistically and culturally different individuals. One result has been the improvement and expansion of bilingual education to provide for the educational needs of the students with limited proficiency in English. But the bilingual student with special learning needs, including authentic disabilities, continues to be improperly identified and inappropriately served in many school districts

across this country. It is on this group of learners that we focus our attention in this text. By interfacing the common knowledge base, programs, and methodologies of bilingual education and special education, we believe that those learners can achieve success and maximize their potential.

Dewey's famous dictum that what the best and wisest father wants for his child, the state should want for all its children continues to have special significance today. By "all," we mean Anglo, Asian, Hispanic, Native American, African-American, the poor, the rich, and all other linguistic, ethnic, cultural, and socioeconomic groups in the United States.

Objective of the Book

We have written this book as a resource for both regular and special education teacher trainers, staff developers, consultants, and others engaged in the preparation of ancillary school personnel, such as school counselors, psychologists, and speech and language specialists. It is designed to familiarize educators with the major needs of the exceptional child with limited skills in English. We provide information on inclusion, model programs, curriculum, and strategies for better educating this unique population of students.

Organization and Flexibility of the Book

We organized the book to emphasize the interface between bilingual and special education. We carefully sequenced the chapters to familiarize you with key issues from the two areas and to demonstrate the creative convergence that can result when these two educational approaches are meaningfully integrated in an inclusive and collaborative environment. The major issues within the emerging field of bilingual special education have all been included in the text. We have tried to strike a balance between the theoretical and the practical dimensions of the material.

The book is written to promote maximum flexibility as well as breadth of coverage. While it is designed as a text for courses in special education, bilingual education, and bilingual special education, certain chapters can also be used as supplementary material for many other education courses. By using the reference list and appendices, you can achieve greater depth and breadth of treatment.

Features of the Third Edition

In response to comments from users of the first and second editions and from our reviewers, we have made some important changes and additions to the third edition of this text. First, we have completely reconstructed the conceptual framework and assumptions undergirding bilingual special education. We have also updated the material in keeping with the growing body of research in this area, the current state of "best" professional practice, and current legislation and regulatory requirements. Furthermore, we have added new material and current references to all the chapters. We have totally revised the chapters on language acquisition and assessment to reflect the current research in these areas. The revised chapter on

consultation greatly strengthens the text and helps situate it in the context of collaborative inclusion.

ACKNOWLEDGMENTS

We are greatly indebted to the many colleagues and individuals, as well as exceptional children, who have motivated and assisted us in numerous ways. One person who was very instrumental is Julia de Valenzuela, and we are most thankful for her contributions in conceptualizing and designing the third edition and in writing several of the major chapters. We would also like to acknowledge the fine assistance and excellent work of our contributing authors: Rudy Chavez, Roberto Torres, Rocky Hill, Joann Starks, James Yates, Alba Ortiz, Catherine Collier, John J. Hoover, Kathy Harris, and Jim Bransford. In addition we wish to thank Robert W. Ortiz, New Mexico State University; and Patricia J. Peterson, Northern Arizona University, who reviewed the text at various stages of its development. We extend our gratitude to Ann Davis, our administrative editor at Merrill/Prentice Hall, for her support and assistance. Many friends and colleagues assisted with typing, proofreading, and technical editing.

Finally, we wish to extend our sincere appreciation to our wives, Eleanor Baca and Cecilia Cervantes, as well as to our children, who provided constant and immeasurable encouragement and support while this text was in preparation.

Leonard M. Baca
Hermes T. Cervantes

CONTRIBUTORS

James Bransford
Director, Multicultural Education Center
College of Education
University of New Mexico
Albuquerque, New Mexico

Rudy Chavez
Associate Director
BUENO Center for Multicultural Education
University of Colorado, Boulder
Boulder, Colorado

Catherine Collier
Director of CrossCultural Developmental
  Education Services
Vancouver, Washington

J. S. de Valenzuela
Graduate Assistant
BUENO Center for Multicultural Education
University of Colorado, Boulder
Boulder, Colorado

Kathleen Harris
Professor, Education
Arizona State University West
Phoenix, Arizona

John J. Hoover
Director of Pathways Project
Boulder, Colorado

Alba Ortiz
Dean for Academic Affairs and Research
Ruben E. Hinojosa Regents Professor in
  Education
University of Texas, Austin
Austin, Texas

Joann Starks
Research Specialist
Southwest Educational Development
  Laboratory
Austin, Texas

Roberto Torres
Graduate Assistant
BUENO Center for Multicultural Education
University of Colorado, Boulder
Boulder, Colorado

James R. Yates
Chairman, Department of Educational
  Administration
University of Texas, Austin
Austin, Texas

The Bilingual
Special Education
Interface

CHAPTER 1

Background and Rationale for Bilingual Special Education

Leonard Baca
J. S. de Valenzuela

- Equal Educational Opportunity
- Right to an Appropriate Education
- Cultural Pluralism and Education
- Bilingual Education as a Worldwide Phenomenon
- Language Policy in the United States
- Incidence Figures on Bilingual Students
- Overrepresentation of Bilingual Students in Special Education
- Call for Bilingual Special Education
- Definition of Bilingual Special Education
- Summary

OBJECTIVES

To introduce the concept of equal educational opportunity

To present information on the right to an appropriate education

To discuss cultural pluralism as it relates to bilingual education

To review language policy in the United States

To present incidence figures on bilingual students

To propose a rationale for bilingual special education

Bilingual students, including those with disabilities, have finally established their right to be educated in their stronger or more proficient language. However, in practice, many culturally and linguistically diverse (CLD) students still do not receive the type and quality of education to which they are legally guaranteed. In the past, these students have been referred to as "triple threat students," because they are presumed to have three strikes against them before they even start school (Rueda & Chan, 1979). The first "strike" is their disability. The second is their limited English proficiency. The third is their lower socioeconomic status. While it is very true that all of these factors are associated with lowered academic achievement, as any beginning student in statistics knows, correlation does not prove causality. We need to rethink the idea that poverty and limited English proficiency *cause* academic difficulties and question why these factors are related. After all, when our schools teach these students in their native language, they build on their cultural and linguistic strengths and foster achievement. Building on strengths is compatible with sound educational practice (Krashen & Biber, 1988) and demonstrates why the strong belief that all children can learn is more beneficial than a deficit perspective.

A major impetus for this third edition of *The Bilingual Special Education Interface* is the need for a critical examination of commonly held assumptions about CLD students, both with and without disabilities, and current educational practices. We will examine how shifts in our own belief systems, as well as metatrends in general education, are influencing how we envision the future for all students. You will notice five major themes woven throughout this book: inclusion, collaboration, prereferral intervention, and new models for assessment and intervention. In the brief history of the field of bilingual special education, we have come to the conclusion that without concurrent change at all levels, in all areas, real systemic change will not occur. Special education, as is, simply provided in the student's native language, is not and will not provide students with the education they need to succeed in the 21st century.

During the past half century special education has developed into a strong and influential part of our overall public school system. Special education reached its peak with the passage in 1974 of PL 94-142, which is known as the Education for All Handicapped Children Act (Haring & McCormick, 1986). A review of recent national legislation and appropriations provides evidence that the education of students with disabilities continues to be a strong national priority today; in 1997 the United States Congress reauthorized the Individuals with Disabilities Education Act (PL 101-476). In fact, the U.S. Department of Education, Office of Special Education and Rehabilitative Services reports that the percentage of students in federally supported programs for disabilities has increased from 8.5% of the total student population in 1977 to 11.7% in 1992 (National Center for Educational Statistics, 1994a).

In contrast, bilingual education is not a new phenomenon; it is as old as education itself (Noboa, 1987). But the past 25 years have seen both a renewed interest in bilingual education in the United States as well as increasingly strong attacks on it as an effective and appropriate educational pedagogy. Congress passed the Bilingual Education Act (PL 90-247) in 1968. This law made it possible for local school districts to receive federal funding through a competitive grant process for the implementation of bilingual programs designed to meet the needs of students with limited English proficiency (LEP). Reauthorizations since that time have both expanded the population of eligible students and increased the emphasis on the development of proficiency in English (Weinberg & Weinberg, 1990). Additionally, since 1984, funds have been available for programs that use alternative instructional methods to traditional transitional bilingual programs, such as English language immersion and English as a Second Language instruction (ESL).

More recent developments in litigation and educational research dealing with exceptional children with limited proficiency in English suggest that educators must seriously address the issues related to designing and implementing bilingual special education programs. This book addresses the complex issues and challenges related to merging the currently decoupled and isolated programs of bilingual education, special education, and general education. The remainder of this chapter discusses the major issues related to the establishment of bilingual special education.

EQUAL EDUCATIONAL OPPORTUNITY

The development of bilingual special education can be viewed as an extension of the equal educational opportunity movement. Equal educational opportunity has a long and rich history that can be traced back to the founding of our nation. For example, the Declaration of Independence asserts that "all men are created equal." In addition, the Fourteenth Amendment to the Constitution ensures equal protection under the law. At one time Thomas Jefferson proposed a plan to promote equal educational opportunity. Steiner, Arnove, and McClellan (1980) state:

> Equalitarian rhetoric first came to be attached to formal education in the Revolutionary era when Thomas Jefferson, among others, proposed a national system of schooling that would provide scholarships for talented youngsters of modest means who might otherwise have little chance to achieve social prominence. Such a system, thought Jefferson, would bring a measure of equality of opportunity to a society where social station and access to education had so often depended solely on the accidents of birth.

The concept of equal educational opportunity has continued to evolve to the present day. Two factors have substantially influenced educational policy regarding equal educational opportunity. They are the *Brown v. Board of Education of Topeka* (1954) decision and the *Coleman Report*. In the *Brown v. Board of Education* decision, the U.S. Supreme Court ruled:

> . . . in these days it is doubtful that any child[7] may reasonably be expected to succeed in life if he is denied the opportunity of an education. Such an opportunity, where the state has undertaken to provide it is a right which must be made available to all on equal terms. (*Brown v. Board of Education*, 347 U.S. 483, 74 S.Ct. 686, 91 L.Ed. 873)[7]

The Court set a precedent by ruling that the segregation of Black and White children in state public schools on the basis of race denied Black children equal protection guaranteed by the Fourteenth Amendment (Jarolimek, 1981). In effect, the Court held that the doctrine of separate but equal education was inherently unequal. According to Jarolimek, for a period of 25 years this landmark decision was followed by one judicial decision after another extending the concept of equal educational opportunity.

The *Coleman Report,* entitled "Equality of Educational Opportunity," was commissioned by the U.S. Office of Education, as mandated by the 1964 Civil Rights Act. In defining equal educational opportunity, Coleman (1968) identifies these components:

1. Providing a free education up to a given level that constituted the principal entry point to the labor force.

2. Providing a common curriculum for all children, regardless of background.

3. Providing that children from diverse backgrounds attend the same school.

4. Providing equality within a given locality, since local taxes provided the source of support for schools.

This approach to equal educational opportunity stresses that all students be treated the same and places the responsibility for achieving equality upon the students. Another approach to equality emphasizes the school as the agent in providing what is fitting and appropriate for the student (Komisar & Coombs, 1974). According to Jarolimek (1981), the concept of individualized instruction, which has been an accepted part of educational thought, if not practice, for at least 50 years, is the embodiment of the "equality as fitting or appropriate" principle. Deciding what is fitting or appropriate for a given student or group of students is the responsibility of school personnel. However, what school officials think is the appropriate program for a child may not really be what the child needs at all.

Another approach, called the "equality of outcomes," protects students from placement in programs not suited for their needs (Sue & Padilla, 1986). This approach was mandated by law with the *Lau v. Nichols* unanimous Supreme Court decision of 1974, which ruled that equal treatment does not necessarily lead to equality of educational opportunities (Nieto, 1996). Jencks (1972) refers to this approach not as equal opportunity but as equal results. Nieto (1992) refers to this approach as equity, rather than equality, because she finds that this term "includes equal educational opportunities while at the same time demanding fairness and the real possibility of *equality of outcomes* for a broader range of students" (p. 2). She also states that multicultural education, recognizing the validity of the experiences, skills, and talents that all students bring to school, is fundamental to educational equity. Therefore, this equality/equity issue becomes the responsibility of the school rather than that of the student. It also allows the school to use a variety of teaching methods and approaches to ensure that the student learns the required material.

Nieto (1992) lists three educational implications of educational equity—the recognition

that equality of opportunities is not the same as equality of results:

1. Acknowledging the differences that children bring to school.
2. Admitting the possibility that such differences may influence how students learn.
3. Accepting differences also means making provisions for them. (p. 110)

The establishment of bilingual special education programs to meet the needs of exceptional children of limited English proficiency is an extension of this equal educational opportunity and equal educational benefits movement. But, as with all social-movement legislation, it is an example of *law* before *consciousness*. In other words, it is advocates for certain social issues—in this case, bilingual special education—using the country's legal system and popular support for equality and equity to legislate rights and services for a previously undefined, albeit marginal, group of students. We are now in the uncomfortable period between mandated social change and the time when girls playing on Little League teams or kids being taught in their native language is standard operating procedure. We are in that period when laws have changed, but the structures, procedures, and attitudes have not yet followed suit. The arduous task of operationalizing the bilingual special education mandate falls to all in the theoretical, preservice and applied fields.

RIGHT TO AN APPROPRIATE EDUCATION

Only within the last 25 years has the right of children with disabilities to an education appropriate to their needs been recognized and at least tacitly accepted by our society (Heward & Orlansky, 1986). Former U.S. Commissioner of Education Sidney Marland (1971) addressed this issue at the international convention of the Council for Exceptional Children:

The right of a handicapped child to the special education he needs is as basic to him as the right of any other young citizen to an appropriate education in the public schools. It is unjust for our society to provide handicapped children with anything less than a full and equal educational opportunity they need to reach their maximum potential and attain rewarding, satisfying lives.

Providing this appropriate education in a language that is intelligible to the student would appear to be a basic prerequisite. It should indeed be an integral part of what could be considered "appropriate education." However, it required the ruling of the United States Supreme Court, in the 1974 *Lau v. Nichols* case, to recognize language rights as a civil right and the relationship of equal educational opportunities to the language of education (Carrasquillo, 1991; Garcia, 1991; Nieto, 1996). Fifteen years ago it would have been impossible to find a school district that provided a bilingual special education program. Today, however, this type of program can be found in most major school districts across the country.

The right to an appropriate education should be viewed as an extension of a more basic concept and fundamental right referred to by the courts as the "right to education." The development of the right-to-education policy has its roots in the Fourteenth Amendment to the U.S. Constitution, which provides that no state may deny to any person within its jurisdiction the equal protection of the law. According to Hockenberry (1979), case law has advanced a series of interpretations of the Fourteenth Amendment preventing government from denying governmental benefits to people because of their unalterable characteristics, that is, because of age, sex, race, or disability. The *Brown v. Board of Education* case of 1954 established an important precedent for subsequent right-to-education cases for all children, including those with disabilities.

If a state agrees to provide a free public education for all school-aged children, it cannot exclude those with disabilities. When such exclusion has been found, court rulings have declared that equal protection of the law was denied to the disabled on the basis of their unalterable trait—their disability (Turnbull & Turnbull, 1978).

The most significant cases dealing with a right to an education are the *Pennsylvania Association for Retarded Children (PARC) v. Pennsylvania* (1971) and *Mills v. Board of Education of D.C.* (1972). Both cases involved equal protection arguments. The plaintiff class in the *PARC* case consisted of all school-age, mentally retarded children excluded from the public schools. The plaintiff class in the *Mills* case consisted of all school-age children with any form of disability who were excluded from public education. In both cases the court ruled in favor of the plaintiffs and mandated that a free public program of education appropriate to the child's capacity be provided. It is interesting to note the court's use of the word *appropriate*. According to Hockenberry (1979), subsequent cases involving the right to education for children with disabilities have closely followed the arguments made in the *PARC* and *Mills* cases, with similar decisions and relief granted by the courts. In addition to court cases, right-to-education policy has been further strengthened by the Rehabilitation Act of 1973. Section 504 of this act is particularly important and includes the following stipulations:

- The child must be furnished an individualized education program (IEP) (Sec. 121a.342).
- The child is entitled to a due process hearing if educational appropriateness is in doubt (Sec. 121a.506).
- The parents (or guardians) are entitled to be included in the development of the IEP (Sec. 121a.344).
- The student is entitled to appropriately and adequately trained teachers (Sec. 121a.12).

- The child has the right of access to school records (Sec 121a.562).
- The student's representatives (parents or others) are entitled to participate in and be given notice of school actions affecting special education programs and the student's own education (Sec. 121a.345).

Using this detailed procedural definition of "appropriate education," one could argue that a special bilingual program of instruction could easily be called for under certain circumstances. A series of cases in New York has raised this very issue. The most significant of these cases was *Dyrcia S. et al. v. Board of Education of New York* (1979). This case was filed on October 2, 1979, on behalf of LEP Puerto Rican and other Hispanic LEP children with disabilities residing in New York City who require bilingual special education programs. On December 14, 1979, a judgment was issued calling for the provision of appropriate bilingual programs for all children with both high- and low-incidence disabilities. Clearly, the issue of the right to an appropriate education is at the heart of any discussion of bilingual special education.

CULTURAL PLURALISM AND EDUCATION

Bilingual special education, as has been pointed out thus far, is closely related to equal educational opportunity and the right to an appropriate education. It is also closely related to cultural pluralism. The National Coalition for Cultural Pluralism (1973) has defined pluralism as:

A state of equal co-existence in a mutually supportive relationship within the boundaries or framework of one nation of people of diverse cultures with significantly different patterns of belief, behavior, color and in many cases with different languages.

Contemporary American society is made up of people from many different cultural backgrounds. Any effective educational program in today's schools should reflect this cultural pluralism (Garcia, 1982). As Hunter (1974) has stated:

It is therefore apparent, if education in the United States is to meet the needs of its peoples, then it must have a life blood of multicultural content in order to be sociologically relevant, philosophically germane, and pedagogically apropos.

Cultural pluralism is not a concept that enjoyed strong support in the early years of the United States. On the contrary, there was strong support for cultural assimilation. This approach has come to be known as the "melting pot" theory. According to the melting pot theory, individuals of all nations should be melted down into one common new "race" of Americans. In other words, all immigrants to this country were expected to relinquish their native language and culture and adopt the new American way of life. This attempt to Americanize all immigrants was strongly reinforced by nationalistic feelings heightened during World War I. At that time, there was concern that some immigrants would support their native countries against the United States. According to Kopan (1974), World War I led to a crash program of Americanization in schools, factories, and churches, much like that subsequent to the Civil War. The purpose of the Americanization program was to assert Nordic superiority by encouraging immigrants to abandon their native cultures and become "American." During this time other languages were excluded from the curriculum. This forced Americanization created an atmosphere of suspicion and mistrust (xenophobia) that has never been completely eliminated.

Israel Zangwill (1909) first used the term *melting pot* as the title of a play that became an instant success on Broadway in 1908. The following excerpt from the play illustrates the thinking upon which the melting pot theory is based.

America is God's Crucible. The great Melting Pot where all the races of Europe are melting and reforming! Here you stand, good folk, think I, when I see them at Ellis Island, here you stand in your fifty groups with your fifty language histories, and your fifty hatreds and rivalries, but you won't be long like that, brothers, for these are the fires of God. A fig for your feuds and vendettas! Germans and Frenchmen, Irishmen and Englishmen, Jews and Russians—into the Crucible with you all! God is making the American . . . . The real American has not yet arrived. He is only in the Crucible, I tell you—he will be the fusion of all races, the coming superman.

Actually the "real American," the "coming superman," has never arrived. To a large extent, the melting pot theory has failed to work. The existence of a myriad of distinct racial and ethnic subgroups within the United States is a confirmation of this failure. Despite the fact that the melting pot approach has failed in many ways, it has nonetheless had a strong influence on American educators. Kobrick (1972) sums it up as follows:

America's intolerance of diversity is reflected in an ethnocentric educational system to "Americanize foreigners or those who are seen as culturally different." America is the great melting pot, and, as one writer recently stated it, "If you don't want to melt, you had better get out of the pot." The ill-disguised contempt for a child's language is part of a broader distaste for the child himself and the culture he represents. Children who are culturally different are said to be culturally "deprived." Their language and culture are seen as "disadvantages." The children must be "remodeled" if they are to succeed in school.

This monocultural and ethnocentric approach to education has been gradually changing toward a pluralistic multicultural model. According to Carpenter (1974), in 1909 an educator wrote that a major task of education in American cities was to "break up these immigrant groups or settlements, to assimilate and amalgamate these people as part of our American race, and to implant in their children, so far as can be done, the Anglo Saxon conception of righteousness, law and order, and popular government . . . ." However, 60 years later the Congress of the United States passed the Ethnic Heritage Studies Act, giving official "recognition to the heterogeneous composition of the nation and the fact that in a multiethnic society, a greater understanding of the contributions of one's own heritage and those of one's fellow citizens can contribute to a more harmonious, patriotic, and committed populace. . . ."

This change in thinking in favor of cultural pluralism has been long overdue. Ethnic and cultural diversity are finally beginning to be viewed as positive aspects of American society. According to Trueba, Guthrie, and Hu-Pei-Au (1981), cultural pluralism is gaining momentum among educators and social scientists. To visualize this shift in perspective, the analogy of a salad bowl has been suggested to represent the contributions of each ethnic group to a multicultural society while still retaining its unique identity (Baruth & Manning, 1992; Garcia, 1991). In describing this analogy, Garcia states that "each ingredient adds to the overall taste and flavor of the salad, yet each retains its individual identity" (p. 26). Garcia also proposes the metaphor of a symphony, with each instrument belonging to a group, which is interdependent with all other groups, and adds to the overall musical harmony, to describe his vision of a pluralistic society. Carlos Cortez (1986) has suggested that the metaphor of a mosaic be used instead of the melting pot metaphor. He refers to it as a "constantly-shifting mosaic in which the multi-hued pieces do not always fit together perfectly, as if an on-going historical earthquake has been challenging the society to attempt to resolve the unresolvable" (p. 6). And unresolvable it seems to be if we allow ourselves to repeat the history of past generations and failed social innovations without learning from their mistakes.

When translated into the schools, cultural pluralism becomes multicultural education. Multicultural education teaches children to recognize and appreciate the contributions of all cultural groups to the development of this nation. However, Nieto (1996) states that it is not sufficient to "sensitize" children to other cultures "without tackling the central but far more difficult issues of stratification, empowerment, and inequity" (p. 1). Baruth and Manning (1992) state that the goals of multicultural education are: (1) to promote changes in the total educational environment, such that all groups experience equitable educational experiences and that respect for all groups is fostered; and (2) to develop the cross-cultural competence needed to function successfully within one's own culture, as well as in the mainstream American and other ethnic cultures. Baruth and Manning also identified seven assumptions underlying their philosophical approach to multicultural education:

1. Cultural diversity is a positive, enriching element in a society because it provides individuals with increased opportunities to experience other cultures and thus to become more fulfilled as human beings.

2. Multicultural education is for all students.

3. Teaching is a cross-cultural encounter.

4. Multicultural education should permeate the total school curriculum rather that taking a "one-course" approach or a teaching unit approach.

5. The educational system has not served all students equally well.

6. Schools will continue to experience and reflect increasing cultural diversity due to influxes of immigrants and refugees and due to the high birthrates of some culturally-diverse groups.

7. It is the responsibility of elementary and secondary schools to implement appropriate multicultural education programs that contribute to better understandings of cultural differences, show the dangers of stereotyping, and reduce racism, sexism, and classism.

In their attempt to promote multicultural education, Stone and De Nevi (1971) stressed these points:

1. We possess in America diverse and linguistic heritages, a tremendous untapped natural resource which is worth preserving and extending. Diversity of culture and language enriches all of us.

2. We ought to consciously encourage bilingualism in our schools. Teachers must become adept at interweaving non-Anglo contributions and material into the curriculum, using such material to enrich all students.

3. Non-White literature, music, art, dance, sports, and games should become part of the curriculum.

4. Non-White teachers must be sought, recruited, trained, retrained, and supported in opportunities to work with non-Anglo pupils.

5. School information (and school meetings) intended for parents of minority group children should be made available in all appropriate languages. (pp. 150–151)

Support for cultural pluralism and multicultural education continues to grow. Not only minority group members advocate a multicultural approach to education; many supporters of this concept are members of the dominant society. Even national educational associations have adopted strong statements in support of multicultural education. However, one difficulty in the implementation of multicultural education has been the lack of appropriate training for teachers. It is interesting to note the National Council for the Accreditation of Teacher Educators (NCATE) established a special standard in 1980, requiring accredited teacher training institutions to include training in multicultural education for all prospective teachers.

One of the most eloquent statements in support of multicultural education was issued by the American Association of Colleges for Teacher Education (AACTE) in 1973. This statement, entitled *No One Model American,* serves as a guide for addressing the issue of multicultural education. In part, it reads;

> Multicultural education is education which values cultural pluralism. Multicultural education rejects the view that schools should seek to melt away cultural differences or the view that schools should merely tolerate cultural pluralism. Instead, multicultural education affirms that schools should be oriented toward the cultural enrichment of all children and youth through programs rooted to the preservation and extension of cultural diversity as a fact of life in American society, and it affirms that this cultural diversity is a valuable resource that should be preserved and extended. It affirms that major education institutions should strive to preserve and enhance cultural pluralism. (p. 264)

Other observations, explicit in the AACTE statement and crucial to an understanding of multicultural education, are summarized here:

> Cultural pluralism does not acknowledge the concept of a model American. Rather, it is a movement and an idea that endorses the health of the entire society, based on the strengths of its unique parts. Cultural pluralism rejects assimilation and separation. No single group lives in isolation. Education, if it is to be meaningful to the ideals of the multicultural movement, must include: (1) the teaching of diverse cultural values, (2) the incorporation of ethnic cultures into the mainstream of economic and political life, and (3) the exploration of alternative lifestyles. A commitment to multiculturalism must be established at all levels of educa-

tion in order for the concept to become a social reality. This is especially true for teacher education. Above all, multicultural education acknowledges the right of different cultures to exist.

As can be seen from the preceding remarks, multicultural education is not the addition of an instructional unit or a course on multiculturalism. Rather, it is a philosophical orientation or attitude that permeates the entire curriculum. Multicultural education is not limited to elementary or regular education but applies to all educational programs. Thus, multicultural education should be a part of special education. The Council for Exceptional Children (CEC) has promoted this position through topical conferences sponsored by The Division for Culturally and Linguistically Diverse Exceptional Learners (DDEL). Additionally, the 1996 CEC convention in Orlando, Florida featured multicultural education as a major focus. The establishment of bilingual special education programs may be viewed as part of a larger movement attempting to infuse multiculturalism into the schools.

BILINGUAL EDUCATION AS A WORLDWIDE PHENOMENON

The concept of bilingual education requires a detailed explanation, which will be provided in the following chapter. At this point, however, we would like to present a broad and generally accepted definition that was developed by Parker (1978): "Bilingual education refers to some configuration of instruction through the medium of two languages." In the U.S., this has meant teaching skills in English as well as another language and teaching content through the medium of both languages. Attempts to put this definition into practice have resulted in a wide variety of programs.

Almost all countries in the world have bilingual populations. Many of these countries have bilingual education programs (Noboa, 1987).

Although many individuals assume that the challenge of educating a large multilingual population is greater in the United States than in other areas of the world, this is not the case. In fact, of the 32 countries participating in an international reading achievement study, all of the following reported a larger percentage of students at ages 9 and 14 who speak a different language at home than at school than in the United States: Belgium, Canada, Italy, Netherlands, New Zealand, Singapore, Spain, Sweden, Switzerland, Trinidad/Tobago, West Germany, and Venezuela (National Center for Educational Statistics, 1994a). Approaches to bilingual education throughout the world show much diversity. Some countries have mandatory bilingual policies while others do not. Because bilingual education may be found in most countries, it is considered a universal phenomenon.

Whether or not a country provides bilingual education for its students is not closely linked with official language status. Some countries are multilingual. For example, Singapore and Switzerland have four official languages. Many other countries are legally designated as bilingual. Among these are Afghanistan, Belgium, Canada, Finland, India, Ireland, and South Africa. Most countries that have only one official language still have bilingual schooling. Such is the case in France, Denmark, Norway, West Germany, Greece, Jordan, Mainland China, the Philippines, Egypt, Mexico, and Guatemala (Fishman, 1976). From these facts we can conclude that bilingual education is considered appropriate education on an international level. Therefore, the establishment of bilingual special education is in keeping with this worldwide tradition of bilingual education.

LANGUAGE POLICY IN THE UNITED STATES

Because the issue of language policy is usually raised in any discussion involving bilingualism, it seems appropriate to discuss briefly the history and status of language policy in the United States.

This nation is made up of more than 230 million people who have come from or have ancestral ties to hundreds of different countries where a vast number of different languages were spoken. Since the founding of this country, multiple languages have been used in both the public and the private sectors. According to Castellanos (1985), "the immigration traffic was so diverse that eighteen different languages were being spoken by people of twenty different nationalities in New Amsterdam (Manhattan Island) in 1664 when it was captured from the Dutch by the English." Uniting a large number of immigrants through the use of a common language was a critical concern for America in 1776. Interestingly enough, however, the nation chose not to initiate language planning. According to Heath (1977), many language policies were proposed in those early days but none was accepted. Instead of a mandatory national language policy being established, a permissive language policy evolved.

From the outset, bilingual education programs were implemented at the local level in several different regions of the country. According to Andersson and Boyer (1970):

> Before 1800 German schools flourished throughout the country. Also this period saw the beginning of many French schools in New England and many Scandinavian and some Dutch schools in the Midwest. Many of these schools were not actually bilingual in their curricula; they were non-English schools where English was taught as a subject.

According to Zirkel (1978), an estimated 1 million students were in bilingual public school programs during the 19th century. This does not include the thousands of students who were in private schools. For example, there were many French-English parochial school programs in Louisiana and Spanish-English parochial school programs in New Mexico.

No official language policy existed at the federal level during the early history of the country. At the state level, most of the early school laws and administrative policies were silently permissive as to the languages of instruction. According to Zirkel (1978):

> Some states specifically authorized using a language other than English as a medium of instruction. For example, a Pennsylvania statute passed in 1837 and an Ohio statute passed in 1839 specifically permitted German-English public schools. Similarly, the California and New Mexico constitutions were drafted in the context of linguistic equality between Spanish and English.

By not adopting an official language policy, the United States chose a permissive language policy (Dozier, 1956). According to Heath (1977), during this early period language was viewed as a social matter, not a political one. It was felt that legislation of social and cultural habits would restrict the guaranteed basic freedoms.

World War I ushered in a new era of language policy in the United States. During this period bilingual instruction was prohibited in most states as a result of a national paranoia that set in with the outbreak of the war. During this time everything foreign became suspect. Immigrant groups who were in any way associated historically with the enemy were under scrutiny regarding their loyalty. This national fear continued into World War II and ultimately led to the internment of thousands of Japanese-Americans in concentration camps. The "English-only era" continued until the mid-1960s. The passage of Title VII of the Elementary and Secondary Education Act of 1968, known as the Bilingual Education Act, finally ended this era and initiated a new period of a permissive bilingual policy. This policy has been supported by a number of court decisions, which are discussed in Chapter 4.

This brief era of support for bilingual education and accommodation for the needs of language minority communities and individuals began to wane in the 1980s. According to Crawford (1992), "Bilingual education had become a lightning rod for tensions about demographic and cultural change, increased immigration from the Third World, reforms in civil rights, and the political empowerment of minorities" (p. 4). In 1981, Senator S. I. Hayakawa introduced a constitutional amendment to make English the "official" language of the United States. Although this "English Language Amendment" never reached the floor of the Senate, it can be seen as the beginning of the English-Only movement. In 1983, the now-retired senator founded a national organization known as U.S. English, which has been diligently lobbying to make English the official language at both the national and state level. In response to a ground swell of popular support, in 1987 alone, 37 states considered making English the official state language (Crawford) and by 1995, 22 states had adopted such statutes or constitutional amendments (Starrick, 1995).

Historical analysis reveals that every large wave of immigration into this country evokes a reaction that, like the English-Only movement, tries to limit language freedom in this country. During the 1990s, such a backlash against immigrants influenced other policies at the state level. In addition to efforts begun in the 1980s to establish English as the official language, other legal measures affecting immigration were considered. In 1994, California passed Proposition 187, which, in addition to other restrictive measures, barred the children of undocumented workers from attending public schools. The issues surrounding immigration even took a prominent position in the 1996 presidential race.

Regardless of periodic shifts in public sentiment regarding immigration and the education of language minority children, there is a strong and consistent bilingual tradition in this country that began long before the first European settlers arrived on this continent and continues to this day. The designation of English as the official language of any state or the nation as a whole has and will have little real effect on educational policies, because students have a legal right to equal educational opportunity, which includes language appropriate services. The development of bilingual special education programs is certainly compatible with best practices in education and our strong legal commitment to human civil rights.

INCIDENCE FIGURES ON BILINGUAL STUDENTS

Available data sources show that the population of limited English proficiency (LEP) students continues to grow at a brisk pace. Results of the 1990 census (National Center for Educational Statistics, 1994a) indicated that 31.8 million people (14% of the population) in the United States speak a language other than English at home. These figures represent an increase from 23.1 million people (11% of the population) reported in 1980 (National Center for Educational Statistics). Perhaps the best example of this increase comes from California, where the number of LEP students has increased dramatically in the past few years. According to the California Department of Education, the number of LEP students in that state rose from 487,800 in 1984 to 1,263,000 in 1995. Based on the 1990 census, there are an estimated 10 million school-age language minority children in the United States (Waggoner, 1994).

According to the U.S. Department of Commerce (U.S. Bureau of the Census, 1994), this bilingual population is distributed throughout the United States, with heavier concentrations in the Southwest and Northwest and with slightly more than half of all speakers of a language other than English residing in California (8,600,000), Texas (4,000,000), and New York (3,900,000). Table 1–1 provides the breakdown of estimated population, aged 5–17, by language background and state. However, Waggoner (1995) reported that, as of 1990, 31 states had at least 25,000 children and youth who speak a language other than English at home. Statistics such as this clearly indicate that the needs of students with linguistically diverse backgrounds must be addressed across the United States.

We have presented statistics from the U.S. Department of Commerce, rather than from the U.S. Department of Education. We do so because the Department of Education provides much lower estimates of LEP students because of using much more stringent criteria than does the Census Bureau, such as only counting students who score below the 19th percentile in overall achievement (Crawford, 1987). Waggoner, as cited in Crawford, believes that the Department of Education figures are a significant underestimate of the actual LEP population. In addition, we are interested in knowing how many students come from a diverse language background, rather than the number classified as limited in English language proficiency, since the issues in assessment and intervention do not apply only to LEP students, but rather to all learners who come from a bilingual background. A passing score on an oral language proficiency test simply does not remove the need for consideration of that student's sociolinguistic background when academic difficulties arise. Indeed, studies suggest that scores on oral proficiency tests are not indicative of students' abilities to understand and use English in academic contexts (Cummins, 1984).

Considering the overall culturally learning disabled (CLD) population in the United States, a critical question for bilingual special educators is: How many of these students are also disabled? If the U.S. Office of Special Education figure of 12% is combined with the estimated 9,985,000 language minority students aged 5–17 from the 1990 census, the result indicates that 1,198,200 children are both linguistically diverse and disabled. This figure constitutes a substantial population who could benefit from bilingual special education services.

Table 1–1
Breakdown of Population Aged 5–17 by Language Background and State

State	Total	Eng. only	Spanish	All Other
Total	44,993,000	35,083,000	5,884,000	4,027,000
Alabama	771,000	715,000	27,000	28,000
Alaska	116,000	93,000	4,000	20,000
Arizona	682,000	430,000	179,000	73,000
Arkansas	452,000	417,000	19,000	15,000
California	5,333,000	2,794,000	1,742,000	797,000
Colorado	605,000	487,000	79,000	38,000
Connecticut	522,000	401,000	57,000	65,000
Delaware	112,000	98,000	6,000	7,000
District of Columbia	79,000	65,000	9,000	6,000
Florida	2,014,000	1,505,000	351,000	158,000
Georgia	1,228,000	1,109,000	56,000	63,000
Hawaii	197,000	125,000	5,000	67,000
Idaho	223,000	194,000	19,000	10,000
Illinois	2,085,000	1,641,000	258,000	187,000
Indiana	1,057,000	951,000	48,000	59,000
Iowa	519,000	476,000	20,000	23,000
Kansas	767,000	414,000	29,000	24,000
Kentucky	697,000	650,000	21,000	26,000
Louisiana	888,000	737,000	30,000	121,000
Maine	225,000	192,000	3,000	29,000
Maryland	806,000	679,000	46,000	81,000
Massachusetts	937,000	715,000	81,000	141,000
Michigan	1,754,000	1,549,000	73,000	132,000
North Carolina	1,142,000	1,033,000	56,000	53,000
North Dakota	127,000	113,000	3,000	11,000
Ohio	2,008,000	1,803,000	78,000	127,000
Oklahoma	612,000	545,000	33,000	34,000
Oregon	517,000	447,000	35,000	36,000
Pennsylvania	1,981,000	1,731,000	93,000	157,000
Rhode Island	159,000	118,000	12,000	29,000
South Carolina	660,000	606,000	26,000	28,000

continued

Table 1–1 *(cont.)*
Breakdown of Population Aged 5–17 by Language Background and State

State	Total	Eng. only	Spanish	All Other
Total	44,993,000	35,083,000	5,884,000	4,027,000
South Dakota	144,000	125,000	3,000	15,000
Tennessee	874,000	810,000	31,000	33,000
Texas	3,428,000	2,074,000	1,190,000	163,000
Utah	455,000	385,000	33,000	38,000
Vermont	100,000	91,000	1,000	8,000
Virginia	1,055,000	913,000	56,000	85,000
Washington	884,000	740,000	61,000	83,000
West Virginia	336,000	314,000	9,000	13,000
Wisconsin	923,000	820,000	43,000	60,000
Wyoming	100,000	88,000	7,000	4,000

Note. From *Needs and Numbers*, 4 (4), by U.S. Bureau of the Census (1994, July), Washington DC: U.S. Government Printing Office.

Although children in the public schools of our country represent diverse language backgrounds, the largest group is composed of native Spanish speakers. At present this population comprises approximately 75% of the children of limited English proficiency (Special Issues Analysis Center, 1995). Additionally, Hispanic students, Spanish-speaking or otherwise, increased from 9.9% of the public school student population in 1986 to 12.3% in 1992 (National Center for Educational Statistics, 1994b). The data in Table 1–2 list the states with Hispanic populations of at least 5% in 1992 and the increase from 1986.

Table 1–3 shows that all ethnic minority groups have steadily increased as a percentage of the total student population, except for African-American students, who have shown a small decline in enrollment over the past 20 years (National Center for Educational Statistics, 1994a). Table 1–4 shows the top ten languages represented in the California public

school population, as of Spring, 1995 (California Department of Education).

OVERREPRESENTATION OF BILINGUAL STUDENTS IN SPECIAL EDUCATION

Even a cursory review of the literature of the past 30 years indicates that bilingual children have not had a positive experience with special education. It has been well established that bilingual children and minority children in general have historically been misplaced and thus overrepresented in special education programs (Bernstein, 1989; Beaumont & Langdon, 1992; Figueroa, Fradd & Correa, 1989; Maldonado-Colón, 1983; Ortiz & Yates, 1984). Mercer (1973) reported that Mexican-American children were placed into classes for the mentally retarded at a rate that was much larger than would have been expected. According to this classic study, Mexican-Americans were 10 times as likely to be placed

Table 1–2
States with Hispanic Population of at Least 5% in 1992

State	Percentage of Student Population (Hispanic)— Fall, 1986	Percentage of Student Population (Hispanic)— Fall, 1992
Arizona	26.4	26.9
California	27.5	36.1
Colorado	13.7	16.8
Connecticut	8.9	10.7
District of Columbia	3.9	5.6
Florida	9.5	13.4
Hawaii	2.2	5.2
Illinois	9.2	10.7
Kansas	4.4	5.0
Massachusetts	6.0	8.5
Nevada	7.5	13.1
New Jersey	10.7	12.6
New Mexico	45.1	45.8
New York	12.3	16.1
Oregon	3.9	5.3
Rhode Island	3.7	8.0
Texas	32.5	34.9
Washington	3.8	6.4
Wyoming	5.9	6.1

Note. From *Digest of Educational Statistics,* by National Center for Educational Statistics, 1994, Washington, DC: Office of Educational Research and Improvement, U.S. Department of Education.

in special education as were their White counterparts. In the *Journal of Mexican American Studies,* Chandler and Plakos (1971) reported that they found that Mexican-American students are placed in classes for the educable mentally retarded at rates two to three times higher than their White peers. According to Garcia and Yates (1986), "eighty percent of Hispanic handicapped students are in LD and speech programs, with three times as many students in LD as might be expected from their representation in the school environment" (p. 126).

Although overrepresentation continues to be an issue, in some school districts, underrepresentation is also problematic. Ortiz and Yates (1983) found that Hispanic students in Texas were underrepresented in all special education categories except learning disabilities. In that category, Hispanic students were significantly overidentified.

An analysis of the 1994 draft of the 1992 elementary and secondary school civil rights compliance report indicates that previously reported patterns of both over- and underrepresentation are continuing (U.S. Department of

toward the goal of a more concerted effort on behalf of those students who are having a tough time in school. The course of the development of a professional discipline does not generally lead to a broadening of perspective, nor toward cooperative and collaborative ventures with other professionals. But special educators are being pushed by legislation, intellectual fashion, perhaps "the times," and most certainly the realities experienced by teachers, students, and families to change the way we do business. At a very fundamental level, special educators are being asked to change the way we think about disabilities, students, appropriate education, and our role in the schools.

Bilingual special education asks us to stretch yet further to accommodate, not by exclusion but by inclusion, another given difference in the general population of students. In the traditional special education model, a "program" would have been created if enough pressure and circumstances came together. That program would then be de-coupled from the regular education program and in many cases physically decoupled as well, by being housed in the temporary buildings out back. The professional special education staff, almost exclusively nonbilingual, would then have exclusive responsibility for programming. This old model no longer fits the needs of our students.

The inclusion/cooperative model (post PL 94-142 and critiques of implementation) potentially lends itself to a greater sensitivity and accommodation of differences, such as languages, cultures, and abilities, within a myriad of cooperative and collaborative systems between regular and special education. These systems should be more supportive of thoughtful and coordinated acculturation experiences for the non-English speaking and nondominant culture students and should include a consciousness about kids which encompasses language and culture as part of a person to be honored and accommodated, given the wishes of the student and family and the realities of the adopted culture.

☙ DISCUSSION QUESTIONS

1. Based on legislative mandates and court rulings, discuss the meaning and implications of equal educational opportunity. What is the underlying rationale for equal education?
2. What factors contribute to the right for an appropriate education?
3. Upon what concepts is the notion of cultural pluralism based?
4. Numerous factors contributed to a tradition of bilingual education in the United States. Identify the historical trends and discuss their implications in terms of the statistics presented in Tables 1–1 through 1–4.
5. The educational needs of LEP and LEP exceptional children have increased with the population. Discuss the projections and their implications for the classroom teacher and school districts.
6. The emphasis on bilingual education during the latter part of the 20th century has been an outgrowth of legislation during the past 50 years. Discuss the development, intent, and application of legislation over this period.
7. The purpose of multicultural education is implicit in the AACTE statement on p. 11. Discuss the rationale for the position taken.

☙ REFERENCES

American Association of Colleges for Teacher Education (1973). No one model American. *American Journal of Teacher Education, 24,* 264.

Andersson, T., & Boyer, M. (1970). *Bilingual schooling in the United States.* Austin, TX: Southwest Educational Development Laboratory.

Baruth, L. G., & Manning, M. L. (1992). *Multicultural education of children and adolescents.* Needham Heights, MA: Allyn and Bacon.

Beaumont, C., & Langdon, H. W. (1992). Speech-language services for Hispanics with communication disorders: A framework. In H. W. Langdon & L. L. Cheng (Eds.), *Hispanic children and adults with communication disorders* (pp. 1–19). Gaithersburg, MD: Aspen.

Bernal, E. (1974). A dialogue on cultural implications for learning. *Exceptional Children, 40,* 552.

Bernstein, D. K. (1989). Assessing children with limited English proficiency: Current perspectives. *Topics in Language Disorders, 9*(3), 15–20.

Brown v. Board of Education of Topeka, 347 U.S. 483, 74 S.Ct. 686, 91 L.Ed. 873 (1954).

California Department of Education (1995). *Languages from around the world: 1995.* Sacramento, CA: California Department of Education, Educational Demographics Unit.

Carpenter, J. (1974). Educating for a new pluralism. In J. Herman (Ed.), *The scholar and group identity.* New York: Institute on Pluralism and Group Identity.

Carrasquillo, A. L. (1991). *Hispanic children and youth in the United States: A resource guide.* New York: Garland Publishing.

Castellanos, D. (1985). *The best of two worlds: Bilingual-bicultural education in the U.S.* Trenton, NJ: New Jersey State Department of Education.

Chandler, J. T., & Plakos, J. (1971). An investigation of Spanish speaking pupils placed in classes for the educable mentally retarded. *Journal of Mexican American Studies, 1,* 58.

Coleman, J. S. (1968). The concept of equality of educational opportunity. *Harvard Educational Review, 38,* 1.

Cortez, C. (1986). The education of language minority students: A contextual interaction model. In *Beyond language: Social and cultural factors in schooling language minority students* (pp. 30–33). Los Angeles: Evaluation, Dissemination and Assessment Center, California State University.

Crawford, J. (1987, April 1). Bilingual education: Language, learning and politics. *Education Week, 6* (27), 19–49.

Crawford, J. (1992). Editor's introduction. In C. Crawford (Ed.), *Language loyalties: A source book on the official English controversy* (pp. 1–8). Chicago: The University of Chicago Press.

Cummins, J. (1984). *Bilingualism and special education: Issues in assessment and pedagogy.* Clevedon, England: Multilingual Matters.

De Leon, J. (1986). An investigation into the development and validation of an assessment procedure for identifying language disorders in Spanish/English bilingual children. *Monograph of the BUENO Center for Multicultural Education, 7*(2), 93–108.

Dozier, E. (1956). Two examples of linguistic acculturation: The Yaqui of Sonora and the Tewa of New Mexico. *Language, 32*(1), 146.

Dyrcia S. et al. v. Board of Education of New York, 79 C. 2562 (E.D.N.Y. 1979).

Figueroa, R. A. (1989). Psychological testing of linguistic-minority students: Knowledge gaps and regulations. *Exceptional Children, 56,* 145–152.

Figueroa, R., Fradd, S. H., & Correa, V. I. (1989). Bilingual special education and this issue. *Exceptional Children, 56,* 174–178.

Finn, J. D. (1982). Patterns in special education placement as revealed by the OCR surveys. In K. A. Heller, W. H. Holzman, & S. Messick (Eds.), *Placing children in special education: A strategy for equity* (pp. 322–381). Washington, DC: National Academy Press.

Fishman, J. A. (1971). Testing special groups: The culturally disadvantaged. In L. C. Delighton (Ed.), *The encyclopedia of education* (Vol. 9). New York: Macmillan.

Fishman, J. A. (1976). *Bilingual education: An international sociological perspective.* Rowley, MA: Newbury House.

Flanigan, P. J., & Schwarz, R. H. (1971). Evaluation of examiner bias in intelligence testing. *American Journal of Mental Deficiency, 56,* 252.

Garcia, R. (1982). *Teaching in a pluralistic society: Concepts, models, strategies.* New York: Harper & Row.

Garcia, R. L. (1991). *Teaching in a pluralistic society: Concepts, models, strategies.* New York: Harper-Collins.

Garcia, S. B., & Yates, J. R. (1986). Policy issues associated with serving bilingual exceptional children. *Reading, Writing, and Learning Disabilities, 2,* 123–137.

Haring, N. G., & McCormick, L. (1986). *Exceptional children and youth: An introduction to special education.* Upper Saddle River, NJ: Merrill/Prentice Hall.

Harry, B. (1994). *The disproportionate representation of minority students in special education: Theories and recommendations.* Alexandria, VA: National Association of State Directors of Special Education.

Heath, S. (1977). Viewpoint: Social history. In *Bilingual education: Current perspectives* (Vol. 2). Arlington, VA: Center for Applied Linguistics.

Heward, W. L., & Orlansky, M. D. (1986). *Exceptional children: An introductory survey of special education*. Upper Saddle River, NJ: Merrill/Prentice Hall.

Hockenberry, C. (1979). *Policy issues and implications on the education of adjudicated handicapped youth*. Reston, VA: Council for Exceptional Children.

Hunter, W. A. (1974). *Multicultural education through competency based teacher education*. Washington, DC: American Association of Colleges for Teacher Education.

Jarolimek, J. (1981). *The schools in contemporary society*. New York: Macmillan.

Jencks, C. (1972). *Inequality: A reassessment of the effect of family and schooling in America*. New York: Basic Books.

Jones, R. L. (1976). *Mainstreaming and the minority child*. Minneapolis: Council for Exceptional Children.

Kobrick, J. W. (1972, April 19). The compelling case for bilingual education. *Saturday Review* (pp. 54, 58).

Komisar, P., & Coombs, J. (1974). The concept of equality in education: Studies in philosophy and education. In C. Tesconi & E. Hurwitz (Eds.), *Education for whom?* New York: Dodd, Mead & Co.

Kopan, A. (1974). Melting pot—myth or reality? In E. Eppr (Ed.), *Cultural pluralism*. Berkeley, CA: McCutchan.

Krashen, S., & Biber, D. (1988). *On course: Bilingual education's success in California*. Sacramento, CA: California Association for Bilingual Education.

Larry P. v. Wilson Riles, C-71-2270 FRP Dis. Ct. (1979).

Linden, E. W., & Linden, K. W. (1968). *Tests on trial*. Boston: Houghton Mifflin.

Maldonado-Colón, E. (1983). The communication disordered Hispanic child. *Monograph of the BUENO Center for Multicultural Education, 1*(4), 59–67.

Maldonado-Colón, E. (1986). Assessment: Interpreting data of linguistically/culturally different students referred for disabilities or disorders. *Journal of Reading, Writing, and Learning Disabilities International, 2*, 73–83.

Marland, S. (1971). Papers presented at the International Convention of the Council for Exceptional Children, Miami, FL.

Mercer, J. R. (1973). *Labeling the mentally retarded*. Berkeley, CA: University of California Press.

Miller-Jones, D. (1989). Culture and testing. *American Psychologist, 44*, 360–366.

Mills v. D.C. Board of Education, 348 E Supp. 866 (D.D.C. 1972)

National Center for Educational Statistics (1994a). *The condition of education*. Washington, DC: Office of Educational Research and Improvement, U.S. Department of Education.

National Center for Educational Statistics (1994b). *Digest of education statistics*. Washington, DC: Office of Educational Research and Improvement, U.S. Department of Education.

National Coalition for Cultural Pluralism (1973). Cultural pluralism defined. In M. Stent, W. Hazard, & N. Rivlin (Eds.), *Cultural pluralism in education: A mandate for change*. New York: Appleton-Century-Crofts.

Nieto, S. (1992). *Affirming diversity: The sociopolitical context of multicultural education*. New York: Longman.

Nieto, S. (1996). *Affirming diversity: The sociopolitical context of multicultural education*. (2nd ed.). New York: Longman.

Noboa, A. (1987). Bilingualism: An important imperative. *Family Resource Coalition Report, 6*(2), Chicago.

Norris, M. K., Juárez, M. J., & Perkins, M. N. (1989). Adaptation of a screening test for bilingual and bidialectal populations. *Language, Speech, and Hearing Specialists in Schools, 20*, 381–390.

Ortiz, A. A., & Yates, J. R. (1984). Incidence of exceptionality among Hispanics: Implications for manpower planning. *NABE Journal, 7*(3), 41–53.

Ovando, C., & Collier, V. (1985). *Bilingual and ESL classrooms: Teaching in multicultural contexts*. New York: McGraw-Hill.

Palomares, U. H., & Johnson, L. L. (1966, April). Evaluation of Mexican American pupils for educable mentally retarded classes. *California Education, 3*, 27.

Parker, L. (1978). *Bilingual education: Current perspectives, synthesis*. Arlington, VA: Center for Applied Linguistics.

Pennsylvania Association for Retarded Citizens (PARC) v. Pennsylvania, 334 E Supp. 1257 (E.D. Pa. 1971)

Rueda, R., & Chan, K. (1979). Poverty and culture in special education: Separate but equal. *Exceptional Children, 45*(7), 422–431.

Special Issues Analysis Center (1995). *Digest of educational statistics for limited English proficient students.* Washington, DC: U.S. Department of Education, Office of Bilingual Education and Minority Languages Affairs.

Starrick, R. (1995). Three more states enact English-only legislation. *NABE News, 19*(1), 42.

Steiner, E., Arnove, R., & McClellan, B. E. (Eds.). (1980). *Education and American culture.* New York: Macmillan.

Stone, S. C., & De Nevi, D. P. (Eds.). (1971). *Teaching multicultural populations: Five heritages.* New York: Van Nostrand Reinhold.

Sue, S., & Padilla, A. (1986). Ethnic minority issues in the U.S.: Challenges for the educational system. In *Beyond language: Social and cultural factors in schooling language minority students* (pp. 35–72). Los Angeles: Evaluation, Dissemination and Assessment Center, California State University.

Trueba, H., Guthrie, G., & Hu-Pei-Au, K. (1981). *Culture and the bilingual classroom: Studies in classroom ethnography.* Rowley, MA: Newbury House.

Turnbull, H., & Turnbull, A. (1978). *Fact appropriate public education-law and implementation.* Denver: Love Publishing Co.

Umbel, V. M., Pearson, B. Z., Fernández, M. C., & Oller, D. K. (1992). Measuring children's receptive vocabularies. *Child Development, 63,* 1012–1020.

U.S. Bureau of the Census (1994, February). *Census questionnaire content, 1990 (CQC-16).* Washington, DC: U.S. Department of Commerce, Economics and Statistics Administration.

U.S. Department of Education, Office for Civil Rights (1994). *1992 elementary and secondary school civil rights compliance report: Reported and projected enrollment data for the nation.* Washington, DC: U.S. Department of Education, Office for Civil Rights.

Waggoner, D. (1994, July). *Numbers and needs: Ethnic and linguistic minorities in the United States, 4*(4).

Waggoner, D. (1995). Language information from the 1990 Census. *NABE News, 19*(1), 7–8, 30.

Weinberg, C., & Weinberg, L. (1990). Equal opportunity for bilingual handicapped students: A legal historical perspective. *NABE Journal, 14*(1, 2 & 3), 17–40.

Zangwill, I. (1909). *The melting pot.* New York: Macmillan.

Zirkel, P. (1978). The legal vicissitudes of bilingual education. In H. Fontaine, B. Persky, & L. Golubchick (Eds.), *Bilingual education.* Wayne, NJ: Avery Publishing Group.

CHAPTER 2

Bilingualism and Bilingual Education

Leonard Baca

- Clarification of Terms
- Goals of Bilingual Education
- Rationale for Bilingual Education
- Impact on Cognitive Development
- Impact on Language Arts Skills
- Impact on Attitude and Self-Concept
- Bilingual Program Designs
- Program Staffing
- Effectiveness of Bilingual Education
- Summary

OBJECTIVES

To present an overview of the field of bilingual education

To clarify issues related to the goals of bilingual education

To discuss the rationale for bilingual education

To provide information on the impact of bilingual education on cognitive development, language arts skills, and self-concept

To discuss program design and methodology

To present information on the effectiveness of bilingual education

A better understanding of the types of services needed by culturally and linguistically diverse exceptional (CLDE) students requires familiarity with the services provided by bilingual education and special education. The next two chapters provide a comprehensive overview of these two important programs.

The main purpose of this chapter is to acquaint the reader with the principal issues and practices in the field of bilingual education. This includes a review of the basic concepts and terms related to bilingual instruction and with the various goals of bilingual programs. Aspects of curricular design, methodology, and staffing are explored and discussed as well. Finally, research data that describe the effectiveness of bilingual education in different contexts are presented.

CLARIFICATION OF TERMS

The terms *bilingualism* and *bilingual education* appear frequently in the literature. However, there is a great deal of variation with regard to the meaning of these terms. To be considered bilingual generally means an individual has the ability to use two different languages. The confusion arises when the degree of proficiency in each language is discussed. Some authorities claim that a bilingual person must have native-like fluency in both languages. Other experts maintain that minimal competency is two languages is sufficient to be called bilingual. This problem is best resolved by following the advice of Hornby (1977), who maintained that bilingualism is not an all or none property. Rather, it is an individual characteristic that may exist to varying degrees from minimal ability to complete fluency in more than one language. Additionally, individuals may also have differing degrees of competency in different components of each language, such as grammar, vocabulary, or pronunciation. The term "balanced bilingual" is used frequently in the literature and refers to someone who is equally competent in both languages. However,

this designation is not very useful, as most individuals tend to be more proficient in one language or have variations in competency according to the linguistic or situational context.

The issue of "African-American English" is raised occasionally in the context of bilingualism. Is an African-American child who speaks a combination of standard English and African-American English bilingual? Most authorities would say no. However, Taylor (1976) defines a bilingual person as one who speaks two or more "languages, dialects, or styles of speech that involve differences in sound, vocabulary, and syntax." According to this definition, the African-American child could be considered bilingual. However, as the issue of "African-American English" is very complex and requires extensive discussion, it will not be included within the scope of this text.

Bilingual education is another term requiring clarification because of its variation of meaning in different circles. According to Cohen (1975), bilingual education may fall into the category of terms that are much talked about but little understood. A commonly accepted definition of bilingual education is Cohen's, which is as follows: "Bilingual Education" is the use of two languages as media of instruction for a child or a group of children in part or all of the school curriculum" (p. 18). The U.S. Congress in Public Law (PL) 95-561, which is known as the Bilingual Act, defines the term *program of bilingual education* as follows:

A program of instruction, designed for children of limited English proficiency in elementary or secondary schools, in which, with respect to the years of study to which the program is applicable, there is instruction given in, and study of, English and, to the extent necessary to allow a child to achieve competence in the English language, the native language of the children of limited English proficiency, and such instruction is given with appreciation for the cultural heritage of such children, and of other children in American society, and with respect to elementary and secondary school instruction, such instruction shall, to the extent necessary, be in all courses or subjects of study which will allow a child to progress effectively through the educational system.

The basic definition of bilingual education, generally agreed upon by both scholars and laymen, is the "use of two languages as media of instruction." However, according to Ovando and Collier (1985), because it is impossible to totally separate language from culture, the term *bilingual education* also includes the concept of bicultural education. As can be seen by these definitions, while there is agreement regarding what the process of bilingual education is, confusion arises when the philosophy and goals of bilingual education are discussed.

GOALS OF BILINGUAL EDUCATION

The goals of bilingual education may be organized into four categories: cognitive development, affective development, linguistic growth, and cultural enrichment. According to Blanco (1977), the consensus of experts in the field of bilingual education is that its primary goals are in the areas of cognitive and affective development rather than in the linguistic and cultural realms. In other words, the primary goal of bilingual education is not to teach English as a second language per se, but to teach children concepts, knowledge, and skills through the language they know best and to reinforce this information through the second language. The definition proposed by Andersson and Boyer (1970) stresses this approach. Accordingly, bilingual education is:

A new way of conceiving the entire range of education especially for the non-English child just entering school. Bilingual learning necessitates rethinking the entire curriculum in terms of a child's best instruments for learning, of his readiness for learning various subjects, and his own identity and potential for growth and development. (p. 63)

When educators, legislators, or parents lose sight of cognitive and affective development as the primary goals of bilingual education, confusion, controversy, and disagreement are likely to be the outcome. What occurs most often is that the linguistic and cultural goals are taken out of context and made the primary purpose of the program. For example, legislators might say: "The main purpose of this program is to teach them English as soon as possible and get them into the mainstream of education." On the other hand, parents might say: "The main purpose of this program should be to maintain their native language and culture while they learn English." The issue of transition to English versus native language maintenance is certainly an important one, but it should not become the central issue when the primary goals of the program are discussed.

The linguistic and cultural goals of bilingual education can be viewed from four different philosophical perspectives: transition, maintenance, restoration, and enrichment. These, however, should not be confused with methodologies. For example, a program with an overt transitional goal, as described below, might teach beginning literacy in the native language, if the directors of that program believed that this pedagogy is the most efficient for acquisition of well-developed literacy skills in English.

A bilingual program with a *transitional* linguistic and cultural goal is one that uses the native language and culture of the student only to the extent necessary for the child to acquire English and thus function in the regular school curriculum. This program does not typically teach the student to read or write in the native language.

A bilingual program with linguistic and cultural *maintenance* as a goal also promotes English language acquisition. In addition, it endorses the value of linguistic and cultural diversity. Therefore, linguistic and cultural maintenance encourages children to become literate in their native language and to develop bilingual skills throughout their schooling even into their adult lives. All state and federal legislation supports the transitional approach to bilingual education. These laws, however, do not prohibit local districts from going beyond the law into a maintenance program, using local resources. Although legislation favors the transitional approach, local districts are free to implement a maintenance approach if they so desire.

A bilingual program with linguistic and cultural *restoration* as a goal would restore the language and culture of the student's ancestors, which may have been lost through the process of assimilation. For example, if a group of Lakota Indian children had lost the ability to speak the Lakota language, an appropriate bilingual program could help them revitalize their ancestral language and culture.

A bilingual program with linguistic and cultural *enrichment* as a goal concerns itself with adding a new language and culture to a group of monolingual children. A good example would be a program for monolingual English-speaking children designed to teach them the Spanish language and culture simply as an enrichment of their education.

Another program sometimes confused with bilingual education is English as a Second Language (ESL). The learning of English is an essential part of every bilingual program in this country (Troike, 1986). The teaching of English as a second language, however, does not, in and of itself, constitute a bilingual program. A good bilingual program, however, will include an ESL component (Ovando & Collier, 1985).

Bilingual and ESL education share a common objective: both strive to promote English proficiency on the part of limited English proficient (LEP) students (Krashen, 1985). The major difference between the two programs is the approach. Bilingual education accepts and develops the native language and culture in the instructional process. ESL instruction relies exclusively on English as the medium of teaching and learning. Bilingual education is more comprehensive in orientation. It teaches not only English, as does ESL, but also cognitive skill development and subject matter concepts throughout the regular school curriculum in the general areas of math, science, language arts, and social studies. Bilingual education and ESL are compatible. However, when either approach is used to the exclusion of the other, it is the LEP students who are slighted.

RATIONALE FOR BILINGUAL EDUCATION

The concept of bilingual education is supported by the idea that schools may use the culture and language of the home to maximize learning for LEP children. At the same time, bilingual education enriches learning for children of the dominant culture. It is an instructional strategy to help the LEP child to achieve maximum cognitive development. It is also an approach for providing a fuller educational experience for the non-LEP child of the majority culture.

At the center of the bilingual education movement is the conviction that the country is best served by preserving the varied contributing cultures that make up this nation instead of seeking to reduce cultures to a monochromatic, homogeneous amalgam. Bilingual education may be justified as: (1) the best way to attain the maximum cognitive development of linguistically different students, (2) a means of achieving equal educational opportunity and/or results, (3) a means of easing the transition into the dominant language and culture, (4) an approach to eventual total educational reform, (5) a means of promoting positive interethnic relations, and (6) a wise economic investment to help linguistic minority children to become maximally productive in adult life for the benefit of themselves and society.

According to Andersson and Boyer (1970), the rationale for bilingual education in the United States rests on the following propositions:

1. American schooling has not met the needs of children coming from homes where non-English languages are spoken; a radical improvement is therefore urgently needed.

2. Such improvement must first of all maintain and strengthen the sense of identity of children entering the school from such homes.

3. The self-image and sense of dignity of families that speak other languages must also be preserved and strengthened.

4. The child's mother tongue is not only an essential part of his sense of identity; it is also his best instrument for learning, especially in the early stages.

5. Preliminary evidence indicates that initial learning through a child's non-English home language does not hinder his learning English or other school subjects.

6. Differences among first, second, and foreign languages need to be understood if learning through them is to be sequenced effectively.

7. The best order of learning basic skills in a language—whether first or second—needs to be understood and respected if best results are to be obtained; for children this order normally is listening comprehension, speaking, reading, and writing.

8. Young children have an impressive learning capacity especially in the case of language learning; the young child learns the sound system, the basic structure, and the vocabulary of a language more easily and better than adolescents or adults.

9. Closely related to bilingualism is biculturalism, which should be an integral part of bilingual instruction.

10. Bilingual education holds the promise of helping to harmonize various ethnic elements in a community into a mutually respectful and creative pluralistic society. (pp. 43-44)

Additional insights on the rationale for bilingual education may be gained from a review of information presented by Garrader (1975). Accordingly, an appropriate bilingual education will:

1. Avoid retardation when the child's English is not adequate.

2. Establish mutually supporting relationships between home and school.

3. Defend and strengthen the child's self-concept.

4. Exploit the career potential of the non-English language.

5. Conserve cultural (including linguistic) heritage of our people.

6. Uphold the basic right of every people to rear and educate their children in their own image.

7. Establish the superiority of foreign medium instruction over foreign language instruction.

8. View bilingualism and bilingual education as instruments of politics.

The rationale for bilingual education is clearly multifarious and comprehensive. Many different variables enter into the rationale, and the reasons for bilingual education are not only pedagogical but also social, psychological, and economic.

IMPACT ON COGNITIVE DEVELOPMENT

The basic and primary goal of bilingual education is the promotion of the maximum cognitive development of the student. Proponents of bilingual education advance a logical and pragmatic argument supporting this contention. Basically, they claim an LEP child is able to learn more effectively in a language the child understands (Cummins, 1981; Garcia, 1982). Moreover, these proponents find that children are able to learn new concepts and skills at a normal rate at the same time as they are learning English. They argue that if the same children were in an English-only program, they would fall behind in concept and skill acquisition until English was learned. For many children this would mean falling behind their peers in cognitive skill development and achievement by at least one or two years. Unfortunately, this initial disadvantage generally becomes more pronounced as the children progress through school. Nieto (1992) affirms that "bilingual education is generally more effective than other programs such as ESL alone, not only in learning content through the native language but also in learning English" (p. 161).

Before discussing the research related to the impact of bilingual education on cognitive development, it is important to understand the notion of cognitive development as a complex one with a long academic history. Many definitions and theories have sought to describe cognition and cognitive development. Flavell (1979) describes three general approaches: traditional, information processing, and developmental. The *traditional* position views cognition as a state involving the higher mental processes. This would include thinking, problem solving, imagination, and conceptualization. The *information processing* position considers cognition analogous to a highly sophisticated computer that stores, retrieves, transforms, and processes information. Finally, the *developmental* position, influenced by Piaget, stresses the gradual development of cognitive abilities through a constant interaction, assimilation, and accommodation with the environment.

The early studies conducted during the 1920s and 1930s used a more traditional approach to cognition when examining the effects of bilingualism on cognitive development. This movement was characterized by emphasis on intelligence test scores as dependent measures. Summarizing the findings of these early studies, Lambert (1977) stated:

The largest proportion of these investigators concluded that bilingualism has a detrimental

effect on intellectual functioning; a smaller number found little or no relation between bilingualism and intelligence; and only two suggested that bilingualism might have favorable effects on cognition. (p. 5)

Ben-Zeev (1979) has written that the majority of the early studies have demonstrated that bilingualism has a negative impact on intelligence. However, these early studies have not been without criticism. Ramirez (1977) noted that the period was dominated by attempts to relate bilingualism to performance on IQ tests. MacNamara (1966) emphasized the important distinction between intelligence and IQ, arguing that many studies measured IQ rather than intelligence. Additionally, there were serious methodological problems with the early studies, as Lambert (1977) has noted. For example, control for social and economic influences was lacking, in addition to control for educational opportunity and the student's degree of bilingualism.

Beginning in the 1960s, studies influenced by the developmental approach to cognition have shown a much more positive impact of bilingualism on cognitive development (Lambert, 1977). In a development-oriented study with over 200 subjects, Duncan and De Avila (1979) found that:

Proficient bilingual children significantly outperformed all other monolingual and bilingual children on cognitive perspectivism tasks as well as on two cognitive perceptual components of field dependent/independent cognitive style. This finding is clearly supportive of the (1962) Peal and Lambert study, as well as the subsequent empirical and theoretical work of Ianco-Worrall, De Avila and Duncan, Cummins, and others regarding the potential cognitive advantages of bilingualism. The extent of the advantages revealed in this study is significant across a series of tasks. The nature of these differences or advantages can be described in terms of superior development of perspectivism or ability to intellectually restructure or reorganize a three-dimensional display; in relative use of separating out part of an organized field from the field as a whole, and in level of development of articulation of body concept . . . . (p. 43)

The results of this study also revealed a positive, monotonic relationship between degree of relative linguistic proficiency (RLP) and cognitive functioning. In other words, the more proficient the children were in each of their languages, the better they performed on the dependent measures (cognitive tasks). Contrary to commonly held views, the results of these studies suggest that the "deficiencies" of limited bilingual children appear to be linguistic rather than intellectual.

Cummins (1979) has argued that the discrepancies found between studies investigating the cognitive and academic benefits of bilingualism can be explained by a "threshold" hypothesis. This theory posits that "there may be threshold levels of linguistic competence which bilingual children must attain both in order to avoid cognitive deficits and to allow the potentially beneficial aspects of becoming bilingual to influence their cognitive growth" (p. 229). He states that adequately developed first language skills are a requirement for academically and cognitively beneficial bilingualism and that if the goal is for minority language children to develop to their full academic and cognitive potential, then additive bilingualism, with literacy in both languages, must be fostered by the school.

A review of the research on bilingualism and cognitive development shows that bilingual education has a positive effect on cognitive development. Barik and Swain (1974) suggest that immersion programs may contribute to the bilingual student's cognitive development. Lambert (1977) maintains there is a definite academic advantage enjoyed by bilingual children in the domain of cognitive flexibility. Supporting a similar position, Duncan and De Avila (1979) argue that bilingual children are poten-

tially advanced with respect to metalinguistic awareness and conclude that their research supports the hypothesis of a cognitive advantage for the bilingual child. Krashen (1985) concludes that continued first language development has practical benefits, helps develop a healthy sense of biculturalism, and can result in superior cognitive development. Nieto (1992) reported several studies that found a positive impact of fluent bilingualism on educational achievement. Even though the literature is not conclusive on the cognitive advantage of students participating in bilingual programs, possibly due to variations in instruction and quality, it does strongly indicate that fluent bilingualism has a positive effect on cognition and academic abilities.

IMPACT ON LANGUAGE ARTS SKILLS

It is well documented that linguistically different students generally do poorly in school when compared to their White peers. This is especially true in the areas of reading and writing proficiency, which are so crucial to academic success. In compiling national statistics on reading proficiency and other aspects of education, the editors of *The Condition of Education* concluded that:

> A student's ability to read is essential to the educational process. If students fall behind in reading proficiency, they may find it difficult to benefit from other aspects of the curriculum. In the future, poor readers may also find it difficult to participate effectively in an economy requiring increasingly sophisticated job skills. (National Center for Educational Statistics, 1994, p. 50)

They also presented the following statistics, derived from the National Assessment of Educational Progress: For all years reported between 1975 and 1992, the average reading proficiency of Hispanic children was significantly lower than that of White children, at all ages reported.

The average writing proficiency of Hispanic children was also lower than that of White children, at all ages reported, for all years reported between 1984 and 1992. They did find some positive signs in their analysis. The gap in reading scores has diminished for older Hispanic students and there has been strong improvements in writing scores since 1990.

It has been argued that at least some of these deficits are due to inappropriate instruction. Many bilingual children do poorly in English language arts because they were taught to read before they had mastered the language. In good bilingual programs, reading is taught in the child's native language to ensure initial reading success. Rather than assuming cultural and linguistic experiences the child does not have in reading instruction, bilingual education capitalizes on the familiar experiences and knowledge of the child's own language. This, according to Nieto (1992), is what Lambert describes as "additive" rather than "subtractive" bilingual education—building on a child's present skills and cultural background to assist in further learning. Thus, with this approach, children are not being taught reading skills and a new language at the same time (U.S. Commission on Civil Rights, 1975).

Once children have learned to read in their native language, they can also learn to read English much more easily, because basic reading skills are transferable from one language to another (Reyes, 1987). Several studies conducted with widely disparate populations (Indians in Mexico, Blacks and Puerto Ricans in New York, Irish students in Ireland) reveal positive indications that bilingual instruction does not hinder reading ability in the second language. Actually, children in bilingual programs appear to be able to read the second language at grade level or above when compared with control groups (Parker & Heath, 1978; Reyes, 1987).

However, some studies are not so unequivocally positive on the effects of bilingual reading instruction. Cohen's findings (1975) on this topic are negative. According to his Redwood City study, Spanish-speaking children in a bilingual program scored lower in English reading than the control group. However, it is of particular note that in this program children were taught to read English and Spanish simultaneously. This practice no longer enjoys strong support by bilingual educators.

A more recent ethnographic study confirms the positive value of teaching reading in the native language to LEP students. Moll and Diaz (1985) hypothesized that the advanced reading skills that the students acquired was a result of their participation in the Spanish language classroom. Their results provide strong support for native language reading instruction. The 1987 Government Accounting Office (GAO) report also supports the claim that the extant research evidence in the field of bilingual education upholds the positive impact of native language instruction on the development of enhanced language arts skills.

Although the research findings on second language reading are somewhat mixed, ample evidence supports the teaching of reading in the native language before the introduction of English reading. Thonis (1981) concurred when she wrote:

> The case for native language reading instruction for language minority students is strong. The rationale can be defended on logical grounds and empirical evidence. The perceptual, sensory-motor, and cognitive processes learned and practiced in any language have tremendous potential for transfer when developmental and learning principles are not violated. Once language minority students have learned to read well and have understood strategies for obtaining meaning from print, these abilities provide a solid foundation for literacy skills in the second language. The essential characteristic of first language skills available for supporting the additions of the

second language is strength. Only strong learning transfers. Lastly, premature introduction to the second writing system may result in two weak sets of skills, neither of which serves well enough to be the carrier of content in school subjects. (p. 178)

IMPACT ON ATTITUDE AND SELF-CONCEPT

To maximize learning potential, children must have a positive attitude and a positive self-concept. Educational research has demonstrated a positive correlation between self-concept and academic achievement. A goal of bilingual education is to improve the self-concept of students in the program. According to Cummins (1989), bilingual education can increase student empowerment and help to reverse students' school failure by becoming "anti-racist education," rather than simply native language instruction. Advocates of bilingual education argue that a program that accepts and shows respect for the language and culture of its students will do more to enhance the self-concept of its students than a program that does not accept and respect the language and culture of its students. These proposed fundamentals of effective bilingual education are similar to those suggested for multicultural education: that it should be anti-racist and affirm the pluralism represented within the school and community (Nieto, 1992). However, it is important to caution that even though many parents and program directors claim self-concepts are improved through bilingual education and although the conclusions appear reasonable, there is not yet sufficient research data to conclusively support this position. Some studies have reported improved self-concept as a result of participation in bilingual programs; however, these findings are tentative due to the many difficulties involved in the measurement of self-concept. Nonetheless, one thing is certain: bilingual education does not harm the self-concept of students. This is more than can be said of English-only programs.

BILINGUAL PROGRAM DESIGNS

Although bilingual education is defined as the use of two languages as media of instruction, programs may be designed and implemented in many different ways. The critical factors determining the design of the programs include (1) student needs, (2) linguistic ability of staff, and (3) program philosophy. School administrators must carefully assess these areas before establishing a program model. Regardless of the program model selected, it is imperative that the students in the process of acquiring English as a second language be provided the opportunity to learn the same curriculum as native English speakers. Bilingual education is not remedial education—these students deserve the same quality and rigor of programs as any other student.

There are three primary types of bilingual education programs in the United States: *transitional, maintenance,* and *two-way enrichment* (Ovando & Collier, 1985). Although there are many variations of these models, almost all programs that use two languages as media of instruction for students who speak a home language other than English can fit into these categories. A consistent feature of all of these models is the use of native language instruction in content areas, instruction for English language development, and explicit modifications designed to make the language of instruction accessible to all students. According to Krashen (1992):

Subject matter classes taught in the first language contribute indirectly but powerfully to the acquisition of English. First, such classes result in knowledge, knowledge that helps make the English input more comprehensible. A limited-English-speaking child who has a good math background will acquire more English and more math in the English-language math class than the limited-English-speaking child whose math background is poor. This is because the former child has more context, more background information that makes the input easier to understand. (p. 355)

Transitional Bilingual Education Programs. These programs initially provide content area instruction in students' native language as well as ESL instruction. Students are exited from these programs as soon as they are deemed sufficiently proficient in English to receive all academic instruction in this language. Typically, students in transitional programs are exited within two to three years. For this reason, these programs are sometimes also called "early-exit" bilingual programs.

Maintenance Bilingual Education Programs. Maintenance programs primarily differ from transitional programs in the length of time that students are in the bilingual program. Maintenance programs typically provide native language content area instruction throughout the elementary grades—from kindergarten through sixth grade. Frequently, the amount of native language instruction decreases as students progress through the program and their proficiency in English increases. In contrast to transitional programs, maintenance bilingual programs are referred to as "late-exit" models.

Two-Way Enrichment Bilingual Education Programs. These programs differ significantly from both of the above programs, in that native English speakers are acquiring a second language in an integrated program with native speakers of that language who are acquiring English. Two-way programs are designed to foster bilingualism and biliteracy in individuals from both language backgrounds. The methodology is different for dominant language students than for those acquiring English, as native language attrition is not a concern for

native English speakers. Due to the strong environmental presence of English, active measures must be taken to support the fluent acquisition of the second language by native English speakers and to prevent native language attrition by native speakers of the nondominant language. Typically, content area instruction is provided primarily in the non-English language for both groups of students, with additional instruction in their second language. Therefore, the program for students from non-English backgrounds is similar to a maintenance bilingual program and for native English speakers it is similar to the Canadian immersion programs. Scheduling is more difficult with this program, as the needs of both groups must be balanced for language use and integrated instructional time.

At times, it is not possible to provide bilingual instruction for students who speak a home language other than English. When there is a very limited number of speakers of a given language, or when personnel fluent in that language are not available, content area instruction in the native language cannot be provided. For these students, an ESL program and modifications to make the language of instruction accessible may be the only option. However, whenever possible, resource materials and people (teachers, aides, and tutors) who speak the student's language should be identified and placed on call to assist the student in or out of the classroom through tutoring in subject areas and to help teach the student skills (such as reading, writing, and computation) in the home language. This option has been termed a *bilingual support model.*

At times, a *language immersion program* is inappropriately recommended for these children. For language minority children, instruction in the language of the dominant culture, without ESL instruction or attempts to make content area instruction accessible through techniques such as Sheltered English is better termed *submersion* than *immersion* (Ovando & Collier, 1985). It was exactly this type of sink-or-swim program that was found inequitable under the *Lau v. Nichols* ruling in 1974.

For native speakers of the language of the dominant culture, an immersion bilingual program may be appropriate. This model has been used extensively in Canada to help dominant culture students acquire French. In this model, students receive most instruction in the second language, with varying amounts of instruction in the first language, depending on the specific adaptation of the model. This model has been found to be successful with English-speaking students in the United States. Additionally, a modified version of this model can be used with native English speakers in a two-way bilingual program, as described above.

Regardless of which bilingual education model is adopted, a school must decide how languages will be distributed across the curriculum. There are two common ratios used for balancing native and second language instruction (Bilingual Education Office, California State Department of Education, 1990). The first option consists of providing a consistent 50:50 ratio of English to the native language throughout the duration of the program. Another option provides for a gradual increase in the amount of instruction in English from a 90:10 ratio of the native language to English in kindergarten to a 50:50 ratio by the last year of the program. Whenever possible, abrupt transitions from primarily native language instruction to all-English instruction should be avoided.

After the decision is made regarding the amount of instruction to be provided in each language, it is necessary to decide when each language should be used and in what contexts. It is generally regarded as good teaching practice to maintain separate contexts for each language through monolingual lesson delivery (Bilingual Education Office, California State Department of Education, 1990). Mixing languages during a discrete time frame or within a single lesson, as with direct translation or code-switching, should be avoided. The following are methods used to provide specific amounts of content area instruction in two languages:

Alternate day plan. One language is used one day and the other is used the next day, as deemed appropriate by the instructional staff. Variations of this method could be the alternate week or month approach.

Half day plan. The home language is used for instruction during one part of the day and English for the other part of the day (similar to the alternate day plan).

Mixed. Some subjects are taught in one language, while other subjects are taught in the second language. In some programs the different lessons in the same subject are provided in each language.

Preview-review method. With the preview-review method, the first lesson is presented in the home language, followed by another in English, and then by a summary in the home language.

With any of these methods, creative and thoughtful scheduling will be necessary to assure that students receive instruction in all content areas in both languages, without needless repetition of lessons. According to the Office of Bilingual Education of the California State Department of Education (1990), "The critical point here is that students need to develop the appropriate vocabulary and language structures for the subject matter about which they are learning so that they can express the content in both languages" (pp. 42–43).

No bilingual education program should be designed without a comprehensive needs assessment of the students who will be involved in the program. This needs assessment should focus on first and second language proficiency, on academic needs, and on affective needs. This information should be provided for both the linguistically different as well as the nonlinguistically different students who wish to participate in the program. Once the school district knows the needs of its students, it can then begin to review and select an appropriate educational program.

The linguistic ability of the staff is another factor to consider before selecting a program design. Answers should be given to such critical questions as these: Are sufficient numbers of bilingual aides available? Are they sufficiently skilled in assisting teachers in reinforcing instruction? Are they fluent enough to teach in the native language?

In summary, the program design is selected when compatibility exists between the needs of the students, the linguistic ability of the staff, and the philosophy of the school district.

PROGRAM STAFFING

As with most other programs, there are several ways of staffing a bilingual program. Creativity and flexibility are needed to provide students with appropriate language models in the ratio of first and second languages desired. Team teaching with a bilingual and a monolingual teacher working together is the most acceptable model. Both teachers can provide monolingual content area lessons which provides natural contexts for each language. Several variations of team teaching can be implemented, as well as forming multi-age classes to capitalize on limited bilingual resources and balance the number of dominant and nondominant language students. Due to the limited number of qualified bilingual teachers, many schools use bilingual teaching aides. However, using an aide to provide the majority of instruction to bilingual students can reinforce the lower status of non-English languages and the image of bilingual education as remedial education. Therefore, the general classroom teacher should also work with the students. Removing children from their regular classes and placing them in resource rooms for brief periods during the day is not considered a quality approach and is not acceptable in some school districts.

EFFECTIVENESS OF BILINGUAL EDUCATION

The following review of the literature on bilingual education discusses the findings of studies conducted in a variety of bilingual program settings. It presents information about some of the bilingual projects that exist or have existed in the United States, as well as those from other countries.

Modiano's study (1968) of the comparison of Spanish direct teaching and the Indian language approach in Chiapas, Mexico, indicates that after three years, students who had been initially taught in their native language and then in Spanish had higher reading comprehension, as measured by a Spanish reading test, than those children who had been taught only in Spanish. Modiano's findings supporting the use of the child's native language in initial reading tasks are substantiated by other studies, such as those of Barrera-Vasquez (1953) with Tarascan Indians, Burns' study (1968) of Quechua Indians, and Osterberg's findings (1961) from his study on dialect-speaking Swedish children.

Gudschinsky (1971) studied the native language approach used in the mountains of Peru. The children in this project were exposed to Quechua, their native language, as the medium of instruction for the first two years and then were moved into Spanish. Gudschinsky found that more children remained in schools under this system, and the work done was superior to that done by comparable students who were not in the bilingual program.

Worrall (1970) studied Afrikaans-English bilingual students, ages 4 to 6 and 7 to 9, in Pretoria, South Africa. She matched each bilingual child with two monolingual children—one Afrikaans-speaking and the other English-speaking—on intelligence, age, sex, school grade, and social class. On a phonetic preference test, the preschool bilingual children showed greater ability to separate the sound of a word from its meaning than did either of the monolingual groups. She concluded that bilingual children are aware that different words can mean the same thing earlier than monolinguals, because they are used to giving the same object two names, one for each of their languages. Blank (1973) claims that a major characteristic of low-functioning preschool children is that they have not developed what she calls the "abstract attitude" acquired by the more successful preschool children. Blank concludes that the primary goal of teaching children who function poorly should be to develop the precursors of abstract thinking, so that they will have an internalized, readily available symbolic system. She believes that if "learning sets" have any value in preschool education, they should be the "metaset" or the learning set par excellence. The metaset is a step beyond specific learning sets. It is a more abstract or sophisticated skill that enables the child to adapt and transfer other learning sets as needed. Worrall's findings (1970) appear to be one instance in which this hypothesis is substantiated.

Malherbe (1969) reported that children involved in the bilingual schools in South Africa performed significantly better in language attainment (in both languages), geography, and arithmetic when compared with comparable monolingual children. Malherbe's study is one of the few that controlled for student's intelligence, and as a result of his investigation, he stated:

> There is a theory that while the clever child may survive the use of the second language as a medium the duller child suffers badly. We, therefore, made the comparison at different intelligence levels and found that not only the bright children, but also the children with below normal intelligence do better school work all around in the bilingual school than in the unilingual school. What is most significant is that the greatest gain for the bilingual school was registered in the second language by the lower intelligence groups. (p. 78)

Richardson's findings (1973) about the Coral Way Elementary School in Florida support Mal-

herbe's findings regarding the benefit of bilingual education. The Coral Way program was similar to that used in the South Africa study, because the subject matter was taught in both languages and the student population was mixed. After a three-year study, his findings indicated:

> . . . that while the students, English-speaking and Spanish-speaking, were not yet as proficient in their second language as in their native language, they had made impressive gains in learning their second language. The study also indicated that the bilingual curriculum was as effective as the traditional curriculum in helping the students progress in paragraph meaning, word meaning, spelling, arithmetic, reasoning, and computation.

The alternate days' approach in the Philippines' bilingual program was similar in structure to the South African bilingual schools. At the end of the first year, the bilingual class performed equally as well as the Filipino class on tests, conducted in Filipino, of reading, science, and nonverbal social studies, as did the English class. Both control and experimental groups performed equally well on oral English (Tucker, Otanes, & Sibayan, 1970).

The San Antonio, Texas, bilingual study was designed to test the effectiveness of intensive oral language instruction in English and Spanish. Taylor's assessment (1976) of oral language skills at the fourth and fifth grades showed that the intensive Spanish group scored the highest on the English oral test. Arnold (1969) also found these children had better reading retention. This finding is similar to those reported by Lambert and Tucker (1972), indicating transfer and learning in the other language without direct teaching. A five-year longitudinal study of the Santa Fe, New Mexico, bilingual program (Leyba, 1978) found children in the bilingual program performed better consistently on academic achievement tests than the nonbilingual control group. The cumulative effect after the five-year period was statistically significant.

Cohen (1975), in his study of the Redwood City, California, bilingual program, reported:

1. That Mexican-American children who are taught in the academic curriculum in Spanish and English for several years are as proficient in English language skills as comparable Mexican-American children taught only in English.

2. Bilingually schooled children are, to a limited extent, more proficient in Spanish language skills than comparable children taught only in English.

3. A bilingual program promotes a greater use of Spanish among its Mexican-American participants than found among comparable nonproject participants.

4. Mexican-American children, following a bilingual program, perform at least as well—and at one group level significantly better—in relation to the comparison group on tests of a non language matter such as mathematics.

5. Students in the bilingual program perform better than the comparison students at one level and the same at the other two levels on measures of academic aptitude.

6. Mexican-American students in the bilingual program gained more positive appreciation of Mexican culture than the comparison group. This positive gain in cultural appreciation was not achieved at the expense of their esteem for the Anglo culture.

7. The school attendance of the Mexican-American students in the bilingual program was much better than that of Mexican-American students in the comparison group.

8. Those students who had been in the bilingual program the longest had more positive attitudes toward school than did comparison students who had been schooled conventionally for the same period of time.

9. The bilingual group parents were more positive than the comparison parents about the virtues of the Spanish language, not only as a means of preserving their heritage but also for practical reasons such as enhancing their children's education and helping them to get a job. (p. 261)

In 1976 the U.S. Government Accounting Office (GAO) issued a report on bilingual education entitled *Bilingual Education: An Unmet Need*. The report indicated that the gains made by the English dominant students on the average were better than those of the non-English dominant students. For example, the data showed that 45% of the English dominant students made normal or better reading progress. But only 33% of the non-English dominant students made normal or better progress in reading. The report goes on to state that two possible causes for these results are not enough native language instruction and too many monolingual English speakers in the program. While these reasons may be valid, it should be pointed out that testing the students in English only is not consistent with the principles of bilingual education. Students in these programs should be evaluated in both languages. A more current GAO report (1987), however, claims that federal bilingual programs have been found effective for educating LEP students. It appears that bilingual education programs are improving with age.

A study by Troike (1978) cited several programs that have documented success. Included among the programs are:

1. **Philadelphia, PA (Spanish).** In a third-year program, English- and Spanish-speaking kindergarten students in the bilingual program exceed the citywide mean and a control group on the Philadelphia Readiness test (a criterion-referenced test), and attendance records were better than in the control group.

2. **San Francisco, CA (Chinese).** Chinese-dominant students in the Title VII bilingual program in 1975–76 were at or above district

and national norms in English and math in three of six grades, and only .1 (one month) below in two others, as measured by the Comprehensive Test of Basic Skills (CTBS). In addition, English speaking students in the program performed at or above national and district norms in all grades, demonstrating that the time spent learning Cantonese did not detract from the English language development.

3. **San Francisco, CA (Spanish).** The Spanish Title VII bilingual program students in the seventh grade showed two months' greater gain than regular district students on the CTBS during 1975–76, and were only .1 below other district students in the same schools. Additionally, the absenteeism among bilingual program students was less than one-third that of the regular program students (3.6% compared to 12.1%).

4. **Lafayette Parish, LA (French).** Students in grades K-3 in the French-English bilingual program performed as well or significantly better than a control group of students in the regular program in all areas tested, including reading and reading readiness, linguistic structures, writing, math concepts, and social science. Instruments used included the Primary Abilities Test, the Metropolitan Achievement Test, and a criterion-referenced test for French.

5. **Artesia, NM (Spanish).** On the Comprehensive Test of Basic Skills, Spanish-dominant children in the bilingual program scored significantly higher than the control group in grades three and four in English and reading, while even English-dominant children in the program scored higher than their control group. In general, the control group children continued to lose positive self-image while the bilingual program children maintained or increased it. (pp 5–6)

In a more recent article, Troike (1986) points out that bilingual programs have demonstrated that they can raise achievement scores to or above the national norms and that the effect of the program is cumulative, with the greatest gains made after five and six years of participation in the program.

The most thoroughly conceived, carefully conducted, and academically respected longitudinal study in the literature on bilingual education was the one conducted by Lambert and Tucker (1972) in Canada. This study differed radically from other studies in these respects:

1. It was not a comparison of two models but rather a demonstration of the value of the Direct Approach.

2. The children in this study were speakers of the dominant language (English) and were learning the nondominant language (French) in Montreal. In all other studies, the subjects have been minority groups who were to learn the language of the majority.

3. The parental input differed. The parents were middle class and active in the education of their children. Parents conceived this project and supported it through six years.

This well-designed and tightly controlled study indicated that:

1. Children in the pilot group were identical to the English control group on achievement and intelligence. Their achievement is apparently unhampered by learning in a weaker language for four years.

2. Retesting in the sixth grade showed that the children in the program were equivalent to English speakers on English exams.

3. The children in general had a high self-concept, and they identified fairly completely with the English-Canadian set of values. However, in a questionnaire given to fourth and fifth graders, the children rated themselves as both English and French Canadian. Thus, they may be gaining some qualities of biculturalism.

4. The experimental program resulted in no native language or subject matter deficit or retardation of any kind.

5. The experimental students appear to be able to read, write, speak, understand, and use English as competently as students in the English control group.

6. During the same period of time and with no apparent personal or academic costs, the experimental children developed a competence in reading, writing, speaking, and understanding French that could never be matched by English students following a standard French as a Second Language program. (p. 71)

In reference to the St. Lambert experimental program, Peal and Lambert (1962) stated:

The picture that emerges of the French/English bilingual in Montreal is that of a youngster whose wider experiences in two cultures have given him advantages, which a monolingual does not enjoy. Intellectually, his experience with two language systems seems to have left him with a mental flexibility, superiority in concept formation, and a more diversified set of mental abilities, in the sense that the patterns of abilities developed by bilinguals were more heterogeneous . . . . In contrast, the monolingual appears to have a more unitary structure of intelligence which he must use for all types of intellectual tasks. (p. 27)

The research discussed and other bilingual studies demonstrate the success of bilingual education. Children involved in learning environments employing two languages are performing at a level equal to or higher than their monolingual counterparts. Dulay, Burt, and Zappert (1976), in their summary of research findings, state:

Contrary to widespread belief, the research contracted to date is not contradictory with regards to the effects of bilingualism and bilingual education on student performance. If one applies objective criteria for applicability and soundness of research design, most of the stud-

ies show a significant positive effect, or a nonsignificant effect, on student performance. Of the 66 studies reviewed only 1% was negative; 58% were positive and 41% were neutral.

Troike (1986), in the *Compendium of Papers on the Topic of Bilingual Education of the 99th Congress,* prepared for the Committee on Education and Labor of the 99th Congress, states that the increased use of the native language in the classroom results in higher academic achievement, as measured in English, and in better language skills.

Hakuta and Snow (1986) conclude that bilingual education is indeed superior to submersion, that poorly conducted evaluation research has observed this fact, and that evaluation research conducted with greater rigor would bear out the superiority of bilingual education as an instructional method in many educational contexts.

Willig (1985), in her meta-analysis study of bilingual education, concluded that the bilingual programs she examined were more effective than nonbilingual programs.

Krashen (1985) and Krashen and Biber (1988), experts in English as a Second Language, also concluded that well-organized bilingual programs are very effective in teaching English as a second language, often more effective, in fact, than all-day English programs that "submerse" the child in English.

Ramirez, Yuen, and Ramey (1991) reported on the results of a four-year, longitudinal study comparing early-exit transitional bilingual programs, structured English immersion programs, and late-exit transitional bilingual programs in nine school districts in five different states. Although the programs did not differ significantly in the type of instructional strategies used and the quality of the language learning environment, they did vary significantly in the amount of English used for instruction. Increased parental involvement was noted in the late-exit bilingual programs, as compared to the other two program types. The researchers noted the following implications of their research:

1. Students in all three programs types improved their academic skills in math, English, and reading as fast or faster than students in the general population. The structured English immersion programs were as effective in promoting academic skills as the early-exist bilingual program.

2. Limited English proficient students remained in immersion and early-exit programs much longer than expected and may need prolonged assistance to succeed in a mainstreamed English-only classroom.

3. Improvements in the quality of instruction at training institutions for teachers who will be serving language minority students need to be made so that they can provide an improved learning environment for their students.

4. Schools with a significant minority language student population need to explore ways to use the home language of their students to encourage parental participation.

5. Some evidence suggests that students who receive most of their instruction in their native language should not be abruptly transferred into an English-only program.

August and Hakuta (1997) indicate that empirical studies have established the beneficial effects of native language instruction within bilingual programs. They see little value in conducting research that attempts to determine which type of program works best, and believe it is more important to find a set of program components that work well in a given unique community.

From this brief review of literature, one can clearly see that bilingual education has been established as an effective educational methodology. There are still arguments as to what instructional type works best with which students and how to best provide quality services. However, it is clear that encouraging fluent, additive bilingualism is a strategy that promotes increased cognitive and academic development. Bilingual education not only works well with the average child, but it has also been shown to be effective with children of limited intellectual ability (Malherbe, 1969) and children with language disabilities (Bruck & Hebert, 1982). This finding suggests that bilingual special education is also an effective method of providing an appropriate education for bilingual children with disabilities.

☺ SUMMARY

This chapter attempted to familiarize the reader with the basic concepts related to bilingual education. Various terms were defined and classified. The philosophy and goals of bilingual education were discussed at some length. It was pointed out that the basic and primary goal of bilingual education is the cognitive and affective development of the student. Various designs and teaching methodologies were described. Finally, research evidence on the effectiveness of bilingual education was presented.

Although there is a great need for additional research, enough studies have been conducted to establish the positive effects of bilingual instruction. It is anticipated that these same positive results will also be encountered in bilingual special education programs. Bilingual special education is based on many of the same theoretical principles as bilingual education. The crossover between bilingual education and bilingual special education will be discussed in Chapter 5.

☺ DISCUSSION QUESTIONS

1. Compare and contrast the definitions of bilingual education. Which seems the most comprehensive? the most appropriate? Why?

2. The primary or central goal of bilingual education is frequently misunderstood. Given the various goals, determine how this misunderstanding occurs.

3. Describe and compare the three types of bilingual programs, as categorized by Ovando and Collier (1985). Then choose the most appropriate and provide a rationale for the choice.

4. What are the critical factors that influence the design of a bilingual program?
5. What evidence supports the cognitive and affective effectiveness of bilingual education?

◎ REFERENCES

Andersson, T., & Boyer, M. (1970). *Bilingual schooling in the United States*. Austin, TX: Southwest Educational Development Laboratory.

Arnold, R. (1969, January). Reliability of test scores for the young bilingual disadvantaged. *Reading Teacher*, 341–346.

August, D., & Hakuta, K., Eds. (1997). *Improving schooling for language minority children: A research agenda*. Washington, DC: National Academy Press.

Barik, H., & Swain, M. (1974). English-French bilingual education in the early grades: The Elgin study. *Modern Language Journal, 54*, 392.

Barrera-Vasquez, E. (1953). The Tarascan project in Mexico. In *Use of vernacular languages in education*. Paris: UNESCO.

Ben-Zeev, S. (1979). Mechanisms by which childhood bilingualism affects understanding of language and cognitive structures. In P. Hornby (Ed.), *Bilingualism: Psychological, social and educational implications*. New York: Academic Press.

Bilingual Education Office (1990, January). *Bilingual immersion education: A program for the year 2000 and beyond*. Sacramento, CA: Bilingual Education Office, California State Department of Education.

Blanco, G. (1977). *Bilingual education: Current perspectives*. Arlington, VA: Center for Applied Linguistics (p. 60).

Blank, M. (1973). A tutorial language program to develop abstract thinking in socially disadvantaged preschool children. *Child Development, 39*, 379.

Bruck, M., & Hebert, M. (1982). Correlates of learning disabled students' peer interactions. *Learning Disability Quarterly, 5*, 353–362.

Burns, D. (1968). Bilingual education in the Andes of Peru. In J. Fishman (Ed.), *Language problems of developing nations*. New York: John Wiley & Sons.

Cohen, A. (1975). *A sociolinguistic approach to bilingual education*. Rowley, MA: Newbury House (pp. 18, 261).

Cummins, J. (1979). Linguistic interdependence and the educational development of bilingual children. *Review of Educational Research, 49*(2), 222–251.

Cummins, J. (1981). The role of primary language development in promoting educational success for language minority students. In *Schooling and language minority students: A theoretical framework* (pp. 3–49). Sacramento, CA: Office of Bilingual Bicultural Education, California State Department of Education.

Cummins, J. (1989). *Empowering minority students*. Sacramento, CA: California Association for Bilingual Education.

De Avila, E. & Duncan, S. (1979). Bilingualism and the metaset. *Journal of the National Association for Bilingual Education, 3*(2), 1.

Dulay, H., Burt, M., & Zappert, L. (1976). *Why bilingual education? A summary of research findings*. Berkeley, CA: BABEL/LAU Center.

Duncan, S., & De Avila, E. (1979, Fall). Bilingualism and cognition: some recent findings. *NABE Journal, 4*(1), 43.

Flavell, J. (1979). The cognitive and affective development of children. In H. Trueba & C. Barnett Mizrahi (Eds.), *Bilingual multicultural education and the professional: From theory to practice*. Rowley, MA: Newbury House.

Garcia, R. (1982). *Teaching in a pluralistic society: Concepts, models, strategies*. New York: Harper & Row.

Garrader, B. (1975). The rationale behind bilingual bicultural education. In E. Von Moltitz (Ed.), *Living and learning in two languages* (pp. 66–67). New York: McGraw-Hill.

Gudschinsky, S. (1971, November 22–24). *Literacy in the mother tongue and second language learning*. Paper presented at the Conference of Child Language, Chicago.

Hakuta, K. & Snow, C. (1986). The role of research in policy decisions about bilingual education. In *Compendium of Papers on the Topic of Bilingual Education of the 99th Congress*. Washington, DC: U.S. Government Printing Office.

Hornby, P. (1977). *Bilingualism: Psychological, social, and educational implications*. New York: Academic Press.

Krashen, S. D. (1985). *Inquiries and insights: Second language teaching, immersion and bilingual education literacy*. Hayward, CA: Alemany Press.

Krashen, S. D. (1992). Sink-or-swim "Success Stories" and bilingual education. In J. Crawford (Ed.), *Language Loyalties*. Chicago: The University of Chicago Press.

Krashen, S., & Biber, D. (1988). *On course: Bilingual education success in California.* Sacramento, CA: California Association for Bilingual Education.

Lambert, W. (1977). The effects of bilingualism on the individual: Cognitive and sociocultural consequences. In P. Hornby (Ed.), *Bilingualism: Psychological, social, and educational implications.* New York: Academic Press.

Lambert, W., & Tucker, R. (1972). *Bilingual education of children; The St. Lambert experiment* (pp. 144–152). Rowley, MA: Newbury House.

Leyba, C. (1978). *Longitudinal study, Title VII bilingual programs, Santa Fe Public Schools.* Los Angeles: National Dissemination and Assessment Center.

MacNamara, J. (1966). *Bilingualism and primary education: A study of Irish experience.* Edinburgh: Edinburgh University Press.

Malherbe, E. (1969). Commentary to N. M. Jones: How and when do persons become bilingual. In L. Kelley (Ed.), *Description and measurement of bilingualism* (p. 78). Toronto: University of Toronto Press.

Modiano, N. (1968). Bilingual education for children of linguistic minorities. *America Indigina, 28,* 405.

Moll, L., & Diaz, S. (1985). Ethnographic pedagogy: Promoting effective bilingual instruction. In E. Garcia & R. Padilla (Eds.), *Advances in bilingual education research.* Tucson, AZ: University of Arizona Press.

National Center for Educational Statistics (1994). *The condition of education.* Washington, DC: Office of Educational Research and Improvement, U.S. Department of Education.

Nieto, S. (1992). *Affirming diversity: The sociopolitical context of multicultural education.* New York: Longman.

Osterberg, T. (1961). *Bilingualism and the first school language.* Umea, Sweden: Vasberbottens Tryekeri.

Ovando, C. J., & Collier, V. P. (1985). *Bilingual and ESL classrooms: Teaching in multiculutral contexts.* New York: McGraw-Hill.

Parker, L., & Heath, S. (1978). *Bilingual education current perspective-synthesis.* Arlington, VA: Center for Applied Linguistics.

Peal, E., & Lambert, W. (1962). The relation of bilingualism to intelligence. *Psychological Monographs—General and Applied 75*(27).

Ramirez, J. L. (1977). *Chicano psychology.* New York: Academic Press.

Ramirez, J. D., Yuen, S. D., & Ramey, D. R. (1991). *Final report: Longitudinal study of structured English immersion strategy, early-exist and late-exit transitional bilingual education programs for language-minority children.* San Mateo, CA: Aguirre International.

Reyes, M. de la L. (1987). Comprehension of content area passages: A study of Spanish/English readers in third and fourth grade. In S. R. Goldman & H. T. Trueba (Eds.), *Becoming literate in English as a second language.* Norwood, NJ: Ablex Publishing Corp.

Richardson, J. (1973). Two patterns of bilingual education in Dade County, Florida. In I. Bird (Ed.), *Foreign language learning: Research and development.* Meneska, WI: George Banta Co.

Taylor, I. (1976). *Introduction to psycholinguistics* (p. 238). New York: Holt, Rinehart & Winston.

Thonis, E. (1981). Reading instruction for language minority students. In *Schooling and language minority students: A theoretical framework* (p. 178). Los Angeles: Office of Bilingual and Bicultural Education, California State Department of Education.

Troike, R. (1978). *Research evidence for the effectiveness of bilingual education* (pp. 5–6). Rosslyn, VA: National Clearinghouse for Bilingual Education.

Troike, R. C. (1986). Improving conditions for success in bilingual education programs. In *Compendium of papers on the topic of bilingual education of the 99th Congress.* Washington DC: U.S. Government Printing Office.

Tucker, G., Otanes, F. T., & Sibayan, B. P. (1972). An alternate days approach to bilingual education. In J. Alatis (Ed.), *Report of the 21st annual round table meeting on linguistics and language studies.* Washington, DC: Georgetown University Press.

U.S. Commission on Civil Rights (1975). *A better chance to learn: Bilingual bicultural education.* U.S. Commission on Civil Rights Clearinghouse Publication No. 51. Washington, DC: U.S. Government Printing Office.

U.S. Government Accounting Office (1976). *Bilingual education: An unmet need.* Washington, DC: U.S. Government Printing Office.

U.S. Government Accounting Office (1987). *Bilingual education: A new look at the research evidence.* Washington, DC: U.S. Government Printing Office.

Willig, A. C. (1985). A meta-analysis of selected studies on the effectiveness of bilingual education. *Review of Educational Research, 55*(3), 269–317.

Worrall, A. (1970). *Bilingualism and cognitive development.* Doctoral dissertation, Cornell University, Ithaca, NY.

CHAPTER 3

The Education of Children with Exceptional Needs

Rocky Hill
J. S. de Valenzuela
Hermes Cervantes
Leonard Baca

- History and Transition
- "Exceptional" Children and Language as a Way to Think
- Exceptional Children Defined
- Special Education Services
- Summary

OBJECTIVES

To be introduced to special education as a way to think about students and a system of services delivered within certain contexts

To understand how children are classified within the school setting and labeled as exceptional

To explore the changing numbers of students identified as exceptional, in total and within different disability categories

To review the historical development of special education programs and some of the contributing individuals

To explore some of the validity issues regarding special education knowledge, processes, classes, and intervention strategies

HISTORY AND TRANSITION

Special education is in a period of transition, "between stories" as Tom Skrtic says (1988, p. xvi). The early history of "special education" found society responding to the needs of two groups of citizens with disabilities, people who were blind and/or deaf, through state and local agencies in the form of institutional placement and services. Additionally, institutional services were available on a smaller scale for people with severe physical and mental disabilities. Technological advances in the areas of assessment and diagnosis—spurred by the development of the Army Alpha and Beta tests during World Wars I and II and the growing field of psychology—portended the growth of special education in the second half of the 20th Century. But advances in the scientific community alone were not sufficient factors in and of themselves to expand the response of the public education system to the needs of people with disabilities. The real push for the phenomenal growth of special education as a force in the public school system came about as a result of the Civil Rights movement in the 1950s and 1960s.

Fundamentally, special education is a civil rights issue: the right of *all* citizens to receive an education. Heretofore, many people were denied access to public schools because of handicapping conditions deemed inappropriate to be served by the public schools. With a civil rights consciousness pervading our society in the '50s and '60s, advocates for people with disabilities began to secure legislation at national and state levels to increase access to public school services and to provide extra funding for districts to serve students with disabilities. The late 1950s and early 1960s began the era of burgeoning services to students with disabilities in the public school system using the "special class" (segregated) service delivery model, based on categories of disabilities, such as "educably mentally retarded." Although the service delivery model for special education

was categorical and segregated, the focus of the special educator was the individual child. You see, many of the differences between special and regular education can be traced to student-focus. Because of the perceived needs of these "special" students, special education was allowed to focus on individual children and their needs. Regular education, on the other hand, has and continues to have a student-focus which is based on grade level (e.g., preschool, 3rd grade, 8th grade) and/or content area (e.g., 11th grade biology, 9th grade English) rather than on individual characteristics and needs. This very different student-focus, which helps to define the roles and relationship of teacher and student, significantly affects attempts to build collaborative programs for students.

Still, during this time, many students were denied access to public schools and instead were served by the private sector (mostly through programs set up and run by parents of these students) and other governmental-sponsored agencies outside the public school system. Concerns regarding the efficacy of services offered and lack of access to services for some students resulted in serious debate among special educators, legislators, and parents around reforming special education.

Over the past 30 years, the field of special education has been engulfed in two major rounds of self-criticism and reform (Skrtic, 1991). The first round took place in the late 1960s, when the traditional special classroom model was criticized for being racially biased, instructionally ineffective, and psychologically and socially damaging to students (Dunn, 1968). This round of self-criticism largely ended in 1975 with the enactment of PL 94-142, the Education For All Handicapped Children Act (now Individuals with Disabilities Education Act, or IDEA) and the introduction of the mainstreaming model. Although the IDEA and mainstreaming were seen as solutions to the problems associated with the special classroom model, a second round of self-criticism and reform emerged in the 1980s when mainstreaming was criticized for merely reproducing these problems in a new form rather than resolving them (Skrtic, 1987, 1988).

Participants in the current round of self-criticism and reform question the efficacy of the mainstreaming model and the rigid procedural-ism of the IDEA and call for yet another new approach to special education programming (Will, 1986). The new approach, first known as the "Regular Education Initiative" (REI) and more recently as "inclusion" or "inclusive edu-cation," rejects the pull-out approach of main-streaming and calls for educating virtually all students with special educational needs in gen-eral education classrooms on a full-time basis with appropriate in-class support services pro-vided by special educators and other special needs professionals (see Gartner & Lipsky, 1987; Pugach & Lilly, 1984; Reynolds & Wang, 1983; Stainback & Stainback, 1984; Will, 1986).

Advocates of inclusion propose to create such an approach to special education by restructur-ing the separate general and special education systems into a new "unitary" system of public education. The new system of public education is characterized as "flexible, supple and respon-sive" (Gartner & Lipsky, 1987, p. 72), a "totally adaptive system" (Reynolds & Wang, 1983, p. 199) in which professional practice is premised on "group problem solving . . . shared responsibility, and . . . negotiation" (Pugach & Lilly, 1984, p. 52). The idea behind inclusive education is to restructure schools so that all students are educated in integrated, het-erogeneous classrooms where they receive per-sonalized instruction through collaborative problem solving among professionals and con-sumers (see Skrtic, 1991 for a discussion of school restructuring). Although opponents of inclusion recognize the problems with the cur-rent system of special education and admit that, in principle, the notion of a unitary sys-tem is an attractive proposition, they are con-cerned about the wisdom and feasibility of inclusive education. Pointing to public educa-tion's demonstrated inflexibility and the virtual absence of meaningful collaboration in schools, ultimately they are concerned that the push for inclusion could result in a loss of hard-won rights and resources and, in the worst case, a return to the unacceptable conditions of the 1960s (Kauffman, 1988; Kauffman, Gerber, & Semmel, 1988; Skrtic, 1991).

As Skrtic (1991) has noted, there are a num-ber of parallels between the debate that led to mainstreaming and the current debate over inclusion, including the fact that in the early 1970s doubts also were raised about the wis-dom and feasibility of mainstreaming (see Keogh & Levitt, 1976; MacMillan & Semmel, 1977). More important for present purposes, however, are the differences between the two debates, particularly with respect to their impli-cations for special education policy and prac-tice. One difference, of course, is that the cur-rent round of self-criticism and reform is more contentious and divisive, largely because there is far more to lose today than in the 1960s in terms of past policy achievements (established rights and targeted resources) for students with special educational needs and their parents (Skr-tic, 1995).

A second difference is that the push for inclu-sion is coming from the bottom up, from local and state practitioners and consumers, rather than from a top-down federal mandate. Even though questions were raised about the feasi-bility of mainstreaming, after the enactment of PL 94-142 in 1975, virtually the entire field of special education became proactively engaged in implementing the new special education pol-icy that was encapsulated in the procedural requirements of the law and in the administra-tive logic of the mainstreaming model. In this sense, the debate over the wisdom and feasibil-ity of mainstreaming ultimately increased the field's certainty in its (new) administrative poli-cies and professional practices, even though in retrospect that certainty largely was misplaced

(Skrtic, 1991). Today, however, the debate over inclusion is unfinished; the question of the wisdom and feasibility of the approach remains unanswered. The result is that special education professionals, policymakers, and consumers are less certain about the field's policies and practices than ever before, particularly since there is far more at stake today than there was in the 1960s.

Finally, a third and related difference stems from the fact that there is no mutually agreed-upon definition of inclusion. This has meant that school districts across the country have begun to implement their own locally-determined inclusive education programs, ranging from "full inclusion" approaches to somewhat less inclusionary or "discretionary" models (see Skrtic & Sailor, 1993; Skrtic, Sailor, & Buchele-Ash, 1995). The fact that inclusive education is being defined from the bottom up has advantages and disadvantages. One advantage is that locally-determined educational policy has more legitimacy to local stakeholders than top-down mandates and thus is more likely to be implemented successfully. In addition, decentralization of authority and decision making is more likely to produce innovation than standardized prescriptions from above, a situation that is particularly true in cases where best practices have yet to be determined (Skrtic, 1988, 1991). On the negative side, however, there is a great deal of concern over the current state of affairs in the implementation of inclusive practices. As Skrtic and Sailor (1993) have noted in this regard:

> The existence of multiple models or definitions of inclusion is making it more difficult for stakeholders to agree on a "philosophy of inclusion" to guide policy development and diffusion of inclusionary special education practices. At a minimum, the lack of consistency complicates communication and increases misunderstanding, which together only add to the inherent uncertainty and confusion that attend most new ideas and practices. Perhaps the greatest

concern at this point in the bottom up development of the inclusive education concept, however, is accountability. On one hand, the existence of multiple definitions of inclusion means that students with similar needs are receiving different services, depending on the district in which they live and the school they attend. Although this was probably the case for some students before the push for inclusive education, it nonetheless places policy makers in a politically difficult situation, particularly since [the IDEA] was meant to equalize special education services across and within states and districts. (pp. 3–4)

"EXCEPTIONAL" CHILDREN AND LANGUAGE AS A WAY TO THINK

In a real sense, all children are exceptional and therefore have exceptional needs. However, in this chapter we focus on children whose needs, behavior, and/or lack of academic success, compared to both empirical and subjective norms, occasion their being served by the special education system. For these children, physical, emotional, cognitive, and/or social factors make it difficult for them to respond appropriately in the general education classroom. Many of these children seem to need extra intervention and care to have a successful school experience, given the ways schools are set up to reward pupils and teachers.

Such exceptional children include students with hearing and vision impairments, physical disabilities, mental retardation, learning disabilities and children and youth with serious emotional and behavioral disorders. Students identified as gifted and talented are recognized under federal and state educational laws as *exceptional* and generally receive a modicum of special (education) services. The purpose of this chapter is to provide the reader with a context with which to consider current educational issues affecting students with disabilities, such as those discussed in the following chapters.

Classification of Children

Over the years many terms have been used to refer to children with exceptional needs, such as *dysfunctional, disabled, handicapped,* and *gifted.* The educational literature in general and the special education literature in particular frequently debate the problematic nature of special education nomenclature and definitions. The questionable connections between assessment-diagnosis-definitions and instructional and intervention strategies is a frequent topic of debate in the literature (see, for example, Stainback & Stainback, 1992). As a result of this debate and changes in society's view of the social professions (Skrtic, 1995), the emphasis seems to be shifting somewhat from developing new definitions and disability categories to focusing on the consequences of applying definitions to children and looking at new ways of determining how and where services should be provided and to whom.

Unlike the case of children in "regular" education (who are generally defined by grade level), the definitions of disability categories have become central to the funding and educational placement of children with exceptionalities and, in turn, to the design of program options and instructional activities. Definitions have been justified as necessary and important for a number of reasons, including:

1. They provide a means to distinguish those students whose abilities and needs dictate more individualized instructional approaches.
2. They allow us to group student characteristics for development of intervention strategies.
3. They provide a common vocabulary and so are a form of communication for personnel at local, district, state, and federal levels who provide funding and services for children identified as exceptional.

Professionally useful as it may be, defining people is always a two-edged sword (Foucault, 1970). Just as terminology and the rhetoric of special education can be explicatory on the one hand, on the other they can become a professional tautology serving primarily to reconfirm the status of special education knowledge and practice. Professional terminology at one level serves to reify conditions and concepts that may or may not have an objective/clinical existence. John Stuart Mill, as cited in Gould (1995), explains this all too human phenomenon as follows:

> The tendency has always been strong to believe that whatever received a name must be an entity or being, having an independent existence of its own, and if no real entity answering to the name could be found, men did not find that reason to suppose that none existed, but imagined that it was something particularly abstruse and mysterious. (p. 22)

The difficulty here is the need for a way to think and talk about students as capable and self-directed individuals, given that the "language" we have chosen in special education—primarily the language of psychology—is a "language" which is medically/pathologically based. Special education is therefore married to a theoretical discipline and means of communication about "clients" which predisposes the types of pathologically-tinged categorical services and dialogue in which special education engages.

Nonetheless, the use of definitions has had some positive benefits. The development of specific special education programs based on definitions of student "disabilities" contributed to mandated education for all exceptional children. Without definitions or significant reform of the general educational system, many children probably would not be receiving specialized assistance and would be required to succeed or fail in a classroom with little consideration of their individual characteristics or needs. Additionally, categorical labels allow us to compare identification rates for different groups of students, such as Hispanic or

African-American, between school districts and states. Although some see labeling as a means to exclude many diverse students from the general education environment, it is unclear whether reversing the institutionalized process of formally labeling students will translate directly into inclusive education for all children. We tend to romanticize the memory of the "one-room schoolhouse" when "all" students were educated together by forgetting that historically, the student population, even when mixed age classes were the norm, was ethnically segregated and homogeneously educated. Although definitions and formal special education categories can be legitimately criticized on a variety of fronts, it should be considered that labels may not be the only, or even the primary, barrier to equitable and inclusive education for *all* students.

EXCEPTIONAL CHILDREN DEFINED

The term *exceptional* is often interpreted by the public to refer to gifted and talented students. However, parents of a child with mental retardation, for example, might associate the term *exceptional* with *handicapped* or *disabled*. Although many teachers, administrators, psychologists, and other professionals apply the term *exceptional* without explanation, it does not communicate the same meaning to everyone and therefore should be used with conscious understanding of the complexities involved. As with all terminology used to refer to groups of individuals who have suffered discrimination, terms such as *exceptional, disabled,* and *handicapped* remain controversial. Scriven (1976) has suggested that the term "exceptional" is misleading, stating that:

> I cannot condone the euphemistic use of the term "exceptional children" to refer to handicapped children. There are exceptional pupils whose problems we are not discussing; they happen to be the ones from whom the term "exceptional children" was stolen because of its

honorific connotations. We will not help children by misrepresenting them . . . and it is a terrible foundation for such an effort to begin by misrepresenting the entire group of such children. (p. 61)

And it *is* in order to capitalize on the "honorific connotations" of the term that *exceptional* has been codified as a way to refer to children receiving special education services. Benjamin Whorf (1956) and feminist writers (see, for example, Gilligan, 1982) have reminded us about the way that language and thought go together in the adage, "we think like we talk." S.I. Hayakawa (Mercer, 1973) echoes John Stuart Mill in the following:

> The question, "What is it really?" "What is its right name?" is a nonsense question . . . one that is not capable of being answered.
>
> . . . the individual object or event we are naming, of course, has no name and belongs to no class until we put it in one. . . . What we call things and where we draw the line between one class of things and another depend upon the interest we have and the purposes of classification. Most intellectual problems are, ultimately, problems of classification and nomenclature. (p. 1)

Language—what we call people—is important. How we refer to people, coupled with our own history of that word and all that goes with that word, in large part sets up many of our reactions and feelings toward people. To think that words are neutral, and merely explicatory, is to miss the power of language in our lives (McCrum, Cran, & MacNiel, 1986).

One of the changes in special education that is reflective of the debate over the language we use is the move to *people-first* language. Whereas for many years children with disabilities were referred to by categorical name first, e.g., mentally retarded student, learning disabled child, emotionally disturbed kid, the field has adopted a new arrangement of words; putting the person-word first. The field now refers to the children noted above as "student with mental retardation," "child with learning disabilities," "kid with an emotional disturbance." Some may think this move is superficial and petty, and it does beg the issue of the pathological nature of the modifiers, but it more humanely places the modifiers (the categorical designations of special education) in *reference to* the person rather than the other way around. In the long haul, person-first language is likely to have a significant effect on how people think and feel about people who are different from the norm. The authors ask that those of you reading this book please carefully think about the language that you use to talk and therefore think about people. Individuals with disabilities suffer greatly from our words and attitudes; person-first language is a gentle start to building more accepting relationships among all people.

Given the range of students included under the umbrella term of *exceptionality,* it is important that we understand how authors in the field define it. Hallahan and Kauffman (1991) emphasize only the unique educational needs of this group of students, stating that "exceptional children are those who require special education and related services if they are to realize their full human potential" (p. 6). However, most definitions include two key points: the child differs in some way from his/her peers and special educational services are needed. These well-known textbook authors define the exceptional child as:

1. . . . . a child who deviates from the average or normal child in (1) mental characteristics, (2) sensory abilities, (3) communication abilities, (4) social behavior, or (5) physical characteristics. These differences must be to such an extent that the child requires a modification of school practices, or special education services to develop to maximum capacity. (Kirk & Gallagher, 1989, p. 5)

2. Exceptional children are those whose differences from the norm are large enough to require an individually designed program of instruction—in other words, special education—if they are to benefit fully from education. (Heward, 1996, p. 9)

3. Exceptional children are children who have physical, mental, behavioral, or sensory characteristics that differ from the majority of children so that they require special education and related services to develop to their maximum capacity. (Blackhurst & Berdine, 1993, p. 7)

Federal Definitions. Although it may not be easy to define general terms such as *exceptional,* and examination of the literature, including state rules and regulations, indicates little substantive variance in how the specific categories of exceptional children have been defined. The language used to describe the different categories varies but, in general, overall definitions have been similar.

The *Federal Register* (1982) includes definitions that are accepted by the U.S. government as well as by most school districts, particularly if they wish to continue to receive financial assistance. Because these definitions are included in the Handicapped Children's Act (PL 94-142) and the subsequent Individuals with Disabilities Education Act (IDEA, 1990) they are pertinent. Section 300.4 of the proposed rules for PL 94-142 includes the following definitions:

A. As used in this part, the term "handicapped child" means a mentally retarded, hard of hearing, deaf, speech impaired, visually handicapped, seriously emotionally disturbed, orthopedically impaired, other health impaired, deaf-blind, or multi-handicapped child, or a child with a specific learning disability whose impairment adversely affects the child's ability to benefit from a regular education program, and who by reason thereof requires special education and related services after an evaluation in accordance with 300.142.

B. The terms used in this definition are defined as follows:

1. "Deaf" means having a hearing impairment which is so severe that the child is impaired in processing linguistic information through hearing, with or without amplification.

2. "Deaf-blind" means having concomitant hearing and visual impairments, the combination of which causes such severe communication and other developmental and educational problems that the child cannot be accommodated in special education programs solely for deaf or blind children.

3. "Hard of hearing" means having a hearing impairment, whether permanent or fluctuating, which is not included under the definition of "deaf" in this section.

4. "Mentally retarded" means having significant sub-average general intellectual functioning existing concurrently with deficits in adaptive behavior and manifested during the developmental period.

5. "Multi-handicapped" means having concomitant impairments (such as mentally retarded-blind, mentally retarded, orthopedically impaired, etc.), the combination of which causes such severe educational problems that the child cannot be accommodated in special education programs solely for one of the impairments. The term does not include a deaf-blind child.

6. "Orthopedically impaired" means having a severe orthopedic impairment. The term includes an impairment caused by a congenital anomaly (e.g., clubfoot, absence of some member, etc.), an impairment caused by disease (e.g., poliomyelitis, bone tuberculosis, etc.), and an impairment from any other cause (e.g., cerebral palsy, amputations, and fractures or burns which cause contractures).

7. "Other health impaired" means having an (a) autistic condition which is manifested by severe communication and other developmental and educational problems, or (b) limited strength, vitality or alertness due to chronic or acute health problems such as a heart condition, tuberculosis, rheumatic fever, nephritis, asthma, sickle cell anemia, hemophilia, epilepsy, lead poisoning, leukemia, or diabetes.

8. "Serious emotionally disturbed" means having a condition exhibiting one or more of the following characteristics over a long period of time and to a marked degree:
   a. An inability to learn which cannot be explained by intellectual, sensory or health factors;
   b. An inability to build or maintain satisfactory interpersonal relationships with peers and teachers;
   d. Inappropriate types of behavior or feelings under normal circumstances;
   d. A general pervasive mood of unhappiness or depression; or
   e. A tendency to develop physical symptoms or fears associated with personal or school problems;
   f. Being schizophrenic.

9. "Specific learning disability" means a disorder in one or more of the basic psychological processes involved in understanding or in using language, spoken or written, which may manifest itself in an imperfect ability to listen, think, speak, read, write, spell, or to do mathematical calculations. The term includes such conditions as a perceptual handicap, brain injury, minimal brain dysfunction, dyslexia, and developmental aphasia. The term does not include a learning problem which is primarily the result of a visual, hearing or motor handicap, of mental retardation, or of environmental, cultural, or economic disadvantage.

10. "Speech impaired" means having a communication disorder, such as stut-

tering, impaired articulation, a language impairment, or a voice impairment.

11. "Visually handicapped" means having a visual impairment with or without correction. The term includes both partially seeing and blind children. *(Federal Register,* 1982, p. 33845)

Incidence of Exceptional Children

The IDEA requires that each child with disabilities be identified and that districts report data on children with disabilities served. This information has been systematically collected nationally since the 1970's and the following excerpt from PL 94-142 specifies the manner in which the data must be reported:

In its report, the State education agency shall include a table which shows (1) The number of handicapped children receiving special education and related services on December 1 of that school year; (2) The number of those handicapped children within each disability category, as defined in the definition of "handicapped child" in Section 300.4(b)(4); and (3) The number of those handicapped children within each of the following age groups: (a) three through five; (b) six through seventeen; and (c) eighteen through twenty-one. *(Federal Register,* 1982, p. 33849)

The number of students receiving special education services consistently increased from the academic year 1976–77 to 1991–92, even though the total student enrollment decreased during the late 1970s and mid 1980s, as can be seen in Table 3–1. The total includes students served under both Chapter 1 and the Individuals with Disabilities Education Act. The increase in the number of students receiving special education services, as a percentage of the general student population, is depicted in Table 3–2. As this table shows, the percentage of students enrolled in special education rose

from 8.33% in 1976–77 to 11.77% in 1991–92. A closer examination of this table shows that although some categories, such as hearing, orthopedic, and visual impairments, did not significantly change during the period covered by this table, other categories, principally specific learning disabilities and mental retardation, did. According to this national data, whereas only 1.8% of the student population was diagnosed as learning disabled in 1976–77, by 1991–92, this percentage had risen to 5.31% of the total student population. Significantly changing percentages of students diagnosed under certain disability categories has led to charges that either our current diagnostic criteria are inadequate or that these disabilities are not so clearly defined or definable as we would have the public assume.

Table 3–3 even more clearly demonstrates the instability of certain disability categories over time. Of the total number of students identified as requiring special services, only 21.6% were identified as learning disabled in 1976–77. This proportion climbed to 45.1% of all students identified as disabled in 1991–92. During this same period, the proportion of students identified as speech or language impaired or mentally retarded decreased as a percentage of the total number of students identified as disabled, from 35.3% to 20.2% and from 26% to 10.9%, respectively.

Problems with Categorical Definitions of Disabilities

The use of categorical disability labels are problematic for many reasons. Reynolds, Zetlin, and Wang (1995) identify six common criticisms and issues:

1. There has been parental and public resistance and resentment to the use of special education labels and segregation into separate programs.

2. Eligibility criteria require the student to demonstrate significant problems before

Table 3–1
Number of Students Served in Special Education from 1976–77 to 1991–92 (in thousands)

Type of Disability	1976–77	1979–80	1980–81	1981–82	1982–83	1983–84	1984–85
All disabilities	**3,692**	**4,005**	**4,142**	**4,198**	**4,255**	**4,298**	**4,315**
Specific learning disabilities	796	1,276	1,462	1,622	1,741	1,806	1,832
Speech or language impairments	1,302	1,186	1,168	1,135	1,131	1,128	1,126
Mental retardation	959	869	829	786	757	727	694
Serious emotional disturbance	283	329	346	339	352	361	372
Hearing impairments	87	80	79	75	73	72	69
Orthopedic impairments	87	66	58	58	57	56	56
Other health impairments	141	106	98	79	50	53	68
Visual impairments	38	31	31	29	28	29	28
Multiple disabilities	-	60	68	71	63	65	69
Deaf-blindness	-	2	3	2	2	2	2
Autism and other	-	-	-	-	-	-	-
Preschool disabled	-	-	-	-	-	-	-

Type of Disability	1985–86	1986–87	1987–88	1988–89	1989–90	1990–91	1991–92
All disabilities	**4,317**	**4,374**	**4,447**	**4,544**	**4,641**	**4,762**	**4,949**
Specific learning disabilities	1,862	1,914	1,928	1,987	2,050	2,130	2,234
Speech or language impairments	1,125	1,136	953	967	973	985	997
Mental retardation	660	643	582	564	548	534	539
Serious emotional disturbance	375	383	373	376	381	390	399
Hearing impairments	66	65	56	56	57	58	60
Orthopedic impairments	57	57	47	47	48	49	51
Other health impairments	57	52	45	43	52	55	58
Visual impairments	27	26	22	23	22	23	24
Multiple disabilities	86	97	77	85	86	96	97
Deaf-blindness	2	2	1	2	2	1	1
Autism and other	-	-	-	-	-	-	5
Preschool disabled	-	-	363	394	422	441	484

Note: From *Digest of Educational Statistics,* by National Center for Educational Statistics, 1994, Washington, D.C.: Office of Educational Research and Improvement, U.S. Department of Education.

Table 3–2
Percentage of Students Receiving Special Education Services as a Function of the Total Student Enrollment
from 1976–77 to 1991–92

Type of Disability	1976–77	1979–80	1980–81	1981–82	1982–83	1983–84	1984–85
All disabilities	8.33	9.62	10.13	10.47	10.75	10.95	11.00
Specific learning disabilities	1.80	3.06	3.58	4.05	4.40	4.60	4.67
Speech or language impairments	2.94	2.85	2.86	2.83	2.86	2.87	2.87
Mental retardation	2.16	2.09	2.03	1.96	1.91	1.85	1.77
Serious emotional disturbance	0.64	0.79	0.85	0.85	0.89	0.92	0.95
Hearing impairments	0.20	0.19	0.19	0.19	0.18	0.18	0.18
Orthopedic impairments	0.20	0.16	0.14	0.14	0.14	0.14	0.14
Other health impairments	0.32	0.25	0.24	0.20	0.13	0.17	0.14
Visual impairments	0.09	0.08	0.08	0.07	0.07	0.07	0.07
Multiple disabilities	-	0.14	0.17	0.18	0.16	0.17	0.17
Deaf-blindness	-	0.01	0.01	<0.005	0.01	0.01	<0.005
Autism and other	-	-	-	-	-	-	-
Preschool disabled	-	-	-	-	-	-	-

Type of Disability	1985–86	1986–87	1987–88	1988–89	1989–90	1990–91	1991–92
All disabilities	10.95	11.00	11.11	11.30	11.44	11.55	11.77
Specific learning disabilities	4.72	4.81	4.82	4.94	5.06	5.17	5.31
Speech or language impairments	2.85	2.86	2.38	2.41	2.40	2.39	2.37
Mental retardation	1.68	1.62	1.45	1.40	1.35	1.30	1.28
Serious emotional disturbance	0.95	0.96	0.93	0.94	0.94	0.95	0.95
Hearing impairments	0.17	0.16	0.14	0.14	0.14	0.14	0.14
Orthopedic impairments	0.14	0.14	0.12	0.12	0.12	0.12	0.12
Other health impairments	0.14	0.13	0.11	0.11	0.13	0.13	0.14
Visual impairments	0.07	0.07	0.05	0.06	0.06	0.06	0.06
Multiple disabilities	0.22	0.24	0.19	0.21	0.21	0.23	0.23
Deaf-blindness	0.01	<0.005	<0.005	<0.005	<0.005	<0.005	<0.005
Autism and other	-	-	-	-	-	-	0.01
Preschool disabled	-	-	0.91	0.98	1.04	1.07	1.15

Note: From *Digest of Educational Statistics,* by National Center for Educational Statistics, 1994, Washington, D.C.: Office of Educational Research and Improvement, U.S. Department of Education.

Table 3–3
Percentage of Students within each Disability Category, as a Function of the Total Number of Students Receiving Special Education Services from 1976–77 to 1991–92

Type of Disability	1976–77	1979–80	1980–81	1981–82	1982–83	1983–84	1984–85
All disabilities	100.00	100.00	100.00	100.00	100.00	100.00	100.00
Specific learning disabilities	21.6	31.9	35.3	38.6	40.9	42.0	42.4
Speech or language impairments	35.3	29.6	28.2	27.0	26.6	26.2	26.1
Mental retardation	26.0	21.7	20.0	18.7	17.8	16.9	16.1
Serious emotional disturbance	7.7	8.2	8.4	8.1	8.3	8.4	8.6
Hearing impairments	2.4	2.0	1.9	1.8	1.7	1.7	1.6
Orthopedic impairments	2.4	1.6	1.4	1.4	1.3	1.3	1.3
Other health impairments	3.8	2.6	2.4	1.9	1.2	1.2	1.6
Visual impairments	1.0	0.8	0.7	0.7	0.7	0.7	0.7
Multiple disabilities	-	1.5	1.6	1.7	1.5	1.5	0.6
Deaf-blindness	-	<0.05	0.1	<0.05	<0.05	0.01	<0.05
Autism and other	-	-	-	-	-	-	-
Preschool disabled	-	-	-	-	-	-	-

Type of Disability	1985–86	1986–87	1987–88	1988–89	1989–90	1990–91	1991–92
All disabilities	100.00	100.00	100.00	100.00	100.00	100.00	100.00
Specific learning disabilities	43.1	43.8	43.4	43.6	44.2	44.7	45.1
Speech or language impairments	26.1	26.0	21.4	21.1	21.0	20.7	20.2
Mental retardation	15.3	14.7	13.1	12.7	11.8	11.2	10.9
Serious emotional disturbance	8.7	8.8	8.4	8.3	8.2	8.2	8.1
Hearing impairments	1.5	1.5	1.3	1.3	1.2	1.2	1.2
Orthopedic impairments	1.3	1.3	1.1	1.1	1.0	1.0	1.0
Other health impairments	1.3	1.2	1.0	1.0	1.1	1.2	1.2
Visual impairments	0.6	0.6	0.5	0.5	0.5	0.5	0.5
Multiple disabilities	2.0	2.2	1.7	1.8	1.9	2.0	2.0
Deaf-blindness	<0.05	<0.05	<0.05	<0.05	<0.05	<0.05	<0.05
Autism and other	-	-	-	-	-	-	0.1
Preschool disabled	-	-	8.2	8.7	9.1	9.3	9.8

Note: From *Digest of Educational Statistics,* by National Center for Educational Statistics, 1994, Washington, D.C.: Office of Educational Research and Improvement, U.S. Department of Education.

qualifying for services. This leads to a neglect of prevention efforts for learning and behavior problems.

3. Excessive regulatory processes have become problematic for teachers and shift the emphasis from attention to student learning to compliance with regulations.

4. A lack of coordination among categorical programs leads to students often receiving less help in problematic areas than if they had remained in the general education class.

5. Narrow role definitions leads to misuse of specialists, such as restricting educational psychologist to assessment and placement activities.

6. The lack of evidence that categorical programs are effective.

However, these six are not the only issues discussed regarding labels. Another frequent criticism is that most definitions emphasize limitations and weaknesses rather than strengths. The criteria included in most focus on physical limitations; low intelligence; unusual, bizarre, or inappropriate behavior; or communication difficulties. Children are classified on the basis of what they cannot do, rather than on what they can. In the process of being identified as a student with special needs, the child acquires a label that provides eligibility for a special education program, but also includes a stigma that frequently follows him or her far beyond the school setting. This can lead to decreased expectations for student performance and, worse yet, feelings *within* the child which may have a self-limiting effect.

This perspective is in contrast to the long recognized observation that students' performance can vary according to the situational context. Dunn brought this to attention in the publication *The Six Hour Retarded Child* (Presidential Commission on Mental Retardation, 1969). He observed that students who were not functioning well in the academic environment could do so in other settings. This report questioned the appropriateness of the label "mentally retarded" for many students.

The above criticisms of the use of categorical definitions focus on the negative repercussions of labeling for the students, their teachers, and their families. Another way of critiquing the use of special education categories is to discuss how the definition of what constitutes a disability functions within a social context, is culture specific, and reflects our perspective on linguistic diversity. The interaction of these three contexts has important, and often very negative, consequences for students of diverse ethnic and linguistic backgrounds. Later in this section, we will expand on these three themes, using specific disability categories as exemplars, as well as discuss two additional issues that are emerging as problematic in the debate about labeling and inclusion, namely gender and learning styles.

However, before examining the three contexts highlighted above, let us visit another context. We can call this part of the human context—the propensities we all have to be human. Over the years there has been extensive dialogue and debate regarding the knowledge base of special education: to what extent it constitutes a scientifically-based knowledge and theoretical foundation, to what extent it is anti-human, and to what extent it presages the policies and practices of special education. Bogdan and Kugelmass (1984) suggest that, rather than special education having a clear and coherent knowledge and theory base, what we have are "assumptions" about human beings and the way the world works—in particular, schools and services to students experiencing difficulty in classrooms. The assumptions that they have identified are:

1. That *disability* is a condition that individuals have.

2. That *typical/atypical* is a useful and objective distinction.

3. That special education is a rationally conceived and coordinated system of services that help children labelled "disabled."

4. That progress in the field is made by improving diagnosis, intervention, and technology.

The first two assumptions about the nature of *disability* and human and organizational nature are what interest us for the present discussion. These assumptions guide and drive not only the field of special education, but also the fields of psychology, counseling, teacher preparation, and social work, to name just a few. More importantly, these assumptions underlie the thinking and reactions of most of us in our daily lives toward people who are in one way or another "different" from us. The point here is to understand that what we take as *internal* feelings and thoughts (about many if not all things in our lives) are, to some extent, set up by *external* circumstances and assumptions.

Disabilities as a Social Construction. Labels are problematic because they reify disability categories as objective realities that exist outside of any situational, historical, or cultural context. Definitions suggest that a disability is something that a child has; that the disorder can be objectively and reliably diagnosed and numerically quantified; and that its identification leads to effective and appropriate treatment and intervention. They lend an air of legitimacy to the assumptions presented in the preceeding section, that "disability" is a condition that individuals have and that "typical/atypical" is a useful and objective distinction. Categorical definitions obscure the very real debate about the existence of certain disability categories. They also locate the problem within the individual, isolating the student's "disability" or "impairment" from environmental interactions and influences.

The category "learning disability" serves as an example of how disabilities can be viewed as a social construction. This disability category

has been controversial since it was first proposed in the early 1960s. A review of the demographic data presented earlier in this chapter demonstrates that it is also the one disability category that has experienced the most significant increase over the past 20+ years. Sleeter (1986, 1987) suggests that we need to look at the historical development of this category and how specific educational practices and reform movements produce disabled students. In 1957, when the Soviet Union beat the United States in the race to become the first nation in space with the launch of Sputnik, there was a call for raising educational standards and student achievement. We saw a similar reaction to the Japanese domination in global markets, starting in the late 1980s. Schools were blamed for producing graduates who were seen as poorly equipped to compete with foreign students, and higher academic standards were seen as the cure. According to Sleeter (1986), following the escalation of standards after Sputnik, "Many children were unable to keep up, but few blamed the raising of standards. Instead, students who scored low on reading achievement were personally blamed for their failure" (p. 49).

Sleeter (1986) claims that during its first 10 years of existence, "learning disabilities" was a category into which white, middle-class students who were failing academically could be placed. Unlike the other categories existing at that time, such as "slow learners," "mental retardation," "emotional disturbance," and "cultural deprivation," learning disabilities were not thought to be related to environmental (i.e., low socioeconomic background and ethnicity) or emotional factors. Additionally, the requirement of a discrepancy between intelligence (IQ) and achievement for diagnosis of learning disabilities "suggested its members 'really' belonged in the middle or upper tracks or ability groups" (p. 50).

Sleeter's historical critique of the formation of this category gains further support as we investigate how the type of students placed in learning disability programs has changed since the early 1970s. As the overrepresentation of African-American students in classes for the mentally retarded in the 1960s and 1970s became more publicized, litigation, such as *Larry P. v. Riles,* forced school districts to modify their placement procedures. Although African-American students continue to be overrepresented in the disability categories of mild and moderate mental retardation, these categories as a whole have declined significantly in terms of the number and percentage of students identified. Tables 3–1 and 3–2, presented earlier, document these trends. These tables also show that, at the same time that the percentage of students identified in the category of mental retardation were declining, the category of learning disabilities was increasing significantly. These changes suggest that as it became more difficult to justify the placement of significant numbers of African-American learners in classes for the mentally retarded, these students were simply shifted into a more politically palatable disability category—learning disabilities. Currently, this category accounts for over 45% of all students placed in special education (National Center for Educational Statistics, 1994). This suggests that social pressures have greatly influenced the development of this disability category.

Disabilities as a Cultural Construction. We can also examine how disability categories are constructed within a particular cultural context. This is to say, that which is considered normal is defined with reference to cultural norms. Not all cultures define behaviors considered problematic in U.S. schools as deviant or abnormal, and certain behaviors and activities which are valued in our schools may be considered problematic or of little or no value in other cultures. It needs to be understood that the federal definitions for disabilities highlight those behaviors which are considered problematic in schools and incorporate the values of the dominant culture in the United States—the def-

inition of disabilities is inextricably linked to cultural norms and does not define a *generic* normal and abnormal.

Emotional and behavioral disorders can serve as a case in point. In data compiled in the 1994 Office for Civil Rights (OCR) compliance report, it was noted that almost 19% of all the students identified as severally emotionally disturbed were African-American *boys.* Yet, out of the general student population, African-American males comprise little over 8%. (See Chapter 14, Table 14–1, for this information in tabular form.) This means that African-American boys are found in classes for the severely emotionally disturbed (SED) at over twice their representation in the population as a whole. Analyzing the OCR data in another way, we find that while an African-American boy has 16 chances in a thousand of being diagnosed as SED, this percentage drops to 7 in a thousand for the general population. (A special education wag commented that if we want to reduce the disproportion of pubescent Black males in SED classes, we need to teach those kids how to act more like 35 year old white women.)

Some might argue that this disproportionate representation of African-American boys in the SED category (as well as all other disability categories for which statistics along ethnic groups are collected) is merely a reflection of the difficult social circumstances in which many minority children live. However, we fail to find a corresponding national trend among Hispanic boys, who also tend to be exposed to those factors commonly cited as a cause for emotional disturbance, namely, drugs, gangs, and poverty. Additionally, the representation of African-American girls is similar to that of the total student population, both as a whole and as broken down by gender. Therefore, it appears likely that the disparity in classification rates is inappropriate and does not suggest a true (physiologically-based) higher incidence of this disorder within this segment of the population.

Why would the behavior of one group of students be consistently judged as inappropriate at a higher rate than other groups? One argument is that what is considered "normal" behavior differs significantly cross-culturally; what is acceptable in one culture might be considered unacceptable in another. This is not to play down teachers' concerns about the effects of some students' behavior on the classroom environment, but rather to question whether those behaviors constitute a disorder. This "cultural construction of disability" emphasizes the need to involve family and community members in diagnosis and placement proceedings as local experts. These individuals can provide experienced judgments as to whether problematic behaviors are typical within the group of the student's peers.

Disability as a Linguistic Construction. The use of more than one language within a community and the influence of bilingualism on the developing child are controversial issues within the United States. Linda Chavez, an outspoken opponent of bilingual education and former president of *English Only,* an organization dedicated to promoting English as the official language of the United States, recently used the controversy surrounding the recognition of Black English Vernacular (Ebonics) as a language by the Oakland, California, school district to once again deny the efficacy of native language instruction. She wrote, "Lately, Hispanic parents have caught on that bilingual education may actually be harming their kids" (Chavez, 1996, p. 3D). Similarly, Robert Dole, speaking as a presidential candidate before the American Legion Convention on September 4, 1995, stated, "If we want to ensure that our children have the same opportunities in life, alternative language education should stop and English should be acknowledged once and for all as the official language of the United States." These statements from national political figures demonstrate how bilingualism is framed as problematic and as a deficit that must be remedied.

Another example of this deficit perspective about the acquisition of languages other than English can be seen in the all too often heard and extremely misguided advice to CLD parents to refrain from speaking their native language to their children, so as not to "confuse" them. It is within this social and political context that CLD students are educated, and all too frequently, referred for special services. Specialists are frequently unsure of how to assess the language competency of bilingual children. When assessments are administered in both languages, typically, students' performance is compared to that of monolingual speakers. Therefore, understandably given the social context and negative perspectives about bilingualism held by the vast majority of Americans, many CLD students are judged as deficit in both languages. The poor understanding of normal patterns of bilingual language acquisition among children in the United States can explain the very inconsistent and disproportionate representation of Hispanic students in special education programs. These patterns of both over- and under-representation of Hispanics in special education programs was discussed in greater detail in Chapter 1. In some districts, students are either placed in bilingual or English as a Second Language (ESL) programs or in special education, based on the erroneous assumption that students are ineligible for both types of programs. Other times, teachers in strong bilingual education programs may be hesitant to refer students to a monolingual special education program. Both of these situations can lead to underrepresentation. In other districts, a lack of knowledge about the normal process of second language acquisition can lead to an overrepresentation of Hispanic and other bilingual students to special education programs.

We can also see this linguistic construction of ability and disability in the percentages of LEP students in programs for the gifted and talented (GATE). This group of students has, by far, the lowest representation in GATE programs, with very slightly over one in a hundred identified as gifted or talented, as compared to more than five in a hundred in the general population.

Culturally and linguistically diverse students are affected by all types of disability construction—social, cultural, and linguistic, as depicted in Figure 3–1. Therefore, we must be especially careful with CLD students of viewing disability labels as objective identifiers of an intrinsic disability that is isolated from social, cultural, and linguistic influences.

Emerging Issues in the Labeling Debate. In addition to the recognition that disability categories are social, cultural, and linguistic constructions, new issues have arisen. Concerns have been raised about the influence of gender and learning styles in how disabilities are defined and diagnosed.

The controversy surrounding Attention Deficit Disorder (ADD) and Attention Deficit Hyperactivity Disorder (ADHD) is a case in point. Categorical terminology suggests that ADD and ADHD are real physiological disorders, as real as pneumonia or cancer, and implies much more agreement than actually exists about ADD and ADHD. In reality, experts in the field disagree as to whether this disorder in fact exists as a purely biologically determined problem (see, for example, Armstrong, 1995; Pellegrini & Horvat, 1995), which behaviors or clusters of behaviors differentially distinguish ADD and ADHD from other disorders (Sabatino & Vance, 1994; McKinney, Montague, & Hocutt, 1993), and what intervention or treatment is most appropriate or effective (Fiore, Becker, & Nero, 1993; Swanson, et al., 1993). Additionally, significant gender differences in diagnosis rates, varying from as low as 1:2 to as high as 1:20 for girls versus boys (Armstrong, 1995; Pellegrini &

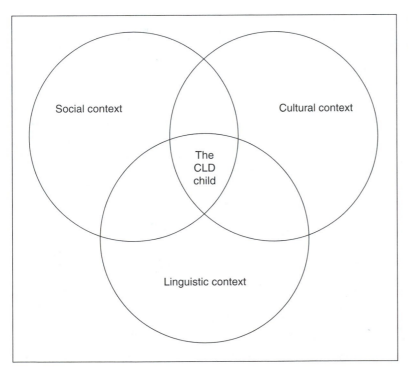

Figure 3–1
The Interaction of Social, Cultural, and Linguistic Contexts in the Construction of Disability in CLD students

Horvat, 1995), are problematic. There is much disagreement as to whether gender differences in diagnosis rates are due to physiologically based differences or a gender bias in diagnosis stemming from social and cultural beliefs about what constitutes "normal" behavior. According to Armstrong, "Some boys may be at risk to be identified as hyperactive or ADD simply because their gender-appropriate activities clash with the expectations of a highly verbal, highly schedule-oriented, and usually female-dominated classroom environment" (pp. 31–32). Clearly, there is not an overwhelming consensus about most aspects of this disorder, which further supports the idea of disability categories as situational constructions.

The controversy over ADD and ADHD also raises concerns about disability and ability as a construction of which learning styles are most valued in academic contexts. Gardner (1983) has discussed seven different kinds of "intelligences." He found that the vast majority of activities in the academic context rely upon what he terms the "linguistic and logical-mathematical intelligences." Armstrong (1995) provides the following description of how students diagnosed with an attention deficit disorder can act within the typical school context:

> many ADD students who attend schools that are based on "central-task," verbal, nonspontaneous learning will be at a distinct disadvantage compared to other students and may have learning difficulties and/or attentional or behavioral problems. That, in fact, is what the research reveals: that as many as 90 percent of students labeled ADD have learning problems. The boundary line between learning difficulties and behavior problems is rather fuzzy for these kids. Because they have trouble learning in traditional ways, they become inattentive, restless, and disruptive. These behaviors make it even more difficult for them to learn material covered in class. If these students were provided with opportunities to learn in environments that embraced their personal learning style, they might well experience success. This is what the research shows. ADD students are almost indistinguishable from so-called normal students in classroom environments that use activity centers, hands-on learning, self-paced projects, films, games, and other highly stimulating curricula. (pp. 33–34)

ADD/ADHD is the new growth industry in special education and a glimpse into the way a special education category is created, nurtured, and codified. With a history of some 50 years and 25 name changes (Armstrong, 1995), ADD is gaining political currency in this country. ADD is a classic example of how categorical special education has grown over the years: (1) identify a "disorder," (2) gather scientific evidence for the disorder, and (3) legislate the disorder into existence. This pattern has been followed by virtually all of the categorical conditions accepted—legally—by the special education establishment. ADD is on the one hand, a response by parents, educators, and the medical profession to "help" kids, mostly boys. ADD advocates have the "disorder"—sanctified by the American Psychiatric Association in its *Diagnostic and Statistical Manual of Mental Disorders* (1994)—and a plethora of scientific evidence. Yet unrecognized by the IDEA as a "handicapping condition," ADD is being codified by using the provisions of Section 504 of the Rehabilitation Act of 1973 to force school districts to respond to ADD/ADHD much as any special education need.

Again, the phenomenon of ADD is an example of the creation of a special education category, thus expecting schools to respond in some way to the "unique" needs of students with this "disability." Most people walking around assume that ADD is in fact some kind of disease-like condition that a lot of kids seem to have nowadays. Thomas Armstrong (1995) sees other factors at work:

> And the discovery of "attention deficit disorder" represents not so much the unveiling of a malady that has been waiting for decades to be

discovered, as much as it does the confluence of complex social, political, economic, medical, and psychological factors coming together at just the right time. (p. 8)

The fact that we operate with our assumptions, both personally and organizationally, intact, ends up, at one level, pathologizing a very large number of little boys in our school systems. Additionally, the treatment of choice for this disability is the administration of a powerful psychotropic drug. Special education is serious business.

SPECIAL EDUCATION SERVICES

Along with the changes in how we view students with disabilities, there have been changes in the methods used in public schools to provide services to exceptional children. Reynolds (1989) sums up these changes as follows:

> The history of special education delivery services can be summarized quite well in two words: *progressive inclusion.* Children with disabilities, in the Western world, moved first from total neglect into residential schools. Then came special day schools and classes and, more recently, fast-growing resource rooms (with pull-out procedures) and mainstreaming. The story is one of gradual change, not one of wide pendulum swings. It is, indeed, a story of quite steady or progressive inclusion. (p. 7)

Cascade of Services

With the passage of PL 94-142, the concept of the "least restrictive environment" (LRE) was codified in federal legislation. In keeping with the provisions of this act and its later amendments, it is the responsibility of the public schools to place each special child in as normal an instructional environment as possible, given the child's disability. Placement in the general education classroom within the public school

setting is generally considered to be the *sine qui non* of the LRE. One way of looking at how students should be placed, given the federal mandate of the LRE, was developed by Deno (1971). Figure 3–2 presents an adaptation of their schemata of what has been termed the "cascade system of special education services."

This cascade is a series of optional placements in the schools and in environments outside of the school context, such as hospitals and residential care facilities. Any of these placements may be the LRE for a student with disabilities at some time, depending on the child's unique needs. Deno (1971) captures the fluid interaction of student needs and the LRE with the following statement about the cascade system of services:

> It assumes that the characteristics of children who fall outside mainstream provisions will change continuously as mainstream provisions, medical practice, and social conditions change, because learning problems are presumed to be the product of the interaction between the child and the kind of "education" impinging on him at home, on the streets, and in school. Where regular education responsibilities should end and special education's begin is definable only in terms of the individual case in its particular situation. (p. 15–16)

The LRE in this model is the general education classroom. Each subsequent step upward becomes increasingly more restrictive. Basic to the placement cascade is the notion that the child should be moved only as far as necessary from the general education classroom to obtain the specialized assistance necessary and then returned to the general education classroom or to a less restricted environment as soon as feasible (Reynolds & Birch, 1977). Additionally, inherent to this model is the assumption that the general educational classroom is the LRE for the greatest number of students. According to Deno (1971),

Figure 3–2
The Special Education Cascade of Services

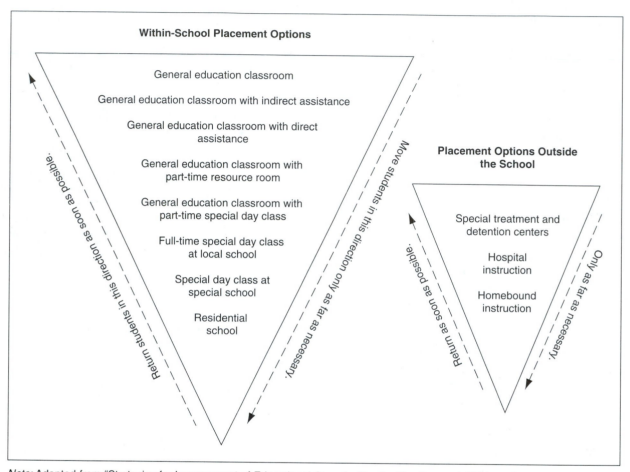

Note: Adapted from "Strategies for Improvement of Educational Opportunities for Handicapped Children: Suggestions for Exploitation of EPDA Potential," by E. Deno, 1971, in *Exceptional Children in Regular Classrooms* (pp. 12-20), M. C. Reynolds and M. D. Davis (Eds.). Washington, DC: Leadership Training Institute/Special Education. Sponsored by the Bureau for Educational Personnel Development, U.S. Department of Education.

The tapered design is used to indicate the considerable difference in the numbers of children anticipated at the different levels. . . . The most specialized facilities are likely to be needed by the fewest number of children on a long-term basis. (p. 14)

The following section describes program options for special education services available within the cascade system of services. Though one finds a variety of terms used in describing special education services across different school districts, an effort will be made to use the most commonly used terms. Table 3–4 presents the percentage of students with various disabilities served in these different educational environments. As this table shows, the majority of students, 71.5%, receive services either in the general education classroom or with resource room support.

1. *Regular class placement.* Placement in a general education class becomes a service option when it can meet the exceptional stu-

Table 3–4
Percentage of Students with Disabilities Age 6 through 21 Served in Different Educational Environments, by Disability: School Year 1992–93

Disability	Regular Class	Resource Room	Separate Class	Separate School	Residential Facility	Homebound/ Hospital
Specific learning disabilities	34.8	43.9	20.1	.8	0.2	0.2
Speech or language impairments	81.8	10.7	6.0	1.4	0.1	0.1
Mental retardation	7.1	26.8	56.8	7.9	0.9	0.5
Serious emotional disturbance	19.6	26.7	35.2	13.7	3.5	1.3
Multiple disabilities	7.6	19.1	44.6	23.6	3.4	1.8
Hearing impairments	29.5	19.7	28.1	8.3	14.0	0.4
Orthopedic impairments	35.1	20.0	34.1	6.7	0.6	3.5
Other health impairments	40.0	27.4	20.6	2.5	0.5	9.1
Visual impairments	45.5	21.1	18.0	5.6	9.4	0.5
Autism	9.0	9.6	50.0	27.6	3.2	0.6
Deaf-blindness	12.3	9.7	31.4	21.2	24.6	1.0
Traumatic brain injury	16.4	19.8	28.4	28.4	4.4	2.6
All disabilities	39.8	31.7	23.5	3.7	0.8	0.5

Note: From *Seventeenth Annual Report to Congress on the Implementation of the Individuals with Disabilities Education Act,* by U.S. Department of Education, 1995, Washington, DC: U.S. Department of Education.

dent's specific needs. It is assumed that in such a placement, the general education classroom teacher has specialized training in adapting instructional materials for the specific needs of the exceptional child. It is also assumed that the teacher has the necessary curriculum and resource materials.

2. *The consulting teacher.* In this option the consulting teacher provides consultation to teachers and other school staff members involved in the exceptional child's program. Consulting teachers do not provide direct services to students with disabilities. Their basic purpose is to assist the general education classroom teacher in understanding the exceptional children in their room and to aid them in adjusting their instruction accordingly.

   With the growing emphasis on the least restrictive environment, the general educator is being called upon more and more to assume responsibility for the educational needs of exceptional children. This service model is becoming an important major option as more and more exceptional children are educated in the general education classroom. Additionally, when the dominant language of the exceptional student is not one in which the consultant is fluent, indirect service provision, through demonstration lessons and assistance to the classroom teacher in curriculum adaptation, is the most appropriate approach.

3. *The itinerant teacher.* In the itinerant teacher option, the direct services to children with disabilities are provided by a special education teacher who is not responsible for a classroom. Such teachers provide tutorial assistance as a supplement to instruction provided by the student's general education

classroom teacher. It is important to note here that itinerant teachers provide instructional assistance to students with disabilities while the student remains in the general education classroom. A requirement for implementation of the itinerant teacher option is the cooperation and coordination of instruction between the general education classroom teacher and the itinerant teacher. This is the most common service delivery method for speech- or language-impaired students.

4. *Resource room placement.* Resource room placement has become a favorable mode of service delivery of special education for the learning disabled. Generally, students are referred to a special education teacher on the basis of assessed academic deficiencies. In addition, instruction is typically provided on an individualized basis, depending on the student's particular skills. The primary concern of the special education teacher is the delivery of remedial and supplemental instruction based on objectives and prescribed activities for individual students.

    Placement in the resource room is on a short-term basis; that is, it is expected that the student will be returned to the general education classroom when sufficient academic progress is realized. For a majority of exceptional children, the combination of the resource room and the general education class placement is seen as an appropriate, less restrictive alternative to special class placement.

5. *Resource center.* The resource center option has been a popular service delivery model for children with disabilities. One finds resource centers organized into one or two classrooms and staffed by at least two special education teachers. Teachers are assigned to the resource center as a team to work with students that have a variety of disabilities. Resource centers are most frequently found in junior and senior high schools. Students

are assigned to the resource center between one and three periods a day and seldom for more than three periods or three hours a day. Again, instruction is provided by the team teachers based on specific objectives and activities for individual students' academic needs.

6. *Part-time special class placement.* Another option is part-time placement in a special class. In this option, the child is assigned to the special class for at least half the school day. Generally, the students receive special educational instruction in basic skill areas and then are mainstreamed into general education classes for other subjects.

7. *Self-contained special class placement.* Full-time placement in a self-contained special class becomes an option for a student when specialized assistance is required for the majority of the day. However, the self-contained special class is becoming less and less of a primary option for most students with disabilities.

    Generally, in the self-contained special classroom, a group of children with similar disabilities is assigned to a teacher responsible for their educational program. In addition to the teacher, one might find a classroom aide, parent, or other paraprofessional. The option of a self-contained special classroom generally is considered for students with moderate to severe handicapping conditions.

8. *Homebound instruction.* When a student's education is interrupted by a short- or long-term illness, homebound instruction is routinely employed. Special education teachers visit the student at home on a regular basis, generally every day. These teachers provide individualized instruction and also coordinate the instruction with the student's general education teacher. This option is designed to function on a short-term basis and is rarely a student's primary source of instruction. Homebound instruction is used

most frequently for health reasons, such as illnesses or accidents, as well as for some behavioral disorders.

9. *Hospital instruction.* Hospital instruction is an option for students who are confined to a hospital. Instruction here is similar to home-bound instruction. An important condition, as in homebound instruction, is that educational activities be adjusted according to the child's physical and emotional state. In some large school districts, there is a cooperative effort between the district and children's hospitals such that special education teachers are part of the hospital staff. However, as health care reforms, such as managed care, are reducing the average length of stay, there is becoming less of a need for full-time hospital-based special educators on rehabilitation wards.

Mainstreaming, Inclusion, Full Inclusion

The history of special education in the public schools shows a proliferation of segregated service delivery options after World War II, with federal and subsequent state policy initiatives regarding mainstreaming becoming popular in the late 1960s and early 1970s. Between the first real support for integrated programming—special and regular education—and now, we have seen two major movements, mainstreaming and inclusion.

The special education cascade "assumes that there will always be some children who require the help of specialists" (Deno, 1971, p. 15). Although many people would agree that specialists can contribute much to the education of students with disabilities, exactly how, when, and where these specialists function, both with regard to students as well as in relation to general educators and the general education system, is hotly debated (Stainback & Stainback, 1992; Fuchs & Fuchs, 1994). As was noted, the history of special education in this country has

been one of initial "defining out" of individuals, a relegation to the "other" (Pagels, 1995; Foucault, 1970) with a commensurate "decoupling" (Skrtic, 1991) and segregation of the organizational systems set up to provide services to these people (training institutions and schools). From this, there has been a continuous move since the late 1960s to involve identified special education students in various ways back into what we call the "general education" system via *mainstreaming, inclusion,* and now *full inclusion.*

This idea of progression by the field has been occurring within a larger societal context which has seen a significant increase in the "pathologizing" of many aspects of Western life. The past 30 years in America has witnessed the ever encroaching sense of a sort of psychological pall over life histories and personal characteristics. Our society has managed to secularize guilt about families, eating, sex, drinking, exercising, being exuberant, and many other activities associated with being in the world. Special education is, to some extent, an extension of this search for the non-normal. Heretofore in America, and still the case in many countries of the world, special education services were/are offered to a relatively small percentage of the population (approximately 2-5%). Because of the numbers of students associated with mild and moderate handicapping conditions, our present numbers approach 12% (National Center for Educational Statistics, 1994). These are the "conditions" most sensitive to societal norms for behavior and academic achievement. We have many states and the federal government working on "standards," at one level a practice which can only end in the pathologizing of greater numbers of students and more pressure on the special education system to provide services.

Yet the inclusion movement is happening in light of and in spite of the trend toward referring increasing numbers of students to special education. Some see inclusion as a civil right (Ferguson, 1995), segregated services in the public sector being immanently nonequitable and non-American in a political sense. Even more important, though, is that the idea and the philosophy of inclusion is a better way, a more humane way to treat people. As a people, we often strive for a sense of fairness when it comes to how we treat each other. Segregation for the sense of efficiency of services is not a defensible position when stacked against the sequelae of that kind of practice.

Inclusion is an idea—a democratic idea in the vein of John Dewey (1980; Skrtic, Sailor, & Gee, 1996)—that strikes at human nature and the affiliations we seemingly choose throughout our lives. Inclusion is a way to rearrange some of those affiliations, some of our relationships with people. At a very substantial level, special educators are aligned with the idea of inclusion as a way to facilitate the development of relationships—and hence, more accepting attitudes—among the very diverse students in schools. Inclusion seems to many a step up in the teleology of special education, more of a right way of treating all our people.

Now, working out the many kinks in a system and attitudes which have been specifically designed to segregate programs for marginal students is a difficult process. Again, as noted earlier, the many facets of inclusion and the varying attempts to define and implement inclusive education manifest in local programs based on local interpretations of the dialogue in the field and in the absence of concerted federal or state direction.

Special and "regular" education have formed a strong symbiotic relationship over the past 40 years; this relationship is largely based on each system taking care of its own business. Mainstreaming, and now inclusion, are forcing these two systems to somehow share students in a way not required up to now. Mainstreaming was relatively easy for the systems to deal with since students from special education programs were just "visiting" general education classrooms. "Belonging" is qualitatively different from visiting, and the systems, attitudes of individuals notwithstanding, are in the throes of attempting to operationalize a philosophy which is in many ways antithetical to the way that special education has grown and worked out a place in the overall educational structure.

And "place" is at the center of the debate regarding inclusion: the place of where the student spends time, the place of special education service delivery, the place of the responsibilities for implementing IEP provisions, and the place of being accountable for the student's program. Although mainstreaming and inclusion have ushered in an era of identified special education students spending more time in regular classrooms, there is still great concern among all parties affected as to the efficacy of this practice. And no wonder. We have educational systems and professional development institutions which have been operating and training teachers as separate entities—"regular" education and "special" education—for almost 50 years. The move to serve diverse student populations in the mainstream system started by *Brown v. The Board of Education,* and extended to other student populations over the years (such as culturally and linguistically diverse students, students with disabilities, and female students), flies in the face of how schools are set up and designed to function efficiently (Skrtic, 1987). Inclusion asks schools to do its business in a fundamentally different way; schools generally respond by making nonfundamental adjustments while expecting teachers to effectively instruct a greater diversity of students. Approaches to the practice of inclusion at the local level are varied and at times creative. Local school systems are reacting to local pressure and community norms for inclusive programs and developing philosophies and delivery systems in light of their local context. Inclusion is a difficult process, because we have built our schools and the special and regular education systems to be noninclusive; in many ways, we have trained our teachers to be noninclusive.

Reframing the System of Services Debate

The inclusion debate has typically been framed as a dichotomy between those that support a range of placement options and "full inclusionists," who support the placement of all students within the general education environment. In this section, however, we would like to reconsider whether these positions are indeed exclusive of one another and whether this debate would better be cast in terms of (1) considering inclusion as a philosophy rather than a placement option, and (2) viewing inclusion within the perspective of students as lifelong learners.

Inclusion as a philosophy asks educators to go beyond our conditioning and perhaps our biology in terms of how we define people in our hearts and minds and therefore how we treat students in our schools. Differentiation and categorization, as noted, serve many purposes, some of which can be positive. However, most of those purposes are subsumed by the inherently noninclusionary nature of these processes. Some archaeologists (Pagels, 1995) believe that the first human differentiation point is *human* and *nonhuman,* after which we differentiate by *us* and *them.* Our tendency seems to be to create the "other" in many varied ways. Gordon Allport (1954) suggests the human species differentiates by the sense of sight—you look different, you are different. Benjamin Whorf (1956) and others suggest that we differentiate by the language we use, and Fussell (1983) speaks about our differentiation by class. The point here is to question the extent to which these definitions/differentiations set us up to exclude someone from our sense of *me* and *us* and, therefore, to possibly treat them in a less than fair way, a less than inclusive way.

The human condition seems to dictate that we remain uncomfortable with people with whom we are unfamiliar, and we tend to define them as somehow outside ourselves. *Familiar-ity,* then, appears to be a necessary biological, sociological, and psychological condition for learning to live together in more humane ways, in ways which affirm and honor each person. Schools which allow students to become familiar with each other, to learn about each other, to help and be helped by each other—these schools are inclusive. The schools that encourage critical debate regarding what we call students and how that informs our thinking and feelings; how delivery systems define us as professionals and thereby define the students and their needs—those schools are inclusive. Schools which support the creative efforts of teachers to respond to the unique characteristics of each child—those schools are inclusive.

The perspective of students as lifelong learners chides those of us in education to have a broader, more inclusive view of a student's day and life. The fact that academic placement options represent a small portion of a person's day and an even smaller portion of his or her life needs to be recognized by the educational community. Schools can become to an even greater extent a coordinator of community services and supporter of inclusive environments for people with disabilities by more fully involving ourselves in the lives of our students. Life happens all around us while we are in schools teaching; the lives of our students reach outside the classroom to the rest of the school, their family, and the community. Take responsibility for looking at all aspects of a student's life for inclusive opportunities. Situations which enhance familiarity can expand the scope of influence of the educational program.

☺ SUMMARY

All children are exceptional. Some, however, differ from other children in a significant way, such as giftedness, deafness, blindness, mental retardation, or some other disability. Defining *exceptional* is a difficult and complex task that has been made more difficult by state regulations, guidelines, and federal and state statutes. Definitions have their advantages and disadvantages, including (1) facilitating legislation, (2) enhancing referrals, (3) labeling, and (4) affecting the student's self concept. In this chapter we discussed how disability categories are not really objective, isolated constructs, but rather, social, political, historical, and cultural constructions that carry inherent perceptions about language use, gender differences, and preferred learning styles.

In addition to discussing various ways that we can look at students, we also examined ways to look at programs. The cascade of special education services model was discussed and placement options defined. The controversy surrounding the inclusion and the REI movement was elaborated. This was contrasted with an attempt to somewhat reframe the debate, namely, in terms of lifelong and community learning and inclusion as a philosophy.

The field of special education as a whole is peopled by parents, families, professionals, and others who genuinely care about kids who tend to get short-changed by schools and many other aspects of life. Special education is a way to gain recognition, services, and maybe acceptance of people considered the "other." We also know that special education can create the "other" and inform our thinking and feeling about human beings . . . little human beings.

☺ DISCUSSION QUESTIONS

1. Applying definitions to exceptional children has positive and negative points. Discuss some of these.
2. Present a definition of exceptionality from those included in the chapter or prepare your own. Explain how this definition differs from the others presented.
3. Discuss what "social, cultural, and linguistic disability construction" means and how it

influences how we perceive disability categories.
4. Discuss why disability categories, when used with CLD students, have been criticized.
5. Program options for special education services can be provided in several ways. Explain several different program options.
6. Compare and contrast the LRE and REI positions as stated in this chapter and from outside readings. Take a position and defend your perspective in light of the current controversy.

☺ REFERENCES

Allport, G. W. (1954). *The nature of prejudice*. Reading, MA: Addison-Wesley.

Armstrong, T. (1995). *The myth of the A.D.D. child*. New York: Dutton.

Blackhurst, E. A., & Berdine, W. H. (1993). *An introduction to special education* (3rd ed.). New York: HarperCollins College Publishers.

Bogdan, R., & Kugelmass, J. (1984). Case studies of mainstreaming: A symbolic interactionist approach to special schooling. In L. Barton & S. Tomlinson (Eds.), *Special education and social interests* (pp. 173–191). New York: Nichols Publishing.

Chavez, L. (1996, December 29). The bilingual boondoggle. *The Denver Post*, p. 3D.

Deno, E. (1971). Strategies for improvement of educational opportunities for handicapped children: Suggestions for exploitation of EPDA potential. In M. C. Reynolds & M. D. Davis (Eds.), *Exceptional children in regular classrooms* (pp. 12–20). Washington, DC: Leadership Training Institute/Special Education, sponsored by the Bureau for Educational Personnel Development, U.S. Department of Education.

Dewey, J. (1980). Democracy and education. In J. A. Boydston (Ed.), *John Dewey: Vol. 9. The middle works, 1899–1924* (pp. 1–370). Carbondale: Southern Illinois University Press. (Original work published 1916.)

Diagnostic and statistical manual of mental disorders IV (1994). Washington, DC: American Psychiatric Association.

Dunn, L. M. (1968). Special education for the mildly retarded—Is much of it justifiable? *Exceptional Children, 35*, 5–22.

Federal Register (1982, August). Part 11. No. 150 (p. 33845). Washington, DC: Department of Health, Education and Welfare.

Ferguson, D. L. (1995, December). The real challenge of inclusion: Confessions of a "rabid inclusionist." *Phi Delta Kappan.*

Fiore, T. A., Becker, E. A., & Nero, R. C. (1993). Educational interventions for students with attention deficit disorder. *Exceptional Children, 60*(2), 163–173.

Foucault, M. (1970). *The order of things: An archeology of the human sciences.* New York: Random House; trans. by Alan Sheridan-Smith of *Les mots et les choses: Une archéologie des sciences humaines.* Paris: Gallimard, 1966.

Fuchs, D., & Fuchs, L. S. (1994). Inclusive schools movement and the radicalization of special education reform. *Exceptional Children, 60*(4), 294–309.

Fussell, P. (1983). *Class: A guide through the American status system.* New York: Touchstone.

Gardner, H. (1983). *Frames of mind: The theory of multiple intelligences.* New York: Basic Books.

Gartner, A., & Lipsky, D.K. (1987). Beyond special education: Toward a quality system for all students. *Harvard Educational Review, 57*(4), 367–390.

Gilligan, C. (1982). *In a different voice: Psychological theory and women's development.* Cambridge, MA: Harvard University Press.

Gould, S. J. (1995). Curveball. In S. Fraser (Ed.), *The bell curve wars.* New York: Basic Books.

Hallahan, D. P., & Kauffman, J. M. (1991). *Exceptional children: An introduction to special education* (5th ed.). Upper Saddle River, NJ: Prentice Hall.

Heward, W. A. (1996). *Exceptional children: An introduction to special education* (5th ed.). Upper Saddle River, NJ: Merrill/Prentice Hall.

Kauffman, J. M. (1988). Revolution can also mean returning to the starting point: Will school psychology help special education complete the circuit? *School Psychology Review, 17,* 490–494.

Kauffman, M. C., Gerber, M. M., & Semmel, M. I. (1988). Arguable assumptions underlying the regular education initiative. *Journal of Learning Disabilities, 21*(1), 6–11.

Keogh, B. K., & Levitt, M. L. (1976). Special education in the mainstream: A confrontation of limitations? *Focus on Exceptional Children, 8,* 1–11.

Kirk, S. A., & Gallagher, J. J. (1989). *Educating exceptional children* (6th ed.). Boston: Houghton Mifflin.

MacMillan, D. L., & Semmel, M. I. (1977). Evaluation of mainstreaming programs. *Focus on Exceptional Children, 9*(4), 1–14.

McCrum, R., Cran, W., & MacNiel, R. (1986). *The story of English.* New York: Penguin Books.

McKinney, J. D., Montague, M., & Hocutt, A. M. (1993). Educational assessment of students with attention deficit disorder. *Exceptional Children, 60*(2), 125–131.

Mercer, J. R. (1973). *Labeling the mentally retarded.* Berkeley, CA: University of California Press.

National Center for Educational Statistics (1994). *Digest of education statistics.* Washington, DC: Office of Educational Research and Improvement, U.S. Department of Education.

Pagels, E. (1995). *The origin of Satan.* New York: Random House.

Pellegrini, A. D., & Horvat, M. (1995). A developmental contextualist critique of attention deficit hyperactivity disorder. *Educational Researcher,* 13–19.

Presidential Commission on Mental Retardation (1969). *The six hour retarded child.* Washington, DC: Presidential Commission on Mental Retardation.

Pugach, M., & Lilly, M. S. (1984). Reconceptualizing support services for classroom teachers: Implications for teacher education. *Journal for Teacher Education, 35*(5), 48–55.

Reynolds, M. C. (1989). An historical perspective: The delivery of special education to mildly disabled and at-risk students. *Remedial and Special Education, 10*(6), 7–11.

Reynolds, M. C., & Birch, J. W. (1977). *Teaching exceptional children in America's schools.* Reston, VA: The Council for Exceptional Children.

Reynolds, M. C., & Wang, M. C. (1983). Restructuring "special" school programs: A position paper. *Policy Studies Review, 2*(1), 189–212.

Reynolds, M. C., Zetlin, A. G., & Wang, M. C. (1996). Categories beyond the evidence: An introduction to the issues. *Education and Urban Society, 27*(4), 371–378.

Sabatino, D. A., & Vance, H. B. (1994). Is the diagnosis of attention deficit/hyperactivity disorders meaningful? *Psychology in the Schools, 31,* 188–196.

Scriven, M. (1976). Some issues in the logic and ethics of mainstreaming. *Minnesota Education, 2,* 61–67.

Skrtic, T. M. (1987). An organizational analysis of special education reform. *Counterpoint, 8*(2), 15–19.

Skrtic, T. M. (1988). The organizational context of special education. In E. Meyen & T. Skrtic (Eds.), *Exceptional children and youth* (3rd ed., pp. 479–517). Denver: Love Publishing.

Skrtic, T. M. (1991). *Behind special education: A critical analysis of professional culture and school organization.* Denver: Love Publishing.

Skrtic, T. M. (1995). *Disability and democracy: Reconstructing (special) education for postmodernity,* New York: Teachers College Press.

Skrtic, T. M., & Sailor, W. (1993). *Bridges and barriers to inclusive education: An analysis of Louisiana special education policy.* Lawrence, KS: University Affiliated Programs.

Skrtic, T. M., Sailor, W., & Buchele-Ash, A. (1995). *Bridges and barriers to inclusive education: An analysis of Georgia special education policy.* Lawrence, KS: University Affiliated Programs.

Skrtic, T. M., Sailor, W., & Gee, K. (1996). Voice, collaboration and inclusion: Democratic themes in educational and social reform initiatives. *Remedial and Special Education, 17*(3), 142–157.

Sleeter, C. E. (1986). Learning disabilities: The social construction of a special education category. *Exceptional Children, 53*(1), 46–54.

Sleeter, C. E. (1987). Literacy, definitions of learning disabilities, and social control. In B. M. Franklin (Ed.), *Learning disabilities: Dissenting essays* (pp. 67–87). London: The Falmer Press.

Stainback, S., & Stainback, W. (1992). Schools as inclusive communities. In W. Stainback & S. Stainback (Eds.), *Controversial issues confronting special education: Divergent perspectives* (pp. 29–43). Needham Heights, MA: Allyn and Bacon.

Stainback, W., & Stainback, S. (1984). A rationale for the merger of special and regular education. *Exceptional Children, 51*(2), 102–111.

Swanson, J. M., McBurnett, K., Wigal, T., Pfiffner, L. J., Lerner, M. A., Williams, L., Christian, D. L., Tamm, L., Willcutt, E., Crowley, K., Clevenger, W., Khouzam, N., Woo, C., Crinella, F. M., & Fisher, T. O. (1993). Effect of stimulant medication on children with attention deficit disorder: A "review of reviews." *Exceptional Children, 60*(2), 154–162.

U.S. Department of Education (1995). *Seventeenth annual report to Congress on the implementation of the Individuals with Disabilities Education Act.* Washington DC: U.S. Department of Education.

Whorf, B. (1956). *Language, thought and reality.* Cambridge, MA: Technology Press of Massachusetts Institute of Technology.

Will, M. C. (1986). Educating children with learning problems: A shared responsibility. *Exceptional Children, 52*(5), 411–416.

CHAPTER 4

Bilingual Special Education:
A Judicial Perspective

Leonard Baca

- Federal Legislative History of Special Education
- State Education Laws for Students with Disabilities
- Special Education and the Courts
- Federal Legislative History of Bilingual Education
- Evolution of Federal Bilingual Education Policy
- State Bilingual Education Laws
- The Official English Movement
- Bilingual Education and the Courts
- Bilingual Special Education: The Law and the Courts
- Summary

OBJECTIVES

To review federal legislation for special education

To analyze state education laws for students with disabilities

To review landmark special education court cases

To present the federal legislative history of bilingual education

To discuss state legislation related to bilingual education

To review landmark bilingual education court cases

To present a bilingual special education interface from a juridical perspective

This chapter discusses the legal background and history of bilingual special education. It also describes the impact of the major court decisions related to bilingual special education. Finally, it presents the current status of bilingual special education from a legislative and judicial point of view.

At the present time no laws have been formulated to deal specifically with bilingual special education. What does exist is a legal history dealing with bilingual education and a legal history dealing with special education. In order to discuss the legal perspective of bilingual special education, it will be necessary to treat these two areas separately and point out where they interface.

FEDERAL LEGISLATIVE HISTORY OF SPECIAL EDUCATION

Legislation specifically designed to protect the rights of students with disabilities is a fairly recent phenomenon. There was no legislation of this type until the second half of this century. The period of 1776 to 1817 is referred to as the period of neglect of the disabled. During this time people with disabilities were rejected and removed as far as possible from society. The period from 1817 to 1869 is known as the age of the asylum. A sense of pity characterized this period. During this time individuals with disabilities were "stored away" and isolated from society in large institutions. The establishment of these large asylums was a practice imported from Europe. The years from 1869 to 1913 are referred to as the period of day school classes. In this period many states began to provide special day schools for these students. From 1913 to 1950, public school programs for students with disabilities were established throughout the United States. The years since 1950 can be referred to as the age of equity for people with disabilities. During this time a recognition has begun to emerge that people with disabilities deserve the same rights and opportunities enjoyed by all other American citizens. Since 1950 a great deal of legislation designed to implement various forms of special education programs began to emerge, both at the state and at the national level. More has been done to promote the rights of citizens with disabilities in the past 45 years than ever before in the history of this country.

Federal legislation dealing with the education of students with disabilities was passed in 1864. This law established Gallaudet College, a national college for the deaf. In 1879 additional legislation created the American Printing House for the Blind. This was the only federal legislation that benefited individuals with disabilities until the middle of the twentieth century. In 1958 the Congress passed PL 85-905, the Captioned Films for the Deaf Act. This law provided educational as well as recreational films for the deaf on a loan basis. This same year Congress also passed PL 85-926, which was a law that provided for the training of teacher trainers for the mentally retarded. Three years later, in 1961, the Congress passed PL 87-276, the Act to Train Teachers for the Deaf. This legislation was amended in 1963 to include the training of educational personnel for all disability groups. This law, PL 88-164, was called the Mental Retardation Facilities and Community Mental Health Centers Construction Act. It was signed into law by President Kennedy, a staunch supporter of special education. This same law also provided for research and demonstration grants to explore problems relating to the education of exceptional children.

The federal government's most extensive involvement in education came with the passage of PL 89-10, which is known as the Elementary and Secondary Education Act of 1965 (ESEA). This measure provided large sums of money for the educationally disadvantaged and students with disabilities. Several other laws were passed in 1965 that benefited the educational opportunities for students with disabilities. One of the most significant of these was PL 89-313, which was called Aid for Education of Handicapped Children in State Operated Institutions. This measure provided monies for the education of students with disabilities who were in state-operated institutions.

In 1966 the U.S. House of Representatives formed a subcommittee to assess the educational needs of students with disabilities and the extent to which the federal government was involved in meeting these needs. The major findings of the subcommittee were incorporated into the 1976 amendments to the ESEA. These amendments established ESEA Title VI, a program of grants-in-aid to the states for special education. Under the program's provisions, each state could submit to the Office of Education a plan established by a state advisory committee, detailing the special education needs of the state and priorities for meeting these needs. In addition, Congress mandated the Office of Education to establish the Bureau of Education for the Handicapped to administer all federal programs for children with disabilities (Weintraub, 1971).

The 90th Congress took another bold step toward providing better educational services for children with disabilities when it passed PL 90-538, the Handicapped Children's Early Education Assistance Act in September 1968. With minor exceptions, this law represents the first time that Congress passed specific legislation for special education. In the past, federal legislation for special education was tied to the coattails of general education or health. The 1968 law provides for the establishment of experimental demonstration centers for the education of preschool students with disabilities and reflects a clear concern on the part of the federal government about meeting the unique needs of all students with disabilities.

In addition, the 90th Congress amended three major general education laws to assure special education's access to their provisions. Title III of the ESEA, which provides for the establishment of innovative regional centers, was amended by the earmarking of 15% of the funds for special education purposes. In addition, Congress required that state and national Title III advisory councils have special education representation. A similar approach was followed in the 1968 amendments to the Vocational Education Act of 1963 by the requirement that 10% of state grant funds be used for special education purposes and that special education be represented on state and national advisory councils. The 1968 amendments to the Higher Education Facilities Act of 1963 reflected Congress's concern that many academically capable students with disabilities were not being given access to higher education because of varying secondary effects of their disabilities.

In 1969 the Congress, through PL 91-61, established a National Center on Educational Media and Materials for the Handicapped to facilitate the use of new educational technology in programs for people with disabilities. The 1970 ESEA amendments, PL 91-230, extended the major aid programs for the disabled under ESEA and in addition created a program of special grants for research, training, and establishment of model centers for the education of children with specific learning disabilities. In the past such children had not been included in existing programs for individuals with disabilities, and for the first time, with this legislation they began receiving the more appropriate educational assistance that their problems demand (Carey, 1971).

In 1974 the Congress passed PL 93-380, the Educational Amendments of 1974. This law required that the states, in order to remain eligible to receive federal funds for the education of students with disabilities, adapt amendments to existing state plans for fiscal year 1975. These amendments included provisions such as a full services goal, priority to unserved children, and evaluation-placement safeguards. Evaluation safeguards included a provision for nondiscriminatory testing, which applied directly to bilingual children. This was the first time that special education legislation included initial provisions for limited English proficient (LEP) children.

In 1975 the Congress passed PL 94-142, The Education of All Handicapped Children Act, which was without any doubt the most significant legislation on behalf of students with disabilities to date. In terms of the bilingual exceptional child, this legislation not only included a provision for nondiscriminatory testing, but also called for appropriate education for each child through an individualized educational program (IEP). With the passage of this law, the legal foundation for bilingual special education was initiated.

In 1978 President Carter signed the Educational Amendments of 1978 (PL 95-561), which reorganized and extended for 5 years the existing ESEA programs, including services for students with disabilities. In 1990 the Individuals with Disabilities Education Act (IDEA) was passed. At this time transitional programming and assistant technology were incorporated into the legislation. In 1990 the Americans with Disabilities Act (ADA) was also passed. This is the major civil rights statute for people with disabilities (Rothstein, 1994). In summary, special education legislation now exists that mandates a free and appropriate education for all students with disabilities. For the bilingual exceptional child, this means that testing must be done in a nondiscriminatory manner and that an individualized educational program must be set up, which could require that the instruction be carried out in a bilingual manner and definitely would require an ESL approach.

In 1996 Congress took up the challenge of updating and reauthorizing the Individuals with Disabilities Act (IDEA). A great deal of discussion and debate occurred, but consensus was not reached. In 1997 Congress finalized its work on reauthorization and President Clinton signed the latest version of IDEA into law. It is important to note that before IDEA, special education practices were inconsistent and haphazard. Through the use of questionable tests and procedures, students could be labeled "special education" and placed in dead-end pro-

grams; frequently, students from culturally and linguistically different backgrounds were inappropriately labeled "mentally retarded" and "learning disabled" and placed in special education. Parents were often not involved in any of these decisions and sometimes did not know that their children had been removed from regular classrooms. Students with disabilities and, in particular, those who come from culturally and linguistically diverse backgrounds have much to gain from an improved and updated federal law.

The U.S. Department of Education (1997) had set the tone for the reauthorization of IDEA by establishing six key principles which guided the reauthorization process. They were as follows:

1. Align IDEA with state and local education improvement efforts, so that students with disabilities can benefit from them.

2. Improve results for students with disabilities through higher expectations and access to the general curriculum.

3. Address individual needs in the least restrictive environment for the student.

4. Provide families and teachers—those closest to students—with the knowledge and training to effectively support students' learning.

5. Focus on teaching and learning.

6. Strengthen early intervention to help ensure that every child starts school ready to learn.

According to the National Parent Network (1997), the 105th Congress, under the leadership of Senate Majority Leader Trent Lott, presented on February 21, 1997 a list of eight proposed changes to IDEA that had been agreed to by both the legislative and administrative staff. They are as follows:

1. Add orientation and mobility training as related services.

2. Require participation of children with disabilities in state- and district-wide assessments of student progress.

3. Require states to have placement-neutral state funding formula.

4. Require parent participation in placement decisions regarding their child.

5. Require performance goals and indicators for children with disabilities.

6. Expand the provisions of current law regarding nondiscriminatory testing procedures.

7. Allow "incidental benefits" to children without disabilities.

8. Require noneducational agencies to reimburse schools to pay for services.

These proposed legislative changes have now been enacted and should promote the improvement of programs and services for all students with disabilities, including students from culturally and linguistically different backgrounds.

STATE EDUCATION LAWS FOR STUDENTS WITH DISABILITIES

Since education is primarily the responsibility of the state, every state has formulated a comprehensive code of school law. For students who do not have disabilities, this regular school law is generally sufficient and provides the basis for an equal educational opportunity in the theoretical domain. However, this has not been the case for the exceptional children of the United States. Advocates for students with disabilities have fought for and acquired additional legal provisions on behalf of these students in our schools. In order to protect children who have various physical, mental, emotional, and learning impairments, legal provisions have been established that facilitate the provision of specialized aids and services designed to ameliorate the barriers these students face in school. Every state has enacted some form of special education legislation. This state-sponsored legislation is the basis on which students with disabilities are able to gain access to free public education, which is the responsibility of each state to provide (Abeson, 1973).

State laws relating to the education of students with disabilities vary from state to state. It is beyond the scope of this chapter to provide a comprehensive analysis of these many laws. An attempt will be made, however, to deal with general patterns and trends in state legislation. According to Abeson (1973), four patterns are used by the states to determine which children are eligible for special education programs. The essential difference in the laws is the degree of specificity in the descriptions of the various categories of disability. The most specific laws create and define specific disability categories. A case in point is a statute from South Carolina. This law defines emotionally handicapped children very specifically as children with demonstrably adequate intellectual potential who, because of emotional, motivational, or social disturbance, are unable to benefit from the normal classrooms of the public schools but who can benefit from special services suited to their needs.

The second most common pattern in state eligibility laws lists the actual categories of children. For example, the Kansas statute names nine disability categories, including children who (1) are crippled; (2) are visually defective; (3) are hard of hearing; (4) are speech impaired; (5) have heart disease; (6) have tuberculosis; (7) have cerebral palsy; (8) are emotionally or socially maladjusted or intellectually inferior or superior; or (9) are physically or mentally defective.

The third type of law is more flexible. An example is the New York law, which defines the handicapped child as "one who, because of mental, physical or emotional reasons, cannot be educated in regular classes but can benefit by special services . . . ." (Sec. 4401 N.Y. Stats.).

The fourth type of law establishes authority for special education and designates a state agency to develop definitions of children who are eligible for services. The following excerpt from Maryland law is an example: "It shall be the duty of the State Board of Education to set up standards, rules and regulations for the examination, classification and education of such children in the counties of the state who can be benefited under the provisions of this subtitle" (Sec. 77-241 ACM).

The issue of mandatory or permissive legislation has been one of high priority in the struggle to provide an appropriate education for students with disabilities. There are various forms of mandatory and/or permissive legislation. This issue is sometimes referred to as the "shall" or "may" controversy. Mandatory legislation does not by any means guarantee an adequate or even better education for students with disabilities. In fact, it has been argued that some states with permissive legislation provide better services. All things being equal, however, mandatory legislation of some type is more effective, since such mandates for services are more readily available for direct judicial review. This is certainly the trend in most states.

It is apparent from this review of state and federal legislation that there is a strong legal basis for the appropriate education of students with disabilities. Both the federal and the state governments have passed numerous laws ensuring that students with disabilities have an equal educational opportunity. None of these laws are aimed directly at bilingual exceptional children. The current IDEA legislation does, however, require nondiscriminatory assessment as well as the establishment of an individualized educational program for each student with a disability, including LEP children. This individualized program will require bilingual education in some instances and ESL special education in all instances.

SPECIAL EDUCATION AND THE COURTS

Legislation in behalf of students with disabilities has had a strong positive impact on the improvement of educational opportunity. Added to this is another very important advocacy force: litigation through the courts. The American educational system has not always been responsive to the needs of students with disabilities. Much of the progress that has been made in the past 45 years has come as a result of litigation. Most of the impetus for the various court cases came from parent groups. A comprehensive set of class action suits became the vehicle for reform. These suits can generally be grouped into three categories. The first group has dealt with the right of students with disabilities to acquire an appropriate tax-supported education. The emphasis here has been on "appropriate" as well as on "tax-supported." The plaintiffs have argued that for a student with a disability to have access to just any education program is not enough. The education of a learner with a disability must be appropriate to his/her unique needs. Parents have maintained that they should not have to pay high tuition in order to get an appropriate and quality education for their children with disabilities, but rather the proper program should be provided through the public schools at taxpayers' expense.

The second group of suits is referred to as the "right to adequate treatment" cases. These lawsuits have demanded that students with disabilities who are institutionalized receive proper services, including education. The third category of suits are those that concern the improper classification and placement practices that have resulted in the restriction of opportunities for the appropriate education of students with disabilities.

These many suits, according to Abeson (1977), have occurred because the appropriate remedies did not come through legislative and administrative channels. Although litigation is very costly and time consuming, it has been a highly effective way of obtaining positive public policy changes for students with disabilities. It is interesting to note that the plaintiffs and the defendants in many of these cases have often agreed regarding the needed remedies but had to use the courts to bring about the desired changes. For example, Abeson (1977) states that "in some cases the defendants have spent days preparing defenses for the suit, and nights assisting the plaintiffs to prepare their arguments."

The concept of a right to an appropriate education was introduced in Chapter 1. From the standpoint of legal history, the establishment of this basic concept that no child can be denied or excluded from a publicly supported education because of a disability comes from two cases: *Pennsylvania Association of Retarded Children v. Commonwealth of Pennsylvania* (PARC), 334 F. Supp. 1257 (E.D. PA 1971), and *Mills v. the Board of Education of the District of Columbia*, 348 F. Supp. 866 (DDC 1972). Although PARC ended in a consent agreement and was not fully litigated, *Mills* did go to trial and the opinion by Judge Waddy represents the leading case in the area. *Mills* was a class action suit that established the constitutional right of students with disabilities to a public education commensurate with their ability to learn. The problem behind this suit was that the city was not providing the necessary funds for children who needed special education. Many of the children were being forced to remain at home without any formal education. In August of 1972 Federal Judge Joseph Waddy ruled in favor of the plaintiffs and ordered the District of Columbia to provide an appropriate education for all students with disabilities in 30 days.

A good example of a "right to adequate treatment" case is the precedent case of *Wyatt v. Aderholt*, 503 F.2nd. 1305 (1974). This case involved institutionalized adults and children with disabilities. It was found that two state hospitals for the mentally ill and a home for the mentally retarded were understaffed and that the services provided were extremely inadequate. As a result of this suit, a set of treatment standards was adopted and the state was ordered to hire 300 new employees. Included in the treatment standards were educational standards dealing with teacher-student ratios and length of school days. Another aspect of

this case established the right of the mentally retarded to receive services in the least restrictive setting. Abeson (1973) describes the precedent-setting value of this case. He indicates that this was the first time a court has ruled that the institutionalized mentally retarded have a constitutional right to adequate treatment. It also represents the first time measurable and judicially enforceable standards for adequate treatment have been established. The minimum standards established in the case included the implementation of individual treatment plans, length of school days, and teacher-student ratios. Also included were detailed physical standards, minimum nutritional requirements, and the requirement that the mentally retarded person be provided the least restrictive setting for habitation.

There has been a great deal of discussion in the litigation literature related to the improper classification and placement of LEP children into special education programs and classes. Three of the more significant cases originated in California from 1968 through 1970. In chronological order they were *Arreola v. Board of Education, Diana v. State Board of Education,* and *Covarrubias v. San Diego Unified School District*. All three cases challenged the validity of using IQ tests to measure the mental ability of linguistically and culturally different children. *Arreola* established the due process rights of parents and children to have a hearing before placement into classes for the educable mentally retarded (EMR). In the *Diana* agreement the school districts agreed to several procedures to ensure improved placement practices. These included testing in the children's primary language, the use of nonverbal tests, and the collection and use of extensive supporting data.

A unique issue raised in the *Covarrubias* case was the requirement of informed parental consent before EMR placement. In this class action suit, the plaintiffs were predominantly Spanish-speaking Chicano parents and students. However, there were a few Chinese and

African-American parents and children included in the class.

According to Casso (1973), each of the three lawsuits had the plaintiff children retested and found they were not retarded and should never have been placed into EMR classes. Each of the three lawsuits also demonstrated the damage that was caused the children as a result of misplacement. During the late 1960s and 1970s the educational community became painfully aware of these testing and placement problems and abuses through the action of the above-mentioned courts and others throughout the country involving Hispanics. In Arizona, *Guadalupe Organization v. Tempe Elementary School District No. 3* (1972) was settled by consent agreement. In Chicago, *Parents in Action on Special Education (PASE) v. Redmond* (1974) challenged the misplacement of both Black and Latino students. The Detroit school system was challenged by *Hernandez v. Porter* (1976), which also terminated by consent decree.

Once the problem was exposed and acknowledged, educators as well as legislators and policymakers began to take steps toward the improvement of the testing and classification procedures of all children in general and minority and LEP children in particular. In the early and middle 1970s, several states, including Arizona, California, and Texas, began making legislative, regulatory, and educational changes that promoted more accurate assessment and placement procedures for these children. Likewise, the federal government began to make provisions for ensuring that minority and LEP children be evaluated in a nondiscriminatory manner and instructed in a more appropriate way. A good example of this can be seen in the following excerpt from the U.S. Office of Education, Bureau of Education for the Handicapped guidelines of 1974. It reads as follows:

A procedure also should be included in terms of a move toward the development of diagnostic prescriptive techniques to be utilized when for reasons of language differences or deficiencies, non-adaptive behavior, or extreme cultural differences, a child cannot be evaluated by the instrumentation of tests. Such procedures should ensure that no assessment will be attempted when a child is unable to respond to the tasks or behavior required by a test because of linguistic or cultural differences unless culturally and linguistically appropriate measures are administered by qualified persons. In those cases in which appropriate measures and/or qualified persons are not available, diagnostic-prescriptive educational programs should be used until the child has acquired sufficient familiarity with the language and culture of the school for more formal assessment.

The problem of misplacement and overrepresentation of minority, as well as LEP, children has been ameliorated but not yet resolved to the complete satisfaction of many parents and educators. As this problem of overrepresentation has been addressed and partially resolved, a new problem of underrepresentation has also developed in some areas of the country. It appears that some students who have a disability and are also limited in their use of English are not being referred and placed into the special education programs they need. This seems to be to a certain extent the result of an overreaction to the misplacement issue. This phenomenon, along with related litigation, is addressed later in this chapter.

FEDERAL LEGISLATIVE HISTORY OF BILINGUAL EDUCATION

It was pointed out in Chapter 2 that bilingual education is not a new educational innovation. Bilingual education has a long-standing, rich historical tradition worldwide. Federal support for bilingual education in the United States is, however, a relatively new phenomenon. The federal government's involvement in bilingual education came about through the passage of the Bilingual Education Act (PL 90-247). This occurred on January 2, 1968. This Act is known as Title VII of the Elementary and Secondary Education Act. The Act in part states:

The congress declares it to be the policy of the United States, in order to establish equal educational opportunity for all children (A) to encourage the establishment and operation, where appropriate, of educational programs using bilingual educational practices, techniques, and methods, and (B) for that purpose, to provide financial assistance to local education agencies, and to State education agencies for certain purposes, in order to enable such local educational agencies to develop and carry out such programs in elementary and secondary schools, including activities at the preschool level, which are designed to meet the educational needs of such children; and to demonstrate effective ways of providing, for children of limited English speaking ability, instruction designed to enable them, while using their native language, to achieve competence in the English language.

When this initial law was passed, it carried with it a miniscule appropriation of $7.5 million to fund 76 local school district programs. In order to qualify for the programs, children had to be identified as having limited English speaking ability (LESA) and as coming from low-income families who lived in environments where the dominant language was not English. The primary purpose of the law was to assist students in developing greater competence in English. It also promoted native language improvement, the study of the history and culture associated with the student's mother tongue, and the enhancement of the child's self-esteem. The passage of this law marked the first time that a lack of English proficiency was acknowledged at the federal legislative level as a barrier to equal access to educational opportunities.

The 1968 Bilingual Education Act, once implemented, was found to be limited in certain areas. Therefore, Congress amended it with the passage of PL 93-380 in 1974. The requirement that a LESA child be from a low-income family was removed. This increased the population of students who qualified to receive services. Additional language groups became eligible for services. Some of these language groups included the French, Portuguese, Italian, and Greek. Another weakness in the 1968 legislation was its failure to provide a means of assessing the success of the bilingual program. This was remedied in the 1974 amendments. The Secretary of the Interior was given the responsibility of reviewing and evaluating bilingual education programs. The 1974 legislation did not take a definitive position on the transitional approach versus the maintenance approach to bilingual education. This can be seen from the language used in the project application manual published after the passage of the 1974 legislation. According to this manual, both the maintenance as well as the transitional approaches to bilingual education are acceptable:

It is intended that children participating in this program will develop greater competence in English, become more proficient in their dominant language, and profit from increased educational opportunity. Though the Title VII, ESEA program affirms the primary importance of English, it also recognizes that the use of the children's mother tongue in school can have a beneficial effect upon their education. Instructional use of the mother tongue can help to prevent retardation in school performance until sufficient command of English is attained. Moreover, the development of literacy in the mother tongue as well as in English should result in more broadly educated adults.

In 1978 the Bilingual Education Act was further amended as PL 95-561. Through these amendments, the definition of the target population changed from LESA (limited English speaking ability) to LEP (limited English proficient). This again expanded the population of eligible participants. Limited English proficiency was defined to include children with limited English reading, writing, speaking, and understanding. The 1978 statute formally included the Native American and Native Alaskan language groups. In order to promote a multicultural environment and to protect the LEP student from segregation, the law set up a 60:40 ratio requirement. This meant the monolingual English speaker could participate in the program but only up to a maximum of 40% of the total number of children.

The uses of the native language and culture in bilingual education were maintained in the 1978 legislation, but as Leibowitz (1980) points out, they were subordinated to a stronger English language emphasis. Another strong emphasis included in the 1978 legislation was the support included for research. The Act itself states: "The Commissioner [of Education] is charged to carry out a research program through competitive contracts with institutions of higher education, private and nonprofit organizations, state educational agencies, and individuals."

The research activities to be funded are set forth in the statute and are wide-ranging. Almost all arose in a 1978 Senate initiative:

1. Studies to determine and evaluate effective models for bilingual bicultural programs.
2. Studies to determine
   a. language acquisition characteristics and
   b. the most effective method of teaching English within the context of a bilingual bicultural program.
3. A five-year longitudinal study to measure the effect of bilingual education on students who have non-English language proficiencies.
4. Studies to identify the most effective and reliable method of identifying students entitled to bilingual education services.
5. Studies to determine the most effective methods for teaching reading to children

and adults who have language proficiencies other than English.
6. Studies to determine the effectiveness of teacher training preservice and inservice programs funded under this title.
7. Studies to determine the critical cultural characteristics of selected groups of individuals in order to teach about culture in the program.
8. The operation of a clearinghouse of information for bilingual education.

In 1984 the Bilingual Education Act was again amended and signed by the president as PL 98-511. Other related pieces of legislation also support bilingual education. These include the bilingual vocational training provisions of the Carl Perkins Vocational Education Act of 1984, the refugee education provisions of the Refugee Act of 1980, and provisions of the Emergency Immigrant Education Act of the Education Amendments of 1984.

The 1984 Bilingual Education Act reauthorized bilingual education for four years through September 30, 1988. According to Stein (1984), the following are the key funding provisions of the Act:

1. At least 60% of the funds for the Act as a whole are to be set aside for financial assistance for bilingual education programs (Part A).
2. At least 75% of the Part A amount is to be reserved for transitional bilingual education programs.
3. From 4 to 10% of the overall funds are to be set aside for special alternative instructional programs. (These are English-only programs)
4. At least 25% of the funds are to be reserved for training and technical assistance (Part C).
5. The National Advisory and Coordinating Council for Bilingual Education is to receive

up to 1% of the funds not reserved for Parts A and C.

6. State education agencies are eligible for grants of at least $50,000, not to exceed 5% of the funds received under Part A the previous fiscal year.

The 1984 amendments introduced several new program options. Included among these are the following six types of programs:

1. Transitional bilingual education programs. These programs combine structured English language instruction with a native language component. These programs also incorporate the students' cultural heritage into the curriculum.

2. Developmental bilingual education programs. These are programs of English- and second-language instruction designed to help children achieve competence in English and a second language.

3. Special alternative instructional programs. These are specially designed programs in which native language instruction need not be used.

4. Academic excellence programs. These are transitional bilingual education developmental bilingual education, or special alternative instruction programs that have an established record of providing effective, academically excellent instruction for limited English proficient (LEP) students. These programs must be designed to serve as models of exemplary bilingual education programs and to disseminate information on effective bilingual education practices.

5. Family English literacy programs. These are programs designed to help adults and out-of-school youth achieve English language competency. Preference will be given to the immediate families of LEP students in programs funded under this act. The program curriculum includes instruction on how parents and family members can assist LEP children with educational achievement.

6. Preschool, special education and gifted programs. Under the Act, one- to three-year grants may be awarded to conduct preschool, special education, and gifted and talented programs. The programs, however, are to be "preparatory or supplementary to programs such as those assisted under this Act."

In 1994 the 103rd Congress undertook a major reform of our federal education legislation. This extensive and far-reaching reform has impacted all of education, including bilingual education. The two most significant pieces of legislation enacted in 1994 were H.R. 1804, entitled Goals 2000: Educate America Act; and Public Law 103-382 Improving America's Schools Act of 1994. With this legislation the Congress abandoned the compensatory and categorical model for both Title I and bilingual education that had been the norm since the Elementary and Secondary Education Act of 1965. For the first time in the history of the United States, our legislators acknowledged that children with limited English proficiency as well as children living in poverty could and should be expected to achieve at high and rigorous academic standards.

The Goals 2000: Educate America Act was designed specifically for the following purposes: to improve learning and teaching by providing a national framework for education reform; to promote the research, consensus building, and systemic changes needed to ensure equitable educational opportunities and high levels of educational achievement for all students; to provide a framework for reauthorization of all federal education programs; and to promote the development and adoption of a voluntary national system of skill standards and certifications.

PL 103-382 Improving America's Schools Act of 1994 was also passed in 1994. The purpose of this legislation is to enable schools to provide opportunities for children to acquire the knowledge and skills contained in the challenging state content standards and to meet the challenging state performance standards developed for all children. According to the law, this should be accomplished by:

1. Ensuring high standards for all children and aligning the efforts of states, local educational agencies, and schools to help children served under this title to reach such standards.

2. Providing children an enriched and accelerated educational program, including, when appropriate, the use of the arts, through schoolwide programs or through additional services that increase the amount and quality of instructional time so that children served under this title receive at least the classroom instruction that other children receive.

3. Promoting schoolwide reform and ensuring access of children (from the earliest grades) to effective instructional strategies and challenging academic content that includes intensive complex thinking and problem-solving experiences.

4. Significantly upgrading the quality of instruction by providing staff in participating schools with substantial opportunities for professional development.

5. Coordinating services under all parts of this title with each other, with other educational services, and, to the extent feasible, with health and social service programs funded from other sources.

6. Affording parents meaningful opportunities to participate in the education of their children at home and at school.

7. Distributing resources, in amounts sufficient to make a difference, to areas and schools where needs are greatest.

8. Improving accountability, as well as teaching and learning, by using state assessment systems designed to measure how well children served under this title are achieving challenging state student performance standards expected of all children.

9. Providing greater decision-making authority and flexibility to schools and teachers in exchange for greater responsibility for student performance.

The latest version of Title VII which is a sub part of Improving America's Schools Act of 1994 makes funding available for the purpose of increasing the capacity of Local Education Agencies (LEAs) and State Education Agencies (SEAs) to meet the educational needs of linguistically and culturally diverse students. It provides educators with the flexibility to implement and expand programs that build upon the strengths of linguistically and culturally diverse students with the goal of helping them achieve to high academic standards.

The Improving of America's School Act of 1994 reauthorizes Title VII in a new configuration (U.S. Department of Education, 1997). The reauthorized Title VII strengthens the comprehensive approach of funded programs, streamlines program definitions to enhance flexibility, strengthens the state administrative role, improves research and evaluation, and emphasizes professional development. The new Title VII:

• Establishes four functional discretionary grant categories aligned with the department's comprehensive educational reform efforts. The restructured programs are (1) three-year development and implementation grants to initiate new programs, (2) two-year enhancement grants to improve existing programs, (3) five-year comprehensive school grants to develop projects integrated with the overall school program, and (4) five-year system-wide improvement grants for district-wide projects that serve all or most LEP students.

- Improves local program evaluations and promotes the use of appropriate assessments linked to instructional practices that build upon the strengths of linguistically and culturally diverse students to help them achieve to high standards. It supports field-initiated research, enhanced national dissemination efforts, and growth in academic excellence programs.

- Strengthens the state role by requiring SEAs to review Title VII applications within the context of their state reform plans. The new Title VII promotes partnerships between SEAs, LEAs, and other entities for purposes of improving program design, assessment of student performance, and capacity building to meet the educational services of linguistically and culturally diverse students.

- Redesigns and strengthens professional development programs and ensures their integration with broader school curricula and reforms to improve the knowledge base and practices of educational personnel serving linguistically and culturally diverse students.

- Authorizes the Foreign Language Assistance Program as a discretionary grant program to help local educational agencies establish and improve foreign language instruction in elementary and secondary schools. This program aims to develop the foreign language proficiency of our students to face the challenges, as a nation, of the increasingly competitive global economy.

- Incorporates the Emergency Immigrant Education Act, which provides funds to assist in supporting educational services in local educational agencies that experience large increases in their student enrollment due to immigration.

- Incorporates the Uniform Provisions Section of Title XIV to provide for the participation of eligible children attending private schools, including timely and meaningful consultation procedures.

As you can see, the original Bilingual Education Act of 1968 has gone through a number of significant changes over the past 30 years. The changes have gradually expanded the population of eligible students. The changes have also opened up many new program options and have put much more emphasis on the acquisition of English language proficiency as well as on the development of the native language.

While the federal bilingual legislation has played a key role in shaping the federal policy toward bilingual education, civil rights legislation and juridical case law has also had a major role in shaping this policy. The list of court cases and legislation in Table 4–1 summarizes the gradual evolution of federal policy regarding bilingual education.

STATE BILINGUAL EDUCATION LAWS

Since education is a state responsibility, it is not surprising that most states have addressed the broader issue of the use or prohibition of non-English languages in the school. As mentioned in Chapter 1, bilingual education flourished in many states during the 1880s. During the post-World War I era, however, the trend throughout the country was for states to pass laws that prohibited the use of non-English languages for purposes of instruction, with the exception of foreign language education at the secondary level. This anti-second language legislative trend began to reverse itself with the advent of the Civil Rights Movement in the 1960s.

In 1971, 20 states did not permit bilingual instruction in the public schools (Cordasco, 1976). These states included Alabama, Arkansas, Connecticut, Delaware, Idaho, Indiana, Iowa, Kansas, Louisiana, Michigan, Minnesota, Montana, Nebraska, North Carolina, North Dakota, Oklahoma, Oregon, South Dakota, West Virginia, and Wisconsin. Five years later, in 1976, 7 of the above-mentioned states repealed their English-only legislation.

Table 4–1
Evolution of Federal Bilingual Education Policy

1920s-1960s	English immersion or "sink-or-swim" policies are the dominant method of instruction for language minority students. Few or no remedial services are available, and students are generally held at the same grade level until enough English is mastered to advance in subject areas.
1963	Success of a two-way bilingual program for Cuban refugee children in Dade County, FL inspires implementation of similar programs elsewhere.
1964	Civil Rights Act: Title VI prohibits discrimination on the basis of race, color, or national origin in the operation of all federally-assisted programs.
1968	The Bilingual Education Act, Title VII of the Elementary and Secondary Education Act of 1968, establishes federal policy for bilingual education for economically disadvantaged language-minority students, allocates funds for innovative programs, and recognizes the unique educational disadvantages faced by non-English speaking students.
1974	*Lau v. Nichols* suit by Chinese parents in San Francisco leads to Supreme Court ruling that identical education does not constitute equal education under the Civil Rights Act. School districts must take "affirmative steps" to overcome educational barriers faced by non-English speakers. Congress passes the Equal Educational Opportunity Act, extending the *Lau* decision to all schools.
1978	Amendments to Title VII emphasize strictly transitional nature of native language instruction, expand eligibility to students who are limited English proficient (LEP), and permit enrollment of English speaking students in bilingual programs.
1982	*Plyler v. Doe* Supreme Court case denies the state's right to exclude the children of illegal immigrants from public schools.
1984	Amendments to Title VII allow for some native language maintenance, provide program funding for LEP students with special needs, support family English literacy programs, and emphasize importance of teacher training.
1988	Amendments to Title VII include increased funding to state education agencies, expanded funding for "special alternative" programs where only English is used, a three-year limit on participation in most Title VII programs, and the creation of fellowship programs for professional training.
1994	Comprehensive education reforms entail reconfiguration of Title VII programs. New provisions reinforce professional development programs, increase attention to language maintenance and foreign language instruction, improve research and evaluation at state and local level, supply additional funds for immigrant education, and allow participation of some private school students.

These states were Connecticut, Indiana, Kansas, Michigan, North Dakota, Oregon, and South Dakota. By 1981 only 5 states prohibited bilingual education. These are Alabama, Arkansas, Delaware, Nebraska, and West Virginia. The types of bilingual education statutes passed by the various states were similar to the special education laws in terms of their permissive and mandatory provisions. According to the Center for Applied Linguistics (1981), 30 states had bilingual education legislation that was either mandatory (18 states) or permissive (12 states). Interestingly, states such as Texas, California, New Mexico, Illinois, and New York, which have large numbers of LEP students, all have mandatory statutes. Florida, however, which also has a high concentration of LEP students, has permissive legislation.

THE OFFICIAL ENGLISH MOVEMENT

The movement to declare English the official language of the U.S. started in 1981 when Senator S.I. Hayakawa of California introduced a constitutional amendment to Congress. Since that time, 20 states have made English the official language either by legislation or through a constitutional amendment (Crawford, 1995). This movement has had a negative impact on legislation supporting bilingual education at both the state and the national level. For example, in 1986 California, the state with the largest number of LEP students, had the strongest and most prescriptive bilingual education legislation in the country. One year later, after English was declared the official language of California, bilingual education legislation was completely eliminated. In 1995, Congressman King of New York introduced a bill to make English the official language of the United States. A provision of this proposed legislation called for the repeal of the federal Bilingual Education Act.

BILINGUAL EDUCATION AND THE COURTS

The legislative and, to an extent, the executive branches of our government have had a significant role in advancing the cause of equal educational opportunity for all citizens, including people with disabilities as well as the limited English proficient. The role of the judicial branch of government, however, is perhaps the most critical in guaranteeing that the rights of these individuals are not only protected but facilitated. The decisions of the courts at both the state and the federal levels in bilingual education are therefore of utmost importance to the field of bilingual special education. These decisions are even more significant to the parents and children directly affected by them.

Any contemporary discussion of bilingual education litigation should be centered around the 1974 unanimous U.S. Supreme Court decision in *Lau v. Nichols,* 44 U.S. 563, 1974. This is without question the landmark case in this field of study. The *Lau* case was a class action suit brought before the highest court of the United States in behalf of 1,800 Chinese students. The Court did not involve itself directly in the specifics of school curriculum by mandating bilingual education. It did, however, state that "there was no equality of treatment merely by providing students with the same facilities, textbooks, teachers, and curriculum, for students who do not understand English are effectively foreclosed from any meaningful education." The Court went on to further stipulate that special language programs were necessary if schools were going to provide equal educational opportunity. According to Teitelbaum and Hiller (1977), the *Lau* decision is significant because, even though it did not expressly endorse bilingual education per se, it "did legitimize and give impetus to the movement for equal educational opportunity for non-English speakers as only a unanimous Supreme Court ruling can."

Before getting into the implications of the *Lau* decision and a discussion of the other related cases subsequent to *Lau,* we will discuss briefly the rationale upon which *Lau* was based as well as the trend of the cases before *Lau.* A careful analysis of the decision itself shows that the Court relied exclusively on Title VI of the Civil Rights Act of 1964. The decision states:

> We do not reach the Equal Protection Clause argument which has been advanced but rely solely on section 601 of the Civil Rights Act of 1964, 42 U.S.C. 200d to reverse the Court of Appeals. That section bans discrimination based "on the ground of race, color or national origin," in "any program or activity receiving Federal financial assistance."

Another factor that highly influenced the Court in its decision was the so-called May 25th Memorandum of 1970. This was a regulatory document published by the U.S. Department of

Health, Education and Welfare in an attempt to assist school districts to comply with the Civil Rights Act of 1964. This directive told school districts that they must correct English language deficiencies by taking affirmative steps that go beyond the provision of the same books and teachers to all students.

Only a few cases before *Lau* dealt with the use of non-English languages. Teitelbaum and Hiller (1977) discuss three significant cases in this regard. They are *Meyer v. Nebraska* (1923), *Yu Cong v. Trinidad* (1925), and *Cardona v. Power* (1966). In the *Meyer* case a teacher had been convicted for giving German instruction in a private school; the Court ruled in favor of the teacher and overturned the conviction. The *Yu Cong* decision upheld the use of foreign languages in commerce by striking down a Philippine criminal statute called "Chinese Bookkeeping Act," which permitted only the use of English and Spanish. The final case, *Cardona v. Power,* challenged the use of a literacy test for a Spanish-speaking Puerto Rican from New York. It was declared moot because of the passage of the Voting Rights Act of 1965. Nonetheless, both Justice Douglas and Justice Fortas went on record supporting Spanish literacy as a basis for voting.

It can be seen from this discussion that before the *Lau* decision, bilingual education related issues had never been directly considered by the courts. In these early cases, the rights of individuals to use non-English languages in private schools, in commerce, and, to an extent, in the exercise of one's civic responsibilities were upheld. It is also important to note that although *Lau* is closely related to the *Brown v. Topeka Board of Education,* 347 U.S. 483, 1954, in terms of equal educational opportunity, it was not argued directly on the equal protection principle of the Fourteenth Amendment of the Constitution, as was the *Brown* case. The *Brown* case was decided by the Supreme Court some 44 years ago. It is also an extremely important landmark decision in the area of school desegregation and civil rights

generally. It in effect outlawed socially segregated systems of public education as inherently unfair and unconstitutional (Baca and Chinn, 1982). The *Brown* case is important both to those with disabilities as well as to English language learners, because it played such a major role in the development of our current social and educational policy. It helped create the climate that made the passage of the Civil Rights Act of 1964 and the Education of All Handicapped Children Act of 1975 and IDEA possible.

The impact of *Lau* on the public schools, on subsequent legislation, and on the courts has been very significant as well as controversial. Teitelbaum and Hiller (1979) point out that *Lau* raised the nation's consciousness of the need for bilingual education and in so doing, encouraged both federal and state legislation, motivated federal enforcement efforts through the U.S. Office of Civil Rights, and set the stage for a number of additional lawsuits.

According to Applewhite (1979), the aftermath of *Lau* can be more easily interpreted by examining the cases that spell out what he calls the "legal dialect" of bilingual education. The critical cases are *Keyes v. School District #1,* Denver, Colorado; *Serna v. Portales Municipal Schools,* New Mexico; *Aspira of New York, Inc. v. Board of Education of the City of New York; Otero v. Mesa County Valley School District No. 51;* and *Rios v. Reed,* New York.

In the *Serna* case, segregation was not an issue. According to Applewhite (1979), the court voted that although an equal education was provided to the Spanish-speaking student, in terms of teachers, classrooms, and textbooks, the district did not address the English language deficiencies of the students. The court mandated the adoption of a bilingual program. Both *Serna* and *Keyes* relied heavily on the principle of equal protection under the law taken from the Fourteenth Amendment in arriving at their final decision (Teitelbaum and Hiller, 1979). The Tenth Circuit Court of Appeals upheld the *Serna* decision and held that the students had a right to a bilingual education.

The *Aspira* case is another very significant case dealing with bilingual education. Puerto Rican, as well as other Hispanic students, sued the New York City Board of Education for not living up to its publicly stated commitment to provide bilingual education. Tens of thousands of students were getting no instruction related to their language and cultural needs, and many were receiving instruction in English as a Second Language (ESL) only. At the same time that the *Aspira* case was being argued, the *Lau* decision was handed down. Seven months later, in August of 1974, the parties consented to a decree. The decree requires the district to design and implement an approved method for assessing the English and Spanish language skills of students to determine who is eligible for bilingual education. The decree also addresses teacher qualification and recruitment and explicitly forbids the use of a pull-out program that would remove children from their regular classroom.

Teitelbaum and Hiller (1979) point out that *Aspira* is perhaps the most far-reaching court-ordered bilingual program ruling since *Lau*. They also point out, however, that *Aspira*, unlike *Lau*, is limited to Spanish-speaking students only and to Spanish speakers who are more proficient in Spanish than they are in English.

The *Otero* case is important because it is the only case that was decided in favor of the defendants and that did not require the district to provide bilingual education. The court found that the low level of achievement of Chicano students was caused by socioeconomic factors rather than by the type of educational program. According to Applewhite (1979), the low number of affected students was an important factor in this decision. The right to bilingual education was not upheld.

The *Rios v. Reed* case of 1977 is also very significant because it introduced for the first time the issue of effectiveness or quality of a

district's bilingual program. In this case a school district in Long Island, New York, was told that the critical question is not simply the provision of a bilingual program, but rather whether the program is effective. "An inadequate program is as harmful to a child who does not speak English as no program at all" (*Rios v. Reed*, 75 C.296 at 15).

Finally, *Casteneda v. Pickard* (48 F.2nd.989, 1981) set up court standards for reviewing remediation plans and said that, although a school policy for programs may have once been appropriate, nevertheless, it is subject to review in the future if, in practice, it has failed to remediate.

BILINGUAL SPECIAL EDUCATION: THE LAW AND THE COURTS

Up to this point we have reviewed the major legislation and litigation relative both to special education and to bilingual education. No laws have been passed up to this time that specifically mandate bilingual special education for bilingual exceptional students. Existing laws, however, in both bilingual education and special education do apply to bilingual exceptional children. This is so because both Title VI of the Civil Rights Act of 1964 as well as Section 504 of the Rehabilitation Act prohibit discrimination based on race, national origin, and handicapping conditions under any program receiving federal financial assistance. In practice, this means is that a bilingual exceptional child qualifies for services under both special education as well as bilingual education. *Just because a bilingual exceptional child qualifies for services under special education does not mean that he/she is automatically disqualified for services under bilingual education or vice versa.* For some bilingual exceptional students, the ideal situation would be to receive bilingual special education services through one teacher who has the training and expertise to provide the special education services within an inclusive bilingual instructional environment.

Bilingual special education services for bilingual exceptional children are not just guaranteed through Title VI of the Civil Rights Act and Section 504 of the Rehabilitation Act. IDEA as well as the *Lau* remedies also support the provision of bilingual special education services when a student's needs call for it. Bergin (1980) also supports this position. She puts it this way: "The law guarantees minority language handicapped students equal access to education. Special education and bilingual education must come together within the administrative structure of a school system to provide, in practice, what the law requires."

In terms of litigation, issues related to bilingual special education have been addressed in several New York court cases. In *Lora v. Board of Education*, New York, which was settled in 1978, a program of Hispanic and Black students in a day school for the emotionally disturbed was found to be inadequate. *Jose P. v. Ambach* was filed in 1979. It charged that students with disabilities were being denied a free and appropriate education because of a lack of timely evaluation and placement in an appropriate program. Later in 1979, the case of *United Cerebral Palsy (UCP) of New York v. Board of Education* charged that children who have disabilities resulting from brain injury or other impairments to the central nervous system were not receiving appropriate special education services.

The most significant of these cases was *Dyrcia S. et al v. Board of Education of the City of New York et al*. This case was also filed in 1979. The plaintiffs were Puerto Rican and other Hispanic children living in New York City who were LEP and had a disability, and who required bilingual special education programs for which they were not being promptly evaluated and placed. Because these cases were all so closely related to one another in terms of location, content, and timing, a consolidated judgment was issued in the *UCP* and *Dyrcia S.* cases, which incorporated the provisions of the *Jose P.* case. In summary, the relief that was

ordered affects all special education programs and procedures in the city of New York. What follows is a brief summary of the court order, particularly as it relates to the bilingual provisions. The relief included these provisions:

1. Identification of children needing special education services with the inclusion of an outreach office with adequate bilingual resources.

2. Appropriate evaluation through the establishment of school-based support teams to evaluate children in their own environment with a bilingual, nondiscriminatory evaluation process.

3. Appropriate programs in the least restrictive environment, including a comprehensive continuum of services with the provision of appropriate bilingual programs at each level of the continuum for children with limited English proficiency.

4. Due process and parental student rights, including a Spanish version of a parent's rights booklet, which explains all of the due process rights of children and parents. Also included is the hiring of neighborhood workers to facilitate parental involvement in the evaluation and development of the individualized educational program.

A subsequent bilingual special education case, which is classified as an educational malpractice suit, was filed on Nov. 12, 1981 in the U.S. District Court of New Jersey. It is known as *Carrasquillo v. Board of Education of the City of Plainfield*, No. 81-3503 (D.N.J. 1981). According to Moran (1981), the 17-year-old plaintiff claimed she was misclassified by a school psychologist and placed in a class for the educable mentally retarded. According to the plaintiff, this occurred after one school psychologist evaluated her as having a severe learning disability and after the physician of the New Jersey Association for Retarded Citizens indicated that her problems centered around her language barrier. The relief the plaintiff was seeking included concentrated and specialized tutorial educational assistance, psychological counseling from a bilingual psychologist, and compensatory and punitive damages and attorney's fees.

The most recent bilingual special education court case is currently in litigation in the state of New York. It is referred to by professionals in New York as the "baby *Jose P.* case" because it is similar to the *Jose P.* case. The "baby" designation is due to the fact that it is at the early childhood level of birth through age five. The official name of the case is *Ray M. v. Board of Education of the City of New York. Ray M.* was filed in 1994 and is still in process. Nonetheless, the city and state of New York have already responded to some of the issues raised by this case. The New York Department of Education, for example, has recently published a set of guidelines for bilingual special education services at the early childhood level.

☺ SUMMARY

This chapter has discussed the legislative history of special education at both state and federal levels. The early period from 1776 to 1817 was known as the period of neglect of people with disabilities. The age of the asylum followed from 1817 to 1869. The period of day schools for the disabled followed from 1869 to 1913. From 1913 to 1950 was the age of public school programs for the disabled. The final period from 1950 to the present is called the age of equity for individuals with disabilities. Most of the major legislation authorizing education services for students with disabilities has been formulated during this age of equity. The most significant pieces of legislation were PL 99-10, which is known as the Elementary and Secondary Education Act of 1965; PL 94-142, the Education of All Handicapped Children Act of 1975; Individuals with Disabilities Education Act of 1991 (IDEA); and Improving America's Schools Act of 1994. Through these major pieces of legislation, LEP students with disabilities are entitled to nondiscriminatory bilingual assessment and an individualized educational program that warrants ESL support and could require bilingual instruction. The bilingual legislation at the federal level was instituted in 1968 with the passage of PL 90-247, which is known as the Bilingual Education Act. The law was amended in 1974, 1978, 1984, and 1994. The law provides financial support to school districts for the provision of bilingual instruction to children who are limited English proficient. There is nothing in the law that precludes the participation of bilingual exceptional children in these programs. State legislation in bilingual education has followed the general pattern that occurred in state special education legislation. Many of the states historically had statutes that excluded students with disabilities from the schools. Similarly, many states had statutes that forbade the use of non-English languages for instruction. The next trend in state legislation was to initiate permissive legislation, which allowed school districts to provide programs for both students with disabilities and LEP students. The final trend was the passage of mandatory legislation, which compelled districts to provide both special education services and bilingual education services.

In terms of litigation, the suits related to special education can be grouped into three categories. The categories are (1) right to an education, (2) right to adequate treatment, and (3) improper classification and placement. The decisions have all favored plaintiffs; their rights have been established and more appropriate services have been provided. In the area of bilingual education, the rights of the LEP students to special services, including bilingual education, have been firmly established. In some instances, bilingual programs have been mandated and the issue of the quality of the programs has been raised and upheld. The litigation dealing specifically with bilingual special education has also established the rights of bilingual exceptional children and their parents to receive bilingual instruction and supportive services.

☺ DISCUSSION QUESTIONS

1. Discuss the salient cases that have upheld the rights of plaintiffs in the area of bilingual education.
2. Discuss the salient cases that have upheld equity for students with disabilities.
3. Discuss the impact of current laws and mandates in the areas of bilingual and special education in your local school district.
4. What impact has the *Lau v. Nichols* case of 1974 had on your local school district?
5. Discuss the issue of over- and underrepresentation of LEP students in special education.
6. Select any two cases mentioned in this chapter and show their relation to the concepts of equal and adequate treatment of children.
7. What is the Official English movement and what impact has it had on bilingual education?

☺ REFERENCES

Abeson, A. (1973). *Legal chance for the handicapped through litigation.* Reston, VA: The Council for Exceptional Children.

Abeson, A. (1977). Litigation. In F. J. Weintraub et al. (Eds.). *Public policy and the education of exceptional children.* Reston, VA.: The Council for Exceptional Children.

Applewhite, S. R. (1979). The legal dialect of bilingual education. In R. V. Padilla (Ed.). *Bilingual education and public policy in the United States.* Ypsilanti, MI: Eastern Michigan University.

Baca, L., & Chinn, P. (1982, February). Coming to grips with cultural diversity. *Exceptional Children Quarterly, 2,* 4.

Bergin, V. D. (1980). *Special education needs in bilingual programs.* Rosslyn, VA: National Clearinghouse of Bilingual Education.

Bilingual Education Act, as amended by the Elementary and Secondary Education Amendments of 1978, PL 95-561, 92 Stat. 2268 (Nov. 1, 1978).

Bureau of Education for the Handicapped, U.S. Department of Health, Education and Welfare, Office of Education. State plan amendment for fiscal year 1975 under part B, Education of the Handicapped.

Carey, H. L. (1971, August). Education services for the handicapped: The federal role. *Compact, 5,* 4.

Casso, H. (1973). *A descriptive study of three legal challenges for placing Mexican American and other linguistically and culturally different children into educably mentally retarded classes.* Unpublished doctoral dissertation, University of Massachusetts, Amherst.

Center for Applied Linguistics. (1981). *Papers in applied linguistics, Bilingual Education Series: 9. The current status of bilingual education legislation: an update.* Washington, DC: Author.

Cordasco, F. (1976). *Bilingual schooling in the United States: A sourcebook for educational personnel.* New York: McGraw-Hill.

Crawford, J. (1995). *Bilingual education: History, politics, theory, and practice.* Trenton, NJ: Crane Publishing Company.

Lau v. Nichols (1974). 414 U.S. 563; 39L Ed 2d 1, 94 S. Ct. 786.

Leibowitz, A. H. (1980). *The Bilingual Education Act: A legislative analysis.* Rosslyn, VA: National Clearinghouse for Bilingual Education.

Lessow-Hurley, J. (1991). *A commonsense guide to Bilingual Education.* Alexandria, VA: Association for Supervision and Curriculum Development.

Lyons, J. (1988, revised 1992). *Legal responsibilities of education agencies serving national origin language minority students.* Washington, DC: The Mid-Atlantic Equity Center, The American University.

Moran, D. (1981). Educational malpractice suit filed. *NOLPE Notes.* Topeka, KS. vol. 16, no. 12, National Organization on Legal Problems of Education.

National Parent Network. (1997, February 28). *The Friday News,* No. 32.

Padilla, A. et al. (Eds) (1990). *Bilingual Education: Issues and strategies.* Newbury Park, CA: Sage Publications.

Rothstein, L. F. (1994). *Special Education Law.* New York: Longman Publishers.

Stein, C. B. (1984). *The 1984 Bilingual Education Act.* Rosslyn, VA: The National Clearinghouse for Bilingual Education.

Teitelbaum, H., & Hiller, R. (1977). The legal perspective. In *Center for applied linguistics, bilingual education: Current perspectives/law.* Arlington, VA: Center for Applied Linguistics.

Teitelbaum, H., & Hiller, R. J. (1979). Bilingual education: The legal mandate. In H. T. Trueba, & C. Barnett-Mizrahi (Eds.). *Bilingual multicultural education and the professional: From theory to practice.* Rowley, MA: Newbury House Publishers.

U.S. Department of Education (1994). *The Improving America's Schools Act of 1994: Summary Sheets.* Washington, DC.

U.S. Department of Education (1997). What does Title VII in the new Improving America's Schools Act authorize? *World Wide Web Site.*

U.S. Office of Education, Office of Bilingual Education (1980). Manual for application for grants under bilingual education, 1974. In A. H. Leibowitz, *The Bilingual Education Act: A legislative analysis.* Rosslyn, VA: National Clearinghouse for Bilingual Education.

Weintraub, F. J. (1971). *The encyclopedia of education.* New York: Macmillan.

Weintraub, F. J., Abeson, A. R., & Bradock, D. L. (1971). *State law and education of handicapped children: Issues and recommendations.* Reston, VA: The Council for Exceptional Children.

CHAPTER 5

Development of the Bilingual Special Education Interface

Leonard Baca
J. S. de Valenzuela

- Current Trends in Special Education
- Unanswered Calls for Change
- Avenues for Change
- Summary

OBJECTIVES

To introduce a new direction for bilingual special education

To present a historical perspective of this field

To provide a rationale for needed changes

To discuss the areas in need of change

To review potential avenues for change

To discuss how the roles of those involved will need to change to effect reform efforts

In the previous four chapters you have been exposed to four important topics in bilingual special education: the development of this field, its legal foundations, and the complementary disciplines of bilingual education and special education. The purpose of this chapter is to build upon this knowledge to present a new direction for bilingual special education.

In the past 20 years, educators have come to recognize the unique needs of culturally and linguistically diverse students with exceptionalities (CLDE). The purpose of the first edition of this text was to call for a needed interface between bilingual and special education to adequately address the educational needs of these CLDE students. The fundamental beliefs and adequacy of these separate systems were not challenged; it was assumed that what was needed was simply a merger of these two special programs to form a third—bilingual special education.

However, as this idea of an interface between bilingual and special education was coming to consciousness, significant changes were emerging within special education. The inherent "specialness" of special education was being challenged, with individuals questioning whether special education actually provided intervention techniques and strategies that were truly "special" (Stainback & Stainback, 1984). Secondly, evidence began to mount that once a student is placed in special education, he or she typically remains there. Also, questions were raised about the validity of the diagnostic categories which determined what services were needed (Algozzine & Ysseldyke, 1983; Shepard & Smith, 1983). Therefore, special educators began to ask "what is so special about special education?"

The efficacy of maintaining two (or more) separate educational systems was also challenged. Special education and general education have their own budgets, administrators, teachers, certification systems, and educational programs. The formalization of bilingual special education as an additional specialized program that does not interact with other programs augmented this problem. These divisions of students and personnel into separate and compartmentalized programs is the antithesis of the collaborative consultative model, revolving around the general education classroom, that we are supporting. This consultative model will be discussed in greater detail later in this chapter.

Skrtic (1988) finds that "decoupled" programs provide barriers to adoption of recommended best practices. Decoupled programs are those in which two incompatible bureaucratic structures co-exist to fulfill the frequently incongruent responsibilities of education: (1) compliance with public standards, and (2) doing complex, professional work. Skrtic posits that "formal" and "informal" structures exist to comply with these disparate responsibilities. The "formal" structure of rules and regulations and the "informal" structure that influences how teachers really perform the complex work of teaching are many times in conflict. This uneasy co-existence of two different bureaucratic structures forces many teachers to simply close their doors and teach as they feel is best.

The existence of these decoupled systems can hinder attempts at collaboration as teachers may feel uneasy about exposing their actual practices to close scrutiny. This conflict can also be seen in assessment practices, where, due to the perceived constraints of district guidelines, assessment personnel often fail to report the legitimate modifications they make during the administration of standardized test batteries. To resolve these problems caused by decoupled programs, Skrtic proposes that schools bypass these bureaucracies to become "adhocracies," or problem-solving organizations, in which unique solutions are created for each problem or situation as it arises. For schools to become adhocratic as Skrtic recommends, many changes will be required. Foremost is the development of a forum for open and honest dialog about actual practices and beliefs without fear of recrimination. We hope that this text can be used as the basis for such a dialogue, rather than as a cookbook or prescription for requisite practices.

Due to these concerns, as well as others that will be discussed later, we have come to a point where we need to question our original vision of a bilingual special education interface. While it is still apparent that CLD students, with and without exceptionalities, do have unique needs that must be addressed, we do not believe that separate, decoupled educational programs adequately and appropriately meet their needs. Therefore, we propose that the bilingual special education interface become a merger of the unique talents of general education with those of special programs. We are advocating that CLDE students remain part of the general education system with the support and collaboration of specialists who are knowledgeable about and sensitive to their needs and abilities. This interface depends not only on the full inclusion of students with exceptionalities into general education, but also the inclusion of special educators and special programs into general education.

With this emphasis on programmatic inclusion and away from decoupled, disjointed programs, we need to examine how CLDE students will be treated, both programmatically as well as philosophically. Currently, when a general education teacher identifies a student experiencing difficulties, he or she refers the student for assessment. After a staffing meeting, the assessment results are reviewed and a placement determination is made. If that student is diagnosed as requiring special education services, then the student becomes the responsibility of special education. The student's individual educational plan (IEP) specifies what he or she should be learning and by when. Typically, the special education evaluation is carried out by assessment personnel, with little or no input from the general education teacher once the initial referral is made. Similarly, the teaching provided by special educators frequently is unrelated to that provided within the classroom. This intervention is also separate from the assessment process. Standardized test scores, although useful for stating percentile ranks and eligibility for services for placement, give little useful information about how a particular student will best learn what material. In this context, then, we can also say that assessment and instruction are decoupled, each from the other as well as from general education. Therefore, this new bilingual special education interface also will require the merger of assessment and intervention and the integrated use of current best practices that have developed from both areas.

In addition to procedural changes, the new bilingual special education interface also implies a shift in how we think about CLD students, both with and without disabilities. We envision the interface to include the awareness of the interaction of the student with his or her environment and the educational process within the greater social context. We can no longer condone remedial practices that respond only to "within-child" disabilities. The focus of attention must shift from the individual student to a critical examination of the student's interaction with the world.

CURRENT TRENDS IN SPECIAL EDUCATION

There have been three major trends in special education reform: the movement toward inclusion, adoption of the collaborative consultation model for intervention, and prereferral intervention. Although many other areas have been suggested in the literature as needing reform, inclusion, collaboration, and prereferral intervention have become actualities, at least to some extent, in many schools. As discussed in Chapter 4, PL 94-142 was instrumental in beginning the move from placement of students with special needs in separate classes to the regular classroom. The legislation introduced the concept of the "least restrictive environment." The different possibilities for placement within this philosophy of the least restrictive environment have been described as a cascade of services (Reynolds & Birch, 1977). This cascade is provided in Chapter 3. Within this philosophy, the least restrictive environment refers to a placement location, such as whether the student receives services at a special school, in a special day class, partially in a special class, or in the general education classroom with pull-out or consultation services.

Inclusion

In this book, we would like to contrast the idea of the least restrictive environment with inclusion. The definition of *inclusion* is difficult to specify, as it means different things to different people. For example, for those who think of inclusion as a placement issue (as discussed in Chapter 3), it refers to the full-time enrollment of students with special needs in the general education classroom. "Full inclusionists" are those individuals that share the belief that *all* students with disabilities should be enrolled full-time in general education classes.

At present, almost 70% of all students with disabilities in the United States receive assistance within the general education classroom or in a combination of the general education classroom and resource room (National Center for Educational Statistics, 1994). Although we strongly believe that a much larger percentage of students can and should be served in the general education classroom, our current focus is on whether "mainstreamed" students are truly included in the general education classroom environment. We contest that simply adding more students to the general education classroom will not bring about the fundamental changes needed for true inclusion. Our primary focus must shift from asking how many students are educated in general education classrooms to questioning how those students are educated. Through changes in how educators view the function of the general classroom and the participation of different types of teachers in the education of CLD youth, with and without exceptionalities, we believe that true inclu-

sion can become a reality for greater numbers of students with a wide range of disabilities.

This stated focus reveals our philosophy that inclusion implies much more than the full-time attendance of a student with disabilities in a general education class. We suggest that inclusion refers to the amount of involvement, or active participation, of students with exceptionalities in the general education curriculum. Collier and Baca (1994) define this participation as including all of "the planned and guided learning experiences under the direction of the school and teachers." From this perspective, the curriculum is clearly viewed as much more than the content covered in specific subject areas. All school experiences, both in and out of the classroom, comprise the curriculum. This implies that inclusion must incorporate a wide range of possible school experiences. For high school students, inclusion, or access to the curriculum, may include opportunities to participate in after-school clubs and activities, such as music or sports.

Our vision of inclusive environments questions the practice of "mainstreaming" students by placing them in the general education classroom for the majority of their day, but giving them different, nonrelated lessons and either intentionally or unintentionally excluding them from full and active participation in whole group projects and activities. Students who spend time in general education classes yet are perceived of as "special ed kids" and still the responsibility of the special education department are not "fully included." We also question the inclusion of students with disabilities who receive unadapted instruction in the general education classroom. While this common practice may appear to be equitable on the surface, as we learned in the *Lau v. Nichols* case, equal treatment does not guarantee equitable treatment. If the unadapted curriculum is not accessible to students with disabilities, then we cannot claim that they are fully included in the classroom curriculum.

This definition of an inclusive environment does not necessarily exclude the possibility of some out-of-classroom instruction or activities for students with exceptionalities, although we do not endorse "pull-out" programs that seek to provide the majority of a student's "special" instruction in a noninclusive and segregated environment. This idea that it is the philosophy of inclusion, rather than the location of instruction, that is crucial can be seen in the example of the student who is not identified as needing special education but who receives out-of-classroom instruction in music or another type of "enrichment" program. The "inclusion" of this student would never be questioned as he or she is assumed to be a full participant in the general curriculum. Therefore, inclusion refers to the extent of access by students with diverse needs to the general curriculum of a classroom and/or school rather than the location of their instruction. To be fully included, students must: (1) be in the general classroom for the vast majority of the day, (2) have access to the general curriculum, (3) participate actively and fully in whole group classroom activities, and (4) be viewed as full members of the general classroom community.

Collaborative Consultation

Part of the move away from pull-out programs where special and regular education are decoupled involves the use of collaboration and consultation. Although true collaborative environments are hard to find, this practice is being actively promoted in many schools. A key factor in truly collaborative professional relationships is the willingness of all parties to listen and respect the needs and wants of others, rather than attempting to impose their perspective of what is needed on their peers. Through collaboration, the work that students do in special education can be closely related to that done in the regular classroom.

Consultation takes this idea a step further. Rather than special educators being responsible for direct provision of services to students with special needs, specialists work as consultants to general educators. This idea stems from the realization that unless the special education intervention will actually eliminate the students' academic problems, they will still experience difficulties during that part of the day when special help is not available. Therefore, consultation seeks to modify the students' classroom experiences on a full-time basis by collaboration between specialists and classroom teachers. Ideally, this will help not only the students with special needs in particular but also will provide indirect assistance for other students who are not officially eligible for special services and direct support for the teacher. In reality, pull-out programs that function without collaboration and consultation do no more for the classroom teacher than provide a respite when the students with special needs are removed from the class. Typically, they do not help the teacher learn how to better assist the students when they are in the regular classroom or work with those students who might have been referred for assessment but not found to be eligible for special education.

Collaboration allows classroom teachers to define their needs, with respect to particular students, and request and receive the help that they need and want. For this to succeed, special educators need to allow classroom teachers to define their needs. One way that special educators can approach general educators is by asking, "What can I do to help you?" Classroom teachers will not be receptive to collaborative consultation if it is viewed as a one-way process during which they are expected to implement the activities and modifications that the special educator has designed in isolation. Collaborative consultation must be a two-way relationship, with all participants viewed as equally competent and expert in their domain of knowledge.

Consultation provides an additional function when the special educator does not speak the dominant language of the student. Rather than providing direct services in the student's less proficient language, the monolingual special educator can teach demonstration lessons in the general classroom and consult with the teacher on ways to adapt the curriculum to the student's unique needs. In a bilingual classroom, these demonstration lessons can be part of the English as a Second Language (ESL) instructional component. The bilingual general educator would still provide primary language instruction to his or her students with exceptionalities, with assistance provided through collaboration and consultation with the special educator. Chapter 13 provides more information about theories and models of collaborative consultation, as well as sample schedules illustrating how different staff members can most effectively structure their schedules to incorporate collaborative consultation.

It is our contention that without a true philosophy of inclusion, the placement of students with special needs in the general education classroom is doomed to failure, especially for those students with severe or profound needs. We need to change our ideas about our roles as special educators involved in the schooling of students with and without identified disabilities. Perhaps we can come to view all students as being jointly served by general and special educators in a two-way collaboration. However, without this shift, in-classroom services will continue to be as decoupled and decontextualized as before, except now they will be delivered at the back of the class instead of in the broom closet or resource room. This certainly is not what people have in mind when they advocate for inclusion. It is our belief that through successful adoption of a truly inclusive philosophy, based on collaborative consultation, teachers and administrators will feel empowered to place more students on a full-time basis in the general education program.

Prereferral Intervention

Prereferral intervention is a cyclical process of assessment, hypothesis formation, intervention, and re-assessment. According to Graden, Casey, and Christenson (1985), the first authors to describe prereferral intervention in the literature:

> It consists of procedures for problem solving (consultation) and intervention as the first stage in the special education process. Thus, resources traditionally used to test and place large numbers of students are redirected toward providing assistance for students and their teachers in the regular classroom, where the problems first arise. The goal of the prereferral intervention model is to implement systematically intervention strategies in the regular classroom and to evaluate the effectiveness of these strategies before a student is formally referred for consideration for special education placement. A major goal of the prereferral intervention model is to identify successful interventions to help students remain in the least restrictive environment, the regular classroom. As a consequence, inappropriate referrals and placements in special education will be reduced. Another goal of the model is to aid in making the decision-making process more instructionally relevant and data-based by using data on the effectiveness of interventions as a major component of the decision-making process. (p. 377–378)

Ideally, prereferral intervention should be a teacher-directed and teacher-owned process which need not involve a formal team meeting for the resolution of most routine problems. This should be outgrowth of informal professional collaboration between a given teacher and the teacher's trusted and respected colleagues. In this sense, prereferral intervention is "action research," with the general educator acting as researcher, collaborating with colleagues to gather data, form hypotheses, implement and supervise the "treatment condition," and obtain data on the results of the "treatment."

Many teachers feel that the inclusion of students with diversities into the general education classroom constitutes an expectation of excessive knowledge and ability on the part of regular educators. We feel that the situation is really just the opposite. In the past, general educators have been solely responsible for all students in their classes and therefore those students that could not perform adequately in the environment that the teacher was able to provide were referred out to special programs. Now we recognize that no individual is capable of knowing how to effectively instruct all students. This is not a failure on the part of any teacher, rather a recognition of the need for collaboration to increase our knowledge base. Collaboration with colleagues and modifications of the instructional environment according to the unique needs of individual students should be seen as a natural and necessary part of education. The idea that any one teacher can be self-sufficient for providing an adequate learning environment for all students is absurd and must change.

Some of the key elements of prereferral intervention are teacher ownership, informality, flexibility, teacher support, creativity, student advocacy, consistency, documentation, focus on curricular modification, planning time, and staff development. One example of a successful inservice teaching model is the EXITO assessment program. This intensive staff development model was developed in response to the specific needs of the Special Education Local Planning Area (SELPA) of Monterey County, California, by Candace Clark and Leonard Baca. After several attempts to effect systemic change in assessment procedures that were found to be insufficient, a formal year-long series of eight training sessions was developed. The goals of this program were threefold:

1. To refine school district policies and procedures regarding special education referrals of CLD students.

2. To develop a student needs-based assessment environment.

3. To empower referral and assessment team members with the skills needed to make clinical judgments regarding the needs of CLD students. (Clark, 1994)

In order for educators to make sound clinical judgments regarding CLD students, they must receive information about cultural and linguistic diversity, alternative assessment paradigms and procedures, and the selection and use of specific assessment techniques. Therefore, the EXITO staff development model provides the following components:

- Cultural differences and second language acquisition theory.

- Prereferral intervention, emphasizing portfolio data collection, structured classroom observations, curricular interventions and modifications, and evaluation of student/teacher interactions.

- Special education assessment, including reliability and validity of standardized tests, informal assessment techniques, the use of interpreters and translators, and the development of clinical judgment and team dynamics.

UNANSWERED CALLS FOR CHANGE

Even in light of the progress made to date, there are still significant areas requiring change. Despite efforts to the contrary, most attention directed at prevention of disabilities emphasizes early diagnosis and intervention. This approach continues to locate the problem within the child or in the child's "deprived" background. Much has been discussed regarding assessment reform; however, there is still a significant problem of disproportionate representation of CLD students receiving special education services, continued overreliance on standardized tests, the lack of inclusion of bilingual personnel in assessments and staffings, and the lack of a strong bilingual component in most special education training programs. Special education intervention still continues to function under a remedial perspective, and the curriculum is frequently unrelated to that of the general education classroom. Also, even though "collaboration" has become a very popular concept, special education and regular education still remain decoupled, and many specialists still function within noncollaborative models of consultation. Figure 5–1 summarizes these unanswered calls for change.

Need for Prevention of Disabilities

Traditionally, the focus of efforts to prevent disabilities emphasized early identification and intervention. However, if we consider that disabilities may, at least in part, be socially constructed, then we must focus our efforts at disability prevention toward correcting the misconceptions that lead to misdiagnosis. Cummins' (1986) framework for empowering minority students is useful for our discussion of the prevention of "constructed" disabilities in CLD students. In this framework, he identifies four characteristics of schools that can function to either empower or disable CLD students. Cummins posits that "these characteristics reflect the extent to which (1) minority students' language and culture are incorporated into the school program; (2) minority community participation is encouraged as an integral component of children's education; (3) the pedagogy promotes intrinsic motivation on the

part of students to use language actively in order to generate their own knowledge; and (4) professionals involved in assessment become advocates for minority students rather than legitimizing the location of the 'problem' in the students" (p. 21).

By focusing our attention on prevention of disabilities through amelioration of those factors that operate in our schools to disempower CLD students, we are adopting a student advocacy orientation. We are recognizing that there are conditions that exist in the school, independent of any one particular student, that can function to create an educational environment that virtually guarantees poor academic achievement for many CLD students. However, there are specific things that teachers can do to address those institutional characteristics that Cummins (1986) delineates.

Cummins (1986) suggests that the language and culture of CLD students be incorporated into the school program. Even when bilingual programs are not available, use of students' native language can be encouraged and valued. Educational catalogs are full of books, posters, and other instructional materials in a variety of languages. The incorporation of a student's language requires only that the teacher be

Figure 5–1
The Unanswered Calls for Change

- Emphasis on prevention of disabilities
- Continued disproportionate representation of CLD students in special education
- Continued biased assessment practices
- Continued overreliance on standardized tests
- Failure to include bilingual personnel in assessment team meetings and staffings
- Lack of a bilingual component to most special education training programs
- Failure to adopt best practices in intervention
- Lack of continuity between special and regular education curriculums
- Minimal interaction and collaboration between special and general education programs

encouraging and value other languages and cultures as equal to that of the dominant society. With a positive attitude and a modicum of creativity, teachers can find many avenues to incorporate languages other than English into the curriculum. When possible, native language instruction and primary language instructional support can facilitate the learning of academic knowledge by second language learners. However, it is essential that primary language instruction be provided by fluent, proficient speakers of that language only. This use of the native language for instruction is not and should not be regarded as remedial instruction—second language learners are as capable of school success as native English speakers.

Multicultural Education. Multicultural education can also be an excellent avenue for incorporating students' native language and culture into the classroom. Nieto (1996) identifies multicultural education not as an add-on program, but as a pervasive alternative to what she terms "monocultural" education. She provides the following definition:

> Multicultural education is a process of comprehensive school reform and basic education for all students. It challenges and rejects racism and other forms of discrimination in schools and society and accepts and affirms the pluralism (ethnic, racial, linguistic, religious, economic, and gender, among other) that students, their communities, and teachers represent. Multicultural education permeates the curriculum and instruction strategies used in schools, as well as the interactions among teachers, students, parents, and the very way that schools conceptualize the nature of teaching and learning. Because it uses critical pedagogy as its underlying philosophy and focuses on knowledge, reflection, and action (praxis) as the basis for social change, multicultural education promotes the democratic principles of social justice. (p. 307)

In this definition, Nieto identifies seven critical elements of multicultural education: (1) anti-racist education, (2) basic education, (3) important for all students, (4) pervasive, (5) education for social justice, (6) a process, and (7) critical pedagogy. Viewed in this manner, multicultural education certainly can influence the institutional characteristic identified by Cummins (1986) as the extent to which students' cultural background is incorporated into the school program.

Multicultural education, defined in this manner, is also important for fostering the true inclusion of "mainstreamed" students with disabilities, in addition to preventing "constructed" disabilities. We as educators need to work very hard to overcome the stereotypes that can limit the participation of individuals with disabilities in general classroom activities. Following Nieto's (1996) criteria, we can see that education in inclusive environments must be anti-racist if we want our students with exceptionalities to be judged on their individual merits, rather than on preconceived notions about "the disabled." It must be basic education in inclusive environments, because our youth growing up today will and do find themselves in situations where they must interact effectively with individuals with disabilities. This education is important for *all* students; inclusion will not happen if the entire class is not involved. Multicultural education must be pervasive because beliefs and stereotypes are pervasive, and relegating discussions and activities about diverse individuals to isolated teaching units further reinforces the idea that disabilities and individuals with disabilities are not a part of "normal" life. Education for social justice is important for creating real inclusive environments, as, according to Nieto (p. 316), "developing a multicultural perspective means learning to think in more inclusive and expansive ways, reflecting on what we learn, and putting our learning into action." Education for inclusion must be recognized as a process; changes in philosophies and long-held beliefs will not change overnight. We need to foster a critical pedagogy that identifies and seeks to change those elements that disable our students with exceptionalities and that, furthermore, empowers the students to seek and demand change. We not only want to provide inclusive environments for our students, but we also want to teach them to create inclusive environments.

Parental Involvement. Cummins (1986) also posits the extent of real participation of CLD community members in the education of their children as either empowering or disabling. Without active encouragement, real participation will not occur. However, for this to happen, the parental role must be re-envisioned to incorporate educational responsibilities. Real participation does not occur when the role of parents is restricted to parent-teacher conferences and baking cookies for students' birthdays. Parents must be assured that their input is valued, that their participation in meetings is more than just superficial, and that their knowledge and abilities as co-teachers will be respected. Without this, parents cannot take an active, collaborative role in the education of

their youth—their participation is restricted to either a passive or adversarial relationship with the school. Chapter 14 provides an in-depth discussion of ways that parents of students with disabilities can be actively involved in their children's education.

Instructional Principles for Student Empowerment. Tharp (1997) has been concerned with the extent to which the educational environment is compatible with CLD students' cultural patterns of social organization, sociolinguistics, cognition, and motivation. He has identified five instructional principles that can facilitate increased cultural compatibility between CLD students and the mainstream educational setting. These principles, which are summarized in Figure 5–2, emphasize purposeful conversation and instructional conversation, and are consistent with Cummins' (1986) institutional characteristics that he identifies as empowering.

Through instructional conversations, students' acquisition of English can be facilitated and use of language for generation of knowledge can be modeled and cued by the teacher. The key to effective instructional conversations

Figure 5–2
Instructional Principles that Characterize Cultural Compatibility

1. The development of linguistic competence in the language of instruction through functional language use and purposeful conversational interactions should be an instructional metagoal.

2. Schooling should be contextualized at all levels—pedagogical, curricular, and policy—in the skills and experience of the students' home and community.

3. Joint productive activities, shared by teachers and students and with opportunities to converse interactively, should be implemented as a way of creating a common context of school experiences for students of varying backgrounds.

4. Instructional conversation, teacher-student dialogue that helps develop students' abilities to form, exchange, and express ideas interactively through oral and/or written means, should be used as the basic form of teaching.

5. Effective and appropriate instruction for students should challenge them toward cognitive complexity.

Note: From "At Risk to Excellence: Research, Theory, and Principles for Practice," by R.G. Tharp, 1997, Santa Cruz, CA: Center for Reseach on Education, Diversity and Excellence.

is that these dialogues be purposeful and functional; artificial interactions, without a real conversational purpose, are neither realistic nor appropriate. The instructional activity or expression of ideas should be the primary motivation for engaging in these dialogues, rather than engaging in "instructional conversation" just for the sake of doing "instructional conversation."

The Prevention and Enhancement Programming (PEP) Model

Prereferral intervention has been criticized for its special education focus. Although Graden (1989) contends that this should not be a special education owned process, the involvement of special educators in a partnership with general educators is reinforced. The original definition of prereferral intervention as "the first step in the special education process" (Graden, Casey, & Christenson, 1985, p. 377) reinforces for many the idea that this process inherently involves special educators. Additionally, prereferral intervention is designed to ameliorate difficulties that students are already exhibiting. In contrast, a disability prevention approach seeks to identify ways in which the curriculum may be inappropriate for CLD students prior to the development of significant and pervasive difficulties. "Prereferral" indicates that there are already *significant* concerns about the performance of a particular child. A preventative approach "examines the appropriateness of the learning environment (rather than trying to fit the child to the program) and seeks to improve the 'match' between learner needs/characteristics and instruction. . . . Prevention efforts seek to systematically develop general education programs that will enhance the performance of CLD population" (S. Garcia, personal communication, March 28, 1996). It is exactly this shift from prereferral to prevention that we are advocating with the Prevention and Enhancement Programming (PEP) model.

This problem-solving framework should *not*

been seen as the initial step toward a formal referral to special education. It is a process that is initiated by and owned by general educators. In contrast to prereferral intervention, that "first step" of the special education referral/ assessment/staffing process, PEP is a general education, problem-solving process, where the "problem" is not student academic failure, but a systematic mismatch between learners and the classroom environment. It can be an individual process that a sole teacher engages in, as a form of action research in the classroom. Through PEP, the teacher makes systematic assessments of the interaction between the learner (or a group of learners) and the educational environment, attempts modifications in activities, materials, or instruction, and documents the results. This process enhances the academic environment for students and increases the ongoing learning of the teacher. Some of the factors that should be assessed have already been discussed in this section. Others will become apparent through collaboration, observation of and reflection on teaching practices, and continuing education.

The teacher should cycle repeatedly through the model, with additional resources available to the teacher on each rotation. During the first cycle, the teacher may attempt to assess the situation and modify the instructional environment without collaboration. This systematic approach may be sufficient to highlight the changes necessary to bring about a better student/classroom fit. If not, then the teacher might consider collaborating informally with a colleague during the second cycle. This colleague could be a respected fellow classroom teacher, a friend in special education, or that knowledgeable bilingual specialist that gave a dynamite inservice on second-language acquisition.

Very early in this process, the student's parents should be involved. They may be able to provide insights that those inside the school had not considered. They can serve as informants, teaching the teacher about the normal and appropriate patterns of behavior of their community and alerting the teacher to special cultural knowledge that can enhance classroom instruction. When involving parents in the PEP process, it is necessary to establish a positive, mutually respectful relationship. Parents care whether their child is doing well in school and may feel intimidated by the authority of school personnel. This is especially true of CLD families. Therefore, care should be taken so that they are not given the impression that there is something wrong with their child. The truth that should be communicated is that the teacher wants to learn more about the student so that the classroom instruction is as effective as possible. Parents need to be viewed as authorities on their children and as potentially valuable teaching resources. These attitudes must be overtly communicated to parents during every contact with the school.

At some point, the teacher may find that the classroom modifications developed and attempted as a result of informal collaboration with a peer are not sufficient to accommodate the diversity in the class. PEP is designed as a disability prevention mechanism, but it can also function to resolve academic or behavior difficulties demonstrated by the student. However, as a general education model, it assumes that the locus of even pervasive difficulties is an instructional mismatch between the learner and environment. If more assistance is required, additional individuals may need to be involved in a team format. The name and composition of this team will vary according to the school and district. However, the core members should include the student's general education teacher; the student's parents or primary caretaker; the student, if old enough to participate effectively; and a team support member, who can be either a general or special educator. If the student speaks a home language other than English, a bilingual specialist should also be a core member of the initial team. If the student's parents are not fluent and proficient in English, then a translator or interpreter should be pro-

vided. It is not appropriate to ask the bilingual specialist or bilingual special educator to assume a dual role in the meeting. A trained interpreter should be made available for the sole purpose of translating information for the parents. Additional personnel who might be included are an administrator, resource specialist, counselor, social worker, nurse, educational psychologist, speech-language specialist, community members, child advocate, members of outside agencies, and extended family members, among others.

The critical features for effective team meetings are:

- A problem-solving rather than diagnostic intent.
- A willingness by all team members to maintain an open mind.
- A respect for the knowledge and input of all team members.
- Avoidance of blame or insistence on individual expertise.
- Consistent follow-up and documentation of results.
- Willingness to consider and attempt alternatives.
- An emphasis on creative and feasible solutions.
- A willingness to attempt multiple modifications without jumping to the conclusion that the problems lie in the child.

Need for Assessment Reform

CLD students are still disproportionately represented in special education programs, regardless of the plethora of research studies detailing the problem and the amount of legislation and litigation designed to promote equity. We use the term *disproportionate representation* because there are problems of both over- and underrepresentation of CLD students in special education, as detailed in Chapter 1. This problem indicates that current assessment practices are insufficiently sophisticated to distinguish between academic difficulties resulting from true physiologically-based disabilities and those resulting from environmental, social, experiential, linguistic, or cultural factors. There has been much discussion regarding assessment reform. These criticisms appear to revolve around three main areas: selection and use of specific assessment techniques, the make-up and procedures of assessment and staffing teams, and the training received by assessment personnel in institutions of higher education.

Standardized tests continue to form the backbone of most special education assessments. Regardless of the availability of many alternative assessment techniques and measures, many special educators continue to believe that standardized test scores are necessary and valid for diagnosis and placement of CLD students. An in-depth discussion of alternative assessment practices can be found in Chapter 8. At this point, suffice it to say that overreliance on standardized tests is a continuing and serious problem that leads to the inappropriate placement of CLD students in special education.

Another major problem that is currently being debated deals with how assessments should be carried out and by whom. Traditionally, evaluations have been performed solely by identified assessment personnel, such as an educational psychologist or a speech-language pathologist. Information presented by parents and teachers, other than that related to the child's medical or educational history, was frequently disregarded as "subjective." Now, many schools have begun to implement prereferral and assessment teams, with the purpose of widening the perspectives from which the student or situation is viewed. Unfortunately, bilingual specialists are not always included on teams, especially if the student in question is considered to be "proficient" in English. Hopefully, with the inclusion of more people, such as bilingual educators and parents, the results of evaluations will begin to demonstrate consideration of factors other than whether that specific student "has" a disability. For example, assessments should include more information regarding how a student learns best and how the instructional environment can be modified to best suit the student's needs. Chapter 7 provides more information on issues in assessment reform.

Need for Instructional/ Intervention Reform

General education has also undergone considerable changes, in terms of what are considered best practices in teaching. Whole language, cooperative learning, and contextualized instruction are all examples of educational techniques now used widely in the general education classroom. We recommend that special educators begin to incorporate these ideas into their intervention practices. Also, if our long-term goal in intervention is for students to increase their academic performance and eventually need little or no modification of the educational environment for success, then our short-term goals should focus on the general education curriculum. Regardless of whether we must modify our instructional strategies to accommodate differences in learning styles and abilities, that instruction must be integrated with that of the general education curriculum. It is no longer acceptable for students to be working on projects and activities with the resource specialist, speech/language pathologist, or other special educator that are unrelated to the curriculum in the student's general education setting. That is contrary to the philosophy of inclusion that we are encouraging. It is the curriculum of the general education classroom which should be central in every student's educational plan. The goals on the student's individualized educational plan (IEP) must be somehow related to the instruction in the general education classroom, or the intervention will be irrelevant to the student's education.

Several model programs have obtained excellent results teaching culturally and linguistically diverse children identified as requiring specialized educational assistance or experiencing academic difficulties. The Optimal Learning Environment (OLE) program (Figueroa and Ruiz, 1994; Ruiz, 1989) is one such program. Initially, the researchers looked at how children were being taught in the California Resource Specialist Program. It was determined that, as in many programs across the country, most instruction was broken down into incremental, sequential segments which were taught in repetitive drills. This type of instruction is called *reductionist,* as learning is reduced to small components. Unfortunately, this type of teaching leaves many learners with fragmented knowledge and skills which they are unable to apply in diverse contexts. Therefore, the OLE researchers devised a curriculum which emphasizes holistic teaching strategies and biliteracy. They found that students receiving this instruction gained an average of one year in reading, in comparison to the average student in the resource specialist program, who scored at or below the second percentile. The instructional principles of the OLE curriculum, as identified by Ruiz and Figueroa, are as follows:

- Awareness of students' sociocultural background and what effect it may have on native and second language acquisition, both oral and written.

- Awareness of possible learning disabilities and their effects on language development.

- The developmental process of literacy acquisition.

- A meaningful context for curriculum and a clear and authentic communicative purpose.

- The integration of students' personal experiences into lessons.

- Active parental involvement in instruction.

- Experience with whole texts during lessons.

- The incorporation of collaborative learning activities, when possible.

The Assessment and Intervention Model for Bilingual Exceptional Students (AIM for the BESt) also emphasizes holistic, reciprocal, and interactionist teaching, in place of reductionist and transmission oriented approaches (Ortiz & Rivera, 1990). Teaching strategies that recognize and value students' language background, experiences, and interests and those that encourage active student participation are considered important. In the pilot program, Shared Literature and the Graves Writing Workshop were used as examples of effective teaching practices. Teacher training and prereferral intervention were emphasized, with the results indicating that student and teacher assistance teams that encourage and support teachers' use of "best practices" can be effective in resolving problems without the need for a special education referral. These researchers reported that 73% of the requests for assistance in the pilot program were resolved without special education placement of the student experiencing difficulties.

Both of these model programs for CLD students identified the traditional curriculum as problematic. In both programs an enrichment rather than remedial approach was found to be beneficial to the students. Therefore, we strongly recommend that practitioners consider a "gifted," or enrichment, curriculum as appropriate for students experiencing academic difficulties. Those same techniques that have been demonstrated as effective for "gifted" students should not be reserved only for that type of "exceptionality." *All* students can benefit from a stimulating, interactive, and holistic teaching environment.

Need for Collaborative Consultation

There have been changes in the way we look at consultation also. We have moved from an expert model of consultation to a collaborative consultation model. Within the expert model of consultation, specialists are seen as possessing an inherent expertise that qualifies them to make judgments, recommendations, and decisions. In contrast, collaborative consultation recognizes the value of the contributions made by all participants. Idol, Paolucci-Whitcomb, and Nevin (1986) defined collaborative consultation in the following manner:

> Collaborative consultation is an interactive process that enables people with diverse expertise to generate creative solutions to mutually defined problems. The outcome is enhanced, altered, and produces solutions that are different from those that the individual team members would produce independently. The major outcome of collaborative consultation is to provide comprehensive and effective programs for students with special needs within the most appropriate context, thereby enabling them to achieve maximum constructive interaction with their non-handicapped peers. (p. 1)

This definition emphasizes the problem-solving nature of the process and the goal of inclusive instruction. Others have characterized collaborative consultation by the voluntary nature of participation, parity, reciprocity, and shared goals, accountability, responsibility, and resources (Cook & Friend, 1991; Laycock, Gable, & Korinek, 1991). Other important characteristics found in strong collaborative programs include the following (Evans, 1991; Male, 1991): (1) active involvement of students and their parents; (2) lack of any expectation for special education outcomes; (3) communication strategies on the part of the consultant that include asking, rather than telling, the classroom teacher how to identify and use resources; and (4) joint development of plans with incorporation of suggestions from the consultee as well as the consultant. This recognition of the knowledge and expertise of the classroom teacher is essential to the success of collaborative consultation. Johnson, Pugach, and Hammittee (1988) provide the following caution:

> As long as consultation exists in a hierarchical organizational structure in which classroom teachers are perceived to have less expertise, its success is likely to be limited, especially in a climate of reform in which classroom teachers are rightfully searching for the professional respect due them in light of the difficult job they perform. If consultation were conceptualized more as a two-way relationship in which special educators perceived that they had much to gain professionally from the classroom teacher, not just with respect to a specific student but in terms of large group organization and general education curricula, its chances for success would increase. But as long as special education consultants believe that their techniques are superior, it is inevitable that resistance will occur. (p. 44)

In addition to the above needed areas for changes—prevention of disability, assessment, intervention, and collaborative consultation—we must also address the continuing problems of the failure of students to be exited from special education and the continued poor academic progress of CLD students in comparison to dominant culture students (Skrtic, 1991). We suggest that there are three fundamental causes to these identified problems: (1) the decoupled nature of schooling and the existence of compartmentalized, disjointed special programs, (2) the failure to adopt instructional strategies known to be effective with CLD students and to integrate assessment and instruction, and (3) the assumptions we hold about CLD students and their families and students with exceptionalities.

AVENUES FOR CHANGE

Rueda (1989) identified three avenues for change available to special education: system maintenance, system improvement, and system restructuring. *System maintenance* focuses on improving compliance with the existing system of regulated practices. *System improvement* seeks to improve current practices within the existing system. *System restructuring* questions the underlying assumptions of special education and looks to a reconstruction of the general and special education systems as a means of addressing broader social and educational issues.

Significant energy has been expended in attempts to better the education of students with disabilities via system maintenance and system improvement. Quality assurance measures, adopted from business models, have been attempted. These systems were implemented in hopes that stricter adherence to guidelines would produce better education. In reality, however, most of what is produced by these systems is simply more bureaucracy and more paperwork. Much research has focused on "best practices," which is a type of system improvement. Newer and better instructional strategies have been proposed and a whole industry has been built around developing and publishing newer and better tests. In the end, however, system improvement also fails to provide an adequate framework for fundamental change. The recent realization that 10 years of large-scale implementation of "whole language" in California classrooms have failed to produce the increase in literacy rates and standardized test scores that had been predicted is an example of how system improvement is inadequate.

We suggest that significant improvements in the education of students will only come through pervasive and systemic change. Considering the unanswered calls for change that we identified in the previous section and our postulated causes for these problems, a system reconstruction approach is the only feasible avenue for change. We assert that changes in the procedures, practices, and goals of special education, the roles of all participants, and our basic assumptions are necessary for meaningful systemic improvements. By taking this stance, we imply that current regulated best practices are inappropriate or inadequate and therefore reject system maintenance. We also reject system improvement as inadequate for changing some of the fundamental problems in schools;

system improvement does not address programmatic integration, role redefinition, or changing assumptions about diversity and how that should best be addressed by our schools today.

Procedures, Practices, and Goals. Prereferral intervention has been suggested as a means of reducing inappropriate referrals to special education, identifying and implementing effective instructional strategies in the regular classroom, and making the assessment process more instructionally relevant (Graden, Casey, & Christenson, 1985). Since this process was first suggested, it has been implemented in a variety of forms across the country with good results. In Pennsylvania, a reduction of 40% of special education placements has been achieved during the initial implementation of the state-wide Instructional Support Team (IST) program.

The most critical aspect of this model is the emphasis on collaborative consultation to formulate a problem solving approach to instructional development (Graden, 1989). Without this collaboration, the prereferral team becomes merely one step in the inevitable progress toward special education assessment and placement. This never was the intent of the proponents of prereferral intervention, and we recommend that emphasis return to the use of informal collaborative consultation as a means of individualizing and adapting the curriculum to fit the needs of individual students. The shift in emphasis is explicit in the PEP model that we introduced earlier in this chapter.

One way of changing this emphasis is through modification of our goals. We tend to see assessment and intervention as separate activities, with distinct objectives. We suggest that, as in the original intent of prereferral intervention and as explicit in the PEP model, educational activities be used with an evaluative intent and that a student's responses to instruction should provide information about the effectiveness and appropriateness of the activities, suggest alternative instructional strategies, and tell us more about how that particular student learns best. The instructional context, the student, and the interaction between the two are all evaluated under this paradigm. This type of analytic teaching, as with all forms of assessment, should be used with the underlying assumption that there is nothing inherently wrong or deficient with the student, but rather that the manifest problem lies in the interactions between the student and the educational context. The overt goal should be maintaining students in the regular educational setting and increasing academic performance, rather than diagnosis and exclusion.

This shift in our thinking about teaching away from purely instructional to evaluative teaching parallels our thinking about assessment. Even when additional personnel are consulted and involved in evaluation activities, the purpose of assessment must shift from diagnosis of disability to a description of students' strengths, knowledge, abilities, and learning preferences that will have direct implications for modifications of the learning environment. In other words, student evaluation should be more formative than summative. After all, even if a student does have a physiologically-based condition, such as Down's Syndrome, there is nothing that we can do to alter that reality. We can, however, reduce the disability that the condition imposes on the student by altering the academic context. A student who is blind, who does not have access to reading materials in Braille, is disabled by that lack of access, not by the physical condition. In this sense, it is the unadapted curriculum that is disabled, and disabling, not the student.

Roles of Participants. For these changes in procedures, practices, and goals to become a reality, the roles of those involved in the education of CLD students must change. We are advocating an interface of general and special programs. This means that general classroom educators and specialists must change how they view their roles. No one individual can be totally responsible for the education of any one student and no one individual can be perceived of as the ultimate expert on the child.

Parents and general educators must be actively involved in assessment activities. Specialists must become involved in the adaptation of the regular education curriculum. Students must have a real voice in making curricular decisions. Parents must be encouraged and allowed to assume a substantial role as co-teachers and colleagues in the lifelong education of their children. Just as programs can no longer remain compartmentalized and disjointed, neither can professional domains.

Underlying Assumptions. Bogdan and Kugelmass (1984) identified four basic assumptions underlying the current practice of special education. These assumptions are that:

- Disability is a condition that individuals have.
- "Disabled" and "typical" are useful and objective distinctions.
- Special education is a coordinated and rationally conceived system of services that helps children identified as disabled.
- Progress in special education is made through improvements in diagnostics, intervention, and technology.

Clearly, these assumptions are coming under critical scrutiny. For example, Cummins (1989) disagrees with the assumption that a disability is an inherent condition specific to an individual. He states that "the causes of minority students' academic difficulties are to be found in the ways schools have reinforced, both overtly and covertly, the discrimination that certain minority groups have historically experienced in the society at large" (p. 111). Sleeter (1986; 1987) also disagrees with this assumption, arguing that mild learning disabilities are to a great extent socially constructed. She discusses how she believes school reform efforts that raise performance standards and the emphasis on literacy as the primary avenue for acquisition of academic knowledge "create" disabilities in otherwise normal children.

Many researchers have argued with the assumptions that (1) we are able to make objective discriminations between students with disabilities and those without, and that (2) those students so identified are helped by this process of assessment and intervention (for example, see Hilliard, 1992; Skrtic, 1991; Stainback & Stainback, 1984; Reynolds, Wang, & Walberg, 1987). These researchers, as well as others, also argue that the lack of coordination of services is one of the major difficulties in providing appropriate education to all students. Given these critiques, the assumption that change is made only through the avenues of diagnostics, intervention, and technology appears incomplete. Clearly, assessment reform is needed. Progress in improving pedagogy is also important. Adapting to and implementing new forms of technology is also necessary. However, without changing how regular and special education programs interact and cooperate, we cannot implement these needed reforms.

Baca (1993) has suggested five conscious assumptions that should be considered fundamental to special education reconstruction. These new assumptions are provided Figure 5–3 and should provide a more useful and equitable foundation for the new Bilingual Special Education Interface that we are proposing.

In addition to the assumptions underlying special education practices, there are other assumptions that we need to critically examine. We need to question whether CLD students come to school ill-prepared to learn, or we as educators come to school ill-prepared to teach *all* students. We need to ask whether specialists are the only experts on students with special needs, or parents and general classroom teachers are experts on their children and students. We need to ask if "education" is restricted to the classroom and the context of the school, or diverse experiences outside of the classroom can lead to knowledge and learning that has value and importance. We need to ask whether those factors that were once seen as a "triple threat," poverty and cultural and linguistic differences, are tantamount to a deficit, a difference, or a source of unique and rich learning experiences. Does old and ragged clothing put a child at a disadvantage for learning, or is it the reaction of others to that child that puts him/her at a disadvantage? Why does a refugee child come from a "deprived" background, while a middle-class student who studies abroad undergoes an "enriching" experience? These are all questions we need to continually ponder as we

Figure 5–3
Conscious Assumptions for Bilingual Special Education

1. All children can learn.
2. Early intervention in the students' native language can prevent disabilities.
3. Native language and culture are strengths to be built upon.
4. Students who are not succeeding academically need a gifted, rather than a remedial, curriculum.
5. Students who are differentially abled and/or culturally and linguistically diverse should be educated in inclusive environments.

Note: From *Bilingual Special Education's Conscious Assumptions,* by L. Baca, 1993, August. Presentation at the Bueno Center for Multicultural Education Bilingual Special Education Institute, Boulder, CO.

attempt to measure the effects of our preconceived notions on the schooling of CLD students and identify locus of disabilities.

⊛ SUMMARY

In this chapter, we have attempted to provide for the reader a clear description of our vision for the changing Bilingual Special Education Interface. We have discussed the need to interface or integrate special programs with general education. We proposed a philosophical definition of inclusion that incorporates the idea that programs as well as students need to be included, and that active participation and access to the general education curriculum is key to educating "mainstreamed" students in inclusive environments. Continuing problems that CLD students, with and without disabilities, confront in our schools were detailed, and the fundamental causes of these problems were identified. The system reconstruction approach was identified as the most plausible avenue for improving education. Finally, we recommended changes in the procedures, practices, and goals of special education, the roles of all participants, and the basic assumptions held by many about CLD students, their families, and the validity and value of their life experiences.

⊛ DISCUSSION QUESTIONS

1. Discuss why change is needed in current bilingual special education "best practices."
2. Compare and contrast the three avenues for change identified by Rueda and discussed in this chapter. Which do you think is the most appropriate avenue for change? Why?
3. Identify the principal components of effective collaborative consultation.
4. Compare and contrast prereferral intervention and disability prevention approaches.
5. Discuss how Cummins' (1986) disability prevention framework differs from or is similar to the PEP model.

⊛ REFERENCES

Algozzine, B., & Ysseldyke, J. (1983). Learning disabilities as a subset of school failure. *Exceptional Children, 50,* 242–246.

Baca, L. (1993, August). *Bilingual special education's conscious assumptions.* Presentation at the Bueno Center for Multicultural Education Bilingual Special Education Institute, Boulder, Co.

Bogdan, R., & Kugelmass, J. (1984). Case studies of mainstreaming: A symbolic interactionist approach to special schooling. In L. Barton & S. Tomlinson (Eds.), *Special education and social interests* (pp. 173–191). New York: Nichols.

Clark, C. (1994). *EXITO: A dynamic team assessment process for culturally diverse students.* Monterey, CA: Special Education Local Plan Area of Monterey County.

Collier, C., & Baca, L. (1994). *Classroom management and curriculum implementation* (Module No. 5). Boulder, CO: BUENO Center for Multicultural Education.

Cook, L., & Friend, M. (1991). Principles for the practice of collaboration in schools. *Preventing School Failure, 35*(4), 6–9.

Cummins, J. (1986). Empowering minority students: A framework for intervention. *Harvard Educational Review, 56*(1), 18–36.

Cummins, J. (1989). A theoretical framework for bilingual special education. *Exceptional Children, 56*(2), 111–119.

Evans, S. B. (1991). A realistic look at the research base for collaboration in special education. *Preventing School Failure, 35*(4), 10–13.

Figueroa, R. A., & Ruiz, N. T. (1994). The reconstruction of bilingual special education II. *Focus on Diversity, 4*(1), 2–3.

Graden, J. L. (1989). Redefining "prereferral" intervention as intervention assistance: Collaboration between general and special education. *Exceptional Children, 56*(3), 227–231.

Graden, J. L., Casey, A., & Christenson, S. L. (1985). Implementing a prereferral intervention system: Part I. The model. *Exceptional Children, 51*(5), 377–384.

Hilliard, A. G. I. (1992). The pitfalls and promises of special education. *Exceptional Children, 59*(2),

168–172.

Idol, L., Paolucci-Whitcomb, P., & Nevin, A. (1986). *Collaborative consultation*. Austin, TX: PRO-ED.

Johnson, L. J., Pugach, M. C., & Hammittee, D. (1988). Barriers to effective special education consultation. *Remedial and Special Education, 9*(6), 41–47.

Laycock, V., Gable, R. A., & Korinek, L. (1991). Alternative structures for collaboration in the delivery of special services. *Preventing School Failure, 35*(4), 15–18.

Male, M. (1991). Effective team participation. *Preventing School Failure, 35*(4), 29–35.

National Center for Educational Statistics. (1994). *The condition of education*. Washington, DC: Office of Educational Research and Improvement, U.S. Department of Education.

Nieto, S. (1996). *Affirming diversity: The sociopolitical context of multicultural education* (2nd ed.). New York: Longman.

Ortiz, A. A., & Rivera, C. (1990). *AIM for the BEST: Assessment and intervention model for bilingual exceptional students* (Contract 300-87-0131). Washington, DC: Office of Bilingual Education and Minority Education Affairs.

Reynolds, M. C., & Birch, J. W. (1977). *Teaching exceptional children in all America's schools*. Reston, VA: The Council for Exceptional Children.

Reynolds, M. C., Wang, M., & Walberg, H. J. (1987). The necessary restructuring of special and regular education. *Exceptional Children, 53*(5), 391–398.

Ruiz, N. T. (1989). An optimal learning environment for Rosemary. *Exceptional Children, 56*(2), 130–144.

Shephard, L. A., & Smith, M. L. (1983). An evaluation of the identification of learning disabled students in Colorado. *Learning Disability Quarterly, 6,* 115–127.

Rueda, R. (1989). Defining mild disabilities with language-minority students. *Exceptional Children, 56*(2), 121–128.

Skrtic, T. M. (1988). The organizational context of special education. In E. L. Meyen & T. M. Skrtic (Eds.), *Exceptional children and youth: An introduction* (3rd ed., pp. 479–517). Denver: Love Publishing.

Skrtic, T. M. (1991). Students with special educational needs: Artifacts of the traditional curriculum. In M. Ainscow (Ed.), *Effective schools for all* (pp. 20–42). London: David Fulton Publishers.

Sleeter, C. (1987). Literacy, definitions of learning disabilities, and social control. In B. M. Franklin (Ed.), *Learning disabilities: Dissenting essays* (pp. 67–87). London: The Falmer Press.

Sleeter, C. E. (1986). Learning disabilities: The social construction of a special education category. *Exceptional Children, 53*(1), 46–54.

Stainback, W., & Stainback, S. (1984). A rationale for the merger of special and regular education. *Exceptional Children, 51*(2), 102.

Tharp, R. G. (1997). From at-risk to excellence: Research, theory, and principles for practice. Santa Cruz, CA: Center for Research on Education, Diversity and Excellence.

CHAPTER 6

Language Acquisition and the Bilingual Exceptional Child

J. S. de Valenzuela

- Defining Language
- Language Acquisition
- Second Language Acquisition
- Summary

OBJECTIVES

To emphasize the importance of understanding language acquisition in bilingual children

To discuss popular fallacies about bilingual children with exceptionalities

To define basic concepts of language

To overview language acquisition as a general process

To define second language acquisition

To compare and contrast first and second language acquisition

To examine some models of second language acquisition

To discuss current controversies in second language acquisition

Understanding the process of language acquisition is crucial to the appropriate education and assessment of culturally and linguistically diverse (CLD) students. The purpose of this chapter is to provide a framework for considering how language development is different for bilingual children. This will hopefully lead educators to consider how bilingualism can affect the academic performance and assessment of bilingual students and how it plays a part in the education of CLD students with exceptionalities.

In this chapter, "language acquisition" is used as a central concept, rather than "second language acquisition." This is done so with the intent of shifting the focus from examining how English is acquired to a more general examination of how bilingual students acquire language. There are several reasons for this shift in focus: (1) many bilingual students in this country begin the process of developing English before their native language is fully established, and their language development can most accurately be called "bilingual"; (2) understanding the effects of second language development on first language development, and vice versa, will help us understand where students are, in terms of their overall language competence; and (3) incorrect assumptions about students' native language competence and development can lead to inappropriate referrals and erroneous assessment procedures. We cannot simply talk about acquisition of English as a second language without considering the total process of language acquisition for bilingual students.

There are many popular misconceptions about bilingualism, language acquisition, and bilingual students. Some people erroneously believe that students with exceptionalities cannot learn two (or more) languages. Others believe that encouraging the parents of CLD students, with and without exceptionalities, to speak with their children at home in English, is in the best interests of the students. Another common fallacy is that acquiring more than one language is "difficult" and can lead to academic problems. Some teachers have been heard to suggest that their bilingual students don't speak any language to a real extent and are "semilingual." We will return to these myths at the end of this chapter. By then, the intervening information will have provided you with enough understanding about the normal process of language acquisition that the faulty logic of these beliefs should be obvious.

Regardless of whether the above beliefs lack grounding, they are very common and can influence how educators assess and educate CLD students. Without understanding how language acquisition works, the continuation of these fallacies is understandable. Therefore, educators working with bilingual students must understand the language acquisition process for effective implementation of assessment and selection of appropriate intervention techniques.

DEFINING LANGUAGE

Language is a Dynamic Construct

What is "language"? The answer to this question is both extremely simple and extremely complex. Although we all know what it is, we may have a hard time defining it exactly. In simple terms, we can say that language is how we communicate with one another. *Webster's Unabridged Dictionary* (1986) defines language in the following ways:

- The body of words and systems for their use common to a people who are of the same community or nation, the same geographical area, or the same cultural tradition.

- The system of linguistic signs or symbols considered in the abstract (as opposed to *speech*).

- Any set or system of such symbols as used in a more or less uniform fashion by a number of people, who are thus enabled to communicate intelligibly with one another.

- Any system of formalized symbols, signs, gestures, or the like, used or conceived as a means of communicating thought, emotion, etc.

These definitions convey the important concepts that language is systematic (rule governed), symbolic, abstract, culturally relevant, and social. We can also say that language is a dynamic construct, as it means different things to different people and in different contexts and because it is ever changing, both in terms of individual languages and as a generic concept. These definitions recognize that the word "school" in English means "a place where children go to learn" only because our community has agreed that this is what it means. There is no inherent relationship between this particular group of sounds and the concept "school." Rather, the relationship is socially agreed upon.

Language is also culturally defined. "School" means "school" because of how our culture defines what the institution of schooling is. Although individuals from other cultures may understand in general the use of the term "school," they may not have the same cultural understandings about school that Americans do. For example, "school" in the United States conveys the idea of a particular age group—young children through adolescents. However, in other countries, not all children are expected to participate in "schooling" nor is "school" restricted to a particular age group. A "third grader" might be an adult who simply had not completed this grade earlier in life. The term "school" also conveys ideas about particular behaviors and activities that can vary from culture to culture. Just as our cultural background influences our behaviors and beliefs, it also shapes how we use language.

Different Ways of Looking at Language

When we talk about language, we can talk about it in different ways. As described above, we can discuss the social and cultural components of language. More commonly, when we think about language acquisition in schools, we think about the *form* of language. We can also talk about the *content* of language and about language *use*.

We use terms such as *syntax, morphology,* and *phonology* when we talk about linguistic form. Syntax and morphology refer to the grammatical system of a language. Syntax governs the use of different word classes (such as nouns and verbs) and how these words are combined into intelligible and grammatical sentences. Morphology refers to the rule system that governs how words are put together from smaller grammatical parts, such as root words, prefixes, and suffixes. We refer to the internalized rule system for putting together sounds as our phonological system. For example, the phonological system of English prohibits certain types of consonant clusters in the beginning of words, which makes it difficult for native English speakers to correctly pronounce the names of the following cities: Mbandake (Zaire); Mtwara (Tanzania); and Mpika, Mzimba, and Shiwa Ngandu (Zimbabwe). These rules also govern whether the plural -s sounds like an "s" or a "z," as in "dogs" and "cats." No one consciously learns the rules of phonology, morphology, and syntax of their native language. In fact, most people would be hard pressed to explain why they form words and sentences in the way they do—most of our knowledge about language is unconscious.

We can also talk about the *content* of language. When we talk about word meanings, we are talking about *semantics*. Semantics refers to more than just vocabulary knowledge or the meaning of words. Semantics also refers to the function of words. Understanding how words function is very important in child language research, as many times one word will assume many functions, depending on the context. An example is "daddy go," which could mean a variety of different things. Also, there is a relationship between content and form—what you want to say can influence the form you select to use, just as the form of an utterance can affect the content.

More recently, people have also started talking about language use, or *pragmatics*. This area is concerned with the multitude of ways that people can say things and how this varies in different situations. Pragmatics involves language form and content, as well as other facets of language, such as intonation, hesitancies, pauses, loudness, and rate. Speakers should be able to switch styles of speech according to different communicative contexts. An analysis of language use will identify how well speakers can accommodate their speech production to different contexts. For example, the way students address their peers is most likely different from how they would greet the school principal. Pragmatic language skills are acquired along with knowledge and use of syntax, morphology, phonology, and semantics. Children learn very quickly the language use rules of their community and dialect, although, as with any linguistic ability, full competence takes a matter of years to develop.

Important Concepts in Linguistics

Linguistics has provided us with a framework for understanding language in a variety of contexts: historically, cross-culturally, developmentally, and theoretically, to name just a few. Regardless of the different ways that we can talk about language, there are a few basic concepts that most language specialists hold in common. These concepts are: (1) the understanding that no one language is intrinsically better than another, (2) the difference between prescriptive and descriptive grammars, (3) the difference between linguistic competence and performance, (4) the difference between receptive and expressive language abilities, and (5) commonalties among all living languages, called *linguistic universals*.

Is the English spoken by educated university professors in England intrinsically better than that spoken by blue-collar workers in the Appalachian Mountains of the United States? Socially, Standard English, and especially the form known as RP ("received pronunciation" after the dialect "received" in the royal court of England), is more prestigious than Appalachian English. But is RP really "better" or more "correct" than other dialects of English? From a purely linguistic perspective, all languages and dialects are able to convey equally complex information and are equally able to adapt for new situations, such as developing vocabulary for computer technology. Speaking on a functional level, the question of "better" depends on the social situation. Clearly it would be awkward, less effective, and really quite inappropriate to use RP at a family party among working-class people who were raised in the Appalachians. So "better" depends upon the social situation and the ability to effectively convey a message, including the relevant social information. In fact, the mark of a truly accomplished communicator is the ability to vary speaking styles according to the social situation. Although acquiring Standard English (or Standard Spanish, for that matter) may be an appropriate academic goal, it is imperative that teachers understand that students' native dialects are as valid, functional, appropriate, and grammatical as the standard dialect. Nonprestige forms should never be considered "broken" or "corrupt"—they are legitimate and appropriate forms of speech in the students' home community. Educators *must* demonstrate respect for their students' native dialect/language if they want them to acquire another.

The goal of linguists is to describe the underlying rules and regularities of languages, without making judgments about the value of particular forms. They want to understand how language functions under different circumstances and how to best describe the interaction of linguistic forms and their functions. That goal, the goal of language *description*, is very different from language *prescription*, which seeks conformity with a linguistic standard. Linguists recognize that while "ain't" and "gonna" are not considered "correct" in formal Standard English, these verb forms are appropriate in informal speech for most speakers of Standard English and follow a definite pattern of rules for the formation and use of these forms (I'm gonna, you're gonna, we're gonna, etc.). Although these words may not be socially correct in some circumstances, from a linguistic perspective, they are grammatically correct and well-formed. Whether a specific grammatical construction is considered "correct" by the public has more to do with the social context and the prestige of a particular dialect than with any intrinsic value. Standard English is considered correct English because it is the dialect associated with the dominant social culture, not because it is inherently any better than any other dialect of English. As teachers, we need to distinguish between dialectally inappropriate and grammatically incorrect productions. "Don't have none" is dialectally inappropriate in Standard English but is not grammatically incorrect—the use of double negation is rule-governed and "grammatical" in many dialects and languages. However, using "goed" instead of "went" is grammatically incorrect—there is no dialect of English that uses that grammatical form.

In fact, whether or not individuals use "ain't" or "aren't" or "gonna" or "going to" when talking informally to friends does not tell us whether they could or would use the prestige form under different circumstances. Observations of linguistic *performance* do not always indicate individuals' linguistic *competence*. This distinction between competence and performance is important for teachers of CLD students to understand. Many constraints can operate to influence how students produce language in the school context. Sometimes the situation will influence a student to use a different language, dialect, or speech style. Other times, the situation will inhibit the student from using forms correctly (grammatically). This may especially occur under pressured situations when the student is in the process of acquiring English as a second language. This type of production error is akin to the common errors we all make when we are tired or under stress. For example, an ice skater may not be able to carry out a complicated jump during competition, even though he or she had no difficulty with it during practice.

Related to this idea that performance does not always give an accurate representation of linguistic competence is the understanding that expressive language skills do not always indicate accurately the level of receptive language skills. Students may understand a grammatical form or vocabulary item even though they do not or cannot use it independently in speech. Sometimes second-language learners undergo what is termed a "silent period"—a period of time during which the students produce little or no spontaneous oral speech for communication with others. During this time, which can vary from days to months, the students may understand more of what they hear than they are able to demonstrate through their speech. Conversely, young children and second language learners may produce words or phrases that they have heard without evidence of real comprehension. Research indicates that repetition (either immediately or at a later time) of overheard utterances, even without comprehension and in inappropriate contexts, can be a strategy used by children in the process of learning a second language (Hakuta, 1986; Saville-Troike, 1988).

Linguists have developed over the years a set of *linguistic universals*—facts that are believed to pertain to *all* languages. The following are from Fromkin and Rodman's introductory text on linguistics (1988):

1. Wherever humans exist, language exists.
2. There are no "primitive" languages—all languages are equally complex and equally capable of expressing any idea in the uni-

verse. The vocabulary of any language can be expanded to include new words for new concepts.

3. All languages change through time.

4. The relationships between the sounds and meanings of spoken languages and between the gestures (signs) and meanings of sign languages are for the most part arbitrary.

5. All human languages utilize a finite set of discrete sounds (or gestures) that are combined to form meaningful elements or words, which themselves form an infinite set of possible sentences.

6. All grammars contain rules for the formation of words and sentences of a similar kind.

7. Every spoken language includes discrete sound segments like *p, n,* or *a,* which can all be defined by a finite set of sound properties or features. Every spoken language has a class of vowels and a class of consonants.

8. Similar grammatical categories (for example, noun, verb) are found in all languages.

9. There are semantic universals, such as "male" or "female," "animate" or "human," found in every language in the world.

10. Every language has a way of referring to past time, negating, forming questions, issuing commands, and so on.

11. Speakers of all languages are capable of producing and comprehending an infinite set of sentences. Syntactic universals reveal that every language has a way of forming sentences such as:
- Linguistics is an interesting subject.
- I know that linguistics is an interesting subject.
- You know that I know linguistics is an interesting subject.

- Cecilia knows that you know that I know that linguistics is an interesting subject.
- Is it a fact that Cecilia knows that you know that I know that linguistics is an interesting subject?

12. Any normal child, born anywhere in the world, of any racial, geographical, social, or economic heritage, is capable of learning any language to which he or she is exposed. The differences we find among languages cannot be due to biological reasons. (p. 18–19)

LANGUAGE ACQUISITION
Theories of Language Acquisition

Why do we study language acquisition? Depending on the orientation of the researcher, the study of language acquisition can be either important in and of itself or as a mechanism for understanding other areas of research, such as theoretical linguistics, cognitive psychology, neuroscience, or child development. Some want to know what the process of first and second language acquisition tells us about human development, learning, and organization of the brain. Others want to know about language acquisition so they can make recommendations about educational programs. Regardless of their research focus, all of these researchers must take a position on some fundamental arguments about the development of language and its relationship to other mental functions.

Linguistic theory can be divided into several main camps, depending on (1) whether language is viewed as either separate from or as an outgrowth of cognition and (2) whether language acquisition is believed to be directed by a preprogrammed, language-specific area of the brain or guided primarily by experiential factors. Noam Chomsky (1965) addressed both of these issues when he proposed that human brains are "hardwired" for language acquisition via what has come to be called the "Language Acquisition Device" or LAD. This is considered a "nativist" theoretical position. The development of this theory was in direct opposition to B. F. Skinner's (1957) ideas about the development of language as shaped by behavioral reinforcement received from a child's environment. Chomsky demonstrated that the language available in a child's environment is far too complex and the reinforcement (i.e., praise) far too inconsistent to account for a behavioral model of language development. Although the extent to which grammatical structures are specifically preprogrammed is still hotly debated (Bowerman, 1994), most child language specialists today agree that, at least to some extent, the human brain is predisposed to (1) attend differentially to language input, (2) process that input according to some preset principles, and (3) formulate unconscious rules for language comprehension and production.

This perspective of language as biologically driven has been traditionally considered diametrically opposed to sociocultural perspectives that recognize the role of the environment in shaping language development. However, many child language researchers are coming to the conclusion that this does not necessarily need to be the case. Some have come to take the position that "it is perfectly consistent to believe that, while much of language development is governed by the operation of powerful innate principles, some important aspects of early language development are significantly influenced by the child's language experience" (Harris, 1992, p. XI). These researchers, while acknowledging the existence of the biological basis of language acquisition, also acknowledge that "interpretation and meaning are necessarily embedded in cultural systems of understanding. If language is a meaning-making system and speaking and listening are meaning-making activities, then accounts of these phenomena must at some point draw on accounts of society and culture" (Ochs, 1988, p. 4). In recognition of the influence of culture, Schieffelin and Ochs (1986) refer to the process of lan-

guage acquisition in the sociocultural context as "language socialization." Ochs defines socialization as "the process by which one becomes a competent member of society" (p. 5) and language socialization as "socialization through language and socialization to use language" (p. 14). This perspective recognizes that linguistic competence involves much more than the ability to comprehend and produce grammatically correct utterances. Language competence involves the ability to select between a variety of possible options of linguistic form and content according to the social context and cultural norms, as well as interpreting subtle meanings that require extensive social and cultural knowledge. An example is knowing when the sentence "Would you like to sit down?" becomes an indirect command, a real question, or a comment on inappropriate behavior.

The study of second language acquisition clearly fits within the above theoretical debate. Understanding how second language learners best acquire a new language may shed more light on the relative influence of cognition, language-specific brain functions, and environmental influences. Unlike the process of first language acquisition in young children, the process of second language acquisition can be observed under a variety of circumstances. The relative influences of age, personality, social context, type of language input, and other factors can be better isolated and explored. This information can, in turn, inform our understanding of how language acquisition as a generic process unfolds.

The Process of First Language Acquisition

It is a remarkable fact that, without special training or carefully sequenced linguistic input, every normal child acquires a natural language. The universality of language in our species stands in glaring contrast to the much more selective attainment of comparable cognitive skills, such as the ability to perform arithmetic calculations. A related fact is that every child in a linguistic community succeeds in converging on a grammatical system that is equivalent to everyone else's, despite considerable variability in linguistic experience. Moreover, children acquire language quite rapidly and with few wrong turns, considering the number of potential pitfalls that exist. (Crain, 1994, p. 364)

Precursors to Language Production. Language acquisition is indeed a remarkable process. Children acquire the language(s) heard around them and seem to do so in strikingly similar ways the world over. This process is even more remarkable when we consider what children must know and be able to do to produce their first word, for example, "mama." To answer this question, we need to distinguish between the real use of a word for communicative purposes and the imitation of a string of sounds. It is easy for first-time parents, eagerly anticipating Joey's first word, to interpret "mama" as "mother" and "dada" for "daddy" when the child is really just engaging in babbling or sound play. In order to call "mama" or "dada" a word, it should occur in consistent contexts, spontaneously (without imitation), and appear to indicate a communicative intent. Clearly, this can be difficult to determine. However, if Joey says "dada" when repeating sounds made during play with his mother and produces this consonant-vowel combination along with others, such as "baba," "gaga," and "dadada," then we can probably suspect that it is not a real word. On the other hand, if Joey sees his father coming into the room and spontaneously looks at him and says "dada," and also has done this before in a similar context, then there is a good likelihood that for him, "dada" is now a word that means "daddy."

For Joey to do this, what must he know and be able to do? He must have a variety of linguistic, cognitive, social, and perceptual competencies. It is amazing to consider all that a child must be capable of to produce even one

real word. This is as true for the child acquiring a second language as it is for the first.

Linguistically, Joey has already developed quite a bit of knowledge about the phonology of his first language. Studies have indicated that within the first year of life, children have already learned what sounds and sound combinations are possible in their native language. Using the example presented in the beginning of this chapter, native-English speaking infants learn that a word cannot start with "mb." Joey has also learned how to produce a variety of sounds correctly in English. Although his pronunciation is not adult-like, it is well-enough developed that many early words are grossly intelligible.

Joey has also started understanding how language functions. Although first words can assume a variety of grammatical functions, young children have at least a basic understanding of what a word is and what different functions they can perform. Joey also understands the meaning of various words, even though his understanding may not be exactly like that of an adult. To at least some extent then, Joey understands the words "mama" and "daddy."

In addition to understanding the early words that he produces, Joey understands their underlying concepts. To identify a mother, Joey has to understand what a mother is. His understanding of this concept, again, may not be exactly like that of an adult (he may conceive of a mother as any female adult caregiver rather than one unique individual), but he clearly does have some idea. This means that Joey can also differentiate between individuals and can typically differentiate between genders and age groups. Joey must be able to understand a lot of what goes on around him and differentiate and interpret relationships between objects, actions, sounds, and people in his environment.

To produce one word, a child must also have acquired quite a bit of social and cultural knowledge. Words have social functions—they can be used to label, request, greet, query, and deny, to name just a few. Therefore, by saying "mama," Joey demonstrates his knowledge about the social functions of language and his understanding of social relationships. He knows that words are to be used interactively with others, and he knows when and how to initiate and continue communicative interactions. He knows how to take conversational turns, and he expects that others will respond to him in specific ways.

Joey must have some useful auditory capabilities if he is producing his first words orally. Although children who are deaf and severely hearing impaired do begin to babble, they stop doing so around the age of six months. Therefore, production of oral speech is dependent on the ability to hear. Joey is also able to process auditory input. He can distinguish between human speech and environmental sounds. Visual acuity is not necessary to the development of oral language; however, the language development of children who are blind has been studied and found to be affected by their blindness. Clearly, children can do and know a lot, even before they ever produce their first words.

Language Comprehension. What does it mean to understand a word? Language comprehension is not an all-or-none phenomenon. This idea is important for educators to understand. Children may be able to "comprehend" a word or phrase in some contexts and not in others. Children may first comprehend a word within a specific routine or context (such as "jacket" during a getting-dressed-for-going-outside routine) and with an accompanying gesture or linguistic cue (such as pointing to or naming an item using known words, such as "doggie book"). We can say children really understand a word when they are able to follow a direction or identify an item, when the item(s) involved are not present and the context is not routine. For example, children demonstrate some amount of comprehension when they put their shoes on after being asked to during a dressing routine. They demonstrate greater comprehension when they are asked to "show me how you put your shoes on" during a nondressing situation, such as play testing. With second language learners, we must be careful that we do not either over- or under-estimate their receptive language abilities by failing to analyze the linguistic, social, situational, and/or gestural context of comprehension.

The Process of Language Acquisition. Language acquisition does not progress randomly. Although there is significant individual variation, children appear to acquire language in a fairly systematic fashion. The sequence of acquisition of syntax and morphology, the manner in which these develop, and the development of phonology all appear to proceed in a somewhat consistent and systematic fashion.

Evidence for the biological foundation of grammatical acquisition came with the discovery that grammatical morpheme acquisition appears to progress in an orderly fashion (Brown, 1973). Brown observed the grammatical development of three children, Adam, Eve, and Sarah, over a period of several years and discovered that the order of appearance of the first 14 grammatical morphemes was the same for all three children. Figure 6–1 lists these morphemes in their order of appearance. Another classic study also found striking similarities in the sequence of morphological acquisition among native-English speaking children (deVilliers & deVilliers, 1973).

In addition to determining the sequence of acquisition of grammatical morphemes in English, the research by Brown (1973) and deVilliers and deVilliers (1973) was also important in establishing parameters for when these morphemes should appear, in terms of stage of language development. This research described children's level of language development according to a measure of utterance length—Mean Length of Utterance (MLU). A determination of MLU is made by analyzing a 100 utterance language sample for the average

Figure 6–1
Brown's First 14 Morphemes

1. present progressive -ing (without auxiliary)
2. "in"
3. "on"
4. regular plural -s
5. irregular past
6. possessive -s
7. uncontractible copula (to be as main verb)
8. articles
9. regular past -ed
10. regular 3rd person -s
11. irregular 3rd person
12. uncontractible auxiliary
13. contractible copula
14. contractible auxiliary

length of child-produced utterances, in terms of morphemes. For example, the utterance 'Bobby hitting' has a morpheme count of 3, as 'hitting' includes both the verb 'to hit' and the present progressive morpheme -ing. This type of measure of language development, rather than age, is considered a better predictor of grammatical development, as children of similar chronological ages can vary greatly in their language acquisition. Therefore, researchers have attempted to determine in what order and at what stage of linguistic development different language forms should appear.

Until recently, most research has focused on similarities in grammatical development, with the accompanying perception that all normal children follow a relatively fixed and stable pattern of grammatical development. However, more recently, investigators have begun to question this assumption, with research that indicates a greater variability than previously assumed (Lahey, Liebergott, Chesnick, Menyuk, & Adams, 1982). Given the original research indicating very consistent patterns of grammatical acquisition among middle-class native-English speakers, this trend was assumed to hold for nondominant culture En-

glish speakers as well as for children acquiring languages other than English.

A considerable amount of research on the grammatical development of native-Spanish speakers has been performed, with the goal of finding a consistent order of acquisition of morphemes such as that found among middle-class, native-English speakers (e.g., González, 1978; Kvaal, Shipstead-Cox, Nevitt, Hodson, & Launer, 1988; Olarte, 1985; Vivas, 1979). However, in a meta-analysis of these studies, Merino (1992) found that no more than very gross generalities could be found, such as the acquisition of the present tense before the subjective. These findings have important implications for the language assessment of bilingual and non-English speaking children.

These studies that indicate that the order and developmental age of appearance of morphemes may not be as consistent as previously thought should warn educators and assessment personnel against making judgments about grammatical development for the purposes of determining special education placement. We need to be very cautious when making comparisons of individual children against assumed benchmarks of "normal" development. These guidelines of morphological development should be seen as generalities, and deviance from this observed progression should not be taken as indications of a language problem.

In addition to research focused on the stage and sequence of grammatical development, researchers have also looked at the process by which children acquire grammatical forms. This process was assumed to be a matter of modeling, imitation, and reinforcement when Skinner's behavioral model of language development was in vogue. However, researchers have since observed that children seem to go through a process of hypothesis testing. Children may acquire a form of a word, such as "went," without acquiring the rule for irregular past tenses. Late, when they acquire the rule for formation of regular past tenses, they may overgeneralize the rule, forming productions such as "goed." As they fine tune their system of grammatical rules and acquire the irregular past tense, they will once again correctly produce "went." During this period of over-extensions, children may be very resistant to corrections of forms that they have not yet acquired. Figure 6–2 provides an example of a hypothetical, but typical, mother-child interaction that demonstrates children's attention to the truthfulness, rather than the grammatical correctness, of the input. In fact, observations of mother-child dyads indicate that parents respond more to the truthfulness of the child's productions, rather than to the grammatical form. This is more evidence of why the behavioral model of language learning has been rejected as untenable.

Similar to grammatical acquisition, phonological acquisition appears to follow a general pattern of development, with some sounds typically appearing earlier than others. In general, sounds such as *p, b,* and *m* appear very early, even across different cultures. Other sounds, such as *s, th, r,* and *l,* typically appear much later. However, as with all generalities, these patterns may not hold for individual children. Although a normally developing English-speaking child may not correctly produce *r* in all phonological contexts until age 5 or 6, some 3-year-olds can produce this sound without difficulty. This is one more reason that we must take a child's total language abilities into consideration when evaluating their language competence: language form, content, and use all must be assessed.

Input Influences.   Even if we accept a strong nativist position, the influence of external input

on the process of language acquisition is undeniable. A child growing up in China learns to speak Chinese, not because of a physical predisposition, but because that is the language of the child's environment. If that same child had been born in the United States, of monolingual English speaking, Chinese-American parents, the child's native language would be English. Obviously, the language of input is the language that will be acquired.

A child raised in a home where American Sign Language (ASL) is the dominant language will acquire that code. In addition to the language of input, the mode of input, signed or spoken, will determine the language acquired. Sign language, just like spoken language, is a complex, systematic, rule-governed code. The linguistic universals discussed in the beginning of this chapter apply to sign languages just as to oral languages.

The language and mode of input are unarguable examples of the influence of external factors. The influence of other factors, though, are more questionable. Some researchers have found that the way parents speak to their children may affect early vocabulary development (Beals & Tabors, 1995; Harris, 1992). However, what long-term effect different maternal styles will have is still unknown. At one time, the typical way that middle-class English-speaking mothers communicate with their children was thought to be a universal pattern. The elevated pitch, expressive intonation, and tendency to treat even very young infants as capable communicative partners has been termed "motherese." However, by the 1980s evidence from cross-cultural studies had begun to reveal that what was once considered a universal communication style with young children and necessary for facilitation of language acquisition is not found in all cultures (Ochs, 1982, 1988; Schieffelin & Ochs, 1986). Although there are considerable differences in the ways that adults communicate with young children and the expectations they have for children's participation in conversation, children the

Figure 6–2
Example of Grammatical Over-extension

Child:	he falled down
Mom:	no Timmy, he *fell* down
Child:	yeah, he falled down

world over acquire language fluently and competently.

SECOND LANGUAGE ACQUISITION

The focus of this chapter has been on language acquisition as a general process and on first language acquisition as providing fundamental understandings about the development of language. Although in many important ways second language acquisition differs from first language acquisition, it is an error with CLD students to focus only on their development in English. The extent to which they have had a chance to develop their native language can have important implications for second language acquisition (Cummins, 1991). Studies indicate that students acquire their second language better if they have a firm foundation in their native language. Also, the acquisition of a second language for very young children may be more similar to first language acquisition than to the second language acquisition process of an adult.

Different Types of Language Acquisition

Second language acquisition has typically been divided into two categories, depending on the age of acquisition of the second language. Second language acquisition before the age of 3 has been considered *concurrent* or *simultaneous* language acquisition. The simultaneous development of two languages from birth is also sometimes called *bilingual language acquisition*. Many of the early second language acquisition studies fall into this category, as they typically involved the observation of a researcher's own child who was acquiring two languages concurrently (see Redlinger, 1979, for a review of this research). Summarizing the research regarding bilingual language development, Garcia (1983) drew the following tentative conclusions:

1. Children can and do acquire more than one language during early childhood.

2. The acquisition of two languages need not hamper the acquisition of either language.

3. The acquisition of two languages can be parallel but need not be. That is, one language may lag behind, surge ahead, or develop simultaneously with the other language. (p. 7)

Exposure to the second language after the age of 3 has been considered *sequential language acquisition* (Kessler, 1984). However, there is no evidence that age 3 is a magical number, at which point the acquisition process changes dramatically. This division is an artificial one, which best serves to emphasize that early exposure to two languages is different from acquisition at a later stage of development. Sequential language acquisition is also sometimes divided into different categories, such as early and late sequential bilingualism (Kessler). However, it might be most realistic to view these different categories of second language development (bilingual, concurrent/simultaneous, early sequential and late sequential) along a continuum, ranging from true bilingual language acquisition to second language acquisition in adulthood.

The Process of Bilingual/Second Language Acquisition

Depending upon the age of acquisition of the second language, there will be more or fewer similarities to first language acquisition. Currently, there is much debate about the extent to which the processes of first and second language acquisition are similar. According to Kessler (1984, p. 33), "While research does not support the hypothesis that the acquisition of a second language is identical to that of the first language, neither does it support the position that the two processes are different." Part of the difficulty differentiating between these two processes is that there is still much disagreement between researchers as to the exact nature of first language acquisition. As discussed earlier in this chapter, the extent to which a language dedicated function of the brain, such as a LAD, or general cognitive development is responsible is still hotly debated. Also, the literature is not consistent in supporting the importance of other factors, such as parental input, in first language acquisition. Without agreement as to how first language acquisition proceeds, it will be very difficult to achieve consensus about the similarity or difference of this process to second language acquisition. Nevertheless, it is possible to draw some tentative conclusions.

Similarities to First Language Acquisition. In general, we can say that the process of grammatical development, the relationship of comprehension to production, and the role of hypothesis testing and formulaic speech are somewhat similar in first and second language development. Although we cannot specify the exact order of morphological development for second language learners (i.e., Brown's first 14 morphemes), we can observe that the process is not random. Grammatical forms develop, just as in first language acquisition, in a relatively orderly and systematic fashion. Depending upon the individual's native language and learning context, some grammatical forms will be acquired before others. Second language learners will not begin to use all forms correctly at once; the process will be incremental and reflect common language use patterns of the language being acquired. For example, the passive grammatical construction will most likely not be the first to be used correctly in the speech of either a first or second language learner.

Second language learners, depending upon the environment in which they are acquiring their second language, may undergo a similar process of hypothesis testing, in which they first acquire a non-productive grammatical form. "Non-productive" refers to an utterance that may appear grammatically correct, but which the learner has acquired as an unanalyzed whole. An example would be the student who uses "it's mine" to indicate possession of an object. However, if the student has not acquired the contractible copula, he probably cannot produce other phrases using the components of this utterance, such as "it's not yours," "it's all right," or "that's mine." These unanalyzed whole utterances, called *prefabricated utterances* (Hakuta, 1986) or *formulaic speech* (Wong Fillmore, 1994), play a role in the acquisition of first and second language. When learners acquire the grammatical rule for formation of a particular construction, they may over-extend its usage to inappropriate contexts. Just as the first language learner may begin to use "goed" in place of "went," second language learners may also begin to over-extend their grammatical rules.

When using formulaic utterances, second language learners may generally understand the social context for their use, without really understanding what the utterance means. Diaz, Padilla, and Weathersby (1991) observed their research subjects using English words in contexts where it was clear the students did not understand the word meaning, such as in imitation of native speakers or in sound play. This type of production without corresponding competence can also be observed in first language learners.

Just as production does not necessarily imply competence, comprehension does not always imply production. First language learners may understand more than they are able to produce. Likewise, second language learners may exhibit a period of time during which they do not actively engage in verbal communication. This "silent period" does not indicate that students have a lack of comprehension—they may be actively acquiring language competence even though they are not yet ready to speak.

Differences from First Language Acquisition. Studies indicate that social interaction is important for second language acquisition (Chesterfield, Hayes-Latimer, Chesterfield, & Chávez, 1983) just as it is for first language learners. However, the contexts under which second language learners acquire their second language may vary greatly. Snow (1992) concurs, finding that "the social and the cultural situatedness of language learning and use . . . constitute a much greater source of variation in second- than first-language acquisition" (p. 17). Second language learners may not be exposed to their second language outside of a formal learning environment. They may not be exposed to as wide a range of social experiences. Therefore, we can say that the amount, type, and variation of input may differ greatly between first and second language acquisition and that this can influence the rate and quality of second language acquisition.

The simple fact of already having acquired a language is different for second language learners. According to Kessler (1984), for second language learners, "increased age, cognitive maturity and more extensive language experience are variables which can serve to enhance the process" (p. 49). They may be able to draw upon information about language structures and language use from their native language experiences. Although the use of native language grammatical forms in the second language may be looked at as errors or "native language interference," it can also be seen as a resource that learners can call upon to increase their communicative competence. Although the structures may not be grammatically correct, they may allow the speaker to achieve some level of fluency early in the acquisition process.

With increased age and experience, learners may also be able to capitalize on cognitive strategies unavailable to first language learners. Second language learners may be able to use conscious learning strategies, such as mnemonics, to remember new vocabulary. They may already have native language literacy skills, making it easier to acquire second language literacy. Due to greater knowledge and life experiences, they may be better able to anticipate and interpret the context of utterances, thereby facilitating comprehension.

Unlike monolingual first language acquisition, where the language acquired is the language of the child's environment and commu-

nity, bilingual or second language acquisition may involve issues of differential language status. When a child's native language is not that of the dominant culture, it may not be considered a high-status language. This is the case in the United States for many immigrant languages, such as Spanish, Hmong, and Vietnamese. The social devaluing of a student's native language may have repercussions for both continued native language development as well as second language development. These second language learners are at risk for native language loss and/or difficulty acquiring English as a second language.

Critical Periods.   Related to the issue of similarities and differences between first and second language acquisition is the notion of critical periods for language development. This idea comes from the neurosciences, where it has been discovered that some parts of the brain must receive stimulation for development. For example, studies of critical periods in the development of the visual system have been performed with cats. Researchers have found that if kitten's eyes are covered with eye patches for a specific period of time during infancy, then after the patches are removed, the kittens will be blind. This type of experiment has shown that certain functions of the brain must be activated by stimulation and, furthermore, that this stimulation must occur during a specific period of development. Up until a certain point of development, the brain is considered to be "plastic," that is, receptive to new input (Hoffman, 1991).

Following this research, linguists hypothesized that there may be a critical period for language acquisition as well. This is a multifaceted issue that incorporates several different subquestions:

1. Is there a critical period for exposure to a first language?

2. Is there a critical period only during which a "Language Acquisition Device" (LAD) functions, after which the LAD ceases to func-

tion, affecting continued language acquisition (i.e., second language acquisition)?

3. Are adults or children "better" at acquiring language?

Research with individuals who have been deaf since birth or who became deaf before acquiring their first language indicates that there may be a critical period during which time exposure to a first language is necessary for well-developed language. Some deaf individuals have been raised in homes where they were not exposed to sign language until they were 5 or 6 years old and subsequently began attending a school where sign language was used. As adults, these individuals' language abilities have been found to be different from those of other deaf adults who were exposed to sign language at an earlier age (Newport, 1993). This research seems to indicate that acquisition of language during early childhood is important to the end result and supports the idea of a possible critical period for exposure to a first language.

However, even if we accept that early exposure to language is necessary to trigger the language specific portions of the brain, this does not necessarily imply that a LAD only functions during a specific time period, once triggered. After all, adults clearly can learn a second language, under optimal conditions. However, some research suggests that a critical period may exist for some features of grammatical acquisition (Newport, 1993). Additionally, it is a common observation that children acquire native-like accents much more readily than adults. Some have taken this as evidence that there may be a critical period for the establishment of neuro-muscular patterns (Hoffman, 1991). However, according to Hoffman, this issue has clearly not been resolved.

Many times, what people really want to know when they discuss critical periods is whether adults or children learn language better. First, it is important to clarify a popular misconception—that young children acquire language at a rapid pace unmatched by second-language learners. Consider the grammatical, semantic, and pragmatic development of a 2-year-old. A toddler is just beginning to put two and three words together and, although competent in communicating most basic needs, is not nearly as functional as we expect a second language learner to be after two years of exposure to English. Many second language learners in our school are "transitioned" to English-only classes after only two years of bilingual instruction, if they are lucky enough to have received this much native language instruction. We clearly have much greater expectations of linguistic competence for our school-aged second language learners than we do of toddlers.

Whether or not first language learners have an advantage in terms of a critical period, older learners may also have certain advantages in terms of better-developed cognitive abilities and greater social and linguistic experiences. Additionally, discussions of the best time to learn a second language cannot be placed within the context of "all things being equal, are younger or older learners better at acquiring a second language?" The problem with this type of discussion is that all things are not equal for all individuals. When considering the best time to expose a student to a second language, factors other than age must be considered, such as level of development of the native language, type of educational programs available, support for the first and second languages in the environment, and student motivation. These factors may far outweigh any physiological or cognitive advantage experienced during a specific developmental stage.

Models of Second Language Acquisition

In this section, we will consider three well-known models of second language acquisition, those proposed by Krashen (1994), Wong Fillmore (1991a), and Cummins (1994). Although all of these models have been criticized to some extent, and no one alone is sufficient to explain the process of second language acquisition in all contexts, they have had a significant impact on our understanding of how second language learners function in academic contexts and have greatly influenced pedagogy. Perhaps the greatest impact of these models has been the recognition of how both factors internal to the students as well as the environment can influence the pace and quality of language development. Previous pedagogical styles, such as the audio-lingual method, became much less popular after the introduction of these models. Other teaching methods, emphasizing the natural acquisition of language in real communicative contexts and attention to learner motivation, have been developed and implemented.

Krashen.   Krashen's model of second language acquisition has five primary hypotheses: (1) the acquisition learning hypothesis, (2) the natural order hypothesis, (3) the monitor hypothesis, (4) the input hypothesis, and (5) the affective filter hypothesis. This model, along with Cummins', was originally presented in 1981 in a text produced by the Evaluation, Dissemination, and Assessment Center at California State University, Los Angeles, as well as in other publications. This text has recently been updated, although the primary tenet of the original proposals remains. Readers are encouraged to use this as a resource for further understanding of these theories. Krashen summarizes all five hypothesizes with the following statement:

> People acquire second language when they obtain comprehensible input and when their affective filters are low enough to allow the input in. In other words, comprehensible input is the only causative variable in second language acquisition. All other factors thought to encourage or cause second language acquisition only work when they are related to comprehensible input. (1994, p. 58)

With this statement, Krashen emphasizes two primary parts of his model, namely, *comprehensible input* and the *affective filter*. The input hypothesis postulates that learners acquire language from input that is just above their current competence, which Krashen symbolizes as i + 1. This idea of facilitative input being just beyond the learner's current level is somewhat similar to Vygotsky's Zone of Proximal Development (ZPD). Learners' ZPD is just beyond their current independent level, but within their grasp with assistance from another. This "scaffolding" of learners' current competence with assisted performance has influenced teaching techniques in many different areas, not only second language instruction.

The second important part of Krashen's model involves what he calls an "affective filter." This filter is composed of those affective variables that have been found to influence second language acquisition. These variables are: (1) anxiety, (2) motivation, and (3) self-confidence. According to this theory, these learner variables can block access to the learner's LAD. By referring to a LAD, Krashen is taking an implicit stance on two theoretical issues in language acquisition: that the brain is biologically predisposed to acquire language and that it is not significantly influenced by maturational factors (critical period).

Wong Fillmore.   Wong Fillmore's model of second language learning in social context does not contradict Krashen's model. This researcher identified three components necessary for second language learning that interact with three types of processes. The necessary components are the learners themselves, speakers of the target language, and a social setting that allows second language learners and proficient speakers to interact. The processes identified in this model are (1) social, (2) linguistic, and (3) cognitive. These three processes are interrelated with each other, as well as with the three components. The social skills of the second language learner, as well as competent speakers of the target language, will influence the social setting. Linguistic processes influence how second language learners and target language speakers use and interpret language. Using one of

Krashen's ideas, we can say that the assumptions that target language speakers hold about language will influence whether they produce comprehensible input when communicating with second language learners. The linguistic expectations that second language learners hold will influence how they interpret that input. Cognitive processes "involve the analytic procedures and operations that take place in the heads of learners and ultimately result in the acquisition of that language" (Wong Fillmore, 1991a, p. 56). This idea that second language learners can draw upon cognitive skills is one of the hypothesized differences between first and second language acquisition and may help compensate for the decreasing importance or effect of a critical period for a functioning LAD, if indeed such as maturational decrease does occur.

Cummins. Cummins (1981) postulates three principles related to second language acquisition: (1) the conversational/academic language proficiency principle, (2) the linguistic interdependence principle, and (3) the additive bilingual enrichment principle. The issue of how to define language proficiency will be addressed in greater detail in Chapter 7. Cummins proposed an interesting dichotomy between communicative skills, what he terms basic interpersonal communication skills (BICS) and the language proficiency required for academic success, cognitive academic language proficiency (CALP). He postulates that educators can make false assumptions about students' total language proficiency when they rely primarily on observations of students' ability to participate in social conversation.

The linguistic interdependence principle posits "a common underlying proficiency" (CUP) model in which the literacy-related aspects of a bilingual's proficiency in L_1 and L_2 are seen as common or interdependent across languages" (Cummins, 1981, p. 18). This principle is consistent with Wong Fillmore's postulated linguistic and cognitive processes, which

second language learners originally develop via their native language but which they can access for second language acquisition.

The additive bilingual enrichment principle draws upon Lambert's (1975) idea of *additive bilingualism* as the acquisition of a second language without detriment to the first. *Subtractive bilingualism,* in contrast, is the replacement of the first language by the second. Cummins' principle suggests that additive second language acquisition has a positive cognitive benefit for learners, when they are able to acquire a high degree of proficiency in both languages. He summarizes the research on the cognitive effects of bilingualism with the following statement:

> The development of additive bilingual and biliteracy skills entails no negative consequences for children's academic, linguistic, or intellectual development. On the contrary, although not conclusive, the evidence points in the direction of subtle metalinguistic, academic, and intellectual benefits for bilingual children. (Cummins, 1994, p. 27)

Saville-Troike. As Cummins stated, research does not support the hypothesis that bilingualism is tantamount to a cognitive deficit. Many research studies and literature reviews have supported the idea that additive bilingualism is a cognitive benefit (for example, see Ben-Zeev, 1984; Bialystok & Cummins, 1991; Diaz & Klingler, 1991; Malakoff & Hakuta, 1991; and Ricciardelli, 1992).

Other research has focused on more applied dimensions of these theories. A group of researchers investigated the effects of different language competencies on the academic performance of second language learners from a variety of linguistic backgrounds (Saville-Troike, 1984). The results indicated the following five generalizations:

1. In English, a well-developed vocabulary is the most important aspect of oral English proficiency for academic achievement.

2. Oral practice may not be necessary for the development of English proficiency and in some instances may retard acquisition. An emphasis on interpersonal communication may therefore inhibit academic achievement.

3. A focus on structural patterns, especially grammatical inflections, appears to contribute little toward meeting students' immediate academic needs. When participating in real communicative interaction, most beginning students do not use grammatical inflections.

4. Social interaction between students is not sufficient for development of English language skills.

5. Students who had opportunities to discuss academic concepts in their native language with other children or adults obtained the highest performance in content area knowledge, as measured by tests in English.

What Does This Mean for Students with Exceptionalities?

To understand how all of this information applies to students with or suspected as having disabilities, we now return to the fallacies introduced at the beginning of this chapter.

1. **Fallacy:** *Students with exceptionalities cannot learn two (or more) languages.*

The reality is that many CLD students with disabilities *must* learn a second language. If children with disabilities speak a home language other than English, they must acquire a second language to participate in the school environment. Although research does suggest that some children may acquire a second language more slowly, especially if they exhibited language difficulties in their native language (Kessler, 1984), this should not dissuade educators from assisting their students' second language acquisition as much as possible. Therefore, the real question becomes, should the

language of instruction for CLD students with disabilities be the students' first or second language? Studies suggest that, just as for students without disabilities, a second language is best acquired from a firm and well-developed first language foundation (Perozzi, 1985; Perozzi & Sanchez, 1992). This research suggests that grammatical forms are most quickly and accurately acquired in English when they have first been taught in the students' native language. This supports a bilingual approach to special education with CLD students.

2. **Fallacy:** *Parents of CLD students, with and without exceptionalities, should speak with their children at home in English.*

This advice, although popular, is incorrect for several reasons. As discussed above, students will best acquire a second language if their first language is well-established. Second, asking parents who may not be able to provide an adequate language model in English to restrict the use of their more proficient language is absurd. Parents will neither be able to stimulate their child's language development nor will they be able to communicate easily for social purposes with their child. Wong Fillmore (1991b, p. 343) makes the following poignant observation:

> When parents are unable to talk to their children, they cannot easily convey to them their values, beliefs, understandings, or wisdom about how to cope with their experiences. They cannot teach them about the meaning of work, or about personal responsibility, or what it means to be a moral or ethical person in a world with too many choices and too few guideposts to follow. What is lost are the bits of advice, the *consejos* parents should be able to offer children in their everyday interactions with them. Talk is a crucial link between parents and children: It is how parents impart their cultures to their children and enable them to become the kind of men and women they want them to be. When parents lose the means

for socializing and influencing their children, rifts develop and families lose the intimacy that comes from shared beliefs and understandings.

3. **Fallacy:** *Acquiring more than one language is "difficult" and can lead to academic problems.*

Cummins' additive bilingualism enrichment principle and the research on the cognitive benefits of bilingualism clearly suggest that bilingualism is not a burden for students. In fact, in many parts of the world, it is a common part of daily life. When fluently bilingual parents are encouraged to raise their children monolingually, as in the case of a 1995 child custody case in which Texas State District Judge Samuel C. Kaiser equated raising the child of a bilingual mother in a Spanish-speaking home as tantamount to child abuse, beliefs about bilingualism as a cognitive deficit are reinforced. Regardless of the cognitive benefits, bilingualism is of social benefit in our global village and can only have positive outcomes when students leave school and seek employment.

4. **Fallacy:** *Some bilingual students don't speak any language to a real extent and are "semilingual."*

This idea of "semilingualism" can be compelling when we do not understand language acquisition. Educators may confuse students undergoing a "silent period" as demonstrating a lack of ability to communicate. Consider all that children have to know to be able to say even one word in their first language. Even those children who demonstrate little expressive language in the school environment (in their first or second language) bring with them a wealth of information about the phonology, morphology, syntax, lexicon, and language use patterns of their native language. Also, standardized tests developed based on standard dialects in English and the students' native language may fail to identify their communicative competence.

There are three important concepts that relate to this issue of language competence in bilingual children: *language attrition, semilingualism,* and *code-switching.* Language attrition is a recognized phenomenon in which individuals lose all or part of their native language competence. It can happen naturally as a result of immigration and the lack of opportunities to communicate in a particular language. For adults who have immigrated without their families to a new country and rarely return for visits, this may occur over time. It can also happen to young children who are exposed to a new language at school before their first language has been well established or where there is a significant discrepancy between the social prestige of the two languages. Language attrition is a common phenomenon in the United States among children from discriminated and dominated ethnic groups, such as Hispanics. The preliminary results of the National Association for Bilingual Education (NABE) No-Cost Study on Families indicate that the early exposure to English, by enrollment of non-English background children in preschool programs that are not conducted exclusively in the children's home language, results in a shift in use of the native language at home and leads to language attrition (Wong Fillmore, 1991b). Merino (1982) found that among the native Spanish speaking children in her research project, language attrition occurred by the fourth grade, and sometimes even earlier. She also found that language attrition initially affects later developing skills and abilities. The dynamic relationship between increasing second language proficiency and first language loss can result in a temporary stage in which the child appears limited in both languages.

The problem with applying the label of "semilingualism" to these children is twofold: (1) this term suggests a difficulty in acquiring language and does not recognize that children may have lost language skills they once possessed, and (2) this term implies a resultant *cognitive deficit.* Although bilingual children from nondominant culture backgrounds do have a higher percentage of below-average academic performance, there is no evidence that this stems from a cognitive problem brought about by their bilingualism. Inappropriate academic programs and home-school incongruities have been suggested as reasons for these academic problems. In fact, one of the major problems facing our school system today is the lowered academic achievement of all culturally diverse youth, regardless of whether they speak a home language other than English or not.

Sometimes the term *semilingual* is applied because educators observe students speaking what they consider to be a mixture of two languages. However, research has indicated that what may appear to a monolingual speaker to be a random hodgepodge of two different languages is in fact a systematic and socially governed interplay between two separate and well-developed linguistic systems (Genishi, 1981). In fact, that students are able to switch back and forth between two distinct codes is a sign of linguistic maturity. Code-switching refers to "the use of two or more linguistic varieties in the same conversation or interaction" (Scotton & Ury, 1977, p. 5). This can involve switching between social styles or registers or between different languages. Most people code-switch as a regular part of social interactions, but we don't even recognize what we are doing because it is such a normal part of communication. When we are talking with a friend and using informal speech and then start speaking more formally when the boss walks by, we are engaging in "code-switching." Research suggests that bilingual children are able to differentiate between their two languages at a very early age, even as young as age 2 (Lindholm & Padilla, 1978; Meisel, 1987). Therefore, we can conclude that the use of two different languages, as well as a range of social styles, merely makes a bilingual individual able to communicate in a wider range of social contexts. Depending on the social situation and the community norms, bilingual code-switching may be more or less prevalent. However, regardless of the frequency of code-switching, it should not be taken as evidence that a child is "semilingual."

☺ SUMMARY

In this chapter, the foundations for first and second language acquisition were reviewed. Central concepts in linguistic and child language were presented and discussed in terms of their implications for second language acquisition. The similarities and differences between first and second language acquisition were delineated. Three current theories of second language acquisition, those developed by Krashen (1981), Wong Fillmore (1991a), and Cummins (1981) were summarized and their central tenets were compared with the research literature for feasibility. In light of the information presented on linguistic fundamentals and first and second language acquisition, the four common fallacies which were presented at the beginning of the chapter were revisited. These were considered with regard to CLD students both with and without disabilities. The information presented in this chapter should allow you to make more informed observations and assessment and intervention decisions regarding CLD students in the schools.

☺ DISCUSSION QUESTIONS

1. Discuss the relevance of important concepts in first language acquisition to our understanding of second language acquisition.
2. Define *simultaneous* and *sequential bilingualism*.
3. Discuss some of the similarities and differences of first and second language acquisition.

4. Elaborate on why the term "semilingualism" is not appropriate for the description of the majority of CLD students.
5. Propose and discuss other common fallacies about second language acquisition and second language learners that you have heard.
6. Synthesize the four theories of second language acquisition presented in this chapter.

☺ REFERENCES

Beals, D. E., & Tabors, P. O. (1995). Arboretum, bureaucratic and carbohydrates: Preschoolers' exposure to rare vocabulary at home. *First Language, 15,* 57–76.

Ben-Zeev, S. (1984). Bilingualism and cognitive development. In N. Miller (Ed.), *Bilingualism and language disability: Assessment and remediation* (pp. 55–80). San Diego: College-Hill Press.

Bialystok, E., & Cummins, J. (1991). Language, cognition, and education of bilingual children. In E. Bialystok (Ed.), *Language processing in bilingual children* (pp. 222–232). Cambridge, MA: Cambridge University Press.

Bowerman, M. (1994). Learning a semantic system: What role do cognitive predispositions play? In P. Bloom (Ed.), *Language acquisition: Core readings* (pp. 329–363). Cambridge, MA: MIT Press.

Brown, R. (1973). *A first language: The early stages.* Cambridge, MA: Harvard University Press.

Chesterfield, R., Hayes-Latimer, K., Chesterfield, K. B., & Chávez, R. (1983). The influence of teachers and peers on second language acquisition in bilingual preschool programs. *TESOL Quarterly, 17*(3), 401–419.

Chomsky, N. (1965). *Aspects of the theory of syntax.* Cambridge, MA: MIT Press.

Crain, S. (1994). Language acquisition in the absence of experience. In P. Bloom (Ed.), *Language acquisition: Core readings* (pp. 364–409). Cambridge, MA: MIT Press.

Cummins, J. (1981). The role of primary language development in promoting educational success for language minority students. In Bilingual Education Office (Ed.), *Schooling and language-minority students: A theoretical framework* (pp. 3–47). Los Angeles: Evaluation, Dissemination and Assessment Center, California State University.

Cummins, J. (1991). Interdependence of first- and second-language proficiency in bilingual children. In E. Bialystok (Ed.), *Language processing in bilingual children* (pp. 70–89). Cambirdge, MA: Cambridge University Press.

Cummins, J. (1994). The role of primary language development in promoting educational success for language minority students. In Bilingual Education Office (Ed.), *Schooling and language-minority students: A theoretical framework* (2nd ed., pp. 3–46). Los Angeles: Evaluation, Dissemination and Assessment Center, California State University.

de Villiers, J., & deVilliers, P. (1973). A cross-sectional study of the acquisition of grammatical morphemes in child speech. *Journal of Psycholinguistic Research, 3,* 267–278.

Diaz, R. M., & Klingler, C. (1991). Towards an explanatory model of the interaction between bilingualism and cognitive development. In E. Bialystok (Ed.), *Language processing in bilingual children* (pp. 167–192). Cambridge, MA: Cambridge University Press.

Diaz, R. M., Padilla, K. A., & Weathersby, E. K. (1991). The effects of bilingualism on preschoolers' private speech. *Early Childhood Research Quarterly, 6,* 377–393.

Fromkin, V., & Rodman, R. (1988). *An introduction to language* (4th ed.). New York: Holt, Rinehart and Winston.

Garcia, E. E. (1983). Bilingual acquisition and bilingual instruction. In T. H. Escobedo (Ed.), *Early childhood bilingual education: A Hispanic perspective* (pp. 3–17). New York: Teachers College Press.

Genishi, C. (1981). Codeswitching in Chicano six-year-olds. In R. P. Durán (Ed.), *Latino language and communicative behavior* (pp. 133–152). Norwood, NJ: Ablex.

González, G. (1978). *The acquisition of Spanish grammar by native Spanish speaking children.* Rosslyn, VA: National Clearinghouse for Bilingual Education.

Hakuta, K. (1986). *Mirror of language: The debate on bilingualism.* New York: Basic Books.

Harris, M. (1992). *Language experience and early language development: From input to uptake.* Hillsdale, NJ: Lawrence Erlbaum Associates.

Hoffman, C. (1991). *An introduction to bilingualism.* New York: Longman.

Kessler, C. (1984). Language acquisition in bilingual children. In N. Miller (Ed.), *Bilingualism and language disability* (pp. 26–54). San Diego: College-Hill Press.

Krashen, S. D. (1981). Bilingual education and second language acquisition theory. In Bilingual Education Office (Ed.), *Schooling and language-minority students: A theoretical framework* (pp. 51–79). Los Angeles: Evaluation, Dissemination, and Assessment Center.

Krashen, S. D. (1994). Bilingual education and second language acquisition theory. In Bilingual Education Office (Ed.), *Schooling and language-minority students: A theoretical framework* (2nd ed., pp. 47–75). Los Angeles: Evaluation, Dissemination and Assessment Center, California State University.

Kvaal, J. T., Shipstead-Cox, N., Nevitt, S. G., Hodson, B. W., & Launer, P. B. (1988). The acquisition of 10 Spanish morphemes by Spanish-speaking children. *Language, Speech, and Hearing Services in Schools, 19,* 384–394.

Lahey, M., Liebergott, J., Chesnick, M., Menyuk, P., & Adams, J. (1982). Variability in children's use of grammatical morphemes. *Applied Psycholinguistics, 13,* 373–398.

Lambert, W. E. (1975). Culture and language as factors in learning and education. In A. Wolfgang (Ed.), *Education of immigrant students* (pp. 55–83). Toronto: OISE Press.

Lindholm, K. J., & Padilla, A. M. (1978). Language mixing in bilingual children. *Journal of Child Language, 5,* 327–335.

Malakoff, M., & Hakuta, K. (1991). Translation skill and metalinguistic awareness in bilinguals. In E. Bialystok (Ed.), *Language processing in bilinguals* (pp. 141–166). Cambridge, MA: Cambridge University Press.

Meisel, J. M. (1987). Early differentiation of languages in bilingual children. In K. Hyltenstam & L. K. Obler (Eds.), *Bilingualism across the lifespan: Aspects of acquisition, maturity and loss* (pp. 13–40). Cambridge, MA: Cambridge University Press.

Merino, B. J. (1982). Order and pace of syntactic development of bilingual children. In J. A. Fishman & G. D. Keller (Eds.), *Bilingual education for Hispanic students in the United States* (pp. 446–464). New York: Teachers College Press.

Merino, B. J. (1992). Acquisition of syntactic and phonological features in Spanish. In H. W. Langdon & L. L. Cheng (Eds.), *Hispanic children and adults with communication disorders: Assessment and intervention* (pp. 57–98). Gaithersburg, MD: Aspen.

Newport, E. L. (1993). Maturational constraints on language learning. In P. Bloom (Ed.), *Language acquisition: Core readings* (pp. 543–560). Cambridge, MA: MIT Press.

Ochs, E. (1982). Talking to children in Western Samoa. *Language in Society, 11,* 77–104.

Ochs, E. (1988). Culture and language development: Language acquisition and language socialization in a Samoan village. Cambridge, MA: Cambridge University Press.

Olarte, G. (1985). *Acquisition of Spanish morphemes by monolingual, monocultural Spanish speaking children.* Unpublished doctoral dissertation, University of Florida.

Perozzi, J. A. (1985). A pilot study of language facilitation for bilingual, language-handicapped children: Theoretical and intervention implications. *Journal of Speech and Hearing Disorders, 50,* 403–406.

Perozzi, J. A., & Sanchez, M. L. C. (1992). The effect of instruction in L_1 on receptive acquisition of L_2 for bilingual children with language delay. *Language, Speech, and Hearing Services in Schools, 23,* 348–352.

Redlinger, W. E. (1979). Early developmental bilingualism: A review of the literature. *The Bilingual Review, 6*(1), 11–30.

Ricciardelli, L. A. (1992). Bilingualism and cognitive development in relation to threshold theory. *Journal of Psycholinguistic Research, 21*(4), 301–316.

Saville-Troike, M. (1984). What *really* matters in second language learning for academic achievement? *TESOL Quarterly, 18*(2), 199–219.

Saville-Troike, M. (1988). Private speech: Evidence for second language learning strategies during the "silent" period. *Journal of Child Language, 15,* 567–590.

Schieffelin, B. B., & Ochs, E. (Eds.). (1986). *Language socialization across cultures.* Melbourne, Australia: Cambridge University Press.

Scotton, C. M., & Ury, W. (1977). Bilingual strategies: The social functions of code-switching. *Linguistics, 193,* 5–20.

Skinner, B. F. (1957). *Verbal behavior.* New York: Appleton-Century-Crofts.

Snow, C. E. (1992). Perspectives on second-language development: Implications for bilingual education. *Educational Researcher, 21*(2), 16–19.

Vivas, D. M. (1979). Order of acquisition of Spanish grammatical morphemes: Comparison to English and some cross-linguistic methodological problems. *Kansas Working Papers in Linguistics, 4*(3), 77–105.

Webster's Encyclopedic Unabridged Dictionary of the English Language. (1989). New York: Gramercy Books.

Wong Fillmore, L. (1991a). Second-language learning in children: A model of language learning in social context. In E. Biaylstok (Ed.), *Language processing in bilingual children* (pp. 49-69). Cambridge, MA: Cambridge University Press.

Wong Fillmore, L. (1991b). When learning a second language means losing the first. *Early Childhood Research Quarterly, 6,* 323–346.

Wong Fillmore, L. (1994). The role and function of formulaic speech in conversation. In A. Grimshaw (Ed.), *What's going on here? Complementary studies of professional talk* (pp. 230–269). Norwood, NJ: Ablex.

Issues and Theoretical Considerations in the Assessment of Bilingual Children

J. S. de Valenzuela
Hermes Cervantes

- What's the Problem with Testing?
- The Purpose of Assessment
- Theoretical Considerations
- Assessment Paradigms
- Cautions When Assessing CLD Students
- Summary

OBJECTIVES

To present the need to redefine assessment and evaluation

To describe some of the problems associated with assessment in special education

To give a historical perspective of evaluation

To discuss the theoretical bases underlying assessment practices

To introduce several contrasting assessment paradigms

To present cautions regarding the assessment of CLD students

Assessment is a major component of special education services in the schools today and can consume a major portion of a district's special education budget. In Colorado, Shepard and Smith (1983) found that almost half of special education funds were spent on assessment and staffing. The primary goal of these assessments is the diagnosis and placement of students in special programs. We suggest that this is neither cost effective nor practical. In this chapter, we will propose alternative ways of looking at assessment so that the information obtained will be more useful, less expensive, and less biased than with the current procedures that have caused so many culturally and linguistically diverse (CLD) children to be inappropriately placed in remedial educational programs.

Another purpose of this chapter is to provide a theoretical foundation for understanding the assessment procedures and techniques which are discussed in some detail in Chapter 8. We strongly feel that it is not sufficient for individuals involved in the education of culturally and linguistically diverse exceptional (CLDE) children to know how to administer and score evaluation measures; they must also be able to interpret the results and draw programmatic conclusions. Without an understanding of the purposes of assessment and the underlying theoretical frameworks of different assessment techniques, those involved in assessment cannot interpret evaluation results and draw conclusions in an appropriate and knowledgeable manner.

Traditionally, assessment has been primarily equated with testing. In this chapter, we will redefine assessment as a much larger and more complex task. As with the proposed integration of special and general education, the bilingual special education interface also implies the merging of assessment and intervention. All too often, the purpose of assessment has been to diagnose disability and determine appropriate placement. In an era of tightened budgets, our assessments need to do far more than tell us

that Emilio has a learning disability and needs to work with Mrs. Jones in the resource room twice a week. We need to know how Emilio learns best and how the regular classroom can be modified so that he can participate fully and with maximum success. We want to know how Emilio came to be experiencing academic difficulties and what his strengths are. We want to know a lot about his family and how we can empower them to become effective team participants in his educational planning and intervention program. We want an assessment rich in descriptive information that will be useful in planning academic activities, both in special education and in regular education. Finally, we want the assessment process to be educational, just as we want instructional activities to yield valid information for assessment.

Assessment encompasses the use of both formal tests and informal measures (Baca & Almanza, 1991), and although testing can be part of the assessment process, the term "assessment" is a more general one that calls into consideration a variety of factors to yield a more holistic and complete picture of the individual. According to Midgette (1995):

> Assessment refers to the gathering of relevant information to help individuals make well-informed decisions. Assessment in education and psychology involves the collection of information that is relevant in making decisions regarding appropriate goals and objectives, teaching strategies, and program placement. Meaningful assessment ought to be an ongoing process, individualized and programmatic. (p. 3)

The process of assessment includes compiling a wide variety of information about a student and his/her abilities, observations of performance patterns, and diagnostic conclusions into a complete picture of the child. Multiple evaluation techniques should be used and information about a child's performance should be gathered from multiple sources and take into consideration multiple contexts. For example, a student's language performance in academic contexts should not be considered as representative of her/his total linguistic competence. That student may demonstrate far greater linguistic abilities during nonacademic activities. This observation, in conjunction with other information, might rule out a language disability. Those additional factors which should be considered when assessing CLD students are cultural and linguistic background, experiential and academic background, stage and pattern of acculturation, and patterns of language development (Collier, 1988).

WHAT'S THE PROBLEM WITH TESTING?

At this point, it might be useful to ask why we should bother changing how we assess students. What's so wrong with traditional assessment practices? There are several principle complaints. As mentioned before, traditional special education evaluations are not very practical. The results may indicate the presence of a specific disability and assumptions about appropriate educational placements and educational goals may be drawn. But rarely do these evaluations provide the type of descriptive information necessary to plan an effective educational program. Additionally, many researchers have concluded that the results of diagnostic evaluations are not very reliable and many clinical labels are arbitrary (Collier, 1988; Stainback & Stainback, 1984). Whether a student is diagnosed as language impaired or learning disabled may depend more on who is performing the assessment than on a real disability that can be differentially diagnosed from other related disorders. Others even question the physiological reality of many mild disabilities, arguing that they are socially constructed rather than objective conditions. For example, Sleeter (1986) contends that "learning disabilities is in part an artifact of past school reform efforts that have escalated standards for literacy" (p. 47). Taking a futuristic perspective on this criticism, we can

predict that those now-considered "normal" students who cannot work with computers due to the triggering of epileptic seizures by flashing computer screens would be considered "disabled" in a society dependent on computer use.

The above criticisms hold for all students, but for the CLD student, traditional assessment practices have an even greater risk. These type of assessments are heavily biased against students from cultural, linguistic, and economic groups other than the mainstream, and there is good evidence that LEP students, Spanish speaking or otherwise, have been and continue to be misplaced with regard to special education services (Bernstein, 1989; Beaumont & Langdon, 1992; Figueroa, Fradd, & Correa, 1989; Harry, 1994). According to Garcia and Yates (1986), "eighty percent of Hispanic handicapped students are in LD [learning disabilities] and speech programs, with three times as many students in LD as might be expected from their representation in the school environment" (p. 126). Maldonado-Colón (1983) states that "discrepancies in the norm representation of Hispanics in these categories [learning disabled and speech handicapped] suggests that educators are unable to distinguish when problems are the result of handicapping conditions and/or whether speech and language behaviors are characteristic of students who learn English as a second language" (p. 59). Collier (1988) additionally finds that educators frequently confuse the normal side effects of acculturation with indicators of disability.

Carpenter (1986) states that speech-language pathologists are frequently responsible for making the decision of whether learning problems are due to a language difference or language disorder; however, Damico and Nye (1990) find that "the profession is poorly trained to deal with students from diverse backgrounds" (p. 127). Campbell (1992), in reviewing her prior research on American Speech-Language-Hearing Association (ASHA) certified speech-language pathologists, found that greater than 79% "reported that they did not feel competent to evaluate and/or to treat communication disorders in persons with limited proficiency in English" and that "greater than 66% did not feel competent to evaluate and/or treat communication disorders in individuals from culturally and linguistically diverse backgrounds" (p. 28). Although these practitioners may have a primary responsibility for making assessment decisions regarding LEP students, the vast majority of speech pathologists report having received no formal training in issues involved in serving LEP students (Roseberry-McKibbin & Eicholtz, 1994).

In the past, educators could choose whether they would work with CLD students by limiting their employment to certain geographical regions. This is no longer the case. Yates (1994) predicts that by the mid- to late-21st century, there will be no definable majority group in the country. Even though this change is occurring faster in some areas than others, such as the East and West Coasts, the Southwest, and the Pacific Northwest, all parts of the country are being affected. Therefore, all educators in all fields must be aware of how to appropriately educate students with a wide range of diversity.

Spanish is one of the primary targets for bilingual education and bilingual special education programs due to the large number of native Spanish speakers in this country. Spanish language background children currently comprise the majority of CLD students, with projections that this group will grow to 77% of the total number of students speaking a home language other than English by the year 2000 (Garcia, 1989). Macías (1993) found that Spanish speakers increased from 48.4% of all those who speak a language other than English in the United States in 1980 to 54.5% in 1990. Additionally, due to the rapidly increasing and relatively young age of this population, Latino student enrollment is projected to increase faster than all other segments of the population. According to the California Department of Finance, as cited in Macías, the number of Hispanic students is predicted to grow 112%

between 1991 and 2005. A significant number of these children will be native Spanish speakers. Macías provides additional information from California school enrollments, finding that 45.9% of all Hispanic students were classified as not proficient enough to effectively participate in an English-only classroom. As of the spring of 1995, 78.4% of the California total LEP count was composed of Spanish language background students (California Department of Education, 1995).

If we agree that traditional evaluation practices are inappropriate, especially for CLD students, and that we must specifically address the unique needs of these students, then we have to ask why questionable practices continue in our schools. One of the problems faced by practitioners when evaluating the language, cognitive, or academic abilities of CLD students is the assumption that it is necessary to use standardized tests to comply with mandated criteria for special education placement. Another difficulty is the equation of assessment with testing. Additionally, pervasive misunderstandings about the impact of the acculturation process on students, with or without disabilities, influences educators' continued use of standardized test batteries (Collier, 1995).

To understand the argument against the use of standardized test scores with CLD students for diagnostic purposes, it is necessary to define what we mean by "standardized tests." *Standardized tests* are those published assessment instruments that have a uniform method of administration and have been normed on a given representative population of students. Although many school districts do have a blanket requirement for the administration of standardized tests for placement in special education, waivers can be obtained if the available tests are not appropriate for the student being assessed. In 1991, the American Psychological Association cautioned that people administering standardized tests must be aware of the limitations of their use with individuals who are not represented in the norm referencing population. It is our strongly held position that if the normative population does not apply to the child, if the test items are culturally or linguistically inappropriate, or if the test must be modified during administration, then it is unethical to use standardized test scores to qualify that student to receive special education services. Due to the prevailing belief held by many educators that standardized test scores are indicative of a student's true abilities, regardless of the evidence to the contrary, we suggest that these scores should not be reported for CLD students, even if they are not to be used for placement decisions. This position is consistent with that held by leaders in the field of bilingual special education (Ortiz, 1995; Valdés & Figueroa, 1994). This does not mean that standardized tests cannot be used during the assessment of CLD students; there are several good techniques for using the materials of these tests in a nonstandardized way. However, it is essential that the student not be compared to others on the basis of scores obtained with these tests and that the examiner be very aware that these now nonstandardized tests are no more legitimate than any other informal assessment technique. Two methods for using published tests in a nonstandardized manner will be discussed in Chapter 8.

THE PURPOSE OF ASSESSMENT
Historical Purpose

As noted in the previous sections, assessment has historically been used in our schools to diagnose disabilities and make determinations about educational placements. However, as a general field, psychological testing has a much more nefarious history. The first example of the use of an intelligence test in the United States for sorting purposes occurred on Ellis Island in 1913 (Gould, 1981). Many immigrants were returned to their certain death in Europe, based upon the determination that they were mentally deficient. According to Gould, Goddard, the individual responsible for bringing Binet's work to the United States and for initiating the test-

ing of immigrants, reported that "deportations for mental deficiency increased 350 percent in 1913 and 570 percent in 1914 over the average of the five preceding years" (p. 168). Restrictive immigration quotas by national origin were implemented as a result of this mass testing and the identification of many poor, non-English speaking immigrants as "morons" (Mercer, 1992). During World War I, the first mass-produced version of the intelligence test was used to determine which soldiers would make good officers and which were destined to be cannon fodder. Many illiterate and/or non-English speaking Americans died in the trenches of Europe, having first been administered an early version of the standardized intelligence test, the Army Mental Test.

Clearly, the early developers of standardized intelligence tests in this country, such as Goddard, Yerkes, and Terman, had preconceived notions about the hereditability of intelligence and the differences between racial groups. This bias can be seen clearly in the following statement made by Terman in 1916:

A low level of intelligence is very, very common among Spanish-Indians and Mexican families of the Southwest and also among Negroes. Their dullness seems to be racial, or at least inherent in the family stocks from which they come. The fact that one meets this type with such extraordinary frequency among Indians, Mexicans, and Negroes suggests quite forceably that the whole question of racial differences in mental traits will have to be taken up anew and by experimental methods. The writer predicts that when this is done there will be discovered enormously significant racial differences in general intelligence, differences which cannot be wiped out by any scheme of mental culture.

Children of this group should be segregated into special classes and be given instruction which is concrete and practical. They cannot master abstractions but they often can be made efficient workers, able to look out for themselves. There is no possibility at the present in convincing society that they should not be allowed to reproduce, although from a eugenic point of view they constitute a grave problem because of their unusually prolific breeding. (pp. 91–92)

Clearly, the historical roots of our profession should give us great caution when considering using standardized tests, or any other assessment measure, to make determinations about the inherent abilities and intellectual potential of any individual.

Differing Theoretical Perspectives

Mercer and Rueda (Mercer, 1992; Mercer & Rueda, 1991) have developed a framework for describing assessment paradigms and theoreti-

cal models in special education. This framework is depicted in Figure 7–1. This model is based on Burrell and Morgan's (1979) proposal of two dimensions which can be used to differentiate between scientific paradigms: the assumed nature of reality and the assumed nature of society. Assumptions about the nature of reality range from the belief that reality is objective and knowable to the belief that all knowledge is inherently subjective. The nature of society refers to the belief in the heterogeneity or homogeneity of society and whether one perceives differences as a source of conflict.

Members of the educational community have fundamental differences in these basic assumptions, and these differences frequently underlie debates regarding best practices. Because these

Figure 7–1
Competing Assessment Paradigms

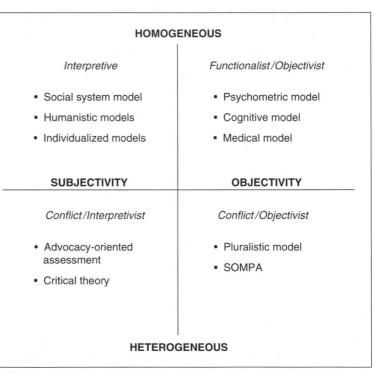

Note: Adapted from "The Impact of Changing Paradigms of Disability on Mental Retardation in the Year 2000," by Mercer, 1992. In L. Rowitz (Ed.), *Mental Retardation in the Year 2000,* New York: Springer-Verlag.

are assumptions, no one perspective can be proven or disproved—these are the underlying beliefs, or epistemologies, that individuals hold and that can be identified in any theoretical position in any academic discipline.

The major theories in assessment and learning can be placed in this framework according to their underlying world views. The psychometric model of assessment is based upon the assumptions that (1) disabilities are an objective, knowable reality and that (2) society is homogeneous. Without either one of these assumptions, the current statistical definition of disability would not be possible. Given the current controversy about the nature of learning disabilities are socially constructed and the reality of our heterogeneous, multicultural society, clearly these assumptions are no longer tenable.

The pluralistic model of assessment, upon which the System of Multicultural Pluralistic Assessment (SOMPA) (Mercer, 1979) was based, questions the homogeneous nature of society. However, this conflict/objectivist assessment model does not question the assumed reality of disabilities as intrinsic to the individual. It assumes that an objective perspective of the individual can be obtained via use of a less-biased standardized assessment instrument. Therefore, this paradigm relies on a modification of the psychometric model to account for diversity in society.

In contrast to the conflict/objectivist paradigm, researchers who argue that disability is a socially constructed phenomenon hold an interpretive perspective. Supporters of this paradigm disagree that reality is objective and hold that behavioral norms develop through societal consensus which can change over time and context. Mercer (1992) contrasts the interpretive and psychomedical models as follows:

Where the psychomedical model sees "mental retardation" as an objective, empirical fact, the social system model sees it as a social construction. Because the definition of "mental retardation" is socially negotiated, it not only varies from society to society but changes over time. Where the psychomedical model sees "mental retardation" as a disability that one "has," the interpretive model sees it as a status that one holds as a result of a variety of social contingencies. A person can be "retarded" in one group and not in another. Retardation is a social enactment. (p. 25)

Only recently have theoretical paradigms from the conflict/interpretive quadrant begun to influence special education theories. The work of Jim Cummins (1986a) is an example of this shift in thinking. In his theoretical framework for empowering minority students, disability is located not only as a societal construct, but also as a result of social inequalities. "The central tenet of the framework is that students from 'dominated' societal groups are 'empowered' or 'disabled' as a direct result of their interactions with educators in the schools" (p. 21). The influence of institutionalized social structures and intergroup status and power relationships are seen as crucial factors influencing the academic success of CLD students. Out of this framework has come the idea of advocacy-oriented assessment, which will be discussed in more detail later in this chapter.

New Purposes

After considering the historical and current purposes of assessment and the Mercer/Rueda assessment framework, we can better describe the new focus that we are proposing for assessment with CLD students. Given the diversity we face in schools today, assessment must be descriptive, instructional, and useful for designing ongoing intervention and instruction. They must evaluate not only the student but the educational context as well. Figueroa and Garcia (1994) made the following point that exemplifies our position well:

The same student with the same academic task can use many different cognitive strategies depending on the day, the teacher, or the mood. Only assessments that recognize that contexts often influence or define outcomes actually begin to work under a different paradigm, and under a more contextualist and constructivist view of human functioning and human measurement. Such assessments are by nature longitudinal and bifocal. That is, they inherently measure the individual's work and the context in which it happened. (p. 19)

Our recommended framework for assessment comes from the constructivist/interactionist perspective and recognizes that societal inequalities exist and can negatively influence the education of CLD students. When performing assessments, the heterogeneity of society must be forefront in our minds, and we must consistently doubt those who would argue that our knowledge of any particular child can ever be objective. We must recognize that our beliefs, biases, and prejudices are so ingrained in each of us that no human endeavor can ever be completely objective; it will always be influenced by our unique perspective, or lens. Only through constant and critical examination of our fundamental assumptions and by obtaining input from multiple individuals can we hope to dilute our individual biases. Therefore, assessments must use multiple techniques, in multiple contexts, and incorporate multiple perspectives.

The basis for the disability categories that are currently used in schools to qualify students to receive special education services came about with the legislation of PL 94-142 (The Education for All Handicapped Children Act) in 1975. Although this act was beneficial in directly addressing the educational needs of students with disabilities, it has also single-handedly promoted the industry of differential diagnosis of disabilities, which many today find to be so problematic. However, in 1973, there was another piece of legislation, PL 93-112 (the Rehabilitation Act), which has also influenced how we think about specifying disability categories. Section 504 of this act guarantees nondiscrimination on the basis of a disability and provision of equitable services. Also, this section allows for provision of services without specification of a disability category. This provision for noncategorical assessment in PL 93-112 is important as it provides a model for what many are advocating for all students with disabilities. Additionally, PL 99-457, which is the 1986 amendment to PL 94-142 that extends the right to a free and appropriate education to preschool children, does not require states to report preschool students by disability category. Therefore, preschool children also do not have to be labeled to receive services. According to DeMers, Fiorello, and Langer (1992, p. 48), "such an approach also allows for services to be designed around the specific needs of individual children rather than all children with the same label being treated the same." Many educators are calling for a noncategorical approach to assessment for all students, not only for those under 5 years of age or who fall under the provisions of section 504 of the Rehabilitation Act.

Assessment activities have not typically provided a direct instructional benefit for students. Any benefit derived is secondary to the determination of an appropriate educational placement. We recommend that assessment and instructional activities become more integrated. The reasons for this are multiple and varied:

1. Instructional activities in the regular classroom can yield valuable and valid information for assessment.
2. Assessment activities should be ongoing and the academic environment is well-suited to this new purpose.
3. Integrating assessment and intervention will ensure the involvement of regular educators in assessment.
4. This new interface will help refocus the purpose of assessment on intervention rather than diagnosis and placement.

The prereferral process, with its emphasis on curricular modifications of the regular educational environment, is a good example of how assessment and intervention can be merged. The information gathered from these modifications provides a better picture of the possibilities of that particular learning environment as well as learning strategies that may or may not be successful for that particular student.

This merger of assessment and intervention should, as mentioned above, make the assessment process more practical, in terms of designing an effective educational program. It does not help the language arts teacher to know that Laura has an expressive language disorder. What would help is to know exactly which cueing strategies are helpful and which curricular modifications would be more effective in this particular language arts classroom. For an assessment to have a practical value, there must be specific detail about how the student will acquire what knowledge. Specification of general educational goals is not sufficient. Rather than just providing an end destination, we want the assessment process to provide an individualized road map that takes into consideration the student, the student's unique history and background, family support, cultural and linguistic factors, as well as the instructional environment, which includes the classroom, school, surrounding community, and general society. This type of holistic and comprehensive assessment will provide educators with instructionally meaningful information.

THEORETICAL CONSIDERATIONS
What Are We Assessing?

Construct validity refers to how well an assessment instrument measures what it purports to measure. But to have good construct validity, there must be general agreement about the "construct" being measured. While it is generally agreed upon that "height" refers to how much distance there is between the bottom of an individual's feet and the top of the head, the constructs of "intelligence," "language," or "language proficiency" are not so easily defined. Even so, all assessment instruments do have an implied theoretical basis. The individuals that construct tests have a framework for or a definition about that which they are measuring. However, if that theoretical framework is not the same as that held by the examiner, then the test fails its designed purposes. For example, the Peabody Picture Vocabulary Test originally provided a mental age equivalency and intelligence quotient (IQ) from the raw score. For those individuals who believe that "intelligence" comprises much more than the receptive knowledge of vocabulary items, it would have been inappropriate to use this test for such purposes.

In this section, we will examine the major theoretical paradigms important to special education assessment. This should allow you to make more critical decisions regarding how to assess language, language proficiency, and intelligence. Considerable detail is provided on linguistic theories, as any type of assessment with a bilingual student is inherently a measure of language abilities. Even those individuals who only administer intelligence and achievement tests need to be aware that linguistic abilities can significantly influence how a student performs on any given measure.

Defining "Language"

The definition of language is central to the debate surrounding assessment. Erickson and Iglesias (1986) stated:

> How language is defined dictates how it is measured. If an individual defines language as knowing names of colors, body parts, animals, or shapes or using embedded phrases, wh-/questions, conjunctions, tense and plural markers, then that is what is measured. (pp. 192–193)

In general, language is assumed to be composed of form, content, and function. *Form* refers to the phonology (sound system), syntax (grammar), and morphology (bound morphemes, such as root words, prefixes, and suffixes) of a language; *content* refers to semantics (vocabulary); and *function* refers to the combination of content and form for the functional and socially appropriate use of language in communication (ASHA, 1993). Some linguistic universals have been accepted, although this is not always apparent during language testing and assessment (see Chapter 6 for a more in-depth discussion of language universals). According to Gonzalez (1974), it is a given that all languages are systematic, constantly changing, and equally good. This can be said to hold true for dialectal variations as well. These universals have important implications for the assessment of CLD students, as they force us to re-examine our criteria for "good" or "correct" answers.

Structuralist and Nativist Paradigms. Currently, most assessments focus on discrete, structural components of language (Damico, Oller & Storey, 1983; Langdon, 1989; Vaughn-Cook, 1986). This method is based on the pre-Chomskian structuralist model of language (Mattes & Omark, 1984), which was concerned with describing the grammatical structures of different languages. Nativists, who adhere to Chomsky's 1965 theory of the innate hardwiring of the brain for language, do recognize the important role of the environment in triggering these structures. However, as this paradigm is most concerned with grammatical structures, which are believed to be preprogrammed in the brain, nativists also use a structural analysis for language assessment (Beaumont & Langdon, 1992).

This type of assessment, called the *discrete point approach*, functions under the assumption that the analysis of discrete components of language will yield valid information regarding an individual's communication skills as a whole (Damico, 1991). Critics of discrete point testing contend that these assessments provide a limited picture of an individual's true communicative abilities (Mattes & Omark, 1984). Others argue that an inaccurate view of language abilities may be formed via the use of discrete point testing. Damico points out that studies have not demonstrated an accurate correlation between these tests and actual language dominance or proficiency in language usage. He sums up his concerns with the statement that "language is too complex to be described in this manner" (p. 173).

In addition to concerns that within a homogeneous population of speakers of a single language or dialect, discrete point assessments may yield a limited or inaccurate picture of true communication abilities, we must also question how well these evaluation measures function with a heterogeneous population of speakers. Students in our schools today speak many different languages and dialects. Yet, commonly used discrete point assessments compare the observed linguistic performance of an individual against the assumed competence of those who speak that language fluently. According to Chomsky (1965), "linguistic theory is concerned primarily with an ideal speaker-listener, in a completely homogeneous speech community, who knows its language perfectly and is unaffected by such grammatically irrelevant conditions such as memory limitations, distractions, shifts of attention and interest, and errors (random or characteristic) in applying his knowledge of the language in actual performance" (p. 3). This perspective can be placed in the Mercer/Rueda framework in the functionalist/objectivist quadrant, which was criticized as untenable in the prior section.

Even though test designers can attempt to define what is "normal variation" in a population of real speakers or listeners through the use of a normative population, the use of a theory of language as described by Chomsky for assessment purposes raises some fundamental concerns, especially when examiners are confronted with a very heterogeneous student population. One might argue that the use of a normative population to define "normal" within a homogeneous population is valid. This position is consistent with the nativist paradigm. However, once language variation is considered, we need to ask if the rationale still holds. We would dispute this claim. Even if the use of a grammatical structure occurs in very low incidence in the general population, and therefore also in the normative population, should it be considered outside of the normal range? Grammatical structures, such as "I be," are grammatically correct in African-American English, although not in Standard English. If a language assessment is based on the assumed linguistic competence of Chomsky's ideal listener-hearer and then normed on a representative population of American speakers, a truly normal and functional speaker of a dialect other than Standard English will obtain a score significantly below that of an "average" speaker. This example illustrates one way in which standardized tests are biased against CLD students.

Sociolinguistic Paradigm. The sociolinguistic perspective is that language must be viewed as an integrated whole (Damico, 1991) and that language use is context-bound and varies with participants, setting, topic, and purpose (Brinton & Fujiki, 1992; Erickson & Iglesias, 1986; Gavillán-Torres, 1984; Kovarsky, 1992). This epistemology implies an approach to assessment that takes into consideration language form, content, and use in natural contexts, and allows for cultural variation according to topic, situation, and speaker. The awareness of the communicative context is crucial to this dynamic view of language. When assessing individuals within this framework, the evaluator must be knowledgeable and aware of cultural and individual variations in communication and language use (Cummins, 1984). Proponents of descriptive, or ethnographic, assessments argue that analysis of pragmatic criteria is more effective in distinguishing actual language disorders from differences, in addition to

having a higher construct validity. Damico et al. (1983) found that pragmatic criteria were more effective than surface-oriented criteria in diagnosing language disorders among bilingual children.

Within the paradigm of language use as socially, contextually, and culturally situated is the implication that communicative incompetencies are situationally constructed (Kovarsky, 1992). According to Cummins (1986), this perspective "involves locating the pathology within the societal power relations between school and communities, and in the mental and cultural disabling of minority students that has taken and still does take place in classrooms" (p. 15). Rueda (1989) disagrees with the prevailing belief that disabilities can be identified without taking into consideration the context in which the skills are measured, and that "true" disabilities exist independent of context. These theoreticians postulate that focusing on the individual and locating the problem in intrinsic traits or characteristics of the individual assures discriminatory assessment of minority students.

Defining Language Proficiency

The question of language proficiency deals with the above issues involved in defining language, as well as the question of what it means to be proficient in a language. This latter question remains quite controversial and lacks a clear solution. This difficulty in defining language proficiency leads to practical problems, as it is frequently necessary to determine in which of two languages the students are most proficient (language dominance) as well as their level of functioning in each language (language proficiency).

Attention has been focused on the identification of linguistically different students based on their English language proficiency by the passage of the Bilingual Education Act of 1986, the confirmation of the *Lau v. Nichols* decision in 1974, and the "Remedies" Task Force in

1975. These legal decisions, combined with the requirement to test pupils in their native language as mandated by PL 94-142, have made it necessary to determine both language dominance and language proficiency. Commonly used language proficiency tests include the Bilingual Syntax Measure (BSM) and the Language Assessment Scales (LAS). The problem with this requirement is that proficiency is commonly determined in discrete levels rather than in a continuum from nonspeaker to proficient speaker. Also, determination of language dominance typically fails to take into consideration a variety of contexts and recognize that "proficiency" and "dominance" can vary according to the conversational context. A student may be dominant in English, in terms of academic vocabulary, but dominant in Spanish in conversation contexts revolving around home and community.

The determination of language dominance can influence whether language assessments will be provided in English, the student's native language, or in both languages. According to Rivera and Simich (1981), a difficulty with this practice is that "research has not provided evidence that would allow valid and reliable weighting of language skills as indicators of different levels of proficiency" (p. 20). Olmedo (1982) has also expressed concerns with the need to make this type of determination, whether based on the results of standardized tests or on information regarding the home language. Additionally, Merino and Spencer (1983) found little comparability in the commonly used oral language measures across languages and strongly suggested that these results not be used for placement determination.

One of the issues concerning these researchers is this idea of levels of language proficiency or a proficiency hierarchy. Different tests give different proportional weights to the various components of language—pronunciation, comprehension, grammatical structure, vocabulary, etc. Also, these tests frequently fail to take under consideration that individuals can perform differently under different contexts. According to Lantolf and Frawley (1988):

> the proficiency of a given speaker can never be characterized in any absolute sense, with everyone having the same fit between form and function. To use another analogy, not only do different people have different driving styles in different circumstances, but different people may have different driving styles under the same circumstances.

Given that it may be impossible to define language ability in an absolute sense, we return to the question of what it means to be proficient in a language. Clearly, that differs according to the situation. Continuing with Lantolf and Frawley's driving analogy, a proficient driver of California's congested multilane freeways may not be proficient in navigating the backroads of Wisconsin during a snowstorm.

Cummins (1980) has proposed that we can think of language proficiency in two levels: Basic Interpersonal Communicative Skills (BICS) and Cognitive Academic Language Proficiency (CALP). According to Cummins, BICS includes the ability to participate in complex context-embedded face-to-face communication and typically takes two years to master. CALP requires the ability to understand and produce language typical of academic instruction and has a higher cognitive load than BICS. Cummins postulates that it requires five to seven years to acquire CALP. Although BICS and CALP may be in some ways an artificial dichotomy delineated for purposes of discussion that ignores the importance of other linguistic/cognitive skills necessary to communicate proficiently in different contexts, this framework is important in that it focuses on specifying the communicative proficiencies required in common academic contexts. CALP answers the question of "What is language proficiency?" by defining the linguistic skills necessary to function well in the classroom.

Defining Intelligence and Achievement

Underlying the debate surrounding the use of standardized IQ tests is the lack of consensus about a definition of intelligence. Initially *intelligence* was considered a single entity that could be measured and that predicted an individual's intellectual ability or aptitude. This was considered distinct from an individual's academic achievement. This distinction was critical, as aptitude was seen as having a biological basis, while achievement was indicative of what an individual had been exposed to or had learned. The construct of learning disabilities is based on this assumption of a distinction between ability (intelligence) and achievement.

Although popular belief in this distinction continues today, most academics have abandoned this approach. Many theoreticians have simply abandoned the attempt to define and measure intelligence apart from achievement. According to Mercer (1992), there are no longer any major defenders in the scientific community of the idea that intelligence can be measured. She predicts that by the year 2000, psychometric measures will only attempt to measure "achievement," with no illusion of measuring "intelligence" as a separate entity.

Clearly, intelligence as a construct separate from achievement is difficult to define. It has been even harder to test. On the Weschler Intelligence Scale for Children (WISC), aptitude was divided into verbal and non-verbal intelligences. This subdivision of intelligence into various components has had several manifestations ranging from Cattell's two or three factors to Guilford's 120 (Miller-Jones, 1989). Gardner (1983) has delineated seven "intelligences": logical-mathematical, linguistic, musical, spatial, interpersonal, intrapersonal, and bodily kinesthetic. Currently, this theory of intelligence is much in vogue among educational practitioners, although has received scant attention from the major developers of standardized IQ tests.

Theories of cognitive processing or human information processing are prevalent in cognitive psychology. These theories, such as those based on Luria's (1966; 1973; 1980) work in neuropsychology, attempt to define intelligence in a broader sense. However, these theories also have not significantly influenced the construction of IQ tests. Naglieri, Das, and Jarman (1990) reviewed the available studies that compared current measures of intelligence and found as follows:

> These findings and the analysis of separate scale intercorrelations across tests, lead to the conclusion that the field of intelligence assessment, as represented by these tests, has shown very little growth or innovation over time. The result has been that "new" tests have only appeared different. (p. 425)

Reschly and Wilson (1990) made a similar observation:

> Item types, around which current tests are organized, have not changed significantly since the 1920s. The various subtests and scales represent an amalgamation of cognitive processes varying from simple memory to abstract problem solving. However, the items are not organized nor constructed to facilitate observation of cognitive processes. (p. 447)

This failure to incorporate newer theories of intelligence and achievement into older tests lends support to the claim that standardized IQ tests lack construct validity.

Newer paradigms in cognitive psychology and education emphasize theories of learning rather than models of innate "intelligence." The work of Vygotsky and Piaget have greatly influenced these theories, which share a constructivist/ interpretivist foundation. According to Shepard (1991), these new theories share the following principles:

1. Intelligence and reasoning are developed abilities.

2. Developed abilities and learning-to-learn strategies are largely context specific.

3. Learning is a constructive process.

4. Meaning is socially constructed.

Reconsidering the framework developed by Mercer and Rueda presented earlier in this chapter, these newer theories fall into the subjective-homogeneous consensual quadrant. The frameworks within this interpretive paradigm do not emphasize clearly any one particular assessment protocol. They do, however, lend themselves well to rich description of the uniqueness of individual students and the analysis of the teaching environment.

ASSESSMENT PARADIGMS

So far in this chapter, we have discussed the need for improved assessment practices with CLD students, argued for a new purpose driving assessment, and described competing theories in psychology and linguistics that can inform our perspective on how cognitive, academic and linguistic abilities can be described and compared.

Traditionally, arguments in the field of assessment have been limited to these areas and, therefore, have boiled down to the question of which assessment technique is better than others. Recently, special education as a field appears to be beginning to recognize that these discussions are moot. The question should no longer be "Which technique is better?" but "How we should approach assessment as a whole?" The rise of prereferral intervention is a good example of the changing approach to assessment. In theory, this new procedure should force any later formal special education assessment procedures to incorporate multiple perspectives, address the educational environment, and consider students within the context of their classroom, school, family, community, and culture. In reality, this does not always happen, and the prereferral process becomes simply another hoop to jump through before

the students in question can be tested with traditional standardized measures and placed in special education. This perspective must change.

Within the traditional assessment paradigm, standardized assessments are judged to yield real and accurate information regarding a student's abilities. The context of the assessment, who tests the child and where the testing takes place, is regarded as irrelevant. The authority of the expert examiner is paramount. The purpose of assessment within this paradigm is to discover whether the child does indeed have an underlying disorder and, if so, what exactly that disability or disorder might be. The assumptions underlying this assessment paradigm are that it is possible to determine the existence of a disability separate from experiential, cultural, and linguistic factors and that determination of this disability is necessary and useful. These assumptions are being critically challenged in the literature, and new assessment paradigms are being proposed. In the following section, four new perspectives on assessment will be described: ecological, descriptive, bi-level, and advocacy-oriented assessment. Although each of these frameworks is unique, they are not mutually exclusive. As a whole, all of these proposed assessment paradigms offer a more in-depth view of students within their unique contexts and seek to provide a foundation for more equitable assessment procedures.

Ecological Assessment

Ecological assessment is consistent with our recommendation that both the students and the educational context be assessed. According to Bulgren and Knackendoffel (1986), "ecological assessment takes both the student and the environment into consideration and focuses upon resultant interactions" (p. 23). This model is appropriate for educators who operate under social-interactionist theories of learning. This is because "the overriding focus of ecological assessment is the awareness of a constant inter-action between people and their surroundings" (Bulgren & Knackendoffel, p. 24). Also, these authors suggest that within this framework, evaluation is an ongoing process that interacts cyclically with intervention to provide a greater view of the total situation. This is consistent with the disability prevention/prereferral inter-vention process and the blending of assessment with intervention that were proposed in Chap-ter 5.

An ecologically-based view of a student locates the child within nested settings, such as the immediate family, extended family, friends, school, and the greater context of the stu-dent's culture, social class, and larger society (Vazquez Nuttal, 1992). The techniques for gathering the information necessary to perform an ecological assessment must include multiple sources, methodologies, and settings.

Descriptive assessments are difficult to quan-tify and therefore may not be as helpful for making categorical diagnostic decisions. How-ever, with the emphasis shifting away from diagnosis and toward providing information useful for educational planning, ecological assessment can be seen as a useful framework. Also, ecological assessment can help shift the focus of educators from students' "deficits" to the idea that they can learn. Linehan, Brady, and Hwang (1991) found that educators had significantly higher expectations for students with severe disabilities when provided with ecological assessment reports than with reports containing developmental information. They also found that these reports provided more functional information that was useful in pro-gram planning.

Descriptive Assessment

Descriptive assessment is an approach that incorporates the use of a variety of evaluative techniques to achieve a more holistic view of the students within their environments. Proto-cols for descriptive assessment are becoming more common in the literature. A variety of nomenclature is used: descriptive (Damico, 1991), pragmatic (Bernstein, 1989), ethno-graphic (Kovarsky, 1992), interactive analysis (Creaghead, 1992), naturalistic (Bernstein, 1989), and natural language interaction (Ber-dan & Garcia, 1982), among others. Each of these terms have somewhat different meanings; however, all are concerned with the holistic view of language use in context. This is in sharp contrast to discrete point measures. The basic ideas of descriptive assessment can also be used for the analysis of learning and achievement, as well as behavior.

With descriptive assessment, a variety of data collection methods can be used, including language sampling (Prutting, 1983), narrative analysis (Westby, 1992), rating scales (Damico, 1991), dynamic assessments (Peña, Quinn, & Iglesias, 1992), and criterion-referenced assess-ments (Damico & Nye, 1990), as well as other techniques. The difference lies not with the type of information collected, as much as with how it is obtained and with what perspective it is analyzed. A language sample, which is com-monly cited as a descriptive analysis technique, can very easily be used as a discrete point assessment, if the sample is analyzed only for grammatical accuracy. In fact, an analysis based on language form and content is the most frequent manner in which language sam-ples are used (Kayser, 1986). This is inappro-priate within the descriptive assessment para-digm.

The common criteria cited as important for maintaining the ecological and construct valid-ity of descriptive assessments are observations of children in natural settings, multiple obser-vations, cultural sensitivity and knowledge on the part of the examiner, and collaboration with others, such as bilingual personnel, the student's family members, and the student's classroom teacher. Given the sociolinguistic model of language acquisition upon which descriptive assessments are based, observa-tions of the student's language performance in natural settings is mandatory. Damico, Secord, and Wiig (1992) state that "language must be assessed in naturally occurring situations where it is influenced by numerous contextual variables and where it can function optimally" (p. 2). Creaghead (1992) suggests that the classroom is an appropriate setting for making language observations, as she finds that "analysis of what the teacher is saying at the moment that the child fails to understand may reveal more about the child's language problem than a formal language test" (p. 68). This applies to all academic difficulties, as well as to possible language problems.

When assessing linguistically and culturally different children, Cheng (1987) finds that "it is extremely helpful to observe how well children communicate with speakers of their native language, within the framework of ongoing interactions rather than to focus on the end product (i.e., speech phenomenon) alone" (p. 131). Damico and Nye (1990) assert that multiple observations are important, stating that "assessment should take place over several time periods so that a true sample of the student's communicative behavior can be obtained for analysis" (p. 129). Researchers have also argued that the examiner should have a familiarity with the cultural mores and the linguistic characteristics of the child's ethnic or regional group (Terrell & Terrell, 1983). De Leon (1986) found that, in fact, familiarity with the language community, rather than expertise in identifying language disorders with Spanish/English bilingual children, was more important for the consistent and appropriate differentiation between language differences and disorders.

Many assert that collaboration provides the soundest means of assuring ecological validity with descriptive assessments (Chamberlain & Medinos-Landurand, 1991; Damico & Nye, 1990; Mattes & Omark, 1984). Creaghead (1992) suggests that collaborative assessment has an additional benefit in creating a less-threatening environment for the classroom teacher, if the teacher is involved in the evaluation process. Kovarsky (1992) also suggests that data can be gathered more efficiently if multiple sources are used.

Considerations with Descriptive Assessments. As with all assessment techniques, descriptive assessment has not been discussed without some criticism. Concerns stem from the paucity of developmental data on languages and dialects other than English, as well as a lack of information regarding cross-cultural child socialization patterns (Erickson & Iglesias, 1986). Without such knowledge, certain linguistic and behavioral patterns might be judged to be universal, although, in fact, only representatives of middle-class White Americans. Pragmatic criteria for linguistic competence typically include dysfluencies, hesitations, revisions, poor topic maintenance, use of nonspecific vocabulary, inappropriate responses, and the frequent need for repetition (Oller, 1983). However, in a 1985 position paper, the American Speech-Language-Hearing Association noted that "hesitations, false starts, filled and silent pauses, and other dysfluent behavior may be exhibited by a bilingual speaker due to lack of familiarity with English" (p. 30).

Bi-Level Assessment

Damico (1991, 1992) and Damico et al. (1992) have recommended the use of bi-level analysis with descriptive assessments, especially when evaluating language minority students. In this framework, the descriptive data are analyzed twice. Initially, the data are evaluated to determine whether the student is experiencing difficulty performing in the context of interest. No judgments as to whether difficulties are the result of a language/cultural/experiential difference or a disability are made at this time. At this level, descriptive information about a student's performance in different contexts is collected. For example, the assessment of communicative proficiency is focused on the effectiveness of the student's communication, the fluency of the interaction, and the appropriateness of how meaning is communicated. This method of analyzing communicative interactions takes into account all components of language, as well as the situational context. If no difficulties are revealed at this stage of analysis, then the assessment is stopped. If difficulties are determined, then an explanatory analysis is performed to determine possible causal factors.

Damico (1991) stresses the need for the examiner to take the role of an advocate for the student, beginning with the belief that factors other than an intrinsic disorder are the cause of the apparent difficulties. Appropriate strategies for intervention, if needed, are also discussed at the explanatory analysis level.

Advocacy-Oriented Assessment

Cummins (1986) introduced advocacy-oriented assessment in his well-known article, "Empowering Minority Students: A Framework for Intervention." He suggests that "power and status relations between minority and majority groups exert a major influence on school performance" and therefore recommends that "professionals involved in assessment become advocates for minority students rather than legitimizing the location of the 'problem' in the students" (p. 21). This entails challenging the traditional role of assessments and advocating a critical examination of the social and education context of the student.

This philosophical approach to assessment works well with the ecological approach, descriptive methodologies, and bi-level process. All of these frameworks have in common the recognition that we must approach assessment as skeptics. Educators should need to be soundly convinced that there are no possible alternative explanations for a student's academic difficulties before identifying a disability. After all, even if there does exist an underlying physiological difference in a child, that reality will continue to

exist notwithstanding any of our interventions. Therefore, the only reasonable solution available to an educator is to modify the educational environment to maximize learning. These alternative assessment frameworks provide the guidance needed to obtain the information that will make our teaching effective.

CAUTIONS WHEN ASSESSING CLD STUDENTS

Throughout the literature on assessment practices with CLD children, the need for caution in interpreting assessment results has been raised repeatedly. Figueroa and Garcia (1994) reviewed reports from the National Academy of Sciences and the many national organizations for testing professions, such as the American Psychological Association and the American Educational Research Association. From these articles and text, they compiled the following cautions:

- The quality of the student's learning experience in the classroom should be evaluated.
- Tests given in English to students who have not had sufficient exposure to English becomes, to at least some extent, a test of English proficiency.
- The linguistic background of a bilingual individual must be taken into account.
- The psychometric properties of a test do not hold when a test is translated.
- Multifactorial language tests, including communicative competence, in both the student's native language and English are necessary to make an appropriate placement decision.
- Language proficiency includes that required in both formal and informal communication contexts.
- The testing context itself may lead to culturally directed patterns of responding which may be misinterpreted.

In the area of language assessment, cautions have been raised due to lack of sufficient developmental information with which to set criteria or compare developmental sequences. However, this assumes that there are consistent developmental sequences of language acquisition for all Spanish language background children living in the United States. This assumption is based on research with White, middle class, English speaking children, for whom syntactic acquisition is highly predictable (Seymour & Wyatt, 1992). However, Merino (1992) performed an extensive review of language acquisition studies involving monolingual and bilingual Spanish speaking children, both in the United States and elsewhere, and concluded that it is not possible to make generalizations regarding relative order or age of acquisition of grammatical markers. She found that the only conclusion that could be drawn is that certain grammatical forms are mastered, in general, earlier than others. Even within the Mexican-American community, there is evidence for considerable variation in acquisition of grammatical forms (González, 1991). These differences in language acquisition patterns of Spanish language background children have been credited to a variety of factors: differences between distinct groups within the United States Hispanic community, in terms of national origin, socio-economic standing, and cultural differences (Sole, 1979); relative language abilities and language attitudes of the mother (Redlinger, 1979); the degree of bilingualism and contextual use of language (Kessler, 1984; Laosa, 1975; Padilla & Liebman, 1975); and the child's personality and child-caretaker interaction (Miller, 1984). Based on the above information, it is clear that reliable and predictable patterns of language acquisition for monolingual and bilingual Spanish speaking children have not been identified and most likely will never be. This evidence should encourage educators to approach assessment with CLD students with great caution.

Chamberlain and Medinos-Landurand (1991) question the validity of traditional assessments with bilingual students who regularly, appropriately, and predictably code-switch. They suggest that evaluators may penalize these students when testing is performed in only one language, based on the prior determination of language dominance. Due to these concerns, some researchers have suggested that testing be performed in both languages (Juárez, 1983; Langdon, 1989). However, others have argued that traditional bilingual assessment, testing separately in the native language and in the second language, fails to take into consideration "the labile interplay between language loss and language acquisition in bilingual children in the United States" (Figueroa, 1989, p. 148). They point out that discrete point tests administered in each language separately could falsely demonstrate a learning or language disorder with these students. Umbel, Pearson, Fernández, and Oller (1992) contest that "from a theoretical perspective, monolingual norms may be inherently unfair to bilingual children" (p. 1013). Concerns also exist regarding the appropriateness of using formal tests in English with bilingual students. Maldonado-Colón (1986) found that bilingual and LEP Spanish-speaking students were compared with native English speakers when evaluated with language assessment instruments in English, and that furthermore, their errors were interpreted without consideration of the errors resulting from acquiring English as a second language. The information provided by these researchers presents a strong argument for exhibiting extreme caution when assessing and interpreting assessment results with CLD students.

☺ SUMMARY

In this chapter, we have redefined assessment as an ongoing interface of intervention and assessment that evaluates students within the context of their school, family, experiences, and culture. The academic context is assessed as well as the students, and all educators are encouraged to approach assessment with a philosophy of student advocacy. The historical and new purposes of assessment were discussed, as well as the theoretical constructs underlying psychoeducational assessment. Four alternative frameworks for assessment were introduced: ecological, descriptive, bi-level, and advocacy-oriented. Cautions and considerations for assessing CLD students were presented in the hope that readers will approach assessment with a more skeptical and open mind. Assessment is a major part of the special education enterprise and will require thoughtful changes on the part of all individuals involved for it to become more useful for educators and more equitable for all students.

☙ DISCUSSION QUESTIONS

1. Describe some of the problems (historical and current) associated with assessing CLD students.
2. Compare and contrast the psychomedical, pluralistic, interpretive, and critical interpretive models of assessment.
3. Discuss why it is important to understand the theoretical bases underlying different assessment practices.
4. Compare several perspectives of language and how they affect assessment practices.
5. Describe some of the cautions that should be acknowledged when assessing CLD students.

☙ REFERENCES

American Speech-Language-Hearing Association. (1985). Clinical management of communicatively handicapped minority language populations. *ASHA, 27*(6), 29–32.

American Speech-Language-Hearing Association. (1993). Definitions of communication disorders and variations. *ASHA, 35*(suppl. 10), 40–41.

Baca, L. M., & Almanza, E. (1991). *Language minority students with disabilities.* Reston, VA: The Council for Exceptional Children.

Beaumont, C., & Langdon, H. W. (1992). Speech-language services for Hispanics with communication disorders: A framework. In H. W. Langdon & L. L Cheng (Eds.), *Hispanic children and adults with communication disorders* (pp. 1–19). Gaithersburg, MD: Aspen Publishers.

Berdan, R., & Garcia, M. (1982). *Discourse-sensitive measurement of language in bilingual children.* Los Alamitos, CA: National Center for Bilingual Research.

Bernstein, D. K. (1989). Assessing children with limited English proficiency: Current perspectives. *Topics in Language Disorders, 9,* 15–20.

Brinton, B., & Fujiki, M. (1992). Setting the context for conversational language sampling. *Best Practices in School Speech-Language Pathology, 2,* 9–19.

Bulgren, J. A., & Knackendoffel, A. (1986). Ecological assessment: An overview. *The Pointer, 30*(2), 21–30.

Burrell, G., & Morgan, G. (1979). *Sociological paradigms and organizational analysis.* Portsmouth, NH: Heinemann.

California Department of Education. (1995). *Languages from around the world: 1995.* Sacramento, CA: Educational Demographics Unit, California Department of Education.

Campbell, L. R. (1992). Meeting the speech and language needs of minority children in rural settings. *Rural Special Education Quarterly, 11*(2), 26–30.

Carpenter, L. (1986). The influence of examiner knowledge base on diagnostic decision making with language minority students. *Monograph of BUENO Center for Multicultural Education, 7*(2), 159–168.

Chamberlain, P., & Medinos-Landurand, P. (1991). Practical considerations for the assessment of LEP students with special needs. In E. V. Hamayan & J. S. Damico (Eds.), *Limiting bias in the assessment of bilingual students* (pp. 112–156). Austin, TX: Pro-Ed.

Cheng, L. L. (1987). *Assessing Asian language performance.* Rockville, MD: Aspen Publishers.

Chomsky, N. (1965). *Aspects of the theory of syntax.* Cambridge, MA: MIT Press.

Collier, C. (1988). *Assessing minority students with learning and behavior problems.* Lindale, TX: Hamilton Publications.

Collier, C. (1995, August). *Alternative assessment with CLD students.* Paper presented at the BUENO Center for Multicultural Education Trainer of Trainers Institute, Boulder, CO.

Creaghead, N. A. (1992). Classroom interactional analysis/script analysis. *Best Practices in School Speech-Language Pathology, 2,* 65–72.

Cummins, J. (1980). The entry and exit fallacy in bilingual education. *NABE Journal, 4*(3), 25–59.

Cummins, J. (1984). *Bilingualism and special education: Issues in assessment and pedagogy.* Avon, England: Multilingual Matters.

Cummins, J. (1986). Empowering minority students: A framework for intervention. *Harvard Educational Review, 56*(1), 18–36.

Damico, J. S. (1991). Descriptive assessment of communicative ability in limited English proficient students. In E. V. Hamayan & J. S. Damico (Eds.), *Limiting bias in the assessment of bilingual students* (pp. 158–217). Austin, TX: Pro-Ed.

Damico, J. S. (1992). Systematic observation of communicative interaction: A valid and practical descriptive assessment technique. *Best Practices in School Speech-Language Pathology, 2,* 133–143.

Damico, J. S., & Nye, C. (1990). Collaborative issues in multicultural populations. *Best Practices in School Speech-Language Pathology, 2,* 127–137.

Damico, J. S., Oller, J. W., & Storey, M. E. (1983). The diagnosis of language disorders in bilingual children: Surface-oriented and pragmatic criteria. *Journal of Speech and Hearing Disorders, 48,* 385–394.

Damico, J. S., Secord, W. A., & Wiig, E. H. (1992). Descriptive language assessment at school: Characteristics and design. *Best Practices in School Speech-Language Pathology, 2,* 1–8.

De Leon, J. (1986). An investigation into the development and validation of an assessment procedure for identifying language disorders in Spanish/English bilingual children. *Monograph of BUENO Center for Multicultural Education, 7* (2), 93–108.

DeMers, S. T., Fiorello, C., & Langer, K. L. (1992). Legal and ethical issues in preschool assessment. In E. V. Nuttall, I. Romero, & J. Kalesnik (Eds.), *Assessing and screening preschoolers* (pp. 43–54). Needham Heights, MA: Allyn and Bacon.

Erickson, J. G., & Iglesias, A. (1986). Assessment of communication disorders in non-English proficient children. In O. Taylor (Ed.), *Nature of communication disorders in culturally and linguistically diverse populations* (pp. 181–217). San Diego: College-Hill Press.

Figueroa, R. A. (1989). Psychological testing of linguistic-minority students: Knowledge gaps and regulations. *Exceptional Children, 56*(2), 145–152.

Figueroa, R. A., & Garcia, E. (1994). Issues in testing students from culturally and linguistically diverse backgrounds. *Multicultural Education, 2*(1), 10–19.

Figueroa, R., Fradd, S. H., & Correa, V. I. (1989). Bilingual special education and this issue. *Exceptional Children, 56,* 174–178.

Garcia, E. (1989). Issues in assessing children with limited English proficiency. In E. O. Werner & J. D. Kresheck. *Spanish structured photographic expressive language test* (preschool and II) (pp. 3–4). Sandwich, Ill. Janelle Publications.

Garcia, S. B., & Yates, J. R. (1986). Policy issues associated with serving bilingual exceptional children. *Reading, Writing, and Learning Disabilities, 2,* 123–137.

Gardner, H. (1983). *Frames of mind: The theory of multiple intelligences.* New York: Basic Books.

Gavillán-Torres, E. (1984). Issues of assessment of limited-English proficient students and of the truly disabled in the United States. In N. Miller (Ed.), *Bilingualism and language disability* (pp. 131–153). San Diego: College-Hill Press.

Gonzalez, G. (1974). Language, culture and exceptional children. *Exceptional Children, 40,* 565–570.

González, G. (1991). Spanish language acquisition research among Mexican-American children: The sad state of the art. *Early Childhood Research Quarterly, 6,* 411–425.

Gould, S. J. (1981). *The mismeasure of man.* New York: W. W. Norton and Company.

Harry, B. (1994). *This disproportionate representation of minority students in special education: Theories and recommendations.* Alexandria, VA: National Association of State Directors of Special Education.

Juárez, M. (1983). Assessment and treatment of minority-language-handicapped children: The role of the monolingual speech-language pathologist. *Topics in Language Disorders, 3*(3), 57–66.

Kayser, H. G. (1986). An ethnography of three Mexican-American children labeled language disordered. *Monograph of BUENO Center for Multicultural Education, 7*(2), 23–42.

Kessler, C. (1984). Language acquisition in bilingual children. In N. Miller (Ed.), *Bilingualism and language disability* (pp. 26–54). San Diego: College-Hill Press.

Kovarsky, D. (1992). Ethnography and language assessment: Towards the contextualized description and interpretation of communicative behavior. *Best*

Practices in School Speech-language Pathology, 2, 115–122.

Langdon, H. W. (1989). Language disorder or difference? Assessing the language skills of Hispanic students. *Exceptional Children, 56*(2), 160–167.

Lantolf, J. P., & Frawley, W. (1988). Proficiency: Understanding the construct. *Studies in Second Language Acquisition, 10,* 181–195.

Laosa, L. (1975). Bilingualism in three Hispanic groups: Contextual uses of languages by children and adults in their families. *Journal of Educational Psychology, 67,* 617–627.

Linehan, S. A., Brady, M. P., & Hwang, C. (1991). Ecological versus developmental assessment: Influences on instructional expectations. *Journal of the Association for Persons with Severe Handicaps, 16* (3), 146–153.

Luria, A. R. (1966). *Human brain and psychological processes.* New York: Harper & Row.

Luria, A. R. (1973). *The working brain: An introduction to neuropsychology.* New York: Basic Books.

Luria, A. R. (1980). *Higher cortical functions in man* (2nd ed.). New York: Basic Books.

Macías, R. F. (1993). Language and ethnic classification of language minorities: Chicano and Latino students in the 1990's. *Hispanic Journal of Behavioral Sciences, 15,* 230–257.

Maldonado-Colón, E. (1983). The communication disordered Hispanic child. *Monograph of BUENO Center for Multicultural Education, 1*(4), 59–67.

Maldonado-Colón, E. (1986). Assessment: Interpreting data of linguistically/culturally different students referred for disabilities or disorders. *Journal of Reading, Writing, and Learning Disabilities International, 2,* 73–83.

Mattes, L. J., & Omark, D. R. (1984). *Speech and language assessment for the bilingual handicapped child.* San Diego: College-Hill Press.

Mercer, J. R. (1979). *SOMPA: Technical and conceptual manual.* NY: The Psychological Corporation.

Mercer, J. R. (1992). The impact of changing paradigms of disability on mental retardation in the year 2000. In L. Rowitz (Ed.), *Mental retardation in the year 2000* (pp. 15–38). New York: Springer-Verlag.

Mercer, J. R., & Rueda, R. (1991). *The impact of changing paradigms of disability on assessment for special education.* Paper presented at the Annual Meeting of the Council for Exceptional Children, November, 1991.

Merino, B. J. (1992). Acquisition of syntactic and phonological features in Spanish. In H. W. Langdon & L. L. Cheng (Eds.), *Hispanic children and adults with communication disorders* (pp. 57–98). Gaithersburg, MD: Aspen Publishers.

Merino, B. J., & Spencer, M. (1983). The comparability of English and Spanish versions of oral language proficiency instruments. *NABE Journal, 7*(2), 1–31.

Midgette, T. E. (1995). Assessment of African-American exceptional learners: New strategies and perspectives. In B. A. Ford, F. E. Obiakor, & J. M. Patton (Eds.), *Effective education of African-American exceptional learners* (pp. 3–25). Austin, TX: Pro-Ed.

Miller, N. (1984). Language problems and bilingual children. In N. Miller (Ed.), *Bilingualism and language disability* (pp. 81–103). San Diego: College-Hill Press.

Miller-Jones, D. (1989). Culture and testing. *American Psychologist, 44*(2), 360–366.

Naglieri, J. A., Das, J. P., & Jarman, R. F. (1990). Planning, attention, simultaneous, and successive cognitive processes as a model for assessment. *School Psychology Review, 19*(4) 423–442.

Oller, J. W. (1983). Testing proficiencies and diagnosing language disorders in bilingual children. In D. R. Omark & J. G. Erickson (Eds.), *The bilingual exceptional child* (pp. 69–88). San Diego: College-Hill Press.

Olmedo, E. L. (1982). Testing linguistic minorities. *Monograph of BUENO Center for Multicultural Education, 1*(3), 1–20.

Ortiz, A. (1995, February). Roundtable on assessment practices with LEP students. In L. Baca (Chair), Bilingual Special Education Half Day Institute. Symposium conducted at the Annual National Association for Bilingual Education Conference, Phoenix, AZ.

Padilla, A., & Liebman, E. (1975). Language acquisition in the bilingual child. *The Bilingual Review/La Revista Bilingüe, 2,* 34–55.

Peña, E., Quinn, R., & Iglesias, A. (1992). The application of dynamic methods to language assessment: A nonbiased procedure. *Journal of Special Education, 26,* 269–280.

Prutting, C. A. (1983). Assessing communicative behavior using a language sample. In D. R. Omark & J. G. Erickson (Eds.), *The bilingual exceptional child* (pp. 89–102). San Diego: College-Hill Press.

Redlinger, W. E. (1979). Early developmental bilingualism: A review of the literature. *The Bilingual Review/La Revista Bilingüe, 6*(1), 11–30.

Reschly, D. J., & Wilson, M. S. (1990). Cognitive processing versus traditional intelligence: Diagnostic utility, intervention implications, and treatment validity. *School Psychology Review, 19*(4), 443–458.

Rivera, C., & Simich, C. (1981). Issues in the assessment of language proficiency of linguistic minority students. *NABE Journal, 6*(1), 19–39.

Roseberry-McKibbin, C. A., & Eicholtz, G. E. (1994). Serving children with limited English proficiency in the schools: A national survey. *Language, Speech, and Hearing Services in Schools, 25*(3), 156–164.

Rueda, R. (1989). Defining mild disabilities with language-minority students. *Exceptional Children, 56,* 121–128.

Seymour, H. N., & Wyatt, T. (1992). Speech and language assessment of preschool children. In E. V. Nuttall, I. Romero, & J. Kalesnik (Eds.), *Assessing and screening preschoolers: Psychological and educational dimensions* (pp. 193–212). Needham Heights, MA: Allyn and Bacon.

Shepard, L. A. (1991). Negative policies for dealing with diversity: When does assessment and diagnosis turn into sorting and segregation. In E. Heibert (Ed.), *Literacy for a diverse society: Perspectives, practices, and policies* (pp. 279–298). New York: Teachers College Press.

Shepard, L. A., & Smith, M. L. (1983). An evaluation of the identification of learning disabled students in Colorado. *Learning Disability Quarterly, 6,* 115–127.

Sleeter, C. E. (1986). Learning disabilities: The social construction of a special education category. *Exceptional Children, 53*(1), 46–54.

Solé, C. (1979). Selección idiomatica entre la nueva generación de cubano-americanos. *The Bilingual Review/La Revista Bilingüe, 6,* 1–10.

Stainback, W., & Stainback, S. (1984). A rationale for the merger of special and regular education. *Exceptional Children, 51*(2), 102.

Terman, L. M. (1916). *The measure of intelligence.* Boston: Houghton-Mifflin.

Terrell, S. L., & Terrell, F. (1983). Distinguishing linguistic differences from disorders: The past, present, and future of nonbiased assessment. *Topics in Language Disorders, 3*(3), 1–7.

Umbel, V. M., Pearson, B. Z., Fernández, M. C., & Oller, D. K. (1992). Measuring bilingual children's receptive vocabularies. *Child Development, 63,* 1012–1020.

Valdés, G., & Figueroa, R. (1994). *Bilingualism and testing: A special case of bias.* Norwood, NJ: Ablex.

Vaughn-Cook, F. B. (1986). The challenge of assessing the language of nonmainstream speakers. In O. Taylor (Ed.), *Treatment of communication disorders in culturally and linguistically diverse populations* (pp. 23–48). San Diego: College-Hill Press.

Vazquez Nuttall, E. (1992). Introduction. In E. V. Nuttall, I. Romero, & J. Kalesnik (Eds.), *Assessing and screening preschoolers: Psychological and educational dimensions* (pp. 1–7). Needham Heights, MA: Allyn and Bacon.

Westby, C. (1992). Narrative analysis. *Best Practices in School Speech-Language Pathology, 2,* 53–63.

Yates, J. (1994, February). Demographics on cultural diversity. In L. Baca (Chair), Bilingual Special Education Half Day Institute. Symposium conducted at the Annual National Association for Bilingual Education Conference, Phoenix, AZ.

CHAPTER 8

Procedures and Techniques for Assessing the Bilingual Exceptional Child

J. S. de Valenzuela
Hermes Cervantes

- The Purpose of Assessment
- Assessment Techniques: Selection Criteria
- Current Assessment Techniques
- Summary

OBJECTIVES

To review the legal requirements for assessment

To discuss the information collected during assessment

To delineate the process of assessment

To explain criteria for selection of assessment measures

To describe multiple assessment techniques

With the advent of Public Law (PL) 94-142, the Education For All Handicapped Children Act of 1975, the requirement for nondiscriminatory assessment provided in the pupil's native language was mandated at the federal level (Cervantes & Bieber, 1981; DeMers, Fiorello, & Langer, 1992; Langdon, 1983). According to DeMers et al., this legislation has affected how schools provide special education services, as it addressed the constitutional rights of children and is considered by some to constitute a civil rights mandate. Although exact statistics are not available, there is considerable agreement that the number of children affected by this portion of PL 94-142 is significant. O'Malley, as cited in Erickson and Iglesias (1986), found that in six states, Arizona, California, Colorado, New Mexico, New York, and Texas, the linguistic minority population comprised more than 15% of the total student population. Speech-language pathologists in California responding to a survey reported that 20% of the students they served were limited-English proficient (LEP) or non-English proficient (NEP) (Carpenter, 1983). This percentage has undoubtedly increased over the last decade, even though the number of bilingual practitioners has not appreciably increased (Roseberry-McKibbin & Eicholtz, 1994).

It is easy to lose sight of the idea that the bilingual special education interface refers to the appropriate education of *all* culturally and linguistically diverse students, not only those with limited proficiency in English. The LEP student population is concentrated in a minority of states, with almost 60% of the nation's LEP population located in California, Texas, and New York (National Center for Educational Statistics, 1994a). Therefore, some may assume that only the teachers in these states need to be involved in bilingual special education. However, even in the six states that reported that less than 2% of the student population speaks a language other than English at home, significant increases were reported between 1980 and 1990, with the percentage change in that decade ranging from 71.7% in

Mississippi to 108.1% in Alabama (National Center for Educational Statistics). Additionally, although these states report having few students with a non-English background, the total nonwhite student population in four out of these six states ranges from almost 25% in Tennessee to more than 50% in Mississippi (National Center for Educational Statistics, 1994b). This high percentage of nonwhite students can be attributed to the relatively higher population of African-American students in these states. Although this text does not deal specifically with the unique problems these students face in the schools, they are clearly included in the population that we are concerned about. Therefore, we can unequivocally state that the need for personnel trained in the appropriate assessment of culturally and linguistically diverse (CLD) students is great and is not restricted in geographic location. Bilingual special education is concerned with the appropriate assessment and education of *all* culturally and linguistically diverse students. This includes those proficient English speakers who speak a home language or dialect other than Standard English, as well as those who are still in the process of acquiring English as a second language.

THE PURPOSE OF ASSESSMENT

The purpose of assessment should determine the type of techniques selected, and this purpose should be explicit and clearly apparent from the methodology used. For example, the traditional purpose of assessment has been diagnostic, with a strong belief in the validity of a statistical definition of "disability." With this purpose and underlying assumption, psychometric tests were the most feasible option. However, this assumption and purpose were critically examined in Chapters 5 and 7 and found to be inappropriate for our current student population. We suggested that assessments should be richly descriptive and have clear pedagogical implications. Therefore, we can say that our new purposes in assessment are:

1. To describe the student.
2. To describe the educational context.
3. To describe the interaction between the student and the educational context.
4. To describe the apparent difficulties.
5. To propose several possible reasons for the difficulties, reserving the assumption that the problem lies in the student until all other possibilities have been exhausted.
6. To develop several potential teaching strategies and modifications of the curriculum based upon the prior descriptive information and hypothesized locus of the problem.

When we describe individual students, we must include a description of their cultural and linguistic background, their prior experiences, level of acculturation, sociolinguistic development, and preferred cognitive learning styles (Collier & Thomas, 1988). If we use an ecological approach to assessment, we must also think of how the students function within different contexts. This implies providing information on their participation in the family, community involvement and activities, and interactions with friends. We want to know what academic and linguistic skills each student demonstrates and in what contexts.

When we describe the educational context, we want to know what is being taught in the classroom and what instructional strategies are being employed. We want to describe how the teacher and other students interact with the students in question and with each other. We want to understand what the expected patterns of behavior and performance in the classroom are and how they are communicated to the students. We want to understand how the school environment supports and discourages different activities, ideas, values, and behaviors that the students exhibit.

The difficulties that students are experiencing need to be described in an objective fashion, without interpretation of cause or attachment of a value. As with the other areas, description of the context is crucial. It is not enough to know what the students can do independently, what they cannot do, or what behaviors they exhibit. We also need to understand under what conditions or in which contexts the problems arise and what the students can do with what type of assistance. This information is necessary for developing appropriate teaching strategies and relies on the idea of scaffolding instruction for active learning.

After we have described the students, the academic environment, and the difficulties experienced by the students, we want to form some hypotheses. These hypotheses should initially focus on the idea of a mismatch between the students and the academic environment. With a critical examination of the students' academic history, it may be apparent that they had received inconsistent native-language support and English as a Second Language (ESL) assistance. Their assumed English-language proficiency may be based upon their basic interpersonal communication skills (BICS), rather than on their cognitive academic language proficiency (CALP). Another possibility is that the students respond better to hands-on activities than to highly linguistically-loaded instruction. Our very last assumption should be that the students "have" a disability (Damico, 1991).

All of this information should allow us to draw programmatic conclusions. If our assessment suggests that the students have received insufficient English-language development assistance, then we can focus on developing this area with proven teaching strategies. If we assume that there is a mismatch in the predominate teaching style in the classroom and the students' dominant learning styles, then we can modify instruction and learning activities. These programmatic conclusions are the result of and should be the primary focus for our assessment.

The Holographic and Culturally Responsive Informal Assessment (HCRI) model (Baca & Metz, 1993) suggests that our purpose in assessment must be to consider individual students in terms of their total abilities, development, and life history and take into account their sociocultural experiences and identity. There-fore, when we describe the students, as sug-gested earlier in this section, our assessment must reflect a holistic picture or perspective. We must remember the old adage that "the whole is more than the sum of the parts." The HCRI model includes seven areas of con-cern, or distinct goals, for the assessment process:

- Identification of specific area of instruc-tional/behavioral concern
- Identification of the sociocultural context impinging on the area(s) of concern
- Delineation of assessment parameters
- Selection of assessment techniques and data collection
- Data analysis and formulation of hypotheses
- Formation of initial conclusions about needed instructional modifications
- Implementation of recommendations

This assessment model can be implemented in a circular process to continually adapt the instruc-tional environment to each students' changing needs. This model is an example of how we can incorporate our multiple assessment purposes in an ongoing problem-solving framework. Although not specifically a special education assessment model, the Prevention and Enhance-ment Programming (PEP) model introduced in Chapter 5 also provides a framework for con-sidering alternative assessment.

ASSESSMENT TECHNIQUES: SELECTION CRITERIA

Selecting Assessment Measures

The selection of specific assessment techniques depends on the purpose of the assessment, the competencies of the examiner, and the psycho-metric properties of a given measure. With the current view of assessment as requiring multi-ple techniques, multiple inputs, and multiple contexts, we need to be careful to select the

right methodologies, in the appropriate con-texts, and assure their use by the correct indi-viduals. With more people involved in assess-ment, the individual burden for administering assessment measures and collecting informa-tion is lessened. However, we want to be cer-tain that all of the required information is obtained in the appropriate manner and by individuals who are qualified to do so.

Integrating Technique Selection with Assessment Purposes

The assessment paradigm recommended and described in this text includes multiple pur-poses for evaluations, with the meta-goal of developing appropriate and specific program-matic conclusions. Each of these individual objectives can be achieved through careful selection of assessment techniques, many of which would be considered "informal" mea-sures. When we consider what techniques to use, we must determine whether our focus of assessment at that time is a description of reported difficulties, the student, the educa-tional context, or the interaction of the student and the environment.

Much of the information needed to describe both the student and the apparent academic or behavior difficulties can be obtained through interviews, observations, and a thorough review of records. This data should be compared with the information gathered through additional sources, such as work samples, and curriculum-based and criterion-referenced assessments. All of these techniques can provide useful infor-mation about the student's performance in the classroom and other school contexts. It should be remembered during the selection of techniques used to describe the student that the goal is a holistic and culturally-referenced description.

When describing the context of the class-room, observations are also very useful. Other techniques include interviews with the class-room teacher and/or paraprofessional, a review of lesson plans, analysis of work samples from other students that includes written feedback from the teacher, and documentation of attempted curricular modifications.

The interaction between the student and the educational environment can be described by comparisons of observations made during different school contexts, such as lessons or activities using different kinds of teaching materials or methods, during interactions with different people, and in different settings. Interviews with the student, parents or caretakers, and school personnel can yield a multifaceted picture that can suggest how the interaction between the student and environment may be influencing the behavior or performance in question. This type of analysis can suggest ways in which the environment can be altered to allow the student to perform at his or her potential.

Tests also have their place in this new assessment paradigm. Sometimes it is informative to use a teacher-made measure, criterion-referenced test or curricular-based assessment to document a student's progress prior to and following instructional modifications. Dynamic assessment, which is described later in this chapter, is a way of using tests to document the effectiveness of intervention. Rating scales can also be used to obtain information from the classroom teacher or the student's parents. A comparison of rating scales completed by the parents and school personnel can often reveal discrepancies between the student's ability to perform in different contexts or indicate assumptions on the part of educators that may not be correct or consistent with the parent's perceptions. These are all ways that can be used to gather different types of information to provide a more multifaceted or holistic picture of a student's abilities.

Also, standardized tests can be used in *non-standardized ways* to demonstrate the effectiveness of attempted teaching strategies or to indicate new avenues for intervention. *These tests, however, should not be used to compare CLD*

students to the general population. Even those normed on linguistically similar groups, such as students in Mexico City, are often inappropriate for our students in the United States, due to differences in dialect, economic status, educational experiences, and exposure to more than one language. Therefore, the comparative information that one can get from standardized tests, such as age-equivalency scores or percentile ranks, *should not* be used with CLD students for diagnostic purposes. Some of the types of assessment techniques that can be used include:

- analytic teaching
- criterion-referenced tests
- curriculum-based assessment
- dynamic assessment
- interviews
- language samples
- narrative analysis
- testing to the limits
- observations
- rating scales
- review of records
- work samples

Examiner Competencies

Before administering any type of assessment measure, the examiner's qualifications should be considered. Simply put, you need to ask yourself, am I the right person to administer this measure? Time and financial constraints are not sufficient reasons for unqualified personnel to be responsible for data collection.

One area of concern involves language proficiency. If you are not fluently proficient in the language of the assessment measure, you should not be responsible for administration and interpretation of results. A summer in Mexico does not qualify anyone to administer a test, regardless of whether they think they can read the directions and test items clearly or whether they can pass a basic proficiency test in that language. Basic competence in a language is insufficient for assessment purposes. If you are not very fluent in a language, you can all too easily misinterpret students' answers. Many times, students' responses are correct, even though they differ from those provided by test manufacturers. Published tests are based upon standard dialects, and many times students will respond in their regional dialect.

Another area of concern involves the use of translators and interpreters. It is not appropriate to use just anyone who is available to translate. During both testing and interviews, the knowledge and beliefs of the person involved in translation can have a significant impact on the outcome. That individual must be educated about the purposes of the assessment and aware of the role of a translator. If not, inappropriate and incorrect information can be transmitted. Mr. Tran, the custodian, should not be asked to step in for a minute and help out with an evaluation. He will not know what type of answers are considered right and wrong, will not know whether to "coach" an answer or not, and may not interpret the information as you assume he will. *If a trained interpreter is not available ahead of time, the assessment should not proceed.* If the school district does not have a trained interpreter, community members can be recruited. However, time and effort *must be* expended in training that individual to ensure that the translation is correct and free from excess interpretation bias. Again, financial and time constraints do *not* justify an inappropriate assessment process.

Psychometric Criteria

As discussed in the preceding chapter, the term *assessment* encompasses both formal tests and informal approaches. However, regardless of the means used to evaluate cognitive abilities, academic achievement, linguistic competence, or language proficiency, confidence in the real-

ity of the assessment rests with the selection of reliable and valid measures, with careful consideration of the context of the evaluation. Lack of awareness of the potential weaknesses in any one of these areas can invalidate the results obtained during the assessment. Damico, Secord, and Wiig (1992) state that "it is equally important for descriptive assessment procedures to demonstrate reliability, validity, and clinical utility. Without such qualities, the results of these assessment procedures may be inaccurate" (p. 2).

Reliability. *Reliability* refers to the extent to which the attribute or construct assessed is being measured in a systematic and repeatable manner (Walsh & Betz, 1990). Psychometricians discuss test-retest and interrater reliability and internal consistency. These concepts are as important for descriptive assessments as they are for standardized tests. Factors that can influence test-retest reliability are poor test instructions, subjective scoring, and guessing (Kline, 1993). Clearly, all three of these factors can be problematic for standardized tests in a clinical setting. Investigators have also found differences in children's performance on standardized tests, depending on examiner's race (Norris, Juárez, & Perkins, 1989) and on examiner familiarity (Fuchs, 1987; Fuchs & Fuchs, 1986; 1989). The robust demonstration of these effects clearly calls into question the reliability of standardized tests with CLD children. The factor which may influence the reliability of descriptive assessments most is the possibility of subjective scoring. This can be controlled for by the use of multiple observations, collaborative assessments, and observer training.

Validity. In general, *validity* refers to "the extent to which a test measures what it purports to measure" (Walsh, 1989, p. 26). Typically, three types of validity are discussed when evaluating the quality of a measure: criterion-related, content, and construct validity. *Criterion-related validity* compares performance on an assessment against some standard or measure. For example, as stated in Chapter 7, researchers have found that pragmatic criteria are more highly predictive of actual language competency than syntactic measures. This indicates a higher concurrent criterion-related validity for descriptive assessments. Oller (1983) states that "there is no evidence that the superficial problems examined [in discrete point assessments] are directly linked with general learning difficulties" (p. 81). With this criticism, he questions the predictive criterion-related validity of these measures.

Content validity refers to whether a measure covers the material that it claims to cover (Walsh, 1989). Therefore, tests which purport to assess language, but which only cover a few components, such as syntax or vocabulary, can be criticized for poor content validity. Similarly, intelligence tests that use limited question types or rely on only a few cognitive processing functions have poor content validity. Descriptive assessments are designed to increase content validity by examining all components of language (form, content, and function) within a broad variety of contexts. The careful selection of assessment instruments, with consideration of their underlying theoretical framework, as described in the preceding chapter, is critical to maintaining content validity.

Construct validity is concerned with how well an assessment measures the theoretical construct or characteristic that it is designed to assess (Walsh, 1989; Walsh & Betz, 1990). Therefore, the construct validity of an assessment depends heavily on the theoretical paradigm current at the time the measure was designed. For example, intelligence tests which rely on outmoded theories of cognition and learning lack construct validity. As the idea of a single intelligence is increasingly disputed, researchers have critically questioned the construct validity of traditional IQ measures. The validity of discrete point assessments, which measure isolated areas of language abilities, has also been strongly called into question since the

advent of sociolinguistic and ethnolinguistic theory, as these tests are based on previous paradigms of language and language development. Damico (1991), discussing discrete point assessments, bluntly states that "this approach lacks construct validity" (p. 177).

Descriptive measures are also concerned with ecological validity (Damico, Secord, & Wiig, 1992; Westby, 1992). This type of validity reflects the extent to which a particular behavior is produced in natural settings and contexts. Achievement tests that fail to take into consideration the contexts under which a student can or cannot perform have poor ecological validity. The same applies to behavioral rating scales that are only used in one context, such as the classroom. Standardized language tests that require students to answer in grammatically correct, but pragmatically inappropriate, ways also violate ecological validity. Similarly, language samples obtained during interactions in an unfamiliar environment with an unfamiliar examiner have poor ecological validity. Although this is a new form of validity to be discussed, it is nonetheless a very important concern during the assessment of CLD students.

Norm-Referencing. Considerable controversy exists regarding the use of standardized, norm-referenced tests. Most experts in the field of multicultural assessment agree that significant difficulties exist with current assessment instruments. The poor reliability and weak validity of these tests has been well-described (Merino & Spencer, 1983; Langdon, 1992; Schiff-Myers, 1992). Some measures even fail to provide norms for the Spanish version of the test, in which case the English norms are inappropriately used. Also, the theoretical basis upon which these tests have been developed has been strongly questioned (Damico, 1991; Kovarsky, 1992). Nevertheless, standardized tests continue to prevail over all other methods of obtaining information regarding language ability (Langdon, 1989) and in qualifying students to receive special education services. Also, many of the same researchers who question the reliability, validity, and theoretical basis for these tests continue to recommend their use, albeit with qualifications and in conjunction with other methods of assessment (see, for example, Burt & Dulay, 1978; Garcia, 1989; Gavillán-Torres, 1984; Juárez, 1983; Langdon, 1983, 1989, 1992; Mattes & Omark, 1984; Mercer, 1983; Miller, 1984). Far fewer are those that, recognizing the limitations of standardized tests and the widespread misuse of the results of such assessments, state unequivocally that normative tests should not be used in the diagnosis or placement of CLD students (for example, Fuchs et al., 1987; Merino & Spencer, 1983; Ortiz, 1995; Ruiz & Figueroa, 1995; Valdés & Figueroa, 1994). The common justification for including such proven unreliable and invalid tests in special education assessments is that alternative procedures have not yet been validated (Langdon, 1992) or that better measuring devices do not yet exist (Rivera & Simich, 1981). We feel that these arguments do not provide sufficient justification for the continued use of such proven unreliable and invalid tests for diagnostic and placement purposes.

CURRENT ASSESSMENT TECHNIQUES

Analytic Teaching

Analytic teaching is an assessment technique that uses the systematic modification of instruction, objective observation, and documentation of results. This technique is a key part of curricular modification, which was discussed earlier in this chapter. This method allows the teacher to identify which teaching strategies are most effective for a particular student and is an excellent means of analyzing and individualizing instruction. Collier and Thomas (1988) have identified the following 14 steps involved in analytic teaching:

1. Identify the current instructional condition or baseline performance.
2. Identify an activity which will assess the student's problem(s).
3. Identify the steps necessary to successfully complete the activity.
4. Construct a sequence and completion checklist based on this sequence for the student to complete.
5. Construct a self-analysis checklist based on this sequence for the student to complete.
6. Develop and implement an instructional activity which incorporates the steps and sequence to be assessed.
7. Observe the student during the activity, noting the results, and have the student complete his self-analysis.
8. Analyze the results obtained from the checklists.
9. Identify and select a new instructional strategy to evaluate.
10. Implement new instructional strategy for a brief period.
11. Continue to regularly assess the student's performance.
12. Implement a second new instructional strategy if desired.
13. Continue to regularly assess the student's performance.
14. Plot the student's performance data. (p. 52)

As can be seen from this description, analytic teaching is a circular process, without a clearly defined end point. Ideally, this process will be repeated multiple times as a means of continually adapting the instructional environment to the student's needs.

Criterion-Referenced Tests

Criterion-referenced tests have also been suggested as an alternative for standardized tests (Damico & Nye, 1990; Nelson, 1992; Taylor

& Payne, 1983). Unlike norm-referenced tests, which compare children to the mean performance score of the normative population, criterion-referenced tests are designed to determine if a student does or does not meet a predetermined set of criteria (Aylward, 1991; Erickson & Iglesias, 1986). Many different assessment techniques can fall under this heading, including curricular-based assessments, rating scales, and analysis of language and work samples. The key feature is that the student's performance is compared to some preset criteria. The following are some examples of criterion-referenced assessment measures:

- Developmental milestone checklists
- Score on chapter-end science test
- Ability to complete a four-mile run
- Teacher-made rubrics
- Timed math facts test
- Teacher-made checklists of student competencies
- Record of amount of in-class assignments completed
- Driver's license test

Although criterion-referenced measures are frequently used in the classroom and during skills testing, their use in language assessment has been controversial. Although Taylor and Payne (1983) have suggested that this type of assessment would be more appropriate for assessing language development than norm-referenced tests, this suggestion has met with some criticism. Vaughn-Cook (1983) finds that "there is no valid developmental sequence which can be used to specify which linguistic behaviors should be selected as goals for a particular child" (p. 31). Mattes and Omark (1984) state that "without this developmental information, one has no basis for establishing the criteria that will be used to evaluate children's performance on these measures" (p. 99). This lack of information about developmental sequences is especially notable for languages and dialects other than Standard English. Therefore, extreme caution should be used when interpreting criterion-referenced language measures for diagnostic and placement purposes, especially with CLD students.

An alternative use of criterion-referenced measures has been proposed by Nelson (1989, 1992). She suggests the use of curriculum-based, criterion-referenced language assessments as a means of evaluating language abilities relative to what a student must know to be successful in school. As such, curriculum-based language assessments cannot be used to differentiate between second language learners and language impaired learners. Nonetheless, Nelson contends that the information provided by these measures is important to comprehensive speech-language evaluations. This might also be an effective technique for evaluating relative language proficiency in bilingual students. Damico and Nye (1990) also suggest that curriculum-based assessments can help determine a student's language and communicative needs, as the environmental demands of the classroom context are taken into consideration. In this respect, criterion-referenced, curriculum-based assessment has strong ecological validity.

Curriculum-Based Assessment

Curriculum-based assessment (CBA) is quite similar to analytic teaching and is typically a form of criterion-based assessment. However, unlike analytic teaching, which can be used to assess all types of difficulties observed in the classroom, including behavior problems, CBA is focused on the student's interaction with specific content materials. This type of assessment will provide the teacher with specific information about what curricular content or instructional strategies present the student with most difficulty. The following steps are necessary when using CBA (Collier, 1988; Idol, Nevin, & Paolucci-Whitcomb, 1986):

1. Select the content area to be assessed from the curriculum.

2. Arrange the material in order of difficulty.

3. Administer the CBA to the whole class.

4. Repeat the CBA with different items from the same content area.

5. Conduct this assessment across curricular levels.

6. The performance of the class as a whole should be recorded.

7. Acceptable levels of typical performance should be determined.

8. The CBA should be conducted immediately prior to instruction.

9. The results should be studied to determine which students:

   - have mastered skills
   - possess preskills
   - ack skills

10. The CBA should be re-administered after instruction.

11. The CBA should then be modified to reflect students' performance.

12. The CBA should be re-administered periodically to assess long-term retention.

Interviews

Interviews are an essential part of the assessment process and can serve several different functions. Although interviews may be primarily perceived as vehicles for gathering information about a student, they can also be an excellent forum for problem-solving. Many different individuals can be interviewed, including the student, the student's parents or extended family members, current and former teachers, other school personnel that are in contact with the student, and outside individuals who know the student or are knowledgeable about the community.

Interviews should be conducted with respect for the knowledge of the participants and cultural sensitivity. Interviewers should not hold the information or suggestions provided by fellow educators in greater value than those provided by parents or other family members. It has been a common occurrence in the past that assessment personnel discounted parental reports of students' ability to perform competently at home by judging their observations as biased. We must question that assumption critically and accept parental reports as valid, unless there is a significant and overwhelming reason to doubt their veracity.

When we inquire about a student's ability to perform a given skill, it is not enough to know whether the student can or cannot do something. We need to know when, how, under what conditions and with what type of assistance a student can be successful. This information is important for planning curricular modifications as it gets right to the heart of "assisted performance" and the student's "zone of proximal development."

Luis Moll and colleagues have written about their success drawing upon families' "funds of knowledge" (1992). This term refers to the wealth of skills, abilities, strengths, information, and knowledge that every family possesses. Those families outside of the dominant culture may have unique funds of knowledge from that typically available to educators. This can be investigated during interviews and used by schools to enrich their teaching. Additional information about "funds of knowledge" is provided in Chapter 14.

In summary, educators need to recognize the following: (1) many different people can be interviewed to provide information; (2) interviews can have a problem-solving as well as information gathering focus; (3) parents' reports of students' performance and behaviors at home should be taken seriously; (4) information about *when* and *how* students perform best should be gathered, in addition to information about what they can and cannot do;

and (5) information obtained from parents through interviews can be used as a rich resource for curricular modification.

Language Samples

Language sampling is the most extensively selected and taught method of language assessment, after the use of standardized tests. Prutting (1983) has been a strong advocate for the use of language samples with CLD children. She states that "the language sample is the only procedure which provides an opportunity to assess communication in real live contexts with real live communicative partners who need to communicate" (p. 90). Research has shown that language samples are sensitive to linguistic differences between normal and language-disordered Spanish speaking children (Linares-Orama & Sanders, 1977). However, most speech-language pathologists collect the language sample from an interaction with the child, using picture description tasks or engaging the child in conversation (Holland & Forbes, 1986). This clearly does not fit the requirements for ecologically valid descriptive assessment. Prutting recommends that the child's communication partner be familiar, such as a friend or family member, and she cautions against attempts to prompt or pressure for answers during conversation. Holland and Forbes also express concern that the setting be representative of the child's natural environment, stating that "the clinical environment itself appears to have a limiting effect on the language sample" (p. 53).

In spite of this support for the use of language samples, there is some controversy regarding the use of language sampling with CLD students. The concerns are focused on the criteria used for analyzing the samples. As language samples are typically judged for form and content, some researchers feel that insufficient information is known about the developmental sequences of minority languages and dialects to perform appropriate interpretations

of the data collected (Mattes & Omark, 1984; Vaughn-Cook, 1986). Therefore, the following recommendations should be taken seriously by individuals collecting and analyzing language samples:

- Collect languages samples in natural and multiple contexts.
- Use a familiar and culturally appropriate conversational partner.
- Do not attempt to "elicit" specific language forms.
- Do not prompt or pressure for answers during conversation.
- Videotape or audiotape conversations for later analysis—concurrent note-taking may interfere with the naturalness of the interaction and will miss subtleties in language use.
- Analysis should focus on language function (use), not only on form and content.
- Caution should be used when comparing the language performance of CLD students to published developmental norms or sequences.

Narrative Analysis

Narrative analysis has also been advocated as a valid form of descriptive assessment (Westby, 1992). It is used for the analysis of oral and written narratives and is frequently used to assess students' writing skills. However, the appropriateness of this technique with CLD students for diagnostic purposes is still questionable, due to significant cultural differences in narrative production.

Narrative analysis is similar to language sampling, in that a speaker's productions are transcribed or a written sample is collected, which is later analyzed for form, content, and function. However, narrative analysis differs in that a child's extended oral or written monologue, usually obtained by storytelling, is used rather than a dialogue. Some of the features that can be assessed with narrative analysis include referencing, cohesion, elaboration, organization, topic maintenance, and coherence. Westby (1992) finds that the ability to comprehend and produce extended narratives is a requirement in the school environment, which lends ecological validity to this method. However, as there are significant cultural differences in the development and use of narratives, further research needs to be performed prior to the use of this technique with CLD students for diagnostic purposes. It would, however, be useful as a criterion-referenced, rather than comparative, or norm-referenced measure. In this way, the student is assumed to have normal narrative abilities according to the communicative rules of the student's cultural group. This type of analysis would simply indicate which skills need to be developed for success in the academic environment.

Norm-Referenced Tests

As mentioned earlier in this text, standardized tests can be modified to provide more relevant and valid information regarding the abilities of CLD students. We feel that it is necessary to reiterate our firm position that it is unethical to use standardized test scores as a basis for comparing CLD students to the normative population for diagnostic and placement purposes. These test scores should *not* be interpreted as indicative of a nondominant culture student's abilities or potential for learning or achievement.

Modified standardized tests are appropriate tools for comparing a student's current performance against that knowledge demanded in an academic environment. They can indicate potentially effective curricular modifications and provide data documenting the effectiveness of attempted curricular adaptations. These tests, when used in a dynamic format, can indicate the student's ability to acquire the specified knowledge under certain conditions. These tests by themselves cannot indicate whether demonstrated problems are the result of an underlying

"disability" or the result of acculturation, acquisition of English as a second language, a mismatch between the student and the educational setting, or any one of a number of factors that can negatively impact a student's ability to learn. They can, however, supply important information that can be used in conjunction with other assessment techniques to build a holistic picture of the student within her/his environment.

Developing Local Norms. Even tests which do provide language specific norms have been criticized as not being representative of local populations. This is because frequently they are normed on monolingual Spanish-speaking populations outside of the United States (Langdon, 1992). Therefore, some individuals have suggested that the development of local norms would render such tests more appropriate (Garcia, 1989; Tornoto & Merrill, 1983). The rationale for providing local norms appears sound. It is based on the argument that the requirement for a nationally normed test is a homogeneous national population and that, therefore, locally normed tests will be more representative of any one student within the local norming area (Toronto & Merrill). However, the argument against the development of local norms can also follow directly from this supposition; just as minority groups vary too widely nationally to validate national norms, local communities are equally heterogeneous. Also, local norms would not be appropriate for students moving into the community from another area. Vaughn-Cook (1983) presents the concern that the standardization of existing tests on nonmainstream speakers can result in lower norms. These are potentially dangerous, as they invite comparisons between groups. She also expresses concern that renorming tests will not improve validity if the test does not represent the student's dialect, but rather compares his/her speech to the standard dialect. *For all of these reasons, we do not support the use of local normative populations, if the result of the* *renormed tests will be used for diagnosis of disability, for statement of achievement potential, or for placement purposes.*

Dynamic Assessment. Dynamic assessment is the process of using standardized tests or set criteria in a test-teach-retest format over a period of several weeks. As can be seen in the following description provided by Lidz (1991), this assessment strategy is consistent with the emphasis on modification of instructional strategies and use of alternative methods for identifying students' potential to learn that we are advocating in this text.

> Although models of dynamic assessment vary, most share the incorporation of a test-intervene-retest format, as well as a focus on learner modifiability and on underlying metacognitive processes that facilitate learning. The role of the assessor as active interventionist rather than passive recorder is also a common ingredient. Thus, the response to the question of what is "dynamic" about dynamic assessment is threefold:
>
> 1. The assessor actively works to facilitate learning and induce active participation in the learner.
> 2. The assessment focuses on process rather than product—in this case, the process of metacognition.
> 3. The assessment produces information about learner modifiability and the means by which change is best accomplished. (p. ix)

Although this technique is best associated with the assessment of learning potential for academic materials, it may also be useful for the evaluation of behavior and language difficulties. Peña, Quinn, and Iglesias (1992) recommend this technique for language assessments and suggest that this procedure is appropriate for use with CLD students, as they believe it is an inherently nonbiased method. Their research indicates that it is a reliable procedure for discriminating between language disordered and normal second language learning children. One possible concern with the methodology remains with the use of discrete point tests that purport to measure language competence as a whole, as were used in the research performed by Peña et al. Nonetheless, if used in conjunction with descriptive measures, dynamic assessment could provide a strong and predictive analysis of students' learning, language, and behavioral abilities.

Testing to the Limits. This technique, termed "testing to the limits," is frequently used in conjunction with dynamic assessment, and many authors do not explicitly differentiate between the two. However, if we think of dynamic assessment as a complete and systematic test-teach-retest process and "testing to the limits" as a cluster of strategies for modification of standardized tests that are designed to elicit students' best performance without an overt test-teach-retest cycle, then the distinction becomes clearer and more functional. Although this distinction is not universally agreed upon, we will use this section to discuss some of the test modification techniques that can be used to explore a student's performance under a variety of conditions. These modifications seek to identify conditions under which the student performs best and reduce possible sources of test bias. *It is imperative that any modification in test administration be documented and clearly discussed in the assessment report.* Testing to the limits can include the following modifications, among others:

- Substitution of dialectally/culturally appropriate vocabulary.
- Deletion/modification of culturally inappropriate items.
- Modification of scoring criteria (correct/incorrect), according to examiner's knowledge of student's culture/dialect/language.
- Use of cues.
- Explicit instruction, beyond that allowed in administration criteria.

- Information about correctness of responses.
- Use of practice items.
- Dual scoring of test protocols, both with and without modifications.
- Allowance of longer response time.
- Probing for reasons behind student responses.
- Modification/substitution of test stimuli.
- Alteration to test format in length or selection of test items.
- Use of alternative methods of establishing ceiling and baseline.
- Translation.
- Administration in alternate location to reduce formality.
- Discussion of test items.
- Overt recognition of correct answers.
- Modification of test stimuli, such as using larger print.

In addition to those modification listed, many others are possible and appropriate. However, it is vital that examiners recognize that *any modification of test administration from that specified in the test manual violates standardization criteria and invalidates the use of normative comparisons.* Therefore, these modifications must be explicitly stated in the assessment report. However, as the normative populations of these tests are not appropriate for the vast majority of CLD students in the United States, we feel that such normative comparisons are invalid, regardless of the testing conditions. Therefore, modification of the test administration and scoring may be the only way to obtain useful information from these tests. As such, they should not be considered "standardized" and have no greater validity than any other informal assessment technique.

Observations

Observations can provide a wealth of information regarding the interaction of the student with her/his environment. Although observations can be carried out in a number of contexts, such as the student's home or the playground, the classroom is also an ideal location for identifying possible factors that may be interfering with the student's ability to perform. The key to good observations is the *objective* documentation of events and the contexts in which events occurred, without interpretation embedded in the observers notes. Table 8–1 provides some examples of different ways that observations can be stated, both objectively and subjectively.

A sketch of the room, description of class activities, and reference to amounts of time in

Table 8–1
Examples of Better and Worse Ways to Document Observations

Subjective (Worse)	Objective (Better)
• The student was working hard.	• The student worked without stopping for a period of 10 minutes.
• The student learned more with visual aids.	• The student received a score of X when the teacher presented the information using visual aids, such as overheads and diagrams.
• The student was off task.	• The student demonstrated off-task behaviors, such as repeatedly leaving his seat (5 ×/30 min), talking loudly to seat mates, and throwing his papers on the floor.

which a particular behavior was observed will help to later make inferences about possible interactions. Repeated quick visits during different times of the day and during different class periods may be more useful than one long observation session. When observing, it is important to remain as nonobtrusive as possible. The goal is to identify under which contexts problems arise and what may be influencing factors. If your observations cause either the student or teacher to alter their performance or routine, then the results may not be particularly helpful for drawing diagnostic and/or programmatic conclusions.

Rating Scales

Rating scales have also been discussed as a potentially useful component of comprehensive assessments. Gronlund and Linn (1990) define *rating scales* as consisting of "a set of characteristics or qualities to be judged and some type of scale for indicating the degree to which each attribute is present" (p. 383). These instruments can be easily and quickly filled out by classroom teachers, parents, and others as a way of documenting demonstrated skills in a variety of areas, such as behavior, academic performance, and language development. If several individuals fill out the same rating scale, such as the classroom teacher and the student's parents, the results can be compared for consistency. Differences in ratings may indicate that the environment, rather than an intrinsic disability, is the precipitating factor in the problems observed. Gronlund and Linn (1990) identified the following six principles for the construction and use of effective rating scales:

1. The characteristics to be rated should be educationally significant.
2. The characteristics to be rated should be directly observable.
3. Both the characteristics to be rated and the points in the scale used for rating should be clearly defined.

4. No more than seven and no less than three rating points should be provided and raters should be allowed to mark between the rating points if they wish.
5. The raters should be told that they should not rate characteristics that they do not feel qualified to judge.
6. The ratings from several people should be combined and compared when possible.

According to McCloskey (1990), a variety of scores can be derived from rating scales; they can be norm-referenced, criterion-referenced, or content-referenced. Depending upon the construction and use of the scale, it can be either a type of holistic assessment, taking into consideration multiple components of performance, or a discrete point evaluation of an isolated component of achievement, behavior, language, or cognitive processing. Therefore, care must be taken with the selection and interpretation of rating scales, as with all other assessment devices. All of the preceding considerations, with regard to reliability, validity, population, judgment criteria, and theoretical basis, must be evaluated prior to the use of a rating scale.

Review of Records

The review of records is frequently an underused assessment technique. Even when records are scanty, as can be the case when students attend a variety of schools, this in itself can provide useful information. A review of records might indicate that documentation of language proficiency testing is absent. This could indicate that a bilingual child was "exited" from a native language instruction program too early. A review might indicate prior educational deficiencies, such as inconsistent ESL or native language support or discontinuities in content matter instruction. Other information that a review of records can reveal includes standardized achievement testing scores, prior testing for special education, home language survey, progression in grade levels, prior concerns regarding behavior, and attendance patterns. Especially with students born outside of the United States, it is wise to verify their age and prior grade placement during the review of records. Currently, many schools compile portfolios of student work. If this is the case, then this would be an excellent source of information as well. From a thorough review of records, documentation about past school experiences may indicate that more information is necessary. This may be obtained by phone interviews with past teachers, an administrator, or other individuals involved with the student. The following should be looked for in a review of records: (1) home language survey, (2) language proficiency test results, (3) previous special education referrals and/or assessment, (4) standardized test results, (5) attendance records, (6) previous schools attended, (7) enrollment in specific educational programs (e.g., bilingual education), (8) evidence of previous grade retention, (9) referrals to social worker and/or counselor, and (10) documentation of previous behavioral problems.

Work Samples

Analysis of work samples can be a very time effective means of understanding the student's performance in relation to the work expected. There are many ways of analyzing work samples—from formalized analyses of writing samples to a more holistic analysis of a compilation of work samples. The crucial factor in the analysis of work samples is to compare student performance under different conditions, analyze teacher expectations, and attempt to form a more in-depth understanding of why the student produces work in the manner demonstrated. Suggestions for collection of work samples include:

- Writing samples
- Spelling tests
- Math tests
- Art work

- Videotaped or audiotaped student performances
- Descriptions or photos of student projects
- Lists of self-selected reading materials
- Printouts of work done on a computer
- Drawings and charts/graphs
- Student journals

Work samples can indicate a student's abilities to reach set criteria of performance. This documentation of a student's ability to achieve certain criteria or perform specific tasks is important information relevant to the assessment process, and general educators can frequently gather this type of information very easily during normal classroom routines.

☺ SUMMARY

The purpose of this chapter has been to redefine the purpose and process of assessment with CLD students and to describe the selection and use of multiple assessment techniques. With this information, you should be able to make more informed choices when designing a unique assessment battery and process for each student. The day when a cookbook approach to special education evaluations was accepted is over. No longer is it considered appropriate to use a set battery of standardized assessments to justify the placement of students in special education. We are now all too aware of the dangers of indiscriminate use of standardized tests with every student—far too many CLD students have been and are being inappropriately labeled as "disabled" without consideration of external factors. PL 94-194 in 1975 guaranteed students the right to nondiscriminatory assessment. It is high time that we begin to seriously implement new and less-biased assessment procedures.

In Chapter 7, we discussed the theoretical frameworks underlying assessment with culturally and linguistically diverse students. A significant paradigm shift has occurred in linguistics, with a radically different view introduced by sociolinguists and anthropological linguists within the past 20 years—that of communicative interaction shaped by contextual, social, and cultural factors. This paradigm is in strong contrast to structural and nativist perspectives, which focus most heavily on discrete, easily describable components of language form. Similar shifts have occurred in education and psychology, with many adopting a constructivist and interactionist perspective of learning.

Unfortunately, these paradigm shifts are only beginning to influence the construction of assessment batteries. Although assessment instruments should reflect the dominant or prevailing definition of the given construct at the time of test construction, this has not been the case. Only recently have new forms of assessment begun to be implemented by some practicing educational psychologists, special educators, and speech-language pathologists. The research is resounding in the support for descriptive assessments with strong reliability, construct and ecological validity, and functionality. Yet, the administration of two or more standardized tests still is the norm for special education assessments. Clearly, much more needs to be done. Much more research on developmental sequences and patterns of language use for dialects and languages other than Standard English is needed. Schools need to become open, welcoming places for the parents and families of CLD students. Cultural and linguistic diversity needs to become viewed as a strength rather than a deficit. Educators need to avail themselves of information regarding appropriate methods of assessment with CLD students. Ignorance and comfort with known practices can no longer be accepted as an excuse for inappropriate and discriminatory assessments. In the words of Cummins (1986):

Those who train psychologists and other educators to use certain tools and fulfill particular roles within social systems have an ethical responsibility to simultaneously train them to question those role definitions and challenge a social system that disables minority students. Discriminatory assessment is carried out by individual people who have accepted a role definition and a socio-educational system that makes discriminatory assessment virtually inevitable. (p. 16)

☺ DISCUSSION QUESTIONS

1. Discuss the legal requirements for assessment and consider how the use of standardized tests fits within these requirements, especially with regard to CLD students.
2. Compare and contrast three or more possible different purposes for assessment.
3. Compare the types of information recommended for collection during assessment with those typically found in special education assessments.
4. Consider the role of the general educator in data collection for assessment purposes. What types of assessment methods would be appropriate for a general educator to implement?
5. Discuss how you think a parent or family member could be actively involved in assessment.

☺ REFERENCES

Aylward, E. H. (1991). *Understanding children's testing.* Austin, TX: Pro-Ed.

Baca, L., & Metz, I. (1993). The holographic and culturally responsive informal assessment model. Unpublished paper, Evaluation Assistance Center, University of New Mexico, Albuquerque.

Burt, M., & Dulay, H. (1978). Some guidelines for the assessment of oral language proficiency and dominance. *TESOL Quarterly, 12,* 177–191.

Carpenter, L. (1983). Communication disorders in limited and non-English proficient children. *Monograph of BUENO Center for Multicultural Education, 4*(1), 46–58.

Cervantes, H. T., & Bieber, B. J. (1981). Non-discriminatory assessment: A school district's response. *Monograph of BUENO Center for Multicultural Education, 2*(2), 39–49.

Collier, C. (1988). *Assessing minority students with learning and behavior problems.* Lindale, TX: Hamilton Publications.

Cummins, J. (1986). Psychological assessment of minority students: Out of context, out of control? *Journal of Reading, Writing, and Learning Disabilities International, 2,* 9–19.

Damico, J. S. (1991). Descriptive assessment of communicative ability in limited English proficient students. In E. V. Hamayan & J. S. Damico (Eds.), *Limiting bias in the assessment of bilingual students* (pp. 155–217). Austin, TX: Pro-Ed.

Damico, J. S., & Nye, C. (1990). Collaborative issues in multicultural populations. *Best Practices in School Speech-Language Pathology, 2,* 127–137.

Damico, J. S., Secord, W. A., & Wiig, E. H. (1992). Descriptive language assessment at school: Characteristics and design. *Best Practices in School Speech-Language Pathology, 2,* 1–8.

DeMers, S. T., Fiorello, C., & Langer, K. L. (1992). Legal and ethical issues in preschool assessment. In E. V. Nuttall, I. Romero, & J. Kalesnik (Eds.), *Assessing and screening preschoolers* (pp. 43–54). Needham Heights, MA: Allyn and Bacon.

Erickson, J. G., & Iglesias, A. (1986). Assessment of communication disorders in non-English proficient children. In O. Taylor (Ed.), *Nature of communication disorders in culturally and linguistically diverse populations* (pp. 181–217). San Diego: College-Hill Press.

Fuchs, D. (1987). Examiner familiarity effects on test performance: Implications for training and practice. In J. T. Neisworth (Ed.), Personnel preparation [special issue]. *Topics in Early Childhood Special Education, 7,* 90–104.

Fuchs, D., & Fuchs, L. (1989). Effects of examiner familiarity on Black, Caucasian, and Hispanic children: A meta-analysis. *Exceptional Children, 55,* 303–308.

Fuchs, D., & Fuchs, L. S. (1986). Test procedure bias: A meta-analysis of examiner familiarity effects. *Review of Educational Research, 56,* 243–262.

Fuchs, D., Fuchs, L. S., Benowitz, S., & Barringer, K. (1987). Norm-referenced tests: Are they valid for use with handicapped children? *Exceptional Children, 54,* 263–271.

Garcia, E. (1989). Issues in assessing children with limited English proficiency. In E. O. Werner & J. D. Kresheck. *Spanish structured photographic expressive language test (preschool and II)* (pp. 3–4). Sandwich, IL: Janelle Publications.

Gavillán-Torres, E. (1984). Issues of assessment of limited-English proficient students and of the truly disabled in the United States. In N. Miller (Ed.), *Bilingualism and language disability* (pp. 131–153). San Diego: College-Hill Press.

Gronlund, N. E., & Linn, R. L. (1990). *Measurement and evaluation in teaching.* (6th ed.). New York: Macmillan Publishing.

Holland, A. L., & Forbes, M. (1986). Nonstandardized approaches to speech and language assessment. In O. Taylor (Ed.), *Treatment of communication disorders in culturally and linguistically diverse populations* (pp. 49–66). San Diego: College-Hill Press.

Idol, L., Levin, A., & Paolucci-Whitcomb, P. (1986). *Models of curriculum-based assessment.* Austin, TX: Pro-Ed.

Juárez, M. (1983). Assessment and treatment of minority-language-handicapped children: The role of the monolingual speech-language pathologist. *Topics in Language Disorders, 3*(3), 57–66.

Kline, P. (1993). *The handbook of psychological testing.* London: Routledge.

Kovarsky, D. (1992). Ethnography and language assessment: Towards the contextualized description and interpretation of communicative behavior. *Best Practices in School Speech-Language Pathology, 2,* 115–122.

Langdon, H. W. (1983). Assessment and intervention strategies for the bilingual language disordered student. *Exceptional Children, 50,* 37–45.

Langdon, H. W. (1989). Language disorder or difference? Assessing the language skills of Hispanic students. *Exceptional Children, 56*(2), 160–167.

Langdon, H. W. (1992). Speech and language assessment of LEP/bilingual Hispanic students. In H. W. Langdon & L. L. Cheng (Eds.), *Hispanic children and adults with communication disorders* (pp. 201–265). Gaithersburg, MD: Aspen Publishers.

Lidz, C. S. (1991). *Practitioner's guide to dynamic assessment.* New York: The Guilford Press.

Linares-Orama, N., & Sanders, L. J. (1977). Evaluation of syntax in three-year-old Spanish-speaking Puerto Rican children. *Journal of Speech and Hearing Research, 20,* 350–357.

Mattes, L. J., & Omark, D. R. (1984). *Speech and language assessment for the bilingual handicapped child.* San Diego: College-Hill Press.

McCloskey, G. (1990). Selecting and using early childhood rating scales. *Topics in Early Childhood Special Education, 10*(3), 39–64.

Mercer, J. R. (1983). Issues in the diagnosis of language disorders in students whose primary language is not English. *Topics in Language Disorders, 3*(3), 46–56.

Merino, B. J., & Spencer, M. (1983). The comparability of English and Spanish versions of oral language proficiency instruments. *NABE Journal, 7*(2), 1–31.

Miller, N. (1984). Language problems and bilingual children. In N. Miller (Ed.), *Bilingualism and language disability* (pp. 81–103). San Diego: College-Hill Press.

Moll, L. C., Amanti, C., Neff, D., & Gonzalez, N. (1992). Funds of knowledge for teaching: Using a qualitative approach to connect homes and classrooms. *Theory into Practice, 31*(2), 132–141.

National Center for Educational Statistics. (1994a). *The condition of education.* Washington, DC: Office of Educational Research and Improvement, U.S. Department of Education.

National Center for Educational Statistics. (1994b). *Digest of education statistics.* Washington, DC: Office of Educational Research and Improvement, U.S. Department of Education.

Nelson, N. W. (1989). Curriculum-based language assessment and intervention. *Language, Speech, and Hearing Services in Schools, 20*, 170–184.

Nelson, N. W. (1992). Targets of curriculum-based language assessment. *Best Practices in School Speech-Language Pathology, 2*, 73–85.

Norris, M. K., Juárez, M. J., & Perkins, M. N. (1989). Adaptation of a screening test for bilingual and bidialectal populations. *Language, Speech, and Hearing Specialists in Schools, 20*, 381–390.

Oller, J. W. (1983). Testing proficiencies and diagnosing language disorders in bilingual children. In D. R. Omark & J. G. Erickson (Eds.), *The bilingual exceptional child* (pp. 69–88). San Diego: College-Hill Press.

Olmedo, E. L. (1982). Testing linguistic minorities. *Monograph of BUENO Center for Multicultural Education, 1*(3), 1–20.

Ornat, S. L. (1988). On data sources on the acquisition of Spanish as a first language. *Journal of Child Language, 15*, 679–686.

Ortiz, A. A. (1995, February). Roundtable on assessment practices with LEP students. In L. Baca (Chair), Bilingual Special Education Half Day Institute. Symposium conducted at the Annual National Association for Bilingual Education Conference, Phoenix, AZ.

Peña, E., Quinn, R., & Iglesias, A. (1992). The application of dynamic methods to language assessment: A nonbiased procedure. *Journal of Special Education, 26*, 269–280.

Prutting, C. A. (1983). Assessing communicative behavior using a language sample. In D. R. Omark & J. G. Erickson (Eds.), *The bilingual exceptional child* (pp. 89–102). San Diego: College-Hill Press.

Rivera, C., & Simich, C. (1981). Issues in the assessment of language proficiency of linguistic minority students. *NABE Journal, 6*(1), 19–39.

Roseberry-McKibbin, C. A., & Eicholtz, G. E. (1994). Serving children with limited English proficiency in the schools: A national survey. *Language, Speech, and Hearing Services in Schools, 25*(3), 156–164.

Ruiz, N. T., & Figueroa, R. A. (1995). Learning-handicapped classrooms with Latino students: The Optimal Learning Environment (OLE) Project. *Educational and Urban Society, 27*(4), 463–483.

Schiff-Myers, N. B. (1992). Considering arrested language development and language loss in the assessment of second language learners. *Language, Speech, and Hearing Specialists in Schools, 23*, 28–33.

Taylor, O. L., & Payne, K. T. (1983). Culturally valid testing: A proactive approach. *Topics in Language Disorders, 3*(3), 1–7.

Toronto, A. S., & Merrill, S. (1983). Developing local normed assessment instruments. In D. R. Omark & J. G. Erickson (Eds.), *The bilingual exceptional child* (pp. 105–121). San Diego: College-Hill Press.

Valdés, G., & Figueroa, R. (1994). *Bilingualism and testing: A special case of bias.* Norwood, NJ: Ablex.

Vaughn-Cook, F. B. (1983, September). Improving language assessment in minority children. *ASHA, 25* (9), 29–34.

Vaughn-Cook, F. B. (1986). The challenge of assessing the language of nonmainstream speakers. In O. Taylor (Ed.), *Treatment of communication disorders in culturally and linguistically diverse populations* (pp. 23–48). San Diego: College-Hill Press.

Walsh, W. B. (1989). *Tests and measurements* (3rd ed.). Upper Saddle River, NJ: Prentice Hall.

Walsh, W. B., & Betz, N. E. (1990). *Tests and assessment* (2nd ed.). Upper Saddle River, NJ: Prentice Hall.

Westby, C. (1992). Narrative analysis. *Best Practices in School Speech-Language Pathology, 2*, 53–63.

CHAPTER 9

Developing Individualized Education Programs for Exceptional Language Minority Students

James R. Yates
Alba A. Ortiz

- Multidisciplinary Teams
- Individual Educational Programs
- Considerations in Language Planning
- Recommendations for Instruction
- Other Considerations in Implementing IEPs
- Continuum of Placement Alternatives
- Obstacles to Effective Service Delivery for English-Language Learners
- Summary

OBJECTIVES

To review the major responsibilities of Multidisciplinary Teams in designing Individualized Education Programs for language minority students with disabilities

To provide a framework for developing IEPs for language minority students, with a focus on students who are also limited English proficient

To consider instructional arrangements for English-Language Learners with disabilities

To understand variables that affect the provision of educational services to language minority students with disabilities

Every region of the country has experienced significant increases in the number of individuals from linguistic, ethnic and racial minority backgrounds (Violand-Sanchez, Sutton, & Ware, 1991). These demographic changes are also reflected in school enrollments. Concomitant with dramatic increases in the number of culturally and linguistically diverse students, schools are also experiencing significant increases in enrollments of language minority students, that is, students who come from homes where languages other than English are spoken. One subset of the language minority student population is *English language learners,* students whose English language skills are so limited that they cannot profit from instruction delivered entirely in English and must have modification in their programs. These students are eligible for special language programs, such as bilingual education or English as a Second Language (ESL) instruction. The number of English language learners is already estimated at more than 3 million students (Townsend, 1995).

Unfortunately, education professionals are generally unprepared to serve language minority students, an issue which is exacerbated when these students have disabilities. To meet the needs of language minority students, general education, special language program, and special education personnel must understand how a native and a second language are acquired and how culture, socioeconomic status, and other factors affect the teaching-learning process. Knowledge and skills in these areas are crucial in determining which students are eligible for special education services and in designing Individualized Education Programs (IEPs) which address both disability-related concerns and language characteristics.

The Individualized Educational Program (IEP) is a powerful document used to describe the educational needs of students with disabilities and the school's commitment to address those needs. The Individuals with Disabilities Education Act (PL 101-476, 1992) defines an IEP as:

a written statement for each child with a disability developed in any meeting by a representative of the local educational agency or an intermediate educational unit who shall be qualified to provide, or supervise the provision of, specially designed instruction to meet the unique needs of children with disabilities, the teacher, the parents or guardian of such child, and, whenever appropriate, such child. (Section 1401)

While federal law does not specify the process to be followed in developing the IEP, it does set forth detailed requirements as to what should be included and conditions under which this plan should be developed. The law's intent is not to standardize instructional planning or to promote particular teaching methodologies but, rather, to establish the IEP as a vehicle for ensuring quality education for exceptional children and youth.

Research (e.g., Schenck & Levy, 1979; Pyecha et al., 1980; Safer & Hobbs, 1980) has shown that IEPs tend to comply with articulated federal requirements. Given that, it is unfortunate that policy and law are silent about specific factors that must be considered in planning instruction for language minority students with disabilities. In the absence of specific mandates, it is not surprising that IEPs fail to address the language needs of these students. For example, Ortiz and Wilkinson (1989) reviewed the goals and objectives selected by IEP committees for Hispanic students who were being served in programs for students with learning disabilities or mental retardation. Of the 203 IEPs they examined, 98% stated that instruction would be carried out in English; none included English as a Second Language goals or objectives, although students were legally classified as limited English proficient. Committee recommendations, almost without exception, assumed that language minority students would profit more from instruction delivered entirely in English than from instruction in the native language with English as a Second Language (ESL) support, as is recommended for English-language learners without disabilities.

This chapter attempts to address these issues by suggesting unique considerations in designing IEPs for language minority students and, specifically, for English language learners who are unlikely to profit from special education instruction unless it accommodates their limited English proficiency. In addition to discussing membership on the Multidisciplinary Teams that develop IEPs, guidelines are given for choosing the language of instruction, and instructional strategies which can help students achieve their potential are recommended. Finally, obstacles encountered in designing and implementing IEPs are identified, underscoring that further research and enhanced personnel preparation efforts are crucial if language minority students are to receive the free, appropriate education they are guaranteed by federal law.

MULTIDISCIPLINARY TEAMS

The determination as to whether a child has a disability and significant educational needs which require special education intervention is made by a *Multidisciplinary Team (MDT)* which has these major responsibilities:

1. Determining eligibility for initial assignment to special education.
2. Designing individual educational plans for eligible students.
3. Evaluating progress toward accomplishment of goals and objectives.
4. Determining which students need continued special education services.

In the case of language minority students, the MDT is also charged with assuring that students are not assigned to special education on the basis of differences of language, culture, socioeconomic status, or lack of opportunity to learn. To fulfill these responsibilities, team members must understand unique considerations in educating language minority students,

must be competent interpreters and/or consumers of evaluation data so they can accurately identify language minority students who have disabilities, and must be skilled in designing instructional programs which address needs associated with the disability and which are also linguistically and culturally sensitive. To ensure that these skills are represented on the MDT, careful attention must be given to the composition of these committees.

The Multidisciplinary Team includes, at a minimum, representatives of appraisal, instruction, and administration; the parent; and the student, if appropriate. Other representatives may be required by law, as is typically the case when students have auditory or visual impairments. Because language minority students with disabilities are also likely to require a wider array of services than those required by monolingual English speakers, still other representatives may need to be included on the MDT. For example, if the parent is not a fluent-English speaker, an interpreter may need to be included so that parents can participate meaningfully in team deliberations and give or withhold consent for services, fully cognizant of the implications of their decision. Because many language minority students will also qualify for services from related programs such as migrant education, Title I, or social, welfare, or health services, including personnel from these areas lends valuable expertise to the committee.

Representative of Administration

The representative of administration must have the power to provide and to supervise services delineated in the IEP. Ideally, this representative is the building principal who has ultimate responsibility for campus personnel, programs, and services and who has the authority to ensure that the team's recommendations are implemented, that resources and personnel are assigned across programs to meet the child's educational needs, and that the IEP is successfully implemented. The principal is also key to creating positive school and classroom contexts in which all children learn because linguistic, cultural, and other student differences are respected and teachers are trained to provide instruction using strategies and approaches which have been shown to be successful with language minority students. The building principal, then, plays a critical role in achieving the coordination and cooperation that are essential for serving language minority students who require a broad range of integrated services. (Moecker, 1989).

Representative of Appraisal

There is evidence from the Moecher (1989) study that the appraisal representative supplies critical information that in some ways drives the rest of the decision-making process for the Multidisciplinary Team. When the child under consideration in the committee meeting is a language minority student, the responsibilities of the appraisal representative become more complex and the information shared must be supported by more detailed information. For example, results of individual or group standardized tests must be accompanied by explanations of issues of norming bias, content bias, and linquistic and cultural biases. These factors from a psychometric standpoint make it almost impossible, with concern for validity and reliability, to report standardized test results in the usual format of raw scores, standard scores, percentiles, and so forth. Therefore, the appraisal representative must have sufficient familiarity with these types of validity and reliability issues and with the specific effects they may have on the results obtained from the testing processes to advise and guide the MDT. Team members will need to consider whether test norms are appropriate to the student being considered and whether standardized procedures were adapted. If an interpreter was necessary, the team needs to consider the probable effects of this alteration of standardization. Sufficient clinical observations must be made to

allow meaningful interpretation of the results. Scores obtained through the use of inappropriate instruments or instruments which have been modified are invalid and thus are of questionable use for educational planning. In addition, the appraisal representative must have familiarity with the issues and procedures of assessment of language proficiency to provide guidance on such issues as whether there is a learning disability or a language difference, what the language of instruction should be, what special language program services are needed, and so forth. Assessment data should be comprehensive enough to allow the MDT to support conclusions that students are not assigned to special education on the basis of performance or behaviors which can be solely attributed to such factors as differences in language, culture, lifestyle, experiential background, or opportunity to learn. To provide this assurance, the MDT should look for evidence that assessments were conducted by personnel trained to assess language minority students and that evaluations were conducted in the student's dominant language. If assessments were administered solely in English, reports should include clinical interpretations of results in light of the student's current level of English proficiency and information about progress as a result of English as a Second Language instruction. Simply reporting test scores is inadequate, and the appraisal representative must assume responsibility for guiding the MDT relative to these matters of assessment.

Representative of Instruction

Bilingual education teachers are excellent resources for Multidisciplinary Teams in that they can provide important information about student progress as a result of native language instruction. Since they usually are also the student's English as a Second Language teacher, they can reflect on how the child's progress in acquiring English compares with that of other students in their classes who are not experiencing academic problems. If students are in general education classrooms and receiving English as a Second Language instruction, the ESL teacher should be a member of the MDT. Like bilingual educators, ESL teachers will be able to provide information about students' language proficiency and their progress as a result of ESL instruction. Well-trained, special language teachers can help the MDT distinguish students who have disabilities from those whose academic problems would be more appropriately attributed to their limited English proficiency.

Parents

Parental participation on the Multidisciplinary Team is crucial. They can provide information to help team members decide whether their child has a disability and needs special education services. Parents can speak about behaviors the child demonstrates in the home and community and share their perceptions as to whether these behaviors are consistent with those expected of same-age peers in their community. They can also indicate whether the same behaviors considered problematic by school personnel are present and considered deviant in these other contexts. Moreover, when assessments have left questions about the child's language dominance proficiency, parents can indicate the language(s) they use in the home and whether the child's native language is developing normally.

To be effective advocates for their children, parents must understand policies and procedures associated with special education. IDEA (1992) requires that parents be provided information, assistance, and/or counsel to ensure that they understand the various proceedings, deliberations, and decisions that affect their children's education. Prior written notice, in the parents' native language, is required in matters relating to identification, evaluation, and any changes in placement being considered. Parental consent forms must include all information rel-

evant to the activity, including a description of any evaluation procedures, tests, records, or other reports that the school will use as a basis for decision making. Parents must be informed that their consent is voluntary and can be withdrawn at any time. Parents should also be advised that they have the right to bring an advocate to Multidisciplinary Team meetings and deliberations.

Advocates and Interpreters

Parents advocates should be familiar with special education law and procedures and able to assist parents in understanding the information being presented and the significance of decisions reached. Parents may also need the services of interpreters in order to be informed participants in the decision-making process. Bilingual educators or other bilingual professionals (e.g., school psychologists or speech pathologists) can often serve very effectively in these roles. In instances where such professionals are not available, then other arrangements must be made to provide these services. Because interpreting and translating are complex tasks, individuals who provide such services have to be carefully selected and receive training in the topics/areas for which they will provide interpretation or translation. Interpreters should have native like oral language skills in the language of the parents; if they will be doing translation, they must also have appropriate literacy skills. As important, individuals who use interpreters should be trained in how to use their services effectively.

Expert in Linguistic and Cultural Diversity

Whatever its makeup, it is essential that the Multidisciplinary Team have the expertise of someone who can interpret performance and make suggestions about instruction or interventions which are congruent with the child's language, culture, and other background characteristics. Too often, individuals are included on MDTs simply because they are bilingual. However, bilingualism without accompanying expertise is of little value. The purpose of having an expert representative is to engage committee members in discussions leading to critical decisions about the language of instruction and recommendations about instructional approaches and strategies which have been shown to be effective for language minority students. For English language learners, this representative could be a member of the special language program placement committee which determines eligibility for bilingual education and English as a Second Language instruction.

INDIVIDUAL EDUCATIONAL PROGRAMS

Failure to recommend native language instruction for English language learners with disabilities may reflect a lack of knowledge about native and second language acquisition. Another explanation may be that IEP forms and related materials used by local education agencies are designed for monolingual English speaking students (Ortiz & Wilkinson, 1989). For example, if districts use objective checklists or computerized IEPs, and these lists or banks do not include goals and objectives specific to native language and ESL development, committees may overlook the need to provide such support. A simple but very helpful solution is to develop IEP forms for language minority students. Figure 9–1 suggests such a format. The sections which follow discuss considerations in designing IEPs for these students.

Student's Present Level of Educational Performance

Assessment data used for educational planning purposes should identify the student's dominant language (i.e., the language in which the student shows the greatest skill) and describe student's language proficiency (level of skill) in the first and in the second language (Ortiz & Garcia, 1990). The MDT should have access to a summary of the student's academic achievement in the native language and in English and to data which speak to other factors (e.g., family and community environment) which may affect student performance (Ortiz & Yates, 1995).

Specific Education Services Needed by the Child

All special education and related services that are needed to meet the child's unique needs, including any special instructional media or materials, must be specified in the IEP. For language minority students, the IEP should indicate (1) the language(s) of instruction for each goal and objective; (2) instructional strategies which take into account language proficiency, academic skills, and modality and cognitive style preferences; (3) curricula and materials designed specifically for linguistically and culturally diverse learners; and (4) motivators and reinforcers which are compatible with the student's cultural and experiential background (Ambert & Dew, 1982). Decisions about services needed by students must be made without regard to cost or availability of these services. This is an important safeguard for language minority students in light of the shortage of trained bilingual special education personnel and the lack of materials, media, and other resources to support instruction in the native language. The committee should specify students' needs and then work toward ensuring that services and appropriately trained personnel are available to meet these needs.

Individuals Responsible for Implementing the IEP

The IEP should specify the duration of services and identify the individuals responsible for implementing the IEP, monitoring progress, and synthesizing information that will be used for

Figure 9–1

Individualized Education Plan for Language Minority Students

Student _____ Sex _____ ID# _____
          (Last)   (First)   (Middle)

Date of Birth _____ Place of Birth _____ School _____ Grade _____

Current Program Placement: Reg Ed _____ Bi Ed _____ Migrant Ed _____ ESL _____ Special Ed _____ Other: _____

If in special education, current disability _____

If applicable, percent of English instruction _____ Native language instruction _____ ESL instruction _____

Number of years in bilingual education program_____ English as a second language program _____

Purpose of meeting: Admission_____ Dismissal _____ Review _____ Other (specify): _____

   Date parent notified of meeting _____ Date of meeting _____

   Language of meeting: English _____ Native language_____ Other_____ Interpreter used: Yes_____ No _____

I. ELIGIBILITY DETERMINATIONS Record language(s) of testing as appropriate: L1 = Native Language; L2 = English

A. Information reviewed by the committee:

Instrument	Language	Date	Score	
	English			*Limited English Proficient (LEP)?* Yes____ No____
	Other Language:			*Dominant Language*

	Date of Report	Lang. of Assessment L1	L2		Date of Report
Parent information				Referral folder	
Group achievement/aptitude				Attendance history	
Language proficiency				Prior school history	
Comprehensive individual assessment				Other:	
Related services assessment				Other:	

B. Summary of Assessment Data:

Area(s) Assessed	Eval. Date(s)	Lang(s). of Evaluation	Evaluation Method/Data Sources	Grade/Age/ Functioning Level L1	L2	Information on Current Functioning (include info. on strengths/weakness in both languages as appropriate)
Mathematics Calculation						
Reasoning						
Reading Word Recognition						
Comprehension						
Spelling/Written Expression						
Speech/Language						
Intellectual/ Developmental						
Social/ Emotional						
Pre Vocational/ Vocational						
Physical						

C. Based on the information indicated above, the committee decided that the student:

   DOES / DOES NOT meet eligibility criteria for_____ / _____

                                  Primary Disability   Other Disability

continued

D. Based on above information, committee ensures that this decision was <u>not</u> primarily due to criteria based on:

	Data Source(s)	Justification
_____ Command of the English language		
_____ Different cultural lifestyle		
_____ Lack of educational opportunity		

II. PLACEMENT DECISIONS: Amount of Time (min/hrs per day/wk)

Voc. Ed. _____ Spec. Ed. _____ Other _____

Reg. Ed. _____ Bi. Ed _____ ESL _____ Migrant Ed _____ Other (specify): _____

Instructional arrangement (Indicate bilingual special education if appropriate):

Resource____Itinerant____Partially Self-Contained____Self Contained____Regular Education ___Other: _____

SUBJECT	TIME/DAY			DATES		MODIFICATIONS NEEDED (IF ANY) (facility, equip. method, material)	*LANGUAGE OF INSTRUCTION*
	Reg	Voc	Sp	Beg	End		

RELATED SERVICES	POSITION RESPONSIBLE	*LANGUAGE OF SERVICE*	AMT TIME PER DAY	DAYS PER WK	DATES	
					Beg	End

B. This educational placement is the least restrictive environment and is appropriate to meet the needs of the student. The student is being educated to the maximum extent appropriate with students who are non-handicapped.

Alternative placements reviewed and reasons rejected: _____
_____

Services reviewed and reasons rejected: _____
_____

III. COMMITTEE SIGNATURES – Indicate area represented (e.g., representative of administration, instruction, appraisal, special education, vocation education). Continue on reverse if necessary.

VOTING MEMBER	AGREE	DISAGREE*	SIGNATURE	POSITION	PROGRAM ASSIGNMENT (e.g., Bi. Ed., ESL)	Bilingual	
						Yes	No
				Parent/Legal Guardian			

*If disagreeing, indicate area(s) of disagreement below.

_____
_____
_____
_____
_____
_____

GROUP ACHIEVEMENT TESTING				
	Yes	No	For Experience Only	Language of Testing
READING				
MATH				
(other)				

continued

Individualized Education Plan for Language Minority Students
Page

Goal: _____

Objectives	Language of Instruction	Criteria	Evaluation Procedure	Recommended Methods/Materials	Date of Review

Goal: _____

Objectives	Language of Instruction	Criteria	Evaluation Procedure	Recommended Methods/Materials	Date of Review

English as a Second Language Goal: _____

Objectives	Criteria	Evaluation Procedure	Recommended Methods/Materials	Date of Review

Related Services Goal: _____

Objectives	Language of Service	Criteria	Evaluation Procedure	Recommended	Date of Review

Developed by: Alba A. Ortiz
Department of Special Education
Bilingual Special Education Programs
The University of Texas at Austin

mandated annual reviews and for planning triennial evaluations. The more personnel are involved in the implementation of the IEP, the more critical it is that services provided students be coordinated. Teachers and other service providers must have a clear understanding of the educational needs of the child and must continuously share information about how each is addressing the child's needs so that interventions are well-coordinated. Some straightforward procedures can be implemented to facilitate this planning and coordination. For example, as the IEP is implemented, observations of student behaviors and progress notes can be shared quickly and efficiently via photo- or electronic copies of monitoring forms.

Annual Reviews

An important aspect of the educational planning process is evaluating student progress toward meeting IEP goals and objectives. Such progress checks help the MDT identify students who are not making expected progress. Ortiz and Wilkinson (1989) found that after three years of special education services, Hispanic students identified as having learning disabilities had actually lost ground. Their verbal and full scale IQ scores were lower then they had been at initial entry into special education and their achievement scores were essentially the same level as at entry. In the majority of instances, special education services were intensified, even though data suggested that the educational program was not yielding intended benefits. These findings underscore the importance of periodic reviews to ensure students' needs are being met. When students are not making expected progress, IEPs can be modified and alternative strategies and procedures recommended to improve student performance. Also, since English language learners are constantly acquiring English, more frequent observations and reviews of their performance may be necessary in order for the students' IEP to maintain accurate specifications of modifications necessary.

CONSIDERATIONS IN LANGUAGE PLANNING

Multidisciplinary Teams must assume the responsibility for designing IEPs for students with very diverse native language and English skills. The complexity of this task demands time, care, and expertise which exceeds the ordinary allocations for admission, review, and dismissal committee meetings.

English-Language Learners

As indicated previously, English language learners are students whose English skills are so limited they cannot profit from instruction delivered entirely in English without modification. Before the advent of bilingual education and other special language programs, these students were almost always destined to fail because they were required to meet two expectations simultaneously: (1) to learn English without the benefit of a structured language program, and (2) to master basic skills taught in a language foreign to them. This "sink or swim" approach is still a common experience for students with limited English proficiency and may explain why Hispanics continue to drop out of school in numbers greater than any other ethnically identified group in the United States (Cardenas, Robledo, & Supik, 1986).

Fortunately, legislation and litigation (e.g., *Lau v. Nichols,* 1974; Bilingual Education Act, 1968) mandate specialized programs for English-language learners so that they are not excluded from participation in school activities. These students are typically served under one of two program models: (1) they are provided academic skill instruction in their native language and receive a structured program of English as a Second Language instruction; or (2) they are placed in a general education program and provided instruction from an English as a Second Language teacher, typically on a pull-out basis for one or two hours per day. The ESL model is prevalent for students from low-incidence language groups and in districts that have difficulty recruiting bilingual education teachers.

Other Language Minority Students

Language minority students who are classified as "English proficient" (that is, not eligible for Bilingual Education or English as a Second Language programs) are usually placed in general education classrooms in which instruction is provided entirely in English. Because these children have managed to acquire conversational English, they impress professionals as having the linguistic abilities necessary to handle the complex, context-reduced language which is used by teachers and found in textbooks and other instructional materials (Cummins, 1984). When they begin to experience difficulty, lack of English proficiency is ruled out as a possible cause of the problem, because these students appear to have no difficulty understanding or communicating in English with teachers or peers. While they demonstrate good interpersonal communication skills, bilingual children may need more time to obtain cognitive academic language proficiency required for mastery of literacy skills (Cummins, 1984).

It is likely that English proficient students, including those who have disabilities, will require a language development program to assure that they make progress toward acquiring language skills commensurate with those of native English language peers. If they have disabilities, IEPs must address the need for such language support.

Figure 9–2 summarizes important considerations in choosing the language of instruction and in planning language-related interventions for language minority students.

Language Assessment

Multidisciplinary Teams must have access to current information about students' language proficiency in the native language and in English. Language assessments must include descriptions of students' conversational skills

Figure 9–2
Considerations in Language Planning

Comprehensive Language Assessment
    Language dominance
    Language proficiency
        Conversational skills
        Academic language proficiency

Type of Language Intervention Required
    Language enrichment
    Language development
    Language remediation

Language of Instruction
    Native language
    English as a Second Language
    English without special language program support

Language Use Plan
    Who?
    Why?
    When?

Recommended Instructional Strategies or Approaches

and their academic language proficiency (Ortiz & Garcia, 1990). Many currently used language assessment instruments and procedures do not provide the data needed by Multidisciplinary Teams to design IEPs for language minority students (Ortiz & Garcia, 1990; Damico, 1991).

Most language assessment instruments used to make decisions about language dominance or proficiency measure students' performance of basic interpersonal communication skills, BICS (Cummins, 1984). Furthermore, many of these tests are based on the misconception that linguistic proficiency is demonstrated by mastery over the surface structures of the language; that is, students are judged primarily on the basis of whether their utterances are grammatically correct (Damico, 1991). Performance on these tests, however, does not predict academic achievement. Many language minority students possess BICS, but experience academic failure because they lack cognitive academic language proficiency (CALP), the literacy-related aspects of language (Cummins, 1991). If a student is being considered for possible placement in a learning disabilities program, it is essential that CALP skills (e.g., narrative skills, story-retelling skills, ability to use language abstractly) be assessed in the native language and in English (Ortiz & Garcia, 1990). Otherwise, achievement difficulties may be inaccurately attributed to a learning disability when they are, in reality, related to language proficiency. Language assessments should provide evidence that the student had developed the cognitive academic language proficiency required for mastery of literacy skills.

The language assessment should indicate the student's language dominance and levels of proficiency in the native language and in English. It is these data that will support the decision as to which language should be given preference in instruction.

Instruction in the Dominant Language

Language minority students should be taught in their stronger or better developed language, that is, in their dominant language. As a rule of thumb, children dominant in a language other than English should receive instruction in that language; children dominant in English should be instructed in English (Ortiz, 1984). If no clear dominance can be established, other variables should be taken into consideration, including (1) the child's age, (2) the child's language preference, (3) motivation, (4) previous language experiences, and (5) attitudes or wishes of the parent. The language of instruction, however, should be the language through which the child learns best.

Type of Language Intervention Required

As suggested, beyond specifying the language of instruction, the IEP should also indicate the type of language intervention students need.

Language Enrichment. Some students will have intact language skills and will simply require that teachers help them refine and expand their linguistic skills. This type of language intervention can be characterized as "enrichment," in that a decision has been made that the student's language proficiency is adequate for academic instruction. In this case, IEPs will focus on disability-specific concerns.

Language Development. Other students will require language development programs, which focus on addressing gaps in students' communication effectiveness. The needs of students who are considered English proficient but who do not have native-like skills have been discussed. However, it is also not unusual for students from lower socioeconomic status environments to experience difficulty because their language skills, although totally adequate for communication in their home and community, do not match the type of language used by teachers and found in school texts and other curricular materials. The task of teachers, in such cases, is to provide a language development program that allows students to handle the language demands of the classroom.

Remediation. Some students will have serious language problems and it will be evident that their language skills are not consistent with those of peers of the same chronological age or developmental level. Too often, educators assume that if students with disabilities have not acquired proficiency in their native language, it will not matter whether English or the native language is used for instruction. Consequently, they opt for instruction in English. Such reasoning, however, ignores the relationship between the native language and English as a Second Language acquisition, a relationship that predicts that disabilities demonstrated in the first language will also be manifested in English (Ortiz & Garcia, 1990). In that case, students who have had difficulty acquiring the language of their parents are likely to encounter even greater difficulties in mastering English. Unless there are intervening factors, the child whose dominant language is other than English should receive instruction in that language.

Students with language-related disorders will need a remedial program aimed at helping students acquire critical language competencies and/or learn strategies to help them compensate for the disability. In ideal situations, English-language learners receive special education and related services in their native language. There will be some circumstances, usually because of lack of bilingual special educators, under which the option of native language instruction is not available. In such cases, special education instruction must be modified using English as a Second Language strategies.

Choosing the Language of Instruction

The IEP should indicate whether students will receive instruction in the native language, be placed in English as a Second Language program, or have adequate levels of social and academic language skills in English to receive instruction in English only, as do their native English language peers.

Native Language Instruction. For English language learners, IEPs must target development of native language conceptual skills to provide the foundation for learning English oral language and literacy skills. This point cannot be overemphasized, given that oral language, reading, writing, and spelling are the goal areas most frequently selected for language minority students with language and learning disabilities (Ortiz & Wilkinson, 1989). Students should be taught basic skills in the native language, so they do not fall behind English-speaking peers in academic areas. Fortunately, most of these students can also profit from ESL instruction. ESL lessons should be consistent with students' native language proficiency and should reinforce concepts and skills that students have already mastered in their native language.

English as a Second Language. Research confirms that the process of second language acquisition conforms to the stages of language development common to children who acquire English as a native language. This process is a lengthy one, estimated to be 5–7 years for students in bilingual education programs and 8–10 years for students who receive ESL support only (Collier, 1996; Krashen, 1996; Cummins, 1984). Research further indicates that the native language is the means through which competence in a second language is acquired (Cummins, 1989). For students being taught in the native language and who are also receiving ESL instruction, and especially for those students for whom ESL instruction is the only available option, it is important that ESL goals and objectives be a part of students' IEPs. Students will not profit from specially designed instruction unless they have adequate English language proficiency to handle task demands.

According to Krashen (1982), language acquisition takes place best when input is provided that is comprehensible, interesting, and relevant, not only grammatically sequenced, and when it is provided in sufficient quantity. Instructional activities that are embedded in real purposes and that incorporate cues and clues to aid comprehension produce higher task engagement and greater success for English language learners with disabilities (Willig, Swedo, & Ortiz, 1987).

Special education teachers should be familiar with ESL strategies that can help make lessons understandable to students with limited English proficiency. For example, these simple modifications can scaffold instruction for English language learners: (1) establish students' prior knowledge and experiences related to the lesson; (2) when possible, review (or have an assistant review) key words, concepts, and ideas in the students' native language; (3) use multisensory approaches and visual and concrete referents; (4) slow the rate of speech, but keep it natural; (5) repeat key ideas; (6) at the end of the lesson, provide a review in the native language, if possible (Northcutt & Watson, 1986; Garcia, 1994). Methods such as the Total Physical

Response Approach (Asher, 1979) or the Natural Approach (Krashen & Terrell, 1983) seem to be effective because they allow students to develop comprehension skills, attempt to reduce student anxiety, and provide comprehensible input. An advantage for students with disabilities is that these methods offer simplified language codes and active involvement in the learning process.

Instruction in English Without Special Language Program Support. Students are transitioned into English instruction without support when it is determined that they have adequate English skills to function in that environment without such support. These transitions should occur when assessments indicate that students' oral language skills are commensurate with those of native English language peers of the same age and when academic skills are grade-appropriate.

It is common practice to reclassify students as English proficient and to exit them from special language programs when they have intermediate (versus native-like) English skills and when they score at or above the 40th percentile on an English language arts achievement test, not a level of true proficiency or competitive with native speakers of English. General education and special education classroom teachers should be aware of this and recognize that they must provide continued language development support for exited students to achieve native-like English proficiency. Without such language support, students will soon begin to experience academic difficulties.

Language Use Plan

Because students with disabilities are likely to receive services from several instructional or related services personnel, it will be important to develop a language use plan as part of the IEP. The *language use plan* essentially describes who will be using which language, for what purpose (why), and in which skill or subject.

For each objective specified in the IEP, a person is designated as responsible for instruction leading to attainment of that objective. For bilingual students, the IEP should specify the language in which instruction or other services will be provided, not only by special education and regular classroom teachers, but also by speech pathologists, counselors, occupational and physical therapists, and so forth. Specifying the language of instruction will assure that instruction is consistent with the student's language status.

RECOMMENDATIONS FOR INSTRUCTION

Instruction for English language learners with disabilities should be consistent with what we know about language acquisition and about native language and English as a Second Language instruction. Teachers should also use instructional strategies which have been shown to be effective for language minority students.

Cultural Relevance

While there is general agreement that adapting curricula and materials to reflect a multicultural perspective is a step toward reducing incompatibilities between characteristics of students and those of school programs, there is disagreement about the nature of cultural differences which must be considered, and about how instruction should be adapted to take these factors into account (Henderson, 1980; Garcia, 1994). Care must be exercised to avoid existing stereotypes. If educational programs are tailored to these stereotypes, they are likely to be inappropriate. While efforts to design instructional programs and to produce culturally relevant instructional materials are well-intentioned, such efforts will be irrelevant if they reflect stereotypes of racial or ethnic groups.

There is no one set of characteristics that can be ascribed to all members of any ethnic group. Instead, one must think of culture as a continuum, with individuals demonstrating traits ranging from characteristics attributed to a traditional group to characteristics that are descriptive of a totally assimilated individual whose behaviors do not reflect membership in an ethnic minority group (Ramirez & Castaneda, 1974). While it is appropriate to incorporate history, heritage, traditions, and lifestyles of diverse cultural groups when developing or adapting instructional materials or curricula, when aspects of the traditional culture are overemphasized, teachers may inadvertently reinforce the very stereotypes they wish to eliminate (Ortiz & Yates, 1995). In addition to a focus on traditional aspects, educators should learn as much as possible about students' contemporary culture, so that learning environments and curricula are compatible with, and build upon, their daily experiences. This, of course, underscores the importance of involving parents and community members in the educational process. A critical analysis of the characteristics of the home and community, as they presently exist, provides a more viable foundation for development of curricula that are relevant to and meet the needs of culturally and linguistically different students.

Approaches and Strategies

Approaches for native and English as a Second Language instruction have been discussed. But, in addition to addressing students' language needs, IEPs must include recommendations for instruction to address academic concerns.

Integration of Higher Order and Basic Skills. Cummins (1984) suggests that instruction provided in special education classrooms may serve to maintain students' low functioning. Too often, instruction is characterized by an emphasis on direct instruction of basic skills (which are sequenced from simpler to more complex), using highly structured drills and independent seat work. These tasks present dif-

ficulty for English language learners, because activities are frequently stripped of context and therefore lose meaning and purpose. When the focus is on language development, lessons which emphasize accuracy of linguistic structures and which rely on patterns and drills, rather than stressing natural communication, may actually interfere with the second language acquisition process.

Instructional activities that are associated with the most intensive and prolonged levels of task engagement for English language learners with disabilities (Willig, Swedo, & Ortiz, 1987): (1) draw heavily upon students' prior knowledge and encourage them to share their experiences; (2) support the use of the native language; (3) are holistic in nature, in that they do not involve rote learning or drilling of isolated, decontextualized segments of information; (4) foster intrinsic motivation and feelings of success and pride in accomplishments; and (5) involve peer collaboration. Such instruction has the characteristics of what Cummins (1989) calls "reciprocal interaction teaching," which involves frequent interactions among teachers and students, meaningful communication, and development of higher-order thinking and problem-solving skills. Teachers consciously integrate language development into all curricular content. For example, reading emphasizes comprehension but includes instruction on word recognition skills. Literacy lessons emphasize approaches such as language experience stories, dialogue journals, shared book experiences, and creative writing tasks, because these approaches help develop students' communication effectiveness in the native language and in English. Direct, specific-skill instruction which is embedded within these approaches (e.g., teaching correct spelling using children's own stories) is more likely to be successful, because sufficient contextual cues are provided to make academic tasks meaningful.

Collaborative Learning. Collaborative learning approaches provide excellent opportunities for students to develop leadership, to learn how to make decisions, to resolve conflicts, and to enhance communication skills, all critical to independent functioning (Slavin, 1988). These approaches are particularly effective for learners who have difficulty operating from a framework of independence and intrinsic motivation, as is oftentimes the case for students with disabilities. Teachers foster positive interdependence by establishing that the goal of the group is to ensure that all its members learn and then by assigning complementary roles to all members and structuring tasks so they require cooperation and coordination among group members in order to achieve the goal. Rewards are based on the overall achievement of the group. An additional benefit for English language learners is that collaborative learning groups offer natural contexts for development of both conversational and academic language proficiency.

Learning Strategies. Some students continuously meet with academic failure because of incompatibilities between the way they learn and the way teachers teach. Various terms have been used to discuss behaviors of these students, including internal versus external locus of control (Walker, 1980); learned helplessness (Henderson, 1980); field independence versus field sensitivity (Ramirez & Castaneda, 1974); and cultural deprivation (Feuerstein, 1980). These authors suggest that, for a variety of reasons, some students exhibit behaviors which predispose them to school failure. Motivation problems are usually linked to poor learning histories, cognitive deficits, and negative attribution states (Borkowski, Weyning, & Turner, 1986).

Learning strategies instruction can provide students with the means of obtaining academic success in school (Chamot & O'Malley, 1994; Chamot, Cummins, Fillmore, Kessler, & O'Malley, 1996). Henderson (1980) suggests that teachers provide opportunities for students to set goals and to help develop their own plans for achieving these goals. Students can be

taught to evaluate tasks, plan various options, select appropriate strategies to achieve goals, and modify their own behaviors as they encounter problems (Paris & Oka, 1986). Teaching students problem-solving strategies increases the likelihood of academic success. In turn, success enhances the student's own perception of competence and helps maintain on-task behaviors. Moreover, success helps foster intrinsic motivation and appreciation of learning for learning's sake. IEPs should recommend reinforcement systems which emphasize task engagement and performance in relation to a standard, rather than systems that focus on tangible rewards and maintain external motivation (Willig, Swedo, & Ortiz, 1987).

OTHER CONSIDERATIONS IN IMPLEMENTING IEPs

Adelman (1970) hypothesized that children's school difficulties are sometimes caused by school programs which do not accommodate individual differences and needs. This explanation is quite different from alternative explanations, which frequently center upon such variables as lack of support in the home, insufficient capabilities on the part of the child, or inadequate resources available within the educational system. The IEP recommends interventions that have, in large part, been selected based on student characteristics and needs identified by assessments and Multidisciplinary Team deliberations. Yet, it is important to consider other factors that may affect the success of these interventions.

Teacher Perceptions and Expectations

Research shows that when they hold positive perceptions and expectations of students, teachers are more likely to provide quality educational opportunities (Rist, 1970; Good & Brophy, 1973; Brophy & Good, 1986). Conversely, when perceptions are negative and expectations are low, the quality of instruction is diminished over time for some children, and this factor alone can explain differences in student achievement.

For example, teachers may have stereotypes of poverty environments that influence their perceptions of children and, ultimately, their own teaching behaviors. Teachers may expect children to come to school with experiences that facilitate learning, including exposure to books, academic orientation, exposure to success models, educational toys and materials, and interactions of an educational nature with parents (Cardenas, 1995). When children have not had such experiences, teachers attribute school problems to the child's having grown up in a "deficient environment." They may determine that they will not be able to help the child because he/she is culturally deprived or disadvantaged (while these terms are not commonly used anymore, the value or the attitudes expressed by the terms seems to continue to exist). Teachers may seek to compensate for deficiencies in home background, but this compensation is offered in the absence of knowledge of precisely what, if anything, is lacking in the home (Benson, Medrich, & Buckley, 1980). Rather than *deficient* or *limited,* many children have had a wealth of experiences that are *different* from those of middle-class children. To ask them to identify with and learn from a curriculum based on experiences that they have not had is to predispose them to failure.

In order for language minority students to be successful, teachers must have high expectations for them. High expectations can be fostered by ensuring that all staff are trained in principles of second language acquisition, in cultural background and experiences of students, and in effective instructional approaches to teaching culturally and linguistically diverse learners (Garcia, 1994). Garcia underscores the importance of having school leaders who make the education of language minority students a priority and who hold teachers accountable for their success.

Classroom Management

Given the diversity of student backgrounds, skills, abilities, and interests that teachers, and especially special education teachers, encounter in their classrooms daily, they must be efficient classroom managers. Brophy and Good (1986) suggest that to maximize learning, teachers must install procedures which insure that students know what work they are responsible for, how to get help when they need it, and what to do when they finish. Effective classroom managers give thorough explanations of assignments and provide guided practice before they ask students to work independently. They then monitor work and provide timely and specific feedback. If students experience difficulty, they reteach or teach prerequisite skills to assure mastery of content. To eliminate having students wait for long periods for teacher assistance, good managers appoint other students, or paraprofessionals if they are available, to act as resources and/or establish buddy or peer tutoring systems or other collaborative approaches to maintain task engagement.

In his study of significant bilingual instructional features, Tikunoff (1982) found that many of the same behaviors identified by Brophy and Good (1986) were also evident in bilingual education classrooms. Effective bilingual education teachers organized instructional activities which created, reinforced, and communicated task demands, monitored students' work, and provided frequent and immediate feedback. In addition, though, teachers mediated instruction using both English and the native language and responded to and/or used cultural clues in teaching. This mediation helped assure that instruction was both linguistically and culturally relevant.

Using procedures such as those described above will increase students' involvement in instruction and increase the likelihood of success. These procedures are especially important for special education teachers who serve language minority students. In addition to various disabilities and academic levels, teachers must also accommodate diversity of linguistic ability and sociocultural backgrounds, factors that also influence the nature and type of instruction provided (e.g., native language instruction versus instruction in English using ESL strategies versus English-only instruction).

Parental Involvement

School personnel commonly complain that parents of minority children do not care about their children, as the parents are perceived not to be involved, supportive, or helpful to the school or education professionals. The problem may actually be a conflict between the values and perceptions of school personnel and those of parents. For example, parents in lower socioeconomic groups may have priorities that supersede their children's education, such as finding ways to provide adequate nutrition, shelter, and clothing. Parents may perceive participation in school conferences as very important but may not have the flexibility or control over their environments (for example, permission to leave work) to allow them to attend such meetings. As a result, school conferences may be a luxury parents can ill afford. Interpreting lack of attendance as lack of interest may well be an injustice to parents.

The following story illustrates that, contrary to the perception of school personnel that parents are nonsupportive and do not assume responsibility for the children's education, parental support may be demonstrated in nontraditional ways.

A Mexican-American child attending a primary school across the street from the intermediate school where one of her brothers was a student was given a five-dollar bill for lunch. Her mother instructed her to give the change to her brother so he might also purchase lunch. When the girl reached the intermediate school campus, she was accosted by the principal, who, without asking questions, spanked the girl's hands for disobeying the school rule prohibiting children from leaving the school ground. At

home, the girl explained to her mother what had happened. The mother spanked her again and for the same reason—disobeying the school rule—despite the fact that the child was trying to do what her mother directed. The message that the mother was conveying to the child was that during school hours, school personnel are the only authority to whom the child should answer, and the school rule outweighed the mother's directive.

Parents want the best possible education for their children but may feel they should not be involved in the education processes or decision making because they lack skill, training, or information. They may very well perceive schooling to be totally the realm of the professional. In addition, their own experiences with school may not have been particularly satisfying and they may resist returning to the school environment, which holds uncomfortable memories. These variables and others may make it extremely difficult for parents to participate meaningfully in the decision-making process associated with special education.

Any attempt to provide parental educational programs must be appropriate to the parent and their child's educational program. Training programs should be consistent with the parent's language, culture, and other background characteristics. If training is not provided in the language of the parent, it will be ineffective, which is unfortunate since providing training was well intentioned. In addition, even if the parents speak English, they may be reluctant to express thoughts, concerns, or doubts in their second language. Requiring interaction with the school representative in a language other than their native language may inhibit their acquisition of the skills that are the goal of parent education.

CONTINUUM OF PLACEMENT ALTERNATIVES

Once the IEP is developed, the MDT must determine the instructional arrangements in which the child will receive the most appropriate education. In reaching such a decision, there must be a determination of the "least restrictive environment," ensuring that:

> to the maximum extent appropriate, children with disabilities, including children in public or private institutions or other care facilities, are educated with children who are not disabled, and that special classes, separate schooling, or other removal of children with disabilities from the regular educational environment occurs only when the nature or severity of the disability is such that education in regular classes with the use of supplementary aids and services cannot be achieved satisfactorily. . . . (IDEA, Section 1412, 1992)

Frequently, the concept of "least restrictive environment" is ignored when placement decisions are made for children who have limited English proficiency and also have disabilities. For example, students may be placed in bilingual education programs on a full-time basis in hope that teachers who speak the student's native language will be able to remediate learning gaps. However, bilingual education without appropriate modifications and additional support is insufficient to overcome school-related difficulties. In other cases, English language learners with disabilities are exited from bilingual education classes and placed in general education classes, so they will not be "confused" by dual language instruction. These instructional arrangements deny English language learners their right to an appropriate education in the least restrictive environment. Exceptional English language learners should have access to a continuum of placement alternatives, including:

- Full-time placement in a bilingual education classroom, with modifications of instruction to accommodate disabilities.
- If bilingual education programs are not available, full-time placement in general education classrooms and a program of English as a Second Language instruction, with mod-

ifications of instruction to accommodate disabilities.

- Inclusive classrooms (bilingual education or general education with ESL support), with assistance from special educators who serve as consultants to special language program and other regular educators in instructional planning for included English language learners.
- Bilingual education classroom, or general education classroom with English as a Second Language instruction, and special education instruction in a resource setting.
- Full-time special education placement in which instruction not only addresses students' disabilities but is also adapted to fit the students' linguistic, cultural, or other background characteristics.

Bilingual education and ESL programs have increased the availability of personnel whose training and experiences can be a valuable resource in instructional planning for language minority students. Also, special language programs provide access to an array of instructional materials and instructional strategies that can be adapted for use by special educators who work with language minority students. Special language program personnel must be trained to adapt or modify curriculum and instruction, such that students with disabilities can be successful in bilingual education inclusive settings. This is an important, but difficult, task given the typical range of student abilities, in the native language and in English, typically found in bilingual education classes. These special language program teachers and students must also have the direct support of special educators.

By the same token, given the dearth of special education teachers skilled in adapting curriculum, instruction, and materials in terms of language and culture, special education intervention is likely to require a collaborative team of special education and special language program specialists. Special education teachers must either be trained to provide bilingual special education instruction or, if they are not bilingual, trained in English as a Second Language methodology, so that they can better support language minority students with disabilities. In the latter case, the bilingual education teacher can provide native language academic instruction, and the special education teacher can provide ESL support in related subject or content areas, as appropriate. Without ESL training, special educators may be setting unrealistic goals by requiring that students master academic skills in a language they neither speak nor understand.

All too often, teacher assistants who are bilingual are given primary responsibility for teaching English language learners. These paraprofessionals are neither certified teachers nor do they have sufficient training in pedagogy, curriculum, or instruction to assume this responsibility. Instructional assistants should be closely supervised by the special education teacher, with the help of bilingual professionals if the special educator is not bilingual. The assistant can preview lessons in the native language (e.g., review key vocabulary, concepts, and ideas) and then the special educator can deliver lessons in English, adapting delivery using ESL strategies to make it comprehensible to the learner. After the teacher's lesson, the assistant can then review important content in the native language. Using this approach, the teacher retains primary responsibility for instruction. However, these lessons are anchored by native language support in the form of previews and reviews provided by the teacher assistant in the student's native language.

OBSTACLES TO EFFECTIVE SERVICE DELIVERY FOR ENGLISH LANGUAGE LEARNERS

Provision of special education services, and the design of IEPs, is complicated by numerous factors. The dramatically changing demography of this country underscores the critical need to address these issues.

Lack of Understanding of Program Purposes

There is growing concern that special language programs, that is, bilingual education and English as a Second Language programs, have become alternatives to special education intervention. For example, it is argued that maintaining a child in a bilingual education class because the teacher speaks the child's language is a better alternative than having services provided by a special educator who is not bilingual. Yet, native language instruction which does not accommodate a child's disabilities does not constitute an appropriate education. Bilingual educators often lack necessary training to determine whether a child has a disability or to provide educational interventions that help exceptional children. Further, bilingual teachers are often no better prepared than regular teachers to prevent inappropriate placement of exceptional children in their classes.

Alternatively, there is concern that special education is being used as a dumping ground for underachieving language minority students. Educators, including special educators, may mistakenly interpret children's language and behavioral characteristics as disabilities or may argue for special education services so that English language learners "will get necessary extra help" to remedy school difficulties.

Inadequate Training of General Education Personnel

There is evidence that even the very best regular educators make only "minimal accommodations for students with learning disabilities" (Garnett, 1996, p. 12). These issues magnify when English language learners are included in general education classrooms, and teachers are expected to respond appropriately to disability-related concerns and to students' language status.

Assessment Practices

As indicated previously, educational programming related to school problems often is based on information of questionable validity, even though IDEA (1992) requires "procedures to assure that testing and evaluation materials and procedures utilized for the purposes of evaluation and placement of children with disabilities will be selected and administered so as not to be racially or culturally discriminatory" (Section 1412). One obstacle to accurate identification of language minority students who have disabilities is the critical shortage of bilingual assessment personnel (Nuttall, 1987). Another is that the majority of school psychologists and other educational evaluators have limited training in assessment of limited English proficient and bilingual students (Ochoa, Rivera, & Ford, 1994). As indicated previously, matters are further complicated by the common practice of modifying instruments and procedures used with second language learners and then reporting results as accurate measures of student abilities.

Lack of Trained Special Education Personnel

Many English language learners and bilingual exceptional children are not provided an appropriate education because of the lack of special educational personnel uniquely trained to serve this population (Wald, 1996). Of particular concern is the lack of personnel who can provide instruction in the child's native language (Ortiz & Yates, 1982) and/or who are skilled in English as a Second Language instruction. Failure to recommend the instructional use of the native language is likely to occur because districts do not have the personnel to provide such instruction. Committees are reluctant to specify services which cannot be delivered, even though federal law clearly states that instructional programs be developed without consideration of cost or availability of such services.

Knowledge Base

There is a paucity of research in the area of special education for exceptional language minority students. Available literature includes theoretical or conceptual treatments of important issues or evidence that is basically deductive or generalized from studies in bilingual education, special education, or general theories of learning. Without systematic, scientific data and resultant knowledge specific to this population, efforts to provide appropriate services will continue to be based on assumptions and intuitions. A related concern, though, is that educators fail to act upon existing evidence about what constitutes recommended practice in educating language minority students. For example, although the literature supports the benefits of native language instructions, most MDTs continue to give preference to English language intervention.

Policy/Law

The complexity of responding to the requirements of federal law are now well established after more than 20 years of experience in developing and implementing IEPs. In some ways, what was originally perceived as a simple, efficient, and effective mechanism for meeting the unique needs of each student with disabilities has been lost in the complexity of the implementation process. Some of this complexity is organizational, in that school districts and state education agencies have an ever-increasing number of suggested procedures and forms to be completed to create the "formal" document. Other difficulties are pragmatic, such as deciding which personnel should be involved in developing the IEP and which of these personnel are "available" for the IEP meeting. Additional difficulties surround the articulation of complex student instructional needs and the difficulty of "knowing" what the student really needs in order to progress. Yet other issues are political and/or quasi-legal, such as determining what should be placed in "writing" that could and does serve as the measure of accountability for progress of the student. The changing student demography has added an additional layer of complexity to the IEP development process.

Existing safeguards in IDEA (1992), if appropriately implemented, greatly improve the services for linguistically and culturally diverse exceptional children. However, administrative costs, personnel dynamics in organizations, concerns for litigation, and political pressure resulting from the general public's lack of knowledge surrounding issues of language and culture constrain the appropriate implementation of policy and law.

☺ SUMMARY

This chapter has highlighted the complexity of developing Individualized Education Programs for language minority students with disabilities. Serving the needs of these students requires specialized knowledge and skills associated with serving linguistically and culturally diverse learners, developing native language and English as a Second Language proficiency, and providing instruction using strategies known to be effective for English language learners. It also requires collaboration among administrators and special language program, general education, special education, and related services personnel. Without such collaboration, language minority students will be denied the free, appropriate education they are guaranteed by law.

☺ DISCUSSION QUESTIONS

1. Conduct simulations of a parent conference wherein you, the teacher, explain to the parents their role in the IEP planning meeting. Discuss how you would incorporate parents' goals for their child into the IEP.

2. Frequently schools lack trained bilingual special educators to effectively implement the student's IEP. Suggest strategies that might be used to serve English language learners under such circumstances.
3. It is recommended that multidisciplinary teams include someone with expertise in linguistic and cultural diversity. What specific types of knowledge and competencies should such an individual possess?
4. Discuss barriers to successfully integrating English language learners into mainstream or inclusive classrooms. Identify strategies that can be used to overcome these barriers.
5. Discuss instructional strategies and practices that you feel are particularly effective for English language learners with disabilities. What characteristics do these strategies and practices seem to have in common?
6. Suggest ideas for building stronger linkages among bilingual educators, special educators, and general education teachers in designing and implementing instructional programs for English language learners.

☺ REFERENCES

Adelman, H. (1970). An interactive view of causality. *Academic Therapy, 6,* 43–52.

Ambert, A., & Dew, N. (1982). *Special education for exceptional bilingual students: A handbook for educators.* Milwaukee: Midwest National Origin Desegregation Assistance Center.

Asher, J. (1979). *Learning another language through actions: The complete teacher's guidebook.* Los Gatos, CA: Skyoak Productions.

Benson, C. S., Medrich, E. A., & Buckley, S. (1980). A new view of school efficiency: Household time contributions to school achievement. In J. W. Guthrie (Ed.), *School finance policies and practices. The 1980's: A decade of conflict* (pp. 169–204). Cambridge, MA: Ballinger Publishing Company.

Bilingual Education Act. Pub. L. No. 90-247, 81 Stat. 783 816 (1968).

Borkowski, J. G., Weyhing, R. S., & Turner, L. A. (1986). Attributional retraining and the teaching of strategies. *Exceptional Children, 53*(2), 130–137.

Brophy, J., & Good, T. (1986). Teacher behavior and student achievement. In M. C. Wittrock (Ed.), *Handbook of research on teaching* (3rd Edition) (pp. 328–375). New York: Macmillan.

Cardenas, J. A. (1995). *Multicultural education: A generation of advocacy.* Needham Heights, MA: Simon & Schuster.

Cardenas, J. S., Robledo, M., & Supik, J. D. (1986, Oct. 31). *Texas school dropout survey project: A summary of findings.* San Antonio: Intercultural Development Research Association.

Chamot, A. U., Cummins, J., Fillmore, L. W., Kessler, C., & O'Malley, J. M. (1996). *ESL program for grades 1–8.* Glenview, IL: Scott Foresman.

Chamot, A. U., & O'Malley, J. M. (1994). *The CALLA Handbook: Implementing the cognitive academic language learning approach.* Reading, MA: Addison-Wesley.

Collier, V. (1996, May). Language-minority student achievement and program effectiveness. *NABE News, 19*(6), 33–35.

Cummins, J. (1984). *Bilingualism and special education: Issues in assessment and pedagogy.* Clevedon, Avon, England: Multilingual Matters.

Cummins, J. (1989). *Empowering minority students.* Sacramento, CA: California Association for Bilingual Education.

Cummins, J. (1991) Interdependency of first- and second-language proficiency in bilingual children. In E. Bialystok (Ed.). *Language processing in bilingual children.* New York: Cambridge University Press.

Damico, J. S. (1991). Descriptive assessment of communicative ability in limited English proficient students. In E. V. Hamayan & J. S. Damico (Eds.), *Limiting bias in the assessment of bilingual students* (pp. 157–217). Austin, TX: Pro-Ed.

Education for All Handicapped Children Act of 1975, 20 U.S.C. 1400.

Feuerstein, R. (1980). *Instrumental enrichment: An intervention program for cognitive modifiability.* Baltimore: University Park Press.

Garcia, E. (1994). *Understanding and meeting the challenge of student cultural diversity.* Boston: Houghton Mifflin.

Garnett, K. (1996). *Thinking about inclusion and learning disabilities: A teacher's guide.* Reston, VA: Council for Exceptional Children.

Gonzales, L., & Watson, D. (1986). *Sheltered English teaching handbook.* Carlsbad, CA: Binet International.

Good, T. L., & Brophy, J. E. (1973). *Looking into classrooms.* New York: Harper & Row.

Henderson, R. (1980). Social and emotional needs of culturally diverse children. *Exceptional Children, 46,* 598–605.

Individuals with Disabilities Education Act (IDEA), Pub. L. No. 101-476, § 33, Sec. 1401 (1992).

Krashen, S. (1982). Bilingual education and second language acquisition theory. In *Schooling and language minority students: A theoretical framework.* Los Angeles: Bilingual Education Evaluation, Dissemination, and Assessment Center.

Krashen, S. (1996, June). A gradual exit, variable threshold model for limited English proficient children. *NABE News, 19*(7), 1, 15–18.

Krashen, S., & Terrell, T. (1983). *The natural approach: Language acquisition in the classroom.* Oxford, England: Pergamon Press.

Lau v. Nichols. 414 U.S. 563;39. L. Ed 2d 1, 94 S. Ct. 787 (1974).

Moecker, D. (1989). *The Argyris-Schon theoretical model applied to special education decision process for Anglo and Hispanic students.* Unpublished doctoral dissertation, Austin, TX: The University of Texas at Austin.

Nuttall, E. V. (1987). Survey of current practices in the psychological assessment of limited-English-proficiency handicapped children. *Journal of School Psychology, 25,* 53–61.

Ochoa, S. H., Rivera, B., & Ford, L. (1994). School psychology training pertaining to bilingual psychoeducational assessment. Paper presented at the 102nd Annual American Psychological Association Convention, Los Angeles, California.

Ortiz, A. (1984). Choosing the language of instruction for exceptional bilingual children. *Teaching Exceptional Children, 16,* 208–212.

Ortiz, A. A. & Garcia, S. B. (1990). Using language assessment data for language and instructional planning for exceptional bilingual students. In A. Carrasquillo & R. Baecher (Eds.), *Teaching the bilingual special education student* (pp. 24–47). Norwood, NJ: Ablex Publishing Corporation.

Ortiz, A. A., & Wilkinson, C. Yelich. (1989, May). Adapting IEPs for limited English proficient students. *Academy Therapy, 24*(5), 555–568.

Ortiz, A. A., & Yates, J. R. (1982). Teacher training associated with serving bilingual exceptional students. *Teacher Education and Special Education, 5* (3), 61–68.

Ortiz, A. A., & Yates, J. R. (1983). Incidence among Hispanic exceptionals: Implications for manpower planning. *Journal of the National Association for Bilingual Education, 7*(3), 41–53.

Paris, S. G., & Oka, E. R. (1986). Self-regulated learning among exceptional children. *Exceptional Children, 53*(2), 103–108.

Pyecha, J., Cox, J. L., Conway, L. E., Hocott, A., Jaffe, J., Pelosi, J., & Wiegerink, R. (1980). *A national survey of individualized programs (IEPs) for handicapped children: Volume III (basic survey findings).* (ERIC Document Reproduction Service No. ED 199 972).

Ramirez, M., & Castaneda, A. (1974). *Cultural democracy, bicognitive development, and education.* New York: Academic Press.

Rist, R. (1970). Student social class and leader expectations: The self-fulling prophecy in ghetto education. *Harvard Educational Review, 40,* 411–451.

Safer, N., & Hobbs, B. (1980). Developing, implementing and evaluation individualized education programs. *School Psychology Review, 9,*(3), 212–220.

Schenck, S. J., & Levy, W. K. (1979, April). *IEPs: The state of the art—1978.* Paper presented at the annual meeting of the American Educational Research Association, San Francisco, CA. (ERIC Document Reproduction Service No. ED 175 201).

Slavin, R. E. (1988). *Cooperative learning and student achievement.* In R. E. Slavin (Ed.). Schools and classroom organization. Hillsdale, NJ: Erlbaum.

Tikunoff, W. (1982). *The significant bilingual instructional features descriptive study: Progress and issues from Part I.* Paper presented at the meeting of the American Educational Research Association, New York.

Townsend, W. A. (1995). *Pocket digest: Digest of educational statistics for limited English proficient students.* Washington, D.C.: Office of Bilingual Education and Minority Language Affairs.

Violand-Sanchez, E., Sutton, C. P., Ware, H. W. (Summer 1991). *Fostering home-school cooperation: Involving language minority families as partners in education.* Washington, D.C.: National Clearinghouse for Bilingual Education.

Walker, C. L. (1980). *Locus of control and attribution responses of bilingual Spanish-English children.* Unpublished Doctoral Dissertation, University of Illinois, Urbana-Champaign.

Willig, A. C., Swedo, J. J., & Ortiz, A. A. (1987). *Characteristics of teaching strategies which result in high task engagement for exceptional limited English proficient students.* Austin, TX: The University of Texas at Austin, Handicapped Minority Research Institute on Language Proficiency.

Yates, J. R. & Ortiz, A. A., (1995). Linguistically and culturally diverse students. In R. S. Podemski, G. E. Marsh II, T. E. C. Smith & B. J. Price, *Comprehensive administration of special education.* Upper Saddle River, NJ: Prentice Hall/Merrill.

CHAPTER 10

Developing Instructional Plans and Curriculum for Bilingual Special Education Students

Catherine Collier

- Conducting the IEP Meeting
- Step 1: Review Initial Intervention Information
- Step 2: List All of the Student's Needs
- Step 3: Identify Appropriate Interventions and Approaches
- Step 4: Identify Appropriate Timeline and Expectations
- Step 5: Identify Monitoring Schedule
- Summary

OBJECTIVES

To describe the curriculum-development process for culturally and linguistically diverse exceptional (CLDE) learners

To develop a clearer understanding of the special learning needs of bilingual-exceptional children, especially as they relate to planning individual education plans

To describe the unique cultural and linguistic considerations the curriculum developer must integrate into the curriculum

To describe the unique acculturation considerations the curriculum developer must integrate into the curriculum

To provide guidelines for the selection and adaptation of curricular materials

To offer appropriate suggestions for teaching in the culturally and linguistically diverse special education classroom

Because the integration of bilingual and special education is a relatively recent phenomenon, there are few curricular materials specifically geared to Bilingual Special Education. It is frequently special education teachers, working in collaboration with other classroom personnel, who must develop new curricula and adapt existing ones.

Over 15 years ago, in a study conducted by McLean (1981), lack of curricular materials and trained personnel were cited as the greatest needs in providing service to bilingual exceptional children. This remains a serious service concern, as noted in Baca, Fradd, and Collier (1990) and Hoover and Collier (1991). The continuing need for curricular adaptation for culturally and linguistically different exceptional (CLDE) students is discussed in Hoover and Collier (1986) as well.

Bilingual education and special education curriculum guides both indicate how to prepare the bilingual student and the student with disabilities to assume a responsible role and to function effectively in a pluralistic society. However, these materials must be integrated for culturally and linguistically diverse (CLDE) learners; it is not enough to send the student with disabilities into a bilingual class part-time and into a special education class part-time. Neither would provide comprehensive instruction to meet the student's special needs. The bilingual teacher rarely has the training to provide for exceptional children, and the special education teacher does not usually have the training to deal with acculturation and second language acquisition.

This makes the task of the team developing the individual education plan (IEP) very challenging. This is true also for the teacher or team developing integrated curricula for diverse learners who will receive all their instruction in a general education setting. It also applies to intervention teams, such as Teacher Assistance Teams (TAT) or Prevention Intervention Period (PIP) teams (Chapter 12). Chapter 10 specifically addresses the IEP process, but the steps described and issues raised apply equally to anyone developing curricular materials for diverse learners.

The individualized educational plan (IEP) is developed after the placement decision is made. An IEP meeting is convened to develop the individualized plan based on the student's strengths and weaknesses in the areas of achievement, aptitude/ability, and emotional/behavioral competence. There are five steps in the IEP process which result in the completion of the IEP document. These steps are summarized in Figure 10–1. An IEP appears as Appendix A at the end of the chapter.

The IEP, developed in consultation with all concerned parties, must be a comprehensive presentation of the student's total learning needs. This includes instructional guidelines and objectives to address the student's acculturation and language acquisition needs, as well as his/her special educational needs. In addition, it should address the integration of these services, indicating *who* is responsible for providing and maintaining culturally and linguistically appropriate instructional interventions within each service setting provided. The IEP should also address *how* culturally and linguistically appropriate instructional interventions will be used in meeting the student's special needs.

CONDUCTING THE IEP MEETING

The parents are invited to participate in the actual IEP meeting. A notice of the IEP meeting must be sent to the parents or legal guardians of the student in their native language early enough to assure their participation. If the parents cannot attend the meeting, other methods need to be used to ensure parent participation, including individual or conference calls.

The IEP meeting for each newly identified exceptional pupil should be conducted as soon as possible. Participants at the IEP meetings for limited English proficient (LEP) students must include:

Figure 10–1
The Five Essential IEP Steps

The five essential steps in developing and implementing a comprehensive IEP or curriculum for bilingual exceptional children are:

1. Review information gathered during the initial intervention period: Review the PreReferral Review Form (PRR), which appears as Appendix B at the end of the chapter, or other evaluation tool findings, being especially attentive to the second language acquisition and acculturation needs of the student in addition to his/her special learning and behavior needs.

2. List all of the student's needs: Determine the specific needs which can be addressed with services available within the school, the district, and the community. Determine the language of instruction and also the sociocultural needs and the linguistic needs of the student, and record this information on the IEP form. Establish goals and objectives. These needs can be determined by using the PRR, the Acculturation Quick Screen (AQS), the Classroom Language Interaction Checklist (CLIC), the Language Assessment Scales (LAS), the Woodcock-Muñoz (WM), or the Sociocultural Checklist (SC). The PRR, AQS, CLIC and SC all appear as appendices B-E at the end of the chapter.

3. Identify appropriate interventions and approaches: This includes developing an IEP and individualizing lessons and interventions for acculturation level, culture and language, and cognitive learning style. Identify the language(s) of instruction. Determine specific instructional strategies, procedures, and personnel to be responsible for addressing each specific need. Identify where referrals to external services are needed.

4. Identify appropriate timeline and expectations. Define specific measurable goals and expectations. Determine a realistic timeline for these outcomes on specific interventions, addressing specific needs within the context of the student's second language acquisition and acculturation needs. Decide who is responsible for implementing each intervention and within what setting. This may be a Teacher Assistance Child Intervention Team (TACIT), a Teacher Assistance Team (TAT), a Student Assistance Team (SAT), etc.

5. Establish a monitoring schedule: Determine an appropriate schedule for monitoring and reevaluating the student's progress with learning and behavior development, including expected benchmarks for second language acquisition and acculturation. Identify specific instruments and procedures to be used. Specify a generalization process as well.

- A representative of the school district or other public agency
- A person knowledgeable about the language and acculturation needs of the student
- The student's general education classroom teacher or special education teacher or therapist
- General education teacher(s) in whose class the student is enrolled
- Parents or legal guardians
- The student
- A member of the Multidisciplinary Team (MDT) or a person knowledgeable about the evaluation procedures
- A person knowledgeable about service options

- Other individuals at the discretion of the district or other public agency

Individual professionals may fulfill more than one of these functions concurrently; i.e., the MDT member may also be knowledgeable about the language and acculturative needs of the student. A translation of the IEP must be provided in the parents' or guardians' native language. The assessment report should be orally translated in the native language of the parents.

STEP 1: REVIEW INITIAL INTERVENTION INFORMATION

The IEP meeting begins with a review of the documentation provided by the team during the prevention and intervention period (PIP) and the MDT, with special attention to the second language acquisition and acculturation needs of the student in relation to his/her special learning and behavior needs. A discussion of the form for documenting PIP findings is provided in Chapter 12. The group develops a statement describing the student's present level of performance in all areas under discussion. This includes a statement of the student's present level of acculturation, including his/her present levels of performance in the native language and in English. This statement of present levels of performance is written in the first portion of the IEP and forms the basis for identifying all of the student's needs.

STEP 2: LIST ALL OF THE STUDENT'S NEEDS

The group next identifies specific needs and sociocultural, linguistic, and cognitive learning styles which can be addressed with the services available within the school, the district, and the community. Among these needs will be a determination of the language of instruction within each area of concern. The guidelines for determining this are described in the PIP discussion in Chapter 12. There may be some areas of concern where the native language of the student is more appropriate and some areas where English is more appropriate, depending upon the LEP student's basic interpersonal communication skills (BICS) and cognitive academic language proficiency (CALP) in both languages and his/her present level of acculturation. The language of instruction in each area should be recorded on the IEP form.

The group develops specific short- and long-term goals and objectives for each identified need. These goals and objectives will include desired proficiency outcomes for the student's acquisition of English as a second language as well. There should also be goals and objectives for facilitating the student's acculturation to the school system.

The group also identifies appropriate objective criteria and evaluation procedures consistent with the student's linguistic abilities in the first and in the second language to measure all desired outcomes. These must be documented on the IEP form. The form in Appendix A at the end of the chapter has examples of how and where to record this information.

Sociocultural and Linguistic Considerations When Planning Instruction for Diverse Learners

Areas of special concern in planning instruction for CLDE are sociocultural needs, language needs, and any special needs of the CLDE student. Sociocultural needs include the student's cultural and linguistic background, experiential background, the stage and pattern of acculturation, and the student's cognitive and learning styles. When the student's language needs are considered, differing patterns of sociolinguistic development and language transfer must be considered. In the area of special needs, the particular identified disability and its manifestation within the context of the student's culture, acculturation, second language acquisition must be considered. These form the foundation for the instruction of culturally and linguistically diverse (CLD) students. Addressing these three factors, as well as the identified disability, will assure the IEP is comprehensive.

Sociocultural Needs: Cultural and Language Background. All human beings grow up within a cultural context. The process of acquiring one's native culture is called "enculturation" and may begin in the womb, but definitely at birth. Adapting to a different culture is called "acculturation." "Culture consists of whatever it is one has to know or believe in order to operate in a manner acceptable to its members" (Goodenough, 1957, p. 167). *Culture* is how we organize our behaviors, communication, values, and emotions; it is the patterns of interaction, communication, socialization, and education held in common by a particular group of people.

The components of culture—language, behavior, and socialization—are not static but are changed continually by the influence of both internal and external circumstances. Where several cultures are in contact, where there is much movement and communication between social groups and geographic areas, some overlapping and blurring of cultural boundaries will occur. However, it is true that both enculturation and acculturation shape an individual's cultural identity.

The way individuals perceive, relate to, and interpret their environment is shaped by their cultural milieu. Culture determines how we think (cognition), how we interact (behavior), how we communicate (language), and how we transmit knowledge to the next generation (education). Since culture has such a comprehensive effect upon the thinking, perceptions, and interaction patterns of individuals, practitioners must become familiar with the cultural and sociolinguistic background of their students, particularly students with learning and behavior problems. Our educational system is founded on culturally based assumptions about what students should learn, how and where they should learn it, as well as why and when they will need this knowledge. Exceptional students reared in a different cultural environment will have learned a different body of knowledge and different ways of manipulating and demonstrating this knowledge. Education professionals must be sensitive to the cultural and sociolinguistic backgrounds of diverse learners and must consider how these differences may affect a student's performance in the classroom. An instructional goal in regard to culture would be: "The student will be able to make analogies between what his family uses [to measure objects] at home and what he is introduced to at school." An instructional goal in regard to language would be: "The student will be able to discuss how his family does something, e.g., bakes bread, in both Spanish and English."

Sociocultural Needs: Experiential Background. Differences in experience may account for much of the discrepancy between achievement and ability seen in diverse learners with learning and behavior problems. Many refugee and immigrant students in this country come from socioeconomic and political situations where they have not had the educational experiences of mainstream American students. This is also true of many Hispanic and Native American students, especially those who live in migrant families (Serrano, 1982). Many of these students are raised in settings with little or no exposure to regular and consistent public school education or to children's educational programs, such as day care centers and educational television. As a result, many diverse learners lack experiences and preskills necessary for learning in American public schools, and which educators usually assume students bring with them. The IEP must address these missing experiential elements. This may mean building in frequent reviews and refresher lessons. In addition, teaching CLDE students to begin each new lesson with an analogy to prior knowledge will bridge this gap.

Differences in experiential background also affect diverse learners' responses to various elements of the curriculum. The use of inquiry techniques, behavior contracting, active processing, and other individualized instructional strategies is very dependent on prior experience. Role expectations and the ability to make quick cause-and-effect associations are necessary prerequisite skills for optimal effectiveness of many strategies. Diverse learners' lack of appropriate response to these commonly used instructional strategies and interventions compounds their learning and behavior problems. The teacher should not use these without demonstrating what is expected of CLDE students and providing guided practice in the activity.

Some of the diverse learners' responses to the school environment may be due to previous school experiences and others to cultural differences. Students who have been in school systems in other countries generally know basic school procedures, such as raising their hands for attention, asking permission to do something, and recess and lunchroom behaviors. However, they may be unfamiliar with particular instructional strategies, such as independent or silent reading rather than group recitation, or discovery learning rather than rote memorization. Their inappropriate responses to silent reading, discovery learning, or other activities may be disruptive or troublesome to the teacher. The teacher should facilitate demonstration of the expected behavior as long as it seems necessary. With exceptional bilingual students, guided practice may need to become a regular part of the daily schedule.

In addition to these experience-based responses to the school environment, differences in school behavior may be due to cultural differences. For example, many cultures value individual achievement only as it enhances a group. More value is placed on individual contribution to the success of the group than on the success of the individual. A student who appears to act apart from the group may be shunned or ridiculed in many Native American and Asian cultures (Hoover & Collier, 1985; Nazarro, 1981; Woodward, 1981). Since much of the focus of the IEP is upon individual performance objectives and individual activities, the diverse learner's actual performance abilities may be obscured. The fear of being seen by peers as different may affect the student's performance during independent instruction activities.

Also, diverse learners from a culture that values indirectness and distance as evidence of appropriate behavior may not respond positively to the use of touching or praise as reinforcement strategies. These students' interpretation of "time out" and other teaching and behavior management techniques may be quite different from the teacher's intent when using those techniques. Inappropriate responses may lead the teacher to inaccurate conclusions about

the student's performance. The IEP should not include these strategies until a baseline of effectiveness and familiarity has been established. An instructional goal in regard to experience would be: "The student will be able to respond appropriately to guided practice and demonstrations."

Sociocultural Needs: Acculturation. Educators who work with diverse learners who have learning and behavior problems also need to address the effects of acculturation. The diverse learner's cultural identity is affected by both enculturation and acculturation. The common concept of acculturation is the "melting pot," the assimilation of one cultural group into another. However, assimilation is only one component of acculturation; assimilation is a very complex process usually occurring over a generational, rather than individual, timespan.

Acculturation is the process of adaptation to a new cultural environment. If the native culture and language is essentially eliminated from the person's cognitive behavior as the second culture takes its place, we say assimilation has occurred. This acculturative response is actually rather rare; a person more frequently integrates new cultural patterns into the cognitive and behavioral framework of the first culture and language. Integrative acculturation can be facilitated by school personnel. This is the most positive acculturative response and enables the learner to deal effectively with the "side effects" of acculturation.

Of special concern to education professionals are the psychological responses to the acculturation experience, which are very similar to indicators of handicapping conditions. These include confused locus of control, heightened anxiety, poor self-image, and withdrawal (Collier, 1985; Padilla, 1980). Another effect of acculturation is acculturative stress. This stress is common, though not inevitable, during acculturation and is characterized by deviant behavior, psychosomatic symptoms, and a feeling of marginality. Berry (1976) found that

Native American groups experience high stress when the traditional cultural is less similar to the second or mainstream culture. Groups experience lower stress when the culture is more similar to the second culture and has greater contact with other cultural groups.

Since students who consistently demonstrate heightened anxiety or stress, confused locus of control, or lack of response are often placed in special services, it is imperative that teachers working with diverse learners who are experiencing acculturation consider the psychological "side-effects" of acculturation when planning instruction intervention. These students may need cross-cultural counseling or acculturation assistance programs rather than or in addition to special education.

Studies of the effect of acculturation upon individuals have looked at the various steps involved and the degree of "culture shock" experienced (Adler, 1965; Juffer, 1983). Major variables which affect acculturation include the amount of time spent in the process, the quantity and quality of interaction, ethnicity or nation of origin, and language proficiency. These variables form the basis of the acculturation screening device, the Acculturation Quick Screen (AQS), which is recommended for the assessment of CLD learners and as a tool to guide educators in making better instructional decisions for diverse learners. This assessment tool appears in the Appendix B at the end of the chapter.

The relationship between degree of acculturation and length of time (1) in school and (2) in an orientation experience was explored in a study by Juffer (1983). She found that the length of time in school and receiving orientation both are highly correlated with degree of adaptation (acculturation). Juffer's findings of fewer problems in school cross-cultural social settings among more highly acculturated students are reflected by Finn (1982). He found that there were fewer referrals of culturally and linguistically different learners to special education in districts with bilingual programs. In addition,

Szapocznik and Kurtines (1980) demonstrated that as bilingualism or biculturalism increased, socio-emotional problems decreased. A study by Albino-Cordero (1981) showed that diverse learners in bilingual programs had fewer behavior problems than diverse learners in general education programs. This has considerable implications for CLDE students and highlights the importance of *bilingual* special education classrooms.

Szapocznik and Kurtines (1980) focused on the importance of strong language skills in both the first language (L_1) and the second language (L_2) as factors in mental health among diverse individuals. The importance of English language proficiency in determining degree of and success in acculturation was documented by Juffer (1983). English ability was significant in three of four subcategories and in predicting a high composite score on the adaptation inventory. Research in bilingual education also indicates the importance of proficiency in the native language as a foundation for proficiency in L_2 acquisition and development, especially in the acculturation context (Krashen, 1994; Skutnabb-Kangas & Toukamaa, 1976; Wells, 1981). Cummins (1986) provides an extensive description of the relationship between L_1 and L_2 development and stresses the vital importance of L_1 in promoting educational success and cognitive development in the diverse student in a cross-cultural learning situation. This further substantiates the critical need for L_1 development and bilingual interventions as part of IEP implementation.

National origin or ethnicity has been examined as a factor in school achievement and referral to special education (Argulewicz & Elliott, 1981). Studies have shown a significant relationship between membership in an ethnically diverse group and likelihood of being referred to special education. In addition, Juffer (1983) identified national origin as a factor which significantly predicted rate of adaptation to a second culture. This factor is one of the elements in the AQS and must be considered by the IEP team as they identify instructional strategies and materials.

Another factor which Juffer (1983) identified as significant in acculturation was the amount of interaction with mainstream American students. This may be interpreted as a function of the diverse enrollment in the school. Finn (1982) indicates that there is a distinct relationship between diverse school enrollment and special education referral and placement. As diverse enrollment in a school district increases, the referral and placement of culturally and linguistically different students to special education becomes more consistent with mainstream referral rates (Collier, 1985; Finn, 1982). With regards to IEP development, educators must consider how they will integrate opportunities for constructive interaction between LEP and English speaking students. This may include guided practice in cross-cultural communication. An instructional goal in regard to acculturation would be: "The student will be able to assist less proficient LEP peers with communication and content acquisition."

Linguistic Needs.   A further basic element of special concern in the instruction of diverse learners is language acquisition and development. Language is the primary medium through which culture and experiences are shared and transmitted from generation to generation and is a primary element in the acculturation of diverse learners. Language occurs within a social and interactive communicative context; the term "sociolinguistic development" is used to describe the comprehensiveness of language development and usage. It is important to identify and assess the diverse learners' sociolinguistic abilities in both the first and the second language, since misunderstandings about sociolinguistic abilities frequently are involved in placement of diverse learners in special education.

Many diverse learners who are placed in special education are described as deficient in or lacking sociolinguistic skills entirely. This usu-

ally means that the student appears to have deficits in both English and the native language or speaks a dialect of English very different from his or her teachers. There is ample evidence that the development of language skills for communication within a social context is a natural process and that human beings are genetically programmed for language acquisition (Chomsky, 1971; Lenneberg, 1967; Slobin, 1979; Snow, 1984). Therefore, a student who is "lacking language" (Grosjean, 1982) would indeed be severely and unusually disabled. Research has shown, however, that many diverse learners have well-established sociolinguistic systems in their first language while limited in English, but they use these systems selectively and nonacademically (Commins, 1986). Commins collected extensive natural language samples outside the school environment and concluded that diverse learners may well have sociolinguistic competence in both languages, but that their limited sociolinguistic performance in the academic setting obscures this underlying competence. The IEP will need to address this instructional need, and teachers working with CLDE students should include language development activities focused upon developing cognitive academic language proficiency (CALP).

Pinker (1994) has shown that all students progress through several stages of language development. By two years of age, children begin to incorporate the unique grammatical structures of their home language and dialect. Even learners with moderate disabilities manage to acquire language. Only the most profoundly physically or mentally disabled students who are subjected to extreme sensory deprivation or isolation fail to acquire language of some sort (Curtiss, 1982; Pinker, 1994). Curtiss cites the case of a child, raised in isolation from human interaction, who learned limited but meaningful verbal communication after exposure to spoken language.

Wells (1981) has demonstrated that the quality and quantity of verbal interaction students receive in the home language, whichever language is used, is the greatest predictor of later academic success in English. Krashen (1994) and Cummins (1986) also cite research that supports the importance of quality first-language development as a precursor to acquisition of English as a second language and later academic success. Those CLD learners who have not received "quality" development in their native language, and who have poor first and second language proficiency, will need additional language development assistance based upon their sociolinguistic proficiency. Chesarek (1981) discusses this in regard to Native American students who have had continuing problems with academic achievement and second language acquisition, even though their language ability in English is better than or equal to their ability in the native language. More and more diverse learners are coming to school with both limited English and limited native language skills; however, as discussed in Chapter 6, limited language skills, particularly as assessed by standardized tests, are not necessarily indicative of a language disorder. This is especially true if this is a typical language acquisition pattern within a particular community or language acquisition context.

Diverse learners who do not have strong language skills in either English or their native language are particularly challenging for special educators. Even with bilingual assistance, these students will need intensive intervention, and the IEP must reflect this need. With students still in elementary school or prior to about 12–14 years of age, rebuilding the L_1 linguistic foundation is recommended. By the end of the student's secondary career, the focus should shift to school-to-work transition, emphasizing functional language use in L_2. As soon as the child acquires and demonstrates skills in L_1, the teacher should use these skills to build comparable skills in L_2. As new knowledge is achieved in L_2, the vocabulary to discuss it in L_1 should be provided. This ratcheting effect should continue as the teacher works with the student to learn and generalize new content and skills. This ratcheting is, in essence, restoring and strengthening the linguistic and cognitive foundations that have been neglected in these children's language development.

An IEP provides a unique opportunity to address the linguistic needs of this particular group of children. Special educators, particularly those who can provide bilingual services, are in a unique position to individualize this L_1–L_2–L_1–L_2 developmental ladder. The ratcheting can be built into the IEP within selected content areas and can be a particular focus of the monitoring plan. An instructional goal in regard to linguistic needs would be: "The student will be able to demonstrate communication structures in English which he acquired in Spanish. He will be able to explain in Spanish how to use particular grammatical vocabulary in English."

Cognitive Learning Styles. *Cognition* is the process of perceiving, attending, thinking, remembering, and knowing (Blumenthal, 1977). It is a continuous process which begins before birth and continues throughout life. Some people have more cognitive capacities than others, and some do not use what they possess. Education can affect the ability to develop and use cognitive processes. As Epstein (1978) notes, education can physically alter the brain, increasing the number of dendrite connections and the level of neural activity. There have been several studies of differences in cognitive style. Many researchers agree that the differences in how we conceptually organize our environment result in characteristic ways of learning from our experiences (Gardner, Jackson, & Messick, 1960; Mann & Sabatino, 1985; Ramirez & Castaneda, 1974).

Keogh (1973) defined *cognitive style* as the stable, typical, and consistent way in which individuals select and organize environmental data. *Learning styles* are the characteristic ways in which individual students respond to the instructional environment. While viewed as a consistent pattern of behavior, learning style has been shown to change with age and experience, especially exposure to cognitive and learning strategies (Stone & Wertsch, 1984).

Culture is the concept of things that a particular people use as models for perceiving, relating, and interpreting their environment. Cognitive development and cognitive learning style depend largely on the diverse student's cultural background and experience (Collier & Hoover, 1987a). The culture shapes and influences the diverse student's cognitive learning style; identifying these styles becomes an instructionally meaningful foundation for the IEP. Identifying the cognitive learning styles of the diverse student contributes directly to the development of appropriate prereferral interventions and individualized education plans.

Cognitive learning styles are the characteristic ways in which individual students respond to the learning task and instructional environment. They include (1) preference for analytic versus global interpretations, (2) broad versus narrow categorizations, (3) tolerance versus intolerance for ambiguous or unusual stimuli, (4) reflective versus impulsive tempo, (5) external versus internal locus of control, and (6) other characteristic learning patterns (Collier & Hoover, 1987a). Refer to Collier and Hoover (1987a) and Mann and Sabatino (1985) for a detailed discussion on the identification of cognitive learning styles. An instructional goal in regard to cognitive learning styles would be: "The student is able to select and use specific cognitive learning strategies when given a new content lesson."

Goals and Objectives

Once the sociocultural and linguistic needs and an indication of learning style are determined, the IEP team should develop specific goals and objectives. Formal planning is a must when developing the individual education plan; short- and long-range goals need to be converted to workable objectives and finally to lesson plans and tasks. Planning ought to begin

with the specific learning objectives, developed from an assessment of the child's exceptionality and specific linguistic needs. Next, alternate ways to meeting the objectives should be developed, building on the unique cultural and linguistic background of the child, and finally, the best means for maintaining and developing mastery of the objective should be selected.

Planning is necessary for converting the curriculum into instruction, especially for preparing and acquiring needed curricular materials and for adapting special education classroom materials to the student language and culture. Teachers should run through the task and think aloud while performing it, so that decisions can be made about the content, scope and sequence, and pace and learnability of the materials. This run-through tells the teacher what is available to work with and how best to present the task to the students. This think aloud method is also called *process tracing* (Shavelson & Stern, 1981) and is similar to the active processing strategy used as an acculturative intervention with CLDE students (Collier & Hoover, 1989). In this form, it is useful for studying the operations involved in diverse students' performance on tasks.

Farnham-Diggory's version (1972) for the student is *protocol analysis,* which is based on what the student is actually doing during the task, that is, thinking out loud. Another version is *stimulated recall* (Shavelson & Stern, 1981), which is used when the process tracing would interfere with the student's performance on the task. After the task is completed, the student is helped (cued) in recalling the covert mental activities that accompanied the performance on the task, that is, the cognitive processes and the operations on the task. *Active processing* is another name for this cognitive learning strategy of having the student "self-talk" through a lesson (Collier & Hoover, 1987a).

It is important to be very clear in describing goals and objectives on the IEP. If the teacher is unclear about what is expected from the students or what will be done in a lesson, then it will also be unclear to the children and interfere with their learning. Goals are the generally or broadly worded outcomes the IEP identifies for the diverse learner. Objectives are more detailed descriptions of what the student will achieve. One method of describing objectives in curriculum and lesson planning is to use performance objectives. This is a way of describing exactly what outcomes are expected. The IEP planning team decides what the student needs to learn and describes it in terms of what the student will be able to do as a result of each particular lesson. The teacher may have broader goals and objectives that have been used in developing the general scope and sequence of the curriculum but then use specific performance objectives for the individual lessons.

A concise way to separate specific task objectives from broader objectives is *task analysis*. The steps of task analysis as outlined by the Center for Innovation in Teaching the Disabled (CITH, 1974) are as follows:

1. Specify main task, consider conditions and standards. How accurate do children have to be? What form should children use? Example: Telling time. Use of wall clock as standard. Children accurate to five minutes.

2. Identify subtasks at preceding levels of complexity. What simpler tasks must the child be able to do to perform the main task? Example: Child needs to be able to tell hour and minutes correct to five minutes, but does not need to be able to discriminate a watch from a clock to tell time.

3. Treat each subtask as a main task and repeat procedure for finding simpler subtasks. Example: Being able to tell hour involves knowing that the short hand points to the hour. The hour is the first number you say when telling time. If short hand is on or after the number, you say that number. The short hand goes around "clockwise" (so "after" means to the right of the number, and the child must be able to discriminate between short and long hands).

4. Determine entry level of students. The entry level is what the learners can already do.

STEP 3: IDENTIFY APPROPRIATE INTERVENTIONS AND APPROACHES

The IEP group uses the list of goals and objectives to identify instructional interventions, strategies, and procedures for addressing each specific need. They also identify the personnel who will be responsible for implementing these approaches and in which language(s) this will occur. The group also identifies appropriate second language acquisition and acculturation interventions and which service providers will be responsible. Documentation is required where referrals to external services are needed. The IEP group generates a statement of the specific special education and related services to be provided. This description of special education and related services to be provided includes:

- The recommended program and level of bilingual special education services to be provided.
- Alternative testing procedures and/or modifications related to both limited English proficiency and disability condition(s).
- Specification of services to meet the linguistic and cultural needs of the LEP student.
- The language(s) in which related services will be provided.
- Degree of participation with English speaking children.
- Specification of language intervention in the native and in the second language (development, enrichment, remediation).
- The facilitation of acculturation.
- Special-education needs.
- The integration of specific cultural and language interventions which address special-education needs.

- The extent of instruction in subject/cognitive areas in the native language or in English, as appropriate.

- Identification of service providers responsible for implementing and monitoring the integration of these services.

- Identification of the extent to which the student will be involved in Chapter 1/Title I, Bilingual/ESL, Migrant Education, and other related services.

- Intensive instruction in English as a Second Language (ESL).

- Instruction which focuses on the student's abilities (linguistic and cognitive) while targeting the area of disability.

- The extent to which the student will participate with nondisabled (both LEP as well as English proficient) peers in a general education setting.

- An explanation of the basis for rejecting specific indicated services.

In considering interventions and approaches, it is important to include time for developing preskills, evaluating progress, and teaching review/remedial lessons when planning the sequence and scope of the instructional plan. The IEP must be coordinated with the scope and sequence of the general programs as well as the bilingual and special education programs. All this planning takes time but makes classroom life, teaching, and learning much easier for both teachers and students.

In considering method of instruction, remember to (1) proceed from the easiest to the most difficult tasks and (2) begin with the most frequently used tasks and move to the unique tasks.

The Language of Instruction

The child's performance on language proficiency tests in L_1 and L_2 is the basis for determining the language of instruction. Both basic interpersonal communication skills and cognitive/academic language proficiency should be assessed in both languages. Until children achieve some cognitive/academic proficiency in English, they should not receive content instruction relying heavily on English. Until children achieve some receptive proficiency in English, they should not receive English-only instruction in academic subject areas. Once they have developed substantial receptive English skills, children's development of English skills may benefit by their participation in English instruction while they receive concurrent review or alternative instruction in their native languages. The use of sheltered instruction techniques is recommended in *both* languages. Sheltered English instruction without L_1 is only recommended at third grade or higher achievement level. Also, use of the ratcheting technique discussed earlier in this chapter is highly recommended.

Teacher Responsibility

Planning should be a collaborative endeavor. However, the practical question may arise of which teacher is responsible for which instructional objectives. This may vary for different instructional objectives and will probably change over time as the student gains proficiency in English or different skill areas. The extreme importance of coordinating the services of all those involved in the planning and implementation of the child's instruction must be kept in mind. All too often, children are referred to special services without preplanned collaboration. This results in disjointed instructional efforts, and the student never receives comprehensive attention to needs. Without reinforcement of the student's new skills in all instructional settings, the child never learns to generalize and apply the skills.

To truly coordinate services and familiarize oneself with cultural and language needs, the teacher of the exceptional bilingual child must work with parents and cultural resource people. However, the teacher may feel concerned about being able to communicate effectively with resource people of these different cultures. Some valuable suggestions in cross-cultural communication are made by Scollon and Scollon (1980).

Scollon and Scollon suggest that the teacher should not dominate the conversation or talk too fast. They emphasize that being too intent, talking down to, and being overly boisterous are all impediments to cross-cultural communication between teachers and parents. Scollon and Scollon recommend the following:

1. Listen until the other person is finished.
2. Allow extra time.
3. Avoid situations with many people interacting at one time.
4. Talk openly about communication and discrimination.
5. Seek help.
6. Learn to accept and appreciate difference.

Whether or not the children in the class are culturally different, whether they speak a different language or a dialect of the dominant language, and whether or not they have some exceptional characteristics, it is important to remember that they are all human children. They feel, eat, and think like any other people.

Phase of Instruction

Different teachers may be responsible for different phases of instruction, that is, initiation, application, remediation, and maintenance. For example, an educable mentally retarded LEP child may be introduced to a new concept by the bilingual specialist in Spanish. After the child understands the general concept, the special education consultant may be able to provide broadening application instruction and assist the general education teacher in maintaining competency in the application of the concept or skill. The special education specialist would also be available for remediation if necessary, and both the bilingual and special education teachers can assist with sheltered instruction.

Learning Style

Teachers should consider the student's tendencies toward various cognitive learning styles and use specific cognitive learning strategies to address these. For example, the teacher could consider whether the student approaches tasks analytically or globally and with field independence or field sensitivity. Table 10–1 shows the relationship between styles and choice of strategy.

Time on Task

The planning team must consider the optimal time for each objective. This includes the consideration of attention span, classroom time available, and student's cultural time frame.

It is also important to identify what preskills are needed for each objective. In addition, the teacher should consider the mode of reinforcement to be used. There are many means of motivating students and reinforcing learning. The key for the bilingual exceptional student, as with all students, is to find out what is especially rewarding to that particular student. Some of these rewards may be praise, a smile, touching, being a student helper (for other students or teacher), free time, or cooperative or group success.

Selecting Methodology

In selecting the appropriate method of instruction, after determining the specific objectives, the IEP team may refer the teacher to specific curricular materials, while keeping in mind the earlier discussion of cultural relevance and transference problems. Other suggestions for techniques and strategies are provided in Chapter 11. The appropriateness and effectiveness of materials and methodology often become apparent only after trail and error, although

Table 10–1
Cognitive Styles, Associated Learning Styles, and Cognitive Learning Strategy Clusters

Cognitive Style	Associated Learning Styles	Cognitive Learning Strategy Clusters
1. FIELD Independent	Tendency to see everything as elements making up a whole: emphasis upon the parts and not the whole.	Evaluation
and Sensitive	Tendency to see the whole: difficulty separating the whole from its parts	Organization
2. TOLERANCE High Tolerance	Tendency to accept experiences that vary markedly from the ordinary or even from reality or the truth.	Analogy
and Low Tolerance	Tendency to show a preference for conventional ideas and reality	Coping Rehearsal
3. TEMPO Reflective	Tendency to take more time and generate more effort to provide appropriate responses	Active Processing
and Impulsive	Tendency to give first answer that comes to mind even if frequently wrong or inappropriate	Evaluation Rehearsal
4. CATEGORIZATION Broad	Tendency to include many items in a category and lessen the risk of leaving something out.	Analogy
and Narrow	Tendency to exclude doubtful items and lessen the probability of including something that doesn't belong	Evaluation Organization

this selection process can be enhanced and speeded up by discussing the adapted curriculum with other teachers, parents, or cultural consultants. Some specific interventions and approaches to consider are provided in the following discussion.

Integrated Curriculum. One method of instruction, which has proved to be useful in exceptional cross-cultural instruction, is the integrated curriculum (Collier & Hoover, 1986; Shoemaker, 1989; Collier, 1989). In the integrated curriculum, the teacher selects focal topics drawn from the lives of the students and develops specific skills and lessons around these general topics, integrating many specific skills and subject lessons into the central topic. For example, the teacher may develop an integrated curriculum around the general unit topic "The Family at Home." The students work on bilin-

Table 10–1 (cont.)
Cognitive Styles, Associated Learning Styles, and Cognitive Learning Strategy Clusters

Cognitive Style	Associated Learning Styles	Cognitive Learning Strategy Clusters
5. PERSISTENCE High	Tendency to work until the task has been completed: seeks any necessary help.	Active Processing
and Low	Tendency to short attention: inability to work on a task for any length of time.	Coping Evaluation
6. ANXIETY High	Tendency to perform less well when challenged by a difficult task.	Coping
and Low	Tendency to perform better when challenged by a difficult task.	Evaluation
7. LOCUS OF CONTROL Internal	Tendency to think of oneself as responsible for own behavior.	Active Processing
and External	Tendency to see circumstances as beyond one's own control: luck or others are seen as responsible for one's behavior.	Coping Evaluation

Note. Copyright 1992. All rights reserved, Dr. C. Collier

gual lessons that develop their skills in various subject areas.

1. Math and science skills: How does your father measure the logs for the corral? How is adobe made? How does your grandfather [or uncle] determine the proper time and season to tell stories? to shear the sheep? to plant the crops or harvest? What about the treatment of illness? Let's make some fry bread, sopapillas, or rice.

2. Language arts skills: Tell us about when you helped your grandmother. Tell or write about where your home is located. How does your mother teach you about what to do in the morning? Let's all read Kee's story about taking the lambs to water.

3. Motor/visual development: Draw a picture of your family, home, or maps of the area; build a model of hoghans or wickiups or make a diorama of the environment. Engage in traditional games and activities that build coordination, such as dancing or drama.

4. Other individualized lessons and activities designed to meet specific needs.

Culture Interventions. The IEP team should ask questions such as the following: Are the words and phrases used to describe the lesson and materials familiar to the child? Are they culturally correct? Are the vocabulary words in the native language or an approved translation? If translated materials are used, are they literal translations or conceptual translations, and are annotations available? If literal, problems in comprehension may result.

The teacher should consult the bilingual specialist about the meaning of materials that seem confusing or peculiar. The teacher must feel confident of the meaning in both cultural contexts. For example, if using Coyote stories, the teacher must understand what these meant in traditional cultures and use the best translations available. The teacher should be aware of seasonal prohibitions or limitations on use (some tribes have a certain time of year they can be told). It may frighten, worry, or otherwise convince students of the teacher's disrespect of their culture if stories are used improperly or in fun when serious. Yet the teacher should use them in the class. In the right context, they are an enriching experience for teacher and students alike.

Whenever materials possibly contradict the child's cultural beliefs, both sides should be discussed. The child may firmly believe that a hearing impairment or physical disability is caused by being out of harmony with the natural order in some way. The child may even have had a native practitioner treat the condition using traditional methods. In teaching the child compensatory techniques such as of movement or hearing, the teacher should acknowledge the positive contributions of the cultural practitioner and explain that learning new ways adds to the child's power to deal with the exceptionality. Nothing is subtracted. The teacher must find ways to integrate cultural practices with teaching. Rarely if ever are native practices and beliefs harmful, and supporting the children's belief in them while teaching new ways to deal with the exceptional condition may give the children more confidence in themselves and their cultural identities.

In many cultures, children are taught that it is improper to volunteer or that it is unwise to speak or answer unless absolutely sure of the answer (no guessing or using make believe). The teacher can teach children to respond this way if it is a necessary part of the classroom, but children cannot be expected to do so without developing the skill. The "pretend" or "what do you suppose" approach may create problems without adequate preparation. The teacher should always start with very real concrete actions and examples from the real life of students. Many students newly arrived in the United States are not familiar with items using electricity and the actions associated with the use of such items. The game/song "This is the way we . . ." (wash our clothes, etc.) is very common in primary classrooms. Yet, ironing, vacuuming, driving a car, or using washing machines would be confusing to children not exposed to the actions. The teacher should stick to common activities, such as walking and running at first.

The use of masks and puppets without adequate preparation should be avoided. Putting on a mask and acting or speaking through the character has more serious meaning in many traditional cultures than in the dominant American culture. It can be a very effective teaching method, but the teacher must be sure of underlying structural meaning in both cultural contexts before using it.

The teacher's own cultural teaching screen should be analyzed. Are competitive or cooperative rewards used in lessons? Is the teacher rewarding or paying more attention to individual behaviors over the whole group's performance or cooperative behavior? Is the teacher rewarding attending to task or achievement at the expense of behavior and vice versa? Many cultures do not prize individual achievement or competition. Children are trained to be cooperative—to help one another in need, to blend into the group—and to believe that the group's success is more important than individual success. By singling out for praise or censure, by identifying individuals by name during lessons, or by using bulletin board displays of the best work or graphing progress publicly (Pat's horse is way ahead of the others; Marty's is way behind), the teacher may be motivating the children to not do their best, to feel ashamed of their best, and to believe that their best means little. Alternate means of rewarding or encouraging achievement can be tried. Participation can be rewarded. Lessons can be organized in such a way that children of various ability are encouraged and rewarded for working together. "Cheating" is in the eyes of the teacher, not in the students helping one another. Everyone will produce something. Careful pairing of children with different skills and complementary learning styles, for example, may benefit all.

Clark and Yinger (1980) propose that routines can increase teacher efficiency and flexibility and can lead to structure in the student's environment. Routines for teachers lead to a style that reduces the need for planning each activity and lead to increased student time on the task, which is a central variable in school learning.

Finally, the teacher's communication to the student of a plan of what to do and how to do it leads to a commitment of cooperation and interaction in the teacher-learning process. Other specific interventions and approaches (Step 3) that need to be considered are those which address differing levels of acculturation, cognitive learning style differences, and specific language acquisition needs.

Acculturation Interventions. Interventions appropriate for students scoring at the less acculturated (below 20 on the AQS) level include translation, interpretation, and modification of normed instruments. Assistance with the acculturation process itself is also recommended. This may be done by providing school survival and adaptation assistance, including the use of bilingual assistance and bilingual materials. Cross-cultural communication strategies and L_1 instruction in the content areas is also recommended for these students, as well as sheltered instruction.

For students in transition (corresponds to a score of between 20 and 30 on the AQS), sheltered English with bilingual/multicultural content is appropriate. Peers tutors and cooperative learning strategies will also be useful with

these students. Access to translation in specific content areas may need to continue. Cross-cultural communication and instructional strategies that enhance the cross cultural competence of all students is also needed at this level. Cognitive learning strategies are an especially useful tool at this level. Authentic assessment is recommended.

Students who are more acculturated (a score on the AQS above 30) may still need cultural adaptation of content area instruction. They can serve as peer tutors, which will enhance their own progress. They may need continued access to translation. Cross-cultural communication and cross-cultural cognitive learning strategies will continue to be useful.

All students experiencing acculturation will benefit from a variety of psychosocial, communicative, cognitive, behavioral, and ethnoecological assistence. The frequency and extent of these interventions will vary according to their level and stage of acculturation and may be monitored by their performance on the AQS. Psychosocial assistance that addresses culture shock, response fatigue, confusion in locus of control, stress reactions, and other psychological side-effects of the acculturation process should also be provided. An example of this is guided practice in constructive, positive quality second culture (C_2)–second language (L_2) interactions. Role plays in constructive, positive quality C_2/L_2 interactions are also helpful, as well as sheltered interactions with variety of C_2 children and adults. Students may need survival strategies regarding rules of C_2 interactions and expectations. Cross-cultural counseling and the peer acculturation process support will help with this. Video tapes in L_1 about interaction patterns in America and guided practice in C_2 interaction strategies could be very helpful. Guidance in rest and relaxation techniques and a reduced level of stimuli will benefit these students. Cross-cultural communication strategies should be used with and taught to these students. First culture (C_1)–second culture (C_2) transition activities will continue to be useful.

Cognitive learning assistance which addresses differences in cognitive learning style, confusion in locus of control, resistance to change, distractibility, response fatigue, limited experience in academic settings, and other cognitive academic needs should be provided. Role play in cognitive academic interaction strategies and cognitive learning strategies, as well as guided practice in these strategies, will benefit the CLDE student. Cooperative learning strategies should be taught. Cross-cultural communication strategies and cognitive learning strategies, which include active processing strategy, organization strategy, coping strategy, evaluation strategy, analogy strategy, and rehearsal strategy, will benefit CLDE students needing cognitive learning assistance. Classroom and school survival strategies, including self-monitoring techniques, would also be helpful. Instruction in L_1/L_2 cognitive academic interactions and guided practice in L_1/L_2 CALP transitions will help as well. This would be followed by L_2 cognitive academic interaction reinforcement. Context embedded instruction (sheltered instruction techniques) along with mediated stimuli in the classroom and concrete demonstrations is also recommended, along with reduced stimuli in the classroom. Videotapes in L_1 about American school procedures, expectations, and rules could also be used.

Communicative assistance that addresses code-switching, stages in second language acquisition, development of BICS and CALP in both languages, comprehensible input, and other communicative needs could include some guided practice in constructive, positive quality interactions with L_2. Role play in L_2 BICS and CALP development, L_1/L_2 CALP instruction and transition, guided practice in L_2 BICS, and L_1/L_2 transition activities will be beneficial to CLDE students needing communicative assistance. Sheltered instruction and peer bilingual tutoring are tools that will be helpful. The use of listening activities is recommended. Guided practice and planned interactions with different L_2 speakers will also be helpful. Cross-cultural survival interaction strategies as well as cross-cultural communication strategies should be used and taught. Sheltered English should be used. Videotapes in L_1 about American speech patterns are helpful for these CLDE students. Interactive language learning strategies should be provided.

Behavioral assistance which addresses distractibility, disorientation, confusion in locus of control, withdrawal, acting out, and other behavioral side effects of the acculturation process might include guided practice in constructive positive quality interactions with children from the dominant culture. Role play in constructive, positive quality interactions with children and adults from the mainstream culture will also help. These students should be taught cooperative behavior strategies. The use of peer support groups and cross-cultural counseling is recommended. Teaching coping strategies will help. Giving guided practice in C_1/C_2 behavior transition activities and in classroom behavior expectations and survival strategies will help. Teaching cross-cultural behavior strategies and guided practice in cross-cultural conflict resolution strategies is recommended. Videotapes in L_1 about behavior patterns and expectations in America would be very helpful as well as filmed observations of various behavior interactions and settings in U.S. schools.

Ethnoecological assistance which addresses the adaptation needs of children within the family and community should be provided. Guided practice in dealing with government services, sponsoring agencies, school, or service providers would be helpful. Family centered learning activities, such as literacy, discipline, and English classes, are recommended. Guided practice in C_1/C_2 interactions in community settings (store, schools, church, government agencies, police, etc.) is needed. Videotapes in L_1 about American schools, communities, social service providers, laws, etc. could be part of teaching survival strategies for families. Cross-cultural counseling for families might include cross-cultural conflict resolution techniques and strategies and cross-cultural communication strategies. C_1/C_2 transition activities should be provided for families and community groups and might cover assistance about school expectations, structures, systems, and laws.

Cognitive Learning Style Interventions. Learning styles differ within both the cultural and the individual context (Kagan, 1965; Cornett, 1983). Some children appear to learn better from auditory rather than visual cues and vice versa. Some seem to learn better in shorter time spans than in long concentrated periods of study or repetition. The ability or inability to distinguish a specific object as a discrete entity within a general pattern may also be a matter of learning style (Collier & Hoover, 1987a). Some children appear to learn better from a global approach rather than from an analytical approach (Mosley & Spicker, 1975). An example of this is use of the whole-word "sight" approach as opposed to the word-analysis "phonics" approach in teaching reading (Chall, 1967). Children may need to be taught how to think analytically before such skills as the "phonics" approach are possible (Almanza & Mosley, 1980). However, an initial inability to distinguish particular phonemes of English may be a sign of the non-English speaking students' second language development and not necessarily an indication of global versus analytical learning style. Woodward (1981) notes that many LEP students from non-Western European cultures learn better from a visual approach.

The majority of LEP students may be visually oriented and accustomed to rote learning. Thus, the "look and say" approach may be more effective than the phonetic approach during the beginning stage. During the initial period their auditory discrimination skills are not at a sufficient level to identify some sound differences in English which do not exist in their primary language.

Major perceptual modalities, as well as cultural and linguistic factors, may affect learning style. The perceptual modes usually considered in special education are visual, auditory, kinesthetic, and tactile (Bolander, Lamb, & Ramirez, 1981). The *visual* and *auditory* modes are the most frequently used in the classroom today. Students are constantly required to use these as they "look and listen" to classroom instruction. The *kinesthetic* mode involves adding movement to the learning process. An example of kinesthetic learning is tracing a letter or word over and over again, so that the student feels the motion required to make that letter or word. *Tactile* means touching. Beaded alphabet cards are an example of a material that makes use of tactile cues to teach letter discrimination.

A particular perceptual cue or modality may not work well with a particular student. Just as there are variations in abilities within any classroom, there are also variations in perceptual styles. Students with perceptual problems may have 20/20 vision and not understand what they see. Students may have normal hearing but be unable to understand or remember all that they hear. Students with limited English proficiency (LEP) may have difficulty relying on the auditory modality for learning because of the phonetic differences discussed earlier.

Cultural learning styles should also be considered in identifying the most appropriate interventions and approaches (Collier & Hoover, 1987a). Does the culture emphasize group achievement and conformity? Does the child react negatively to individual praise and positively to praise as a member of a successful group? Does the child respond better to adult-directed instruction than to individualized seat work or peer tutoring? Is it more culturally appropriate to use physical demonstrations and experience activities rather than diagrams and verbal/visual directions?

The teacher should teach to the student's strengths to maximize the student's chances for success in the classroom. The teacher should teach to strengths in a group setting and to areas that need strengthening in an individual setting. Many educators of exceptional children recommend using a multisensory approach. Bolander, Lamb, and Ramirez (1981) describe the use of this approach in the LEP classroom. A multisensory approach, using several modalities, is very effective for use with LEP students. The teacher uses methods and materials which first teach to the student's strengths. For example, the teacher would address the visual learner's visual style and then involve the auditory, kinesthetic, and tactile modalities.

At times, a teacher may not be able to adapt an instructional program well enough to meet the student's needs. In that case, the teacher should use a different approach. For example, if the teacher is using a reading program that employs a phonetic approach, a visual learner with severe auditory discrimination problems will have difficulty learning to read, even if the teacher makes use of visual aids. The student's needs would be better met with the look-say approach to reading.

Since the student uses all of his or her learning styles in the learning process, a teacher should remember to teach to the student's strengths while remediating the student's weaknesses where possible. This process will provide opportunities for more integrated learning.

A teacher who has limited or no skills in the CLDE child's native language should make greater use of the visual, kinesthetic, and tactile modalities. The auditory modality should not be used with CLDE students who lack the language skills to comprehend auditory information. However, the auditory modality is the most important in the acquisition of language and thus cannot be ignored. The CLDE student should not, however, be kept from progressing in other areas while he or she is working on acquiring competent second language skills.

The use of multisensory approaches coupled with multicultural materials and cross-cultural techniques is a good beginning in bridging the bilingual/bicultural and special learning needs of the CLDE child. In addition to differences in learning styles, the educational needs of these children also differ in regard to exceptionality. Brief guidelines for working with specific dis-

ability conditions, CLDE children, and the use of teaching specific strategies are discussed elsewhere in this book.

Language and Content Reinforcement. Language and content reinforcement activities, such as games and role play, may be used in versatile ways to supplement content lessons at any grade level. Content and language card games (Collier, 1985) are best used as review, reinforcement, or assessment tools. There are three basic games which can be created and used with cards: sets, pairs, and memory. Each of the three basic games can be varied according to specific lesson objectives. Teacher or student created or purchased decks of cards can be tailored to specific content areas or to specific language acquisition needs. The following, adapted from Collier, details the construction and use of language development card decks designed for use in bilingual and ESL programs. Each deck of cards is designed to reinforce or assess specific language learning concepts or content.

Constructing the Cards: Classroom teachers can prepare their own deck of cards to fit the particular content or language skill they wish to reinforce. Cards can be copied or created based upon any curricular content. This is a good substitute use for commercial flash cards. The best size is a $3'' \times 5''$ index card, and they should be laminated or covered with plastic if at all possible. Be careful not to let colors bleed through if students hand color the cards with markers. When possible, having students assist in designing and constructing the cards engages them in the learning process. Complete decks of already designed cards are available from other sources.

The Games: There are three basic games: sets, pairs, and memory. All of these three games can be played to reinforce or assess receptive and expressive language, visual and auditory memory, or content literacy. They can also be used to reinforce or assess cognitive learning balance in tempo, tolerance, persistence, and categorization styles. If students are nonverbal, the games can be played through cognitive visual matching. If students are limited English proficient, the games can be played in their native language, and later bilingually. A set of bilingual cards can be created by starting with native language cards, adding English language captions, and finally adding English language pairs to the set.

By mixing familiar and imaginary images and words, requiring reflection and association, the games can be used to reinforce cognitive learning balance in tempo, tolerance, persistence, and categorization styles. The cards may be used to review basic concepts, vocabulary words, or other content. The games can be played periodically during the school year to provide a review of foundation concepts when making a transition to a new topic or subject matter.

Assessment: The games may be used as an alternate assessment process. By watching the students play the card games, especially when a lot of expressive and receptive language is required, the teacher will be able to observe the extent to which individual students have acquired the learning concepts and content or how well they have retained previously presented information.

SETS: Each group playing should get a deck with 8 to 12 sets of four cards of each concept. There should be two to six in each group playing the game. The object of the game is to collect the most sets of four-of-a-kind. Cards are dealt one at a time with each player receiving five cards. The rest of the pack is placed face down in the center of the table to form the "draw" pile. Have the students choose the first player by names alphabetically, ages, or other device. Starting with the first player, each player calls another by name and requests cards of a specific type, as: "David, do you have any Red?" or "David, kavirliten taiski." The player asking must hold at least one of the type of card requested. The player asked must give up the card requested, saying: "Yes, Kala, I have a Red" or "Eii, Kala, kavirliq tuten." Another

variation of this is to have the player ask for the category first. For example, "David, do you have anyone signing?" David holds up a card and says, "Yes, Kala, I have someone singing. Who/what is it?" If Kala successfully identifies the picture, "That is a bird singing," then she gets the card. Another variation is to have equations on the cards. For example: $4 + 4$, $2 + 6$, $3 + 5$, $9 - 1$. The student asks, "Bahe, do you have any 8s? (Tseebii' hoo'lo?)" Bahe holds up a card with $2 + 6$ on it and says, "Yes, what is it? (Haash woolye?)" David replies, "8" (Tseebii') to receive the card. The player asked does not have to say she has more of the set of cards if she has more than one of the same set of cards. The player requesting has to ask for each individual card, e.g., "David, do you have another card about the Civil War?"

If the player asked does not have any cards of the type requested, then she says "Draw!" and the asker draws the top card from the draw pile. A player's turn to ask continues so long as she is successful in getting the cards requested. If he is told to draw and happens to draw a card of the type requested, the player may show this card, name it, and continue the turn. As soon as the players get a set of all four cards of one type, they must show them and give the names of the cards out loud, placing them on the table in front of them. If played competitively, the player who collects the most sets by the end of the game wins.

PAIRS: Each group playing should get a deck with 8 to 12 sets of four cards of each concept. Three to six players are in each group. The object is to match all the pairs and to avoid getting left with the single one. First one card is taken out of the deck and placed aside; the remaining cards are dealt one at a time. All of the cards are dealt; it does not matter if the distribution is unequal.

Play I: Players look at their group of cards and pick out all the pairs. They place these on the table in front of them while naming out loud the items depicted. When all the hands have been reduced to nonpaired cards, the starting player presents her cards to her left-hand neighbor, making sure he cannot see their faces, saying "Pick a card." If the card drawn matches one in his hand, the neighbor lays the pair down, saying: "These are both about Abraham Lincoln," or "These are a pair of something blue." He then presents his cards to his left-hand neighbor. Play continues in the same way around the table, each player drawing a card from the hand at the right, paired cards being put on the table, until only the odd card remains. The player stuck with the odd card is out of the game. Play continues until one player is left.

Play II: This is best played with two or three, but not more than four players. Players place their pile of cards face down on the table in front of them. All the players simultaneously turn over one card. If two of the cards match, the first player to say "Pair!" gets to keep the pair of cards. Pairs are set aside next to the player winning them. The player must tell the other players how the cards make a pair before placing them in his winning pile, e.g., "These are a pair of 'He is running'" or "These are both about the Rainforest." If she cannot explain how they make a pair, she cannot keep them. Play continues until all the cards are matched. A prize can be given to the player making the most successful matches, if played competitively.

MEMORY: Each group playing should get a deck with 8 to 12 sets of four cards of each concept. There should be two to four players in each group. The object of this game is to match all the pairs and to get the most pairs matched. All of the cards are dealt one at a time, face down on the table. It is easier if they form a symmetrical pattern, i.e., a square or rectangle, and more challenging if placed randomly. The starting player turns two cards face up, one at a time, without moving either away from its position on the table. If the two cards are a pair, she places them in front of her and names them to the other players, e.g., "These are both something blue; this is a blue cat and this is a

blue cup" or "These are both 'She is running.' " She turns up two more cards. When she turns up two cards which are not a pair, she turns the cards face down, without disturbing their location, and the turn passes to her left-hand neighbor. The player who gathers the most cards wins the game. It is important to have the students monitor one another in always giving descriptions of the pairs out loud and in as complete a way as is appropriate for their level of development.

STEP 4: IDENTIFY APPROPRIATE TIMELINE AND EXPECTATIONS

It is also beneficial for the teachers to determine how much time is available to achieve a particular goal, especially if the child is to be exited from special education by a certain date or upon completion of a particular skill. The teachers need to work closely together to assure that the exceptional bilingual child receives the time necessary for the acquisition of the needed skill or intervention program.

After identifying appropriate instructional services, strategies, and approaches, the IEP group determines realistic timelines for each specific intervention and when and how the outcomes will be measured. This measurement must be described within the context of the student's second language acquisition and acculturation needs.

The timeline includes the projected date for the initiation of special education and related services, the amount of time per day the pupil will receive such services, and whether the pupil is eligible for a 12-month educational program. The timeline establishes the time limits for specific interventions and service options, as well as documenting the schedule for specific reevaluations and monitoring meetings.

STEP 5: IDENTIFY MONITORING SCHEDULE

Finally, the IEP group determines an appropriate schedule for monitoring and retesting/

reevaluating the LEP student's progress with learning and behavior development. This schedule should include expected benchmarks for second language acquisition and acculturation for this CLDE student. The IEP group identifies specific instruments and procedures that will be used and records these on their form.

This assessment monitoring is a cyclical process. As prescribed services and interventions are implemented, the service provider keeps track of and documents the LEP student's responses to specific approaches and strategies. In addition, the IEP contains a schedule for annual and triennial monitoring and subsequent reassessment of the CLDE student's overall progress on their prescribed learning and behavior goals.

The plan for monitoring should indicate the individual responsible for each element of the monitoring process and should include: (1) regular assessment and evaluation of the student's level of performance in targeted learning and behavior areas of concern, (2) regular assessment of the CLDE student's second language acquisition, (3) periodic review of his or her degree of acculturation and response to acculturative stress, and (4) monitoring the student's changing responses to the school environment and to the acquisition of new cognitive learning strategies.

Depending upon the CLDE student's response to sociocultural prescriptions and interventions, and to those prescribed to address the student's learning and behavior problem, the monitoring process may result in reassessing the placement decision and the student's return to the general education program. On the other hand, as the CLDE student successfully resolves the identified learning and behavior problems, additional problems may be manifested. In addition, the CLDE student may continue to need assistance with second language acquisition and acculturation.

If it is determined that the LEP student has achieved the goals on his/her present IEP, but new needs have become manifest, monitoring would result in a reassessment of the student's

needs and a subsequent revision of the IEP. The monitoring schedule includes annual and triennial reviews.

Annual Reviews

At a reasonable time, prior to conducting the annual review, the "Parent Notification of Reassessment" is sent to the parents in their native language. All annual review proceedings must be understandable to the parents. For all students receiving special education services, the service provider must attend the conference. If the attendance of a bilingual professional is not possible, a translator must attend the meeting. The participation of bilingual professionals and translators must be documented in the IEP.

At the annual review, the IEP of each LEP student with disabilities must be reviewed. Information that should be available for this review includes:

- Updated language proficiency test results in the native language and in English. This should include both BICS and CALP.

- Updated acculturation level records, e.g., AQS results.

- Current levels of performance as measured in accordance with the student's level of first and second language proficiency.

- A statement concerning the language of instruction that is being used for each IEP goal and objective.

Implementation of the recommendation must occur within 10 calendar days subsequent to the final recommendation or as specified on the IEP. This may include those instances where there has been a change in the services provided from bilingual to monolingual, or monolingual to bilingual.

Triennial Evaluation

The triennial evaluation is a comprehensive reevaluation of a student with a disability condition which is conducted every three years. The same guidelines to determine if a bilingual assessment is needed, as described in Chapters 1 and 2, apply to the triennial evaluation. The purpose of the triennial evaluation for the LEP student is the same as for monolingual students: to update the LEP student's present levels of educational performance (including performance in both languages) and to analyze and document the student's instructional needs.

☺ SUMMARY

This chapter has discussed the five steps involved in developing an IEP for culturally and linguistically diverse exceptional students. Each step has been described and specific examples of implementation have been provided.

There are no simple steps to developing and adapting curriculum materials to meet the special needs of CLDE children. It is a process of consciousness raising; a deliberate, self-directed effort on the part of the concerned teacher to become culturally and linguistically sensitive as well as competent to deal with a range of exceptionalities. The development of cultural sensitivity and comprehensive teaching competencies are at the root of successful bilingual special education curriculum development and adaptation. Without them, all our suggestions and examples are for naught.

The nine considerations for the IEP team to keep in mind while developing the individual educational plan are:

1. Individualize the problem. Consider what the child can and cannot do in particular situations, his/her level of functioning, relevant medical data, cultural/linguistic background, and educational history. Modify curricular materials as necessary.

2. Remember that comprehension precedes demonstration. If the child is unable to perform at a certain level as expected, the child may not have correctly understood and assimilated the concept. It may be advantageous to maintain the use of the native language for additional instruction.

3. Use appropriate cognitive learning strategies.

4. Control the environment. Eliminate distractions. Place the child near the teacher when appropriate. Introduce new materials and concepts gradually.

5. Motivate with success. Create a learning environment that ensures success. Build on the child's success and keep learning steps to attainable size—whatever is appropriate for each child.

6. Remediate needs; teach to strengths. Identify what/where/how a child can do something and use that information to assist the child with what cannot yet be done.

7. Sequence tasks. Present instruction in small structured developmental units. Proceed from the known to the unknown by developmental steps, relating previously learned skills to new tasks. Krashen (1994) refers to this as $i + 1$ learning (i = what the student knows).

8. Use feedback. Feedback is a two-way street. Feedback from students can be used diagnostically to assess progress and modify the individual planning. Students need to receive feedback from teachers. The sooner the child receives feedback about a response, the more learning is facilitated. Feedback from the students to the teacher can facilitate the teacher's learning also.

9. Reinforce learning. Systematic reinforcement must be given as the desired behavior occurs. Reinforcement should be consistent and appropriate at all times. At the beginning stages, reinforcement may be more frequent and gradually become more intermittent as skills are mastered. Students should continue to receive some form of reinforcement upon mastery to encourage the maintenance of the skill.

☺ DISCUSSION QUESTIONS

1. Discuss the instructional implications of three sociocultural considerations covered in the chapter. How will these affect your identification and monitoring process?

2. Using either case studies provided by the instructor or actual students with whom you are working, compare and contrast two identified bilingual special education students following the five IEP steps outlined in this chapter. How do the interventions and approaches recommended for these students differ and how are they similar? Discuss what you think the MDT's reasoning was in each case.

3. Discuss what you can do to address a referred student's acculturation needs for the following identified disabilities:
   a) Hearing impairments
   b) Learning disabilities
   c) Multiple handicaps
   d) Emotional disabilities
   e) Visual impairments
   f) Speech impairments

4. Using one of the student cases you explored in Question 1, develop an appropriate plan of intervention, including at least four elements outlined in the chapter. Provide elaboration on how you would implement this plan of intervention and why.

5. Discuss the cultural and linguistic implications of monitoring timelines typical of IEPs in your local schools.

☺ REFERENCES

Adler, P. S. (1965). The transitional experience: An alternative view of culture shock. *Journal of Humanistic Psychology, 15*, 13–23.

Albino-Cordero, H. P. (1981). *An investigation of the effects of bilingualism and non-bilingual school programs on pupil adjustment.* Unpublished doctoral dissertation, University of Connecticut.

Almanza, H. P., & Mosley, W. J. (1980). *A perspective on curriculum adaptations and modifications for culturally diverse disabled children.* Unpublished paper.

Argulewicz, E. D., & Elliott, S. N. (1981, August). *Validity of the SRBCSS for Hispanic and gifted students.* Paper presented at the meeting of the American Psychological Association, Los Angeles.

Baca, L., Fradd, S. H., & Collier, C. (1990). Progress in preparing personnel to meet the needs of handicapped limited English proficient students: Results of a survey in three highly impacted states. *Journal of Educational Issues of Language Minority Students, 7*, 5–20.

Berry, J. W. (1976). *Human ecology and cognitive style: Comparative studies in cultural psychological adaptation.* New York: Sage/Halsted.

Blumenthal, A. L. (1977). *The process of cognition.* Upper Saddle River, NJ: Prentice Hall.

Bolander, M., Lamb, E., & Ramirez, J. L. (1981). *Coordinated services for disabled LEP students.* Program developed for the Houston Independent School District.

Center for Innovation in Teaching the Disabled (1974). *Tips for Teachers.* Bloomington, IN: Indiana University.

Chall, J. (1967). *Learning to read: The great debate.* New York: McGraw-Hill.

Chesarek, S. (1981, March). *Cognitive consequences of home or school education in a limited second language: A case study in the Crow Indian bilingual community.* Paper presented at the Language Proficiency Assessment Symposium, Airlie House, VA.

Chomsky, N. (1971). *Problems of knowledge and freedom.* New York: Pantheon Books.

Clark, C. M., & Yinger, R. S. (1980). *The hidden world of teaching: Implications of research on teacher planning.* Ann Arbor, MI: Michigan State University, Institute for Research on Teaching.

Collier, C. (1985). A comparison of acculturation and education characteristics of referred and nonreferred culturally and linguistically different children. *Dissertation Abstracts International, 46*, 2993A.

Collier, C. (1989). *Thematic integration.* Unpublished manuscript.

Collier, C., & Hoover, J. J. (1986). *Classroom management through curricular adaptations: Educating minority handicapped students.* Lindale, TX: Hamilton Publications.

Collier, C., & Hoover, J. J. (1987a). *Cognitive learning strategies for diverse disabled students.* Lindale, TX: Hamilton Publications.

Collier, C., & Hoover, J. J. (1987b). Sociocultural considerations when referring diverse children for learning disabilities. *LD Focus, 3*(1), 39–45.

Collier, C., & Hoover, J. J. (1989). Methods and materials for bilingual special education. In L. M. Baca & H. Cervantes (Eds.), *The bilingual special education interface* (2nd ed.) (pp. 231–255). New York: Merrill.

Commins, N. (1986). *A descriptive study of the linguistic abilities of four low-achieving Hispanic bilingual students.* Unpublished doctoral dissertation, University of Colorado, Boulder.

Cornett, C. E. (1983). *What you should know about teaching and learning.* Bloomington, MN: Phi Delta Kappa Education Foundation.

Cummins, J. (1986). The role of primary language development in promoting educational success for language minority students. In *Schooling and language minority students: A theoretical framework* (pp. 3–51). Los Angeles, CA: Evaluation, Dissemination, and Assessment Center, California State University, Los Angeles.

Curtiss, S. (1982). Developmental disassociation of language and cognition. In K. Obler & E. Menes (Eds.), *Exceptional language and linguistics* (pp. 139–159). New York: Academic Press.

Epstein, H. T. (1978). Growth spurts during brain development: Implications for educational policy and practice. In J. Chall & A. Mirsky (Eds.), *Education and the brain* (pp. 343–370). Chicago, IL: University of Chicago Press.

Farnham-Diggory, S. (1972). *Cognitive processes in education.* New York: Harper & Row.

Finn, J. D. (1982). Patterns in special education placement as revealed by the OCR surveys. In K. A. Heller, W. H. Holtzman, & S. Messick (Eds.), *Placing children in special education: A strategy for equity* (pp. 322–381). Washington, DC: National Academy Press.

Gardner, R. W., Jackson, D. N., & Messick, S. J. (1960). Personality organization in cognitive controls and intellectual abilities. *Psychological Issues, 2,* 1–149.

Goodenough, W. H. (1957). Cultural anthropology and linguistics. In P. Garvin (Ed.), *Report of the 7th annual meeting on linguistics and language study* (Monograph series on Language and Linguistics, No. 9, pp. 167–173). Washington, DC: Georgetown University.

Grosjean, F. (1982). *Life with two language: An introduction to bilingualism.* Cambridge, MA: Harvard University Press.

Hoover, J. J., & Collier, C. (1985). Referring culturally different children for special education: Sociocultural considerations. *Academic Therapy, 20,* 503–510.

Hoover, J. J., & Collier, C. (1986). *Classroom management through curricular adaptations: Educating diverse disabled students.* Lindale, TX: Hamilton Publications.

Hoover, J. J., & Collier, C. (Eds.) (1991). Bilingual Special Education [Special Issue]. *Teacher Education and Special Education.*

Juffer, K. A. (1983). Initial development and validation of an instrument to access degree of culture shock adaptation. In R. J. Bransford (Ed.), *Monograph Series* (4), (pp. 136–149). Boulder, CO: BUENO Center for Multicultural Education.

Kagan, J. (1965). Reflection/impulsivity and reading ability in primary grade children. *Child Development, 36,* 509.

Keogh, B. K. (1973). Perceptual and cognitive styles: Implications for special education. In L. Mann & D. Sabatino (Eds.), *The first review of special education.* Philadelphia, JSE Press.

Krashen, S. D. (1994). Bilingual education and second language acquisition theory. In C. F. Leyba (Ed.), *Schooling and language minority students: A theoretical framework* (2nd ed.) (pp. 47–75). Los Angeles, CA: Evaluation, Dissemination, and Assessment Center, California State University.

Lenneberg, E. H. (1967). *Biological foundations of language.* New York: Wiley.

Mann, L., & Sabatino, D. A. (1985). *Foundation of cognitive process in remedial and special education.* Austin, TX: Pro-Ed.

McLean, G. D. (1981). *Bilingual special education programs: A needs study based on a survey of directors of bilingual education and special education in United States school districts receiving Title VII ESEA funds.* Ph.D. dissertation. University of Colorado.

Mosley, W. M., & Spicker, H. H. (1975). Mainstreaming for the educationally deprived. *Theory into Practice, 14,* 73–81.

Nazarro, J. N. (Ed.). (1981). *Culturally diverse exceptional children*. Reston, VA: Council for Exceptional Children.

Padilla, A. (Ed.), (1980). *Acculturation: Theory, models, and some new findings*. Boulder, CO: Westview Press.

Pinker, S. (1994). *The language instinct: How the mind creates language*. New York: HarperCollins.

Ramirez, M., & Castaneda, A. (1974). *Cultural democracy: Bicognitive development and education*. New York: Academic Press.

Scollon, R., & Scollon, S. B. (1980). *Interethnic communication*. Fairbanks, AK: University of Alaska, Alaska Native Language Center.

Serrano, V. Z. (1982). *Migrant handicapped children: A second look at their special education needs*. Report for the Education Commission of the States. Washington, DC: Educational Improvement Center.

Shavelson, R., & Stern, P. (1981). Research on teachers' pedagogical thoughts, judgments, decisions and behavior. *Review of Educational Research, 51,* 455–498.

Shoemaker, B. J. E. (1989). Integrative education: A curriculum for the 21st century. *Oregon School Study Council, October 1989* (33, Whole No. 2).

Skutnabb-Kangas, T., & Toukamaa, P. (1976). *Teaching migrant children's mother tongue and learning the language of the host country in the context of the sociocultural situation of the migrant family*. Helsinki: UNESCO.

Slobin, D. I. (1979). *Psycholinguistics*. New York: Scott Foresman.

Snow, C. E. (1984). Parent-child interaction. In R. L. Schiefelbusch & J. Pickar (Eds.), *The acquisition of communicative competence* (pp. 70–107). Baltimore, MD: University Park Press.

Stone, C. A., & Wertsch, J. V. (1984). A social interactional analysis of learning disabilities remediation. *Journal of Learning Disabilities, 17,* 194–198.

Szapocznik, J. & Kurtines, W. (1980). Acculturation, biculturalism, and adjustment among Cuban-Americans. In A. Padilla (Ed.), *Acculturation: Theory, models, and some new findings* (pp. 139–160). Boulder, CO: Westview Press.

Wells, C. G. (1981). *Learning through interaction: The study of language development*. Cambridge, England: Cambridge University Press.

Woodward, M. M. (1981). *Indiana experiences with LEP students: Primarily with Indochinese refugee children*. Report to the Indiana Department of Instruction.

Individualized Education Program (IEP)

Student's Name ___XX_____JOSE_____   Birthdate ___5/16/88___

　　　　　　　　Last　　　First　　　Middle　　　　　　　　　　　Month/Day/Year

Neighborhood School _____Smith Elementary_____   Age __10__ Grade __4th__

Placement School _____Smith Elementary_____   Initial IEP __X_Yes ___No

Date of Latest Multidisciplinary Team (MDT) Evaluation _____

Surrogate Parent Needed? ___Yes ___No

Date of IEP Meeting _____9/30/97_____ Anticipated Review Date of IEP _____3/31/98_____

　　　　　　　　　Month/Day/Year　　　　　　　　　　　　　　　Month/Day/Year

IEP Participants Present (signature) Please indicate whether you agree (A) or disagree (D) beside your name.

_____　　_____

Parent/Guardian/Surrogate　　　　　　　　Parent/Guardian/Surrogate

_____　　_____

Student　　　　　　　　　　　　　　　　District Representative

_____　　_____

Teacher/Staff　　　　　　　　　　　　　　MDT

_____　　_____

Bilingual/Aide　　　　　　　　　　　　　Name/Role

_____　　_____

ESL Teacher　　　　　　　　　　　　　　Name/Role

Special Education and Related Service	Amount of Service (Hours/Minutes)	Project Start Date	Expected Duration of Service	Person Responsible (indicate position)
EH classroom	3 hours a day	10/1/97	One semester	Special Educator
Needed Additional Services				
ESL	1 hour a day	10/1/97	One year	BE/ESL staff
Bilingual	1 hour a day	10/1/97	One year	Aide in 4th grade
Crosscultural Adaptation	4 hours a day	10/1/97	One year	Classroom teacher

Special media, materials or modifications, if necessary, in special or regular education classes: __Bilingual__ __assistance, crosscultural adaptation of materials and instruction, cross-cultural and accul-__ __turation counseling__

Adaptations necessary in physical education: _____

Adaptations necessary in vocational education: ___Bilingual assistance. ESL in content areas___

Need for extended school year: __Yes __No   Delayed Until (Date) _____

Month/Day/Year

Rationale for decision: _____

_____

If yes, specific goals: _____

_____

Estimated time/duration (i.e., 2 hours/day - 4 days/week): _____

JUSTIFICATION FOR PLACEMENT

Placement Options Considered

Based on current assessment results and recommendations, the following placement options were sequentially considered by the MDT in order to determine the most appropriate placement to meet the student's IEP goals and objectives.

Check each placement option considered:

Reason option rejected:

✓	A. General education class	Cannot meet needs
✓	B. General education class with consulting services	Possible goal, but doesn't meet current needs
✓	C. General education class with in-class special education instruction	Would not meet language needs
✓	D. General education class with pull-out related services	Will combine with BE/ESL adaptations
✓	E. General education class with pull-out special education services	Will have Jose in adapted behavior modification
✓	F. Home instruction	No one home during day & isn't needed
✓	G. Hospital instruction	Not needed
✓	H. Residential school	Not needed
✓	I. Self-contained special education class	ESL not available
✓	J. Special education class with integration into general education class and/or community	Does not meet language and culture needs
✓	K. Other	Not applicable

Individualized Education Program (IEP) *(cont.)*

PLACEMENT DECISION

The recommended program placement is: _____ EH pullout with BE/ESL adaptation _____

Supporting comments: _____ Jose needs some immediate intervention in achieving _____ control over his behavior in class. He also needs assistance in adapting to school culture and language (CALP)

The program placement selected is located at: _____ Smith Elementary _____

Is this the student's neighborhood school? __X__ Yes _____ No

If no, explain: _____

Opportunities are available for integrated extra curricular/non-academic (meals, assemblies, transportation, field trips, sports, other): __X__ Yes _____ No

If yes, identify: _____ Jose will remain with his 4th grade class for non-academic and extra curricular activities

If no, explain: _____

Amount of general education participation: _____ Teacher will have Jose in sheltered English activities during the first half of the day

Parent(s) comments (optional):
_____
_____
_____

PRESENT LEVELS OF PERFORMANCE ANNUAL GOALS AND OBJECTIVES			
Present Levels of Performance	Annual Goals	Short Term Objectives Measurable and include (1) Objective Criteria, (2) Evaluation Procedures and (3) Schedules	Objectives Achieved (Date/Initials)
Reading at first grade level (English)	Continuing progress in English development (L3)	Increase reading level in English to second grade level by 5/30/98	
Fluent Quechua speaker	Maintain native language capacity (L1)	Demonstrate capacity as measured by home interviews	
BICS well established in Spanish	Maintain Spanish language capacity and build upon it (L2) for L3 development	Demonstrate L2-L3 capacity as measured by Woodcock-Munoz 5/30/98	
Some CALP in Spanish-none in English	Build upon L2 CALP for L3 CALP development	Increase L2 and L3 CALP as measured by Woodcock Munoz 5/30/98	
K-ABC is 105 in Spanish	Maintain abilities and transfer to English	By 5/30/98, increase ability performance in English as measured by K-ABC	
Extreme acting out and 'temper tantrums'	Develop self-control over outbursts	Increase use of self monitoring skills and decrease number of outbursts as measured by teacher observation and self-monitoring checklists	

Prereferral Review for Diverse Students

Student: _____ DOB: _____ Age: _____ Date: _____

School: _____ Grade: _____

Person Making Request: _____ Position: _____

Acculturation Quick Screen (AQS) Summary		
Cultural Environmental Factors	Raw Scores	Scaled Scores
1. Number of years in United States		
2. Number of years in School District		
3. Number of years in ESL/Bilingual Education		
4. Bilingual Proficiency Category		
5. Native Language Proficiency		
6. English Language Proficiency		
7. Ethnicity/Nation of Origin		
8. % of Minority in Present School		
AQS Score Total:		
Interpretation Guidelines: 0 - 20 Less Acculturated 21 - 31 In transition 32 - 40 More Acculturated		

Reasons for Concern:		
Physical	Adjustment	Academic
• Vision	• Overly Quiet	• Low for Age
• Speech	• Distractible	• Low for Grade
• Coordination	• Impulsive	• Off-Task Often
• General Health	• Easily Frustrated	• Forgets Day to Day
• Physical Disability	• Acts Out a Lot	• Receptive Language
• Writing	• Disruptive	• Directions
• Restlessness	• Upset Easily	• Comprehension
• Low Energy	• Poor Interaction Skills	• Expressive Language
• Ear Infections	• Low Interaction	• Inappropriate Responses
• Hearing	• Needs Lots of Attention	• Unresponsive
• Other	• Shows Avoidance	• Cannot Apply Learning
	• Withdrawn	• Low Response Rate
	• Poor Response When Corrected	• Other
	• Out of School Factors	
	• Other	

Student: _____ DOB: _____ Age: ____ Date: _____

Health Factors:

Vision: _____ Screen Date: _____ Glasses: Y or N Date: _____

Hearing: ____ Screen Date: _____ History of Ear Infections: Y or N

Developmental Problems: Y or N Other _____

	Academic Interventions Tried	Duration	Comments
	Translation (Languages)		
	Adapted Instructional Materials (Examples)		
	Varied Strategies (Examples)		
	Sheltered Instruction (Examples)		
	Peer Tutors (Examples)		
	Extra Aide Time (Identify Content)		
	Guided Practice (Identify Content)		
	Varied Instructional Settings (Identify)		
	Supplemental Materials (Languages)		
	Extra Parent Conference (Languages)		
	Language and Content Reinforcement (Identify)		
	Consulted Resource People (Identify)		
	Learning Support Services (Identify)		
	Cognitive Learning Strategies (Identify)		
	Varied Instructional Strategies (Examples)		
	Other:		

Student: _____   DOB: _____   Age: ____   Date: _____

	Behavioral Interventions Tried	Duration	Comments
	Planned Positive Reinforcement (Examples)		
	Behavioral Contract (Examples)		
	Parent Conferences (Interpreter)		
	Reduction of Stimuli (Examples)		
	Support Group (Identify Teams)		
	Suggestions for Parents (Examples)		
	Culturally Appropriate Guided Practice (Languages)		
	Acculturation Support (Examples)		
	Counseling Services (Interpreter)		
	Coping/Problem-Solving Strategies (Examples)		
	Self-Monitoring (Examples)		
	Other:		

Academic Information	Grades	Test Scores	How Assessed
In English:			
Math Reading/Writing Oral Language			
In Native Language:			
Math Reading/Writing Oral Language			

Student: _____   DOB: _____   Age: ____   Date: _____

Native Language		
Recommendations	Duration	Outcome
Acculturation: Content: Behavior: Other:		

English		
Recommendations	Duration	Outcome
Acculturation: Content: Behavior: Other:		

AQS: A Guide to Estimating Level of Acculturation

Name: _____ School: _____

Date of Birth: _____ Sex: _____ Grade: _____ Age at Arrival in U.S.: _____

Language(s) Spoken at Home: _____

Acculturation Quick Screen (AQS)		
Cultural/Environmental Factors	Raw Scores	Scaled Scores
1. Number of years in United States		
2. Number of years in School District		
3. Number of years in ESL/Bilingual Education		
4. Bilingual Proficiency		
5. Native Language Proficiency		
6. English Language Proficiency		
7. Ethnicity/Nation of Origin		
8. % of Minority in Present School		
AQS Score Total:		

AQS: A Guide to Estimating Level of Acculturation *(cont.)*

AQS Scale Scoring Guidelines	
1. Number of Years in U.S.	**2. Number of Years in District**
Under one year = .5 One to two years = 1 Two to four years = 2 Four to five years = 3 Five to six years = 4 Over six years = 5	Under one year = .5 One to two years = 1 Two to four years = 2 Four to five years = 3 Five to six years = 4 Over six years = 5
3. Years in ESL/Bilingual Program	**4. Bilingual Proficiency**
Up to one year in directed instruction = .5 One to one and a half years = 1 One and a half to two years = 2 Two to two and a half years = 3 Two and a half to four years = 4 Over four years = 5	Monolingual = .5 Primarily L1, some BICS in L2 = 1 Fluent BICS in L1, Intermediate BICS in L2 = 2 Basic CALP in L1, Intermediate BICS in L2 = 3 CALP in L1, some CALP in L2 = 4 Bilingual BICS and CALP = 5
5. Native Language Proficiency	**6. English Language Proficiency**
Does not speak the language = .5 Has receptive comprehension = 1 Limited fluency or BICS only = 2 Intermediate fluency in BICS and limited CALP = 3 Intermediate fluency in BICS and CALP = 4 Total fluency in BICS and CALP = 5	Does not speak the language = .5 Has receptive comprehension = 1 Limited fluency or BICS only = 2 Intermediate fluency in BICS and limited CALP = 3 Intermediate fluency in BICS and CALP = 4 Total fluency in BICS and CALP = 5
7. Ethnicity/National Origin	**8. Percent of Student's Group in School**
American Indian/Alaska Native = .5 Hispanic/Latino/Chicano = 1 African, East Asian, or Pacific Islander = 2 West Asian or Middle Eastern = 3 Eastern European = 4 Western European = 5	81% - 100% of enrollment = .5 65% - 80% of enrollment = 1 45% - 64% of enrollment = 2 25% - 44% of enrollment = 3 11% - 24% of enrollment = 4 0% - 10% of enrollment = 5

Interpretation Guidelines:

0 - 19 Less Acculturated   20 - 29 In Transition   30 - 40 More Acculturated

Comments:

Classroom Language Interaction Checklist

Native Language:_____

Name of Student:_____ Date:_____

Completed By: _____ Title:_____

Directions: Please check skills which you have observed as having been mastered by the above student in native language or English, as appropriate.

BICS (Basic Interpersonal Communicative Skills)—learned through interaction with other speakers and personal experience:

		Native Language	English
_____	1. Follows general classroom directions	_____	_____
_____	2. Acts out common school activities	_____	_____
_____	3. Gives classroom commands to peers	_____	_____
_____	4. Exchanges common greetings	_____	_____
_____	5. Describes classroom objects; describes people	_____	_____
_____	6. Retells a familiar story	_____	_____
_____	7. Initiates and responds to a conversation	_____	_____
_____	8. Appears to attend to what is going on	_____	_____
_____	9. Appropriately answers basic questions	_____	_____
_____	10. Participates in sharing time	_____	_____
_____	11. Narrates a simple story	_____	_____
_____	12. _____		

Comments:_____

_____

_____

_____

_____

_____

Adapted from L. Baca & H. Cervantes 1993; B. Bernhard & B. Lorea 1989
Dr. Catherine Collier

Classroom Language Interaction Checklist *(cont.)*

Native Language:_____

Name of Student:_____ Date:_____

CALP (Cognitive/Academic Language Proficiency)—learned through academic, structured school instruction and interaction with teacher and peers in the classroom:

		Native Language	English
_____	12. Follows specific directions for academic tasks	_____	_____
_____	13. Understands and uses academic vocabulary appropriately	_____	_____
_____	14. Understands teacher's discussion	_____	_____
_____	15. Distinguishes main ideas from supporting details	_____	_____
_____	16. Understands and uses temporal (first, last, etc.) and spatial (top, bottom, left, etc.) concepts	_____	_____
_____	17. Uses sound/symbol association	_____	_____
_____	18. Asks/answers specific questions regarding topic	_____	_____
_____	19. Asks for clarification during academic tasks	_____	_____
_____	20. Actively participates in class discussions; volunteers to answer questions	_____	_____
_____	21. Adds an appropriate ending after listening to a story	_____	_____
_____	22. Can explain simple instructional tasks to peers	_____	_____
_____	23. Decodes words	_____	_____
_____	24. Understands rules of punctuation/capitalization for reading	_____	_____
_____	25. Follows along during oral reading	_____	_____
_____	26. Reads for comprehension	_____	_____
_____	27. Can discuss vocabulary	_____	_____
_____	28. Uses glossary, index, appendix, etc.	_____	_____
_____	29. Demonstrates an interest in reading	_____	_____
_____	30. Completes simple unfinished sentences	_____	_____
_____	31. Generates simple sentences	_____	_____

Native Language:_____

Name of Student:_____ Date:_____

CALP (contd.):

		Native Language	English
_____	32. Writes from dictation	_____	_____
_____	33. Writes short paragraphs	_____	_____
_____	34. Writes in cursive	_____	_____
_____	35. Uses correct punctuation, capitalization, paragraphing, margins	_____	_____
_____	36. Demonstrates an interest in writing	_____	_____
_____	37. Can discuss aspects of language/grammar	_____	_____
_____	38. Initiates writing activities	_____	_____
_____	39. Composes and edits over one-page papers	_____	_____
_____	40. Can explain complex instructional tasks to others	_____	_____

Comments:_____

_____

_____

_____

_____

_____

_____

_____

_____

_____

Adapted from L. Baca & H. Cervantes 1993; B. Bernhard & B. Lorea 1989
Dr. Catherine Collier

Classroom Language Interaction Checklist *(cont.)*

Native Language:_____

Name of Student:_____ Date:_____

Additional information about student's language usage in the classroom setting:

Norm Referenced Proficiency

Native Language

Test Used: _____	Test Used: _____
Score: _____	Score: _____
Date: _____	Date: _____

English

Test Used: _____	Test Used: _____
Score: _____	Score: _____
Date: _____	Date:_____

Language Use Observed in Non-Classroom Setting

Native Language   Date: _____   Setting: _____

Labeling _____	Explaining to peers _____
Modifying _____	Story telling (abstract) _____
BICS _____	Story telling (concrete)_____
Connecting_____	Language expansion _____

English Language   Date _____   Setting: _____

Labeling _____	Explaining to peers _____
Modifying _____	Story telling (abstract) _____
BICS _____	Story telling (concrete)_____
Connecting_____	Language expansion _____

Adapted from L. Baca & H. Cervantes 1993; B. Bernhard & B. Lorea 1989
Dr. Catherine Collier

Sociocultural Resiliency Checklist

Student:		Date:	Age:	Teacher:
Sociocultural Factors	✔	**Selected Cross-Cultural Adaptation Risk Factors**		
Culture & Language % Checked:		Comes from non-English speaking home. Comes from a culture or ethnic group different from mainstream America. Family emphasis support of family or community/group over individual effort. Comes from non-English speaking geographic area. Has culturally appropriate behaviors that are different from expectations of mainstream America. There is no support in the home for bilingual and bicultural development. Out of 6 Total		
Acculturation Level % Checked:		Recent immigrant, refugee, migrant, or resides on reservation. Doesn't interact much with majority culture peers or majority cultural group. Displays confusion in locus of control. Displays heightened stress or anxiety in cross-cultural interactions. Oral expression contains considerable code-switching. Expresses or displays sense of isolation or alienation in cross-cultural interactions. Out of 6 Total		
Cognitive Learning Style % Checked:		Few cognitive learning strategies appropriate to classroom/school. Cognitive learning style different or inappropriate in relation to teacher's instructional style. Easily frustrated or low perseverance in completing tasks. Retains survival strategies which are no longer appropriate. Displays difficulty with task analysis. Displays difficulty with understanding and applying cause and effect. Out of 6 Total		
Experiential Background % Checked:		High family mobility. Limited or sporadic school attendance. Low socioeconomic status. Little exposure to subject or content or not familiar with material. Disrupted early childhood development. Few readiness skills. Does not know how to behave in classroom. Different terms/concepts for subject areas or materials and content. Retains survival strategies which are no longer appropriate. Out of 9 Total		

Sociocultural Resiliency Checklist *(cont.)*

Student:		Date:	Age:	Teacher:
Sociocultural Factors	**✔**	**Selected Cross-Cultural Adaptation Risk Factors**		
Sociolinguistic Development % Checked:		Doesn't speak English. Limited CALP in native language. Limited BICS in English. Rarely speaks in class. Speaks only to cultural peers. Limited CALP in English. Asks peers for assistance in understanding. Appears to know English but can't follow English directions in class. Out of 8 Total.		

The presence of one or more of these five sociocultural factors contribute to students' experiencing success or difficulty in school. Intervention should be provided in any factor area where more than 40% items are checked before proceeding formal referral of students experiencing learning and behavior difficulties. If more than 14 items are checked overall, assessment/placement decisions must include bilingual and English as a Second Language instruction, cross-cultural modification assistance with the acculturation process as well as specific learning and behavior interventions.

WHAT IS THE SOCIOCULTURAL RESILIENCY CHECKLIST?

The **Sociocultural Resiliency Checklist** was developed as an initial screening tool for educators in American public schools who are concerned about the learning and behavior of a specific student from a culturally or linguistically diverse background. The **Sociocultural Resiliency Checklist** is scored by a teacher or team of education personnel who are familiar with the student's background and classroom behavior. It is recommended as part of the initial information gathering and intervention planning stages that should occur prior to making a formal referral for special services. This corresponds with the "Intake" and "Prevention/Intervention" stages of the CrossCultural Assessment paradigm (Collier 1996).

SCORING THE SOCIOCULTURAL RESILIENCY CHECKLIST

Based upon the teacher's or team's knowledge of the student, the educator(s) complete the checklist by checking off items that are known to be true for this particular student. Items that cannot be answered indicate important information about the student that must be collected before proceeding with a referral or more formal assessment (Baca & Cervantes 1996; Collier 1987). Each of the five sociocultural areas has a box " ☐ Out of — Total". Record the number of items checked in the box. Record the percentile score in the space marked "% Checked".

Culture and Language		Acculturation Level	
1 out of 6 = 17%	4 out of 6 = 67%	1 out of 6 = 17%	4 out of 6 = 67%
2 out of 6 = 33%	5 out of 6 = 83%	2 out of 6 = 33%	5 out of 6 = 83%
3 out of 6 = 50%	6 out of 6 = 100%	3 out of 6 = 50%	6 out of 6 = 100%
Cognitive Learning Style		**Sociolinguistic Development**	
1 out of 6 = 17%	4 out of 6 = 67%	1 out of 8 = 13%	5 out of 8 = 63%
2 out of 6 = 33%	5 out of 6 = 83%	2 out of 8 = 25%	6 out of 8 = 75%
3 out of 6 = 50%	6 out of 6 = 100%	3 out of 8 = 38%	7 out of 8 = 89%
		4 out of 8 = 50%	8 out of 8 = 100%

Experiential Background				
1 out of 9 = 11%	3 out of 9 = 33%	5 out of 9 = 55%	7 out of 9 = 77%	9 out of 9 = 100%
2 out of 9 = 22%	4 out of 9 = 44%	6 out of 9 = 66%	8 out of 9 = 88%	

INTERPRETING THE SOCIOCULTURAL RESILIENCY CHECKLIST

If more than 40% of the items in any of the resiliency areas are checked off, it indicates that the student has substantial strength in this area. These strengths can be supported and used to facilitate further growth and achievement. If less than 40% of the items in any of the five areas are checked off, it indicates that the student needs intervention in this area. This allows the educator or team to target a specific area for early intervention and intensive monitoring and guides them in making better instructional decisions for this student. Some students may have several areas needing attention. In these cases, the teacher or team will need to prioritize the student's intervention needs. To prioritize the student's needs, rank order the five sociocultural resilience areas from highest percentile to lowest. The area with the lowest percentile of resiliency factors should receive attention first.

Sociocultural Resiliency Checklist *(cont.)*

Sociocultural Factors	✔	Selected Cross-Cultural Resiliency Factors
Culture & Language % Checked:		There is quality verbal communication in the home in a language other than English. There is behavioral guidance in the home consistent with a specific cultural/religious world view. The cultural values of the home support cooperative effort. The family maintains communication with their linguistic/cultural community. The family participates regularly in religious/social events within their linguistic/cultural community. There is active support in the home for bilingual and bicultural development. Total
Acculturation Level % Checked:		Student attends events within the mainstream community. Student interacts with 'majority' peers or 'majority' cultural group. Student displays consistent sense of locus of control. Student appears comfortable in cross-cultural interactions. The code-switching in the student's speech shows an emerging understanding of English. Student appears comfortable switching from one linguistic/cultural environment to another. Total
Experiential Background % Checked:		Adults in the home will provide encouragement and support for student's development. Student makes an effort to increase attendance. Adults in family provide for the student's basic needs. Family will provide support for student's learning. Early childhood development was appropriate to culture/language. Student displays curiosity and is ready to learn. Student has prior classroom or formal education experience. Student has developmentally and linguistically appropriate literacy skills or pre-skills. Student demonstrates variety of survival strategies. Total

Sociocultural Factors	✔	Selected Cross-Cultural Resiliency Factors
Socio-linguistic Development % Checked:		Student has good basic interpersonal communication skills in native language. Student has moderate to good cognitive academic language proficiency in native language. BICS in English appears to be emerging. Student attempts to translate for others in the classroom. Student demonstrates emerging cognitive academic language proficiency in English. Student seeks assistance from peers. Code-switching demonstrates emerging English syntax and vocabulary. Student can demonstrate content knowledge in his/her native language. Total
Cognitive Learning Style % Checked:		Student demonstrates consistent cognitive learning strategies. Student responds positively to variations in instructional strategies. Student responds positively to appropriate 'rewards/recognition'. Student can apply cognitive learning strategies when given guided practice. Student can use self-monitoring strategies. Student can assist others in learning a task. Total

The presence of one or more of these five socio-cultural factors contribute to students' experiencing success in American public schools. Intervention should be provided in any factor area where less than 40% items are checked before proceeding with a formal referral of students experiencing learning and behavior difficulties. If less than 14 items are checked overall, further assessment/placement decisions must include bilingual and English as a Second Language instruction, cross-cultural modifications, and assistance with the acculturation process as well as specific learning and behavior interventions.

INTERVENTIONS FOR SOCIOCULTURAL ADAPTATION

After prioritizing the student's intervention needs, select the area with the greatest need to begin interventions. Examples of interventions appropriate for each area needing attention are:

Culture & Language

These interventions address culture and language transition and adaptation needs.
Guided practice in behavior transition between the primary culture (C1) and second culture (C2) activities
Guided practice in transition between the primary language (L1) and second language (L2) activities
Guided practice in constructive positive quality interactions with children from the new language and culture (L2/C2) environment.
Guided practice in classroom behavior expectations and survival strategies
Cross-cultural behavior and communication strategies
Guided practice in cross-cultural conflict resolution strategies
Video tapes in L1 about behavior patterns and expectations in America
Filmed observations of various behavior interactions & settings in US schools
Role play in constructive positive quality interactions with children and adults from the L2/C2 environment.
Cooperative behavior strategies
Peer support groups
Cross-cultural counseling
Coping Strategy and other cognitive learning strategies

Cognitive Learning Style

These address differences in cognitive learning style, confusion in locus of control, resistance to change, distractibility, response fatigue, limited experience in academic settings, and other cognitive academic needs.
Role play in cognitive academic interaction strategies and cognitive learning strategies
Guided practice in cognitive learning strategies and cognitive academic interactions
Cooperative learning strategies
Cross-cultural communication strategies
Active Processing, Organization, Coping, Evaluation, Analogy, Rehearsal strategies
Classroom and school survival strategies
Self-monitoring techniques
Instruction in L1/L2 cognitive academic interactions
Guided practice in L1/L2 CALP transitions
L2 Cognitive academic interaction reinforcement
Context embedded instruction (sheltered instruction techniques)
Mediated stimuli in classroom
Concrete demonstrations
Reduced stimuli in classroom
Videotapes in L1 about American school procedures, expectations, rules.

Acculturation Level

These interventions address culture shock, response fatigue, confusion in locus of control, stress reactions and other psychological side-effects of acculturation process.

Guided practice in constructive positive quality C2/L2 interactions
Role plays in constructive positive quality C2/L2 interactions
Sheltered interactions with variety of C2 children and adults
Survival strategies regarding rules of C2 interactions and expectations
Cross-cultural counseling
Peer acculturation process support
Video tapes in L1 about interaction patterns in America
Guided practice in C2 interaction strategies
Rest & relaxation techniques
Reduced stimuli
Cross-cultural communication strategies
C1/C2 transition activities

Experiential Background

These address the adaptation needs of children with the family and community.
Guided practice in dealing with government services, sponsoring agencies, school or service providers
Family centered learning activities such as literacy, discipline, English classes
Guided practice in C1/C2 interactions in community settings (store, schools, church, government agencies, etc.)
Video tapes in L1 about American schools, communities, social service providers, laws, etc.
Cross-cultural counseling for families
Survival strategies for families
C1/C2 transition activities for families and community groups
Cross-cultural conflict resolution techniques and strategies
Cross-cultural communication strategies
Assistance about school expectations, structures, systems, and laws

Sociolinguistic Development

These address code-switching, stages in second language acquisition, development of BICS and CALP in both
languages, comprehensible input, and other communicative needs.
Guided practice in constructive positive quality interactions with L2
Role play in L2 BICS and CALP development
Sheltered instruction
Peer bilingual tutoring
Guided practice in L2 BICS
Listening activities
L1/L2 transition activities
L1/L2 CALP instruction & transition
Guided practice and planned interactions with different L2 speakers
Cross-cultural survival interaction strategies
Cross-cultural communication strategies
Sheltered English
Video tapes in L1 about American speech patterns
Interactive language learning strategies (SOUL & INREAL)

CHAPTER 11

Methods and Materials for Bilingual Special Education

John J. Hoover
Catherine Collier

- Curricular Elements and Adaptation
- Steps in Interventions
- Adapting the Four Curricular Elements
- Teaching and Behavior Management Techniques
- Educational Materials
- Summary

OBJECTIVES

To describe the curricular environment for Bilingual Special Education

To provide information about methods and materials appropriate for Bilingual Special Education

To describe a variety of instructional interventions and strategies for use with bilingual exceptional children

To provide guidelines for curricular adaptations in the culturally diverse special education classroom

In the preceding chapters on curriculum development and inclusive education, various procedures and adaptation techniques have been discussed. The teacher working with culturally and linguistically diverse (CLD) children who are or may be exceptional (CLDE) needs to apply these suggestions in actual classroom settings in the most effective manner. This necessitates a variety of intervention and instruction techniques, strategies, and materials, and the knowledgeable use of these within the complete curricular environment. This topic is addressed within the framework of the more general definitions of curriculum that emphasize that curriculum is composed of several interrelated elements. We will discuss the curricular environment as a whole and the use of various instructional techniques, strategies, and materials particularly effective with CLDE children. The concept of the interrelationship among curricular elements is discussed relative to intervention from the prereferral level through placement for special education services. The importance of effective curricular adaptations and adapting to meet special needs is addressed in this chapter, which also presents numerous teaching and behavior management techniques appropriate for adapting curriculum for CLDE learners. This chapter concludes with a discussion about criteria and guidelines for evaluating, selecting, adapting, and creating educational materials for CLDE learners.

CURRICULAR ELEMENTS AND ADAPTATION

The specific teaching and behavior management strategies to implement curriculum content, use instructional materials, manage behavior, and, in general, organize classroom instruction assist in determining the whole curriculum. *Curriculum* has been defined in various ways from all activities both school and nonschool (Shubert, 1993) to activities included only in school and classroom environments (Nieto, 1996). For purposes of these discussions, *curriculum* should be understood as all planned and guided learning experiences under the direction of the teacher with intended educational outcomes (Hoover & Patton, in press). Although a general definition of curriculum is accepted and understood by most classroom teachers, the specific aspects that comprise curriculum are not as clear. In fact, many educators view the curriculum as merely the materials used in the classroom. Materials are only one important element in the curriculum process. To effectively implement instruction for CLDE children, all aspects of the curricular environment must be addressed.

The total curriculum and curriculum implementation process involves consideration of four major elements: the *content* that is taught, the *instructional strategies* used, *instructional settings* in the classroom, and the management of *student behaviors* (Hoover & Patton, in press). These four major areas within the whole curriculum must be understood relative to their relationship with one another as well as to individual student needs, linguistic and cultural heritages, and prior instructional experiences. As one acquires a more complete understanding of these four curricular elements, the appropriate selection and use of instructional methods and materials are maximized. A deeper understanding will also facilitate integrated efforts across curricular content areas, as emphasized in integrated curriculum teaching (Brodhagen, 1994; Drake, 1993).

The element of *content* refers to the academic skills and knowledge associated with the various subject areas. This includes prerequisite skills needed to complete academic tasks as well as the expressive and receptive language skills in both languages necessary to comprehend and learn the content. The *instructional strategies* are the methods and techniques selected to assist students to acquire the content as well as manage behavior. The *instructional settings* refer to the settings in the classroom in which learning occurs. These include small- and large-group situations as well as independent work and one-to-one instructional situations. The *student behaviors* aspect of the curriculum refers to the CLDE students' abilities to manage and control their own behaviors under a variety of situations, learning activities, and groupings within the classroom. Each of these four elements is an individual factor that contributes to the success of education for CLDE students. These four elements are distinct aspects of the curriculum and often require adaptations in the total curricular implementation process.

Figure 11–1 depicts the process of effective curriculum implementation for CLDE students through the curriculum adaptation process that will be described in a subsequent section. A circular figure is used to illustrate the continuous interaction among the four elements of curriculum comprising the curriculum implementation process. As shown in the figure, the four

curriculum elements are first illustrated as individual elements. The four elements connect to the circular area depicting curriculum adaptation, which in turn connects with the innermost circle of effective curriculum implementation. *Although these four elements are distinct aspects of the total curriculum, the interrelationship among these elements provides the key to success when the total curriculum is implemented.*

Problems, inconsistencies, and other events within a classroom that inhibit effective implementation of curriculum are frequently the result of problems associated with two or more of these curriculum elements. Although a problem limited to only one element of the curriculum is sometimes encountered, many CLDE students who experience problems within the classroom are having difficulty in more than one element within the total curriculum. However, all too often we concentrate our search for and solutions to academic and behavior problems within the individual elements without thinking through the possible interrelationships among the various elements. By ignoring the interrelationships among the elements, we frequently embark upon a path to improve learning or reduce behavior problems that is doomed to failure from the beginning. Often teachers find themselves saying that they were sure that the problem was due to one of the curriculum elements (e.g., content, strategies), and after spending several weeks modifying or focusing upon the individual area or areas, they realize that something else was also contributing to the learning/behavior problems.

In many situations that "something else" pertains to the interrelationships among elements. As one element is addressed or adapted, each of the other three elements may also be affected. Thus, as one curriculum element is adapted or modified, each of the other three areas must also be addressed to determine the effects of the original adaptations on them, and if necessary, they must also be adapted to address potential problems that may arise.

Figure 11–1
Integrative Model for Curriculum Implementation

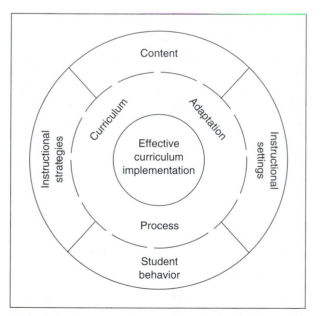

Note. From *Curriculum Adaptation for Students with Learning and Behavior Problems* by J. J. Hoover and J. R. Patton (In press). Austin, TX: Pro-Ed. Reprinted by permission.

STEPS IN INTERVENTIONS

Before proceeding with the discussion of curricular adaptations and methods and materials, a discussion about the topic of *when* these might be most useful in the student's program is necessary. As indicated previously, the use of curricular adaptation techniques and strategies may occur from prereferral through the placement for special services.

Prereferral intervention for CLD students with learning and behavior problems is a preferred method of meeting the needs of these children (see Collier, 1987 for an overview of prereferral intervention). This period of intensive instructional intervention is also referred to as the prevention intervention period (PIP) or as a prevention enhancement program (PEP), as discussed in Chapter 5. The major theme permeating the PIP process emphasizes the need to (1) prevent inappropriate referrals and (2) implement appropriate interventions. Interventions include curricular adaptations to one or more of the four curricular elements and classroom management techniques discussed in this chapter. Other interventions have been discussed in other chapters throughout this book. Within the overall PIP, collaboration and teaming similar to a process discussed by Morsink, Thomas, and Correa (1991) should occur. In the event that prevention efforts are unsuccessful, more formal procedures are initiated to determine if the student requires special education to meet his or her needs. Discussed below is a four-step comprehensive process for referring and evaluating the needs of a CLD student. The questions provided for each step are examples of the types of information to be gathered at that step. These are not all-inclusive and may easily be adapted to specific referral situations.

Step 1: Prevention/Intervention Period

After bringing the CLD child's learning and behavior problems to the attention of a Teacher Assistance Child Intervention Team (TACIT) in the school or district, the referring teacher is assisted in implementing a number of instructional techniques and strategies that may resolve the child's problems. The members of the TACIT should include the classroom teacher, bilingual/English as a Second Language (ESL) specialist, special educator, Chapter I teacher, counselor, social worker, parent/advocate, and others. The TACIT discusses the child's needs with the teacher and proposes appropriate interventions. If the teacher needs assistance in implementing the interventions, the TACIT provides this help.

The suggested intervention techniques and strategies include those described in greater detail in the following section of this chapter. It is important to remember that these techniques and strategies may be used at any time and by any teacher working with a CLD or CLDE student. If implemented before referral, they are considered *preventions* and *interventions*. If implemented after staffing (Step 3) and placement (Step 4), they are considered part of the *Individual Educational Plan* (IEP) discussed in Chapter 10. Any of the service providers may be involved in implementing these intervention strategies, including the bilingual ESL teacher or aide, the regular classroom teacher, the special educator, or other instructional personnel. The recommended intervention areas include:

1. Classroom management assistance
2. Curriculum adaptation
3. Psycho/social assistance
4. Physical assistance
5. Experiential assistance
6. Delayed assistance
7. Language development

These interventions are discussed in this chapter and elsewhere in this book. During the intervention process, diagnostic information is collected about the child's response to the intervention strategies. If the child later must be referred for a formal evaluation and staffing, this information will assist in making an appropriate placement and in identifying instructional goals and objectives. The diagnostic information relating to the CLD child's performance or behavior that is of concern to the TACIT is documented. This includes questions relating to acculturation and language acquisition, examples of what the child can or cannot do in various settings, interventions attempted, how the child responded, patterns observed, and implications for further interventions or a referral to staffing. The TACIT must be able to address seven areas of concern at this point:

- Who receives the initial inquiry for assistance?
- Who monitors the collection of information about the student?
- What instruments or sources of information are used to identify appropriate interventions?
- Who assists the classroom teacher with the interventions?
- Who monitors the implementation of the interventions?
- How are the interventions and their results documented?
- What documentation is considered adequate or appropriate to terminate intervention and who decides this?

Step 2: Referral

"Referral" here means formal referral to evaluation and staffing, as discussed in Chapters 8 and 9. The TACIT members must all be involved in this decision to refer to staffing. Questions to be resolved during staffing may be drawn from a diagnostic intervention document, such as the example shown in Table 11–1. At this point in the process, the TACIT should address six areas of concern:

- At what point in the prevention intervention process do you make a decision to refer?

- Who is involved in the decision to refer to a staffing?
- What documentation is considered adequate or appropriate to terminate intervention and move to a formal referral?
- What documentation is used to certify that the learning or behavior problem is not due to the student's cultural or linguistic difference or to his or her level of acculturation?
- What documentation is used to identify the student's language and acculturation needs in addition to his/her learning or behavior problem?
- What documentation is kept about the intervention results which justifies a formal referral to staffing?

Step 3: Evaluation and Staffing

Step 3 reflects issues related to the formal evaluation and subsequent staffing for a student. At this step, the TACIT must address the following areas:

- Who is involved in the formal evaluation?
- What process or documentation is followed to assure the assessment procedures and instruments are appropriate for this student?
- What documentation is used to certify that the disability is not due to the student's cultural or linguistic difference or to his or her level of acculturation?
- What documentation is used to certify that the student has a disability?
- What documentation is used to identify the student's language and acculturation needs in addition to his/her disability?

Step 4: Placement

After the decision to place is made, the interventions that are used with the student, such as those suggested in Step 1, are incorporated into the individual education plan (IEP). This

Table 11–1
Diagnostic Intervention/Documentation

Questions About Child	Samples of Behavior	Interventions Attempted	Performances Outcomes	Patterns Observed	Conclusions and Recommendations	New Questions
What is present level of functioning in various academic and nonacademic activities?	L_1/L_2 C_1/C_2*	Interactive techniques Cognitive learning strategies	How did child do in various settings?			
What can't child do?	Home and school	Cross-cultural communication strategies	How did child respond to various strategies?			
Appropriate versus inappropriate sociolinguistic behaviors?	Informal and formal Records Observations	Peer tutoring Contracting	What could child do/not do with various behavior expectations?			
What is preferred mode of interaction (verbal and nonverbal)?	Interviews Other interaction settings	Self-monitoring Rewarding task completion Individual instruction Cooperative learning team				
Etc.	Etc.	Etc.	Etc.			

*C_1 = first culture; C_2 = second culture.
Note. Adapted from "Bilingual Special Education Curriculum Trainings," by C. Collier, 1987, *Proceedings of the First Annual Symposium*, Cross-Cultural Special Education Network, p. 47, Boulder, CO: University of Colorado. Reprinted by permission.

includes curriculum adaptations and use of the teaching and behavior management techniques provided in Table 11–2. The following 5 areas should be considered when recommending a placement in special education:

- Who is involved in developing the crosscultural IEP?

- What process or documentation is used to delineate a comprehensive service plan for all the student's learning needs?

- What process is used to identify appropriate language and acculturation interventions for a student in addition to interventions for certified disabilities?

- Who determines the appropriate intersection of diverse services? Who monitors the effectiveness of these?

- How or what documentation is used to monitor the effectiveness of the language and acculturation interventions used for students with disabilities?

If the decision is made to not place the LEP student in special education, these areas of concern should be addressed:

- What process is used to identify appropriate interventions for learning and behavior problems not due to disabilities?

- What process is used to identify appropriate interventions for language and acculturation needs the student may still have?

- How are the student's cross-cultural instructional needs matched to appropriate curricular elements?

- Who or what provides assistance to the classroom teacher in implementing these interventions?

- What documentation is used to monitor the student's language and acculturation development while in inclusive classroom programs?

- What other concerns about this referred but not placed student do you have?

This four-step process supports information presented in other chapters of this book, as it provides educators with an additional approach for meeting the needs of CLDE students in the overall curriculum implementation and adaptation process.

ADAPTING THE FOUR CURRICULAR ELEMENTS

Curriculum adaptation is defined as adapting, modifying, and/or supplementing the curriculum to meet the needs of individual students (Hoover & Patton, in press). The need to adapt curriculum in today's schools becomes readily apparent when one considers the similarities and differences among content, instructional strategies, instructional settings, and student behavior needs within a particular classroom.

Curriculum adaptations need to be an integral part of daily teaching if each CLDE student's needs are to be effectively addressed in the classroom. Because these special learners are educated in both special and inclusive education classrooms, special education teachers may be required to adapt curriculum in their classrooms as well as assist inclusive educators to adapt curriculum in their classrooms. Therefore, the curriculum adaptation issues discussed in this chapter are applicable to both inclusive and special education classroom settings.

As previously discussed, many school districts or state legislatures have established mandated curriculum content that all students are expected to follow. Most, if not all, CLDE students are also expected to follow, to the extent possible, these sequentially oriented, mandated curricula. For the most part, through administrative or legislative mandates, the decisions concerning what to teach have already been made for teachers and students. Thus, for CLDE students who have difficulty functioning within the prescribed curriculum, the issue at hand is not whether the mandated state/district curriculum is appropriate for these learners, but rather how best to help these special learners acquire

Table 11–2
Teaching and Behavior Techniques

Techniques	Desired Outcomes	Examples	Special Considerations
Alternative methods for response	Students respond to questions or assignments in a manner compatible with their needs.	Allow a student who has difficulty with writing activities to tape-record answers in either the first language (L_1) or the second language (L_2).	Ensure that students know varied responses are acceptable.
Clear and concise	Reduce frustration in students due to unclear expectations; minimize ambiguity in classroom expectations.	Modify or break down general classroom rules into specific behavioral expectations to ensure that each student knows exactly what is meant by "acceptable behaviors."	Limited English-speaking students may require pictures of the expected actions or role-played demonstrations of the expectations.
Contingency contracting	Improve motivation; clarify responsibilities, assignments, rewards.	Document in writing that the student will complete 20 math problems with 80% accuracy during the regular math period. Student will receive 10 minutes of extra free time if contract conditions are met.	The rewards for completing the contract must be culturally appropriate.
Individualized instruction	Learners are motivated and complete tasks appropriate to their needs, interests, and abilities.	IEP may state that student will be able to use particular sociolinguistic cues and responses in appropriate first culture (C_1) and second culture (C_2) settings.	IEPs must include language (L_1 and L_2) needs as well as those for identified handicap.
Learning centers	Students are able to reinforce specific skills while working at their own pace; individualization.	Create an area in the classroom where several different activities exist for reviewing sight works in both L_1, and L_2.	The learning center could have visual and auditory stimuli from the students' cultural backgrounds.
Modify presentation of abstract concepts	Students are gradually and systematically introduced to abstract concepts.	Supplement the presentations of abstract concepts with visual aids, manipulatives, examples from students' previous experiences, or other direct hands-on experiences.	This is an application of cognitive/academic development. The concepts as well as the language of cognitive and academic tasks must be taught and built upon students' prior cultural experiences.

Table 11–2 *(cont.)*
Teaching and Behavior Techniques

Techniques	Desired Outcomes	Examples	Special Considerations
Peer tutoring	Learning gains are experienced by both the tutor and the student being tutored.	A student who has mastered a list of sight words or math facts presents these items on flash cards to another student needing assistance in this area.	If the student needing assistance is limited English proficient, it would be most effective to have the peer tutor be bilingual in L_1 and L_2.
Planned ignoring	Reduction of possible confrontations over minor misbehaving; elimination of inappropriate behavior after a few moments.	Teacher elects to ignore some whispering between two students during independent work time.	This must be done consistently and with equal frequency with minority and nonminority students.
Planned physical movement	Prevent or minimize behavior problems in the classroom.	Allow students to move to a learning center or study booth for part of their independent work time instead of remaining seated at their desks for the entire time.	Effective technique if cultural variations in mobility and interaction patterns among students are considered.
Positive reinforcement	Increase the frequency of appropriate responses or behaviors.	Provide the student extra free time when a math or reading assignment has been completed.	Cultural as well as personal relevance must be considered.
Prompting	Increase the students' probability of generating a correct response.	Underline one letter of a pair of letters that a student is studying (e.g., *b* versus *d*). This helps focus the learner's attention on characteristics of both letters, thus reducing confusion.	Cues or prompts must be culturally appropriate and meaningful to the student.
Providing choices	Reduce fears associated with assignments; alleviate power struggles between teacher and student.	Select two reading selections of interest to the student, both of which address the same desired objective. Allow the student to select one of them for the assignment. If student does not select either of these, introduce a third selection and ask student to choose.	Both L_1, and L_2 development should be incorporated into assignments where choices are provided.

continued

Table 11–2 *(cont.)*
Teaching and Behavior Techniques

Techniques	Desired Outcomes	Examples	Special Considerations
Providing success	Improve confidence; student views self as a successful person.	Initially reduce the difficulty level of material and gradually increase the level as easier tasks are met with success.	Must consider L_1 and L_2 development to ensure success with academic tasks.
Proximity control	Increase students' time on task; reassure frustrated students.	Periodically circulate throughout the classroom during group or independent activities, spending time next to particular students.	Cultural implications of proximity must be considered, as personal space varies considerably from culture to culture.
Role-playing	Students learn to confront the reactions of others and ways to deal with the situations similar to the role-play event.	A specific problem, such as discrimination, is identified and described. Students role-play how they would confront the problem and discuss their roles or behaviors upon completion.	This is an effective technique in assisting with the acculturation process.
Self-monitoring	Reduce inappropriate behaviors; increase time on task; students assume responsibility for their own behaviors.	Instruct the students to record a checkmark on a separate sheet of paper each time they catch themselves tapping their pencils on their desks during spelling class.	This may assist minority handicapped students to learn behaviors appropriate to the culture of the school and classroom.
Shortened assignments	Complex or difficult tasks are more manageable to students.	Structure the presentation of weekly spelling words so that two or three new words are introduced and studied each day throughout the week, rather than presenting all words at the beginning of the week.	This technique may assist the teacher to check whether students have the preskills necessary for selected tasks.
Signal interference	Prevent minor inappropriate behaviors from escalating while not providing specific attention to the students' misbehaviors.	Flick the classroom lights on and off when the noise level in the class becomes too loud.	Students experiencing acculturation will have difficulty adjusting to unfamiliar signals.

Table 11–2 *(cont.)*
Teaching and Behavior Techniques

Techniques	Desired Outcomes	Examples	Special Considerations
Simplify reading level	Students study content similar to other classmates but at a level commensurate with their reading abilities.	Provide student with lower level reading material that covers the same topic others are studying.	The materials can be in both L_1 and L_2 with different reading levels for either.
Student accountability	Students become aware of the connection between their actions and the consequences of these actions.	Establish rewards and consequences for completing work or exhibiting appropriate behavior, ensuring that these rewards and consequences are consistently implemented.	Limited English speaking students experiencing acculturation may require some role-playing, mediation, or other teaching of expectations to best understand accountability.
Student input into curricular planning	Facilitate students' ownership in their education.	Allow students to select some specific topics to be covered in an upcoming unit of study.	Ensure that minority learners with disabilities know how to contribute in the planning process.
Time-out	Regain control over self; student thinks about own behavior and behavioral expectations.	Remove a student to a quiet or time-out area for 3-5 minutes when student is unable to respond to a situation in a nonagressive manner.	Sociocultural implications of the time-out must be considered to ensure students understand the purpose of time-out.
Touch control	Increase time on task and awareness of one's behavior.	If a student is looking around the room during independent work time, gently tap student on shoulder as a signal to continue working.	As with proximity control, the cultural implication of the touching must be considered or the effect of this technique will be lost.

Note. Adapted from *Curriculum Adaptation for Students with Learning and Behavior Problems,* by J. J. Hoover and J. R. Patton, in press, Austin, TX: PRO-ED. Reprinted by permission.

what we are required to teach. Within this framework, curriculum adaptations for CLDE students refers specifically to modifying required content as well as adapting instructional strategies, instructional settings within the classroom, and behavior to improve student self-control. Methods for adapting the four curricular elements are the foundation upon which teaching techniques and strategies are built. Adaptations to any of the curricular elements will necessitate some modifications in the others. This continual adjustment is a crucial part of the effective instruction of CLDE students. In addition, when adapting one or more of the curricular elements, issues specific to CLDE students must be addressed and incorporated into the adaptations. Several of these issues within each of the four curricular elements are discussed.

Content

It is possible to use both the primary or home language and English materials in a meaningful manner, either in direct instruction or as content reinforcement. If available, the teacher should obtain materials in both languages, preferably of similar content, and review for CALP (Cognitive/Academic Language Proficiency), relevance, and format. Also, it is important to consider the degree of field independence/field sensitivity necessary for the CLDE students to use the materials. When considering adaptations to content, the teacher should ensure that the selected material enhances subject area growth without penalizing students for gaps in their first and second language and limited English proficiency. The material should allow for integration of language development, home language to English transition, and English acquisition, and be made available in the students' primary language. Material in either the primary language or English should also be appropriate for the proficiency levels in various domains, including vocabulary, syntax, grammar, word attack, and oral paradigms. In addition, the students must possess Basic Interpersonal Communication Skills (BICS) in the primary or home language or English necessary to ask questions about the content, and efforts should be made to ensure that the students do not experience culture shock as new materials and stimuli are introduced.

Instructional Strategies

Strategies that are selected and adapted should exhibit culturally appropriate cues and reinforcements as well as culturally appropriate motivation and relevance to the CLDE students. Some instructional strategies may pro-duce distractions due to children's unfamiliarity with stimuli associated with the strategy. Teachers must also determine whether field-independent or field-sensitive strategies are more appropriate and select strategies accordingly. Additionally, the effects of acculturation experiences pertaining to various strategies must be considered as instruction is implemented for these special learners.

Instructional Settings

Using the setting that is most compatible with the CLDE students' home culture should be most effective in the early stages of instruction. The student is taught how to participate in other less familiar and compatible settings as they become more comfortable with the culture of the public school. The quantity and quality of the verbal and nonverbal interactions that CLDE students are involved in are important elements in their cognitive and academic development and can be enhanced or discouraged by the teacher's selection of the instructional setting. The teacher must also consider the use of space and time in relation to the students' home culture. Depending on the degree of experience and familiarity with particular stimuli in the instructional setting, the teacher will need to adapt the manner in which students are introduced to new settings. Additionally, the selection of an instructional setting should consider the student's different cognitive/learning style as well as cross-cultural communication skills.

Student Behavior

In reference to student behaviors, it is necessary to consider the interaction of culture and language within the acculturation context and the possible effects of a disability on this interaction. Appropriate interventions for culture shock and other side effects of acculturation are discussed in Chapter 10. Teachers of CLDE students should possess cross-cultural communication skills and incorporate these into their instruction. Proficiency in cross-cultural communication facilitates appropriate student behaviors as these skills become effective learning and coping tools in the CLDE students' survival repertoire. Developing a sense of familiarity with the school culture and teaching the students appropriate sociolinguistic skills are important elements in CLDE students' development of self-control in the classroom. When modifications to student behaviors are being considered, these behaviors must be viewed relative to expected socioemotional development within the acculturation context.

Although determining the curriculum elements that require adaptations is difficult, the task of actually implementing the adaptations presents an even greater challenge to teachers of these special learners. The careful selection of various teaching and behavior techniques and cognitive learning strategies that will be used to implement the adaptations is the other main ingredient necessary to consider as one creates effective instruction for CLDE students.

TEACHING AND BEHAVIOR MANAGEMENT TECHNIQUES

Once curricular adaptations are determined to be necessary and the special needs of CLDE students have been considered, the challenge of actually adapting the curriculum while simultaneously meeting the special needs emerges. The appropriate selection and use of teaching and behavior techniques form the base for effective curricular adaptations. This section describes a variety of techniques that may be used to achieve effective instruction through curricular adaptations while meeting the special needs of CLDE students.

Table 11–2 provides a variety of teaching and behavior techniques that may be employed to adapt curriculum elements and address the special needs of these students. Several key aspects about each technique are illustrated in the table. They are the desired outcomes when

using each technique, an example for each strategy, and special considerations when using each technique with CLDE students. Although all the techniques described in this chapter may be used with any learner, they are discussed relative to adaptations particularly appropriate for CLDE students. Some of the techniques may already be an integral part of the whole curriculum process for some teachers. For these teachers, some of the techniques may not represent adaptations in the strict sense of the word. However, the various techniques and strategies described may be appropriately and effectively used to adapt curriculum to address the special needs of CLDE students.

Adapting to Meet Special Needs

Based on the issues discussed elsewhere in this book, several educational needs of CLDE students can be determined. These include needs associated with acculturation, interaction patterns, limited English proficiency, language development, nonverbal communication, language function, attention to task, concept development, locus of control, and perceptions of time and space. The use of teaching and behavior techniques with CLDE students is discussed relative to these special educational needs.

Acculturation. As previously discussed, students experiencing acculturation may find the learning environment in the public schools stressful and relatively unintelligible. The teacher in this circumstance should use teaching and behavior techniques that facilitate interpreting and explaining the learning environment and expectations to the students. The techniques should gradually introduce learners to the new element of activity in their environment through demonstration and explanation of the activity or item. As the students become more familiar with one new activity, they may be introduced to another activity. This is related to the observation that discovery learning techniques may not be effective with students experiencing acculturation without extensive demonstration and explanation of the roles, outcomes, and tasks expected of the student.

In many instances the teacher must lead the students through the process, showing them how to complete the task. This is followed by observing the students' completion of the task and checking for areas in need of further development. Teaching and behavior techniques appropriate for adapting curriculum to address this educational need include peer tutoring, prompting, providing success, positive reinforcement, establishing clear and concise expectations, learning centers, role playing, student input into curricular decisions, self-monitoring, or student accountability.

CLDE students often need to be taught how to behave appropriately in particular settings, as well as why certain behaviors are considered appropriate and others not appropriate. Specifically, the student may need to learn cultural values and behaviors pertaining to proximics (i.e., how close two people stand when interacting in various situations and roles), attitudes toward property and ownership, discrimination, attitudes towards disabilities and status, illustrations of how colors and clothing carry different meanings in different social contexts, and the interaction of sociolinguistic behaviors with other cues to convey meaning in the first culture (C_1) versus the second culture (C_2).

The most basic C_2 cultural values and behaviors must be taught first as survival skills for the CLDE student. These may include dressing appropriately, recognizing dangerous situations, recognizing to whom and where to go to receive assistance, how to ask for assistance, how to order and eat food appropriately, as well as contrasting similarities and differences between appropriate and inappropriate behaviors, in and out of school settings. Teaching and behavior techniques for implementing adaptations to curricular elements that address knowledge of cultural values and behaviors include peer tutoring, role-playing, individual-ized instruction, providing choices, contingency contracting, positive reinforcement, clear and concise expectations, and proximity control.

Interaction Patterns. This educational need refers to assisting students to integrate C_1 and C_2 and to prevent the possible detrimental assimilation or rejection of C_2. This includes lessons in how to communicate without speaking the language, how to participate even when not completely understanding what is going on, the importance of interacting and participating while learning the new language and culture, as well as lessons on multicultural aspects of American society, the pluralistic nature of American heritage, and contributions of the student's culture to American culture and society.

Students should be encouraged to observe others and to respond to them even if they do not fully understand the occurrences. They may also be assigned a peer tutor who will explain the occurrences the student observes. It is also important to teach the students not to hesitate to participate and interact. Students learn to speak by speaking, learn appropriate actions by doing, learn to interact appropriately by interacting, and in turn are interacted with more frequently when they participate. Teaching and behavior techniques such as peer tutoring, student accountability, self-monitoring, role-playing, or student input into curricular decisions may be appropriately used to address interaction needs of CLDE students.

Limited English Proficiency. Research has shown that it takes one or two years for CLDE students without disabilities who do not speak English to learn basic interpersonal communication skills in English. As discussed previously, success in BICS should not be mistaken for proficiency in the type and depth of English used in the classroom. BICS should be fully developed to assist students to develop confidence and experience success in speaking English as a second language. This, in turn, forms the base upon which cognitive academic language skills are developed.

The teacher should use the students' current level of BICS for encouraging greater verbal communication in English through the use of such teaching and behavior techniques as role-playing, prompting, and frequently requesting verbal responses in instructional activities. The content, instructional settings, and strategies of the curriculum must be adapted to allow and encourage this greater verbal discourse. To elicit more frequent and more proficient use of English as a second language, CLDE students must be given more frequent opportunities to use what English they have, even though this may only be BICS-level English.

CALP in English may be developed within five to seven years in non-English speaking children to a level sufficient to succeed academically (Nieto, 1996). This language proficiency is crucial to the academic achievement of the student, and instruction in CALP should be an integral part of the curriculum used with CLDE students. Strategies to use in adapting the curriculum for CALP development also include the use of peer tutoring, role-playing, and frequent use of verbal interactions with the students. Students can role-play particular school activities and personnel to become more familiar with the language used in these situations. Student accountability and self-monitoring are also useful teaching and behavior techniques as CLDE students become more proficient with CALP, but continue to need development.

Language Development. Language development needs of CLDE students include L_1 vocabulary development, L_1 discourse structure and topics, L_1 to L_2 code switching and L_2 and L_1 code switching in planned sequence, translation, contrastive analysis, or transformational grammar. This educational need may also involve revision or clarification, affirmation, acknowledging, commenting, or maintaining a topic in L_1 or L_2. A variety of teaching and behavior techniques and cognitive learning strategies may be used to adapt curriculum to meet these language oriented needs. Some of the effective interventions include peer tutoring, prompting, alternate methods of response, role-playing, modifying presentation of abstract concepts, providing success, positive reinforcement, contingency contracting, or individualized instruction. In addition, various interactive techniques may be used to develop language skills in L_1 and L_2. These include mirroring, parallel talk, self-talk, verbal reflection, and modeling. See Collier and Hoover (1987) for a discussion of these selected strategies.

Nonverbal Communication. Much of expressive communication is nonverbal, and educators often fail to recognize important nonverbal communications found with different cultures (Nieto, 1996). Cooperative learning, alternative methods of response, role-play situations, signal interference, and peer tutoring that focus on the nonverbal elements of the communication and situation are effective techniques to use in implementing adaptations to the curriculum when nonverbal communication skills require assistance. For example, students could act out (without words) the actions of another, depicting a particular situation. The "audience" is instructed to generate a description of the situation and provide appropriate verbal discourse. Peers are instructed to cue CLDE students when their nonverbal communication is inappropriate or misunderstood.

Language Function. Teachers and students use language, but rarely learn how all the elements combine to achieve proficient communication. This does not mean just talking about grammar or syntax, but how grammar, syntax, or vocabulary function in the totality of communication. When the need arises to assist CLDE students to comprehend the function of language and its usage, appropriate curriculum adaptations include use of contrastive phoneme and morpheme (sound/symbol and meaning/symbol) analysis, use of communication with regular patterns, drawing students' attention to these patterns, and teaching how to use these patterns.

Learning centers, modifying presentation of abstract concepts, and self-monitoring are useful techniques to use when adapting curriculum to facilitate comprehension of language function. In addition, role-play situations may be developed in which students ask for directions from a person on the street versus requesting something from another family member. This will assist to illustrate the different functions of language as well as how language itself changes in different situations.

Attention to Task. CLDE students will vary in their willingness to work beyond the required time or to withstand frustration and possible failure. A highly persistent student may work until the task is completed and will seek any necessary assistance. A student with low persistence will demonstrate an inability to work on a task for any length of time or have a short attention span. It should be remembered that an abnormal persistence (i.e., perseveration) is also a learning and behavior problem. Teachers can use monitored observation to determine what, when, where, and with whom appropriate persistence is occurring. To address this educational need, adapt the instructional setting, instructional strategies, and content to continue to elicit the appropriate persistence as observed by the teacher.

Another facet of attention that should be considered is level of anxiety. An individual's level of apprehension and tension under stress conditions will affect attention to the task at hand. Students do better with challenging and difficult tasks if they are in a low-stress situation. Heightened anxiety is one of the side effects of the acculturation process and must be addressed in the instruction of CLDE students. Teachers must adapt their instructional setting and content so that stress for the CLDE student is minimized and must use instructional strategies that do not produce more anxiety in the students.

This may be accomplished by using demonstration techniques and concrete cues to ensure knowledge of expectations, teaching students relaxation techniques before stressful tasks, and always prefacing new lessons with a review of previously successful learning experiences. Other techniques useful in conjunction with attention to task include planned physical movement, clear and concise expectations, time-out, touch control, providing success, prompting, simplifying reading level, alternative methods for response, contingency contracting, or planned ignoring.

Concept Development. This educational need pertains specifically to the ways in which students form and retain concepts. One aspect of this is conceptual tempo (i.e., the speed and adequacy of hypothesis formulation and information processing). Similar to other students, CLDE learners will fall somewhere along the conceptual tempo continuum of reflection versus impulsivity. Cultural factors as well as individual personality factors affect where students fall on this continuum. Some cultures encourage and expect more reflective behavior of learners. Other cultures encourage and expect more impulsive behavior of their children, regarding this as critical to the learning process.

The teacher should adapt the instructional setting, content, and strategies to the current conceptual tempo of the CLDE students and use various techniques and strategies to elicit desired school behavior gradually. The culturally sensitive use of contingency contracting, self-monitoring, and role-play are effective in conceptual tempo development. It is also important for CLDE students to learn which conceptual tempo is appropriate and most effective in a particular setting.

Another consideration in conceptual style is breadth or style of categorization. The broad categorizer likes to include many items in a category and lessens the risk of leaving something out. The narrow categorizer prefers to exclude doubtful items and lessens the probability of including something that does not belong. Cognitive differences are also found when looking at whether students compartmentalize (relatively rigid categories) or differentiate (tendency to conceive of things as having many properties rather than a few). Differences in categorization are to be expected between cultural groups. For example, students from different cultures may group food items in a variety of ways (e.g., color, time of day used, shape, type of utensil used).

To address these differences in concept development, the teacher must very clearly demonstrate the type of categorization that is expected and, if necessary, teach CLDE students how to make the desired categorizations. As previously discussed, some students may be unfamiliar with different "types" of items (e.g., fruit versus vegetable, insect versus animal). These complex categorization skills are common in primary classrooms and are based on assumptions of culturally similar cognitive understanding of concept formation. Teaching and behavior techniques to use in conjunction with development in this area include clear and concise expectations, alternate methods of response, and providing choices.

When considering cognitive development in curricular adaptations for CLDE students, it is important to remember that one of the side effects of acculturation is a resistance to change and new experiences. New activities should always be introduced in relation to previously and successfully learned tasks or skills. Techniques and strategies useful for this conceptual development include providing success, analogy, organization, shortening assignments, or simplifying the reading level of assignments.

Locus of Control.   Locus of control refers to internal versus external perceptions of factors such as responsibility, success, or achievement. Internal people think of themselves as responsible for their own behavior (i.e., their own efforts and abilities resulted in success or failure on a given task). External people, on the other hand, view circumstances as events beyond their control (i.e., luck or other people are responsible for their successes or failures).

CLDE students may display evidence of external locus of control due to the effects of acculturation. They may also display external locus of control due to continued failure to achieve in school no matter how hard they have tried. On the other hand, CLDE students may blame themselves (i.e., display internal locus of control) when failure is really affected by things beyond their control (e.g., their disability).

Confusion in locus of control may be addressed by the teacher in various ways. For example, students may be taught to remind themselves that mistakes are only temporary, that mistakes help show them where they need to put more effort, and that they should congratulate themselves when they are successful. Other techniques that would be useful to address this area of need include student accountability, clear and concise expectations, student input into curricular planning, and self-monitoring.

Perceptions of Time and Space.   Cultures deal with the environment in different ways. These differences must be considered by the classroom teacher when adapting the curriculum. For example, the teacher may adapt seating arrangements and the time of day for particular activities to make maximum use of the CLDE students' particular cultural orientations. The teacher should also be aware of differences in role expectations for males and females and appropriate "personal space." Various techniques and strategies enable the teacher to develop and teach school-appropriate role expectations within the instructional context, without penalizing the student for school or home differences. Role-play, peer tutoring, alternate methods of response, and clear and concise expectations are useful techniques to use as perceptions of time and space require development.

EDUCATIONAL MATERIALS

An integral component within the process of adapting one or more curricular elements is the appropriate selection and use of instructional materials. Materials are vehicles used in class-rooms to study and learn knowledge, skills, and attributes associated with each of the curricular elements. This section provides an overview of criteria to follow when evaluating and selecting different materials, along with ideas for developing and adapting materials if commercial materials are inappropriate for specific situations.

Materials Evaluation and Selection

One primary objective in the materials evaluation and selection process is to select materials that are appropriate for the students who will use them and effective in the particular learning situation for which they are selected. Because an abundant amount of commercial materials exists and because use of some materials may not produce advertised results, careful evaluation of materials must accompany the selection of materials for CLDE students. When evaluating materials for selection and use, the reviewer may use guides or checklists to analyze materials, and/or they may use trial periods with students to determine potential interest and value to a particular group of students. When using materials with students, the evaluation may include pre/post-testing of the learners, observation of student interaction with the material, and reviews with students to gather their feedback about the material.

Criteria for Materials Selection and Evaluation

Criteria important to consider in the materials evaluation and selection process have been identified (Hammill & Bartel, 1995; Lewis & Doorlag, 1995), and some of these are discussed below. In materials selection, educators should consider how materials relate to required content and to student needs. When matching to content, the teacher must consider the match between the structure of the specific

content unit or subject area as well as to the objectives of the particular lesson or activity. Within the content of the subject area, the material must also match the specific objectives for which they are used. Materials must also match student needs. Student needs and abilities that should be considered in materials selection include:

- Difficulty levels relative to language levels of the student
- Pacing of the material
- Format and readability
- Use and control of complex language
- Cultural relevancy and level of interest
- Potential for independent use

These and similar aspects of commercial material must be addressed as particular student needs are considered in the process of evaluating and selecting commercial material for CLDE students.

The following is a list of selected categories to consider when analyzing materials for possible use with students. This information was adapted from Hammill and Bartel (1995) and Affleck, Lowenbraun, and Archer (1980):

Instructional Areas and Skills: Are instruction procedures for each lesson clearly specified? Does the material provide a maximum amount of direct teacher instruction on the skills/concepts presented? Does the direct teacher instruction provide for active student involvement and responses? Are the direct instructional lessons adaptable to small-group/individual instruction? Is a variety of cueing and prompting techniques used to elicit correct child responses? When using verbal instruction, does the instruction proceed in a clear, logical fashion in both languages? Does the teacher use modeling and demonstration when appropriate to the skills being taught? Does the material specify correction and feedback procedures for use during instruction?

Practice: Does the material contain appropriate practice activities that contribute to mastery of the skill/concepts? Are the practice activities directly related to the desired outcome behaviors? Does the material provide enough practice for the slow learner? Does the material provide for feedback on responses during practice? Can the learner complete practice activities independently? Does the material reduce the probability of error in independent practice activities?

Sequence of Instruction: Are the scope and sequence of the material clearly specified? Are facts/concepts/skills ordered in a logical manner from simple to complex? Does the sequence proceed in small steps, easily attainable by the handicapped learner?

Content: Does the selection of the concepts and skills adequately represent the content area? Is the content consistent with the stated objectives? Is the information presented in the material accurate? Is the information presented in the material current? Are various points of view concerning treatment of minorities and people with disabilities, ideologies, social values, sex roles, culture, and socioeconomic class objectively represented? Are the content and topic of the material relevant to the needs of the students with disabilities as well as to the other students in the regular classroom?

Objectives: Are objectives clearly stated for the material? Are the objectives consistent with the goals for the whole classroom? Are the objectives stated in behavioral terms including the desired child behavior, the criteria for measurement of the behavior, and the desired standard of performance?

Entry Behaviors: Does the material specify the prerequisite student skills needed to work with ease in the material? Are the prerequisite student skills compatible with the objectives of the material?

Initial Assessment/Placement: Does the material provide a method to determine initial place-ment into the material? Does the initial placement tool contain enough items to accurately place the learner into the material?

Ongoing Assessment/Evaluation: Does the material provide evaluation procedures for measuring progress and mastery of objectives? Are there sufficient evaluative items to accurately measure learner progress? Are procedures and/or materials for ongoing record-keeping provided?

Review/Maintenance: Are practice and review of content material provided? Are review and maintenance activities systematically and appropriately spaced? Are adequate review and maintenance activities provided for the slow learner?

Motivation/Interest: Are reinforcement procedures built in or suggested for use in the program? Are procedures specified for providing feedback to the student on the student's progress? Has the program been designed to motivate and appeal to students?

Adaptability to Individual Differences: Can the pace be adapted to variations in learner rate of mastery? Can the method of response be adapted to the individual needs of the learner? Can the method of instruction be adapted to the individual needs of the learner? Can the child advance to subsequent tasks when proficiency is demonstrated? Can the learner be placed in the material at an individualized level? Does the material offer alternative teaching strategies for students who are failing to master an objective?

Format of the Material: Is the format uncluttered? Is the format grammatically correct and free of typographical errors? Are photographs and illustrations clear, attractive, and consistent with the content and student experience? Are the type size and style appropriate to the students? Are auditory components of adequate clarity and amplification in both languages? Are the materials durable? Can the materials be easily stored and organized for classroom use?

Teacher Considerations: Is a teacher's manual or set of teacher guidelines provided? Are teacher instructions clear, complete, and unambiguous? Does the material specify the skills and abilities needed by the instructor to work effectively with the material?

Field Test/Research Data: Does the publisher offer research to support the use of the materials for its stated intended purposes? Do the data support the contentions?

Method/Approach: Does the material purport to employ a specific method or approach and is it based on research evidence? Is the method one that is consistent with the educational philosophy used with the students?

In addition to these aspects, when considering materials for selection for CLDE students, the teacher must be cognizant of potential biases that may exist within both the printed and graphic material. These issues include:

- Stereotyping cultures or ethnic groups
- Religious bias
- Sex bias
- Expression of diversity
- Specific material about minority groups
- Portrayal of the interrelationship among diverse groups

As materials evaluation and selection are completed, particular attention must be directed at the potential biases that may exist within materials. Materials should be screened for biases before full evaluation in attempts are undertaken.

When evaluating materials, one method is to complete answers or responses to the questions/items identified above. Another approach is to obtain and use existing evaluation forms to assist with the evaluation process. Yet a third approach is to combine the two methods. The evaluation form in Figure 11–2 was developed by Harris and Schutz (1986) and provides an example of a materials evaluation form. As

illustrated, the form addresses critical areas such as:

- Prerequisite skills
- Thinking abilities
- Required functioning levels
- Individual or group instruction design
- Sequence of materials

This form may be adapted to fit individual needs, be used in conjunction with more comprehensive efforts, or be used as a guide for development of one's own informal material selection guide. Whatever process is followed, particular attention should be paid to individual needs of CLDE students and the four curricular elements previously discussed in this chapter. As a general rule, the more comprehensive the materials, the more thorough and comprehensive the evaluations should be prior to selection and use.

The information described above pertains specifically to the evaluation of curriculum materials. However, in many situations teachers must also become part of the process for appropriately assessing students. Similar to the analysis of curriculum materials, the selection of assessment procedures and devices also requires attention to specific criteria for CLDE students.

Figure 11–3, developed by Collier (1995), provides an example that addresses the student's culture(s), language(s), acculturation level, and experience when selecting assessment devices and procedures. It includes issues to consider, such as: Is the English proficiency necessary for successfully completing the assessment beyond the present CALP of the student? Does this assessment rely heavily on receptive and expressive English-language ability? Is a parallel form of the instrument(s) available in this student's native language or dialect? Is the experience level necessary for success in this assessment directly related to the assessment objectives? Do any items on the instrument(s) represent unfamiliar or misleading content, relative to the

Figure 11–2
Materials Evaluation

Materials Evaluation

Name of material: _____ Copyright date: _____

Publisher and address: _____

Price: _____ Grade level: _____ This analysis by: _____

Subject or content area(s): _____

Structure and time estimates: _____

General goals of the material: _____

What is the cultural orientation of the material? _____

What is the language of instruction? _____

What prerequisite skills are needed? _____

What prerequisite language skills are needed? _____

What is the dominant modality of instruction? _____

What modalities are required for responses? _____

Is convergent or divergent thinking required? _____

Is the level of functioning concrete or abstract? _____

Is the material designed for individual or group instruction? _____

What parts of this material are consumable? _____

Are extra materials required? _____

Are skills logically sequenced? _____

Is there a suggested method for evaluating students' progress and/or performance? _____

Other comments:

Note: Adapted from *The Special Education Resource Program—Rationale and Implementation,* by W. J. Harris and P. N .B. Schutz, 1986, p. 202, Upper Saddle River, NJ: Merrill/Prentice Hall.

Figure 11–3
Cross-cultural Assessment Paradigm

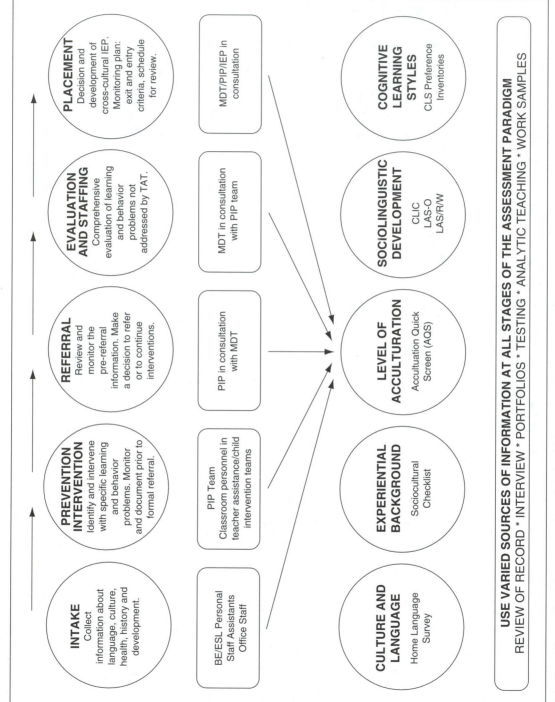

USE VARIED SOURCES OF INFORMATION AT ALL STAGES OF THE ASSESSMENT PARADIGM
REVIEW OF RECORD * INTERVIEW * PORTFOLIOS * TESTING * ANALYTIC TEACHING * WORK SAMPLES

Note. From *Crosscultural Assessment Paradigm,* by C. Collier, 1995, Vancouver, WA.

student's cultural/linguistic background? Does the research or manual for the instrument(s) report any differences in performance related to sociocultural or linguistic background? Is the assessment environment and situation appropriate for this student's cultural and linguistic background? Has the instrument(s) been standardized on a large enough sample from this student's sociocultural group to warrant reliance on the norms or criterion levels? Has the assessment been validated for the specific purpose for which it is being considered?

Creating and Adapting Materials

Although much commercial material exists, teachers of CLDE students may need to adapt material or create their own in an effort to meet prerequisite needs of CLDE students. If possible, commercial material should be used to avoid unnecessary work on the part of the teacher. Using commercial material allows the teacher to concentrate on actual teaching activities with learners and minimizes time required to deal with material once the selection process has been completed. However, the need to adapt or develop materials is not uncommon in today's classrooms for CLDE students. Several guidelines for adapting commercial material or developing teacher-made materials are discussed in the literature (Lewis & Doorlag, 1995). The following list contains suggestions from this and other sources for adapting or developing material. This list is not designed to be all-inclusive, and variations to these ideas may be required in order to meet individual needs.

- Adjust method of presentation of content of material.
- Develop supplemental material.
- Tape record directions or material.
- Provide alternatives for responding to questions in material.
- Rewrite brief sections of material to lower reading level.

- Outline material for student before reading and selection.
- Reduce the number of pages or items on a page to be completed by the student.
- Break tasks into smaller subtasks.
- Provide additional practice to ensure mastery.
- Substitute a similar, less complex task for a particular assignment.
- Develop simple study guides to complement required materials.

These and similar types of adaptations will allow CLDE students to successfully confront various materials used in the classroom. When combined with various curricular adaptation strategies previously discussed in this chapter, the adaptation of materials will allow students to have greater success in all areas within the total curriculum. The development of teacher-made materials, such as study guides, game boards, or other supplemental material, should be carefully completed to avoid unnecessary work for the teacher. However, similar to adapted material, carefully developed teacher-made materials can assist CLDE students successfully to address materials needed in school.

This chapter concludes with the presentation of several guidelines to facilitate the effective use of materials with CLDE students. These guidelines facilitate the effective use of materials with CLDE students, and they represent some of the many considerations teachers should bear in mind when evaluating, selecting, adapting, or developing materials for use by CLDE students:

1. Know specific language abilities of each student.
2. Include appropriate cultural experiences in material adapted or developed.
3. Ensure that material progresses at a rate commensurate with student needs and abilities.
4. Document the success of selected commercial material.

5. Adapt only specific materials requiring modifications and do not attempt to change too much at one time.

6. Attempt different materials and adaptations until appropriate education for all CLDE students exists.

7. Strategically implement materials adaptations to ensure smooth transitions into the new materials.

8. Follow some consistent format or guide when evaluating materials.

9. Be knowledgeable of particular cultures and heritages and their compatibility with selected materials.

10. Follow a well-developed process for evaluating the success of adapted or developed materials as individual language and cultural needs of CLDE students are addressed.

☻ SUMMARY

This chapter has addressed the curricular needs of CLDE students with learning and behavior problems. A procedure for effective instruction through curricular adaptations that address these special needs has been presented. Materials selection and intervention techniques appropriate for meeting the special needs of CLDE students have been described and discussed. Appropriate use of methods and materials within the framework of adapting the four curricular elements will result in improved instruction for culturally and linguistically different students with disabilities. Consider this final thought and challenge—the challenge to look beyond simple solutions to complex curriculum problems through the study of the interrelationship among curricular elements, to achieve and maintain the most effective instruction necessary to promote a positive learning environment.

☻ DISCUSSION QUESTIONS

1. Describe the four curricular elements that must be addressed in the classroom with CLDE students.
2. Explain the purpose of diagnostic intervention.
3. What steps would you go through to document instructional interventions?
4. Develop a simple diagnostic intervention plan for a bilingual child. Document the process you would use.
5. Select one teaching strategy and describe how you would use it with a bilingual exceptional child.

☻ REFERENCES

Affleck, J. Q., Lowenbraun, S., & Archer, A. (1980). *Teaching the mildly handicapped in the regular class.* Upper Saddle River, NJ: Merrill/Prentice Hall.

Brodhagen, B. L. (1994). Assessing and reporting student progress in an integrative curriculum. In *Teaching and Change,* 1, 238–254.

Collier, C. (1987). Bilingual special education curriculum training. In *Proceedings of the First Annual Symposium, Cross-cultural special edcuation network,* 46–47. Boulder, CO: University of Colorado.

Collier, C. (1995). *Crosscultural assessment paradigm.* Vancouver, WA: Cross Cultural Developmental Education Services.

Collier, C., & Hoover, J. J. (1987). *Cognitive learning strategies for diverse disabled students.* Lindale, TX: Hamilton Publications.

Drake, S. M. (1993). *Planning integrated curriculum: The call to adventure.* Alexandria, VA: ASCD.

Hammill, D. D., & Bartel, N. R. (1995). *Teaching students with learning and behavior problems: Managing mild-to-moderate difficulties in resource and inclusive settings.* Austin, TX: Pro-Ed.

Harris, W. J., & Schutz P. N. B. (1986). *The special education resource program—rationale and implementation.* Upper Saddle River, NJ: Merrill/Prentice Hall.

Hoover, J. J., & Patton, J. R. (In press). *Curriculum adaptation for students with learning and behavior problems; Principles and practices* (Second edition). Austin, TX: Pro-Ed.

Lewis, R. B., & Doorlag, D. H. (1995). *Teaching special students in the mainstream.* Upper Saddle River, NJ: Merrill/Prentice Hall.

Morsink, C., Thomas, C. C., & Correa, V. I. (1991). *Interactive teaming: Consultation and collaboration in special programs.* New York: Merrill.

Nieto, S. (1996). *Affirming diversity* (Second edition). New York: Longman.

Shubert, W. H. (1993). Curriculum reform. In *Challenges and achievements of American education,* pp. 80–115. ASCD Yearbook. Arlington, VA: ASCD.

CHAPTER 12

Including Bilingual Exceptional Children in the General Education Classroom

Catherine Collier

- ⊚ Models of Inclusion
- ⊚ The Teacher Assistance Child Intervention Team
- ⊚ Teacher Competencies for Including Bilingual-Exceptional Children in the General Education Classroom
- ⊚ Suggestions for Including CLDE Children
- ⊚ Communication Concerns
- ⊚ Intellectual Concerns
- ⊚ Physical Environment Concerns
- ⊚ Vision Impairment
- ⊚ Summary

OBJECTIVES

To describe various models of inclusion in bilingual and special education programs as well as for exceptional bilingual children

To describe the continuum inclusion model of educational services for exceptional bilingual children

To describe inclusive intervention (II) and prevention and intervention programs (PIP) as effective strategies for bilingual children with language and behavior problems

To describe various teacher competencies for including exceptional bilingual children in the general education classroom

To provide practical suggestions for including bilingual children with various exceptionalities in general education classrooms

Inclusive instruction has come to be the preferred means of providing exceptional children with equal access to appropriate education. In the form of transition and developmental bilingual education programs, it is also the most common type of bilingual education for culturally and linguistically diverse (CLD) children. This chapter discusses the need and justification for inclusive models, teacher competencies for these models, and suggestions for including bilingual children with various exceptionalities in the general education environment.

References to the *mainstream* are meant in the most general sense: the dominant population of a community and its culture and language. In general in the United States, the point of reference is European American and English. *Inclusion* means the integration of all learners into the general education classroom, including those who are exceptional and culturally/linguistically diverse. Inclusive programs integrate all learners to the greatest extent possible and implies a collaborative effort on the part of general educators and specialized staff members. Inclusion is more than enrolling diverse learners in general education classrooms. It involves an education placement procedure for learners based on the belief that each such child is best educated in the least restrictive environment in which the child's needs can be satisfactorily met. The inclusion process recognizes the existence of a wide range of unique learning needs, varying in intensity and duration and the appropriateness of a continuum of educational settings for individual needs. Additionally, to the maximum extent possible, children should receive instruction with their peers, rather than being pulled out for instruction targeting their exceptionality or language.

Inclusion and *least restrictive environment* are not synonymous. Although full instruction in a general education classroom is frequently seen as the most inclusive and as the least restrictive environment for a child with unique learning needs, the diverse learner may benefit from receiving individualized instruction for some of these needs. Because this individual instruction will vary proportionately, depending on the child's special needs, inclusion should be viewed as a continuum of services. This is discussed in greater detail later in this chapter. Removal of the diverse learner from the general education classroom should occur only when particular needs cannot be met satisfactorily in an environment including students without disabilities.

Inclusion means that diverse learners receive the interventions that their own learning needs might merit, while they enjoy the personal and social advantages of life in general education school classes with all the other neighborhood youngsters of their age. It also means that high quality learning is going on at the same time. Further, it means that the general educator coordinates all pupil activities with the assistance of a staff of special educators, aides, the school principal, and other specialists. Together with parents, these personnel make up a team whose central concern is top-flight instruction for all children. In essence, rather than pulling students out to access the resources wherever they are (the classic resource room model), inclusion involves pulling resources in to where the students are. The resources, rather than the children, are moved.

Peck (1993) has identified several factors that facilitate inclusion for students with disabilities. These concern: (1) the underlying ideology and belief about the nature of disability and special education and about education, and (2) whether inclusion is viewed primarily as a valued outcome in itself or just another way to teach. Peck found that underlying beliefs about the nature of disability and special education result in very different approaches to working with students with learning and behavior problems. When school staff have a deficit orientation towards the nature of students' disabilities, they define students' needs in terms of discrepancies from "normal" development. These discrepancies are viewed as "deficits" that will need to be "fixed" or "remediated." Special education would then be the necessary tool to fix the children or their problems. Schools could instead have a support orientation in which children are viewed intrinsically different from each other. These differences require different types and amounts of social support to enable each student to participate meaningfully in his or her own community. Special education in this setting would provide the necessary supports for each student to participate in the community. The underlying beliefs about education within the community and the school itself can have a profound difference on the attitudes and actions of school staff. Diversity in the school is either an expected and valued aspect of children and people in general, or an issue that will need to be "dealt with." Where diversity is valued, each child is expected to differ in his or her pace of development, in style of learning, and background experiences. The schools where diversity is an issue to be dealt with considers different students and their families in terms of how they can fit in with the school culture. Inclusion, when valued for its own merits, creates the sense of community or "belongingness," which is considered an important goal in some schools. Within these contexts, inclusion is viewed as a goal. And while it may not be considered the only important outcome to be achieved, it is not justified primarily in terms of its effects on other outcomes (such as development or academic achievement). In other communities, inclusion is viewed primarily as an educational "treatment," that is, as a means toward other goals—particularly the goal of making kids' social behavior more typical. In these communities the notion of "normal models" is salient in the rationales offered for inclusion, and the success of inclusion is evaluated in terms of the extent to which it produces "outcomes."

Peck (1993) also concluded that the extent to which there is a cohesive philosophy held within and organization which reflects its values and beliefs affects the implementation of inclusion. There are several aspects of education at the structural level which, when modified, can enhance inclusion. When special education is decentralized and there is building-level control, it gives the people closest to the students the flexibility to support their individual needs. Team teaching and consultation models of service delivery enhance inclusion when they replace the concept of special education as a "place." Establishing support services and resources that are designed to support the learning of all children within the inclusive classroom can have profound effects. Even such measures as having classroom aides work with all children can be beneficial. Highly participatory decision making at the district and building level is another factor which can encourage inclusion.

The relationships within the education system, the teaming relationships, support of parent involvement, the transitions between classrooms and building programs, the transdisciplinary practices and shared responsibilities in assessment and instruction, and the extent to which programs developed effective techniques for sharing information across individuals and settings all affected the implementation of inclusion (Peck, 1993). The quality of the teaming relationships and practices has much to do with the level of trust built within the team (the trusting team takes more risks because there is support from within) and the efficiency and effectiveness of task management. Teams that routinely spend time reflecting and modifying their own procedures have more success. In programs where parents are routinely involved in all aspects of building level policy decisions (including staffing and budget decisions), a team relationship is built between parents and staff. When parents are given a more restricted role (such as helping teachers in classrooms), the parent-staff relationship is more often adversarial, administrators and teachers express more concerns about parents being "uninvolved," and legal conflicts are more prominent issues. Transdisciplinary practices (a high degree of "role release" between teacher, child services, special education, etc.)

encourage teams to share disciplinary expertise and plan programs which integrate objectives across disciplines. When assessment, program planning, and instruction are more compartmentalized along disciplinary boundaries, programs struggle more with implementation, since information and responsibility for an array of programs from differing disciplines have to be coordinated. Some programs develop effective techniques for sharing information across individuals and settings by instituting simple, user-friendly information systems. Information in these programs is routinely shared with all members of the team.

Peck (1993) advocates some specific practices to facilitate inclusion. These include roles, activities, and relationships. Roles which facilitate inclusion for children at the individual level are related to the learning process. Children need to participate in a variety of roles related to the learning process in which they have a variety of opportunities to direct their own learning and to learn with the assistance of other children. Adult roles that facilitate inclusion are more generic and involve adults working together in the classroom and sharing a variety of specific and general roles, thereby modeling the inclusive interaction for the children. Activities that are open-ended allow for meaningful participation by children at diverse developmental levels. A variety of activities allow children to select those which are of interest to them. Teachers may encourage children to select activities in which they can participate with some adult guidance or with assistance from a peer. Activities which have personal meaning for children have instruction embedded in them. Relationships which facilitate inclusion include the formation of friendships, and positive social relationships between both culturally and linguistically diverse exceptional (CLDE) and non-CLDE children. Students should be given opportunities to assist each other's learning. Modeling processes can be used to provide learning opportunities for children at developmental levels.

Peck, Mabry, Curley and Conn-Powers (1993) reported some emerging patterns of concern about inclusive classrooms. These concerns fell into six general categories: nonfunctional activities, "sticking out," inappropriate touching, double standard, "out of it," and misplaced responsibility. They found that many of the instructional activities in which students with disabilities participated appeared to have little meaning or functional value for them. They found many examples of students engaging in behaviors that appeared highly stigmatizing (crying, screaming, lying down, and wandering in the classroom). The behaviors were not always disruptive, but they always seemed to make the student noticeable in an undesirable way. Many students with disabilities were observed to touch peers and adults in inappropriate ways. In some cases, this touching violated social norms. In other cases, touching involved aggressive behavior, such as hitting or throwing things at peers. In many cases, peers did not react to these acts directly or clearly, but tended to ignore them and/or avoid the child. In a number of cases, they observed interactions in which peers seemed to allow children with disabilities to "get away with" behavior they would not tolerate from peers without disabilities. There were many examples of students not participating in the general activities of the class. High frequency examples of this included not moving to a new activity signaled by the teacher, refusing to participate in a classroom activity, and failing to attend when the teacher was giving directions. In some examples, individuals were given (or took on) responsibilities which were not appropriate for their role or for which they were unprepared. Examples of this included students who were placed in situations where they had to manage the problematic behavior of a student with disabilities and situations where classroom teaching assistants were given [de facto] responsibility for designing curriculum and instructional strategies for children with disabilities. All of these concerns have parallels in the integration of CLD students–interactions appropriate in one cultural or linguistic context may be inappropriate or out of place in the classroom. Interactions normal in one context may seem strange and unpleasant to the students. LEP students may not participate, because they do not understand or are uncomfortable.

In bilingual and English as a Second Language (ESL) education, several inclusion models are used, including immersion, maintenance, restoration, and transition. As with programs for exceptional children, these programs were developed to provide remedial, compensatory, or special education for culturally or linguistically different children under the impetus of equal educational opportunity and are discussed in greater detail in Chapter 2.

MODELS OF INCLUSION

The goals of inclusion are the complete social, physical, and instructional integration of all children. Reynolds and Birch (1986); Gearheart, Weishahn, and Gearheart (1995); Heward (1996); and Hammill and Bartel (1990) all address various models of including exceptional children in the general education classroom. Peck et al. (1993) discuss the aspects of school systems that allow the total inclusion of exceptional children in every classroom. There are also various models for including bilingual children in the conventional setting which are similar in some respects to those for exceptional children.

Cascade Model

The inclusion model most common in public schools is the *Cascade Model* which is also discussed in Chapter 3 and is presented in Figure 3–2. This model has diversified staffing and offers many forms of individualized instruction to accommodate a variety of students (Reynolds & Birch, 1986). In practice, educational services for exceptional children may take several forms with varying degrees of inclusion, depending on

the resources of the particular school district. Figure 12–1 illustrates some of these.

Models of bilingual/bicultural education programs are quite similar to the various models of services to exceptional children. These may be illustrated as shown in Figure 12–2. As can be seen, all of these models are designed to remediate or compensate for the difference of the learner from the mainstream. In the transition models, the goal is to return the child to the general education classroom as soon as possible, that is, upon the acquisition of English or upon the remediation of the particular learning disability. Maintenance models seek to provide compensatory instruction and/or cultural identification while the child participates in general education to the greatest extent possible.

Frequently, programs in public schools are combinations of these models. In the inclusion process, it is preferable that all children have a place in the general education classroom, that all children begin school with the understanding that they have a place in the general education program, and that a specific general educator is their teacher. As much as possible, special services should be provided to them in the general education classroom setting. This can be accomplished through the use of teacher assistance or instruction support teams, bilingual special education tutors, itinerant bilingual special education teachers, and special consultants to the general educators. If the special services must take place outside the general education classroom for some reason, it should be in the least obtrusive method possible and must be connected to what occurs in the general education classroom.

There is still considerable debate concerning how and where the bilingual exceptional child should be served. Some educators believe that all but the most severely disabled or those with no English should be included in the general education environment. Others advocate continued special class placement for culturally and linguistically diverse children with exceptionalities. In the case of limited English speakers, this

Figure 12–1
Special Education Inclusion Models

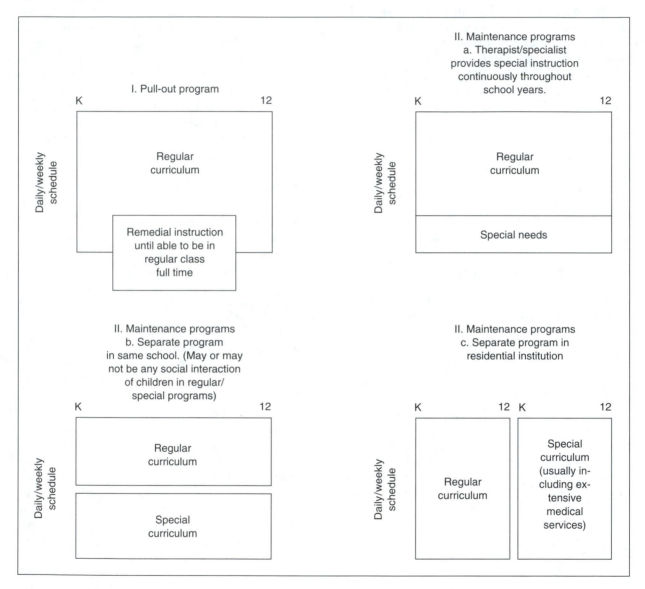

is an especially sensitive issue. Most bilingual/ bicultural education programs are designed to enhance the child's acquisition of English while providing uninterrupted achievement of general curriculum content. This is usually done through a combination of native language instruction in content areas and the ESL program.

However, the bilingual or ESL instructor rarely has the training to adequately serve the special needs of exceptional children. Placing the child with disabilities in the ESL or bilingual education classroom will not adequately serve that child's needs. However, placement part-time or full-time in the special education classroom will

Figure 12–2
Bilingual–Bicultural Inclusion Models: Teacher Competencies for Mainstreaming Bilingual Exceptional Children

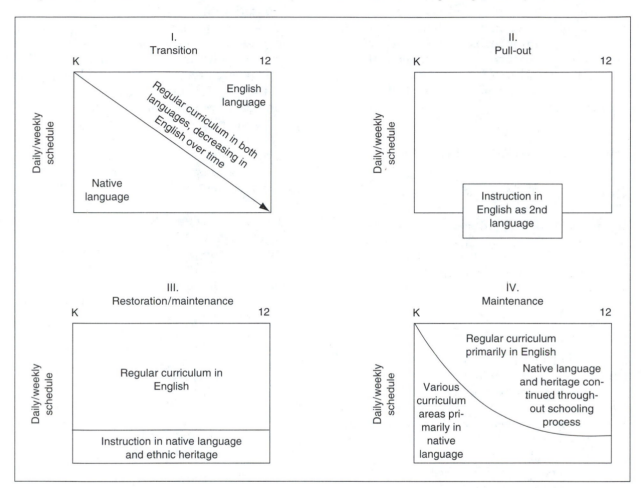

also be inadequate, because few if any special education teachers receive training in second language and the special needs of those undergoing acculturation. Bringing diverse resources to the child is a better solution. To address these concerns for acculturation, language development, and acquisition, and to meet special learning needs of the bilingual exceptional child in a general education setting, an inclusive program with a continuum of services is proposed. The continuum provides a full spectrum of services available at particular periods during the inclusive instruction of the child.

The first level of this continuum of services is a prevention-intervention period (PIP), also referred to as prevention and enhancement programming (PEP, see Chapter 5). These may occur within any of the cascade levels and within any of the transition, general education, and restorative bilingual education models. This process involves the development and interaction of a collaborative team of professionals working with the classroom teacher. This team is sometimes called the Instructional Support Team (IST), a Teacher Assistance Child Intervention Team (TACIT), a Student Assistance

Team (SAT), or a Teacher Assistance Team (TAT). The choice of the term used to describe the intervention period and the name of the team usually reflect the focus and emphasis of the district, e.g., focus is on assisting with instruction, the teacher, or the student with emphasis upon assistance, intervention, support, or something else. Each of these levels is described below.

Hospital or Home Bound

A general educator may assist the home and/or child via video and/or telephone while the student is temporarily at home or in the hospital for a specific medical reason. The home teacher speaks the child's native language or uses an interpreter or a bilingual tutor. This educator teaches ESL as part of oral language development.

Separate Facilities

This type facility may be a place away from the general education building where CLDE students go to participate in a particular activity, such as programs to share in traditional language or cultural events or spend time with students like themselves where they may feel safer and more comfortable for a brief period (e.g., "Newcomers" programs). Teachers and staff in these programs would provide appropriate bilingual special education as needed (also ESL) through the use of bilingual special educators or tutors and would work with the general education staff to develop crossover activities and curriculum that have a direct relationship to the general education program.

TACIT Process

Students may spend most of the day in the general education class with pullout classes for ESL, bilingual, special, and/or bilingual special education classes, as needed. The length of time at-tending each will vary. If teachers do not speak the native language of the child, a bilingual special education tutor should work with the child in the native language to maintain and enhance content achievement. Counselors or tutors fluent in the native language and knowledgeable of effective acculturation process (culture shock) should work with the child to enhance cross-cultural development. This placement option requires close collaboration by all educators to ensure coordination and continuity.

In this option, the student remains in regular classes for all instruction where possible. Pullout sessions may be used for specific interventions. Members of the TACIT may work with the student in pullout sessions, within the regular instructional context, or in a combination of the two settings. Bilingual team members or tutors should work with students in the native language to maintain and enhance content achievement and language acquisition. Use of cross-cultural counselors or peer counseling support sessions may be necessary on occasion for assistance with interventions targeting the acculturation process. Requires close teamwork by all members of the TACIT.

General Education Classroom with Itinerant Services

In this option, the student remains in general education classes. Therapists and ESL bilingual, special, and itinerant bilingual special education tutors and/or teachers work with the student within the general education context. Curriculum comes from the general education sequence, though general education teachers and itinerant teachers/tutors may collaborate on appropriate modifications. The use of native language tutors may be necessary on occasion for maintenance of content achievement. The use of cross-cultural counselors and peer counseling support sessions may be necessary on occasion for assistance with the acculturation process.

General Education Class

This setting requires the use of linguistically and culturally appropriate instruction, with the use of both English and native language. The general educator may consult with bilingual special education staff for assistance with materials. The student may require assistance from a bilingual special education tutor on special occasions. The classroom educator may need to consult with a school counselor knowledgeable in the psychological side effects of acculturation.

THE TEACHER ASSISTANCE CHILD INTERVENTION TEAM

The *Teacher Assistance Child Intervention Team (TACIT)* is a collaborative team assembled to identify limited English proficient (LEP) students whose learning and behavior needs are not being met within general education classrooms (including bilingual/ESL). The intent of a TACIT is to identify and provide appropriate in-class intervention assistance. It is specifically concerned with appropriately and effectively intervening in the general education classroom for students with learning and behavior difficulties caused by acculturation, language or cultural differences, disabilities, or the interaction of all of these. At the end of the 6–10 week TACIT period, the team decides whether to proceed to a formal referral to staffing or to continue monitoring the student's responses to intervention.

The TACIT process provides a collaborative framework for identifying, addressing, documenting, and monitoring this intensive intervention. Research has shown that intensive team intervention over at least six weeks will address 75% to 85% of the student's needs, particularly those related directly to cultural and language differences and acculturation.

To address the concerns, each school and school district should establish a TACIT drawn primarily from general education personnel, both bilingual and non-bilingual, in the building. The first task of the team is to collect preliminary sociocultural and educational information about the student in question, and then to identify appropriate areas of intervention. The team will also assist the presenting teacher in implementing the interventions and will monitor the student's response to the interventions. Depending upon the student's response, the team will then make a decision about alternative educational processes. There are nine steps to the TACIT process.

Step 1: Build the Team

The TACIT is formed within the building from general education personnel, including bilingual and ESL teachers. The most efficient configuration is a core of four or five teachers who meet weekly to consider new issues, plan interventions, or monitor ongoing student concerns. Joining them may be a number of other education professionals with special knowledge or skills useful in the particular student case under discussion. Thus any given meeting may have from five to ten members present. Usually TACIT members are selected by the site based management team or its equivalent, working in conjunction with the principal. Some schools have TACIT members elected by the teaching staff.

The TACIT team should be composed of people knowledgeable in:

- General education curriculum environment
- Cognitive/learning style and classroom performance
- Performance outside of academic settings
- Ethnic and linguistic community
- Family and community environment
- Interventions for specific behavior and learning needs
- Cross-cultural and cross-lingual learning
- Interventions for culture shock and acculturation

- Second language learning
- Interventions for cognitive language development

Step 2: Gather Information

In order to determine the student's needs, the TACIT needs to gather and analyze all appropriate background data on the student. This includes a comprehensive profile of the student's culture and language background, previous experience with public education systems, sociolinguistic development, acculturation level, cognitive learning style, and other information pertinent to the student's case. This information should be recorded in the TACIT file, and should be done on forms developed for this purpose.

The information gathered in this step should come from a variety of settings, not just from the classroom. This means observing the student on the playground, during lunch, and outside the school setting, as appropriate. Information may be gathered through observation, interview, work samples, analytic teaching, portfolios, and classroom informal or other normal performance measures used within general-education classrooms. The information gathered must cover all of the following areas:

Culture and Language. Gathering information about the student's cultural background is crucial to effective intervention. It is especially important to use reliable records and resources to collect this information. Avoid assumptions based upon the student's appearance, name, or language spoken. Interview parents, community members, and siblings for this information. Students have often been listed as "Hispanic" because of their "Spanish-sounding" names. Some of these students were, in fact, Native American and spoke their tribal language, not Spanish, and not even English.

Assessing the student's academic language skills is necessary to determine the student's ability to handle typical classroom tasks in English. These academic materials should reflect authentic classroom demands as much as possible and should assess language in everyday usage. This assessment will help to determine if an LEP student has unaddressed second language acquisition needs. This assessment is also needed with fluent English speakers who have a home language other than English.

It takes only a year or two to acquire the ability to use English in everyday situations and develop *basic interpersonal communication skills (BICS)*. Many students from linguistically diverse backgrounds appear fairly proficient in English in the classroom setting in terms of speaking with peers and adults. But it takes at least five years, with directed assistance, to acquire minimal proficiency in the academic use of English. This means that the students may be speaking English all the time, but not have enough *cognitive academic language proficiency (CALP)* in English to successfully complete or understand assignments, take tests, or develop literacy at their grade level. Therefore, both students already receiving bilingual/ESL services and students exited from these services, but from non-English speaking backgrounds, should receive classroom functional language screening. See Chapter 6 for more information about the language development of bilingual students, both with and without exceptionalities.

Language use information must be gathered in a variety of contexts (e.g., observe casual conversation with peers, interview the student, test, etc.) and provide information about both the BICS and the CALP of the student. Screening tools such as the Language Assessment Scale (LAS) (DeAvila & Duncan, 1986) and the Classroom Language Interaction Checklist (CLIC) (Collier, 1995) are also useful. A copy of the CLIC is provided in Appendix D at the end of Chapter 10. When determining which measures of academic language skills to use, keep in mind that the measure must be developmentally appropriate. Chapters 7 and 8 provide more information about language assessment procedures and measures.

Acculturation Level. *Acculturation* is the process of adaptation to a new cultural environment. It does not mean assimilation, and it is something everyone experiences at various times in their lives. Whenever we move from a known interaction environment into an unknown interaction environment, we acculturate to the new situation. Depending upon how similar the new environment is to what we know, we will experience differing degrees of stress and culture shock as we adapt, acculturate, to the new situation. Research has identified many culture shock or stress related side effects to this process of acculturation. These manifest themselves in behaviors that look a lot like indications of disability, and thus the TACIT must sort out those due to acculturation and cultural and linguistic differences from those due to disability. These side effects may include:

- Distractibility
- Response fatigue
- Withdrawal
- Silence or not responding
- Code-switching
- Confusion in locus of control

The TACIT must determine the student's relative level of acculturation in order to identify appropriate interventions and correctly determine the appropriateness of subsequent instructional approaches, assessment and evaluation procedures, and the language of instruction. One tool for assessing relative level of acculturation is the Acculturation Quick Screen (AQS) (Collier, 1994). A copy of this instrument is provided in Appendix C in Chapter 10. Other instruments and procedures available for use include information from interviews with parents and community members familiar with acculturation issues within the student's cultural and linguistic community.

Experiential Background. Differences in experience may account for much of the discrepancy between achievement and ability seen in LEP students with learning and behavior problems. Many refugee and immigrant students in this country come from socioeconomic and political situations where they have not had the educational experiences of dominant culture American students. This is also true of many Hispanic and Native American students, especially those who live in migrant families. Many of these students are raised in settings with little or no exposure to regular and consistent public school education or early childhood educational programs, such as day care centers and educational television. As a result, many LEP students lack experiences and preskills necessary for successful learning in American public schools and which are significant to public school assessments. Different experiences and backgrounds also affect LEP students' responses to various elements of the curriculum. The use of inquiry techniques, behavior contracting, active processing, and other individualized instructional strategies is very dependent upon prior experience. Role expectations and the ability to make quick cause-and-effect associations are prerequisite skills for optimal effectiveness of many strategies. LEP students' lack of appropriate responses to these commonly used instructional strategies compounds their learning and behavior needs and may be mistaken as an indication of a disability. Some of the LEP students' responses to the school environment may be due to previous school experiences and others to linguistic or cultural differences. Students who have been in school systems in other countries generally know basic school procedures, such as raising their hands for attention, asking permission to do something, and recess and lunchroom behaviors. However, they may be unfamiliar with particular instructional strategies, such as independent or silent reading rather than group recitation, or discovery learning rather than rote memorization. Their inappropriate responses to silent reading, discovery learning, or other activities may appear disruptive to the teacher.

LEP students with no school experience may be unfamiliar with particular instructional strategies as well as the basic operational expectations of the school and classroom. They may not know how or when to ask for assistance or permission, may not be familiar with appropriate school behavior in or out of the classroom, and may not have had any exposure to CALP. Additionally, LEP students from a culture that values indirectness and distance as evidence of appropriate behavior may not respond positively to the use of touching or praise as reinforcement strategies. These students' interpretation of "time out" and other teaching and behavior management techniques may be quite different from the teacher's intent when using those techniques. Inappropriate responses may lead the teacher to incorrectly suspect the presence of a disability.

Sociolinguistic Development. Another basic element of special concern in an assessment of LEP students is language acquisition and development. Language is the primary medium through which culture and experiences are shared and transmitted from generation to generation and is a primary element in the acculturation of LEP students. Language occurs within a social and interactive communicative context; the term "sociolinguistic development" describes the comprehensiveness of language development and usage. It is important to identify and assess the LEP student's sociolinguistic abilities in both first and second languages since misunderstandings about sociolinguistic abilities frequently lead to inaccurate referrals of LEP students.

Many LEP students referred to general education and special education are described as deficient in or lacking sociolinguistic skills entirely. This usually means that the student appears to have deficits in both English and the native language. There is ample evidence that the development of language skills for communication within a social context is a natural process and

that human beings are genetically programmed for sociolinguistic acquisition. Therefore, a student who is "lacking language" would indeed be severely and unusually disabled. Research has shown, however, that most LEP students have well-established sociolinguistic systems in their first language as well as somewhat in English, but they use these systems selectively and nonacademically. LEP students often have sociolinguistic competence in both languages, but their limited sociolinguistic performance in the academic setting obscures this underlying competence. All students, with few exceptions, learn a "home" language. Any student who can speak is not "lacking language," but bilingual students with limited English proficiency are often labeled as such. The quality and quantity of verbal interaction students receive in the home language, whichever language is used, is the greatest predictor of later academic success in English. Those culturally and linguistically diverse (CLD) learners who have not received quality development in their native language, and who have both poor first and second language proficiency, will need additional language development assistance based upon their sociolinguistic proficiency. This sometimes happens in non-English speaking homes, where well-intentioned parents have insisted that children speak only English when they, themselves, are unable to provide adequate interaction models. By doing so, they deny or discourage any use or development of the student's most proficient language. This has resulted in continuing problems with academic achievement and second-language acquisition, even though the student's subsequent language ability in English is better than or equal to their ability in the native language. The identification of LEP students as language disabled when they exhibit auditory perception and expressive problems only in English conflicts with the provisions of PL 94-142 and other legislation and litigation. Only if LEP students demonstrate receptive and expressive language problems both in their native language and in English can they be said to have a linguistic disability. This, both English and native sociolinguistic development must be evaluated during the assessment process. Chapter 6 provides additional information about language acquisition and the bilingual exceptional child.

Cognitive Learning Style. Cognition is the process of perceiving, attending, thinking, remembering, and knowing. It is a continuous process that begins at or before birth and continues throughout life. Some people have more cognitive capacities than others, and some do not use what they possess. Education can affect the ability to develop and use cognitive processes. Many researchers agree that the differences in how we conceptually organize our environment result in characteristic ways of learning from our experiences.

Cognitive style is the stable, typical, and consistent way in which individuals select and organize environmental data. *Learning styles* are the characteristic ways in which individual students respond to the instructional environment. While viewed as a consistent pattern of behavior, learning style changes with age and experience, especially exposure to cognitive and learning strategies. *Cognitive learning styles* are the characteristic ways in which individual students respond to the learning task and instructional environment.

Culture is the concept of things that a particular people uses as a model for perceiving, relating, and interpreting their environment. Cognitive development and cognitive learning style depend largely on the LEP student's cultural background and experience. Culture shapes and influences the LEP student's cognitive learning style; identifying these styles becomes an instructionally meaningful part of the assessment of LEP students. Identifying the cognitive learning styles of the LEP students contributes directly to the development of appropriate TACIT interventions and IEPs.

Step 3: Identify the Needs

At this step, the focus is to analyze the background information collected during Step 2 and identify specific areas of concern to address through interventions. It is critical to address the "reason for referral" question(s) that the teacher posed. The product of Step 3 will be a document outlining the LEP student's needs in priority order, to be addressed within the TACIT activity period.

A useful tool for organizing this stage of the TACIT activities is the Sociocultural Checklist (SC). This single sheet contains all five of the sociocultural question areas discussed in Step 2 and allows the TACIT to organize their focus in these areas. Upon completion of the SC form or some similar documentation process, the TACIT identifies which of the five areas appear to have the most items checked. The areas can be ranked in priority from the one with the most checked to the least. A copy of this form is provided in Appendix E at the end of Chapter 10. If the TACIT is not using the SC form, it prioritizes the student's needs in consultation and based upon their own knowledge of the school based priorities. It is also helpful at this stage to address any additional information and training needs that become apparent. These could include intercultural activities and cross-cultural awareness for the TACIT members, participating teachers, the students, and their classmates. Participating teachers may benefit from cross-cultural communication and cultural competence refresher training. This is also the point at which to determine the best language to use in the interventions and in what balance. The languages of instruction, specific interventions, and that used in various formal and informal assessments and evaluation settings may all vary, depending upon the priority of the specific needs to be addressed.

Step 4: Target One Specific Learning Behavior

The TACIT selects one specific learning or behavior concern to address with specific intervention(s). This is generally the area with the most concerns checked on the SC form, that is, where there is the greatest sociocultural or school adaptation need. It may be the area of most immediate concern for the person initiating the TACIT process for this particular LEP student. Other areas of concern prioritized in Step 3 should be held aside for future attention and review and for future intervention. It is difficult to give quality intervention for more than a few high priority needs at once. When more TACIT members are involved in implementing the interventions, more specific learning behaviors may be addressed simultaneously during the TACIT period of attention. Each intervention should be consistently implemented for at least two weeks, until a positive change is observed or a satisfactory result is achieved. Sometimes and infrequently, the initial response to the intervention is a heightening of the focus of concern, but this response is usually a temporary sign that the learning behavior is accurately targeted and the intervention is having an effect. Change the intervention immediately if the LEP student's response to it is clearly negative and counterproductive.

Within an average TACIT period of eight weeks, several specific learning behaviors may be addressed. The TACIT process usually takes at least six weeks and may last as long as the TACIT observes and documents positive responses to each successive or concurrent intervention.

Step 5: Identify Interventions

The TACIT designs a prereferral intervention plan to address:

- Any academic areas impacted by language difficulties.
- Improvement of verbal skill in one or both languages.
- Improvement of writing skill in one or both languages.
- Any medical, behavioral, or emotional needs.
- Adaptive behavior skills.

- Any cognitive learning strategies which would enhance students' ability to engage in learning.
- Community services needed and outside agencies to access (food, clothing, employment, protective services, counseling, etc.).

The plan should specify who will be responsible for implementing each of the interventions and in what order they will proceed, based upon their prioritization of the student's needs. In designing goals, make sure all goals are specific, measurable, and achievable. Set a summary review date for the plan (six–eight weeks is suggested) and confer weekly to monitor the TACIT process. The plan should identify specific classroom strategies that would be most appropriate to enhance the student's learning and which address the specific learning or behavior of concern. Use a planning and documentation tool, such as the PreReferral Review Form (PRR) (Collier, 1994b), to record and monitor the intervention goals and interventions being implemented. The PRR is useful since it contains lists of appropriate interventions and a means of recording the language of instruction. A copy of this form is contained in Appendix B at the end of Chapter 10.

Examples of appropriate interventions are:

Language Acquisition. Appropriate language acquisition interventions include content instruction in the first language, bilingual assistance in content areas, English as a Second Language, sheltered English techniques, bilingual language and content area instruction, sheltered instruction in both languages, or two-way bilingual instruction.

Acculturation Needs. The LEP student's performance on acculturation measures, such as the AQS, or the advice of expert observers indicates the need for acculturation interventions. An AQS below 19 indicates the need for intensive and extensive acculturation assistance. An AQS between 20 and 30 indicates the student is in transition and is likely still at the height of culture shock. Other indications that the LEP student needs assistance with acculturation are when he/she does not seem to make progress with English acquisition after being exited from the bilingual/ESL program, appears to become less successful in interactions away from cultural and linguistic peers, and suddenly "forgets" how to complete or answer assignments in which he/she was once successful. Appropriate interventions that address acculturation needs and acculturative stress are those which address culture shock, resistance to change, distractibility, response fatigue, limited experience in academic settings, confusion in locus of control, stress reactions, and other psychological side-effects of the acculturation process. These are:

- *Cognitive Learning Assistance:* Addressing cognitive learning needs, including differences between teaching style and the LEP student's cognitive learning style, and other cognitive academic needs, such as CALP acquisition, metacognitive strategies, and cognitive learning strategies.
- *Communicative Assistance:* Addressing code-switching, stages in second language acquisition, development of BICS and CALP in both languages, comprehensible input, and other communicative needs.
- *Behavioral Assistance:* Addressing distractibility, disorientation, confusion in locus of control, withdrawal, acting out, and other behaviors that may be manifestations of culture shock or side-effects of the acculturation process. Interventions providing guided practice for the LEP student in the behavior expectations of this classroom and this school are also beneficial.
- *Ethno-ecological Assistance:* Addressing the adaptation needs of children within the family, school, and community through peer tutoring, cross-cultural communication strategies for both the LEP student and his/her classmates, and increasing family and community involvement in the school program.

Learning and Behavior Difficulties. Appropriate interventions for addressing learning and behavior difficulties are included in the PreReferral Review Form and other sources. These may include:

- Bilingual Materials
- Translation
- Metacognitive Assistance
- Adapted Instructional Materials
- Planned Positive Reinforcement
- Varied Content/Strategies
- Consulted Resource People
- Sheltered English Instruction
- Academic Support Services
- Peer Tutors
- Cognitive Learning Strategies
- Cooperative Learning
- Varied Instructional Setting
- Suggestions for/from Parents
- Parent/Teacher Team
- Structured Self-Monitoring
- Planned Positive Reinforcement
- Varied Instructional Settings
- Behavioral Contract
- Acculturation Support
- Parent Conferences
- Counseling Services
- Reduction of Stimuli
- Varied Outcomes
- Support Group

Step 6: Implement the Intervention

The TACIT advises the referring teacher or staff member about appropriate interventions and provides resources and guided practice in the implementation. Members of the team may go into the classroom and work directly with the student, may team teach with the referring teacher, may pull the student out to implement a specific strategy, or otherwise become directly and collaboratively involved in implementing the recommended intervention for the culturally and linguistically diverse learner with learning and behavior problems. The TACIT's active involvement also facilitates its monitoring of the student's response to the recommended interventions.

Step 7: Evaluate Interventions

The TACIT monitors and evaluates the implementation of each intervention for effectiveness with this particular LEP student. The student's responses to each intervention within the particular context and language in which it is carried out are recorded. As different interventions are implemented within the classroom setting, the student's responses are documented and observed patterns are noted. For example, changing the composition of the peer team in which an LEP student is working, perhaps including one or two bilingual students proficient in the student's native language, would give the student more consistent success in completing assignments. This would be done in a variety of subject areas, and the success or failure in producing differences in the student's behavior would be noted. It could indicate that the LEP student needed additional assistance with language acquisition and CALP in English, it could indicate that the student felt more comfortable working with these peers, or it could mean something else. The positive results achieved by the intervention would be noted on the PRR or other TACIT documentation form.

During the TACIT period it is especially important to document the contexts and content areas or approaches in which the LEP student is successful. These will be helpful in determining further interventions, in guiding the classroom teachers in successful modifications and adaptations, and in building up an accurate learning and behavior profile of the student. This information will also be useful to the mul-

tidisciplinary team (MDT), should the TACIT decide to refer the LEP student.

Step 8: Document the Consultation

Many schools and education professionals are just beginning to establish TACITs. It takes time and effort to build a smooth TACIT process, including the building of good interpersonal communication among team members. TACIT effectiveness relies on members getting to know one another, planning for everyone's schedules, and collaborative, consistent self-reflection upon the TACIT process itself. The TACIT needs to establish clear expectations for each team member and monitor and document each member's contributions to the TACIT process. The team should monitor the effectiveness of the case management process and document the collaborative activities implemented with each LEP student as well as the results of these activities and interventions. The information obtained about the most effective teacher/student interactions and the variation in student response to different teacher styles will be important contributing information in planning further interventions and in obtaining a comprehensive profile of the LEP student's learning needs.

Step 9: Exit TACIT

The decision to move on to another need area on the TACIT priority list may occur after two weeks or less. During the TACIT process and within the average 6- to 10-week TACIT period, whenever the LEP student needs further assistance in learning or behavior areas, the team should return to Step 4 in the TACIT process and select the next need on the priority list. After at least 6 weeks, certainly no longer than 12 weeks, the TACIT should reach a decision about exiting the student from the TACIT process.

There are two likely decisions at this point: (1) The TACIT intervention succeeds and the student exits TACIT monitoring. The student may continue to receive appropriate first language development and second language acquisition assistance. (2) The TACIT decides to refer the student to the MDT. TACIT intervention determines that the student's learning and behavior needs are not due to cultural or linguistic difference or that the student has some other learning and behavior need in addition to those related to second language acquisition, acculturation, and sociocultural adaptation. Therefore, a formal referral to special education is justified and the student is exited from the TACIT.

TEACHER COMPETENCIES FOR INCLUDING BILINGUAL EXCEPTIONAL CHILDREN IN THE GENERAL EDUCATION CLASSROOM

Essential to the effective implementation of inclusion for bilingual exceptional children is an instructionally flexible, culturally competent teacher in every classroom. At best, the teacher should be conversant in the languages and cultures of all children in the class; at least, the teacher should be knowledgeable of and sensitive to children's various cultural and linguistic differences. Because more than two languages/cultures may well be represented in the classroom, the teacher must work with appropriate resource personnel to assist in providing services to all the children in the class and to work as a team to increase information about the languages and cultures present in the classroom, school, and community. Sensitivity and flexibility are two of the competencies teachers of bilingual exceptional children must cultivate.

The ability of a program to provide quality education for the bilingual exceptional child centers on the competence of its education personnel in all classrooms. The majority of certified teachers have received a common core of professional preparation: history and philosophy of education and educational psychology.

Upon these foundation courses are built skills courses that vary with extent and area of specialization. Reynolds (1980) recommends that a body of skills and knowledge be constructed that will prepare teachers to function in the context of social mandates. The content of the knowledge, skill, and practice would be derived, in significant part, from the intent of the mandates to assure equality of educational opportunity for all children, as provided in Public Law 94-142 and other recent laws and adjudications.

As discussed earlier in this book, individualization of education for exceptional children is one such mandate of the current philosophy of education. PL 94-142 provides for an individual instructional plan to be written for each student. An individualized instructional plan should outline specifically what is to be taught by whom, how it is to be taught, and how it will be evaluated. All the teachers/tutors working with the bilingual exceptional child must be aware of and involved in all elements of planning for individualization. It is especially important that the plan include objectives and service information in language, vocational and acculturation needs, and exceptional needs.

The ability to develop and implement individualized instructional plans is a critical competency for all teachers working with bilingual exceptional children in the inclusion process. The development and implementation of these plans for bilingual exceptional children demand instructional flexibility, broad knowledge, and cultural sensitivity. Implementing an individualized instructional plan means adapting the general education curriculum to the needs and abilities of individual CLDE children. This process is also discussed in Chapter 10 in regards to the IEP, particularly. To achieve ongoing individualization, the school must provide teachers with various resources, some of which are outlined in the continuum model discussed earlier in this chapter and some of which are discussed elsewhere in this text, such as in Chapters 3 and 13. In addition to the consultants and special support staff, resources should also include a wide range of differentiated instructional materials and appropriate facilities and space. Given adequate resources, the teacher's ability to develop and implement individualized instructional plans remains the core of an effective individualized program, the heart of inclusion. Specific suggestions for components of individualized instruction are detailed in Chapter 10.

Clusters of capabilities (Reynolds, 1980) may be used to generate the following 12 competencies for achieving effective individualization CLDE children:

- All teachers should have a general knowledge of curriculum principles, guides, and structures from preschool through secondary school levels for diverse learners. The means and procedures by which curriculum is developed and adapted in a cross-cultural setting should be understood.

- All teachers should be culturally competent in teaching the basic skills (defined to include literacy, life maintenance, and personal development skills) and in collaborative practice with other education professionals. Basic skills in cross-cultural contexts must be considered.

- All teachers should be proficient in culturally and linguistically appropriate class management procedures, including applied behavior analysis, cross-cultural communication strategies, acculturation stress intervention techniques, and cognitive affective climate.

- All teachers should be proficient in consultation and other forms of professional communications, as both initiators and receivers, to establish and maintain responsible cross-cultural interactions with parents, bilingual colleagues, and administrators.

- All teachers should have skills and sensitivity for working in collaboration with parents and siblings of CLDE students.

- All teachers should be able to convey to students that they bear some of the responsibility for their social environment and must be willing to help one another within a multicultural environment.

- All teachers should be able to manage the social structure of multicultural classes by generating cooperative, mutually helpful behavior among the students. (Teachers need specific insights into and skills for developing heterogeneously cooperative cross-cultural grouping procedures and peer and cross-age tutoring.)

- All teachers must have an understanding of CLDE children, of school procedures for accommodating children's diverse learning needs.

- All teachers need to learn the procedures for cross-cultural referrals, the responsibilities involved, and ways to capitalize on multicultural resources in behalf of better education for individual pupils.

- All teachers must be skilled in making systematic, cross-cultural observations to provide data and undergird judgments for the referral and individualization process.

- All teachers should be culturally competent in the assessment of the individual student's education needs and in adapting instruction to the individual.

- All teachers, in their personal commitments and professional behavior with pupils, parents, and colleagues, should exemplify the same consideration for all individuals and their educational rights as are called for in the current body of civil rights and educational opportunity laws. These include the right of individual students to due process in all school placement decisions, to education in an inclusive environment, to education in English as a second language, to the use of the native language to facilitate content and achievement, and to carefully individualized education.

Baca (1981) delineated additional teacher competencies for working with CLDE children.

These may be achieved through use of resource personnel and materials, in addition to the individual teacher's abilities, where the existing situation is such that the teacher has not yet mastered all of these competencies. The following five competencies are summarized as ideal recommendations for the bilingual special education teacher working with CLDE children:

1. In the area of language, it is preferable that the teacher be able to (a) understand and speak the native language of the student, (b) read and write the native language at an acceptable level of competency, (c) teach any part of the curriculum in English and in the native language of the student, and (d) communicate with parents in their native language regarding the academic progress of their child.

2. In linguistic competence, it is preferable that the teacher (a) understand the theory and process of first and second language acquisition; (b) deal with specific areas of interlanguage interference and positive transfer; (c) understand phonological, grammatical, and lexical characteristics of both languages and their implications for classroom instruction; and (d) distinguish between local dialects and the standard language.

3. For competence in the assessment area, the teacher should be able to (a) administer a variety of language dominance/proficiency tests, (b) conduct a nondiscriminatory comprehensive diagnostic assessment, (c) evaluate the child from a social/emotional perspective, (d) evaluate the child from a perceptual/motor perspective, and (e) construct and use criterion referenced measures.

4. In the instructional area, teachers should be able to (a) prepare individualized instructional plans based on student needs, (b) individualize instruction of several students and coordinate large- and small-group instruction concurrently, (c) adapt curricula to meet the needs of CLDE students, (d) revise materials and activities to make them more linguistically and culturally appropriate for bilingual children with disabilities, (e) construct instructional materials to enhance the curriculum for bilingual exceptional students, (f) recognize the learning characteristics of various disability conditions, (g) select the proper bilingual instructional approach for each situation, and (h) assess readability levels of materials both in English and in the native language.

5. In the area of culture, the teacher should be able to (a) establish rapport with children from a variety of cultural backgrounds, (b) listen to children and understand the cultural perspective they have, (c) understand the cultural significance of various exceptionalities, (d) take advantage of community resources for CLDE students, (e) advise parents of their due process rights relative to their child's education, and (f) counsel parents regarding various aspects of their child's unique learning needs.

All of the above competencies should become the goals of teachers working with CLDE students. Working with children with special needs is an ongoing learning experience for all professionals. Part of this ongoing learning is sharing suggestions and resources. The following section provides practical suggestions for working with bilingual children with various exceptionalities.

SUGGESTIONS FOR INCLUDING CLDE CHILDREN

Among several things the teacher of CLDE children must keep in mind in inclusion are (1) level of language competence in both native and second languages, (2) degree of cultural identity and acculturation, (3) degree and type of exceptionality, (4) age at onset of exceptionality (birth or acquired) and chronological age, (5) level of achievement, (6) measured intellectual ability in both languages, (7) social maturity in both native and second culture, (8) presence of multiple disabilities, (9) mobility, (10) wishes of student and parents, and (11) availability of services. All of these variables will affect the continuum of services the student needs to receive. Most of this information will come to the teacher through consultation with parents and special support staff members. As mentioned in Chapters 10 and 11, there are also various informal ways to assess some of these. Once the teacher has identified each student's needs and abilities, the teacher should develop an individualized instructional plan for each student in conjunction with parents and other teachers responsible for instructing the child. Other resource people who work with the child are also frequently included in the planning meeting. This team planning process was discussed in Chapter 10 in relation to the IEP meeting.

Taking all of these variables into consideration in the context of the TACIT planning meeting, there are a few additional concerns to address.

Perceptual/Emotional Concerns

Learning and emotional disabilities are grouped under one rubric for several reasons. First, behavior problems are frequently associated with learning disabilities, and in some cases it is difficult to separate the two as "cause and effect." There is a closely integrated relationship between the child's perceptual difficulties (receiving, processing, and expressing information in specific learning tasks) and the child's behavior in the classroom. In addition, cultural factors are especially important in the assessment of an instructional program for these two exceptionalities. Emotional and learning disabilities are probably the areas most affected by cultural interpretation.

What is acceptable behavior in given situations and what and how children are instructed vary considerably from culture to culture. The common identification of a learning disability

is a significant discrepancy between ability and achievement, and because these are usually assessed with reference to English language instruments and Anglo-American cultural expectations, there may be some legitimate questions raised about what this term means in regard to the CLD child (Collier & Hoover, 1987). The same questions may be raised with regard to the identification of emotional disability in the CLD student (Hoover & Collier, 1985). What is unacceptable and aberrant behavior in European American culture may be appropriate in another culture in a particular situation. Also, consideration must be given to the social and psychological difficulties encountered by the culturally different child in the acculturative process.

Emotional Disabilities

All teachers have to handle a variety of behavior problems in class. For example, the aggressive child, the withdrawn child, and the daydreamer all are found in most classrooms. All these behaviors, from passive to aggressive and from manic to depressive, require the teacher to attend to the individual child's emotional needs while at the same time dealing with the less serious, typical, up-and-down behavior of average students. Behaviors characteristic of children with emotional disabilities are seen in all children during stressful moments. It is the frequency and intensity of these behaviors that indicate a serious disturbance. A child may exhibit some of these characteristics temporarily in response to the acculturation process or consistently as a culturally appropriate response within the child's culture (Hoover & Collier, 1985). Assessment and treatment should always be carried out with this in mind.

Hammill and Bartel (1990) provide various strategies for assessing behavior problems, among them direct observation (analysis of the child's work, anecdotal records, and activity checks), behavioral checklists and inventories, procedures for examining interaction in the classroom, and standardized tests. The teacher should also consult with the parents and siblings when appropriate. The general education classroom teacher can generally get assistance in these assessment areas from the support staff, the bilingual special education teacher, and therapists. The teacher should talk to resource people from the same cultural background as the child. Some behaviors that may appear strange in the general education classroom may reflect acceptable behavior in the child's out-of-school environment and not emotional disturbance (Hoover & Collier, 1985). Following are some characteristic behaviors used as indications of emotional disability:

- Depression, hypochondria, regression (such as thumb sucking)
- Overly dependent behavior
- Compulsive behaviors (overly meticulous about arrangement of objects, cleanliness, etc.)
- Being accident-prone (seems to enjoy attention drawn to injuries)
- Feelings and moods that are out of proportion to the provocation or situation in which they occur
- Conversations with self or imaginary figures
- Extreme anxiety
- Refusal to verbalize but ability to do so in native language or English
- Strong uncontrollable fears or frequent crying
- Seeming distracted, dreamy, or extremely withdrawn
- Aggressive behavior

The child's ability to learn may be submerged by emotional disturbance. Remediation involves developing insight, self-esteem, and acceptable social behavior. This must be done within the context of the child's home and community cultural values. Once the emotional disturbance is diminished, the child should be able to benefit from various learning strategies. If the behavior persists, in both the school and the home environment, professional counseling may be necessary. The counselor should understand the child's culture, be able to speak the child's native language, and understand the acculturation experience.

Children experiencing acculturation may exhibit troubling behaviors that are normal side effects of the adaptive process, such as withdrawal or defensiveness in certain situations. These behaviors will diminish as the child receives assistance with and adapts to the cross-cultural situation.

Many teachers ask themselves, "Why me?" when they have an especially troubled or troublesome student in their class. Teachers should keep in mind that there are many positive educational benefits to including a student who is emotionally disabled in the general education environment. Some of these are: (1) the opportunity for the child to observe appropriate behavior within a given cultural context, (2) the opportunity for the child to observe and participate in cross-culturally appropriate emotional expression, (3) the opportunity for the child to see similarities to and differences from other children, and (4) the opportunity for the child to interact with and receive support from peers in a multicultural setting. The main key to working with children with emotional disabilities is showing care and concern about the children. The teacher's approach, positive or negative, is what counts the most. Positive reinforcement of the child's successes and appropriate behaviors should be coupled with a friendly and encouraging attitude.

Techniques useful in managing behavior problems in class include the following:

1. The teacher should not let the situation get out of hand. The teacher should stop the problem behavior before the entire class is disrupted.

2. Appropriate behavior should be positively reinforced, in a culturally appropriate manner.

3. Tasks should be organized to provide a variety of activities and orderly transition from one activity to another. Materials should be culturally and linguistically relevant and interesting.

4. Learning or activity centers, time-out areas, or quiet areas should be used. These are useful when the child has completed tasks early or when the child needs to be alone. (Children might even use a punching bag to let out their frustrations—then be moved to one of the quiet areas before continuing lessons.)

5. The teacher should be consistent.

6. What is appropriate/inappropriate in different situations and the consequences of inappropriate behavior should be demonstrated. Role-play is useful as a way to demonstrate these situations.

Learning Disabilities

Learning disability is not a term used to define temporary or minor learning problems. It refers to severe discrepancies between ability and achievement. PL 94-142, the Education for All Handicapped Children Act of 1975, defines learning disability as follows:

> a disorder in one of the basic psychological processes involved in understanding or in using language, spoken or written, which may manifest itself in an imperfect ability to listen, think, speak, read, write, spell, or do mathematical calculations. The term includes such conditions as perceptual handicaps, brain injury, minimal brain dysfunction, dyslexia, and developmental aphasia. The term does not include children who have learning problems which are primarily the result of visual, hearing or motor handicaps, or mental retardation, or of environment, cultural, or economic disadvantages.

The common and most cited characteristic of children with learning disabilities is a significant discrepancy between achievement and overall ability (intelligence and other measures of ability). As discussed previously, measures of intelligence/ability may be quite inaccurate for the culturally different child. Additionally, the characteristics of the learning disabled are sometimes hard to identify. The following characteristics are intended as general guides. Children with learning disabilities may exhibit several but not all of these:

- Appears to hear but is not able to follow oral instructions or complete tasks assigned orally in both the second and native languages.
- Lacks ability to organize written tasks, speech, or self-care.
- Short attention span, distractible.
- Auditory or visual memory problems.
- Poor perceptual-motor coordination.
- Poor language skills in both native and second languages.
- Sporadic behavior—calm one day, extremely active the next.
- Reverses words, numbers, letters, and phrases in both languages.
- Difficulty in performing mathematical calculations.
- Extreme difficulty in writing in both languages.
- Appears to see and read but is not able to follow written instructions or complete visual tasks.

It must be stressed that none of these characteristics should be taken as single predictors of learning disability. It is important to assess the child in the native language and to consider cultural factors in the testing situation itself. Instruction usually involves presenting materials in a modified step-by-step manner and teaching to the child's strengths. Gearheart, Weishahn, and Gearheart (1995) provide 10 principles as general guidelines for working with children with learning disabilities. These may be summarized for the bilingual exceptional child as follows:

1. There is no single correct method to use. The teacher should try a variety of approaches, methods, and cross-cultural strategies.

2. All other factors being equal, the preferred method should be something new to the child. The teacher may use a method that looks and feels different to the child, but must be sure to explain and demonstrate the procedure.

3. Some type of positive reinforcement and reconditioning should be implemented. Success must be planned. Consultation with a cultural specialist may enhance appropriate teaching.

4. High motivation is a prerequisite to success; deliberate consideration of the affective domain is essential. Cultural differences in this must be accommodated.

5. The existence of nonspecific or difficult-to-define disabilities, particularly with older children, must be recognized. What may exist is significant educational retardation and negative attitudes toward school as a result of earlier problems.

6. Complete accurate information about the child's learning strengths and weaknesses is essential. When one problem is discovered, it should not be automatically assumed that it is the major cause of the learning and behavior problems. A balance of what the child can and cannot do is important information.

7. Symptoms often associated with learning disabilities do not necessarily indicate the presence of learning disabilities or predict future learning disabilities. Many of these symptoms are normal by-products of acculturation.

8. Educational time and effort must be carefully maximized for the child. Specific learning abilities should be developed within a framework of the deficient academic area(s): first language development, second language acquisition, and assistance with acculturation must be a part of this effort.

9. Learning disability planning should be based on a learning theory or theories to be most effective.

10. Both process- and task-oriented assistance and remediation are critically important.

Multisensory technique is a useful approach for the teacher in including bilingual children with learning disabilities in the general education classroom. The teacher presents words or numbers (the approach is primarily used in reading and math remediation) in such a way that the child can hear, see, feel, and then say them alone. The language in which the child has the best oral/auditory proficiency is used. The teacher writes the word or number in crayon (a rougher texture than pencil), clay, glue, or other tactile substance. Cursive script is usually used because it provides a connected "whole" feeling of the word as a single entity rather than a group of separate letters. The teacher says the word aloud while writing it, and the child repeats it. If the teacher does not speak the child's language, a bilingual tutor or peer may assist. The child traces the word or number with a finger in contact with the crayon or substance in which it is written, saying the word or number aloud while tracing it. This activity can be done in the native language and in English as part of teaching the child English as a Second Language. This is done until the child can write the word without referring to the paper.

Teachers may use manipulative objects and methods while talking about what they are doing and then have the children tell what they are doing as they work out the calculation or problem. Again, the use of first the native and then the second language is recommended. In a simpler form, teachers may use many objects illustrative of a particular lesson or topic that the children can feel and talk about with the teacher or tutor. A word of caution about multisensory technique: Some types of neurological dysfunction may lead to a tendency for the brain to "overload" if there are too many stimuli arriving simultaneously. This is not an indisputably established fact, but the possibility of this type of reaction to multiple stimuli should be kept in mind. Feuerstein (1979) suggests that children with learning disabilities must be taught how to respond appropriately to various stimuli in their environment and that this mediated learning can be of great benefit in improving children's academic achievement.

Other approaches to working with children with learning disabilities is the consideration of learning styles as discussed in Chapter 10 and the instructing techniques in Chapter 11. Some children learn more from what they see and touch than from what they hear. Some children learn to read their native language more quickly through phonetics or sound analysis, and some learn through the whole-word or sight-word approach. Some have difficulty seeing the forest for the trees, attend to the individual items, and do not see the underlying similarities and relationships. Some have difficulty seeing the trees for the forest: figure/ground confusion or difficulty discriminating individual objects from a group. Tactile and kinesthetic approaches are useful in singling out objects from a group or background. Activities in taxonomy and categorizing are useful in identifying groups and generalizations, although care must be taken to consider cultural differences in what is similar and different. The oral rhythms and intonations of both languages and the use of native songs are also very useful in teaching bilingual children with learning disabilities. Sometimes song and drama can enhance the multisensory approach and may also greatly assist the development of memory skills.

The comments in Chapters 10 and 11 in regard to the difficulties in identifying and working with learning and emotional disability in CLD students must be carefully considered by all teachers attempting to include these children.

COMMUNICATION CONCERNS
Speech/Language Impairment

The labels of speech impairment and language disorder do not refer to linguistic or language differences or to the problems non-English speaking children have in acquiring English as a second language. Some second language learners may have some problems in pronouncing some sounds when learning a new language, but this is not the same as an articulation disorder or speech impairment (which must be present in the native language as well as English), and the suggestions given later in this section may be helpful in facilitating the student's acquisition of pronunciation skills in English.

Speech and language differences become a disability when (1) they interfere with communication, (2) they cause the speaker to be maladjusted, and (3) they call undue attention to the speech (as opposed to what the person is saying) (Gearheart, Weishahn, & Gearheart, 1995). For a bilingual individual to be considered to have a speech, language, or voice disorder, the problem must be apparent in both languages. Communication disorders may be caused by many different conditions, including cleft lip and/or palate, cerebral palsy, central nervous system damage, certain genetic disorders, and tramatic brain injury.

Some characteristic behaviors that are possible indications of a speech, language, or voice problem are:

- Omission of the initial or final sounds of words in both the native and second language.

- Sound substitutions. (Note: Substitutions occurring as a result of acquiring English as a second language should be eliminated from consideration as an impairment.)

- Hesitancy to participate orally in class in the native language. (Note: The student may not participate in English until more proficiency is gained. This would not be indicative of an impairment.)

- Malformation of the oral cavity with the speech problems apparent in both languages.
- Chronic hoarseness.
- Consistently too loud or too soft speech. (Note: Cultural factors may be involved—loudness level may be appropriate in a given situation in the student's culture.)
- Raspy or gravely-sounding voice.
- Noticeably nasal or de-nasal tone.
- Stuttering or dysfluent communication in both languages. (Note: This behavior may occur temporarily when the student is first learning English, especially if he/she is placed under a lot of stress to speak the unfamiliar language perfectly.)

When a true speech, language, or voice problem exists, the teacher should consult with a speech-language specialist to obtain suggestions regarding classroom activities and procedures that will support and reinforce the objectives of the child's individual educational program in speech. The speech therapist will have the primary responsibility for remediation of the (noncultural) communication disorder. Both the speech therapist and the teacher may work with the ESL specialist on specific second language learning needs (for example, phonemic discrimination, new articulation patterns, and new rhythmic patterns) and bilingual specialist on first language development and transfer skills.

Because speech is closely related to hearing ability, the first step the teacher must take with a child showing speech problems is to find out whether the child has received a recent audiological examination and review the results of the examination. If a hearing problem is indicated, the teacher should follow the suggestions given in the section on children with hearing impairments and work with the audiologist and/or speech pathologist to ameliorate the effects of the hearing impairment as much as possible. Teachers working with bilingual children who have communication disorders should co-ordinate services with the speech-language specialist and bilingual education teacher. In general, the speech therapist will provide the remedial instruction for the speech, language, or voice disorder and the bilingual teacher will assist with pronunciation and language problems which are part of the second language learning process.

Stuttering or Dysfluency

Dysfluency can be a very noticeable speech problem, and the social stigma attached can cause greater difficulty in communication than that actually produced by the hesitancies, repetitions, prolongations, or circumlocutions in the stutterer's speech. There are many theories about the causes and treatments for stuttering, but there is little general agreement. Some specialists believe the problem is organic or neurological and others that it is behavioral. Reynolds and Birch (1986) make several suggestions for working with children with stuttering or other dysfluency problems. The two following points are adapted from their suggestions:

1. Conflict or excitement tends to increase stuttering. The teacher should expect and not be surprised by what happens to speech under such conditions. Students should not be pressured to perform verbally in high stress situations.
2. Children who stutter should be treated like other children. They should have opportunities to ask questions, and the teacher should take the time to listen. The teacher should not fill in words for them any more than for any other child. Such behavior will be a model for the stuttering pupil's classmates.

The speech-language specialist should be consulted when a student is showing signs of stuttering. Even when a formal referral to special education is not warranted, this specialist can provide specific suggestions to help the student and teacher appropriately address the situation. Many folk theories abound about this particular disorder, and it is important to separate fact from fiction. For example, many people believe that you should help a stutterer by telling him/her to "slow down." This, in fact, may just draw attention to the problem and increase the student's anxiety level and exacerbate the problem. Cultural differences also exist with regard to beliefs about stuttering. Advice from those knowledgeable about the student's particular cultural beliefs and the disorder should be actively sought.

Articulation Problems

The following suggestions address articulation problems and apply to instruction in both the native and second languages. When a student has been identified as having an articulation disorder in both languages, collaboration between the general educator and the speech-language specialist is necessary to facilitate the transfer of therapy targets into everyday speech in the classroom.

1. The child must become able to discriminate between accurate and inaccurate pronunciations—he/she must become able to "hear" errors.

2. Teachers should provide good, clear speech models, in both the native and the second languages, if possible. Speech is imitative. Teachers must evaluate their own speech and should work with tutors, parents, and peers to provide good models in both languages.

3. The child must learn to produce correct sounds in both languages. Teachers can motivate learning through culturally appropriate games, songs, and recognition of progressive approximations of the correct sound.

4. The teacher should use culturally appropriate reinforcement to motivate the child to use newly learned sounds in both languages. Puppets, rhymes, and songs, for example,

are all helpful in integrating and encouraging correct speech patterns.

Communication is a basic human faculty necessary for participation in society and culture. It is extremely important that children learn to communicate to the best of their ability and be given the opportunities to use what modes of communication they have. The best thing the classroom teacher can do for children with articulation problems is to give them time to get their thoughts out and plenty of opportunities to initiate and respond to verbal interactions. The teacher in the general education classroom must be careful to provide these opportunities for all children and encourage all children in the classroom to communicate, whether in English or in another language, with whatever means appropriate, including gestures and drawings.

Hearing Impairment

As with speech, hearing becomes a teaching concern when it interferes with social adjustment or communication. Many people have various degrees of hearing impairment. The teacher should watch for:

- Tilting or turning head to hear.
- Cupping hand around ear.
- Hesitancy in participating in oral/auditory activities in native language or talking very little or in brief sentences in native language. (Note: Students may exhibit this behavior in second language situations until greater proficiency is achieved, and this behavior may also be culturally appropriate when speaking to an adult.)
- Complaints of frequent earaches, colds, and similar ailments.
- Watching lips of speakers.
- Failing to respond to loud noises.
- Adequate achievement in small groups, but failure to do well in large groups or space. (Note: This may be due to cultural factors.)

- Confusion in following group activities and discussions in native language.
- Appearing withdrawn, not interacting very much with peers. (Note: Students may exhibit this behavior if new to the culturally different classroom or if few of the children are from the same culture.)

If hearing impairment is diagnosed, the teacher may be working with the assistance of specialists in teaching the child to use a hearing aid, cued speech, sign language, or other technique, depending on the severity of the impairment. The teacher should modify and adapt the curriculum and instruction to include broader academic areas, usually within the general education classroom as much as possible. Attention should also be given to the development of special learning strategies in enhancing memory and generalization from experience. The teacher will need to make certain classroom modifications to accommodate the child with hearing impairment in the general education classroom. To make the appropriate modifications, the teacher should become knowledgeable of the nature of the loss, the amount of residual hearing, and the ways in which the child communicates. The teacher should gain familiarity with the child's unique speech patterns to facilitate communication and decrease the child's embarrassment of being continually asked "What?" or to repeat himself/herself.

It is crucial that the student with hearing difficulties have the best access possible to orally presented material. An important classroom modification is to allow the child to sit as close as possible to the source of sound with an unobstructed view of the speaker's face. This should be within 5 or 10 feet, so that the student can see the speaker's face fully, but also have a view of other important sources of information, such as the blackboard or an overhead, without having to look up constantly. Also, when possible, materials should be presented both visually, such as on an overhead, and orally.

A useful suggestion in working with the child with hearing impairment in the general education classroom is to use another child as a listening partner. This can be a rotating assignment in the room, although the partner should be a child who speaks the same languages as the child needing help, if possible. It is important that the partner provide assistance only when needed; otherwise, the child with hearing impairment may become overly dependent on the classmate. The partner sits next to the child with hearing difficulties and ensures that the child is turning to the correct page and taking accurate notes, or provides other appropriate assistance.

The teacher should be knowledgeable about the care and use of hearing aids. Hearing aids help compensate for hearing loss by amplifying sounds. They cannot replace the natural ability to hear, so the teacher should not expect "normal" hearing ability when the student wears a hearing aid. However, hearing aids are very helpful in allowing the child to use what hearing she or he has, and the student should be encouraged to use one when possible and appropriate. The teacher should be sensitive to possible cultural attitudes toward the hearing impaired within the child's culture. Teachers should also be aware that hearing aids are delicate and expensive devices—care should be taken when students are involved in activities that could expose the hearing aid to foreign materials (such as sand or water). It is also a good idea for the teacher to keep extra batteries and a battery tester at school so the child does not have to go without hearing when the battery goes dead during the school day. Students should be encouraged to check their batteries daily; hearing aids will not help if the battery is dead.

The child should be encouraged to learn to observe face and body gestures, lip formation and movement, and other environmental clues to facilitate understanding of what is going on. This is why it is important that the child sit with an unobstructed view of the speaker. The child should not sit where it is necessary to look into a light source, for example, the windows or a dark or shadowed area. Generally, it is best to have the light source behind the child and on the speaker. In assisting the child to observe and "read" gestures and lip movements, the teacher should not use exaggerated gestures or speech patterns and should be sensitive to cultural differences in body language. The child needs to learn to lip read naturally and appropriately in both native- and second cultural contexts. Gestures should be used, but objects and hands should be kept away from the face whenever possible. Facial hair can obscure facial and lip movement. The teacher should face the group when speaking and should encourage other children to face the child with hearing problems when speaking.

The teacher should consult with the special education staff and hearing specialists about instructional techniques that are appropriate for students with hearing impairments in general education classrooms. Depending upon the resources available, such as wireless amplification systems and sign language interpreters, and the family's decision regarding the use of sign language, instructional techniques can vary widely. With collaboration among the general educator, parents, and specialists, inclusion of students with hearing impairment into the general education classroom can be successfully achieved.

INTELLECTUAL CONCERNS

Mental Retardation

Mental retardation has been defined as "significant subaverage general intellectual functioning existing concurrently with deficits in adaptive behavior and manifested during the developmental period" (Kirk & Gallagher, 1989, p. 132). It should be understood that this discussion relates to the 80% to 90% of the retarded population who may be considered mildly, moderately trainable, or educable retarded. The

care of the severely or profoundly retarded usually is not the responsibility of general educators, although many districts have special self-contained classrooms or separate schools for children needing a highly specialized learning environment. Of the children with mild to moderate retardation found in inclusive schools, the following characteristics may be observed:

- Difficulty in generalizing and understanding abstractions (given in native language).
- Overall academic retardation—significantly below grade level in all subjects.
- Immaturity evidenced in play and other interests both in and out of school.
- Sensory and coordination problems.
- Easily frustrated.
- Vocabulary of a much younger child in the native language (in English this may indicate only the relative proficiency level attained so far).
- Slower growth and development patterns.
- Poor self-help skills (as understood by the particular culture).

Many of these behaviors may be the temporary result of experiential differences and should be carefully assessed in the native language and cultural context of the child. A visit with the parents (with an interpreter, if needed) would provide information about the child's adaptive behaviors and developmental history within the cultural context.

The child with retardation in the general education classroom should be identified by multiple criteria and not by IQ alone. Some of these criteria are level of language development in both native and second languages, level of socialization in both cultures, emotional maturity, and academic achievement, as well as IQ. Most commonly the instruction of children with retardation has been primarily through reduced academic expectations and emphasized functional skills needed for work and community living. Recently, however, their education has included broader academic areas, usually within the general education classroom as much as possible. Attention is also being given to the development of special learning strategies in enhancing memory and generalization from experience.

The general educator who has children with retardation in the classroom should not attempt to require any child to perform tasks for which the child lacks the prerequisite skills. The teacher should provide opportunities for the development of such skills and provide simplified programs and activities. Games and physical activity, such as throwing beanbags or jumping rope, will assist in general motor development and improvement in coordination. Blindfold "guess what it is" games will aid sensory development and language development. Carefully individualized sequenced instruction will assist in all academic areas. Teaching bilingual children with mental retardation cross-cultural associations and generalizations will increase their ability to understand abstractions in both settings. Other cognitive learning strategies are given in Chapter 11. Some frustrations are unavoidable and indeed to some extent are part of growth and development. Learning to deal with difficulties is to be encouraged. However, the teacher needs to reduce the number of possibly frustrating situations that may be of little benefit at that particular time.

Children with mental retardation are capable of learning quite a bit and the teacher should neither underestimate their abilities nor overpower them with unrealistic expectations. Cultural attitudes toward people with developmental disabilities vary, and these differences must be considered in regard to their effect on the bilingual child who is developmentally delayed.

Gifted and Talented Children

Gifted and talented children were generally perceived for many years as able to proceed on their own. Many teachers joyfully hold them up as examples to the rest of their class, to the unhappiness of both the gifted and the not gifted. These children need special opportunities in the general education classroom if they are to develop their great potential and retain their creative and gifted abilities.

Culturally and linguistically different children who are intellectually gifted frequently have their special educational needs overlooked because of their temporary inability to speak the language of the classroom. The characteristics of these children may be summarized here, as adapted from Kirk and Gallagher (1984):

- Has unusually advanced vocabulary and communicative ability in native language.
- Is keen and alert observer, displays a great deal of curiosity.
- Strives toward perfection, is not easily satisfied with own work.
- Often passes judgment on events.
- Displays keen sense of humor.
- Is self-confident with other children as well as with adults.
- Tends to dominate others.

These characteristics must be considered within the child's cultural context and assessed through observation of the child outside of as well as in the classroom and in the native language and cultural setting. Table 12–1 further illustrates characteristics of the gifted or talented child.

The identification of giftedness by the use of IQ alone is currently discouraged and seen as inappropriate, especially for culturally different children. Far more than IQ is involved in identifying and defining giftedness. In addition, serious questions have been raised about the efficacy of IQ and intelligence testing in general (Gould, 1982). As discussed in Jones (1976), standardized intelligence measures have been found to be culturally biased and inappropriate for any child not representative of the dominant culture, especially the bilingual exceptional

Table 12–1
Characteristics of the Gifted

Two Sides to the Behavior of the Gifted	
List A	List B
• Expresses ideas and feelings well	• May be glib, making fluent statements based on little knowledge or understanding
• Can move at a rapid pace	• May dominate discussions
• Works conscientiously	• May be impatient to proceed to next level of task
• Wants to learn, explore, and seek more information	• May be considered nosy
• Develops broad knowledge and an extensive store of vicarious experiences	• May choose reading at the expense of active participation in social, creative, or physical activities
• Is sensitive to the feelings and rights of others	• May struggle against rules, regulations, and standardized procedures
• Makes steady progress	
• Makes original and stimulated contributions to discussions	• May lead discussions "off the track"
• Sees relationships easily	• May be frustrated by the apparent absence of logic in activities and daily events
• Learns material quickly	• May become bored by repetitions
• Is able to use reading skills to obtain new information	• May use humor to manipulate
• Contributes to enjoyment of life for self and others	• May resist a schedule based on time rather than task
• Completes assigned tasks	• May lose interest quickly
• Requires little drill for learning	

Note. From *Exceptional Children: An Introductory Survey to Special Education,* by W. L. Heward and M. D. Orlansky (1980). Upper Saddle River, NJ: Merrill/Prentice Hall. These lists were developed with the assistance of graduate students at The Ohio State University.

child. When intelligence tests are used as part of the identification of giftedness, they must be administered whenever possible in the native language of the child and be used along with a variety of other measures and procedures. These include tests of creativity and achievement and recognition of the student as exceptional by teachers, parents, or other students.

Basic skills need to be taught to the gifted as to all students; however, these should be enriched by such activities as inquiry and research techniques. The lessons should not be repeated over and over in various sequences as may be necessary for other children. The ability to in-

vestigate and pursue meaningful inquiries is a fundamental skill that may enhance the development and education of the gifted and talented. Various cognitive learning strategies are also useful for gifted CLD students (Collier & Hoover, 1987). Two common approaches in the inclusion of gifted and talented bilingual children are enrichment and acceleration, either of which may be done in a direct, indirect, or self-directed manner. As in all individualization and inclusion, the teacher must remain flexible and tolerant of a variety of differences in learning styles. Enrichment occurs when the teacher provides experiences and opportunities for gifted bilingual children to investigate topics of interest in greater detail and depth than in the standard curriculum. These topics of investigation may be built upon the ongoing activities in the general education classroom but allow the gifted bilingual child to go beyond the limits of the general education curriculum. There must be structure and guidance in this investigation; the limits and outcomes expected from the child must be defined. Enrichment in cross-cultural curricular elements is especially useful for bilingual gifted children.

Some of the approaches to acceleration given in Heward (1996) may be summarized as follows:

- Early admission to school
- Grade skipping
- Concurrent enrollment in both high school and college
- Advanced placement tests
- Early admission to college
- Content acceleration (giving youngsters the opportunity to move through a particular curricular sequence at their own rate)

Early acceleration may be possible for the LEP gifted. After the child has a good grasp of English, acceleration may be considered. Heward (1996) notes that acceleration does not cause the problems of social and emotional adjustment often attributed to it. Acceleration combined with enrichment seems to be very beneficial in the inclusion of bilingual gifted children.

PHYSICAL ENVIRONMENT CONCERNS

For both physical and visual disabilities, the child's mobility and ability to physically interact with the environment are very important concerns in the classroom. Another consideration is the cultural attitude toward people with such impairments, which can vary considerably

from culture to culture. Disabilities that affect mobility were and are of special concern in traditionally nomadic or agricultural cultures. Many culturally different children come from such rural cultures and may have special social/psychological needs if visually or physically disabled.

Physical/Neurological Disability

This is an extremely diverse group of children, and it is difficult to characterize them under a single set of criteria. Characteristics vary according to the disability and may include:

- Muscular weakness or paralysis
- Lack of muscle control (may additionally affect speech and communicative ability)
- Poor coordination
- Curved spine
- Inability to walk
- Lack of bowel/bladder control
- Use of orthopedic aids, such as braces or wheelchairs
- Use of prostheses
- Breathing difficulties
- Easily fatigued
- Seizures
- Depression associated with health problems of long duration

Children with physical or neurological disabilities may require modifications in the physical, social, or instructional aspects of the public school environment. Physical modifications may be ramps and wider doorways for wheelchairs. Social and instructional modifications may primarily involve training the students without disabilities to accept and communicate with their peers who are disabled and using special equipment in the classroom. Most commonly included under physically or neurologically disability conditions are:

Cerebral Palsy. Disturbances of voluntary motor function (paralysis, extreme weakness, lack of coordination, involuntary convulsions, and little control over arms, legs, or speech).

Epilepsy. Convulsive disorder characterized by sudden, uncontrollable attacks or seizures during which the child loses consciousness and muscular control. May be grand mal seizures (convulsions), petit mal (brief loss of consciousness), or psychomotor (period of aimless or inappropriate behavior).

Muscular Dystrophy. Fatal disease characterized by progressive gradual weakening of muscle tissue. This slow deterioration of the voluntary muscles ends in a state of complete helplessness and death.

Spina Bifida. Congenital malformation of the spine. The bones of the spine fail to close during fetal development and result in various degrees of paralysis and incontinence, impaired autonomic nervous system, and absence of sensation below the level of the spinal defect.

Paralysis, leukemia, rheumatic fever, allergies, asthma, arthritis, amputation, diabetes, and hemophilia are examples of other physical disabilities that the teacher needs to be prepared for in the inclusion program. The teacher should consult with the school nurse and parents about accommodating these conditions. Cultural attitudes toward the disability should also be considered. Some disabilities are perceived as more or less severe than others. There may be culturally prescribed treatments that the child must follow, as well as medical treatments.

All of these conditions may have to be accommodated within the general education classroom. Sometimes this means physical provisions for wheelchairs, standing tables, walkers, crutches, and other special equipment. It may mean careful preparation of the other children in the class for special aspects of the conditions, such as seizures, incontinence, and disordered speech patterns.

Heward (1996) makes this observation: Some teachers find that simulation or role-playing activities can be useful in building understanding and acceptance of the child with a physical disability. Nondisabled children may, for example, have the opportunity to use wheelchairs, braces, crutches, or other adaptive devices. This may increase their awareness of some of the obstacles faced by the child with the disability. They should learn appropriate terminology and know how to offer the correct kind of assistance when needed.

Reynolds and Birch (1986) provide some guidelines for working with children with physical or neurological disabilities. These may be adapted for culturally and linguistically different children as follows:

1. All children should begin school in general education and bilingual/ESL classes unless there are insurmountable transportation problems.

2. Keep schooling in both the bilingual education/ESL and general education classroom a continuous and full-time process, adjusted in intensity to the child's vitality level and reaction speed.

3. Pupils should attain self-regulation with regard to exertion and scheduling of activities.

4. Organize educational programs in terms of pupils' educational needs; match both short- and long-range instructional designs to the pupils' L_1–L_2 transfer needs, acculturation, cognitive learning styles, and their present and projected cross-cultural educational achievements.

5. Make technology the servant of pupils and teachers.

6. Provide expert cross-cultural educational assessment, instruction, and counseling all along the way.

Many children with physical or neurological disabilities will continue to need a "maintenance" program (see Figures 12–1 and 12–2). That is, they will require a special period of time throughout their school years to work with therapists. This necessitates careful coordination between general educators and special staff members and ongoing consultation with parents and specialists.

VISION IMPAIRMENT

The teacher should refer the child immediately for testing and evaluation of sight when the child shows consistent signs of visual impairment. Some characteristic behaviors the teacher should watch for as indications of possible visual problems are:

- Squinting, covering, or shutting one eye.
- Frequent rubbing of the eyes.
- Difficulty in writing on lines (check native orthography).
- Complaining of eyes itching or burning, dizziness, blurriness.
- Eyes that are crossed, swollen, inflamed.
- Restlessness while working.
- Poor motor coordination, tripping or stumbling a lot.
- Holding book too close or too far from eyes.
- Seeming overly sensitive to light.
- Being unable to distinguish colors (teachers should consider possible different cultural identification of colors).

Upon evaluation and determination of specific need areas, the general education and special education teachers should work together closely to provide a continuum of services as outlined earlier in this chapter. In the early grades or stages of instructing the bilingual child with vision impairment, the child may need extensive assistance from a resource or special education teacher. This teacher can provide intensive instruction and orientation to various ways of writing (such as Braille or typing) and reading (Braille or magnifiers) and means of mobility (the use of a cane, arms, or sounds). If the teacher does not speak the language of the child, a bilingual special education tutor may be nec-

essary. As the child becomes skilled in these areas, the child may need an occasional session with the itinerant teacher to develop and maintain compensatory skills while participating in the general education classroom.

Some special educational materials that may be beneficial with bilingual children with vision impairment are:

- Molded relief maps and globes.
- Abacuses.
- Geometric forms in three dimensions.
- Clocks with raised faces.
- Braille rulers or large/raised numbered rulers.
- Magnifiers of various types.
- Writing guides.
- Raised line writing paper.
- Braille or large-print books and papers.
- Scale models.

The teacher should use open seating and allow the child to sit where necessary to see most clearly for different lessons. Lighting and physical obstacles in travel paths should also be considered in the physical environment. The arrangement of the room may be changed as often as necessary, if the teacher makes sure that the child with vision impairment is oriented to the changes. Other children in the class can assist in this orientation. As the child must depend on sound to a great extent, the noise level in the classroom should be kept reasonably low. A space where the child can store necessary equipment should be provided. Lessons with many visual aids should be supplemented with specific verbal explanation through a native interpreter, if necessary. This should be accompanied by taking the child through the motions, where appropriate, not just by relying on verbal descriptions of what the child has to do. Examples of this are in physical activities and games or in the use and manipulation of concrete objects in math and science lessons.

Lessons should be varied from close to far work, visual to auditory and motor activities. The child should also be allowed to take short rests between visual activities or may even be given a break within an activity requiring long periods of close visual work. The teacher should also be careful always to address the child by name when speaking to aid the child. Also, because the child may not see facial expression or gestures, the teacher should use physical contact (where and how culturally appropriate), such as pats or hugs for positive reinforcement along with verbal praise for a job well done. The general education classroom teacher should be sure not to overprotect or underestimate the bilingual child with impaired vision.

SUMMARY

Working with CLDE children in the general education classroom can be a rewarding experience for both the children and their teacher. This inclusion approach to the education of culturally and linguistically diverse exceptional children has developed over several years, and recently attention is being focused on providing services to children who are both culturally and linguistically diverse and exceptional. The continuum inclusion model is presented here as an appropriate way to provide these services.

The continuum of services proposed provides for bilingual exceptional children to be included in general education classrooms while receiving special assistance via bilingual and special education resource personnel. This special assistance is to be provided proportionate to the child's unique learning needs and continued for as long as necessary. The general educator should coordinate instructional efforts (using the suggestions in the text) with the TACIT.

All children benefit from individual, sensitive, appropriate instruction. As more schools develop inclusion programs, general educators will find more exceptional children from diverse cultural and linguistic backgrounds in their classrooms. A teacher competent in flexible instructional methodology and culturally sensitive interpersonal communication will find working with bilingual exceptional children an enriching and positive teaching experience.

DISCUSSION QUESTIONS

1. Give your own definition of "inclusion."
2. Give your own definition of "least restrictive environment."
3. What do you consider the two most important points in the history of the inclusion effort? Identify and describe them, give dates or eras when they occurred, and tell why you think they are important.
4. Contrast and compare the development of inclusion in bilingual and special education. What are some similarities and differences in their development?
5. Contrast and compare the inclusion models of bilingual and special education programs. What are some similarities and differences in these programs?
6. Using the continuum inclusion model, how would you provide services to a specific bilingual exceptional child? Give two examples of specific children from cultural/linguistic backgrounds different from your own. Identify age/grade, exceptionality, cultural/linguistic background, and level of development in both native and second languages.
7. The continuum model provides for movement in either direction. Give an example of a bilingual exceptional child placed in the general education classroom who may require more specialized assistance. Give an example of a bilingual exceptional child placed in a separate special program who may be moved into a less restricted environment. Identify age, exceptionality, cultural/linguistic background, and level of development in both native and second languages.

8. Select five teacher competencies that you consider most important for effective inclusion of bilingual exceptional children. Identify, describe, and explain why they are essential in the inclusion process.

9. Develop example (single-concept) lesson plans for working with bilingual children with the particular exceptionalities listed. Identify the age, cultural/linguistic background, and level of language development in both languages. Emphasize how you would accommodate for each exceptionality. Be sure instructional objective, methodology, and evaluation procedure are clearly described.

a. Emotionally disturbed
b. Gifted and talented
c. Hearing impaired
d. Learning impaired
e. Mentally retarded
f. Physically/neurologically disabled
g. Speech impaired
h. Vision impaired

☺ REFERENCES

Baca, L. (1981). *Bilingual special education teacher competencies*. Paper prepared for Association of Colleges of Teacher Education, Bilingual Special Education Project.

Bergin, V. (1979). *Special education needs in bilingual programs*. Rosslyn, VA: National Clearinghouse for Bilingual Education.

Collier, C. (1994a). *Acculturation quick screen (AQS)*. Vancouver, WA: Cross Cultural Developmental Education Services.

Collier, C. (1994b). *PreReferral review form (PRR)*. Vancouver, WA: Cross Cultural Developmental Education Services.

Collier, C. (1995). *Classroom language interaction checklist (CLIC)*. Vancouver, WA: Cross Cultural Developmental Education Services.

Collier, C., & Hoover, J. J. (1987). *Cognitive learning strategies for minority handicapped students*. Lindale, TX: Hamilton Publications.

DeAvila, E., & Duncan, S. (1986). *Language assessment scales (LAS)*. Corte Madero, CA: Linguametrics.

Feuerstein, R. (1979). *The dynamic assessment of retarded performers*. Baltimore, MD: University Park Press.

Gearheart, B. R., Weishahn, M. W., & Gearheart, C. J. (1995). *The exceptional student in the regular classroom* (6th ed.). St. Louis, MO: Mosby.

Gould, S. J. (1982). *The mismeasure of man*. New York: Norton.

Hammill, D. D., & Bartel, N. R. (1990). *Teaching children with learning and behavior problems* (5th ed.). Boston, MA: Allyn & Bacon.

Heward, W. A. (1996). *Exceptional children: An introduction to special education* (5th ed.). Upper Saddle River, NJ: Merrill/Prentice Hall.

Heward, W. L., & Orlansky, M.D. (1980). *Exceptional children: An introductory survey to special education*. Upper Saddle River, NJ: Merrill/Prentice Hall.

Hoover, J. J., & Collier, C. (1985). Referring culturally different children: Sociocultural considerations. *Academic Therapy, 20*(4), 503–509.

Jones, R. L (Ed.). (1976). *Inclusion and the minority child*. Reston, VA: Council for Exceptional Children.

Kirk, S. A., & Gallagher, J. J. (1989). *Educating exceptional children* (6th ed.). Boston: Houghton Mifflin.

Lau v. Nichols (1974). 414 U.S. 563.

Peck, C. A. (1993). Ecological perspectives on the implementation of integrated early childhood programs. In C. A. Peck, S. L. Odom, & D. D. Bricker (Eds.), *Integrating young children with disabilities into community programs: Ecological perspectives on research and implementation* (pp. 1–27). Baltimore, MD: Paul H. Brookes.

Peck, C. A., Mabry, S., Curley, L., & Conn-Powers, A. (1993). Integrated early childhood programs: Research on the implementation of change in organizational contexts. In C. A. Peck, S. L. Odom, & D. D. Bricker (Eds.), *Integrating young children with disabilities into community programs: Ecological perspectives on research and implementation* (pp. 134–179). Baltimore, MD: Paul H. Brookes.

Reynolds, M. C. (Ed.) (1980) *A common body of practices for teachers: The challenge of Public Law 94-142 to teacher education*. Minneapolis, MN: University of Minnesota.

Reynolds, M. C., & Birch, J. W. (1986). *Teaching exceptional children in all of America's schools*. Reston, VA: Council for Exceptional Children.

CHAPTER 13

How Educational Consultation Can Enhance Instruction for Culturally and Linguistically Diverse Exceptional (CLDE) Students

Kathleen C. Harris

*Portions of this chapter were adapted from *The educational consultant: Helping profession-als, parents, and mainstreamed students* (3rd ed.), by T. E. Heron and K. C. Harris, (1993). Austin, TX: Pro-Ed; from "Meeting the needs of special education high school students in regular education classrooms," by K. C. Harris, P. Harvey, L. Garcia, D. Innes, P. Lynn, D. Munoz, K. Sexton, & R. Stoica, (1987), *Teacher Education and Special Education, 10*(4): 143–152, and from "Consultation within a multicultural society: Issues for consideration," by K. C. Harris (in press), *Remedial and Special Education*.

- A Definition of Educational Consultation
- The Role of a Educational Consultant
- Developing Collaborative Skills
- Coordinating Services
- A Model of Educational Consultation
- Example of a Collaborative Educational Program
- Summary

OBJECTIVES

To define the term *consultation*

To discuss the roles of an educational consultant

To discuss the skills needed by an educational consultant in a multicultural society

To describe a model of educational consultation

To present an example of a collaborative educational approach for CLDE students

A DEFINITION OF EDUCATIONAL CONSULTATION

As discussed in Heron and Harris (1993), *consultation* has acquired a variety of definitions that vary depending on the setting, target of the consultation, or the intervention used during the consultation (see, for example, Curtis & Meyers, 1988; Friend, 1985; Robinson, Cameron, & Raethel, 1985; Rosenfield, 1987). When individuals engage in consultation, they provide expertise to another party. A *consultant,* therefore, can be anyone who has the necessary expertise for a given situation. For example, if a special educator is developing a unit on study skills and wishes to help students generalize these study skills to the history class, the history teacher could serve as a consultant to the special educator. Similarly, if the bilingual educator wishes to modify instructional materials for a students with learning disabilities who is receiving native language reading instruction, the special educator could serve as a consultant to the bilingual educator. All individuals who work with students can assume the role of a consultant, depending on the needs of the student. Opportunities for consultation exist in a number of different organizational structures within schools. Culturally and linguistically diverse exceptional children (CLDE) are often supported by a variety of professionals, e.g., counselors, bilingual educators, English as a Second Language (ESL) educators, special educators, reading specialists, and general educators. Any of these individuals, as well as the student, the student's family, and significant individuals in the student's community, can serve as consultants to one another.

For approximately the last 20 years, educators have identified educational consultation as a way to facilitate the coordination of programs for exceptional students in the least restrictive environment (see, for example, Adelman, 1972; Bauer, 1975; Evans, 1980; Friend, 1984; Friend & Cook, 1992; Haight & Molitor, 1983; Heron & Harris, 1987; Lilly & Givens-Ogle, 1981; Lilly, 1971; McKenzie et al., 1970; Miller & Sabatino, 1978; Powell, 1982; Reeve & Hallahan, 1994; Spodek, 1982). Therefore, educational consultation is worthy of scrutiny as a vehicle for providing educational services to CLDE students. In this chapter, we will discuss the roles educational consultants can assume, including the methodology for providing direct and indirect services to students; discuss the skills needed by educational consultants in a multicultural society; provide a model of educational consultation; and present an example of a collaborative educational approach for CLDE students.

THE ROLE OF AN EDUCATIONAL CONSULTANT

Effective consultation is a collaborative, voluntary, mutual problem-solving process that leads to the prevention or resolution of identified problems (Heron & Harris, 1993). Collaboration refers to the specific way consultants share their expertise with one another. When consultation occurs as a collaborative process, expertise is shared through a mutual effort. *Collaboration* means that the parties engaging in the consultation share information and work together to plan, implement, and evaluate programs.

Given this definition, the educational consultant assumes three primary and overlapping roles: providing technical assistance, communicating, and coordinating services (Goldstein & Sorcher, 1974). (See Figure 13–1.) Each of these roles will be addressed in the next sections, and we will discuss how consultants can provide technical assistance directly and indirectly.

Technical Assistance

Areas of technical expertise include assessment skills to assist with problem identification and program evaluation, knowledge and skill in instructional and curricular adaptations to ac-

Figure 13–1
The Three Overlapping Roles of a Consultant

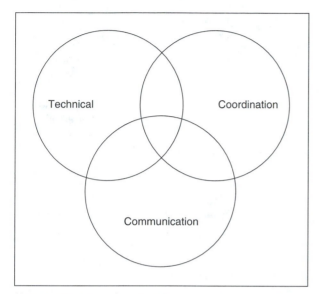

Note. Adapted from *Changing Supervisor Behavior,* by A. Goldstein and M. Sorcher, 1974, New York, Pergamon. Copyright © 1974 by Pergamon. Reprinted with permission.

commodate students with learning problems, and knowledge and skill in behavior and classroom management techniques to accommodate diversity in the classroom. These areas of technical expertise are discussed throughout the text. Technical assistance can be provided in two ways, indirectly and directly, and it can be delivered to, among others, students, teachers, parents, and administrators. In this chapter, we will focus on technical assistance that can be provided to students.

Indirect service to students includes any task where the consultant works with a mediator (e.g., a teacher or family member) who, in turn, works with the student. Indirect services to students are accomplished by providing direct service to the mediator. Generating ideas for interventions as a member of a problem-solving team is an example of an indirect service to a student. The student benefits indirect-

ly from the consultant's intervention with the teacher.

Direct service includes any task where the consultant actually works with an individual without a mediator. Instruction is probably the most common example of direct service to a student. As stated by Meyers, Parsons, and Martin (1979), "When direct service is applied appropriately, it invariably involves consultative aspects; thus to exclude direct service from consultation would be artificial" (p. 89).

Figure 13-2 depicts the types of activities consultants can perform. These activities are not exhaustive but represent activities consultants conduct along a continuum of direct and indirect service to students.

Teacher Assistance Teams

Perhaps the most common indirect service activities in schools are those performed by teams. There are various types of teams using consultation techniques. According to Idol and West (1987), there are six service delivery options which represent the major alternatives available to teachers who want to develop, implement, and evaluate joint programs across general and special education settings. They are teacher assistance teams, prereferral intervention systems, consulting teachers, resource/consulting teacher, special education resource teacher, and resource teacher. While these models have different procedural steps, there is also consensus about their collective emphasis on the consultant's knowledge of content and communication and personal interaction skills (Idol & West, 1987). In addition, with respect to function, consultation with an individual teacher or a core group of professionals and parents is central to each (Graden, Casey, & Christenson, 1985).

Friend and Cook (1992) define a *team* as ". . . a relatively small set of interdependent individuals who work and interact directly in a coordinated manner to achieve a common purpose" (p. 24). There are at least four factors

Figure 13–2
Consultative Services for Students

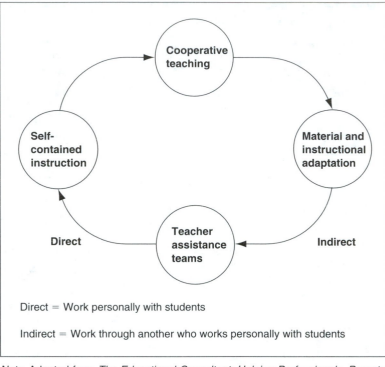

Note. Adapted from *The Educational Consultant: Helping Professionals, Parents, and Mainstreamed Students* (3rd ed.), by T. E. Heron & K. C. Harris, 1993, Austin, TX: PRO-ED.

that characterize effective teams: (1) team goals are clear and members remain focused on the overall requirements of the task at hand, (2) the core group's professional and personal needs are met through the team's interactions, (3) members understand the reciprocal relationship between their behavior and the team's output, and (4) the group works within an organized system of leadership and participation, recognizing shared responsibility in a decentralized process (Friend & Cook, 1992).

Ortiz (1990) discusses the use of teacher assistance teams to address the needs of culturally and linguistically diverse (CLD) students and the importance of involving bilingual educators on these teams. The purpose of these teams is to help teachers develop interventions aimed at improving academic performance in the mainstream before referral to special educa-

tion is considered. Team members consult with colleagues regarding the problems experienced by students in school. Often, the students for whom educators need support are students at-risk for school failure. It is, therefore, important for consultants to identify individuals and resources for appropriate assessment and instructional options for CLD students. This may require consultants to seek the involvement of individuals in formal as well as informal support systems. Special educators usually include parents in their consultations. However, extended family members, unrelated significant individuals in the student's life, neighbors, friends, healers, institutions such as churches, local self-help groups, and community leaders may be among the appropriate resources needed to develop an effective intervention for an at-risk student (Delgado, 1994).

Material and Instructional Modification

When modifying materials and instructional strategies, consultants move along the continuum toward serving students directly. Even if consultants do not use the adapted materials or instructional strategies with students, the materials may still be used to instruct the student by a colleague. When modifying materials for CLDE learners, it is necessary to consider language and culture. The following criteria may be applied when deciding the appropriateness of curriculum material: (1) does it reinforce learning, (2) is the material logically sequenced, (3) is the material comprehensible, and (4) is the material culturally sensitive (Collier & Kalk, 1989; Ortiz & Jones, 1982).

When determining if the material is comprehensible, the consultant must determine if the language level of the material matches the language proficiency of the student. It is also necessary to determine if the language concepts expressed in the material are consistent with the language concept development of the students. For example, in some languages there is no distinction between sexes. Sex is determined by the sensitivity of the culture to different sex roles, not by a word to denote sex. Therefore, the teacher will need to incorporate culturally appropriate activities and teach the concepts of "he" and "she"; otherwise, the student may become confused (Collier & Kalk, 1989).

In addition to determining if the language is comprehensible, the consultant should also determine if the curricular material is culturally sensitive. For example, many materials depicting different cultural groups may present general stereotypes. The teacher should be careful to discuss materials used and note which are indicative of modern-day cultural groups and which are not. The teacher should encourage the students to help identify and explain the cultural values depicted in curricular materials.

The consultant may also be helpful in demonstrating how curricular materials could be used in a culturally sensitive fashion. As discussed by Collier and Kalk (1989), the educator should not assume that what is true in one culture is true in another. For example, the teacher may, in teaching the colors white, black, and brown, use different groups of peoples as examples. However, in many non-Western cultures, the words for white, black, and brown are never applied to human beings.

In summary, the modification of curricular materials requires the educator to be sensitive to the learning, language, and cultural characteristics of students. It requires the educator to know about content area, learning problems, and compensatory strategies as well as language and cultural characteristics. Educators should consult with one another to increase knowledge in areas of weakness as well as determining the individual needs of CLDE students. As stated by Collier and Kalk (1989), "The use of multisensory approaches coupled with multicultural materials and cross-cultural techniques is a good beginning in bridging the bilingual/bicultural and special learning needs of culturally and linguistically different exceptional children" (p. 216).

Tharp & Yamauchi (1994) provide an example of modifying instructional strategies to meet the needs of Native American students in mainstream classrooms. They suggest that educators extend their wait time for student responses to allow students sufficient time to process verbal input. They also recommend that teachers avoid high physical and verbal activity and high volumes of speech, as these are not consistent with cultural expectations for these students. They do suggest that educators present information in a holistic versus an analytic learning style. For example, have Navajo third grade children read or listen to the whole story before discussion. Finally, they suggest that educators organize instruction consistent with home culture. Teachers may want to structure the majority of the school day in individual or small group activities, where peers work together and teachers move around and involve students in quiet discussion. There should also be adequate opportunity for cooperative work to solve problems or make projects which also involve the teacher, as is done in the home culture.

Cooperative Teaching

When teaching cooperatively, consultants can provide a form of direct service to students in collaboration with mediators (e.g., other educators). We shall discuss three types of cooperative teaching techniques: complementary instruction, team teaching, and supportive learning activities (Bauwens & Hourcade, 1995; Bauwens, Hourcade, & Friend, 1989). These three types of cooperative teaching are not mutually exclusive. However, they are offered to help the reader understand different ways educators can co-teach.

Complementary Instruction. In complementary instruction, the general education teacher assumes primary responsibility for teaching the subject matter. The specialist assumes responsibility for each student's mastery of the academic survival skills necessary to acquire the content. This approach is especially appropriate for the secondary level, where content area expertise is essential for effective instruction.

An example is when a specialist instructs students in the use of note taking skills at the beginning of the class and provides a note-taking format for all the students in the class to use. The science teacher provides a classroom lecture on fossils. As the science teacher notes important points during the lecture, the special educator fills in a sample note-taking sheet on an overhead projector. At the end of the lecture, the science teacher reviews the key points from the completed overhead and the special educator reviews the important aspects of the note-taking strategy. While the students follow-up the lecture with independent activities, the science teacher and the special educator circulate among the students and check each student's written notes from the lecture.

Team Teaching. Team teaching is another type of cooperative teaching. It is not a new approach. In a team teaching situation, educators plan and teach academic subject content jointly to all students. This approach is most appropriate when educators have similar areas of expertise. For example, general education teachers and specialists can team teach social studies. They can share responsibility for developing the social studies unit, implementing the activities, and evaluating student mastery of content. By sharing their expertise in social studies, each teacher can help meet the needs of all the children in the class, especially those with special needs.

Supportive Learning Activities. With this approach to cooperative teaching, the mainstream teacher assumes responsibility for delivering the essential curricular content, while the specialist develops and implements supplementary activities. This is different from complementary instruction, in that the specialist's efforts supplement and enrich the specific academic content delivered by the mainstream teacher. In complementary instruction, the specialist provides instruction in new but related content. When providing supportive learning activities, both teachers are present and monitor both types of learning activities cooperatively. For example, in a primary classroom, the teacher provides reading instruction. After reading the story, students identify the key points of the story, summarize it, and then illustrate their summarization. The teacher reads with the students. A specialist, using adapted materials and instruction, helps *all* the students, including those with learning problems, identify the key points of the story using story mapping, generate sentences using sentence starters to summarize the story in an appropriate sequence, and illustrate the story.

An Example of Cooperative Teaching with CLDE Students. In the coordinated services model, the special education teacher and the bilingual education teacher combine their expertise to serve the CLDE student (Baca & Almanza, 1991). In this way, the CLDE student has the benefit of the services of two well-trained individuals. It is also possible that CLDE students can receive these services with peers without disabilities in bilingual classrooms, thereby receiving services in a least restrictive environment. An example is the bilingual teacher providing academic instruction in the student's native language. The special education teacher might assist the bilingual educator by modifying native language and ESL instructional materials for the student with special needs. The special educator may also team teach with the bilingual educator in providing ESL instruction for all students in the class and take greater responsibility for carrying out the IEP when the student is transitioned into all-English instruction.

Self-Contained Instruction

In a self-contained situation, the educator works directly with the student. Ideally for a CLDE student, this should occur in an integrated bilingual special education model (Baca & Almanza, 1991). In this situation, the bilingual special education teacher can provide all the educational services for the CLDE student in a self-contained special program. To offer this program, the teacher must be fluent in the languages of all the children in the class as well as knowledgeable and sensitive to all the children's various cultural and linguistic differences. The teacher's professional training must include bilingual and special education methodologies appropriate for the levels of language proficiency for all the students in the classroom and types of exceptionalities the children represent. However, consultation often occurs even in the self-contained situation. Often, educators consult with each other to problem-solve difficulties they are experiencing in the self-contained situation.

We have come full-circle in considering the services that consultants can provide to stu-

dents. When teaching in self-contained or team teaching situations, educators need the opportunity to consult with one another to meet the individual needs of the students they are teaching. Even though collaborative programs for CLDE students have become more prominent (Ortiz, 1990; Ortiz & Garcia, 1995), few school personnel have had experience working together to meet the needs of CLDE students (Fradd, 1991; Ortiz & Wilkinson, 1991). Therefore, it is important for bilingual, ESL, general and special educators to prepare themselves to work together to develop programs for CLDE students that are appropriate and conducted in least restrictive environments.

DEVELOPING COLLABORATIVE SKILLS

West and Cannon (1988) conducted a national validation study to determine the skills consultants need to acquire expertise as a school consultant. Using a sample of 100 "experts" from around the country, they asked them to rate critical consultation skills. The results of their Delphi investigation showed that 47 skills clustered into eight categories: consultation theory and models, research, personal characteristics, interactive communication, collaborative problem-solving, systems change, equity issues and values, and evaluation. In her review of the literature, Harris (1991) identified interpersonal and communication skills as well as technical skills consultants should have to meet the needs of culturally and linguistically diverse students. Four general competencies emerged from this literature review, i.e., understanding one's perspective; using effective interpersonal, communication and problem-solving skills; understanding the role(s) of collaborators; and using appropriate assessment and instructional strategies. The competencies were identified based on their frequency of appearance in the literature. The competencies selected for discussion in this chapter were chosen considering the specific activities educational consultants might conduct to address the needs of students in a multicultural society.

Understanding One's Culture and Its Relationship to Others' Cultures

Understanding one's perspective is a necessary prerequisite to any collaborative activity. As indicated in the literature (e.g., Kurpius, 1978; West, Idol, & Cannon, 1989), to engage in a consultation activity, it is necessary for educational consultants to understand their attitudes, values, needs, beliefs, skills, knowledge, and limitations. This understanding is necessary to establish a climate for collaboration that will foster growth and change. According to Gibbs (1980), consultants have an ethical responsibility of being aware of their own culture, values, and beliefs as well as understanding how these differ from others. As Jackson and Hughley-Hayes (1993) explain, even in the beginning stages of a consultation, consultants need to have familiarity with the culture of the individuals with whom consultation occurs. The ability to acknowledge cultural differences in communication and relationships helps the educational consultant to be successful. If the educational consultant is not familiar with cultural differences, it is likely that there will be lack of mutual goals, frustration, and disappointment. Gwyn and Kilpatrick (1981) found these to be factors in the termination of consulting before resolution.

Familiarity with culture must precede assessment of the situation. In framing problems during consultation, consultants must avoid conflicts with cultural beliefs. It would not be productive for educational consultants to identify behaviors in need of change that are unlikely to change, given the cultural context. For example, if the educational consultant is working with a team of individuals who embrace high context cultural mores, the use of detailed written referral procedures and plans may be in conflict with cultural values. In some high context cultures, such as Chinese, Japanese, Ara-bian, Latin American, and Mediterranean, less information is contained in the verbal part of the message and more is in the context. So, verbal contracts are binding; procedures are not usually written—they are understood; and there is less of a distinction between social and professional relationships (Hall, 1976).

Recognizing one's culture and how it influences one's behavior is necessary, but not sufficient, for working effectively in a multicultural society. Consultants must also be able to assess how their perspective differs from those with whom they are consulting. Strategies for understanding one's culture and the culture of others are discussed below. Using Hall's (1976) broad view of culture (i.e., personality, modes of expression, ways of thinking, ways of movement, ways of resolving problems), what are some activities consultants can conduct that help them to identify their own culture and how it relates to the cultures of others? According to Lynch and Hanson (1992), "Cultural self-awareness begins with an exploration of one's own heritage. Issues such as place of origin, time of immigration, reasons for immigration, language(s) spoken, and the place of the family's first settlement in the United States all help to define one's own cultural heritage. The political leanings, jobs, status, beliefs, and values of the first immigrants help to paint a cultural picture of one's family as do the economic, social, and vocational changes that subsequent generations have undergone." (p. 37). An example of the influence of culture upon the activities of a Native American counselor is reflected in the following interview excerpt:

In my family, I was socialized to think of the family or community first and myself as part of a larger supportive network. As a descendant of the Miami tribe, I am never alone. I've seen the pain, suffering, and conflict within Native American communities and the movement toward social services is only natural. I was the eldest of 28 grandchildren and Grandmother was at the house every day and later every night for dinner. One of the most beautiful aspects of the Native American Indian tradition is depicted in the Lakota Sioux word Tiospaye. Translated, this means strength through community, everyone working together for the good of the community. This, in turn, leads to a view of counseling which focuses on interdependence and community building as a goal. (Teresa LaFromboise, 1996, p. 5)

Anglo-Europeans, those who make up the mainstream culture in the United States, may be the least aware of the way their culture influences their behavior and interactions. This may be due to the dominance of this culture and the melting pot theory that restricted acknowledgment of diversity among immigrant Americans (Lynch & Hanson, 1992).

Hyun and Fowler (1995) suggest educators ask themselves questions such as, "When I was growing up, what did my family say about people from different cultures?" (p. 25) as a first step in understanding one's culture. They also suggest that educators examine common sayings as a way to understand their culture. As they state: ". . . if you have been raised in beliefs like, 'Where there is a will, there is a way,' your views about disabilities may be very different from those of a person who has heard that 'It's God's will' or 'It's my fate.' (p. 26).

After educators become familiar with their culture and its effects on the ways in which they think and behave, the foundation for learning about other cultures has been established. The next step is to learn about other cultures through readings, interactions, and involvement. However, "assuming that culture-specific information gathered from books, cultural mediators, or language learning applies to all individuals from the cultural groups is not only inaccurate but also dangerous—it can lead to stereotyping that diminishes rather than enhances cross-cultural competence" (Lynch & Hanson, 1992, p. 44). It is best to learn about the culture of collaborators by learning about them as individuals, rather than about them as members of a cultural group. This can be accomplished by effective communication and interpersonal skills.

Using Effective Interpersonal and Communication Skills

Using effective interpersonal and communication skills is essential because the consultation process is based on communication and focuses on the identification, prevention, and resolution of problems. As Daniels and DeWine (1991) suggest, communication can actually be the intervention target. Collaborators can work to establish the same interpretation and meaning. In this way, consultants can use effective communication and interpersonal skills to develop a common culture for the consultation activity.

As Lynch and Hanson (1992) suggest, the general characteristics of cross-cultural communication are influenced by a number of theories. However, there are certain characteristics that emerge in theory and practice. People who are effective cross-cultural communicators tend to respect individuals, make continued and sincere attempts to take others' points of view, be open to learn, be flexible, have a sense of humor, and tolerate ambiguity well. As indicated in Table 13-1, these are characteristics that educational consultants are encouraged to develop, regardless of the cultural diversity of collaborators (see, for example, West et al., 1989). What is most important, according to Lynch and Hanson (1992), is for collaborators to "engage in cross-cultural interactions that explore differences openly and respectfully, interactions that dispel myths and open doors to understanding" (p. 50).

Roberts, Bell, and Salend (1991) extend the above characteristics for educational consultants by suggesting that the following abilities are important to develop in a multicultural society: (1) to understand and appreciate cultural differences in verbal and nonverbal communication styles, (2) to ascertain if organizational

Table 13–1

Generic and Specific Interpersonal and Communication Skills for a Multicultural Society

Interpersonal Skills	
Generic	Specific
• Caring • Respectful • Empathetic • Congruent • Open • Positive self-concept • Enthusiastic attitude • Willingness to learn from others • Calm • Stress-free • Risk-taker • Flexible • Resilient • Manage conflict and confrontation • Manage time	• Make continued and sincere attempts to understand the world from others' points of view. • Respect individuals from other cultures. • Have a sense of humor. • Tolerate ambiguity. • Approach others with a desire to learn. • Be prepared and willing to share information about yourself. • Identify needed multicultural knowledge base. • Move fluidly between the roles of giver and taker of information.

mores tend to privilege or silence different groups of people, (3) to develop a common set of meanings among collaborators, and (4) to analyze the language used by collaborators and change linguistic practices that are disabling to collaborators.

An example of the impact of language practices can be seen in terms used to refer to individuals with disabilities over the years. Words such as "imbecile" and "idiot" are pejorative terms that define the individual to whom they are applied as one who is a substandard human being. As the educational rights of these individuals became acknowledged, terms related to their ability to benefit from instruction became acceptable, e.g., educable mentally retarded. As the recognition that these individuals are, most importantly, human beings with many adjectives that could describe them, the preferred

language pattern became the individual and their disability as one adjective, among many, that described them, e.g., an adolescent with behavior problems. This language usage connotes a different way of viewing individuals and subsequently, developing interventions for them. Now, instead of focusing just on the learning or behavior problem, consultants can encourage participants in the consultation process to focus on individuals and all their characteristics, e.g., an adolescent with bilingual ability and behavior problems.

Being conscious of preferred terms to describe groups of individuals is a necessary step in the development of effective cross-cultural communication. Another communication practice that will facilitate cross-cultural collaboration is to use nontechnical language (Jackson & Hughley-Hayes 1993). This practice will aid

Table 13–1 *(cont.)*

Generic and Specific Interpersonal and Communication Skills for a Multicultural Society

Communication Skills	
Generic	Specific
• Listening	• Work effectively with an interpreter or translator.
• Acknowledging	• Use nontechnical language as an aid in equalizing differences between collaborators.
• Paraphrasing	
• Reflecting	• Acknowledge cultural differences in communication and relationship building.
• Clarifying	
• Elaborating	• Use communication to create systems of meaning among collaborators.
• Summarizing	
• Grasping overt meaning	• Identify language practices that are disabling and change them.
• Grasping covert meaning	
• Interpreting nonverbal communication	• Ensure that problem identification does not conflict with cultural beliefs.
• Interviewing effectively	• Use information regarding socially hidden aspects of power that privilege or silence culturally diverse groups in problem solving.
• Providing feedback	
• Brainstorming	
• Responding nonjudgmentally	
• Developing an action plan	

Note. From "Collaboration Within a Multicultural Society: Issues for Consideration," by K. C. Harris, 1996, *Remedial and Special Education.* Copyright 1996 by PRO-ED, Inc. Adapted and reprinted by permission.

in developing a common set of meanings as well as equalizing differences among collaborators.

Jackson and Hughley-Hayes (1993) also recommend that consultants attend to the concerns of collaborators. Identifying concerns requires trust. Establishing trust, in some cultures, often requires the consultant to share personal information. As discussed by Velez (1980), to establish trust in many Hispanic cultures, collaborators "must be prepared and willing to share of themselves and participate whenever possible in cultural activities within the community. . . . You may be asked personal questions pertaining to place of birth, family background and current marital status" (p. 46). As a consultant, the author experienced this with a teacher assistance team that included Hispanic team members. Following is a recounting of that experience.

Because I attended every team meeting, I assumed that I had membership status, but one incident in particular placed this assumption in doubt. At a team meeting, I summarized comments made by referring teachers to me during unstructured interviews. The overwhelming majority of the comments were positive regarding both team process and content. But, like team members, the referring teachers also had some suggestions for improvement, most of which related to the extension of the team concept to other school issues and the opportunity for more teachers to be members of teacher assistance teams. Despite the positive comments by the referring teachers, the team members reacted very negatively toward the feedback as well as my presentation of it. The team members focused on the negative comments and missed the general support evident in the comments of the referring teachers. A bilingual (Hispanic) resource teacher said: "Evaluation of team activities should really be done by a member of the team." I was surprised. I was operating under the assumption that I was a member of the team, but that was not the perception of the team members. When questioned further, this same bilingual resource teacher said that it would have been preferable to have the director of special education conduct the interviews than to have me conduct the interviews. She hastened to add that the team members like me, but I wasn't really one of them. (Harris, 1995, p. 342)

Understanding the Role(s) of Educational Collaborators

There are many roles that consultants can assume. For example, they might be facilitators of problem-solving sessions among collaborators, catalysts for change, or they might collaborate in designing or implementing educational interventions (e.g., Heron & Harris, 1993; Kurpius & Lewis, 1988). In a multicultural society, consultants might be asked to: (1) facilitate problem solving sessions with individuals with different values and problem-solving styles, (2) promote the use of native language and culture for at-risk students, or (3) collaborate with culturally diverse professionals. For example, in working with CLDE students, educational consultants may be in the position to determine the most effective language of instruction for the student and may need to work with a culturally diverse group of individuals to develop a plan which values the use of native language and culture. The problem-solving session may be conducted with a group of culturally diverse educational professionals (e.g., Latino bilingual teachers and Anglo-European

general and special education teachers) as well as individuals from the student's family and community. Depending on the cultural identity of this culturally diverse group, the consultant may be faced with facilitating a problem-solving session among individuals from "higher context" and "low context" cultures. Individuals from the low-context cultures (e.g., Anglo-Europeans) may focus on precise, direct, logical, spoken communication that quickly gets to the point. They may not easily process the gestures, environmental clues, and unarticulated moods that are central to effective communication in high-context cultures (e.g., among the Latino bilingual educators and family and community members). This may lead to misunderstanding and frustration for both parties (Hecht, Andersen, & Ribeau, 1989).

In her work with bilingual special education teacher assistance teams, Harris (1995) found that team members often approached their roles in the school differently, and the roles assumed were not always dictated by ethnic identity. In one elementary bilingual special education team, the principal of the elementary school, a Mexican-American male, identified his role in the school as "instructional leader." Though he stated that he valued bilingual education advocates, he did not consider that to be a role he played in the school. In a junior high school in the same district, the bilingual and ESL teachers, more than other Hispanic team members, strongly identified with the needs of linguistically diverse students. The Hispanic special education teacher considered her primary role to be "helping teachers." The Title VII specialist, an Anglo-European responsible for bilingual and ESL support, also considered her primary role that of "helping teachers," not advocating for linguistically diverse students. Yet, other bilingual teachers considered themselves bilingual advocates. The teachers in this district struggled with their roles. For some, their roles were clearly influenced by their ethnic identity; for others, their roles were clearly influenced by their job titles. Therefore, consultants are advised to learn about the values of each of the collaborators and not assume that the values and roles of collaborators are based upon identifiable characteristics, such as ethnic identity or job title. Likewise, it is important for consultants to identify the skills of collaborators based on performance and not just ethnic identity. As Ortiz and Garcia (1995) caution, being bilingual does not ensure one has the knowledge of the student's culture or skills in bilingual educational methodology.

COORDINATING SERVICES

In addition to technical expertise and collaboration skills, consultants need to coordinate consultation activities. Since numerous consulting activities can fall within the framework of an individual's job (e.g., a bilingual educator who consults; a science teacher who consults; a special educator who consults), those involved in consultation must manage their time and coordinate their activities effectively with others. Deficiencies in these areas can seriously impede the best conceived interventions.

When scheduling activities, consider incorporating collaborative planning and problem solving time, the activities of all program participants, and flexibility. Collaborative planning and problem-solving time is essential for consultation activities to work. Figure 13–3 provides suggestions for how to arrange time for consultation within a school setting.

Admittedly, scheduling time within a school day can be difficult. Still, with the exception of the fifth suggestion in Figure 13–3—a permanent "floating" substitute—all the remaining recommendations can be implemented by reconsidering supervision assignments or planning periods. Further, having the principal or other support staff teach a class period on a regularly scheduled basis would have the added benefit of increasing their awareness of the specific skills the teacher is attempting to develop with the students. They would experience first hand the challenges that the teacher faces

Figure 13–3
Some Ways to Schedule Time to Consult

- Common planning period.
- Fewer staff supervising large group meetings of students for special types of school experiences (e.g., guest speakers, films, plays).
- Principal or other support staff/supervisor teach a period a day on a regularly scheduled basis.
- When students are working on the same independent assignment or study activity, arrange for them to be clustered in large groups (e.g., in multipurpose room or library).
- A permanent "floating" substitute.
- Aides or volunteers to guide or supervise groups/classes of students at class-changing time, lunch, or recess.
- Specified time each week assigned by principal for staff collaboration.
- Alter the school day to provide staff collaboration without students (e.g., last Friday afternoon each month).
- One day per grading period as "collaboration day" (no other activities can be substituted on this day).

Note. From "Collaborative Consultation in the Education of Mildly Handicapped and At Risk Students," by J. F. West & L. Idol, *Remedial and Special Education, 11* (1), pp. 29-30. Copyright 1990 by PRO-ED, Inc. Adapted and reprinted by permission.

and would experience the importance of consultation as a method for integrating instruction across skills and settings. Finally, the usefulness of a common planning time cannot be understated. When teachers are able to meet together to share ideas, even for brief periods of time, a great deal can be accomplished. The cumulative effect of many short-term meetings can be more efficacious than longer-term meetings conducted sporadically.

A MODEL OF EDUCATIONAL CONSULTATION

The triadic model of educational consultation represents a way in which school consultation can be conceptualized. This model is not intended to be representative of all models that might be used with teachers, parents, or students. Rather, it and the accompanying example illustrate how educational consultation services can be used in a collaborative program for CLDE students.

Historically, researchers in special education have questioned the efficacy of segregated special education placement since at least 1960 (Blatt, 1960). In light of this, the triadic model was developed to provide a basis for specialists to consult with teachers (Tharp, 1975). The triadic model (Figure 13–4), in its most basic form, is a linear sequence that portrays the relationships among the consultant, the mediator or consultee, and the client or target. The bracket that connects the consultant and the mediator represents the collaborative consultation process.

The triadic model describes a functional rather than an absolute sequence for consultation. That is, any teacher, parent, or administrator could serve as the consultant. The only

requirement for serving as a consultant is that the individual possess the knowledge, skills, or abilities needed to work collaboratively with the mediator or the target. A bilingual teacher, paraprofessional, or parent could serve as the mediator. The mediator has access to the target student and has some influence over the student, while the consultant serves as a catalyst to activate the mediator. The target is the individual (or group) for whom the consultative service is intended, or any other person involved with the consultation (Tharp & Wetzel, 1969). According to Idol, Nevin, and Paolucci-Whitcomb (1994), seven principles of collaborative consultation form the basis of the interpersonal, communication, and problem-solving skills of the triadic model.

First, team ownership of the identified problem or issue is necessary for successful collaborative consultation. Both equity and parity must exist among consulting parties for the model to work effectively. Equity is revealed when the ideas of each consulting party are re-

Figure 13–4
The Triadic Model of Consultation Showing Individuals Within Each Role

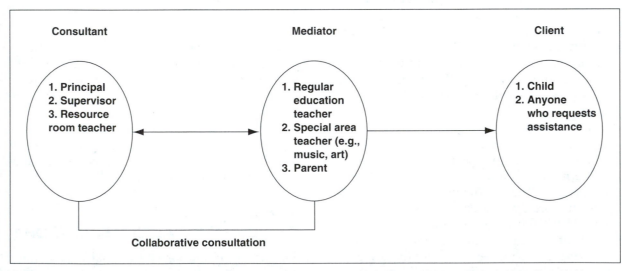

Note. From *Behavior Modification in the Natural Environment* (p. 47), by R. G. Tharp and R. J. Wetzel, 1969, New York. Copyright © 1969 by Harcourt Brace & Company. Adapted and reprinted by permission of the publisher.

spected and used to develop action plans. Parity exists when the knowledge and skills of both parties are blended.

Second, to develop an intervention which necessitates change, there is a need to recognize individual differences in the developmental process. That is, implicit in the implementation of the triadic model is that a change in procedure occurs. For some individuals, making a change in a routine is uncomfortable. The consulting individuals as well as the students they are serving are able to change at different rates, dependent upon different variables. To understand developmental changes in implementing change, refer to the Concerns-Based Adoption Model (CBAM) developed by Hall (1981). This model delineates stages of concern that individuals may experience as they engage in change. The consultant's role in the collaboration process is to be sensitive to effects of change on participating parties and to make transitions as nonthreatening as possible.

Third, situational leadership is a guide to the implementation of collaborative consultation. This implies that leadership is shared among the participating parties rather than having a designated leader. Situational leadership encourages all participating parties to have a commitment to achieving a common goal. It also requires participating parties to support each other as they share leadership responsibilities in achieving their desired goal.

Fourth, cooperative conflict resolution processes underlie collaborative consultation. It is recognized that individuals participating in a consultative relationship will not always agree. Within a cooperative framework, these disagreements are viewed as opportunities. It requires collaborators to be comfortable with controversy and acquire and use skills in negotiating conflict. Participating members should realize that there are two concerns in any conflict: achieving the goal and maintaining positive relationships (Johnson & Johnson, 1995). Not all conflict-resolution strategies attend to both concerns. For example, if an individual

elects to withdraw from the process, then neither the goal nor the relationship(s) is maintained. However, problem-solving is a strategy for addressing both concerns in conflict resolution. Refer to Johnson and Johnson (1995) for a discussion of various conflict resolution strategies and their effects.

Fifth and sixth, consulting parties must use appropriate interviewing skills and active listening techniques. As the intention of the collaborative consultation is to develop a plan that benefits from the best knowledge and thinking of all participants, it is important that all participants are able to elicit the "collective wisdom" from the group through the use of appropriate questioning strategies. Consultants must be able to operate from the cultures from which they have been socialized professionally as well as understand the cultures of the individuals who are part of the consulting process (Raffaniello, 1981). Participants are encouraged to ask themselves the following questions when interviewing: Can I exhibit the ability to be caring, respectful, empathetic, congruent, and open in cross-cultural consultation interactions? Can I exhibit the ability to grasp and validate overt/covert meaning and affect in cross-cultural interactions? (Harris, 1991).

The questions posed above also relate to the seventh principle identified by Idol, Nevin, and Paolucci-Whitcomb (1994)—oral and written communication must rely on common, nonjargon, and positive nonverbal language. As indicated previously in this chapter, the use of nontechnical language facilitates the communication of clear messages as well as the ability of the consulting parties to communicate with equity and parity.

All of the principles discussed above are interrelated. When applied to the consulting process, individuals are likely to experience success in achieving their goals and maintaining positive working relationships. However, the use of these skills on a consistent basis among consulting parties takes time and effort.

Villa (1988) discussed model inservice programs that used these principles and took two years to develop. Consulting parties need to be aware that though successful application of these principles takes time, it is well worth the effort.

EXAMPLE OF A COLLABORATIVE EDUCATIONAL PROGRAM

The following description of a program for CLDE students is an adaptation of a program inplemented at a high school in southern California (Harris et al., 1987). This program is based on a consultation model in that services for CLDE students were provided according to the principles of collaborative consultation and using a combination of direct and indirect services. The program was implemented in five stages: development of the program philosophy, identification of teachers, articulation of the program, program scheduling, and program evaluation.

The consultants in the program were the special educators in the high school (the three resource specialists, the special day class teacher, the speech and language specialist, and the school psychologist). The program was designed to serve all CLDE students in the school (approximately 80). The resources available to implement the program were the special educators, the bilingual educators, ESL educators, the general educators, the special education paraprofessionals, and the bilingual paraprofessionals. Among the staff available to implement the program were a combination of monolingual and bilingual (Spanish) speakers.

Development of Program Philosophy

Before implementing the program, the consultants met to develop their program philosophy. A firm program philosophy was important for the successful implementation of the program. Essentially, the philosophy of the program included the following: a need to serve students with special education needs and with low-ability (those students who were not achieving at a satisfactory level in school but who were not eligible for special education services), a desire to address the development of language proficiency as part of the program, a desire to serve students in mainstream classrooms as the least restrictive environment, and a desire to serve as a resource to the mainstream classroom teacher. Based on this philosophy, the goal of the program was to provide services to CLDE students in mainstream classrooms. These students would only be removed from the mainstream classroom when it was not possible to provide the services they needed in the mainstream classroom. This program was implemented with all the CLDE students in the school.

Identification of Mainstream Teachers

The consultants chose only a portion of all the teachers in the school (approximately 30) to work with during the first year of the program. The consultants chose teachers with the following characteristics: they taught classes in which the CLDE students had been or could be mainstreamed, they were familiar with the consultants, they were willing to work with the consultants, and they and the consultants felt mutual professional respect and credibility. The mainstream teachers who participated in the program taught bilingual and ESL classes in basic reading, English, math, social sciences, and biological sciences.

Articulation of Program

Before program implementation, the consultants met with the mainstream teachers to discuss and refine the program. The meeting was held at the beginning of the school year. The consultants presented themselves as a team. They discussed the philosophy of the program and explained that they wished to serve the CLDE students and the mainstream teachers in the mainstream classroom. The consultants described the services they would be able to implement in this program: (1) student support in the mainstream classroom, (2) student support outside the mainstream classroom, (3) teacher support in the mainstream classroom, and (4) teacher support through collaborative planning. Examples of specific activities in each of these areas can be found in Table 13–2.

During the discussion, the following issues were addressed: difficulty of content, difficulty of material, grading, behavior problems, and collaborating with the consultants. The consultants and the mainstream teachers discussed ways in which these issues could be addressed in this program. By the end of the initial pre-sentation of the program, both consultants and mainstream teachers adopted the philosophy of the program, identified activities that could be conducted to implement the program, and identified procedures that could be used to help meet concerns raised regarding program implementation.

Program Scheduling

This program was a school-wide effort. Therefore, scheduling for program implementation had to reflect how each student in the program would be served by all staff members. The criteria used to develop a preliminary schedule included the following: in-class support for those

Table 13–2
Consultant Activities

Student Support	
In Mainstream Classrooms	Outside Mainstream Classrooms
• Clarifying teachers' directions and instructions	• Counseling students
• Helping students take class notes	• Note-taking/study skills
• Counseling students	• Reading tests to students
	• Coordinating home and school activities

Teacher Support	
Cooperative Teaching	Collaborative Planning
• Team teaching	• Collecting and summarizing student background information
• Developing and implementing behavior management strategies	• Analyzing student behavior
• Teaching small groups of students	• Discussing consultant and teacher roles
• Teaching individual students	• Analyzing teaching
• Establishing cooperative learning groups	• Evaluating lessons
	• Modifying curriculum
	• Developing and supplying materials

Note. Adapted from "Meeting the Needs of Special High School Students in Regular Education Classrooms," by K. D. Harris, P. Harvey, L. Garcia, D. Innes, P. Lynn, D. Munoz, K. Sexton, and R. Stoica, 1987, *Teacher Education and Special Education, 10*(4), pp. 143–152.

mainstream teachers who had the largest concentration of CLDE students, the allocation of most of the consultants' time in the mainstream classrooms, and the allocation of some time for collaborative planning with mainstream teachers as well as among the consultants. Because this was a school-wide program and consultants shared responsibility for students, it was important that consultants have time to discuss among themselves the performance of individuals students as well as their ongoing evaluation of program implementation.

During the initial implementation of the program, the consultants spent time observing and helping the mainstream teachers. This was done so that the role each consultant took in each mainstream classroom could be identified. After weeks, the schedule could be modified, based on the identified needs of the mainstream teachers and the students. For example, some mainstream teachers might want more in-class assistance from the consultants than they were receiving. Therefore, time spent in some mainstream classrooms might be increased, even though there was not a high percentage of CLDE students in those classrooms. Examples of schedules can be found in Figures 13–5 through 13–7.

Figure 13–5 provides a sample student's schedule for a week. This CLDE student was in mainstream classes for all six periods of the school day. The student received support from either consultants or paraprofessionals in the mainstream class every day of the week and in five out of six classes. As can be seen in this table, the student received direct service from four of the six consultants during the course of a week. The student received the most direct service in those classes that were most difficult (e.g., introduction to biological sciences).

Figure 13–6 provides a sample paraprofessional's schedules for a week. This paraprofessional arrived in time for the second period of the school day. Most of the paraprofessional's time was spent in the mainstream classroom (40% of the week) or performing clerical activities (40% of the week). For only 20% of the time did the paraprofessional provide support

Figure 13–5
Sample Student's Schedule

Course	Monday	Tuesday	Wednesday	Thursday	Friday
Applied Math - BL	C1		C1		
Int. Bio. Sci. - BL	P1	P1	P1		C3
ESL	C2		C2		
Reading		C1		C1	
World Cov. - BL			C4		C4
Phys. Ed.					
C = Consultant					
P = Paraprofessional					
BL = Bilingual					

Note. Adapted from "Meeting the Needs of Special High School Students in Regular Education Classrooms," by K. C. Harris, P. Harvey, L. Garcia, D. Innes, P. Lynn, D. Munoz, K. Sexton, and R. Stoica, 1987, *Teacher Education and Special Education,* *10*(4), pp. 143–152.

Figure 13–6
Sample Paraprofessional's Schedule

Period	Monday	Tuesday	Wednesday	Thursday	Friday
2	Int. to Bio. Sci.	Int. to Bio. Sci.	Int. to Bio. Sci.	ESL	ESL
3	RR	RR	RR	RR	RR
4	ESL	Clerical	ESL	Clerical	Clerical
5	Clerical	Clerical	Clerical	Applied Math - BL	Clerical
6	Clerical	Applied Math - BL	Clerical	Applied Math - BL	Clerical

BL = Bilingual

RR = Resource Room

Note. Adapted from "Meeting the Needs of Special High School Students in Regular Education Classrooms," by K. C. Harris, P. Harvey, L. Garcia, D. Innes, P. Lynn, D. Munoz, K. Sexton, and R. Stoica, 1987, *Teacher Education and Special Education,* *10*(4), pp. 143–152.

to CLDE students outside the mainstream classroom (i.e., resource room).

Figure 13–7 provides a sample consultant's schedule for a week. As can be seen by this schedule, half of the consultant's time was spent in the mainstream classroom, working with all students needing assistance (including CLDE students). The consultant spent about 27% of the time in collaborative planning and 17% providing services to CLDE students outside the mainstream classroom. Only 6% of the consultant's time is necessary for the referral

Figure 13–7
Sample Consultant's Schedule

Period	Monday	Tuesday	Wednesday	Thursday	Friday
1	IEP	CP with teachers	World Civ. - BL	CP with consultants	World Civ. - BL
2	IEP	CP with teachers	Reading	CP with consultants	Reading
3	RR	Reading	RR	Reading	RR
4	Applied Math - BL	Applied Math - BL	CP with teachers	Applied Math - BL	CP with teachers
5	Applied Math - BL	RR	CP with teachers	RR	CP with teachers
6	Applied Math - BL	Applied Math - BL	Applied Math - BL	Reading	Applied Math - BL

CP = Collaborative planning

BL = Bilingual

RR = Resource Room

Note. Adapted from "Meeting the Needs of Special High School Students in Regular Education Classrooms," by K. C. Harris, P. Harvey, L. Garcia, D. Innes, P. Lynn, D. Munoz, K. Sexton, and R. Stoica, 1987, *Teacher Education and Special Education,* *10*(4), pp. 143–52.

and classification process (i.e., reserved for IEP meetings).

Program Evaluation

The consultants designed the program evaluation to measure the impact upon the mediators (the mainstream teachers) as well as the targets (CLDE students). This could be done in a number of different ways. In the study conducted by Harris et al. (1987), the consultants administered questionnaires to mainstream teachers and students and also evaluated grades collected from student files. The student questionnaires included the following topics: students' preference for mainstream classrooms, students' comfort with consultants in the mainstream classroom, students' satisfaction with the program, and students' perception of academic and behavioral performance. The teacher questionnaires included the following topics: teachers' comfort with consultants in the mainstream classroom, teachers' satisfaction with the program, and teachers' perceptions of students' academic and behavioral performance. The results of the Harris et al. study (1987), which was an evaluation of a similar program to that described here, was overwhelmingly positive. The students reported that they liked school, they felt as if they were achieving in school, they liked being in mainstream classrooms, and they liked working with consultants in the mainstream classrooms. The mainstream teachers felt comfortable with the consultants in their classrooms. They reported that the consultants were encouraged to work with all the students in the class and to use their own discretion when working collaboratively in the mainstream classroom. In addition, all mainstream teachers felt that collaborative planning with consultants was helpful.

The consultation program described here incorporates several elements discussed in this chapter. Consultants provided teachers and students with direct as well as indirect services. In

addition, this program incorporated components of collaborative consultation as described by Idol, Nevin, and Paolucci-Whitcomb (1994). That is, the consultants worked with the mainstream teachers in clarifying activities that were conducted to implement the program, thereby achieving team ownership. The individual differences of teachers and students were accommodated in the program scheduling and variety of services offered within and outside the mainstream classroom. Consultants shared responsibility for leadership of team meetings. Participants were coached in the use of problem-solving as a conflict resolution strategy, interviewing techniques, active listening, and clear and concrete oral and written communication.

☺ SUMMARY

This chapter discussed how educational consultation can enhance instruction for CLDE students. With the need to provide effective programs for CLDE students within the least restrictive environment, educational consultation becomes viable as a vehicle for providing effective educational services to these students.

Educational consultation is essentially a collaborative, voluntary, mutual problem-solving process that leads to the prevention or resolution of educational problems. Skilled educational consultants capitalize on the knowledge and experiences of those with whom they work, ensuring that the educational program that is implemented is jointly designed and has the widest possible support.

The educational consultant assumes three overlapping roles: providing technical assistance, communicating effectively, and coordinating services. To perform these roles effectively, consultants should be able to collaborate with other educators in cooperative teaching activities as well as planning and problem-solving activities. They need to perform these activities with interpersonal and communication skills appropriate within a multicultural society. Finally, they need to be able to manage time within flexible schedules to conduct these diverse activities.

In this chapter, a model of educational consultation and an application of this model for CLDE students was presented. The components of this model included principles of collaborative consultation and a description of ways in which educational consultants can be involved in providing direct and indirect services. This model was offered as an example. It was not meant to be inclusive of all possible models of educational consultation. Rather, it was provided to assist the reader in conceptualizing a consultation approach for CLDE students. We encourage you to think about different ways in which educational consultation can best meet the needs of CLDE students and develop approaches to meet specific needs. Indeed, one of the key components of collaborative consultation is the ability to recognize and accommodate individual differences.

☺ DISCUSSION QUESTIONS

1. How is the consultation process defined?
2. What are the pros and cons of providing indirect services to CLDE students?
3. What skills must the educational consultant possess to work effectively with personnel who provide services to CLDE students?
4. Discuss how an educational consultant might enhance the cooperation between bilingual educators, ESL educators, special educators, and general educators to provide educational services for CLDE students in mainstream classrooms.
5. Describe a model for educational consultation that would be effective for CLDE students. What are the characteristics of this model that make it particularly appropriate for CLDE students?

☺ REFERENCES

Adelman, H. S. (1972). The resource concept—bigger than a room. *Journal of Special Education, 6,* 361–367.

Baca, L. M., & Almanza, E. (1991). *Language minority students with disabilities.* Reston, VA: The Council for Exceptional Children.

Bauer, H. (1975). The resource teacher—A teacher consultant. *Academic Therapy, 10,* 299–304.

Bauwens, J., & Hourcade, J. J. (1995). *Cooperative teaching: Rebuilding the schoolhouse for all students.* Austin, TX: Pro-Ed.

Bauwens, J., Hourcade, J. J., & Friend, M. (1989). Cooperative teaching: A model for general and special education integration. *Remedial and Special Education, 10*(2), 17–22.

Blatt, B. (1960). Some persistently recurring assumptions concerning the mentally subnormal. *Training School Bulletin, 57,* 48–59.

Collier, C., & Kalk, M. (1989). Bilingual special education curriculum development. In L. M. Baca & H. T. Cervantes, *The bilingual special education interface* (2nd ed., pp. 205–229). Upper Saddle River, NJ: Merrill/Prentice Hall.

Curtis M. J., & Meyers, J. (1988). Consultation: A foundation for alternative services in schools. In J. L. Graden, J. E. Zins, & M. J. Curtis (Eds.), *Alternative educational delivery systems: Enhancing instructional options for all students* (pp. 35–48). Washington, DC: The National Association of School Psychologists.

Daniels, T. D., & DeWine, S. (1991). Communication process as target and tool for consultancy intervention: Rethinking a hackneyed theme. *Journal of Educational and Psychological Consultation, 2*(4), 303–322.

Delgado, M. (1994). Hispanic natural support systems and the AODA field: A developmental framework for collaboration. *Journal of Multicultural Social Work, 3*(2), 11–37.

Evans, S. B. (1980). The consulting role of the resource teacher. *Exceptional Children, 46,* 402–404.

Fradd, S. H. (1991, April). *Developing collaboration in meeting the needs of culturally and linguistically diverse students.* Paper presented at The Research Symposium, State University of New York, University of Buffalo, Buffalo, NY.

Friend, M. (1984). Consulting skills for resource teachers. *Learning Disability Quarterly, 7,* 246–250.

Friend, M. (1985). Training special educators to be consultants. *Teacher Education and Special Education, 8*(3), 115–120.

Friend, M., & Cook, L. (1992). *Interactions: Collaboration skills for school professionals.* New York: Longman.

Gibbs, J. (1980). The interpersonal orientation in mental health consultation: Toward a model of ethnic variations in consultation. *Journal of Community Psychology, 8,* 195–207.

Goldstein, A. P., & Sorcher, M. (1974). *Changing supervisor behavior.* New York: Pergamon.

Graden, J., Casey, A., & Christenson, S. (1985). Implementing a prereferral intervention system: Part II. The data. *Exceptional Children, 51*(6), 487–496.

Gwyn, F. S., & Kilpatrick, A. C. (1981, May). Family therapy with low-income Blacks: A tool or a turnoff? *Social Casework, 259–266.*

Haight, S. L., & Molitor, D. I. (1983). A survey of special education teacher consultants. *Exceptional Children, 49,* 550–553.

Hall, E. T. (1976). *Beyond culture.* Garden City, NY: Anchor Books.

Hall, G. (1981). The concerns-based perspective on personnel preparation program development and dissemination. *Teacher Education and Special Education, 4*(2), 51–60.

Harris, K. C. (1991). An expanded view on consultation competencies for educators serving culturally and linguistically diverse exceptional students. *Teacher Education and Special Education, 14*(1), 25–29.

Harris, K. C. (1995). School-based bilingual special education teacher assistance teams. *Remedial and Special Education, 16*(6), 337–343.

Harris, K. C. (in press). Consultation within a multicultural society: Issues for consideration. *Remedial and Special Education.*

Harris, K. C., Harvey, P., Garcia, L., Innes, D., Lynn, P., Munoz, D., Sexton, K., & Stoica, R. (1987). Meeting the needs of special education high school students in regular education classrooms. *Teacher Education and Special Education, 10*(4), 143–152.

Hecht, M. L., Andersen, P. A., & Ribeau, S. A. (1989). The cultural dimensions of nonverbal communication. In M. K. Asante & W. B. Gudykunst (Eds.), *Handbook of international and intercultural communication* (pp. 163–185). Newbury Park, CA: Sage Publications.

Heron, T. E., & Harris, K. C. (1987). *The educational consultant: Helping professionals, parents, and mainstreamed students* (2nd ed.). Austin, TX: Pro-Ed.

Heron, T. E., & Harris, K. C. (1993). *The educational consultant: Helping professionals, parents, and mainstreamed students* (3rd ed.). Austin, TX: Pro-Ed.

Hyun, J. K., & Fowler, S. A. (1995). Respect, cultural, sensitivity, and communcation: Promoting participation by Asian families in the individualized family service plan. *Teaching Exceptional Children, 28*(1), 25–31.

Idol, L., Nevin. A., Paolucci-Whitcomb, P. (1994). *Collaborative consultation* (2nd ed.). Austin, TX: Pro-Ed.

Idol, L., & West, J. F. (1987). Consultation in special education (Part II). Training and practice. *Journal of Learning Disabilities, 20*(8), 474–494.

Jackson, D. N., & Hughley-Hayes, D. (1993). Multicultural issues in consultation. *Journal of Counseling & Development, 72,* 144–147.

Johnson, D. W., & Johnson, R. T. (1995). *Reducing school violence through conflict resolution.* Alexandria, VA: Association for Supervision and Curriculum Development (ASCD).

Kurpius, D. J. (1978). Consultation theory and process: An integrated model. *Personnel and Guidance Journal, 56,* 335–338.

Kurpius, D. J., & Lewis, J. E. (1988). Assumptions and operating principles for preparing professionals to function as consultants. In J. F. West (Ed.), *School consultation: Interdisciplinary perspectives on theory, research, training and practice* (pp. 143–154). Austin, TX: The Association of Educational and Psychological Consultants.

La Fromboise, T. (1996). Teresa La Fromboise on multicultural issues. *Microtraining and Multicultural Development, 5.*

Lilly, M. S., & Givens-Ogle, L. B. (1981). Teacher consultation: Present, past, and future. *Behavioral Disorders, 6,* 73–77.

Lilly, M. S. (1971). A training based model for special education. *Exceptional Children, 37,* 745–749.

Lynch, E. W., & Hanson, M. J. (Eds.) (1992). *Developing cross-cultural competence: A guide for working with young children and their families.* Baltimore, MD: Paul H. Brookes.

McKenzie, H. S., Egner, A. N., Knight, M. F., Perelman, P. F., Schneider, B. M., & Garvin, J. S. (1970). Training consulting teachers to assist elementary teachers in the management and education of handicapped children. *Exceptional Children, 37,* 137–143.

Meyers, J., Parsons, R. D., & Martin, R. (1979). *Mental health consultation in the schools.* San Francisco: Jossey-Bass.

Miller, T. L., & Sabatino, D. A. (1978). An evaluation of the teacher consultant model as an approach to mainstreaming. *Exceptional Children, 45,* 86–91.

Ortiz, A. A. (1990). Using school-based problem-solving teams for prereferral intervention. *Bilingual Special Education Newsletter, 10*(1), 3–5.

Ortiz, A. A., & Garcia, S. B. (1995). Serving Hispanic students with learning disabilities: Recommended policies and practices. *Urban Education, 29*(4), 471–481.

Ortiz, A. A., & Wilkinson, C. Y. (1991). Assessment and intervention model for the bilingual exceptional student (AIM for the BEST). *Teacher Education and Special Education, 4*(1), 35–42.

Ortiz, S., & Jones, A. (1982). Using bilingual instructional materials for language minority students in special education. Proceedings of the Conference on Special Education and the Bilingual Child (pp. 83–87). San Diego, CA: National Origin Desegregation Lau Center, San Diego State University.

Powell, T. H. (1982). Mainstreaming: A case for the consulting teacher. *Journal for Special Educators, 17,* 183–188.

Raffaniello, E. M. (1981). Competent consultation: The collaborative approach. In M. J. Curtis, & J. E. Zins (Eds.), *The theory and practice of school consultation* (pp. 44–54). Springfield, IL: Carles C. Thomas.

Reeve, P. T., & Hallahan, D. P. (1994). Practical questions about collaboration between general and special educators. *Focus on Exceptional Children, 27*(7), 1–11.

Roberts, G. W., Bell, L. A., & Salend, S. J. (1991). Negotiating change for multicultural education: A consultation model. *Journal of Educational and Psychological Consultation, 2*(4), 323–342.

Robinson, V. M., Cameron, M. M., & Raethel, A. M. (1985). Negotiation of a consultative role for school psychologists: A case study. *Journal of School Psychology, 23,* 43–49.

Rosenfield, S. (1987). *Instructional consultation.* Hillsdale, NJ: Lawrence Erlbaum.

Spodek, B. (1982). What special educators need to know about regular classrooms. *Educational Forum, 46,* 295–307.

Tharp, R. (1975). The triadic model of consultation. In C. Parker (Ed.), *Psychological consultation in the schools: Helping teachers meet special needs* (pp. 133–151). Reston, VA: Council for Exceptional Children.

Tharp. R. G., & Wetzel, R. J. (1969). *Behavior modification in the natural environment.* New York: Academic Press.

Tharp, R. G., & Yamauchi, L. A. (1994). *Effective instructional conversation in Native American classrooms* (Educational Practice Report No. 10). Santa Cruz, CA, and Washington, DC: National Center for Research on Cultural Diversity and Second Language Learning.

Velez, C. G. (1980). Mexican/Hispano support systems and confianza: Theoretical issues of cultural adaptation. In R. Valle & W. Vega (Eds.), *Hispanic Natural Support Systems: Mental Health Promotion Strategies* (p 46). Sacramento: State of California.

Villa, R. (1989). Model public school inservice programs: Do they exist? *Teacher Education and Special Education, 12*(4), 173–176.

West, J. G., & Cannon, G. S. (1988). Essential collaborative consultation competencies for regular and special educators. *Journal of Learning Disabilities, 21*(1), 56–63.

West, J. G., Idol, L., & Cannon, G. (1989). *Collaboration in the schools: An inservice and preservice curriculum for teachers, support staff, and administrators.* Austin, TX: Pro-Ed.

CHAPTER 14

Family Involvement in Bilingual Special Education: Challenging the Norm

J. S. de Valenzuela
R. L. Torres
Rudolfo L. Chavez

- Rationale
- Difficulties in Implementing Parental Involvement Programs
- Considerations for Implementing Parent-Community-Schools Partnerships
- Proposing a Model for Parental and Community Involvement
- Summary

OBJECTIVES

To provide a rationale for increasing and improving family involvement in bilingual special education

To discuss some of the barriers to effective parental involvement

To provide suggestions for reducing these barriers

To describe the type of changes required for increasing family involvement

To present a critical ecological model for family involvement

To discuss several model programs that involved increasing the participation of culturally and linguistically diverse families

The purpose of this chapter is to propose a critical-ecological model for parent and community involvement in bilingual special education. This model is based on the central assumption that active parent and community participation in the education of culturally and linguistically diverse (CLD) students is necessary for a responsive and effective educational system. Increasing student diversity and continuing problems of inappropriate placement of CLD students in special education programs highlight the need to reconsider and challenge the typical exclusion of parents and community members from active involvement and decision making in the general and special education processes. Attendance at yearly parent-teacher conferences and contributions to bake sales will not effect the necessary changes in current practices that can be so detrimental to CLD students.

A successful family involvement program must rest on the establishment of constructive partnerships between schools and families. Partnerships for reform should incorporate an understanding of a community's prevailing attitudes about schooling, cultural influences, socioeconomic environments, and levels of parent education. These variables condition the effectiveness of family involvement programs in education and are the focus of our family/school partnership model. Bilingual educators need to articulate their multiple experiences in education and eagerly embrace the challenge of sharing both the success and failures of our various family involvement efforts. Our own enthusiasm is generated from our constant contacts with parents, students, and school staff. They have expressed a tenacious commitment to building effective partnerships.

RATIONALE

The rationale for promoting increased participation of family and community members in the education of CLD students is threefold: (1) legal requirements for parental involvement in special education procedures, (2) changing demographics that indicate a growing difference between the cultural and linguistic backgrounds of school personnel and the student body and a continuing pattern of disproportionate representation of CLD students in special programs, and (3) demonstrated improvement in academic achievement with increased parental involvement.

Legislation

Parental involvement in special education was mandated with the passage of PL 94-142 (the Education for All Handicapped Children Act) in 1975. Prior to the passage of this bill, "school districts could make placement decisions concerning the child without regard for the parents' wishes" (Osborne, 1995, p. 22). Under PL 94-142 and its later amendments, the following parental rights have been provided for:

- Examination of all records relevant to special education procedures.

- Informed consent prior to evaluation or placement in special education.

- Permission to obtain an independent evaluation if the parents disagree with the school's evaluation.

- Written notification in the language of the home when changes in the student's current placement are initiated.

- Participation in all meetings pertaining to evaluation or placement.

- Procedures for dispute of recommendations or decisions made by the school regarding a student's educational program. (DeMers, Fiorello, & Langer, 1992; Osborne, 1995)

In 1986, the amendment to the Education for All Handicapped Children's Act, PL 99-457, extended the right to a "free and appropriate education" from the previously stipulated age five and above, down to age three. Additionally, a voluntary early intervention grant program targeted at children with special needs from birth to age two was provided for in this legislation. This component contains an important provision—the development of an Individualized Family Service Plan, which expands the role of the family in planning and implementing the child's educational program (DeMers et al., 1992).

Parental involvement has also been provided for in Title I of the Elementary and Secondary Education Act and its later amendments. Title I (also called Chapter 1 from 1981-1994) was developed to provide additional educational assistance for economically disadvantaged and low-achieving students. The 1994 amendment, entitled Improving America's Schools Act, reaffirms parental rights for involvement in planning their children's education. Specifically, under the 1994 amendments, "each local educational agency must have a parental involvement policy, *jointly developed with*, *approved by*, and distributed to parents (Rogers, 1995, p. 22) [emphasis in original].

However, the presence of a legal mandate for parental participation is not without problems. Harry (1992) poses the following concern:

> The definition of parents' roles under PL 94-142 places parents essentially in the role of respondents; that is, the law requires that parents grant permission for the various steps of a process that is conducted under the authority of experts in disability and that parents participate in individualized planning for the child. . . . The language of the law itself makes it clear that its services are conceived within a medical model that casts students in the role of patients, and parents in the role of consumers of services delivered by experts who determine the truth about their children's learning potential and performance. (p. 99)

This legal mandate should be taken seriously. Parents have the right and the responsibility to be involved in the education of their children. However, as Harry has pointed out, we must question the role of the parents in that partici-

pation—will they be passive recipients of information provided by school personnel or will they be active and equal partners in determining the course of their children's schooling?

Demographics

Demographics indicate that CLD students are more likely to live in poverty, repeat a grade, drop out of school, and obtain lower literacy levels (National Center for Educational Statistics, 1994a; National Center for Educational Statistics, 1994b). Additionally, sources indicate that student diversity is increasing at a significant rate (Waggoner, 1995). This increase is occurring at the same time that educator diversity is remaining fairly stagnant. This discrepancy between teacher and student backgrounds argues quite forcibly for parent and community input in designing and implementing programs. Chapter 1 presents a more detailed discussion of changing population demographics.

Student ethnicity also plays a role in placement in special programs. CLD students, aside from Asian students, are significantly underrepresented in classes for gifted and talented (GATE). These students are also overrepresented in certain special education programs. This pattern of disproportionate representation has been repeatedly documented since Dunn's 1968 landmark study that reported the high number of African-American students placed in classes for the "mildly mentally retarded." Although on a national level, representation may not appear disproportionate for all ethnic groups in all categories, significant variation occurs at both the state and district level (Harry, 1994; Robertson et al., 1994). Additionally, lack of adequate reporting on the basis of race/ethnicity and language dominance and proficiency can disguise disproportionate representation trends (Robertson). Nonetheless, available national data does suffice to indicate that students are not placed in special programs in numbers proportionate to their representation in the student population as a whole, based on ethnicity, language status, and gender. Table 14–1 summarizes the data presented in the Department of Education, Office for Civil Rights 1992 Elementary and Secondary School Civil Rights Compliance Report (Office for Civil Rights, 1994), which demonstrates this continuing trend of disproportionate representation.

Increased Academic Achievement

Research has indicated that parental involvement is correlated with increased academic performance, especially in schools with a high percentage of CLD students (Henderson, Marburger, & Ooms, 1986). This positive effect of parental support has been measured using a va-

Table 14–1
Summary of OCR Compliance Report: Reported and Projected

Ethnicity/ Gender	% of Total Population	% in GATE	% in Mild MR*	% in Mod MR*	% in SED**	% in LD***
			Enrollment Data			
Am Ind M	.54	—	.67	.8	1	.9
Am Ind F	.51	—	.53	.6	.3	.4
Am Ind⁺	1	.6	1.2	1.3	1.3	1.3
Asian M	1.8	—	.5	.9	.5	.8
Asian F	1.7	—	.4	.7	.2	.3
Asian⁺	3.4	6.4	.9	1.6	.7	1.1
Hisp M	6.1	—	3.2	5.4	5.6	7.9
Hisp F	5.7	—	2.3	4.1	1.4	3.8
Hisp⁺	11.8	6.5	5.4	9.5	7	11.1
Afr-Am M	8.3	—	19.2	17.3	18.9	12.4
Afr-Am F	8	—	12.5	11.8	4.8	5.4
Afr-Am⁺	16.3	9	31.7	29	23.7	17.8
White M	34.8	—	35.3	34	53.8	47.5
White F	32.7	—	25.5	24.4	13.4	20.4
White⁺	67	77	60.8	58.4	67.3	68
Minority	32.5	22.6	39.2	41.4	32.6	32
LEP	5	1	1.8	3.5	1.2	3.2
Total M	51.4	48.5	58.8	58.4	79.9	69.6
Total Fem	48.6	51.3	41.2	41.6	20.1	30.4

*Mental Retardation
**Serious Emotional Disturbance
***Specific Learning Disability
⁺Combined Genders
Note. Summarized from data compiled in *1992 Elementary and Secondary School Civil Rights Compliance Report: Reported and Projected Enrollment Data for the Nation,* by the Office for Civil Rights, 1994, Washington, DC: U.S. Department of Education.

riety of research techniques and appears to be more important for student achievement than other factors, such as family structure and size, socioeconomic status (SES), ethnicity, parental education, or age of the student (Hidalgo, Siu, Bright, Swap, & Epstein, 1995). This relationship has even been found with children as young as kindergarten age (Klimes-Dougan, Lopez, Nelson, & Adelman, 1992). These robust results strongly suggest that increasing parental involvement should be of primary concern for educators.

Given this information, within the current climate of educational reform, it is important that goals, mandates, standards, assessments, and the multiple list of "educational policy agendas" incorporate the very catalysts of educational attainment: parents and families involved in schools. Initiatives that are not rooted in a recognition of the roles of families and parents in schooling are doomed to be short-lived. Especially with regard to policies regarding the establishment of educational standards, families, and especially parents, are the key to promoting educational equity and educational standards. Since cooperation provides so many benefits for students, families, and teachers, we need to question why more schools are not involved in constructive partnerships (Bransford & Chavez, 1988).

DIFFICULTIES IN IMPLEMENTING PARENTAL INVOLVEMENT PROGRAMS

Although the literature resounds with calls for increased parental and community involvement, there is also significant recognition that implementing and maintaining programs is problematic. America's changing families make traditional methods of recruiting participation difficult for teachers and schools; parents frequently work outside of the home, transportation and child care may be difficult to obtain, and other social concerns may interfere. However, it is naive to believe that parental involvement is restricted only by barriers imposed by

the family's social and physical realities. Schools themselves may impose significant barriers to participation. These barriers can be programmatic and philosophical. Even when we, as educators, call for "increased parental participation," our willingness to allow parents to actively participate in the education of their children is in doubt. We must challenge our own beliefs and procedures that effectively relegate parents to a passive role, by asking ourselves questions such as the following:

- Do I think that parents really know as much about their children's abilities and level of development as I do?
- How much credence do I really give to parents' reports and suggestions?
- Do I think that parents can teach their children with disabilities as well as I can?
- How willing am I to learn from the parents of my students about their unique backgrounds?
- When was the last time that I visited the homes and/or community of my students?
- Do I respect and implement the opinions and suggestions of my CLD and low-SES families as much as those of middle-class White families?
- How often do I make sure that interpreters are available at team conferences for families that are not fluent in English?

Deficit Mentality

Programs aimed at lower SES and CLD students have historically been based on a deficit model of family abilities and functioning. These students have often been characterized as coming from a "deprived" or "disadvantaged" background. Cultural deprivation theories, dominant in the 1950s, explained low school achievement by CLD children based on factors such as parents' failure to stress the educational attainment of their children or inadequate English language skills. Thus, school has the purpose of changing the child's culture and helping them overcome their ethnic handicaps by assimilating them as quickly as possible into the mainstream American culture (Crawford, 1995).

Although differences in child rearing practices, maternal teaching, language use, and social structures have been well documented (see, for example, Heath, 1982, 1983; Philips, 1972; Schieffelin & Ochs, 1986), what is not so clear is whether any one type of family structure or interaction pattern is inherently better than another (Moreno, 1991). However, what is clear is that some types of culturally-based knowledge and behaviors are more like the mainstream patterns found in schools and are therefore automatically valued and respected by educators. In many comparative studies, there is the implicit notion that typical "mainstream American values and behaviors represent the standard against which 'good' parenting should be measured" and "that lower status parents are failing their children linguistically and cognitively by not providing an enriching environment for learning" (Pérez, 1991, p. 802). Moreno suggests that:

> Lower levels of performance by children of "low-status" groups (i.e., blacks, Hispanics, and other low socioeconomic status groups) on school achievement, IQ test, and other related measures have led researchers to conclude that the families of these groups, specifically mothers, are ineffective teachers, and that these families do not provide their children with sufficient cognitive stimulation necessary for cognitive development in comparison to Anglo and middle-class families. (p. 395)

Moreno goes on to question whether we have sufficient evidence to judge one maternal teaching style as better than others and to suggest that the literature is "biased in favor of behaviors and values consistent with highly educated, middle-class researchers" (p. 397). The persistent portrayal of CLD families as deficient in the knowledge, skills, and abilities necessary to prepare their children for school presents a huge barrier to active parental participation. How can we expect schools to welcome and encourage parental input when many are viewed as incapable of rearing their children? This deficit mentality can be seen even in the National Educational Goals, which start with the objective that "all children in America will start school ready to learn." Perhaps we need to reassess our belief that some children are not ready to learn and examine who and what it is that we are ready to teach.

Continuing Myths About Minority Parents

Another barrier to parental involvement is the presence of continuing myths about the lack of concern that minority parents have toward their children's education. It is very easy to excuse failed efforts to increase CLD parent participation by saying "these parents don't really care about their children's education anyway." Just as some may believe that certain parents are not capable, it is also sometimes believed that they do not care. Research on parental attitudes resoundingly demonstrates this to be untrue (Chavkin, 1989; Holloway, Rambaud, Fuller, & Eggers-Piérola, 1995). In fact, the National Education Longitudinal Study revealed very similar patterns for CLD and mainstream parents' involvement with their eighth grade children (reported in National Center for Educational Statistics, 1994a; National Center for Educational Statistics, 1995). These results are summarized in Table 14-2.

Even though research clearly demonstrates that CLD parents are concerned and do participate in the education of their children, these beliefs persist. The persistence of these beliefs may at least partially be attributed to differences in the types of participation in which different groups of parents typically engage. The results of the National Education Longitudinal Study that are summarized above indicate that most parents do engage in behaviors at home to promote student achievement. Additionally,

Table 14–2
Percentage of Eighth-Graders Reporting Parental Involvement—1988

Type of Involvement	Hispanic	African-American	White
Talked about:			
selecting classes	82	80	87
school activities	86	91	92
class studies	84	88	89
Checked homework	90	93	90
Limited TV viewing	67	60	63
Limited going out with friends	89	86	89
Spoke with teacher or counselor	57	68	59
Visited classes	34	36	26

Note. From *The Condition of Education,* by National Center for Educational Statistics, 1994, Washington, DC: Office of Educational Research and Improvement, U.S. Department of Education; and from *The Educational Progress of Hispanic Students,* by National Center for Educational Statistics, 1995, Washington, DC: U.S. Department of Education, Office of Educational Research and Improvement.

similar percentages of parents from different ethnic backgrounds spoke with teachers and counselors and visited their children's schools. However, the types of activities engaged in during school visits and content of the conversations may vary among ethnic and SES groups. Useem (1992, p. 264) found that "well-educated U.S. parents are much more likely than are less-educated U.S. parents to intervene in a lengthy series of small but crucial ways to improve their children's educational opportunities" and that "the impact of social class on achievement is largely mediated by such parental involvement."

Wealthier and more educated parents are able to use what has been termed "cultural capital" (Bennett & LeCompte, 1990) to influence placement and instructional decisions. Some of the resources that these parents can draw upon are financial resources, practical knowledge about schooling, interpersonal/linguistic skills, and informal social networks (Useem, 1992).

These resources can make it easier to find a babysitter, so that parents can attend meetings, ensure adequate transportation, reduce linguistic and cultural barriers to effective communication, and facilitate sharing of information between more and less knowledgeable parents, all of which have been recognized as barriers to active parental involvement (Brantlinger, 1987; Stein, 1983). However, by recognizing how unequal family resources can influence parental involvement and, therefore, student placement and achievement opportunities, schools can take concrete steps to provide more equitable participation.

Barriers to Parental Involvement in Special Education

In addition to recognizing that CLD families have different opportunities for access, schools need to be aware of the unique barriers to parental participation that exist with the special education system. Even though parent involvement in the assessment and placement processes is mandated by law, in actuality very little may occur. Smith (1990) reviewed the available research studies on implementation of Individualized Educational Plans (IEPs), which are the cornerstone of special education legislation and due process procedures. He found these studies indicated "little interaction by parents when they attended the IEP meeting, with parents being perceived by school professionals as recipients of information" (p. 9). This review also indicated little influence by general educators during team IEP meetings.

The minimal influence of general educators and parents during team meetings is not hard to understand, considering the history of educational assessment as dominated by the medical model. In the medical model, the assumption of the reality of physiologically-based disabilities, intrinsic to and isolated within the student, that can be diagnosed with standardized tests, prevails. In this model, the educational psychologist, armed with a battery of standardized tests, is the "expert." This perspective can be clearly seen in research articles that consistently discuss differences between parental and "professional" judgments of children's abilities as the result of *overestimation* on the part of parents (Sexton, Thompson, Perez, & Rheams, 1990). Rarely do researchers consider these differences to occur as a result of professional *underestimation* of students' abilities (Crais, 1992).

Mehan (1983) performed an interesting analysis of the language used by participants during special education team meetings. He found that lay reports had the following characteristics (Mehan, 1983, p. 205):

1. They were elicited.
2. They were made available by people who occupy either low status or temporary positions (both in terms of institutional stratification and distribution of technical knowledge).

3. Their claims to truth were based on common sense.
4. Their reports were based on direct, albeit unguided or unstructured, observations.
5. They offered contingent assessments of student performance.
6. They produced a context-bound view of student disability.

In contrast, reports of attending professionals had these characteristics (Mehan, 1983, p. 205):

1. They were presented, not elicited.
2. They were presented by people who occupy high status and permanent positions.
3. Their claims were based on technical knowledge and expertise.
4. They were based on indirect, albeit guided or structured, observations.
5. They offered categorical assessments of student performance.
6. They produced a context-free view of student disability.

Mehan found that although parents and general educators may provide reports that conflict with the information presented by "professionals" (psychologists, nurses, administrators), their versions had little effect on the decisions ultimately made. These "professional reports" gained their status and authority from the type of language used; Mehan claims that *"the authority of the professional report resides in the very mode of presentation"* (p. 207) [emphasis in original].

Suggestions for Overcoming Barriers to Participation. Considering the information presented above regarding the persistent myths held about CLD parents, unequal resources for facilitating active participation, and significant institutional barriers to participation in special education, we need to think about concrete ways that schools can promote equitable parental involvement. Chavez (1994) suggests schools should:

- Consider the parental involvement programs having numerous other possibilities and options beyond a "volunteer" program.
- Conduct a comprehensive parental needs assessment to determine areas upon which to focus true collaboration.
- Eliminate the "us–them" attitude between parents and educators prevalent in many schools.
- Brainstorm and seek consensus as opposed to mandating.
- Make sincere efforts to help parents feel they are truly partners by informing them and communicating with them personally, and communicating in the family's native language, respect the family's background (cultural, socioeconomic, etc.).
- Consider the parents' goals and desires for their child's future.
- Collaborate in areas that parents know best, such as the interests of their children and the amount of structure or freedom suggested.
- Share decisions about the school's budget, staff selection and general operating procedures with families.
- Include families as members of advisory councils which help set priorities, improve the school, and provide for systemic change.
- Schedule regular communications between the school and parent regarding academic year learning objectives, discipline codes, and student progress reports in the family's native language and in a comprehensible manner. (Chavez, 1994, p. 9–10)

As advocates of the rights of CLD students to receive a world class education, we must invest in effective parent involvement. Parent training should empower a community to discern their own needs while promoting the development of community initiative and leadership (Cummins, 1986; Delgado-Gaitan, 1991).

The following principles guide our commitment to family empowerment:

- The family is a child's first teacher.
- Learning is a life-long endeavor, and we believe all families/children can and want to learn.
- Language is a part of learning in our global world and global economy. Bilingualism is an asset, not a liability.
- All families, regardless of their ethnicity or socioeconomic status (SES), want the best for their children, and they can be a positive impact on their children's education.
- Education must be a shared responsibility, involving both the home and school. The education of the whole child requires a partnership between the school, community, and families.

Empowerment of families through their participation and informed advocacy are the only meaningful ways that our educational institutions can celebrate the diversity of our multicultural, multilingual society. The role of bilingual educators is to validate the diversity in our midst, but most importantly, to build bridges for effective communication and open dialogue so that each voice in our community can be heard. Empowerment provides families with opportunities to express their concerns and to share their hopes and dreams for their children's future.

CONSIDERATIONS FOR IMPLEMENTING PARENT-COMMUNITY-SCHOOLS PARTNERSHIPS

Implementing real parent-community-school partnerships will require much more than superficial changes. Additionally, one blanket program model will not be the best fit for all parents, all communities, or all schools. Implementation of parental involvement efforts must take into consideration the comprehensiveness of the changes required, variation in family and community characteristics and needs, and unique cultural and sociolinguistic resources that each family and community can contribute.

Shifting Paradigms

Fundamental and pervasive changes on the part of parents, educators, and school systems that attempt to link change to individual needs and abilities are necessary to increase active parental involvement. Although changes of this magnitude are time consuming and challenging, they may present the best chance for long-term success (Miller, Lynch, & Campbell, 1991). Miller and her colleagues have suggested six paradigm shifts as fundamental to real parent-professional collaboration. These shifts require us to begin viewing parents of students with disabilities as more capable, supportive, and responsible for making important and informed decisions about their children and their children's education. Our role must shift from that of being the decision makers to being facilitators in the families' decision making processes.

Need to Consider and Accommodate Differences in Families

Although we may have the tendency to view all CLD families as a homogeneous group, we must be aware of the dangers of this myopic perspective (Harry et al., 1995). Individual variations in acculturation, social class, educational background, religion, generational status, gender, geographic location, personality, ability, and idiosyncrasies can be as important as cultural membership in shaping beliefs and practices (Harry, et al.). Previous experiences with schools on the part of parents, particularly negative ones, such as hearing from the school only when there is a problem, can also influence the amount and type of parental involvement (Pérez, 1991). Therefore, educators

need to respond in individually relevant ways to families and community members, rather than making assumptions based on ethnicity or socioeconomic background. Pérez cautions us that "if such variability is ignored, faulty interpretations of findings, and rigid and insensitive approaches to resolving home and school discontinuities could result" (p. 805). Clearly, the historical and current patterns of disproportionate representation of CLD students in special programs should alert us to the danger of making generalized assumptions about students based simply on immediately visible characteristics, such as ethnicity, language background, or SES.

Funds of Knowledge/Community as a Resource

The tendency to view CLD families as disadvantaged or deficient in resources can lead us to ignore important strengths and abilities that can be advantageous to students. An important research effort has come out of the University of Arizona. Luis Moll and colleagues (González et al., 1993; Moll, 1990; Moll, 1992; Moll, Amanti, Neff, & Gonzalez, 1992; Moll & Diaz, 1987) have explored the family resources or "funds of knowledge" that Latino households can contribute to bilingual classrooms. Moll (1992) defines *funds of knowledge* as "the essential cultural practices and bodies of knowledge and information that households use to survive, to get ahead, or to thrive" (p. 21). In this household funds of knowledge project, teachers established relationships with families and identified their unique knowledge and skills through home visits. This information was then used to develop instructional activities, such as thematic units or culturally relevant instructional strategies. Through this collaboration with students' families, the teachers involved in this project have come to see these families and their social networks as a tremendous resource with an impressive wealth of information. Some of the specialized knowledge areas that have been identified are agriculture and mining (such as ranching, farming, animal husbandry, equipment operation, and maintenance); economics (such as accounting, sales, appraisal, labor laws, and building codes); household management (such as budgets, child care, cooking, and appliance repair); material and scientific knowledge (such as carpentry, masonry, design and architecture, and airplane and automotive repair); contemporary and folk medicine; and religion. Clearly the families identified in the research of Moll and his colleagues were both typical of CLD families across the United States and very capable of providing schools with a wealth of information and assistance.

In addition to specialized knowledge such as that described above, researchers are also beginning to recognize other ways in which CLD communities are "rich" in household funds of knowledge. Although low SES, CLD, and immigrant families have typically been considered to provide few early literacy experiences for their children, this may not be an accurate representation (Morrow & Paratore, 1993). According to these authors, there is a "growing body of evidence that many low-income, minority, and immigrant families cultivate rich (though perhaps not school-like) contexts for literacy development and that they, indeed, support family literacy with exceptional effort and imagination" (p. 195). Farr and Guerra (1995) conducted a long-term study of the different types of literacy practices that Mexican immigrant families engaged in during the course of their daily lives. Their research indicated that, although many of the participants have relatively limited literacy skills due to a lack of access to formal education, they nonetheless participated in a wide range of literacy activities in both English and Spanish. However, these practices were found to be embedded in specific contexts. The researchers illustrated the contextualized nature of literacy by describing the types of literate activities that the participants engaged in during interactions with the Immigration and Naturalization Service (INS) and during participation in religious activities. By observing the type and amount of manipulation of written texts necessary to maneuver through the complex bureaucracy of INS, these researchers concluded that "although many members of this social network have relatively limited literacy skills as a consequence of their limited access to quality systems of formal education in both Mexico and the United States, they clearly possess a variety of literacy skills that, to a greater extent than most people are aware, serve their specific literacy needs" (p. 17). The challenge, therefore, for educators is to identify ways in which to make their instruction compatible with the knowledge and skills that students bring with them to school and the funds of knowledge that families and communities possess.

PROPOSING A MODEL FOR PARENTAL AND COMMUNITY INVOLVEMENT

Given the well-documented barriers to active parental involvement and needed shifts in perceptions of CLD families and communities as outlined above, it should be clear that a new model for forming parent-community-school partnerships is needed. The model proposed in this chapter draws upon and integrates two concepts identified in the literature: (1) an ecological model for locating students and families within the wider context of the community, social, and institutional networks (Bronfenbrenner, 1979; Vazquez Nuttall, 1992; Heath & McLaughlin, 1987); and (2) a critical theoretical approach to family empowerment that recognizes differentials in *power, authority,* and *control* (Fine, 1993). Others have already drawn upon these combined frameworks for developing parent-community-school partnership programs as a means of effecting real parental participation and systemic changes in how schools function in relation to CLD students and families (see, for example, Delgado-Gaitan, 1991). Within bilingual special education, the parent training program "Fiesta Educativa" (Rueda & Martinez, 1992) also relies on a critical-ecological framework, although the critical theoretical component is not as explicitly discussed in their conceptual framework as in Delgado-Gaitan's program description. Both of these two model programs will be discussed in greater length in the following sections.

Locating Families and Schools within the Community Context

Bronfenbrenner's ecological systems model (Bronfenbrenner, 1979) has been extremely influential in special education. Alternative assessment paradigms, such as ecological and descriptive assessment, have built upon his concept of mutually influencing "nested" contexts. See Chapter 7 for a more in-depth discussion of ecological assessment. Crais (1992, p. 34) describes the ecological model in the following manner: "This perspective takes into account the mutual influencing factors that surround individuals and families and recognizes that changes in one part of the system affect the entire system." Ecological perspectives place the child at the center of ever-widening concentric circles. For example, in the most basic ecological design, the child occupies the center circle, surrounded by the larger circle of his or her family, and the even larger circle of the school and greater social environment.

This model places the child within the context of her/his unique characteristics, such as language, social-emotional, and cognitive abilities, and the larger contexts of the family, extended family, friends, agencies, and values and culture. Heath and McLaughlin (1987) describe the importance of this ecological model to reframing conventional parent-schools relationships:

The problems of educational achievement and academic success demand resources beyond the scope of the schools and of most families. We believe that promising responses can be crafted by moving from a focus on components of the problem—teachers, texts, families—to a focus on the functional requirements of a healthy, curious, productive, and motivated child. This change in perspective draws attention to the child as an actor in a larger social system and to the institutional networks and resources present in that larger environment. It requires us to look beyond family and school to get a full view of the primary networks that make up a child's environment. We can then think of the school in a new way, as a nexus of institutions within this environment. (p. 579)

This ecological perspective has led Edwards and Young (1992) to make the following recommendations for implementing comprehensive parent-involvement programs: (1) the strengths of families and their perceptions of their children should provide the foundation for home/school strategies, (2) prevention should be the focus of efforts, with an understanding of students' and parents' individual needs, (3) multiple models should be available for family and community involvement, (4) the daily routine of the schools should draw upon community resources to respond quickly to students' immediate needs, and (5) these issues should be presented to preservice teachers during their educational training.

Edwards (1992) drew upon resources in the larger community when designing and implementing a Parents as Partners in Reading project in a low-income African-American community in Louisiana. Community leaders who knew the parents participating in the program assisted in a variety of ways, including recruiting and encouraging participants, providing transportation, coordinating social services, such as babysitting, and organizing a telephone campaign. Edwards states that "the program created a supportive atmosphere and communicated that literacy was important and valued in the community where the parents lived. This made a huge difference in the parents' perceptions of themselves and their ability to help their children" (p. 353). The success of this project is an example of how an ecological model can facilitate greater family and community participation.

Even when recognizing the important role of the community and valuable resources that families can contribute to the education of their children, we must not forget the important role of the school in encouraging, fostering, and maintaining this support. Carter (1994) suggests that strong commitment from the school leadership is crucial in establishing a family-focused approach to education. She recognizes that "parents are rarely in a position to come knocking on the doors of schools and agencies demanding a response, unless they are organized because of concern over a single issue that does not always translate into a different overall approach" (p. 5). Without consistent and ongoing leadership from school personnel, especially administrators and bilingual personnel, family involvement projects are doomed to failure.

A Critical Perspective on Parental Involvement

Critical theory is a way of viewing the world and social interactions that recognizes inequalities in power, privilege, voice and access. According to Bennett and LeCompte (1990):

> Central to critical theory is the notion of power. It is critical of the current structure of society, in which dominant socioeconomic groups exploit and oppress subordinate groups of people. Critical social theory assumes that schools are sites where power struggles between dominant and subordinate groups take place. (p. 26)

These authors go on to contend that it is through the "governmentally imposed system of regulations which prescribe specific curricular and pedagogical models, that dominant, white, male, and middle or upper-class cultural standards are imposed on children" (p. 27). Cummins (1986) also explains how inequalities in power and voice impact parental participation in schools. He states that:

> Although lip service is paid to community involvement through Parent Advisory Committees (PAC) in many educational programs, these committees are frequently manipulated through misinformation and intimidation (Curtis, 1984). The result is that parents from dominated groups retain their powerless status, and their internalized inferiority is reinforced. Children's school failure can then be attributed to the combined effects of parental illiteracy and lack of interest in their children's education. (p. 26)

Delgado-Gaitan (1991) describes a similar situation during a parent organization meeting, in which the parents' goals and objectives were at odds with the administrator's goals for this group. Although the parents' intent was mutual empowerment and building supportive social networks, the principal saw a primary goal for this group as fundraising for the purchase of instructional materials. However, due to the mutually supportive and empowering process that parents had been engaged in through the creation of their organization and their personal ownership during the process, the parents were able to successfully resist the principal's attempt to reconstruct the purpose and goals of their group.

Scenarios such as these have spurred Fine (1993) to assert that issues of power, authority, and control must be directly addressed if we are to avoid the systematic undermining of educational reform. She contends that:

> Without relentless attention to power and critique, parent involvement projects will surface the individual needs of families, which will be-

come the vehicle to express, and dilute, struggles of power. If unacknowledged, power may hide, cloaked in the "needs" or "inadequacies" of disenfranchised mothers, and yet schools will persist in practices that damage. (p. 6)

Harry (1992) takes a similar position, arguing that:

at the heart of parent-professional relationships lie considerations of power and authority. While parental influence may be mediated by social class, parental knowledge and skills, or group influence, there continue to be certain essential differences between the interests of parents and teachers that makes this relationship very complex. (p. 95)

She suggests that the legal mandate for parental involvement is partially responsible for this polemic, suggesting that "the very fact that the impetus for collaboration derives from legal mandate sets the stage for a legalistic framing of parent-school discourse, which is not only likely to describe the relationship in adversarial terms but also means that those already in power will be the ones to define the dimensions, structures, and avenues by which the mandate is implemented" (p. 96). This is not to imply that legal mandates should be revoked. On the contrary, as Harry goes on to explain, the legal support for parental involvement is both essential and powerful. Nonetheless, mandates alone are insufficient to rectify inequalities in power and authority; without a conscious, critical examination of the ways in which schools either foster or inhibit active parental participation, real changes are unlikely to occur.

Family-Community Empowerment

The understanding of how social institutions allow differential access to individuals and groups, based on exiting social stratification, has led to calls for the "empowerment" of CLD students and their families. According to Ben-

nett and LeCompte (1990, p. 176) "empowerment refers to the ability to become conscious of oppression and learn to implement strategies to overcome it." Neuman, Hagedorn, Celano, and Daly (1995, p. 803) add another dimension to this idea of parental empowerment when they argue that "a critical part of the empowerment process, therefore, may be to learn from the parents themselves: their beliefs, values, and practices within their homes and communities." This expanded idea of "empowerment" as an interactive process with mutual negotiation between schools, educators, families, and the community is consistent with the previously discussed ecological model and resonates with calls for the recognition and inclusion of household "funds of knowledge" in the curriculum.

Model Programs: Fiesta Educativa/Parental Mentorship Program Model

Delgado-Gaitan (1991) and Delgado-Gaitan and Ruiz (1992) describe a model parent partnership program that has been implemented in the Carpinteria School District in California. This Parental Mentorship Program Model emphasizes the relationship between parents and their children, acknowledges parents as students' primary teachers of what they term the "home curriculum," and recognizes and challenges the inequalities of power between parents and schools. This is a good example of a critical-ecological model, that views students and families within multiple interactive contexts and recognizes how differences in access to resources, power, authority, control, and voice influence the interactions between contexts. As parents in this study became more empowered through their interactions with other parents via social networks, they were able to change their relationships with the school.

This idea of parents helping other parents to obtain information, formulate strategies for intervening in the school, and develop supportive networks is not unique to this program. The parent special education training program, Fiesta Educativa, also relies on parent advocates to help "scaffold" the participation and knowledge acquisition of other parents. This program originally grew out of a family outreach program that was developed by the East Los Angeles Regional Center for the Developmentally Disabled. Fiesta Educativa has developed into a yearly conference for Latino parents and families of individuals with developmental disabilities (Rueda & Martinez, 1992). According to these authors, important features of this conference that reduce barriers to participation include the following:

1. A family orientation, including provisions for child care and encouragement of attendance by both parents and members of the immediate and extended family.

2. Financial support for registration, housing, transportation, and other related expenses.

3. Parent collaboration in planning and organizing activities, emphasizing and encouraging a sense of "ownership" on the part of parents.

4. Broad-based community sponsorship by a consortium of educational, mental health, and other service agencies.

5. Emphasis on practical information from multiple service agencies with direct application to everyday needs in everyday settings, but with attention to the diversity in levels of sophistication among families.

6. Identification and incorporation of existing formal and informal community networks.

7. A bilingual and bicultural focus.

8. Ready assistance for participants who need help with printed materials (e.g., registration, evaluation forms).

9. Fostering leaderships roles for parents. (p. 99–100)

Although this has been a successful and ongoing event since its inception in 1978, Rueda and Martinez caution about direct transfer of this program to other settings. One of the most powerful aspects of this program has been its ability to respond to the particular needs of the community in which it was developed. Returning to our concept of an ecological context for individuals, families, schools, and programs, we can see that the unique diversity of each situation must be understood and integrated into program development. Additionally, given that these nested contexts will have mutually interactive and continually changing influences on each other, program models must allow for flexibility and change over time.

Integrating the Ecological and Critical Models for Effective Family Involvement

Both of the above described models, ecological and critical, have important implications for involving CLD families in our schools. We propose that it is through the merger of these two frameworks that the most positive and effective programs will be developed. Delgado-Gaitan and Ruiz' Parental Mentorship Program Model is an excellent example of how this interface can work by recognizing the social barriers that work to distance parents from schools (critical) and designing interventions that locate the student and family within multiple and mutually interactive social contexts (ecological). Figure 14–1 illustrates the interactive contexts that must be considered when implementing family involvement efforts.

As can be seen in the schematic, intervention efforts must take into consideration and account for the barriers to parental involvement that are imposed by the larger social context and the school environment. However, educators can also capitalize on support for family involvement that comes from these contexts. For example, legal mandates and changing demographics that make diversity a more usual part of our daily lives may facilitate involve-

Figure 14–1
A Critical-Ecological Model for Family Involvement in Bilingual Special Education

ment. Similarly, not all educators hold negative beliefs about CLD students and their families. Many educators are uncomfortable with existing practices and the accepted roles of participants in the special education process. Chapter 4 discusses some of the changes that have occurred in our schools, such as collaborative consultation, inclusion, and prereferral intervention. Within this model, the family's resources are seen as a strength to be cultivated and incorporated into the school's curriculum, such as has been done in the University of Arizona "household funds of knowledge" project. The student as well is integral to this critical-ecological model. Family participation will depend greatly upon each student's unique amalgamation of personality, knowledge, abilities, disabilities, and likes and dislikes. This model considers the whole child, with his/her surrounding contexts, as a means of developing a uniquely supportive and nurturing family involvement program.

☺ SUMMARY

The purpose of this chapter was to document the need for active parental involvement in the education of CLD students, identify existing barriers to participation and resources that families and communities can contribute to schools, and to propose a framework for conceptualizing and constructing family-community-school partnerships. As most readers will agree, change is difficult, time-consuming, and complex. Nonetheless, it behooves each and every one of us, teachers, parents, administrators, specialists, and members of outside agencies and communities, to deeply consider the ramifications of failure to implement systemic reform.

We as a nation cannot afford to continue to churn out grade after grade of disenfranchised and disempowered youth. We cannot afford to continue supporting the status quo of an educational system that diagnoses African-American boys as mildly and moderately mentally retarded and severely emotionally disturbed at more than twice the rate than their representation in the school-aged population would predict. Change will require a willingness to critically examine the ways in which the educational system in place in each of our neighborhood schools systematically excludes CLD and low-SES families from actively contributing to the educational process. This exclusion is most detrimental and painful when we consider the long-term consequences of potentially inappropriate diagnoses of disabilities. Beth Harry makes the following statement about the complex responsibilities of the educational system in bringing about these changes:

> Styles of child rearing, like styles of participation, will continue to vary with the extent of tradition versus acculturation in families. It is the job of professionals to respect these differences while introducing culturally different families to the expectations of the special education system and the rights accorded parents within that system. It is a question of balance: just as it is unacceptable for us to assume the superiority of mainstream American approaches, so is it unacceptable for us to evade our responsibility to parents by allowing them to remain unaware of their rights and authority within the system. People cannot choose unless they are aware of the choices that exist (Harry, 1992, p. 92–93).

☺ DISCUSSION QUESTIONS

1. What does it mean for families to be defined as partners in education as opposed to merely passive consumers of the advice of the legal, medical, and educational communities?

2. What do teachers need to know about family involvement and how can they be better prepared to help CLD students succeed in schools?

3. Contrast the views of cultural deprivation theories, which explain, respectively, school failure based on parental failure to stress the education of their students, and the position of the authors, who propose that parental involvement is a contributing factor of the educational attainment of students, including CLD students.

4. How would you use the funds of knowledge base, located in the communities of origin of your students, in your classrooms and schools to impact the education of your CLD students?

5. What advantages for CLD students and their families do the ecological model and the critical perspective on parental involvement have over other models such as the cultural deficit?

6. What does family empowerment in education mean and how is it different from what you and your schools do?

⊚ REFERENCES

Bennett, K. P., & LeCompte, M. D. (1990). *The way schools work: A sociological analysis of education.* New York: Longman.

Bransford, J., & Chavez, R. L. (1988). Training for minority language parents: Are we providing them what they want or need? In H. Cortez & R. C. Chavez (Eds.), *Ethnolinguistic issues in education* (pp. 79–89). Lubbock, TX: Texas Tech Press.

Brantlinger, E. A. (1987). Making decisions about special education placement: Do low-income parents have the information they need? *Journal of Learning Disabilities, 20*(2), 94–101.

Bronfenbrenner, U. (1979). *The ecology of human development: Experiments by nature and design.* Cambridge, MA: Harvard University Press.

Carter, J. L. (1994). Moving from principles to practice: Implementing a family-focused approach in schools and community services. *Equity and Choice, 10*(3), 4–9.

Chavez, R. (1994). *Promoting family empowerment: Inclusion through collaboration.* Boulder, Colorado: BUENO Center for Multicultural Education.

Chavkin, N. F. (1989). Debunking the myth about minority parents. *Educational Horizons, 67*(4), 119–123.

Crais, E. R. (1992). "Best practices" with preschoolers: Assessing within the context of a family centered approach. *Best practices in School Speech-Language Pathology, 2,* 33–42.

Crawford, J. (1995). *Bilingual education: History, politics, theory and practice* (3rd ed.). Los Angeles: Bilingual Education Services, Inc.

Cummins, J. (1986). Empowering minority students: A framework for intervention. *Harvard Educational Review, 56*(1), 18–36.

Delgado-Gaitan, C. (1991). Involving parents in the schools: A process of empowerment. *American Journal of Education, 100*(1), 20–46.

Delgado-Gaitan, C., & Ruiz, N. (1992). Parent mentorship: Socializing children to school culture. *Educational Foundations, 6*(2), 45–69.

DeMers, S. T., Fiorello, C., & Langer, K. L. (1992). Legal and ethical issues in preschool assessment. In E. V. Nuttall, I. Romero, & J. Kalesnik (Eds.), *Assessing and screening preschoolers: Psychological and educational dimensions* (pp. 43–54). Needham Heights, MA: Allyn and Bacon.

Dunn, L. M. (1968). Special education for the mildly mentally retarded: Is much of it justifiable? *Exceptional Children, 35,* 5–22.

Edwards, P. A. (1992). Involving parents in building reading instruction for African-American children. *Theory into Practice, 31*(4), 350–359.

Edwards, P. A., & Young, L. S. J. (1992). Beyond parents: Family, community, and school involvement. *Phi Delta Kappan, 74*(1), 72–80.

Farr, M., & Guerra, J. C. (1995). Literacy in the community: A study of Mexicano families in Chicago. *Discourse Processes, 19,* 7–19.

Fine, M. (1993). [Ap]parent involvement. *Equity and Choice, 9*(3), 4–8.

Gonzáles, N., Moll, L. C., Floyd-Tenery, M., Rivera, A., Rendón, P., Gonzales, R., & Amanti, C. (1993). *Teacher research on funds of knowledge: Learning from households.* Santa Cruz, CA: National Center for Research on Cultural Diversity and Second Language Learning.

Harry, B. (1992). Cultural diversity, families, and the special education system: Communication and empowerment. New York: Teachers College Press.

Harry, B. (1994). The disproportionate representation of minority students in special education: Theories and recommendations. Alexandria, VA: National Association of State Directors of Special Education.

Harry, B., Grenot-Scheyer, M., Smith-Lewis, M., Park, H. S., Xin, F., & Schwartz, I. (1995). Developing culturally inclusive services for individuals with disabilities. *Journal of the Association for Persons with Severe Handicaps, 20*(2), 99–109.

Heath, S. B. (1982). What no bedtime story means: Narrative skills at home and school. *Language in Society, 11,* 49–76.

Heath, S. B. (1983). *Ways with words: Language, life, and work in communities and classrooms.* Cambridge, England: Cambridge University Press.

Heath, S. B., & McLaughlin, M. W. (1987). A child resource policy: Moving beyond dependence on school and family. *Phi Delta Kappan, 68*(8), 576–580.

Henderson, A. T., Marburger, C. L., & Ooms, T. (1986). *Beyond the bake sale: An educator's guide to working with parents.* Columbia, MD: National Committee for Citizens in Education.

Hidalgo, N. M., Siu, S.-F., Bright, J. A., Swap, S. M., & Epstein, J. L. (1995). Research on families, schools and communities: A multicultural perspective. In J. A. Banks & C. A. M. Banks (Eds.), *Handbook of research on multicultural education* (pp. 498–524). New York: Simon & Schuster MacMillan.

Holloway, S. D., Rambaud, M. F., Fuller, B., & Eggers-Piérola, C. (1995). What is "appropriate practice": At home and in child care? Low-income mothers' views on preparing their children for school. *Early Childhood Research Quarterly, 10,* 451–473.

Klimes-Dougan, B., Lopez, J. A., Nelson, P., & Adelman, H. S. (1992). Two studies of low income parents' involvement in schooling. *The Urban Review, 24*(3), 185–202.

Mehan, H. (1983). The role of language and the language of role in institutional decision making. *Language in Society, 12,* 187–211.

Miller, L. J., Lynch, E., & Campbell, J. (1991). Parents as partners: A new paradigm for collaboration. *Best Practices in School Speech-Language Pathology, 1,* 49–56.

Moll, L. C. (Ed.). (1990). Vygotsky and education: Instructional implications and applications of sociohistorical psychology. Cambridge, MA: Cambridge University Press.

Moll. L. C. (1992). Bilingual classroom studies and community analysis: Some recent trends. *Educational researcher, 21*(2), 20–24.

Moll, L. C., Amanti, C., Neff, D., & Gonzalez, N. (1992). Funds of knowledge for teaching: Using a qualitative approach to connect homes and classrooms. *Theory into Practice, 31*(2), 132–141.

Moll, L. C., & Diaz, S. (1987). Change as a goal of educational research. *Anthropology and Education Quarterly, 18,* 300–311.

Moreno, R. P. (1991). Maternal teaching of preschool children in minority and low-status families: A critical review. *Early Childhood Research Quarterly, 6,* 395–410.

Morrow, L. M., & Paratore, J. (1993). Family literacy: Perspective and practices. *The Reading Teacher, 47*(3), 194–200.

National Center for Educational Statistics. (1994a). *The condition of education.* Washington, DC: Office of Educational Research and Improvement, U.S. Department of Education.

National Center for Educational Statistics. (1994b). *Digest of education statistics.* Washington, DC: Office of Educational Research and Improvement, U.S. Department of Education.

National Center for Educational Statistics. (1995). *The educational progress of Hispanic students.* Washington, DC: U.S. Department of Education, Office of Educational Research and Improvement.

Neuman, S. B., Hagedorn, T., Celano, D., & Daly, P. (1995). Toward a collaborative approach to parent involvement in early education: A study of teenage mothers in an African-American community. *American Educational Research Journal, 32*(4), 801–827.

Office for Civil Rights, U.S. Department of Education (1994). *1992 elementary and secondary school civil rights compliance report: Reported and projected enrollment data for the nation.* Washington, DC: Office for Civil Rights, U.S. Department of Education.

Osborne, A. G. J. (1995). Procedural due process rights for parents under IDEA. *Preventing School Failure, 39*(2), 22–26.

Pérez, S. M. (1991). Parental involvement and low socio-economic status children in New York city:

An assessment of Camp Liberty. *Journal of Hispanic Policy, 5,* 31–57.

Philips, S. U. (1972). Participant structures and communicative competence: Warm Springs children in community and classroom. In C. B. Cazden, V. P. John, & D. Hymes (Eds.), *Functions of language in the classroom* (pp. 370–394). Prospect Heights, IL: Waveland Press.

Robertson, P., Kushner, M. I., Starks, J., & Drescher, C. (1994). An update of participation rates of culturally and linguistically diverse students in special education: The need for a research and policy agenda. *The Bilingual Special Education Perspective, 14*(1), 1,3–9.

Rogers, M. (1995). Planning for Title I programs: Guildelines for parents, advocates and educators. Washington, DC: Center for Law and Education.

Rueda, R., & Martinez, I. (1992). Fiesta Educativa: One community's approach to parent training in developmental disabilities for Latino families. *Journal of the Association for Persons with Severe Handicaps, 17*(2), 95–103.

Schieffelin, B. B., & Ochs, E. (Eds.). (1986). *Language socialization across cultures.* Melbourne, Australia: Cambridge University Press.

Sexton, D., Thompson, B., Perez, J., & Rheams, T. (1990). Maternal versus professional estimates of developmental status for young children with handicaps: An ecological approach. *Topics in Early Childhood Special Education, 10*(3), 80–95.

Smith, S. W. (1990). Individualized educational programs (IEPs) in special education—From intent to acquiescence. *Exceptional Children, 57*(1), 6–14.

Stein, R. C. (1983). Hispanic parents' perspectives and participation in their children's special education program: Comparisons by program and race. *Learning Disability Quarterly, 6,* 432–439.

Useem, E. L. (1992). Middle schools and math groups: Parents' involvement in children's placement. *Sociology of Education, 65,* 263–279.

Vazquez Nuttall, E. (1992). Introduction. In E. V. Nuttall, I. Romero, & J. Kalesnik (Eds.), *Assessing and screening preschoolers: Psychological and educational dimensions* (pp. 1–7). Needham Heights, MA: Allyn and Bacon.

Waggoner, D. (1995). Numbers and needs: Ethnic and linguistic minorities in the United States. Washington, DC: Numbers and Needs.

CHAPTER 15

Issues in Policy Development and Implementation

Joann Starks
James Bransford
Leonard M. Baca

- General Policy Development
- Models for Policy Development
- Critical Issues Affecting Policy Development
- Federal and State Requirements for Serving LEP Children with Disabilities
- Strategies for Influencing Policies
- Suggested Policy Options
- Planning and Implementation
- Future of bilingual special education
- Summary

OBJECTIVES

To understand the need for and importance of policy development

To become familiar with the process as well as various models for policy development

To be aware of the various federal requirements as they relate to serving LEP students with disabilities

To review and critique various policy options for bilingual special education

To compare and contrast program planning and implementation strategies

To discuss the future of bilingual special education

Many books and articles have been written that attempt to determine a common definition of policy. For instance, Dunn (1981, p. 61) defines *policy* as "a long series of more or less related choices, including decisions not to act, made by governing bodies and officials." In their book for the novice public policy analyst, Patton and Sawicki (1986, p. 38) describe policy as "a course of action to be followed by a government body or institution." They note that the term *policy* is often used synonymously with *plan* and *program*. In his 1984 "state-of-the-art" analysis of education policy, Mitchell cites definitions that range from board and simple statements such as "what governments do and say" to complex lists of characteristics requiring several pages of explanation. Guba (1984, p. 65) identifies eight distinct concepts of policy, three which are particularly relevant to this discussion:

- Policy is an assertion of intents or goals
- Policy is sanctioned behavior
- Policy is a norm of conduct characterized by consistency and regularity in some substantive action area

Duke and Canady (1991, p. 2) define *policy* as "an official action for a specified purpose or purposes." Dye (1992, p. 2) states that public policy is "whatever governments choose to do or not to do." Governments do many things. They regulate conflict within society; they organize society to carry on conflict with other societies; they distribute a great variety of symbolic rewards and material services to members of the society; and they extract money from society, most often in the form of taxes. Anderson (1975) defines policy as a "purposeful cause of action followed by an actor or set of actors in dealing with a problem or matter of concern." Public policy is also described as a definitive course of action adopted or pursued by a government (or other similar body) in response to an articulated or perceived public concern (Lewis & Wallace, 1984). Thus, public policies

may regulate behavior, organize bureaucracies, distribute benefits, or extract taxes—or do all these things at once. Public policies are formally developed by public officials such as legislators, judges, administrators, and board members.

Using this last definition as a point of departure, one can see that there exists today an extensive public policy at both the federal and the state level that addresses the education of all children with disabilities (Ramirez & Pages, 1979). This policy is based on laws such as the Individuals with Disabilities Education Act (IDEA), Section 504 of the Rehabilitation Act of 1973 (PL 93-112), and various state statutes. There is also an officially articulated public policy dealing with the education of limited English proficient (LEP) students. This policy comes primarily from the Bilingual Education Act of 1968 as amended (PL 95-561) and related state statutes. Also important in this context is the 1974 US Supreme Court decision of *Lau v Nichols* (1974). The interpretation of these federal and state directives leads to the conclusion that LEP students with disabilities must be afforded the opportunity of receiving bilingual *and* special education services.

Although many of our nation's school districts have been providing effective special education and bilingual education services for several years, only in the past few years have educators begun to address the complexities involved in merging special education services with bilingual methodology for an increasing number of LEP students with disabilities nationwide. A broad set of policies exists at the federal and, to a limited extent, at the state level. However, there is an absence of well-developed written policies for bilingual special education at the local school district level.

Any new program within a tax-supported institution, such as a public school system, can benefit from the establishment of policies related to that program. Bilingual special education programs and services are no exception. Carefully formulated policies can help provide the support, direction, parameters, and guidelines needed to implement a successful bilingual special education program. The formal establishment of educational policy is of utmost importance. If policy is not planned, developed, and adopted in a formal and systematic manner, it will be established through default rather than through intent. For example, if a school district did not adopt a policy regarding girls' athletics, there would, in fact, be a policy of benign neglect, and consequently little if any formal participation of girls in athletics. Likewise, if a school district has no policy for the provision of bilingual services to LEP children with disabilities, there will probably be no bilingual services for those children.

The purpose of this chapter is to underscore the importance of policy formulation for bilingual special education by discussing various issues related to policy development and implementation. Specifically, this chapter discusses the general background for policy development and provides policy development models. This discussion is followed by the presentation of the critical issues affecting policy development. Federal requirements are discussed along with suggested strategies for influencing policy. A number of policy options and some guidelines for program planning and implementation are presented. The chapter ends with a discussion of the possible future directions of bilingual special education.

GENERAL POLICY DEVELOPMENT

Policy is generally recognized as the outcome of decision-making processes set in motion to respond to existing stimuli or challenges (Dunn, 1986); that is, the sum of the processes in which all the parties involved in and related to a social system shape the goals of the system (Thompson, 1976). The process includes all the factors that tie the various parties together and facilitate their adjustments to one another and to the environmental factors affecting them. Included are structural factors relating to the

more permanent, unchanging elements of the community, such as population characteristics, economic base, and established organizations; cultural factors, or the value commitments of the community at large; and situational factors, or short-term special issues that may arise from time to time in a community. In educational policymaking, these environmental factors are impacted by a number of features that may be unique to the American educational system:

- Decentralization of the educational system, with shared responsibility for developing and implementing educational policy among local, state, and federal governmental and related entities

- Regionalism, or differences in politics and public policies among various states and geographic areas

- Diversity, or the many cultural and economic variances among different American communities

Traditional View

The literature refers to two major views relative to policymaking: the traditional view and the systems approach. The traditional view is a strictly legal perspective. Policymaking is viewed as a responsibility, as stated by law, of elected representatives. In the realm of education the most prominent elected body is the school board. The people elect school board members to serve as their representatives and give them the power to make school policy. The board, in turn, hires a superintendent or other administrator and delegates to that official the authority to administer board policy. The superintendent or other official, with this delegated authority, organizes the work and hires and directs teaching and other staff to carry out specific duties. Policymaking is seen as completely separate from administration (Thompson, 1976).

The traditional view does not take into consideration the many variables that are working constantly and simultaneously to shape policy-making. Many groups both within and outside the schools influence policy development. These groups include students; parents; economic groups (taxpayers); business groups; religious groups; parent organizations; teachers; labor organizations; professional associations; community and college groups; regional education associations; and local, regional, and federal governmental bodies.

Systems Approach

The other major view is the systems approach to educational policymaking. This view considers the many variables that influence policymaking. Besides those groups already mentioned, this view looks at economic factors, demographics, resources, state of technology, and costs. It considers social and cultural factors such as social beliefs, religious beliefs, state systems, individual motivation for education, cultural issues, political administration structures, influence and power structures, degree of governmental stability, and political and administrative organization of the schools. The systems approach also considers social-psychological factors, including attitudes, beliefs, and values of teachers, administrators, and other staff; their educational backgrounds and roles; and the various group affiliations and group strengths that may prevail, in addition to individual motivation and intellectual abilities of the total school population, including the students (Thompson, 1976).

Views of Policymaking

Within these two general views rest two competing images of policymaking: the academic image and the image of policymaking as a pragmatic art. The academic image holds that policymaking is a systematic, rational process of finding the best solution to a social or educational problem. Tremendous importance is placed on the power of information and analysis to influence decisions. The pragmatic art view sees decision making occurring in a context of uncertainty, conflicting values and interests, and incomplete information. Negotiation, compromise, and incremental solutions are considered part of the decision-making or policymaking process (Takanishi, 1981).

This latter image, coupled with the systems approach described earlier, seems to reflect the reality of educational politics better than the other system reviewed. It certainly relates more to the adaptive process described by Bebout and Bredemeier (1963). Policymaking, it contends, goes through a process that involves identification, or feeling of oneness, with other individuals or groups; bargaining, or a system of exchanges in which one attempts to get something from someone by convincing that person that it is beneficial to accede to the request; and using legal bureaucratic mechanisms that, as a last resort, in most cases means getting what one desires by narrowing the alternatives so that the competing individual or group has no choice but to comply.

In effect, in educational policymaking as in politics generally, some individual or group of individuals wants something from government or other agencies and builds a coalition of influences to get it. Other people with different preferences join one another to block or modify the designs of the primary group. They strategize and develop certain tactics that are intended to provoke decision makers and those in power to determine the winners and losers by passing laws and issuing executive and judicial orders. This process is said to be continuous. As soon as a decision is made on a specific issue, new discussion begins on other issues (Thompson, 1976).

The decision-making process leading to policymaking is seen as working in a series of social relationships including both formal and informal decision makers. Individuals who may be pursing their particular interests interact with one another in a series of social situations. From these contacts they come to know and understand one another's attitudes, views, and positions on the various issues. Consensus is established as positions are discussed and negotiated and friendships develop. Because much of the activity leading to formal decisions takes place only in the social milieu, little input is received or considered from individuals or groups not included in these events. As a result, policymaking may reflect the interests of groups or individuals whose influence then extends to major segments of political, economic, educational, and social life (Hughes, 1967).

This process of formulating policy or making decisions in informal and social settings is practiced by government representatives at all levels, state education agency officials, other agencies, various associations and groups, institutions of higher education, and the courts. In education each group must influence the other to influence policy. The process through identification, bargaining, negotiation, accommodation, rules and laws, pressure and coercion, appeals to common loyalties, partnerships, shared ideals, history, and friendships—as well as the use of rational argument—leads directly to specific policy development (Dunn, 1986).

MODELS FOR POLICY DEVELOPMENT

Models are fundamental to policymaking and policy analysis. The creation of precise and manageable processes designed to produce information about the consequences of proposed actions are at the very heart of decision making. Although most models cannot predict the consequences of specific actions with the assurance of some of the best scientific models, they do produce information that assists in understanding situations more clearly (Quade, 1982).

A number of models, theories, views, and approaches have been developed to analyze policymaking and decision making. A model is a simplified representation of some aspect of the real world, whether an actual physical representation—a model airplane, for example, or the tabletop buildings that urban planners use to show how things will look when proposed projects are completed—or a diagram—a road map, for example, or a flowchart that political scientists use to show how a bill becomes a law.

These models and theories are critical to the total process of policy formulation and to the meaningful explanation of policy actions (Anderson, 1984). The models used in studying policy are *conceptual models*—word models that attempt to:

- Simplify and clarify thinking about politics and public policy
- Identify important aspects of policy problems
- Facilitate communication by focusing on essential features of political life
- Direct efforts to understand public policy better by suggesting what is important and what is unimportant
- Suggest explanations for public policy and predict its consequences

Selected Policy Models. Over the years, political science, like other scientific disciplines, has developed a number of models to help us understand political life. Throughout this volume we will try to determine whether these models have any utility in the study of public policy. Specifically we want to examine public policy from the perspective of the following models:

- Group theory
- Elite theory
- Rationalism
- Incremental model
- Systems (Easton) model

Each of these terms identifies a major conceptual model that can be found in the literature of political science. None of these models was derived especially to study public policy. They are not competitive in the sense that any one of them could be judged "best." Each one provides a separate focus on political life, and each can help us to understand different things about public policy (Dye, 1992, pp. 23-24).

Group Model: Policy as Group Equilibrium

The Group (theory) Model as presented by Dye (1992) begins with the proposition that interaction among groups (Fig. 15.1) is the central fact of politics. Individuals with common interests band together formally or informally to press their demands upon government. According to political scientist David Truman, an interest group is "a shared-attitude group that makes certain claims upon other groups in the society"; such a group becomes political "if and when it makes a claim through or upon any of the institutions of government" (Truman, 1951). Individuals are important in politics only when they act as part of, or on behalf of, group interests. The group becomes the essential bridge between the individual and the government. Politics is really the struggle among groups to influence public policy. The task of the political system is to *manage group conflict* by: (1) establishing rules of the game in the group struggle, (2) arranging compromises and balancing interests, (3) enacting compromises in the form of public policy, and (4) enforcing these compromises (Dye, 1992).

Elite Theory: Policy as Elite Preference

Public policy may also be viewed as the preferences and values of a governing elite. Although it is often asserted that public policy reflects the demands of "the people," this may express the myth rather than the reality of American democracy. Elite theory suggests that "the people" are apathetic and ill-informed about public policy—that elites actually shape mass opinion on policy questions more than masses shape elite opinion. Thus, public policy really turns out to be the preferences of elites. Public officials and administrators merely carry out the policies decided upon by the elite. Policies flow "downward" from elites to masses; they do not move up from the demands of the masses (Dye, 1992).

Elite theory suggests, according to Dye, society divided into the few who have power and the many who do not (Fig. 15.2). Only a small number of persons allocate values for society; the masses do not decide public policy. The few who govern are not typical of the masses who are governed. Elites are drawn disproportionately from the upper socioeconomic strata of society. The movement of non-elites to elite positions must be slow and continuous to maintain stability and avoid revolution. Only non-elites who have accepted the basic elite consensus can be admitted to

FIGURE 15.1

The Group Model.

Note: From *Understanding Public Policy* (7th ed.) by T. R. Dye, p. 27, 1991. Reprinted by permission of Prentice-Hall, Inc., Upper Saddle River, NJ.

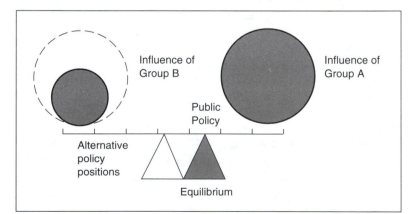

governing circles. Elites share consensus in behalf of the basic values of the social system and the preservation of the system. In America, the bases of elite consensus are the sanctity of private property, limited government, and individual liberty. Public policy does not reflect demands of masses, but rather the prevailing values of the elite. Changes in public policy are incremental rather than revolutionary. Active elites are subject to relatively little direct influence from apathetic masses. Elites influence masses more than masses influence elites (Dye, 1992).

Rationalism: Policy as Maximum Social Gain

A rational policy is one that achieves maximum social gain—that is, one in which gains exceed costs (Fig. 15.3). According to proponents of this model, no policy should be adopted if its costs exceed its benefits. Policy is rational when the differences between the values it achieves and the values it sacrifices are positive and greater than those afforded by any other policy alternatives. Dye suggests that rational policy can be selected only when the policymakers know the society's value preferences and rela-

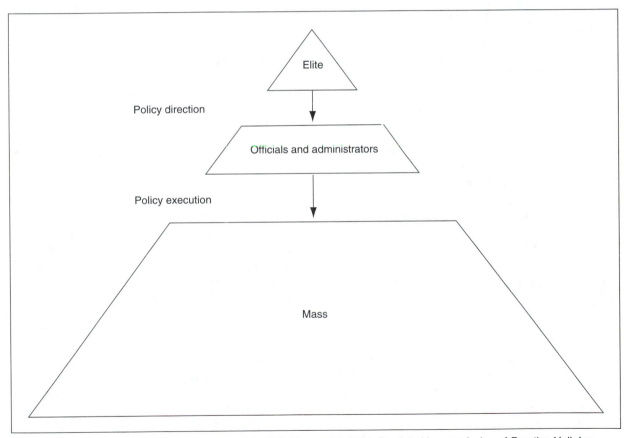

Note: From *Understanding Public Policy* (7th ed.) by T. R. Dye, p. 29, 1991. Reprinted by permission of Prentice-Hall, Inc., Upper Saddle River, NJ.

FIGURE 15.2
The Elite Model

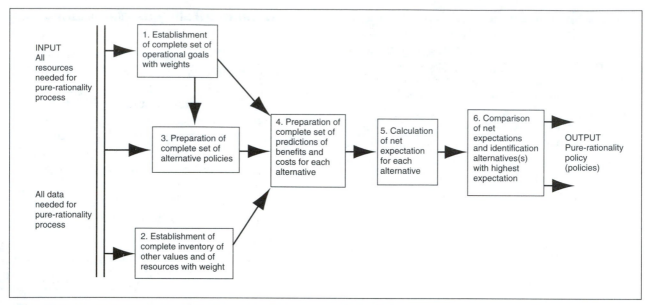

Note: From *Understanding Public Policy* (7th ed.) by T. R. Dye, pp. 30-31, 1991. Reprinted by permission of Prentice-Hall, Inc., Upper Saddle River, NJ.

FIGURE 15.3
A Rational Model of Decision System

tive weights, know all the policy alternatives available, know all the consequences, can calculate the ratio of benefits to costs, and can thereby select the most efficient policy alternative. The rational model is often used when looking at optimal size of government programs. Government spending should increase only until maximum net gain is reached.

Incrementalism: Policy as Variation on the Past

Incrementalism views public policy as a continuation of past government activities with only incremental modifications. Political scientist Charles E. Lindblom first presented the incremental model in the course of a critique of the traditional rational model of decision making. According to Lindblom, decision makers do *not* review the whole range of existing and proposed policies annually, identify societal goals, research the benefits and costs of alternative policies in achieving these goals, rank order of preference for each policy alternative in terms

of the maximum net benefits, and then make a selection on the basis of all relevant information. On the contrary, constraints of time, information, and cost prevent the establishment of clear-cut societal goals and the accurate calculation of costs and benefits. The incremental model (Fig. 15.4) recognizes the impractical nature of "rational-comprehensive" policy making, and describes a more conservative process of decision making (Dye, 1992).

As defined in earlier sections of this chapter, policymaking involves a pattern of actions extending over time and requiring a number of decisions. Policy serves to clarify and organize thought and provides an understanding of policy decisions. Policy is rarely synonymous with a simple decision, which involves, in its simplest form, a choice among competing alternatives. The models identified by Anderson (1984) and Dye (1992) describe a number of "theoretical approaches" that, although not developed specifically for the analysis of policy formulation, have been modified to address policymaking in general and decision making as the logical extension of policy development. Of those models or theories referred to in their analyses—which included group, rational, incremental, and elite theory—the political systems theory provides the most comprehensive perception of general policy development.

Easton Model

Anderson's public policy model mirrors to a great extent the Easton Model developed and refined by David Easton. The Easton Model also identifies the interaction of environmental inputs with outputs and feedback. This model, however, places supreme importance on the understanding of the complexity of the environment. Those interventions through which values are authoritatively allocated for a society, according to Easton, are differentiated from other systems because of the uniqueness of system environments. Easton divided the environment itself into two parts, which he described as the *intrasocietal* and the *extrasocietal* (Easton, 1965).

The first part of Easton's model consists of those systems in the same society as the political system under analysis, but extracted from the system itself. Intrasocietal environmental factors include sets of behaviors, attitudes, and ideas such as the economy, the culture, social structures, and personalities of role players—all of which are functional segments of the society and components of the political system. The extrasocietal environmental factors include all systems that lie outside the society itself and that are functional components of what Easton terms an *international society*. The United Nations is an example of an extrasocietal environmental factor (Easton, 1965).

From these environmental sources arise significant influences that contribute to possible stress on the political system. These influences are termed disturbances emanating from the environment that act upon the environment and attempt to change it. These disturbances or input are raw material, according to Easton, that flow into the conversion process. The process reflects those decisions made by authorities who have special responsibilities for converting demands into outputs in response to demands. Feedback depicts the effects of any decision or change in the environment (Easton, 1965).

Easton's model is presented in Figure 15-5. Because Easton goes into such depth and specificity in describing his model, it is difficult in a few pages to discuss adequately the process he has to a great extent developed and refined. Thompson (1976) has successfully captured Easton's thinking when he describes the political systems theory in the following manner: The political system as part of a broader social system receives input from the environment in the form of demands and support, which are converted through a series of processes into outputs

FIGURE 15.4
The Incremental Model.

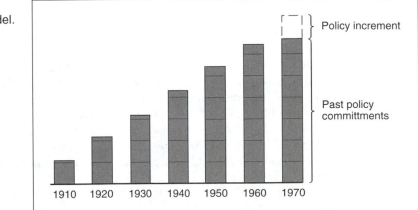

Figure 15.5
Easton's Model. A Dyanmic Response Model of a Political System

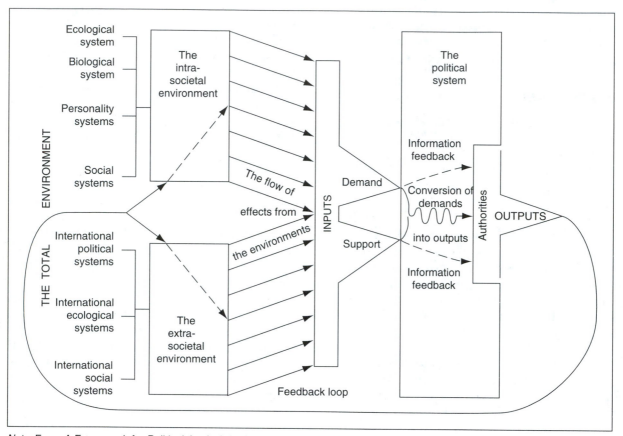

Note: From *A Framework for Political Analysis* by D. Easton, 1979, Chicago: University of Chicago Press. Copyright 1965, 1979 by David Easton. Reprinted by permission

or authoritative rules and actions. In turn, the outputs of the system affect the environment and, as feedback, may result in another demand or input on the system.

Although Easton's model attracts wide attention from individuals supportive of a systems approach to policymaking and decision making, the work of Rakoff and Schaefer (1970) in expanding the Easton Model focuses more directly on the process of policymaking. The fundamental concern behind Rakoff and Schaefer's adoption of Easton's work is the assumption that the process itself matters. They are clearly

concerned with what happens to inputs as they work their way toward becoming outputs.

The creation of public policy involves the environment, procedures, resources, time, and outcomes. To present it simply as inputs/outputs and feedback, they argue, does not seem to enhance a true understanding of how policymaking occurs. Figure 15-6 describes Rakoff and Schaefer's model of the policymaking process graphically.

The environment is recognized as a dominant force. Specific requests for political or government actions go through a two-step

Figure 15.6
A Model of the Policymaking Process

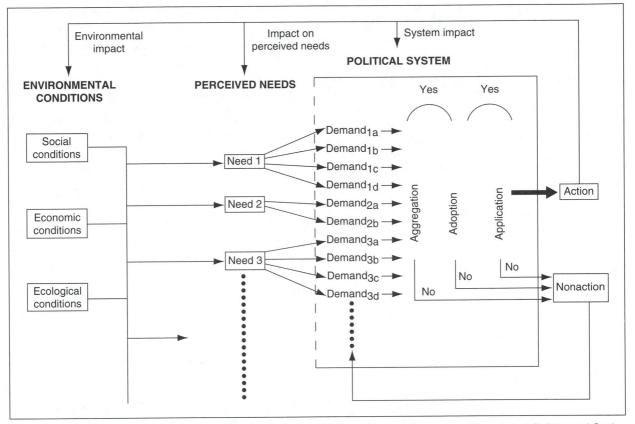

Note: From S. H. Rakoff and G. F. Schaefer, "Politics, Policy, and Political Science: Theoretical Alternatives," *Politics and Society* 1(1), pp. 51-77. Copyright © 1970 by Sage Publications, Inc. Reprinted by permission of Sage Publications, Inc.

process. The first step simply entails some acknowledgment of a condition. The second step identifies a perceived condition of need. The perceived needs can then be transformed into political demands requiring a response from the system. These demands undergo political transformation in three distinct phases: aggregation, adoption, and application.

Aggregation involves the collection, weighing, and ordering of the demands. This is in effect a prioritizing, since no system can deal with all demands imposed on it. Adoption is the formal process by which a decision of "go" or "no-go" is reached on the demand. Application is the actual carrying out of the decision.

In the educational arena a variety of groups interact in an attempt to establish or influence educational policies that they support. These groups are considered components of that environment which Easton, Rakoff, and Schaefer find so important. The composition, size, number, and relative influence of these groups differ depending on the issues, but in education generally, including bilingual special education, one can expect that school-based personnel, state and local government entities, and special interest groups are all playing a particular role as inputs in this policymaking process.

Decisions relating to all program functions or activities in the area of bilingual special education can best be explained by understanding the particular model of policy development and revamping the complex relationship and interaction that occurs in the total environment.

CRITICAL ISSUES AFFECTING POLICY DEVELOPMENT

The critical issues most directly impacting policy development in the area of bilingual special education are those that have the greatest effect on education in general. These issues can be categorized under several major problem areas:

• Economic needs or financing
• States' rights issues or local control
• Planning and implementation
• Training needs
• Effectiveness of bilingual special education

The most visible and critical problem facing special population educational/training programs today relates to the cost of the programs, especially in light of massive cutbacks in federal funding and the inability or unwillingness of state and local governments to assume the costs associated with these programs. The nation is faced with the problem of decreasing gross national product and real net income, along with spiraling budget deficits. High unemployment and underemployment figures, concern over interest rates, increasing costs of government services, reduced federal expenditures for education generally, the shift from categorical funding to block grants, and budget balancing requirements are just some of the issues associated with the problem of financing educational programs for the disadvantaged or disabled.

Related to these economic issues and contributing to the problems of addressing the needs of special student populations are the following conditions (Jones & Ferguson, 1981):

• Radical changes in political party policies and philosophies toward education

• Reduced federal pressures for equity in education and training programs
• Unwillingness of special interest groups to return to spending levels of the past
• Expanding role of state government in educational support
• Support for private school efforts to offer equivalent services at public expense
• Disparities in local funding that result in unequal educational opportunities
• Increased competition from special interest groups for fewer available dollars
• Population shift, resulting in a change in the numbers of people supporting public education
• Decrease in the numbers of children entering the schools, especially in the large urban areas
• Geographic conflict and competition for available funds from sources other than government
• Reduced interest and advocacy for public education from the general population

The issue of who is to pay for the education of bilingual special education students has not undergone extensive study. More information on the costs associated with educating the bilingual child is needed. The Department of Education estimated that bilingual education costs an additional 12 percent over funds appropriated for education generally. The American Institute of Research stated in a highly controversial study that it costs an additional $376 during the school year to educate a child eligible for Title VII funds. A survey of state departments of education by the National Conference of State Legislatures indicated the cost of providing bilingual education programs to be between an additional $10 million and $20 million annually. The costs associated with simply identifying and assessing eligible students was estimated to reach between $6 million and $9 million. Educational programs for limited-English-proficient students with disabilities would add significantly to these costs (Takanishi, 1981).

One additional problem associated with financing bilingual special education relates to the distribution of students. The Education Commission of the States (1979) found that special education students are distributed unevenly throughout the states, and that distribution is not related to the property wealth, population density, or minority populations of the reporting school districts. In essence, the less affluent districts—those situated in the larger urban areas—serve greater numbers of eligible students than do the districts that are better able to support special programs.

States' Rights Issues

The shifting responsibility for the education of special populations from the federal government to states and local agencies does not bode well for bilingual special education students. Although the states have assumed the largest share of the funding responsibility (64%) as compared to the local school district share (30.1%) or the federal share (5.9%), states are apparently unable to pick up any additional costs assumed primarily by the federal government (ECS, 1979).

This inability to assume the additional cost of educating the bilingual special education student produces very special problems for the state and local school districts that have made a major issue of states' rights in the area of education. One of the basic arguments used by states' rights advocates is that educating the young has long been the recognized constitutional responsibility of the states and local school districts (Thompson, 1976).

Using this argument, the states' rightists say that the Tenth Amendment to the Constitution gives the power and responsibility for the education of the populace to the states. The Department of Education, they argue, goes beyond the intent of any laws by issuing specific or prescriptive guidelines to the local school districts, and has therefore usurped the power of the states and local school boards to determine educational methodologies and curriculum policy (Takanishi, 1981).

The intervention of federal governmental entities and the courts in what are perceived to be local educational issues is seen by these defenders of local control as greatly complicating an already serious problem. As one spokesperson for the Center for Applied Legislation stated (Takanishi, 1981): "The proposed rules greatly underestimate and oversimplify the complexity of the task of educating language minority youngsters by attempting to prescribe one educational solution for all."

Planning and Implementation

These problems are exacerbated by the lack of coordination between federal and state agencies in initial planning, implementation, and evaluation of programs. Very little information sharing takes place. Guidelines for program monitoring are usually ambiguous and weak. Federal requirements and court mandates often conflict with existing state laws and, in most cases, funds appropriated for carrying out programs of instruction are inadequate to accomplish the task (Alexander & Nava, 1976). Questions such as the following are rarely addressed:

- What is the rationale for proper services or activities?
- What types of programs are already available?
- What type of teacher is needed?
- What kind of teacher training is necessary?
- How do federal and state requirements interface?
- What changes will current policy need to undergo?
- What are the long-term expectations of the program?
- What costs are associated with the program?

- What kind of community commitment exists?

- What are the long-range financial obligations?

- What alternative funding resources exist?

As a result of this lack of coordination and planning, resources—both human and material—may not even be identified, much less mobilized. Federal and state requirements and expectations run counter to one another, and the schools, caught in the middle of the imbroglio, fail to meet the goals of addressing individual student needs. Students are therefore denied a meaningful opportunity to participate in an appropriate educational experience, resulting in a loss of human potential.

Program Effectiveness

The final issue relates to the effectiveness of both bilingual education and bilingual special education. Little research in bilingual special education has been carried out on a long-term basis. Much research exists, however, on bilingual education generally. Although much of this research provides positive evidence of the effectiveness of such programs (Barrera-Vasquez, 1953; Blank, 1973; Modiano, 1968; Ramírez, 1992; Richardson, 1986; Troike, 1978; Tucker, 1972), highly publicized studies like the 1977 American Institute of Research evaluation of Title VII Programs provide deadly political ammunition to opponents of bilingual education. Many of these antagonists oppose the concept for a variety of political reasons, but base their offense on the question of effectiveness. Thus, as is the case with other highly controversial topics, bilingual education is under constant scrutiny and continuous attack, with only a limited chance of ever receiving unbiased, politically free evaluation.

FEDERAL AND STATE REQUIREMENTS FOR SERVING LEP CHILDREN WITH DISABILITIES

Chapter 4 of this text reviews the legal background related to bilingual special education. The interest here is simply to list and summarize the specific programmatic requirements that are based on the various laws and judicial decisions. Once these basic requirements are established, policy strategies and policy options will then be considered. These were first examined in an ERIC Exceptional Child Education Report (Baca & Bransford, 1982).

1. Every state and its localities shall provide or make available a free appropriate public education for all children with disabilities, aged 3 to 18. (PL 94-142, Section 504 of the Rehabilitation Act of 1973. Section 504 does not refer to specific ages.)

2. Every school district shall conduct a language screening at the beginning of each school year for all new students to determine if there is the influence of a language other than English on the child (*Lau,* 1974).

3. If the initial screening does disclose the influence of a language other than English, then a language assessment shall be made to determine language dominance and proficiency (*Lau,* 1974).

4. If it is determined that a child has both a disability and limited English proficiency, an individualized education plan (IEP) shall be developed that reflects the child's language-related needs (Title VI, PL 94-142, Section 504).

5. When a child is evaluated, the instruments used shall be appropriate and the testing shall be nondiscriminatory (PL 94-142, Section 504).

6. Tests and other evaluation materials must be validated for the specific purpose for which they are used and should be administered by trained personnel in confor-

mance with the instructions provided by their producers (PL 94-142, Section 504).

7. Tests and other evaluation materials must be tailored to access specific areas of educational need. There should not be a total reliance on tests designed to provide a single general intelligence quotient (PL 94-142, Section 504).

8. Tests must be selected and administered to ensure that, when administered to a student with impaired sensory, manual, or speaking skills, the test results accurately reflect the student's aptitude, achievement level, or whatever other factor the test purports to measure, rather than reflecting the student's impaired sensory, manual, or speaking skills (PL 94-142, Section 504).

9. In interpreting evaluation data and in making placement decisions, information shall be drawn from a variety of sources, including aptitude and achievement tests, teacher recommendations, physical condition, social or cultural background, and adaptive behavior (PL 94-142, Section 504).

10. The parents of a child shall be informed of all due process rights in their native language. An interpreter shall be provided at all meetings if the parents cannot communicate in English (Title VI, PL 94-142).

11. The limited-English-proficient child with disabilities shall be provided with a program of instruction that addresses the child's unique needs, including language-related needs (PL 94-142).

In general, the states reflect these same issues in their state plans for education of students with disabilities, state statues, and state rules and regulations. These policy documents were reviewed for all states to determine if they reflected the federal requirements or imposed further requirements on the states to ensure the appropriate education of limited-English-proficient students with disabilities.

Six federal requirements that related to language issues were identified from Part B of the Federal Regulations for the Individuals with Disabilities Education Act:

300.345:	Individualized Education Programs, parent participation
300.500:	Consent (parent informed in native language)
300.505(b):	Content of Notice in native language
300.505(c):	Notice if native language not a written language
300.532:	Evaluation procedures
300.561:	Confidentiality, notice to parents

Table 15-1 indicates whether state documents mirrored the language of the federal requirements (×), were weaker than the federal requirements (−), or exceeded the federal requirements(+). In cases where state requirements were determined to exceed the federal requirements, a code under the category "additional" helps identify the nature of the requirement.

STRATEGIES FOR INFLUENCING POLICIES

As is evident, public policy development and implementation are part of a complex political process. Although the primary developers of policy are elected and appointed officials such as legislators, governors, judges, board members, and administrators of agencies or programs, it is important that they be in communication with their constituents. In other words, policymakers should know the needs and concerns of the people most affected by the policies they are formulating. With this in mind, advocates of LEP children with disabilities can use several strategies in their efforts to shape these policies. In discussing these specific strategies, it is helpful to relate them to the various components of policy development. Anderson (1984) describes five such components, including policy demands,

Table 15–1
Results of State Document Review

State	.345	.500	.505b	.505c	.532	.561	Additional
Alabama	×	×	×	×	+	×	1
Alaska	×	×	×	×	×	×	2
Arizona	+	×	×	×	+	×	3, 5, 6, 7, 10
Arkansas	−	×	×	×	×	×	4
California	+	×	×	×	+	×	1, 3, 5, 6
Colorado	×	×	×	×	+	×	
Connecticut	×	×	×	×	+	×	
Delaware	×	×	×	×	+	×	8
District of Columbia	×	×	×	×	×	×	1
Florida	×	×	−	−	×	×	1, 9, 10
Georgia	×	×	×	×	×	×	8
Hawaii	×		×	×	×	×	5, 10
Idaho	×	×	×	×	+		7
Illinois	+	+	+	+	+	+	PA 87-0995*
Indiana	−	×	×	×	×	×	4, 5
Iowa	×	×	×	×	×	×	
Kansas	×	×	×	×	×	×	2, 3
Kentucky	×	×	×	×	+	×	
Louisiana	×	×	×	×	+	×	
Maine	×	×	×	×	×	+	2
Maryland	×	×	×	×	×	×	3
Massachusetts	+	×	×	×	×	+	2, 3, 9, 12
Michigan	×	+	×	×	×	+	2, 5, 9, 10
Minnesota	×	×	×	×	×	×	9, 10
Mississippi		×	×	×	×	×	

Additional requirements:
1. Problems must not be apparent only in English
2. All notices, awareness information in languages other than English
3. Expanded requirements regarding assessment in home language
4. Surrogate parents must match linguistic and cultural characteristics
5. Hearings require interpreters; provide documents in native language
6. IEPs must specify linguistic goals
7. Multidisciplinary committee for LEP students

State	.345	.500	.505b	.505c	.532	.561	Additional
Missouri	×	×		×	×	×	4,
Montana	×	×	×	×	×	×	3
Nebraska	×	×	×	×	×	×	
Nevada	×	×	×	×	+	×	9
New Hampshire	×	×	×	×	+	×	
New Jersey	×	×	×	×	×	×	
New Mexico	×	×	×	×	×	×	
New York	+	×	×	×	×	×	3, 10
North Carolina	×	×	×	×	×	×	
North Dakota	×				×	×	1, 5
Ohio	×	×	×	×	×	×	2, 4, 5
Oklahoma	×	×	×	×	+	×	2, 3
Oregon	×	×	×	×	×	×	11
Pennsylvania	×	×	×	×	+	×	2, 3
Rhode Island	×	×	×	×	×	×	8
South Carolina	×	×	×	×	×	×	
South Dakota	×	×	×	×	×	×	
Tennessee	×	×	×	×	×	×	1
Texas	+	×	×	×	×	×	7
Utah	×	×	×		×	×	4, 8
Vermont			×				
Virginia	×	×		×	×	×	
Washington	×	×	×	×	×	×	
West Virginia	×	×	×	×	×	×	
Wisconsin	×	×	×	×	×	×	
Wyoming	×	×	×	×	×	×	

8. Prereferral process required
9. Bilingual special education personnel requirements/comprehensive system of personnel development
10. Specific guidelines are available for LEP students with disabilities
11. Prohibition against discrimination based on linguistic background
12. Specific bilingual/special education monitoring goals
* State bilingual special education legislation

policy decisions, policy statements, policy outputs, and policy outcomes.

Policy demands in this context are the policy priorities as perceived by the public. Strategies for teachers and parents include conveying their major concerns or demands to the policymakers. This can be done on an individual basis through letters and through presentations at school board meetings. Another effective strategy in this regard is at the group or organizational level. Professional teacher organizations or parent groups can make their collective concerns known to policymakers.

Policy decisions in this context are the decisions made by public officials and administrators that, in effect, result in policy formulation. Included here is the decision to introduce a bill to the legislature or to seek school board approval for the establishment of program guidelines for bilingual special education services. Possible strategies here include various forms of persuading key officials and administrators of the political and moral value of being an advocate of equal educational opportunity for all children, including LEP students with disabilities.

Policy Statements

The third component of policy development is policy statements. These statements include legislative acts or statutes, executive orders, court decisions, rules and regulations, or even public speeches by key officials (Edwards, 1980). More often than not, these official policy statements are generic and difficult to interpret, and apply at the local school district level. For example, how does *Lau v Nichols* (1974) apply to LEP students with disabilities in Laguna, NM? An important strategy here is to request a clarification of a higher-level policy principle as applied to a local school's practices. For example, a teacher or parent could request that the local director of special education clarify how the district implements the nondiscriminatory testing requirements of PL 94-142 with LEP children.

Likewise, a parent group could request this clarification. Frequently a policy clarification request such as this will highlight the absence of local policy guidelines and thus call attention to the need for developing a local policy.

Policy Outputs

Another phase of policy development is the policy outputs. This refers to what is *actually* done as compared to what the policy says *should be* done. For example, a school district policy might state that the language and cultural needs of an LEP student with a disability should be reflected in the student's IEP. However, a number of LEP students' IEPs may contain very little information on how these students' language and culture needs are to be met. A strategy in this regard is to request a review of existing policy outputs from time to time. This request might be more effective if it came from a state or local advisory committee.

Policy Outcomes

The final aspect of policy development is referred to as the policy outcomes: the actual benefits provided to the LEP child, the child's family, and society at large. In other words, has the policy worked as it was intended to work? This is, in effect, the accountability component of policy development. An important strategy in this regard is to encourage program directors to include this concern in the annual program evaluation. This could also be viewed as a cost–benefit analysis. Are the benefits to the LEP child with disabilities, the child's family, and society at large worth the special education intervention and investment? Although such benefit is difficult to measure, it is advisable to provide such information to policymakers whenever possible.

Training and Coordination

The strategies for influencing policy are addressed to individual teachers, parents, and school administrators, as well as to professional educational organizations. To have maximum impact, these individuals and organizations need training and orientation. Such training can be provided by any number of political action groups. We recommend that training be requested from professional organizations with good track records in governmental relations, such as the Council for Exceptional Children (CEC), the American Speech-Language-Hearing Association (ASHA), and the National Education Association (NEA). It is equally important to seek out training from legal advisory groups such as ASPIRA, the Mexican-American Legal Defense and Education Fund (MALDEF), and the Native American Rights Fund (NARF).

In addition to seeking training on policy shaping, it is important for local groups to support the efforts of organizations such as those listed. In this arena they are the experts. They have highly trained and specialized staff who are well versed in the process of policy formulation. These individuals are also excellent sources of information regarding policy matters.

SUGGESTED POLICY OPTIONS

Bilingual Education Policies Some policy recommendations that focus on bilingual education programs should be reviewed to determine what the implications may be for LEP students with disabilities. Following are recommendations from the Ramírez report (1992):

1. LEP students should be provided with language support services for a minimum of six years, or until such time as they successfully demonstrate the English language skills necessary to function in an English-only mainstream classroom.

2. LEP students should be provided with content instruction in their primary language until such time as they are able to profit from English-only instruction.

3. The optimal instructional program for LEP students appears to be comparable to a developmental bilingual program model that would begin by providing most content instruction in the primary language, with formal ESL instruction, and gradually increasing English content instruction and decreasing primary-language content instruction.

4. In mixed-language settings, efforts should be made to ensure that each student's primary language is used.

5. The home language should be used for instruction and as a means by which to assist parents in helping support their children's learning.

6. University teacher training institutions should be encouraged to upgrade training programs to include elements of good staff development programs (theory, modeling, practicing, ongoing coaching).

7. About two-thirds of the country's LEP students are taught by mainstream, regular credentialed teachers. Teachers should be given a thorough background in language development, particularly content-based ESL instruction. Strategies for using the home language to support English instruction are also recommended (Ramírez, 1992, pp. 46–47).

The Stanford Working Group (1993) prepared a report on *Federal education programs for limited-English proficient students: A blueprint for the second generation.* The group provided several policy recommendations for limited-English-proficient students:

1. The unique needs of LEP students must be specifically addressed in policy.

2. High content and performance standards for LEP students should be established to match those for all other students.

3. Assessments of performance and opportunity-to-learn standards that are appropriate for LEP students should be developed.

4. The state should develop a system or systems of accountability for LEP students that

combine assessment of student outcomes and opportunities to learn.

5. State education agencies should ensure an adequate supply of teachers well prepared to educate LEP students.

Special Education Policies   Special education policy options were suggested by the Federal Resource Center for Special Education at the University of Kentucky. A 1993 task force report on cultural and linguistic diversity in education identified eight state policy issues for change:

1. Restructure relevant state and local laws to ensure that the composition of Board of Education reflect the diversity of the student population.

2. Support the development of policy and regulations for providing primary-language instruction from preschool through graduation.

3. Ensure that administrators participate in specialized training on dealing with cultural diversity, and that they demonstrate competency as part of their certification renewal.

4. Require recertification or license renewal processes for all professional staff, to include linguistic and cross-cultural educational requirements as well as the latest technological advances to facilitate education for diverse learners.

5. Restructure post-secondary education recruitment and admission policies to attract and retain students from culturally and linguistically diverse backgrounds.

6. Support the development of policies and/or administrative directives that provide primary language instruction (including sign language as a primary method of communication) from preschool through graduation.

7. Develop policies that ensure that the curriculum and instructional materials in all schools reflect the value of diverse cultures.

8. Establish policies that ensure that assessment and placement procedures do not follow a medical model—designed to find "and remediate" deficits and pathology (Federal Resource Center, 1993, p. 12).

Bilingual Special Education State Policy   Del Green Associates (1983) looked at policy in the *Review of research affecting educational programming for bilingual handicapped students*. Legislative history and case law in both bilingual and special education as well as the existing policy literature were reviewed. Areas identified as in need of policy development included improved enforcement of already-existing legislation, clarification of such generic terms as "appropriate" and "least restrictive environment," teacher training, testing, evaluation, parent involvement, and organizational models for bilingual special education (Woodson, 1983).

In another component of the Del Green study, specific states were contacted in order to identify their policies regarding bilingual special education. Only 12 of the 21 states contacted offered a response, and of these only four provided any evidence of policy documents, such as guides for non-biased assessment (New Jersey), question-and-answer documents (Maryland, New Jersey, North Carolina), administrative considerations (North Carolina), rules and regulations (Illinois), or goal statements (Illinois) (Woodson, 1983).

Salend and Fradd (1986) contacted 50 state education agencies (SEAs) to request information about the availability of services for *LEP handicapped students*. Of 49 responses, only six states reported that a definition or category for bilingual handicapped students exists; 14 responded that a position at the SEA to address the needs of this population exists; two reported a special funding category; five reported a list of recommended assessment instruments, and two were developing such a list. A total of 35 states reported the existence of procedures regarding language dominance and proficiency before placement; no state reported having a specific curriculum or materials; one state (California) indicated that bilingual special education certification existed; and 16 reported a training program at an Institution of Higher Education (IHE).

A 1987 project of the Council of Chief State School Officers (CCSSO) attempted to gather information about the activities of states in providing educational services for LEP students, including special education services. Surveys were sent to directors of specific program units within the SEAs, including special education, bilingual education, vocational education, migrant education, and compensatory education (Chapter 1). This survey requested information on the number of students served and the types of services provided to LEP students through the various categorical programs, the degree of coordination among the units in the delivery of technical assistance, and state-level barriers to delivery of services to LEP students at the local level. Forty-eight states responded to the survey, although not all surveys were answered completely. One general conclusion of the study indicated that inadequate data due to a lack of national criteria and procedures for identification limits confidence in placements and provision of services, including special education services, for LEP students (CCSSO, 1990).

Bilingual Special Education Policy Options
Every school district is unique in terms of location, size, makeup of student population, teaching staff, financial resources, and many other variables. Because of the unique character of each school district, it is not advisable or possible to design a comprehensive set of model policy statements that would have broad applicability across many districts. The following policy options are presented to highlight issues that may need policy clarification and direction. These policy options may also serve to stimulate a dialogue relative to the need for policy on a number of different topics related to bilingual special education services. These policy options are not meant to be adopted by school districts

as they stand. They must be revised and rewritten to fit the unique needs of a particular school district. Finally, because every policy contains within it both positive and negative implications, an attempt is made to point out the possible positive and negative effects of each option. These policy options are taken in large part from a policy options report prepared for the Council for Exceptional Children (Baca, 1980).

Screening

Every school district shall assure that each of its schools conducts a uniform language screening for all new students at the beginning of each school year to determine if there is the influence of a language other than English on any of the children.

Potential Positive Effects. This option will increase the number of students identified as being in need of special language-related services. It will assure that all schools within the district use the same criteria and procedures for identifying students who may be of limited English proficiency and should assist all school districts in complying with the *Lau* (1974) decision.

Potential Negative Effects. It will add an additional requirement to school districts already burdened with excessive bureaucratic red tape and another level of identification and assessment to an already overly identified and assessed population. It may also take time away from much-needed instruction.

Language Dominance/Proficiency Testing

Every school district will provide language dominance/proficiency testing for students who have been identified through the screening process as needing additional language assessment.

Potential Positive Effects. This option will provide teachers with a better indication of each student's first and second language abilities for instructional purposes, contributing important language proficiency information to the IEP staffing team. It will provide baseline information to help teachers arrive at decisions regarding when to initiate first and second language reading instruction.

Potential Negative Effects. This option will create a requirement for which there are no language dominance/proficiency tests in certain languages, thus creating additional testing requirements for an already-overburdened staff. It will add another financial burden to already-stringent budgets.

Acceptable Tests

Every school district shall adopt a list of acceptable language dominance and proficiency tests in the various languages necessary. In the event that instruments are not available in certain languages, alternate methods of language assessment should be suggested.

Potential Positive Effects. The use of poorer quality instruments or procedures will be minimized. Low-incidence languages will be included.

Potential Negative Effects. Technical data on validity and reliability are not available for some language assessment instruments. The identification of proper instruments and procedures does not ensure that they will be properly administered.

Testing Guidelines

Every school district shall establish guidelines that will assure that appropriate testing instruments are used and that all testing is non-discriminatory in terms of language, culture, and disability.

Potential Positive Effects. The assessment of children with disabilities who have limited English proficiency will be improved. Assessment practices within each school district will be more consistent for this group of students, resulting in more districts being in compliance with PL 94-142.

Potential Negative Effects. There is no assurance that guidelines will be updated from time to time, since the state of the art is not sufficiently advanced to assure that the guideline will be effective. In addition, the personnel needed to do the job may not be available.

Parent Notification

Every school district will assure that parents or guardians of LEP students are notified in their native language regarding permission to test, IEP participation, and due process rights.

Potential Positive Effects. This option will facilitate meaningful parent participation and informed consent. It will help school districts comply with PL 94-142 and will show parents that the school district acknowledges and respects their native language.

Potential Negative Effects. It may be difficult for school districts to find translators who could help formulate parent notices in low-incidence and rare languages. Even though notices are sent in the parents' native language, the parents may not be able to read these notices. In effect, providing information in this manner to parents does not mean that meaningful communication has taken place.

Use of Parents' Language

Every school district shall print parent due process rights in the appropriate target languages and shall compile a list of available interpreters for the various languages.

Potential Positive Effects. Printed material in the various languages will be readily available at the time of the staffings. A pool of interpreters will be available when needed for staffings, and the meaningful involvement of linguistically-different parents will be improved.

Potential Negative Effects. School districts may not hire bilingual staff if they can use community people. In addition, some languages do not have an orthography and, thus, material cannot be printed.

Individualized Education Program Development

Every school district shall assure that each LEP student with a disability and the student's parents or guardians are provided with an IEP in both English and the family's primary language and that an interpreter will be used if necessary to communicate effectively the meaning and content of the IEP to the parents or guardians.

Potential Positive Effects. This option will promote meaningful parental involvement in the educational process and demonstrate the district's willingness to acknowledge the family's primary language. It will help the district document its compliance with PL 94-142.

Potential Negative Effects. Language interpreters in some of the low-incidence languages may be difficult to find. This option may tax an already-overstrained budget and the procedure may slow up the staffing process and delay the implementation of the needed instruction.

Bilingual Advocate

Every school district shall designate a bilingual specialist or specialists who will participate in all staffings for LEP children with disabilities.

Potential Positive Effects. All LEP children with disabilities will have an advocate on the staffing team. Every IEP will include provisions related to language needs, and services for LEP children with disabilities will be improved.

Potential Negative Effects. The specialist may have limited knowledge of the particular disability or of the various languages in the district, adding another expense to an already-strained budget.

Establishing Primary Need

Each staffing team will have the responsibility for determining if the student's principal obstacle to learning in the regular classroom is the disability or the language difference.

Potential Positive Effects. This option will help ensure that the proper remedial emphasis is placed in the area of greatest need, facilitating the proper placement of the student and the development of the IEP.

Potential Negative Effects. It is sometimes difficult to separate the impact of the disability from the impact of the language difference; thus the lesser of the two needs may be considered unimportant and the child may not receive appropriate services.

Establishing Primary Responsibility

When the student's primary need has been established, the student will become the primary responsibility of the appropriate program, that is, bilingual education or special education.

Potential Positive Effects. The lines of responsibility will be clearly established and proper follow-up and restaffing will be assured, promoting the use of the least restrictive environment.

Potential Negative Effects. Additional red tape may not be justified. Special education may view bilingual education as encroaching into its area of responsibility.

Comprehensive Services

Every school district shall design and implement a plan with various alternatives for serving the disabled child with limited English proficiency.

Potential Positive Effects. This option should help ensure that appropriate programs are provided for LEP students with disabilities by providing a variety of alternative programs that will allow the staffing team the opportunity of selecting the most appropriate program. It will assist school districts in complying with *Lau* (1974), as well.

Potential Negative Effects. School districts may not have the expertise and recourses to carry out this policy option. The staff needed may not be available in many parts of the country, and providing a range of alternative programs may be too idealistic.

Use of Existing Services

The school principal will ensure that, whenever possible, students with disabilities in need of bilingual education will use the existing services of the bilingual program in the school building.

Potential Positive Effects. This should help reduce duplication of effort and personnel. It will also keep the student in the local school rather than requiring busing to a special program and will make bilingual programs more accessible to students with disabilities.

Potential Negative Effects. Existing bilingual programs may not be able to meet the students' needs, resulting in a fragmentation of the students' education. It may also encourage matching the student to the program, rather than matching the program to the student.

Accessibility

Every school district with an existing bilingual program will, as a matter of policy, make it available to children of limited English proficiency who have disabilities.

Potential Positive Effects. This option will encourage placement in the least restrictive environment, promote the maximum use of existing resources, and be more cost-effective.

Potential Negative Effects. It may deter some districts from implementing a bilingual special education program because regular bilingual teachers may not be prepared to accept children with disabilities into their classrooms.

Removal of Barriers

Every school district with an existing bilingual program will make every effort to remove any barriers that may prevent meaningful participation of students with disabilities and limited English proficiency.

Potential Positive Effects. This option will promote placement in the least restrictive environment while helping to sensitize teachers and administrators to the needs of people with disabilities. It will make existing bilingual programs accessible to students with disabilities.

Potential Negative Effects. Barriers may be interpreted very narrowly to mean only physical barriers, and some districts may feel their responsibility ends there.

Supplementary Services

Every school district with an existing bilingual program will make every effort to provide supplementary services and materials to make it more responsive to children with disabilities and limited English proficiency.

Potential Positive Effects. This option will serve to improve the quality of services for the student of limited English proficiency who also has disabilities within the mainstream of education, be more cost effective, and encourage more placements in a least restrictive environment.

Potential Negative Effects. It may deter some districts from going a step further to establish a bilingual special education program.

Minimum Services

When no bilingual programs or services are available or accessible, the school district shall, at the very minimum, provide a native language tutor for every LEP child with disabilities.

Potential Positive Effects. LEP children with disabilities will be assured of a minimum level of services because every school district will be accountable for at least a minimum effort in meeting the needs of the disabled child of limited English proficiency.

Potential Negative Effects. This option may deter some districts from providing more comprehensive services. This minimum standard may be too low in certain instances.

Bilingual Special Education

When the number of LEP students with disabilities is large enough, a school district shall design and implement a bilingual special education program.

Potential Positive Effects. Students will be assured of an appropriate educational experience. They will not be relegated to fragmented "pullout" programs (programs that pull or remove children from the regular classroom for supplementary instruction). Teachers in these programs will be trained in both special education and bilingual education methodology.

Potential Negative Effects. Properly trained personnel may not be available to staff such a program. In addition, the term *large enough* is open to a wide range of interpretations.

Parent and Community Involvement

Any school district planning to develop a bilingual special education program shall involve parents and community members in the planning of the program.

Potential Positive Effects. When parents are involved in the planning of the program, they are more supportive of the program and more likely to assist as volunteers for the program, contributing particularly in the areas of language and culture.

Potential Negative Effects. If the role of parents and community members is not clearly defined, conflicts may result. Some parents may act as observers rather than participants.

Exit Criteria

A school district's exit criteria for a bilingual special education program shall be the same as a variety of alternative programs that will allow the staffing team the opportunity of selecting the most appropriate program. It will assist school districts in complying with *Lau* (1974), as well.

Potential Positive Effects. Explicit criteria will assist in assuring compliance with minimal standards.

Potential Negative Effects. School districts may not have the expertise and resourses to carry out this policy option. Necessary staff may not be available in many parts of the country, and providing a range of alternative programs may be too idealistic.

Inservice Training

Every school district shall provide inservice training for the teachers, aides, and administrators who work with LEP students with disabilities.

Potential Positive Effects. The skills of existing staff will be improved, helping to bridge the gap between bilingual and special education and improving the quality of services provided to children.

Potential Negative Effects. Identifying trainers with the proper background may be difficult, and this may deter some districts from hiring new teachers with the appropriate training.

Teacher Certification/Endorsement

State departments of education certification units will set up the criteria for certifying or endorsing bilingual special education teachers in consultation with representatives from local school districts and college or schools of education.

Potential Positive Effects. The establishment of standards will encourage schools of education to begin offering the appropriate training, thereby improving the quality of teacher training and ultimately improving the quality of services provided to disabled children of limited English proficiency.

Potential Negative Effects. The use of existing standards may allow for more flexibility. If such is the case, the additional bureaucratic red tape may not be justified.

Teacher Training

Schools and colleges of education in high-impact areas will revise their training programs to include training experiences for teachers who will work in bilingual special education programs.

Potential Positive Effects. Teachers now in short supply will become more available. Colleges will become more responsive to needs in the field, more easily placing their graduates and thereby leading to improved quality of services to the disabled child of limited English proficiency.

Potential Negative Effects. Colleges may not have the appropriate faculty to accomplish the task. Also, such an approach may add an additional year to the training program.

PLANNING AND IMPLEMENTATION

Earlier in this chapter the current federal requirements for serving LEP children with disabilities were delineated. This section will discuss practical measures for planning and administering services for this population of students. Issues such as student identification, needs assessment, personnel competencies, program implementation, and instructional resources will be treated from a non-theoretical standpoint. This will allow ideas discussed earlier to be viewed from a more practical perspective. Some of this material can be adapted and refined to meet the needs of a local school or school district.

The first step in the planning process is the recognition of the need for this type of program or services. The existence of special learning problems among this population needs to be identified, and steps to solve these learning difficulties should be taken through appropriate program development and correct student placement. The placement and assessment of students into the proper learning environment are of critical importance. The persons responsible for placement should review the referral process and all testing procedures for bias. Cultural and linguistic factors should also be carefully considered in viewing the student's regular program before a referral is made.

After determining that students have been properly identified as needing bilingual special education services, a thorough needs assessment should be completed. This part of the planning process requires a review of existing programs, funding, staff, and materials to see how they can be better used in meeting the needs of these students. Linkages with existing programs such as special education, bilingual education, and remedial reading must be formed to increase effectiveness. Funding sources should also be reviewed to determine length and amount of support in addition to flexibility of allocation.

Along with determining the programs and funding available, it is necessary to determine the existing human resources. To do this, personnel competencies need to be documented. Each staff position involved with the program needs to be evaluated. Questions such as the following need to be answered:

- What are the bilingual abilities of individuals staffing special education and other positions in the district?
- How can personnel with a bilingual and/or special education background be best used?

A thorough evaluation of personnel information is an indispensable part of the planning process. Once the evaluation has occurred, effective use of personnel is an equally vital part of the implementation aspect of the program. It should also be noted that all personnel involved in this program should be aware of their roles. For the program to proceed in a smooth manner, all staff responsible for its success should be informed of their functions.

After the skills of the staff are determined, a plan must account for variables such as student separation time from peers in the standard curriculum, service delivery models, monitoring procedures, instructional techniques, evaluation policies, and exit assurance criteria. The evaluation of the program's effectiveness should be ongoing to make adjustments to improve the program.

Another integral aspect of the planning process is the allocation of material and instructional resources. However, before the acquisition of new materials takes place, an evaluation of available materials should be conducted. This inventory clarifies which items the district already has to assist the program and which items it needs to order. Items in these categories can range from inservice materials to consultants for training. This determination of resources completes the assessment process. Once the needs are understood, the process of planning and implementing the program becomes easier.

Figures 15-7 to 15-10 show planning forms that can be modified and adapted as needed to fit the needs of local schools and districts. These instruments are designed for planning and monitoring a bilingual special education program. With careful evaluation, they can provide effective feedback in the areas of pupil population, personnel skills, program planning, and materials management.

FUTURE OF BILINGUAL SPECIAL EDUCATION

Because bilingual special education is a still-emerging concern within education, it can easily be viewed in a futuristic context. A futurist has been defined as "a person who makes other people's futures more real for them" (Kierstead & Dede, 1979). In this sense bilingual special educators, as well as those involved in bilingual special education policy formulation, are futurists. Dede (1979) has indicated that the field of educational futures resembles a tree. The trunk is the present and the branches are the various alternative futures. As futurists, when we move up the trunk to the branches, or from the present to the future, we have eliminated some alternative futures. The branch we are on becomes the present and many new branches or futures remain ahead of us.

Bilingual special education can be viewed as an emerging branch on the tree of general education. The future direction of bilingual special education depends to a great extent on what happens to general education and to special education as well. On the other hand, the future of bilingual special education will also be affected by the way it is planned for and directed in and of itself. With this in mind, some of the issues that may affect the future of general education as well as bilingual special education will be discussed.

A very common way of relating to the future of education is to analyze some of the past and current practices within the field of education. One obvious historical practice in education has been and continues to be the crisis response to social problems. For example, not many years ago the widespread problem of drug abuse prompted schools to develop drug education programs and classes. The racial and ethnic tensions of the 1960s prompted the implementation of ethnic studies and multicultural education. The pollution of our natural resources resulted in environmental education. The same could be said of many other educational innovations, such as energy education, sex education, and even the back-to-basics movement. Although some of the educational changes that have occurred through this crisis model have been beneficial, a better approach is needed.

Future Trends

Educational futurists stress the importance of planning education in the context of the impact of the major future trends. Shane (1977) stresses that the following factors will influence future educational practices:

1. A continued acceleration in the rate of change

Form 1—Student Identification

CATEGORY	K		1		2		3		4		5		6		7		8		9		10		11		12	
	LEP	NON-LEP	LEP	NON-LEP	LEP	NON-LEP	LEP	NON-LEP	LEP	NON-LEP	LEP	NON-LEP	LEP	NON-LEP	LEP	NON-LEP	LEP	NON-LEP	LEP	NON-LEP	LEP	NON-LEP	LEP	NON-LEP	LEP	NON-LEP
Emotionally disturbed																										
Specific learning disabled																										
Hard of hearing																										
Deaf																										
Deaf-Blind																										
Educable mentally retarded																										
Trainable mentally retarded																										
Severely mentally retarded																										
Speech impaired																										
Orthopedically handicapped																										
Other health impaired																										
Multiply handicapped																										
Gifted and talented																										
Other (specify)																										
Total																										

Figure 15–7
Form I—Student Identification

Form II—Billingual and Special Education Personnel	FULL-TIME EQUIVALENT	
PERSONNEL TYPE	BILINGUAL	NOT BILLINGUAL
Billingual teachers		
Billingual teacher aides		
Teacher of the educationally handicapped		
Teacher of the emotionally handicapped		
Teacher of the hearing impaired		
Teacher of the learning disabled		
Teacher of the mentally retarded		
Teacher of the multiply handicapped		
Teacher of the physically handicapped		
Teacher of the vision impaired		
Vocational teacher		
Special education teacher aides		
Diagnostician		
Psychologist		
Child find coordinator		
Social worker		
Guidance counselor		
Speech and language clinician		
Audiologist		
Billingual special education teacher		
Other (specify)		
Total		

Figure 15–8
Form II—Bilingual and Special Education Personnel

Form III—Program Planning

	CURRENT POLICY		POLICY NEEDED	
	YES	**NO**	**YES**	**NO**
1. The methods your school district uses to contact parents for their participation in the Individual Education Plan meeting are: a. Letter				
b. Home visitations				
c. Telephone				
d. Note home via child				
e. Other (specify)				
2. All written notification is in: a. English				
b. English and oral interpretation/translation				
c. Native language of the parents				
d. Other modes of communication (e.g., sign, braille) if applicable				
e. Other (specify)				
3. The following persons participate in the IEP meeting for a child in your school district: a. Child's teacher				
b. A person from agency other than the child's teacher who is qualified to provide or supervise the provision of special education				
c. One or both of the child's parents				
d. The child where appropriate				
e. Other individuals at the discretion of the parent or agency				
f. A member of the evaluation team or someone knowledgeable about evaluation procedures				

Adapted from Ramirez, B., and Pages, M.: Special education program for American Indian exceptional children and youth, Reston, Va., 1979, Council for Exceptional Children.

Figure 15–9
Form III—Program Planning

Form III—Program Planning—cont'd	CURRENT POLICY		POLICY NEEDED	
	YES	NO	YES	NO
g. Bilingual advocate				
h. An Interpreter where appropriate				
i. Other (specify)				
4. The following are components of the IEP for a child in your school district: a. A statement of the child's present level of educational performance				
b. A statement of annual goals, including short-term instructional objectives				
c. A statement of the specific special education and related services to be provided to the child				
d. The extent to which the child will be able to participate in regular educational programs				
e. The projected dates for initiation of services and the anticipated duration of the services				
f. Appropriate objective criteria and evaluation procedures and schedules for determining, on at least an annual basis, whether the short-term instructional objectives are being achieved				
g. A description of the child's learning style				
h. Intervals for which objectives are written				
i. Explanation of why placement is the least restrictive one feasible				
j. Name and title of IEP meeting participants				
k. Criteria under which the child returns to the regular program or least restrictive alternative				
l. Name and title of personnel required to provide the special services				
m. Designation of responsible person to act as liaison to ensure this plan is followed				

Figure 15–9
continuing

Form III—Program Planning—cont'd

	CURRENT POLICY		POLICY NEEDED	
	YES	NO	YES	NO
n. Other (specify)				
5. If the primary language spoken by the child is other than English, there is a provision made in the IEP as to which language to use for classroom instruction until the child can profit from English instruction				
6. The decision in regard to which language should be used for the child's initial instruction is made by: a. Parents				
b. IEP meeting participants				
c. Other (specify)				
7. If the parents have not participated in the development of the IEP, the following are contained in the parental notice of recommended program: a. A detailed description of the proposed IEP				
b. An explanation of how the IEP was developed				
c. The reasons why the proposed program is deemed appropriate for the child				
d. The reasons why the proposed program is the least restrictive program setting appropriate for the child				
e. A list of the tests, reports, or evaluation procedures on which the proposed program is based				
f. A statement that the school reports, files, and records pertaining to the child are available to them for inspection and copying				
g. A description of the procedures that parent(s) should follow to appeal the placement decisions				
h. A guarantee that the child will be temporarily continued in present placement (unless the child is a danger to himself or others) if proposed action is rejected by parent				
i. An explanation of procedures to be followed if the child cannot remain in his current placement even temporarily				

Figure 15–9
continuing

Form III—Program Planning—cont'd

	CURRENT POLICY		POLICY NEEDED	
	YES	NO	YES	NO
j. Other (specify)				
8. It is the policy of your school district to require written approval of the proposed IEP for their child				
9. If the parents agree to the proposed placement, the child is placed within 14 days				
10. IEPs are reviewed: a. End of each grading period (quarterly)				
b. Twice a year				
c. Once a year				
d. Other (specify)				
11. The following are considered as part of the review: a. Whether the child has achieved the goals set				
b. Whether the child has met the criteria that indicated readiness to enter a less restrictive program				
c. Whether the program the child is in should be modified to render it more suitable to the child's needs				
d. Other (specify)				
12. Your school district's follow-up procedures for billingual children who go from the special education program to the regular program are: a. Monitoring of student progress by the special education teacher				
b. Monitoring of student progress by the billingual administrator, coordinator, or specialist				
c. Written progress reports by regular teacher				
d. Written progress reports by special education teacher				

Figure 15–9
concluding

Form IV—Management of Resources for Bilingual and Special Education

	YES QUANTITY	NO	TO BE ACQUIRED
Your school district or instructional materials center has:			
A. Bilingual curriculum materials			
B. Bilingual special education curriculum materials			
C. Bilingual films			
D. Bilingual literature			
E. Information or referral services			
F. Filmstrips			
G. Audio tapes			
H. Instructional games			
I. Audiovisual materials			
J. Overhead projections			
K. Competency examinations			
L. Pupil evaluations			
M. Basic textbooks			
N. Records			
O. Inservice materials			
P. Supplemental services			
Q. Teacher development materials			
R. Other (specify)			

Figure 15–10
Form IV—Management of Resources for Bilingual and Special Education

2. Greater complexity of life because of new technological breakthroughs

3. A need to reassess our present concepts

4. Continued pressure for human equity in all areas

5. Increased governmental debt and capital deficits

These factors will definitely affect the future of education in our society. Our purpose here is not to discuss them at great length, but rather to illustrate the complexity involved in discussing the future of education. The future financial support of education, for example, is directly related to increased governmental debt and capital deficits. Reynolds and Birch (1982) point out that schools in the United States as well as throughout the Western world are facing a serious problem of meeting expanding educational needs with fewer dollars. Coupled with the declining resources is the changing role of the federal government in supporting education.

This situation can be viewed from the policy perspective of increased emphasis on local control, as well as from the administrative perspective of block granting. In terms of categorical programs like special education and bilingual education, this means that local school administrators will have more flexibility and control in how they choose to design their educational programs. The trend toward block grants means that the hard-fought battles for financial support and quality programs at the federal level will have to be repeated again at the state and local levels.

Another implication of this policy for the future is that services for students with disabilities and the limited-English-proficient will be viewed less as separate categorical programs and more as the responsibility of the local school district. This will be a welcome change, assuming that these services are given adequate support.

Another factor that will influence the future of education is the continued pressure for human equity in all areas. Regardless of what educational changes occur in the future, the principles related to equal educational opportunity as well as the basic educational rights of all children will continue to receive priority consideration.

Projections for Bilingual Special Education

Looking specifically at the future of bilingual special education, some projections can be made.

1. The number of LEP children with disabilities will more than likely increase at a greater rate than the rest of the student population. This increase will be due to a larger number of foreign students coming into the United States. The probable lower socioeconomic background of these students will also be a contributing factor.

2. Psychological and diagnostic testing procedures for LEP students with disabilities will continue to improve as research and training efforts improve and as more bilingual professionals become available.

3. There will be an increasing trend to classify LEP children with disabilities by their educational needs rather than by the current medical model. This change in classification will come about because of the trend away from categorical funding and the increasing concern over the negative stigma attached to the current classification system.

4. Individualized educational plans (IEPs) for LEP students with disabilities will increasingly reflect the language and culture needs of these students. This change will occur because of improved preservice and inservice training and because of continued litigation.

5. Bilingual special education instruction in self-contained classes will be kept to a minimum. Bilingual special education resource

rooms will continue to be used to a limited extent. The majority of LEP children with disabilities will be served in regular classrooms with a variety of support services uniquely designed and based on the resources of each individual school.

6. There will be increased emphasis on early intervention with the LEP-disabled child. This emphasis will be based on demonstrated educational and cost benefits of early childhood education.

7. The use of educational technology with the LEP student with disabilities will become important as the appropriate hardware and software become more readily available.

As mentioned earlier, the future of bilingual special education rests primarily on the future of regular education. The American educational system is in need of reform. The public schools must develop the capacity to respond to an ever-increasing range of individual differences. All students in our schools should be treated as unique individuals. Individualized educational programs should be developed for every child in our schools. When these conditions exist, the future of bilingual special education will be the present.

☺ SUMMARY

The chapter provided a general background on policy development and described various policymaking models that could be used in the development of federal language policy. Critical issues affecting policy development were discussed, as were suggested strategies for influencing policy at the national level. Policy options directly related to bilingual special education were proposed, along with some specific guidelines for bilingual special education program planning and implementation. Several projections on the future direction of bilingual special education were included for reader consideration.

☺ DISCUSSION QUESTIONS

1. Discuss the viability of two bilingual special education service alternatives in your local school district.
2. Select two groups influencing policy development in your local school district and survey their opinions about bilingual special education.
3. Answer, in detail, two of the questions found on pages 385–386.
4. Are any additions or substractions needed to the federal requirements mentioned in the chapter? If so, identify and explain them.
5. Discuss in detail the positive and negative aspects of any three of the oplicy options as applied to your local school district.

☺ REFERENCES

Alexander, D. J, & Nava, A. (1976). *A public policy analysis of bilingual education in California.* San Francisco: R & E Research Associates.

Anderson, J. E. (1975). *Public policy-making.* New York: Praeger.

Anderson, J. E. (1984). *Public policy and politics in America.* Monterrey, CA: Brooks-Cole.

Baca, L. (1980). *Policy options for insuring the delivery of an appropriate education to handicapped children who are of limited English proficiency.* Reston, VA: Council for Exceptional Children.

Baca, L., & Bransford, J. (1982). *An appropriate education for handicapped children of limited English proficiency.* An ERIC Exceptional Child Education Report, ERIC Clearinghouse for Exceptional Children. Reston, VA: Council for Exceptional Children.

Barrera-Vasquez, A. (1953). The Tarascan Project in Mexico. In *Use of vernacular language in education.* Paris: UNESCO.

Bebout J. E., & Bredemeier, H. C. (1963). American cities as special systems. *American Institute of Planners Journal, 29*(2), 64–75.

Blank, M. (1973). A tutorial language program to develop abstract thinking in socially disadvantaged preschool children. *Child Development, 39,* 379–389.

Council of Chief State School Officers. (1990). *School success for limited English proficient students: The challenge and state response.* Washington: Author, Resource Center on Educational Equity.

Council of Chief State School Officers. (1992). *Summary of recommendations and policy implications for improving the assessment and monitoring of students with limited English proficiency.* Washington: Author, State Education Assessment Center, Resource Center on Educational Equity.

Dede, C. (1979). The state of the union in educational theory In E. Kierstead, & C. Dede (Eds.), *Educational futures: Sourcebook, I.* Washington, DC: World Future Society.

Dunn, W. N. (Ed.) (1986). *Policy analysis: Perceptions, concepts, and methods.* Greenwich, CT: Jai Press.

Del Green Associates. (1983). A review of research affecting educational programming for bilingual handicapped students. Final report, Vol. 2. Washington, DC: Author. (ERIC Document Reproduction Services No. ED 267–556)

Dye, T. R. (1992). *Understanding public policy* (7th ed.). Upper Saddle River, NJ: Prentice Hall.

Easton, D. (1965). *A Framework for political analysis.* Upper Saddle River, NJ: Prentice Hall.

Education Commission for the States (ECS). (1979). *Special education finances: The interaction between state and federal support systems.* Denver: Education Finance Center.

Edwards, A. (1980). Policy research and special education: Research issues affecting policy formation and implementation. *Exceptional Education Quarterly,* 2(2),96–102.

Federal Resource Center for Special Education. (1993). Task force report: Cultural and linguistic diversity in education. Lexington, KY: Author, University of Kentucky.

Gallagher, K. S. (Ed.) (1992). *Shaping school policy: Guide to choices, politics, and community relations.* Newbury Park, CA: Sage.

General Accounting Office. (1987). *Bilingual education: A new look at the research evidence.* Washington: Government Printing Office.

Hughes, L. W. (1967, May). Know your power structure. *School Board Journal, 26,* 84–92.

Jones, P., & Ferguson, J. (1981, March). *Trends in school finance at the national, state, and local levels.* Paper presented at the American Education Finance Association, New Orleans, LA.

Kierstead, F., & Dede, C. (Eds.) (1979). *Educational futures: Sourcebook I,* Washington, DC: World Future Society.

Lau v Nichols. (1974). 414 U.S. 563.

Lewis, D., & Wallace, H. (Eds.) (1984). *Policies into practice.* Exeter, NH: Heineman.

Modiano, N. (1968). Bilingual education for children of linguistic minorities. *American Indigena, 28,* 405–414.

Quade, E. S. (1982). *Analysis for public decisions.* New York: Rand.

Rakoff, S. H., & Schaefer, G. E. (1970). Politics, policy and political science: Theoretical alternatives. *Politics and Society,* 1(1), 51–77.

Ramirez, B., & Pages, M. (1979). *Special education programs for American Indian exceptional children and youth: A policy analysis guide.* Reston, VA: Council for Exceptional Children.

Reynolds, M. C., & Birch, J. W. (1982). Teaching exceptional children in all America's schools. Reston, VA: Council for Exceptional Children.

Richardson, M. W. (1986). Two patterns of bilingual education in Dade County, Florida. In E. Bird (Ed.), *Foreign language learning: Research and development.* Menesha, WI: George Banta Co.

Salend, S. J., & Fradd, S. H. (1986). Nationwide availability of services for limited English proficient handicapped students. *Journal of Special Education,* 20(1), 127–135.

Shane, H. G. (1977). *Curriculum change toward the 21st century.* (pp. 16–20). Washington, DC: National Education Association.

Stanford Working Group. (1993). *A blueprint for the second generation.* Manuscript available from Stanford University, Palo Alto, CA.

Takanishi, R. (1981). *Preparing a policy-relevant report: Guidelines for authors.* Los Alamitos, CA: National Center for Bilingual Research.

Thompson, J. T. (1976). *Policymaking in American public education: A framework for analyses.* Upper Saddle River, NJ: Prentice Hall.

Troike, R. C. (1978). *Research evidence for the effectiveness of bilingual education.* Rosslyn, VA: National Clearinghouse for Bilingual Education.

Truman, D. (1951). *The government process: Political interests and public opinion.* NY: Knopf.

Tucker, G. R., et al. (1970). An alternate days approach to bilingual education. In J. E. Alatis (Ed.), *Report of the 21st annual round table meeting of linguistics and language studies.* Washington: Georgetown University Press.

Woodson, C. R. (1983). Educational policy: A review of related research in bilingual special education. In

Del Green Associates, *A review of research affecting educational programming for bilingual handicapped students. Final report, Vol. 2.* (pp. 97–125). Washington, DC: Author. (ERIC Document Reproduction Services No. ED 267–556)

Individuals with Disabilities Education Act of 1990. Public Law 101–476. 34 CFR Ch. V, Part 300, (1991).

Bilingual Education Act, 20 U.S.C. 3281–3341. Title VII of the Elementary and Secondary Education Act, as amended by PL 100–297.

Bilingual Education Act rules and regulations. 34 CFR Ch. V, Part 500–581, pp. 126–185, (1991).

SUBJECT INDEX